Stochastic Claims Reserving Methods in Insurance

For other titles in the Wiley Finance series
please see www.wiley.com/finance

About the authors

MARIO V. WÜTHRICH holds a PhD in mathematics from ETH Zurich (The Swiss Federal Institute of Technology, Zurich). He completed his postdoctoral work on statistical physics in 2000 at the University of Nijmegen in The Netherlands. From 2000 to 2005, he held an actuarial position at Winterthur Insurance, Switzerland where he was responsible for claims reserving in non-life insurance, as well as developing and implementing the Swiss Solvency Test. Since 2005, he has served as senior researcher and lecturer at ETH Zurich with teaching duties in actuarial and financial mathematics. He serves on the board of the Swiss Association of Actuaries (SAA) and is joint editor of the Bulletin SAA.

MICHAEL MERZ has been Assistant Professor for Statistics, Risk and Insurance at the University of Tübingen since October 2006. He was awarded the internationally renowned SCOR Actuarial Prize in 2004 for his doctoral thesis in risk theory. After completing his doctorate, he worked in the actuarial department of the Baloise insurance company in Basel, Switzerland and gained valuable practical working experience in actuarial science and quantitative risk management. His main research interests are actuarial science and quantitative risk management, with special emphasis on claims reserving and risk theory. He is a referee for many academic journals and has published extensively in leading academic journals, including the ASTIN Bulletin and the Scandinavian Actuarial Journal.

Stochastic
claims reserving methods in insurance

"It is astonishing that the methods used for claims reserving in non life-insurance are, even still today, driven by a deterministic understanding of one or several computational algorithms. Stochastic Claims Reserving Methods in Insurance *is tremendously widening this traditional understanding. In this text reserving is model driven, computational algorithms become a consequence of the chosen model. Only with this approach it makes sense to ask how predicted reserves might vary. Stochastic reserving is hence the cornerstone of successful risk management for the technical result of an insurance company. Mario Wüthrich and Michael Merz have to be congratulated for opening the eyes of the non-life-actuary to a new and modern dimension."*

—Hans Bühlmann, Swiss Federal Institute of Technology, Zurich

"Assessing the best estimate of insurance liabilities and modelling their adverse developments are among the new frontiers of insurance under the new IAS and the proposed new solvency regimes. This book makes a leap towards these frontiers. The variegated issue of predicting outstanding loss liabilities in non-life insurance is addressed using the unified framework of theory of stochastic processes. The proposed approach provides valuable tools for tackling one of the most challenging forecasting problems in insurance."

—Franco Moriconi, Professor of Finance, University of Perugia

Stochastic Claims Reserving Methods in Insurance

Mario V. Wüthrich

and

Michael Merz

John Wiley & Sons, Ltd

Published by John Wiley & Sons Ltd, The Atrium, Southern Gate, Chichester, West Sussex PO19 8SQ, England

Telephone (+44) 1243 779777

Email (for orders and customer service enquiries): cs-books@wiley.co.uk
Visit our Home Page on www.wiley.com

Other Wiley Editorial Offices

John Wiley & Sons Inc., 111 River Street, Hoboken, NJ 07030, USA

Jossey-Bass, 989 Market Street, San Francisco, CA 94103-1741, USA

Wiley-VCH Verlag GmbH, Boschstr. 12, D-69469 Weinheim, Germany

John Wiley & Sons Australia Ltd, 42 McDougall Street, Milton, Queensland 4064, Australia

John Wiley & Sons (Asia) Pte Ltd, 2 Clementi Loop #02-01, Jin Xing Distripark, Singapore 129809

John Wiley & Sons Canada Ltd, 6045 Freemont Blvd, Mississauga, ONT, L5R 4J3, Canada

Wiley also publishes its books in a variety of electronic formats. Some content that appears in print may not be available in electronic books.

Library of Congress Cataloging in Publication Data

Wüthrich, Mario V.
Stochastic claims reserving methods in insurance / Mario V. Wüthrich, Michael Merz.
p. cm. — (Wiley finance series)
Includes bibliographical references and index.
ISBN 978-0-470-72346-3 (cloth)
1. Insurance claims—Mathematical models. I. Merz, Michael. II. Title.
HG8106.W88 2008
368′.0140151922—dc22 2008007642

British Library Cataloguing in Publication Data

A catalogue record for this book is available from the British Library

ISBN 978-0-470-72346-3 (HB)

Typeset in 10/12pt Times by Integra Software Services Pvt. Ltd, Pondicherry, India
Printed and bound in Great Britain by Antony Rowe Ltd, Chippenham, Wiltshire

Dedicated to
Alessia, Luisa and Anja

Contents

Preface

For a very long time estimating claims reserves was understood as a pure algorithmic method to determine the insurance liabilities. It was only about 30 years ago that actuaries have realized that also claims reserving includes stochastic modelling. Due to this reason stochastic claims reserving modelling is still only poorly understood and treated in the education and in the industry. At ETH Zurich we have decided to close this gap and give a whole lecture (one term) on the subject stochastic claims reserving methods in insurance. After this decision we went to the library to look for appropriate lecture notes. Soon it became clear that there is no appropriate text for our lecture and we started the ambitious project of writing our own notes.

The present literature on claims reserving can be divided into several subgroups. The first subgroup consists of various claims reserving manuals for practitioners. These manuals mainly belong to the old school and describe the application of different algorithms, how to clean and smoothen data, how to choose appropriate parameters, etc. Most of these guidelines focus on specific data sets and give proposals for the estimation of the expected outstanding claims liabilities. They are mainly based on practical experience and mathematical aspects and stochastic modelling are only poorly treated in these notes.

Another subgroup consists of books on non-life insurance mathematics. There are several books and lecture notes that treat the basic claims reserving methods in a chapter or a section. Mostly, these chapters give only a very short introduction into the subject without going into depth.

Finally, there is an enormous number of recent scientific papers in various different actuarial journals. Some of these papers are based on sound mathematics and statistical methods, others are less rigorous. Most of them use different notations and it is often difficult to see in which aspects two papers are different and in which they are not. In consolidated book form there is only very few literature that focuses on stochastic aspects.

Based on this background we started our project of writing a book on stochastic claims reserving methods. Our goal was to get a correct and consistent text that unifies different notations and approaches and gives an overview on the contributions that have attracted our attention. We initially started our first lecture on stochastic claims reserving methods with a text that had about 150 pages, but which was still growing dramatically. This has soon led to the decision to limit the scope of this book to probabilistic aspects and calculations and not to include other or more advanced questions like data cleaning, statistical topics, solvency considerations, market-values of reserves etc. which itself would make for at least another two books. So in the present book we define several different stochastic models that are used for claims reserving. Stochastic properties of these models are derived and analysed, that is, cashflow prediction is studied within these models and measures for analysing the prediction uncertainties are derived.

Initially, we had in mind an audience having a background typical of someone with a degree in mathematics, statistics or actuarial sciences. But to make the book a valuable reference we have decided to also include more advanced topics and calculations. Still we believe that most results should be understood by a modern trained actuary solving (complex) problems for his company. Furthermore, we recognize that we have learned a lot of new methods and techniques during the writing of this book, which was often very enlightening.

We also recognize that the book does not give a complete survey on the existing literature. Moreover, we would also like to mention that it was often very difficult to track the correct chronological and historical roots to all the results developed. We have tried to be as accurate as possible. For all omissions and also in the light of the fast development of research we apologize to all the authors of such missing papers.

Acknowledgement

Of course the writing of this book was only possible with the support of several individuals. This work would not have been possible without the grant and generosity of our employers, ETH Zurich and University of Tübingen. At ETH Zurich and University of Tübingen we were supported by our departments, our collaborators, our PhD students and, of course, by the students who attended our lectures. At the heart of this encouragement there are the three professors, Paul Embrechts, Hans Bühlmann and Eberhard Schaich, it is only due to them that we have found the fruitful environment (personal, mathematical and methodological) for completing our project. Furthermore, we were assisted by our PhD students Daniel Alai, Matthias Degen, Jochen Heberle, Luis Huergo, Dominik Lambrigger, Natalia Lysenko and Ramona Maier as well as by the diploma students that have completed their thesis during the past years.

However, the beginning of this project was much earlier, before we even knew that we were once going to teach on this subject. Mario started his professional career at Winterthur Insurance (today AXA-Winterthur) where he became responsible for claims reserving for all non-life insurance business lines of Winterthur Insurance Switzerland. The claims reserving group with Alois Gisler, Ursin Mayer, Francesco Pagliari and Markus Steiner introduced him into all the practical secrets of claims reserving, peculiarities of the different lines of business, etc. Michael began his professional career at the actuarial department of the Baloise insurance company in Basel where he gained valuable practical working experience in claims reserving. The non-life group with Marie-Thérèse Kohler, Markus Buchwalder, Hans-Kaspar Britt and Roger Fässler familiarized him with claims reserving and its significance for modern solvency capital requirements, premium calculation, risk management etc. It is only due to our former employers and colleagues that we have learned and realized the importance of claims reserving.

In the process of writing this book we have met many other practitioners and researcher on claims reserving at different universities, conferences, industry, through the actuarial organizations, through the referee processes of actuarial journals, etc. Among all of them, this book has especially profited in some or another form from the knowledge of Gareth Peters, Pavel Shevchenko, Peter England, Thomas Mack, Alain-Sol Sznitman.

Finally, but most importantly, we thank our private environment who has supported us through all these times. Mario thanks his daughters Alessia and Luisa, his parents Rosmarie and Valentin as well as Priska, Andreas, Susan, Fritz, Simon, Stéphane, Peter, Alessandro, Matthias and the Stolz family. Michael thanks his wife Anja and his parents Hannelore and Roland for their endless love and patience as well as Edeltraud, Ludwig and his friends Beppo and Josef.

M.V.W. and M.M.

Acknowledgements

[illegible]

1 Introduction and Notation

1.1 CLAIMS PROCESS

In this book we consider the claims reserving problem for a branch of insurance products known in continental Europe as **non-life insurance**, in the UK as **General Insurance** and in the USA as **Property and Casualty Insurance**. This branch usually contains all kinds of insurance products except life insurance. This separation is mainly for two reasons:

1. Life insurance products are rather different from non-life insurance contracts, for example, terms of contracts, type of claims, risk drivers, etc. This implies that life and non-life products are modeled rather differently.
2. In many countries, for example, Switzerland and Germany, there is a strict legal separation between life insurance and non-life insurance products. This means that a company dealing with non-life insurance products is not allowed to sell life insurance products, and a life insurance company can only sell life-related and disability insurance products. Hence, for example, every Swiss insurance company that sells both life and non-life insurance products, has at least two legal entities.

The non-life insurance branch operates on the following lines of business (LoB):

- motor/car insurance (motor third party liability, motor hull);
- property insurance (private and commercial property against fire, water, flooding, business interruption, etc.);
- liability insurance (private and commercial liability including director and officers (D&O) liability insurance);
- accident insurance (personal and collective accident including compulsory accident insurance and workers' compensation);
- health insurance (private personal and collective health);
- marine insurance (including transportation); and
- other insurance products such as aviation, travel insurance, legal protection, credit insurance, epidemic insurance, etc.

A non-life insurance policy is a contract among two parties: the insurer and the insured. It provides the insurer with a fixed/deterministic amount of money (called premium) and the insured with a financial coverage against the random occurrence of well-specified events (or at least a promise that he or she gets a well-defined amount in case such an event happens). The right of the insured to these amounts (in case the event happens) constitutes a **claim** by the insured to the insurer.

The amount which the insurer is obligated to pay in respect of a claim is known as the **claim amount** or the **loss amount**. The payments that make up this claim are known as

- claims payments
- loss payments
- paid claims, or
- paid losses.

The history of a typical non-life insurance claim may take the form shown in Figure 1.1.

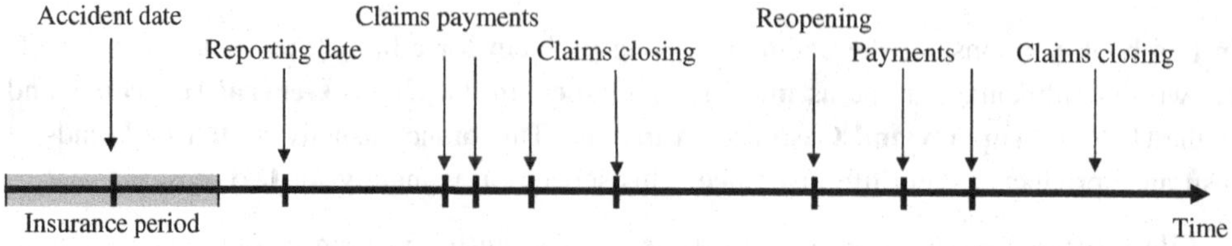

Figure 1.1 Typical time line of a non-life insurance claim

Usually, the insurance company is unable to settle a claim immediately, for three main reasons:

1. There is a reporting delay (time-lag between claims occurrence and claims reporting to the insurer). The reporting of a claim can take several years, especially in liability insurance (e.g. asbestos or environmental pollution claims) – see Example 1.1 and Table 1.1 below.
2. After being reported to the insurer, several years may elapse before the claim is finally settled. For instance, in property insurance we usually have a relatively fast settlement, whereas in liability or bodily injury claims it often takes a long time before the total circumstances of the claim are clear and known (and can be settled).
3. It can also happen that a closed claim needs to be reopened due to (unexpected) new developments, or if a relapse occurs.

1.1.1 Accounting Principles and Accident Years

There are three different premium accounting principles:

1. Premium booked
2. Premium written
3. Premium earned.

The choice of principle depends on the kind of business written. Without loss of generality, in this book, we concentrate on the **premium earned** principle.

Usually, an insurance company closes its books at least once a year. Let us assume that we always close our book on 31 December. How should we show a one-year contract that was written on 1 October 2008 with two premium instalments paid on 1 October 2008 and 1 April 2009?

Let us assume that

- premium written 2008 = 100
- premium booked 2008 = 50 (= premium received in 2008)
- pipeline premium 31.12.2008 = 50 (= premium that will be received in 2009, receivables), which gives a premium booked 2009 = 50.

If we assume that the risk exposure is distributed uniformly over time (*pro rata temporis*), then

- premium earned 2008 = 25 (= premium used for exposure in 2008)
- unearned premium reserve (UPR) 31.12.2008 = 75 (= premium that will be used for exposure in 2009), which gives a premium earned 2009 = 75.

If the exposure is not *pro rata temporis*, then, of course, we have a different split of the premium earned into the different accounting years. In order to have a consistent financial statement, it is important that the accident date and the premium accounting principle are compatible (via the exposure pattern). Hence, all claims that have an accident year of 2008 have to be matched to the premium earned 2008, that is, the claims 2008 have to be paid by the premium earned 2008, whereas the claims with an accident year after 2008 have to be paid by the unearned premium reserve (UPR) 31.12.2008.

Hence, on the one hand, we have to build premium reserves for future exposures and on the other, we need to build claims reserves for unsettled claims of past exposures. There are two different types of claims reserves for past exposures:

1. IBNyR reserves (Incurred But Not yet Reported): We need to build claims reserves for claims that have occurred before 31.12.2008, but have not been reported by the end of the year (i.e. the reporting delay laps into the next accounting years).
2. IBNeR reserves (Incurred But Not enough Reported): We need to build claims reserves for claims that have been reported before 31.12.2008, but have not yet been settled – that is, we still expect payments in the future, which need to be financed by the already earned premium.

This means that the claims payments are directly linked to the insurance premium via the exposure pattern. This link determines the building of provisions and reserves for the claims settlement. Other insurance structures are found, for example, in social insurance where one typically pays claims with the so-called pay-as-you-go system. Such systems require a different legal framework – namely, one has to ensure that the current premium income is at least sufficient to cover present claims payments. This is typically done by legal compulsory insurance, but in this text we do not consider such systems.

1.1.2 Inflation

The following subsection on inflation follows Taylor (2000).

Claims costs are often subject to inflation. This is seldom related to the typical salary or price inflation, but is very specific to the chosen LoB. For example, in the accident LoB, inflation is driven by medical inflation; whereas, for the motor hull LoB inflation is driven by the complexity of car repairing techniques. The essential point is that claims inflation may continue beyond the occurrence date of the accident up to the point of its final payment or settlement.

Example 1.1 (reporting delay, IBNyR claims)

Table 1.1 Claims development triangle for number of IBNyR cases (Taylor 2000)

Accident year i	Number of reported claims, non-cumulative according to reporting delay reporting year j										
	0	1	2	3	4	5	6	7	8	9	10
0	368	191	28	8	6	5	3	1	0	0	1
1	393	151	25	6	4	5	4	1	2	1	0
2	517	185	29	17	11	10	8	1	0	0	1
3	578	254	49	22	17	6	3	0	1	0	0
4	622	206	39	16	3	7	0	1	0	0	0
5	660	243	28	12	12	4	4	1	0	0	0
6	666	234	53	10	8	4	6	1	0	0	0
7	573	266	62	12	5	7	6	5	1	0	1
8	582	281	32	27	12	13	6	2	1	0	
9	545	220	43	18	12	9	5	2	0		
10	509	266	49	22	15	4	8	0			
11	589	210	29	17	12	4	9				
12	564	196	23	12	9	5					
13	607	203	29	9	7						
14	674	169	20	12							
15	619	190	41								
16	660	161									
17	660										

□

If $(X_{t_i})_{i\in\mathbb{N}}$ denote the positive single claims payments at times t_i expressed in money value at time t_1 ($t_k \geq t_l$ for $k \geq l$), then the total claim amount is, in money value at time t_1, given by

$$C_1 = \sum_{i=1}^{\infty} X_{t_i}$$

If $\lambda(\cdot)$ denotes the index that measures the claims inflation, the actual (nominal) claims amount is

$$C = \sum_{i=1}^{\infty} \frac{\lambda(t_i)}{\lambda(t_1)} X_{t_i}$$

Whenever $\lambda(\cdot)$ is an increasing function, we observe that C is larger than C_1. Of course, in practice we only observe the unindexed payments $[\lambda(t_i)/\lambda(t_1)]\ X_{t_i}$ and, in general, it is difficult to estimate an index function such that we can obtain indexed values X_{t_i}. Finding an index function $\lambda(\cdot)$ is equivalent to defining appropriate deflators φ, which is a well-known concept in market consistent actuarial valuation; see, for example, Wüthrich *et al.* (2008).

The basic idea behind indexed values C_1 is that, if two sets of payments relate to identical circumstances except that there is a time translation in the payment, their indexed values will be the same, whereas the unindexed values will differ. For $c > 0$ we assume that we have a second cashflow satisfying

$$\widetilde{X}_{t_i+c} = X_{t_i}$$

Whenever $\lambda(\cdot)$ is an increasing function we have

$$C_1 = \sum_{i=1}^{\infty} X_{t_i} = \sum_{i=1}^{\infty} \widetilde{X}_{t_i+c} = \widetilde{C}_1$$

$$\widetilde{C} = \sum_{i=1}^{\infty} \frac{\lambda(t_i+c)}{\lambda(t_1)} \widetilde{X}_{t_i+c} = \sum_{i=1}^{\infty} \frac{\lambda(t_i+c)}{\lambda(t_1)} X_{t_i} > C$$

That is, the unindexed values differ by the factor $\lambda(t_i+c)/\lambda(t_i) > 1$. However, in practice this ratio often turns out to be of a different form, namely

$$\left[1+\widetilde{\psi}(t_i, t_i+c)\right] \frac{\lambda(t_i+c)}{\lambda(t_i)}$$

meaning that over the time interval $[t_i, t_i+c]$ claim costs are inflated by an additional factor $[1+\widetilde{\psi}(t_i, t_i+c)]$ above the 'natural' inflation. This additional inflation is referred to as superimposed inflation and can be caused by, for example, changes in the jurisdiction or an increased claims awareness of the insured. We will not discuss this further in the text.

1.2 STRUCTURAL FRAMEWORK TO THE CLAIMS-RESERVING PROBLEM

In this section we follow Arjas (1989). We present a mathematical framework for claims reserving and formulate the claims-reserving problem in the language of stochastic processes. This section is interesting from a theoretical point of view but can be skipped by the more practically oriented reader without loss of understanding for the remainder of the book.

Note that in this section all actions related to a claim are listed in the order of their notification at the insurance company. From a statistical point of view this makes perfect sense; however, from an accounting point of view, one should preferably list the claims according to their occurence/accident date; this was done, for example, in Norberg (1993, 1999) as we will see below in Subsection 10.1. Of course, there is a one-to-one relation between the two concepts.

We assume that we have N claims within a fixed time period with reporting dates $T_1, \ldots, T_N$ with $T_i \le T_{i+1}$ for all i. If we fix the ith claim, then $T_i = T_{i,0} \le T_{i,1} \le \ldots \le T_{i,j} \le \ldots \le T_{i,N_i}$ denotes the sequence of dates at which some action on claim i is observed. For example, at time $T_{i,j}$, we might have a payment, a new estimation by the claims adjuster, or other new information on claim i. T_{i,N_i} denotes the date of the final settlement of the claim. Assume that $T_{i,N_i+k} = \infty$ for $k \ge 1$.

We specify the events that take place at time $T_{i,j}$ by

$$X_{i,j} = \begin{cases} \text{payment at time } T_{i,j} \text{ for claim } i \\ 0, \text{ if there is no payment at time } T_{i,j} \end{cases}$$

$$I_{i,j} = \begin{cases} \text{new information available at } T_{i,j} \text{ for claim } i \\ \emptyset, \text{ if there is no new information at time } T_{i,j} \end{cases}$$

We set $X_{i,j}=0$ and $I_{i,j}=\emptyset$ whenever $T_{i,j}=\infty$. That is, we assume that there are no payments or new information after the final settlement of the claim.

With this structure we can define a number of interesting processes; moreover, our claims-reserving problem can be split into several subproblems. For every claim i we obtain a marked point processes.

- ***Payment process of claim*** i $(T_{i,j}, X_{i,j})_{j\geq 0}$ defines the following cumulative payment process

$$C_i(t) = \sum_{j\in\{k;T_{i,k}\leq t\}} X_{i,j}$$

and $C_i(t)=0$ for $t<T_i$. The total ultimate claim amount is given by

$$C_i(\infty)=C_i(T_{i,N_i})=\sum_{j=0}^{\infty} X_{i,j}$$

The total outstanding claims payments for future liabilities of claim i at time t are given by

$$R_i(t)=C_i(\infty)-C_i(t)=\sum_{j\in\{k;T_{i,k}>t\}} X_{i,j}$$

Note that $R_i(t)$ is a random variable at time t that needs to be predicted. As predictor one often chooses its (conditional) expectation, given the information available at time t. This (conditional) expectation is called claims reserves for future liabilities at time t. If the (conditional) expectation is unknown it needs to be estimated with the information available at time t. Henceforth, this estimator is at the same time used as a predictor for $R_i(t)$.

- ***Information process of claim*** i is given by $(T_{i,j}, I_{i,j})_{j\geq 0}$.
- ***Settlement process of claim*** i is given by $(T_{i,j}, I_{i,j}, X_{i,j})_{j\geq 0}$.

We denote the aggregate processes of all claims by

$$C(t)=\sum_{i=1}^{N} C_i(t) \tag{1.1}$$

$$R(t)=\sum_{i=1}^{N} R_i(t) \tag{1.2}$$

$C(t)$ represents all payments up to time t for all N claims, and $R(t)$ is the amount of the outstanding claims payments at time t for these N claims.

Now, we consider claims reserving as a prediction problem. Let

$$\mathcal{F}_t^N=\sigma\left(\{(T_{i,j}, I_{i,j}, X_{i,j}); 1\leq i\leq N, j\geq 0, T_{i,j}\leq t\}\right)$$

be a σ-field, which can be interpreted as the information available at time t from the N claims settlement processes. Often there is additional exogenous information $\mathcal{E}_t$ at time t with

$\mathcal{E}_s \subseteq \mathcal{E}_t$ for $t \geq s$ such as change of legal practice, high inflation, job market information, etc. Therefore, the total information available to the insurance company at time t is defined as

$$\mathcal{F}_t = \sigma\left(\mathcal{F}_t^N \otimes \mathcal{E}_t\right) \tag{1.3}$$

Problem/Task At time t estimate the conditional distribution

$$P[C(\infty) \in \cdot \,|\mathcal{F}_t]$$

with the first two moments

$$M_t = E[C(\infty)|\mathcal{F}_t]$$
$$V_t = \text{Var}\,(C(\infty)|\mathcal{F}_t)$$

1.2.1 Fundamental Properties of the Claims Reserving Process

Since $C(\infty) = C(t) + R(t)$, and because $C(t)$ is $\mathcal{F}_t$-measurable we have

$$M_t = C(t) + E[R(t)|\mathcal{F}_t]$$
$$V_t = \text{Var}\,(R(t)|\mathcal{F}_t)$$

LEMMA 1.2 *M_t is an $\mathcal{F}_t$-martingale. That is, we have for $t > s$*

$$E\,[M_t|\,\mathcal{F}_s] = M_s \quad \text{a.s.}$$

Proof The proof is clear (successive forecasts for increasing information $\mathcal{F}_t$). □

LEMMA 1.3 *The variance process V_t is an $\mathcal{F}_t$-supermartingale. That is, we have for $t > s$*

$$E\,[V_t|\,\mathcal{F}_s] \leq V_s \quad \text{a.s.}$$

Proof Using Jensen's inequality for $t > s$ we get, a.s.,

$$\begin{aligned}
E\,[V_t|\,\mathcal{F}_s] &= E\,[\text{Var}\,(C(\infty)|\mathcal{F}_t)|\,\mathcal{F}_s] \\
&= E\left[E\left[C^2(\infty)|\,\mathcal{F}_t\right]|\,\mathcal{F}_s\right] - E\left[E[C(\infty)|\,\mathcal{F}_t]^2|\,\mathcal{F}_s\right] \\
&\leq E\left[C^2(\infty)|\,\mathcal{F}_s\right] - E\,[E[C(\infty)|\,\mathcal{F}_t]|\,\mathcal{F}_s]^2 \\
&= \text{Var}\,(C(\infty)|\mathcal{F}_s) = V_s
\end{aligned}$$

This completes the proof. □

Consider $u > t$ and define the increment from t to u by

$$M(t, u) = M_u - M_t$$

Then, a.s., we have

$$E[M(t,u)M(u,\infty)|\mathcal{F}_t] = E[M(t,u)E[M(u,\infty)|\mathcal{F}_u]|\mathcal{F}_t]$$
$$= E[M(t,u)(E[C(\infty)|\mathcal{F}_u] - M_u)|\mathcal{F}_t] = 0 \qquad (1.4)$$

This implies that $M(t, u)$ and $M(u, \infty)$ are uncorrelated, which is a well-known property referred to as uncorrelated increments.

First Approach to the Claims Reserving Problem

The use of the martingale integral representation leads to the 'innovation gains process', which determines M_t when updating $\mathcal{F}_t$. Although this theory is well understood, this approach has a limited practical value, since one has little idea about the updating process and (statistically) there is not enough data to model this process. Moreover, it is often too complicated for practical applications.

Second Approach to the Claims Reserving Problem

For $t < u$ we have that $\mathcal{F}_t \subset \mathcal{F}_u$. Since M_t is an $\mathcal{F}_t$-martingale

$$E[M(t,u)|\mathcal{F}_t] = 0, \quad \text{a.s.}$$

We denote the incremental payments from t to u by

$$X(t,u) = C(u) - C(t)$$

Hence, almost surely (a.s.),

$$\begin{aligned} M(t,u) &= E[C(\infty)|\mathcal{F}_u] - E[C(\infty)|\mathcal{F}_t] \\ &= C(u) + E[R(u)|\mathcal{F}_u] - (C(t) + E[R(t)|\mathcal{F}_t]) \\ &= X(t,u) + E[R(u)|\mathcal{F}_u] - E[C(u) - C(t) + R(u)|\mathcal{F}_t] \\ &= X(t,u) - E[X(t,u)|\mathcal{F}_t] + E[R(u)|\mathcal{F}_u] - E[R(u)|\mathcal{F}_t] \end{aligned}$$

Henceforth, we have the following two terms:

1. Prediction error for payments within $(t, t+1)$

$$X(t,t+1) - E[X(t,t+1)|\mathcal{F}_t] \qquad (1.5)$$

2. Prediction error for outstanding claims payments $R(t+1)$ when updating information

$$E\left[R(t+1)|\mathcal{F}_{t+1}\right] - E[R(t+1)|\mathcal{F}_t] \qquad (1.6)$$

this is the change of conditionally expected outstanding liabilities when updating the information from t to $t+1$, $\mathcal{F}_t \to \mathcal{F}_{t+1}$.

In most approaches one focuses on modelling processes (1.5) and (1.6).

1.2.2 Known and Unknown Claims

As in Subsection 1.1.1, we distinguish IBNyR (incurred but not yet reported) claims and reported claims. The process $(N_t)_{t\geq 0}$ defined by

$$N_t = \sum_{i=1}^{N} 1_{\{T_i \leq t\}} \tag{1.7}$$

counts the number of reported claims. We can split the ultimate claims and the amount of outstanding claims payments at time t with respect to the fact of whether we have a reported or an IBNyR claim as follows

$$R(t) = \sum_{i=1}^{N} R_i(t)\ 1_{\{T_i \leq t\}} + \sum_{i=1}^{N} R_i(t)\ 1_{\{T_i > t\}} \tag{1.8}$$

where open liabilities at time t for reported claims are expressed as

$$\sum_{i=1}^{N} R_i(t)\ 1_{\{T_i \leq t\}} \tag{1.9}$$

and open liabilities at time t for IBNyR claims (including UPR liabilities) are expressed as

$$\sum_{i=1}^{N} R_i(t)\ 1_{\{T_i > t\}} \tag{1.10}$$

Remark Here we do not understand IBNyR in a strong sense. Observe that at time t there is, possibly, still a premium exposure (positive UPR liability). Such claims have not yet incurred, and hence are also not yet reported. For the time being we do not distinguish these types of claims for incurred but not yet reported claims – that is, they are all contained in (1.10) (for a more detailed analysis we refer to Subsection 10.1).

Hence, we define the reserves at time t as

$$R_t^{\text{rep}} = E\left[\sum_{i=1}^{N} R_i(t)\ 1_{\{T_i \leq t\}} \middle| \mathcal{F}_t \right] = E\left[\sum_{i=1}^{N_t} R_i(t) \middle| \mathcal{F}_t \right] \tag{1.11}$$

$$R_t^{\text{IBNyR}} = E\left[\sum_{i=1}^{N} R_i(t)\ 1_{\{T_i > t\}} \middle| \mathcal{F}_t \right] = E\left[\sum_{i=N_t+1}^{N} R_i(t) \middle| \mathcal{F}_t \right] \tag{1.12}$$

where N is the total (random) number of claims. Since N_t is $\mathcal{F}_t$-measurable

$$R_t^{\text{rep}} = \sum_{i=1}^{N_t} E\left[R_i(t) \middle| \mathcal{F}_t \right] \tag{1.13}$$

$$R_t^{\text{IBNyR}} = E\left[\sum_{i=N_t+1}^{N} R_i(t) \middle| \mathcal{F}_t \right] \tag{1.14}$$

R_t^{rep} denotes the expected future payments at time t for reported claims. This term is often called 'best estimate reserves at time t for reported claims'. R_t^{IBNyR} are the expected future payments at time t for IBNyR claims including UPR reserves (or 'best estimate reserves at time t for IBNyR and UPR claims').

Conclusions

We can see from (1.13)–(1.14) that the reserves for reported claims and the reserves for IBNyR claims are of a rather different nature:

(i) The reserves for reported claims should/can be determined individually. Often one has a lot of information on reported claims (e.g. case estimates), which suggests estimation on a single claims basis.
(ii) The reserves for IBNyR claims (including UPR reserves) cannot be decoupled due to the fact that N is not known at time t (see (1.12)). Moreover, information on a single claims basis is not available. This shows that IBNyR reserves have to be determined on a collective basis.

Unfortunately, most of the classical claims reserving methods do not distinguish reported claims from IBNyR claims, that is, they estimate the claims reserves for both classes at the same time. In that context, we have to slightly disappoint the reader, since most methods presented in this book do not make this distinction between reported and IBNyR claims. For a first attempt to distinguish these claims categories, we refer to Chapter 10.

1.3 OUTSTANDING LOSS LIABILITIES, CLASSICAL NOTATION

In this subsection we introduce the classical claims reserving notation and terminology. In most cases outstanding loss liabilities are studied in so-called claims development triangles which separate insurance claims on two time axes.

Below we use the following notation (see also Figure 1.2):

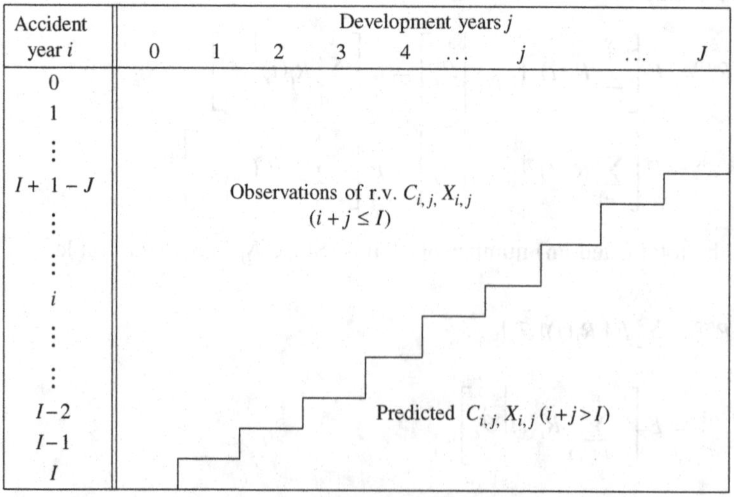

Figure 1.2 Claims development triangle

i = accident year, year of occurrence (vertical axis),

j = development year, development period (horizontal axis).

The most recent accident year is denoted by I while the last development year is denoted by J. That is, $i \in \{0, \ldots, I\}$ and $j \in \{0, \ldots, J\}$.

For illustrative purposes, we assume that $X_{i,j}$ denotes payments. (Alternative meanings for $X_{i,j}$ are given below.) Then $X_{i,j}$ denotes all payments in development period j for claims with accident year i. That is, $X_{i,j}$ corresponds to the payments for claims in accident year i made in accounting year $i+j$. Cumulative payments $C_{i,j}$ for accident year i after j development years are then given by

$$C_{i,j} = \sum_{k=0}^{j} X_{i,k} \tag{1.15}$$

Claims $X_{i,j}$ and $C_{i,j}$ are usually studied in claims development triangles: In a claims development triangle, accident years i are specified on the vertical axis, whereas development periods j are shown on the horizontal axis (see also Figure 1.2). Typically, at time I, the claims development tables are split into two parts: the upper triangle/trapezoid containing observations $X_{i,j}$, $i+j \leq I$, and the lower triangle with estimates or predicted values of the outstanding payments $X_{i,j}$, $i+j > I$. This means that observations are available in the upper triangle/trapezoid

$$\mathcal{D}_I = \{X_{i,j};\ i+j \leq I,\ 0 \leq j \leq J\} \tag{1.16}$$

and the lower triangle $\mathcal{D}_I^c = \{X_{i,j};\ i+j > I,\ i \leq I,\ j \leq J\}$ needs to be estimated or predicted.

The accounting years are then given on the diagonals $i+j=k$, $k \geq 0$. The incremental claims in accounting year $k \geq 0$ are denoted by

$$X_k = \sum_{i+j=k} X_{i,j}$$

and are displayed on the $(k+1)$st diagonal of the claims development triangle.

Incremental claims $X_{i,j}$ may represent the incremental payments in cell (i, j), the number of reported claims with reporting delay j and accident year i, or the change of reported claim amount in cell (i, j). **Cumulative claims** $C_{i,j}$ may represent the cumulative payments, total number of reported claims, or claims incurred (for cumulative reported claims). $C_{i,J}$ is often called the **ultimate claim amount/load** of accident year i or the total number of claims in year i.

Incremental claims			***Cumulative claims***
$X_{i,j}$ incremental payments	$\Longleftrightarrow$	$C_{i,j}$	cumulative payments
$X_{i,j}$ number of reported claims with delay j	$\Longleftrightarrow$	$C_{i,j}$	total number of reported claims
$X_{i,j}$ change of reported claim amount	$\Longleftrightarrow$	$C_{i,j}$	claims incurred

If the $X_{i,j}$ denote incremental payments then the **outstanding loss liabilities** for accident year i at time j are given by

$$R_{i,j} = \sum_{k=j+1}^{J} X_{i,k} = C_{i,J} - C_{i,j} \tag{1.17}$$

$R_{i,j}$ need to be predicted by so-called **claims reserves**. They essentially constitute the amount that has to be estimated/predicted so that, together with the past claims $C_{i,j}$, we obtain the estimator/predictor for the total claims load (ultimate claim) $C_{i,J}$ for accident year i.

General Assumption 1.4

We assume throughout this book that

$$I = J$$

and that $X_{i,j} = 0$ for all $j > J$.

This general assumption, $I = J$, can easily be dropped; however, it substantially simplifies the notation and the formulas. It implies that we have to predict the outstanding loss liabilities for accident years $i = 1, \ldots, I$.

1.4 GENERAL REMARKS

There are several possible ways to consider claims data when constructing loss reserving models, that is, models for estimating/predicting the total ultimate claim amounts. In general, the following data structures are studied:

- cumulative or incremental claims data;
- payments or claims incurred data;
- split small and large claims data;
- indexed or unindexed claims data;
- number of claims and claims averages statistics; etc.

Usually, different methods and differently aggregated data sets lead to very different results. Only an **experienced reserving actuary** is able to tell which is an accurate/good estimate for future liabilities for a specific data set, and which method applies to which data set.

Often there are many phenomena in the data that first need to be understood before applying any claims reserving method (we cannot simply project past observations to the future by applying one stochastic model). Especially in direct insurance, the understanding of the data can even go down to single claims and to the personal knowledge of the managing claims adjusters.

With this in mind, we will describe different methods that can be used to estimate loss reserves, but only practical experience will tell which of the methods should be applied in any particular situation. That is, the focus of this book is on the mathematical description of relevant stochastic models and we will derive various properties of these models. The question of an ***appropriate model choice*** for a specific data set is only ***partially*** treated here. In fact, the model choice is probably one of the most difficult questions in any application in practice. Moreover, the claims reserving literature on the topic of choosing a model is fairly limited – for example, for the chain-ladder method certain aspects are considered in Barnett and Zehnwirth (2000) and Venter (1998), see also Chapter 11. From this point of view we will apply the different methods rather mechanically (without deciding which model to use). We always use the same data set (provided in Table 2.2, which gives an example for cumulative claims $C_{i,j}$). On this data set we will then apply stochastic methods, some of which will be purely data based, while others will incorporate expert opinions and external knowledge.

In classical claims reserving literature, claims reserving is often understood to be providing a best estimate to the outstanding loss liabilities. Providing a best estimate means that one applies an algorithm that gives this number/amount. In recent years, especially under new solvency regimes, one is also interested in the development of adverse claims reserves, and estimating potential losses that may occur in the future in these best estimate reserves. Such questions require stochastic claims reserving models that (1) justify the claims reserving algorithms and (2) quantify the uncertainties in these algorithms.

From this point of view one should always be aware of the fact that stochastic claims reserving models do not provide solutions where deterministic algorithms fail, they rather quantify the uncertainties in deterministic claims reserving algorithms using appropriate stochastic models.

The focus in this chapter is always on estimating total claims reserves and to quantify the total prediction uncertainty in these reserves (prediction errors in total ultimate claims). This is a long-term view that is important in solvency questions; however, there are other views such as short-term views which quantify uncertainties, for example, in profit-and-loss statements. Such short-term views are important if one is to make long term or intertemporal management decisions. We do not consider such short-term views here, but for the interested reader they are partially treated in Merz and Wüthrich (2007a) and Wüthrich *et al.* (2007b).

Moreover, claims reserves are always measured on the nominal scale. From an economic point of view one should also study discounted reserves since these relate to financial markets and market values of insurance liabilities. Unfortunately, market values of non-life insurance run-off portfolios are only barely understood and (probably) their derivation requires a whole set of new mathematical tools, where one needs to understand the influence of financial market drivers on non-life reserves, etc. In the literature there are only few papers that treat the topic of discounted reserves – see, for example, Taylor (2004) and Hoedemakers *et al.* (2003, 2005).

Remark on Claims Figures

When we speak about claims development triangles (paid or incurred data), these usually contain loss adjustment expenses, which can be allocated/attributed to single claims (and therefore are contained in the claims figures). Such expenses are called **allocated loss adjustment expenses** (ALAE). These are typically expenses for external lawyers, external expertise, etc. Internal loss adjustment expenses (income of claims handling department, maintenance of claims handling systems, management fees, etc.) are typically not contained in the claims figures and therefore have to be estimated separately. These costs are called **unallocated loss adjustment expenses** (ULAE). The New York method (paid-to-paid method) is the most popular for estimating reserves for ULAE expenses. The New York method is rather rough as it only works well in stationary situations, and one could therefore think of more sophisticated systems. Since ULAE are usually small compared to the other claims payments, the New York method is often sufficient in practical applications. As we will not comment further on ULAE reserving methods in this text, we refer the reader to Foundation CAS (1989), Feldblum (2002), Kittel (1981), Johnson (1989) and Buchwalder *et al.* (2006a).

2
Basic Methods

We start the general discussion on claims reserving with three standard methods:

1. Chain-ladder (CL) method
2. Bornhuetter–Ferguson (BF) method
3. Poisson model for claim counts.

The goal of this short chapter is to provide a first impression on how to tackle the problem of claims reserves estimation. The chain-ladder (CL) and the Bornhuetter–Ferguson (BF) methods belong to the easiest claims reserving methods; their simplicity makes the CL and the BF methods the most commonly used techniques in practice. Though they are simple, they often give surprisingly accurate results. Each of these methods will be discussed in more detail in Chapter 3, Chapter 4 and Chapter 6, respectively.

The CL method and the BF method can be understood as purely algorithmic methods to set claims reserves. These algorithms are then used as mechanical techniques to predict future liabilities. However, in general, this understanding does not allow for the quantification of the uncertainties in these predictions. Uncertainties can only be determined if we have an underlying stochastic model on which the reserving algorithms can be based. Therefore, although it may not be necessary in this chapter, we will define appropriate stochastic models for the CL and BF methods here since they will be used in later chapters and we wish to develop a well-established mathematical theory.

We assume that the last development period is given by J, hence $X_{i,j} = 0$ for $j > J$, and the last accident year is given by I. Moreover, we refer to our General Assumption 1.4, that is, $I = J$.

2.1 CHAIN-LADDER METHOD (DISTRIBUTION-FREE)

The CL algorithm is probably the most popular loss reserving technique in theory and practice. The classical actuarial literature often explains the CL method as a purely computational algorithm for estimating claims reserves. It was only much later that actuaries started to think about stochastic models that underlie the CL algorithm. There are several different stochastic models that justify the CL method. In this section we present the distribution-free derivation (see Mack 1993). The conditional prediction error of the distribution-free CL derivation is treated in Chapter 3 and the multivariate CL version in Chapter 8. Below, we also give other stochastic models that justify the CL algorithm – see, for instance, Section 2.3.

The distribution-free derivation of the CL method links successive cumulative claims with appropriate link ratios, and is based on the following definition of the model.

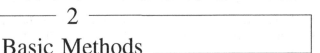

Model Assumptions 2.1 (distribution-free CL model)

- Cumulative claims $C_{i,j}$ of different accident years i are independent.
- There exist development factors $f_0, \ldots, f_{J-1} > 0$ such that for all $0 \leq i \leq I$ and all $1 \leq j \leq J$ we have

$$E\left[C_{i,j} \middle| C_{i,0}, \ldots, C_{i,j-1}\right] = E\left[C_{i,j} \middle| C_{i,j-1}\right] = f_{j-1}\, C_{i,j-1} \tag{2.1}$$

□

Remarks 2.2

- Model Assumptions 2.1 state the first two assumptions of the (distribution-free) CL model proposed by Mack (1993). Note that here we have only an assumption on the first moments (2.1). This is already sufficient for estimating conditionally expected future claims (and hence describe the CL algorithm). Higher moments only come into play when we quantify uncertainties in these estimates and predictions. For the entire Mack model (assumptions on higher moments) we refer to Subsection 3.2.1.
- As will be seen later, the assumption of the independence between the claims in different accident years is common to almost all claims reserving methods. An implication of this assumption is that the effects of accounting years in the data need to be eliminated.
- In addition, we could make stronger assumptions for the sequences $C_{i,0}, C_{i,1}, \ldots$, namely that they form Markov chains. Moreover, observe that

$$C_{i,j} \prod_{k=0}^{j-1} f_k^{-1}$$

  forms a martingale for $j \geq 1$.
- The factors f_j are called link ratios, development factors, CL factors or age-to-age factors. They are the central object of interest in the CL method and describe how we link successive cumulative claims. The main difficulty now is to give appropriate estimators for these CL factors.

In the following $\mathcal{D}_I = \{C_{i,j};\ i + j \leq I, 0 \leq j \leq J\}$ denotes the set of observations at time I (upper triangle; cf. Figure 1.2).

LEMMA 2.3 *Under Model Assumptions 2.1 we have*

$$E\left[C_{i,J} \middle| \mathcal{D}_I\right] = E\left[C_{i,J} \middle| C_{i,I-i}\right] = C_{i,I-i}\, f_{I-i} \cdots f_{J-1} \tag{2.2}$$

for all $1 \leq i \leq I$.

Proof The proof is an easy exercise using conditional expectations, the independence of different accident years, and (2.1)

$$E\left[C_{i,J} \middle| \mathcal{D}_I\right] = E\left[C_{i,J} \middle| C_{i,0}, \ldots, C_{i,I-i}\right]$$

$$= E\left[E\left[C_{i,J} \middle| C_{i,J-1} \right] \middle| C_{i,0}, \ldots, C_{i,I-i} \right]$$
$$= f_{J-1}\, E\left[C_{i,J-1} \middle| \mathcal{D}_I \right]$$

If we iterate this procedure until we reach the diagonal $i+j=I$, we obtain the claim. This completes the proof. Analogously for $E\left[C_{i,J} \middle| C_{i,I-i}\right]$. □

Lemma 2.3 gives an algorithm for predicting the ultimate claim $C_{i,J}$ given the observations $\mathcal{D}_I$. This algorithm is often called the recursive algorithm. For known CL factors f_j, the outstanding claims liabilities of accident year i based on $\mathcal{D}_I$ are predicted by

$$E\left[C_{i,J} \middle| \mathcal{D}_I \right] - C_{i,I-i} = C_{i,I-i}\ (f_{I-i} \cdots f_{J-1} - 1) \tag{2.3}$$

This corresponds to the 'best estimate' reserves for accident year i at time I (based on the information $\mathcal{D}_I$ and known CL factors f_j). Note that in this spirit we use the conditionally expected value (2.3) to predict the outcome of the random variable $C_{i,J} - C_{i,I-i}$, given $\mathcal{D}_I$.

Unfortunately, in most practical applications the CL factors are not known and also need to be estimated. The CL factors f_j, $j=0, \ldots, J-1$, are estimated as follows:

$$\widehat{f}_j = \frac{\sum_{i=0}^{I-j-1} C_{i,j+1}}{\sum_{i=0}^{I-j-1} C_{i,j}} = \sum_{i=0}^{I-j-1} \frac{C_{i,j}}{\sum_{k=0}^{I-j-1} C_{k,j}} \frac{C_{i,j+1}}{C_{i,j}} \tag{2.4}$$

That is, the CL factors f_j are estimated by a volume-weighted average of individual development factors $F_{i,j+1} = C_{i,j+1}/C_{i,j}$.

ESTIMATOR 2.4 (CL estimator) *The CL estimator for $E\left[C_{i,j} \middle| \mathcal{D}_I \right]$ is given by*

$$\widehat{C_{i,j}}^{\mathrm{CL}} = \widehat{E}\left[C_{i,j} \middle| \mathcal{D}_I \right] = C_{i,I-i}\, \widehat{f}_{I-i} \cdots \widehat{f}_{j-1} \tag{2.5}$$

for $i+j>I$.

If we understand the CL method in a purely mechanical way, then (2.5) is the algorithm that leads to the CL reserves. (Note that this algorithm is often used without consideration of an appropriate underlying stochastic model.)

We define (see also Table 2.1)

$$\mathcal{B}_k = \{C_{i,j};\ i+j \le I, 0 \le j \le k\} \subseteq \mathcal{D}_I \tag{2.6}$$

In particular, we have $\mathcal{B}_J = \mathcal{D}_I$, which is the set of all observations at time I.

LEMMA 2.5 *Under Model Assumptions 2.1 we have*

(a) *given $\mathcal{B}_j$, $\widehat{f}_j$ is an unbiased estimator for f_j, i.e. $E\left[\widehat{f}_j \middle| \mathcal{B}_j\right] = f_j$;*

(b) *$\widehat{f}_j$ is (unconditionally) unbiased for f_j, i.e. $E\left[\widehat{f}_j\right] = f_j$;*

(c) *$E\left[\widehat{f}_0 \cdots \widehat{f}_j\right] = E\left[\widehat{f}_0\right] \cdots E\left[\widehat{f}_j\right]$, i.e. $\widehat{f}_0, \ldots, \widehat{f}_{J-1}$ are uncorrelated;*

(d) *given $C_{i,I-i}$, $\widehat{C_{i,J}}^{\mathrm{CL}}$ is an unbiased estimator for $E\left[C_{i,J} \middle| \mathcal{D}_I\right] = E\left[C_{i,J} \middle| C_{i,I-i}\right]$, i.e. $E\left[\widehat{C_{i,J}}^{\mathrm{CL}} \middle| C_{i,I-i}\right] = E\left[C_{i,J} \middle| \mathcal{D}_I\right]$; and*

(e) *$\widehat{C_{i,J}}^{\mathrm{CL}}$ is (unconditionally) unbiased for $E\left[C_{i,J}\right]$, i.e. $E\left[\widehat{C_{i,J}}^{\mathrm{CL}}\right] = E\left[C_{i,J}\right]$.*

Table 2.1 The set $\mathcal{B}_3$

Accident year i	Number of reported claims, non-cumulative according to reporting delay Reporting year j										
	0	1	2	3	4	5	6	7	8	9	10
0	368	191	28	8	6	5	3	1	0	0	1
1	393	151	25	6	4	5	4	1	2	1	0
2	517	185	29	17	11	10	8	1	0	0	1
3	578	254	49	22	17	6	3	0	1	0	0
4	622	206	39	16	3	7	0	1	0	0	0
5	660	243	28	12	12	4	4	1	0	0	0
6	666	234	53	10	8	4	6	1	0	0	0
7	573	266	62	12	5	7	6	5	1	0	1
8	582	281	32	27	12	13	6	2	1	0	
9	545	220	43	18	12	9	5	2	0		
10	509	266	49	22	15	4	8	0			
11	589	210	29	17	12	4	9				
12	564	196	23	12	9	5					
13	607	203	29	9	7						
14	674	169	20	12							
15	619	190	41								
16	660	161									
17	660										

Remarks 2.6

- At first sight, the uncorrelatedness of the CL estimators $\widehat{f}_j$ is surprising since neighbouring estimates of the age-to-age factors depend partly on the same data (once in the numerator and once in the denominator).
- We have proved in Lemma 2.5 that the age-to-age factor estimates $\widehat{f}_j$ are uncorrelated. However, this does **not** imply that they are independent. In fact, they are not independent, and one can show that the squares of two successive estimators $\widehat{f}_j$ and $\widehat{f}_{j+1}$ are negatively correlated (see Lemma 3.8 below). It is this negative correlation that will lead to a number of discussions related to estimation errors of our parameter estimates.
- Lemma 2.5(a) shows that the CL factors f_j are estimated by unbiased estimators $\widehat{f}_j$ (regardless of any underlying distributional assumption). This perfectly motivates the choice (2.4). Of course there are other unbiased estimators, but below we justify the choice of (2.4) because it satisfies an optimality criterion under certain variance assumptions (see Lemma 3.3).

- Observe that Lemma 2.5(d) shows that we obtain unbiased estimators $\widehat{C_{i,J}}^{\text{CL}}$ for the best estimates $E\left[C_{i,J}\middle|\mathcal{D}_I\right]$. This justifies the CL algorithm within the distribution-free CL model framework. In Chapter 3 we will study the properties of these unbiased estimators.

Proof of Lemma 2.5

(a) Using the measurability of $C_{i,j}$ w.r.t. $\mathcal{B}_j$, the independence of different accident years and assumption (2.1) we have

$$E\left[\widehat{f}_j\middle|\mathcal{B}_j\right]=\frac{\sum_{i=0}^{I-j-1}E\left[C_{i,j+1}\middle|\mathcal{B}_j\right]}{\sum_{i=0}^{I-j-1}C_{i,j}}=\frac{\sum_{i=0}^{I-j-1}C_{i,j}\,f_j}{\sum_{i=0}^{I-j-1}C_{i,j}}=f_j$$

This immediately implies the conditional unbiasedness.

(b) This follows immediately from (a).

(c) To show claim (c), consider

$$\begin{aligned}E\left[\widehat{f}_0\cdots\widehat{f}_j\right]&=E\left[E\left[\widehat{f}_0\cdots\widehat{f}_j\middle|\mathcal{B}_j\right]\right]=E\left[\widehat{f}_0\cdots\widehat{f}_{j-1}\,E\left[\widehat{f}_j\middle|\mathcal{B}_j\right]\right]\\&=E\left[\widehat{f}_0\cdots\widehat{f}_{j-1}\right]f_j=E\left[\widehat{f}_0\cdots\widehat{f}_{j-1}\right]E\left[\widehat{f}_j\right]\end{aligned}$$

Iteration of this procedure leads to claim (c).

(d) To show unbiasedness of the CL estimator, consider

$$\begin{aligned}E\left[\widehat{C_{i,J}}^{\text{CL}}\middle|C_{i,I-i}\right]&=E\left[C_{i,I-i}\,\widehat{f}_{I-i}\cdots\widehat{f}_{J-2}\,\widehat{f}_{J-1}\middle|C_{i,I-i}\right]\\&=E\left[C_{i,I-i}\,\widehat{f}_{I-i}\cdots\widehat{f}_{J-2}\,E\left[\widehat{f}_{J-1}\middle|\mathcal{B}_{J-1}\right]\middle|C_{i,I-i}\right]\\&=f_{J-1}\,E\left[\widehat{C_{i,J-1}}^{\text{CL}}\middle|C_{i,I-i}\right]\end{aligned}$$

Iteration of this procedure leads to

$$E\left[\widehat{C_{i,J}}^{CL}\middle|C_{i,I-i}\right]=C_{i,I-i}\,f_{I-i}\cdots f_{J-1}=E\left[C_{i,J}\middle|\mathcal{D}_I\right]$$

(e) This follows immediately from (d).

This completes the proof of the lemma. □

Let us close this section with an example.

Example 2.7 (CL method)

Remark The data set in this example (see Table 2.2) will be used throughout this book to illustrate and compare different claims reserving methods. However, one should always be aware of the fact that it is very unlikely that the same data set will provide the realization of different stochastic models (since they have in general different mathematical properties).

Applying the CL Estimator 2.4 to the data set leads to the CL reserves given in Table 2.3. □

Table 2.2 Observed historical cumulative claims $C_{i,j}$ and estimated CL factors $\widehat{f}_j$

	0	1	2	3	4	5	6	7	8	9
0	5 946 975	9 668 212	10 563 929	10 771 690	10 978 394	11 040 518	11 106 331	11 121 181	11 132 310	11 148 124
1	6 346 756	9 593 162	10 316 383	10 468 180	10 536 004	10 572 608	10 625 360	10 636 546	10 648 192	
2	6 269 090	9 245 313	10 092 366	10 355 134	10 507 837	10 573 282	10 626 827	10 635 751		
3	5 863 015	8 546 239	9 268 771	9 459 424	9 592 399	9 680 740	9 724 068			
4	5 778 885	8 524 114	9 178 009	9 451 404	9 681 692	9 786 916				
5	6 184 793	9 013 132	9 585 897	9 830 796	9 935 753					
6	5 600 184	8 493 391	9 056 505	9 282 022						
7	5 288 066	7 728 169	8 256 211							
8	5 290 793	7 648 729								
9	5 675 568									
$\widehat{f}_j$	1.4925	1.0778	1.0229	1.0148	1.0070	1.0051	1.0011	1.0010	1.0014	

Table 2.3 Predicted cumulative CL claims $\widehat{C_{i,j}}^{\text{CL}}$ and CL reserves $\widehat{C_{i,J}}^{\text{CL}} - C_{i,I-i}$

	0	1	2	3	4	5	6	7	8	9	CL reserves
0											0
1										10 663 318	15 126
2									10 646 884	10 662 008	26 257
3								9 734 574	9 744 764	9 758 606	34 538
4							9 837 277	9 847 906	9 858 214	9 872 218	85 302
5						10 005 044	10 056 528	10 067 393	10 077 931	10 092 247	156 494
6					9 419 776	9 485 469	9 534 279	9 544 580	9 554 571	9 568 143	286 121
7				8 445 057	8 570 389	8 630 159	8 674 568	8 683 940	8 693 030	8 705 378	449 167
8			8 243 496	8 432 051	8 557 190	8 616 868	8 661 208	8 670 566	8 679 642	8 691 971	1 043 242
9		8 470 989	9 129 696	9 338 521	9 477 113	9 543 206	9 592 313	9 602 676	9 612 728	9 626 383	3 950 815
										Total	6 047 061

2.2 BORNHUETTER–FERGUSON METHOD

The BF method is, in general, a very robust method since it does not consider outliers in the observations. We will further comment on this in Chapter 4. The method goes back to Bornhuetter and Ferguson (1972) who published this method in a famous article called 'The Actuary and IBNR'.

The BF method is usually understood as a purely mechanical algorithm to estimate reserves (this is also how it was published in Bornhuetter and Ferguson 1972). There are several possibilities to define an appropriate underlying stochastic model which motivates the BF method. For example, it is easy to verify that the assumptions below are consistent with the BF method.

In Section 6.6 we provide an approach for the estimation of the conditional prediction error of the BF method.

Model Assumptions 2.8

- Cumulative claims $C_{i,j}$ of different accident years i are independent.
- There exist parameters $\mu_0, \ldots, \mu_I > 0$ and a pattern $\beta_0, \ldots, \beta_J > 0$ with $\beta_J = 1$ such that for all $0 \le i \le I$, $0 \le j \le J-1$ and $1 \le k \le J-j$ we have

$$E[C_{i,0}] = \beta_0 \, \mu_i$$

$$E[C_{i,j+k} | C_{i,0}, \ldots, C_{i,j}] = C_{i,j} + \left(\beta_{j+k} - \beta_j\right) \, \mu_i$$

□

Under Model Assumptions 2.8 we have

$$E[C_{i,j}] = \beta_j \, \mu_i \quad \text{and} \quad E[C_{i,J}] = \mu_i$$

The sequence $\left(\beta_j\right)_{j=0,\ldots,J}$ denotes the claims development pattern. If $C_{i,j}$ are cumulative payments, then $\left(\beta_j\right)_j$ reflects the cumulative cashflow pattern (also called the payout pattern). Such a pattern is often used when one needs to build market-consistent/discounted reserves, where time values differ over time (see also Subsection 1.1.2 on inflation).

Based on these discussions we see that Model Assumptions 2.8 imply the following assumptions.

Model Assumptions 2.9

- Cumulative claims $C_{i,j}$ of different accident years i are independent.
- There exist parameters $\mu_0, \ldots, \mu_I > 0$ and a pattern $\beta_0, \ldots, \beta_J > 0$ with $\beta_J = 1$ such that for all $0 \le i \le I$ and $0 \le j \le J$ we have

$$E[C_{i,j}] = \beta_j \, \mu_i \tag{2.7}$$

□

Note that Model Assumptions 2.8 are stronger than Model Assumptions 2.9. Often the BF method is explained with the help of Model Assumptions 2.9 (see, e.g., Radtke and Schmidt

2004, pp. 37ff). However, with Model Assumptions 2.9 we face some difficulties to justify the BF algorithm. Observe that

$$\begin{aligned} E\left[C_{i,J}\middle|\mathcal{D}_I\right] &= E[C_{i,J}|C_{i,0},\ldots,C_{i,I-i}] \\ &= C_{i,I-i} + E\left[C_{i,J} - C_{i,I-i}\middle|C_{i,0},\ldots,C_{i,I-i}\right] \end{aligned} \tag{2.8}$$

If we have no additional assumptions on the dependence structure between incremental claims, we do not exactly know what we should do with the last term in (2.8). If we knew that the incremental claim $C_{i,J} - C_{i,I-i}$ was independent of $C_{i,0},\ldots,C_{i,I-i}$, then this would imply that

$$\begin{aligned} E\left[C_{i,J}\middle|\mathcal{D}_I\right] &= E[C_{i,J}|C_{i,0},\ldots,C_{i,I-i}] \\ &= C_{i,I-i} + E\left[C_{i,J} - C_{i,I-i}\right] \\ &= C_{i,I-i} + (1-\beta_{I-i})\ \mu_i \end{aligned} \tag{2.9}$$

which also follows from Model Assumptions 2.8.

Under both model assumptions, it remains to estimate the last term on the right-hand side of (2.8) and (2.9). In the BF method this is done as follows:

ESTIMATOR 2.10 (BF estimator) *The BF estimator for* $E\left[C_{i,J}\middle|\mathcal{D}_I\right]$ *is given by*

$$\widehat{C_{i,J}}^{\mathrm{BF}} = \widehat{E}\left[C_{i,J}\middle|\mathcal{D}_I\right] = C_{i,I-i} + \left(1-\widehat{\beta}_{I-i}\right)\ \widehat{\mu}_i \tag{2.10}$$

for $1 \le i \le I$, *where* $\widehat{\beta}_{I-i}$ *is an appropriate estimate for* β_{I-i} *and* $\widehat{\mu}_i$ *is a prior estimate for the expected ultimate claim* $E[C_{i,J}]$.

If we understand the BF method in a purely mechanical way, then (2.10) is the algorithm that leads to the BF reserves (note that this algorithm is often used without considering an appropriate underlying stochastic model). The crucial question then is: How should we determine the estimators $\widehat{\beta}_j$ and $\widehat{\mu}_i$?

Comparison of BF and CL Estimators

From the CL Model Assumptions 2.1 we have

$$E[C_{i,j}] = E\left[E\left[C_{i,j}|C_{i,j-1}\right]\right] = f_{j-1}\ E[C_{i,j-1}] = E[C_{i,0}]\ \prod_{k=0}^{j-1} f_k$$

$$E[C_{i,J}] = E[C_{i,0}]\ \prod_{k=0}^{J-1} f_k$$

which implies that

$$E[C_{i,j}] = \prod_{k=j}^{J-1} f_k^{-1}\ E[C_{i,J}]$$

If we compare this to the BF Model 2.9 (cf. (2.7)), we find that

$$\prod_{k=j}^{J-1} f_k^{-1} \quad \text{'plays the role of'} \quad \beta_j \tag{2.11}$$

since $\prod_{k=j}^{J-1} f_k^{-1}$ describes the proportion of $\mu_i = E\left[C_{i,J}\right]$ already paid after j development periods, assuming the CL model. Therefore, the two variables in (2.11) are often related to each other and used as equals. This can be done with Model Assumptions 2.9, but not under Model Assumptions 2.8 (since Model Assumptions 2.8 are not implied by the CL assumptions, nor vice versa). That is, if one knows the CL factors f_j, one constructs a development pattern $(\beta_j)_j$ using an identity in (2.11) and vice versa. Then, the BF estimator can be interpreted as follows:

$$\widehat{C_{i,J}}^{\mathrm{BF}} = C_{i,I-i} + \left(1 - \left(\widehat{\frac{1}{\prod_{j=I-i}^{J-1} f_j}}\right)\right) \widehat{\mu}_i \tag{2.12}$$

On the other hand, for the CL estimator we have

$$\begin{aligned}
\widehat{C_{i,J}}^{\mathrm{CL}} &= C_{i,I-i} \prod_{j=I-i}^{J-1} \widehat{f}_j \\
&= C_{i,I-i} + C_{i,I-i} \left(\prod_{j=I-i}^{J-1} \widehat{f}_j - 1\right) \\
&= C_{i,I-i} + \frac{\widehat{C_{i,J}}^{\mathrm{CL}}}{\prod_{j=I-i}^{J-1} \widehat{f}_j} \left(\prod_{j=I-i}^{J-1} \widehat{f}_j - 1\right) \\
&= C_{i,I-i} + \left(1 - \frac{1}{\prod_{j=I-i}^{J-1} \widehat{f}_j}\right) \widehat{C_{i,J}}^{\mathrm{CL}}
\end{aligned} \tag{2.13}$$

Hence, if we identify the claims development pattern from the CL and BF methods, the difference between the methods is that for the BF method we completely believe in our prior estimate $\widehat{\mu}_i$, whereas in the CL method the prior estimate is replaced by the estimate $\widehat{C_{i,J}}^{CL}$ which is based only on observations. From this point of view the CL and BF methods constitute two extreme positions in the claims-reserving problem and a natural question is: How can we combine these two extreme views? This is the subject of Chapter 4.

Parameter Estimation

- For μ_i we need a prior estimate $\widehat{\mu}_i$. This is often a plan value from a strategic business plan or the value used for premium calculations. This value should be estimated before one has any observations, that is, it should be a pure prior estimate based on expert opinion.
- For the 'still-to-come' factor $(1 - \beta_{I-i})$, one should also use a prior estimate if one strictly applies the BF method. This should be done independently from the observations. However, in most practical applications, one deviates from the path of the pure BF method

and estimates the still-to-come factor from the data with the CL factor estimates. If $\widehat{f_k}$ denotes the CL factor estimates (2.4) for f_k (see also (2.11)), then we set

$$\widehat{\beta}_j^{(\mathrm{CL})} = \widehat{\beta}_j = \widehat{\left(\frac{1}{\prod_{k=j}^{J-1} f_k}\right)} = \prod_{k=j}^{J-1} \frac{1}{\widehat{f_k}} \tag{2.14}$$

In this case, the BF method and the CL method differ only in the choice of estimator for the ultimate claim $C_{i,J}$, that is, *a priori* estimate $\widehat{\mu}_i$ vs CL estimate $\widehat{C_{i,J}}^{\mathrm{CL}}$ because

$$\begin{aligned}\widehat{C_{i,J}}^{\mathrm{BF}} &= C_{i,I-i} + \left(1 - \widehat{\beta}_{I-i}^{(\mathrm{CL})}\right) \widehat{\mu}_i \\ \widehat{C_{i,J}}^{\mathrm{CL}} &= C_{i,I-i} + \left(1 - \widehat{\beta}_{I-i}^{(\mathrm{CL})}\right) \widehat{C_{i,J}}^{\mathrm{CL}}\end{aligned} \tag{2.15}$$

In Section 6.6 we provide an approach for the estimation of the conditional prediction error of the BF method if we use exactly this choice of $\left(\widehat{\beta}_j^{(CL)}\right)_j$ for the estimation of the claims development pattern $(\beta_j)_j$.

Example 2.11 (BF method)

In this example, we illustrate the BF method using the same data set as in Example 2.7, Table 2.2. Table 2.4 shows the BF reserve estimates as well as the corresponding CL estimates for comparison.

Table 2.4 Claims reserves from the BF method and the CL method

	Prior estimate		Estimator		BF reserves	CL reserves
i	$\widehat{\mu}_i$	$\widehat{\beta}_{I-i}^{(\mathrm{CL})}$ (%)	$\widehat{C_{i,J}}^{\mathrm{BF}}$	$\widehat{C_{i,J}}^{\mathrm{CL}}$		
0	11 653 101	100.0	11 148 124	11 148 124		
1	11 367 306	99.9	10 664 316	10 663 318	16 124	15 126
2	10 962 965	99.8	10 662 749	10 662 008	26 998	26 257
3	10 616 762	99.6	9 761 643	9 758 606	37 575	34 538
4	11 044 881	99.1	9 882 350	9 872 218	95 434	85 302
5	11 480 700	98.4	10 113 777	10 092 247	178 024	156 494
6	11 413 572	97.0	9 623 328	9 568 143	341 305	286 121
7	11 126 527	94.8	8 830 301	8 705 378	574 089	449 167
8	10 986 548	88.0	8 967 375	8 691 971	1 318 646	1 043 242
9	11 618 437	59.0	10 443 953	9 626 383	4 768 384	3 950 815
				Total	7 356 580	6 047 061

We can see from this example that the use of different methods can lead to substantial differences in the claims reserves. It seems that the prior estimate $\widehat{\mu}_i$ (expert opinion) is rather pessimistic/conservative compared to the CL estimate (in each year it is more conservative than the CL estimate). □

2.3 NUMBER OF IBNYR CLAIMS, POISSON MODEL

We close this chapter with the Poisson model, which is mainly used for claims counts. The Poisson model is the first claims reserving model we present that is based on explicit distributional choices. These distributional choices allow for the calculation of maximum likelihood (ML) estimators for the parameters that are then used for the estimation of the claims reserves.

The remarkable thing in the Poisson model is that the ML estimators lead to the same reserves as the CL algorithm (see Lemma 2.16). This goes back to Hachemeister and Stanard (1975), which was first published in German by Kremer (1985) and is found in the English literature in a paper by Mack (1991), Appendix A (see also Mack and Venter 2000 and Verrall and England 2000). The conclusions of these findings are that the Poisson model is an alternative stochastic model (in addion to the distribution-free CL Model 2.1) that can be used to motivate the CL reserves. Indeed, there is a controversial discussion about the choice of the 'right' stochastic model for the CL algorithm because various models can be used (which are based on rather different methodologies), see also Mack and Venter (2000) and Verrall and England (2000). The difference in the models turns out to be relevant, especially if we calculate higher moments. This will be highlighted in Chapters 3 and 6. Hence we derive different estimates in different models which, in common, result in reserve estimates that coincide.

Model Assumptions 2.12 (Poisson model)

There exist parameters $\mu_0, \ldots, \mu_I > 0$ and $\gamma_0, \ldots, \gamma_J > 0$ such that the incremental claims $X_{i,j}$ are independently Poisson distributed with

$$E[X_{i,j}] = \mu_i\, \gamma_j, \quad \text{for all} \quad 0 \le i \le I, 0 \le j \le J$$

and

$$\sum_{j=0}^{J} \gamma_j = 1 \qquad \square$$

For the definition of Poisson distribution, see Appendix A.1.2.

Note that the Poisson Model 2.12 immediately implies that the increments $X_{i,j}$ are non-negative. However, in many practical applications we also observe negative increments, which indicates that the Poisson model is not appropriate for these examples.

The cumulative claim in accident year i, $C_{i,J}$, is again Poisson distributed with

$$E[C_{i,J}] = \mu_i$$

Hence, μ_i is a parameter that stands for the total expected claim in accident year i (exposure), whereas γ_j defines an expected reporting/cashflow pattern over the different development periods j. Moreover, we have

$$\frac{E[X_{i,j}]}{E[X_{i,0}]} = \frac{\gamma_j}{\gamma_0}$$

which is independent of i.

LEMMA 2.13 *The Poisson model satisfies Model Assumptions 2.8.*

Proof The independence of cumulative claims of different accident years follows from the independence of $X_{i,j}$. Moreover, we have $E\left[C_{i,0}\right] = E\left[X_{i,0}\right] = \mu_i\ \beta_0$ with $\beta_0 = \gamma_0$, and

$$
\begin{aligned}
E\left[C_{i,j+k}\middle| C_{i,0}, \ldots, C_{i,j}\right] &= C_{i,j} + \sum_{l=1}^{k} E\left[X_{i,j+l}\middle| C_{i,0}, \ldots, C_{i,j}\right] \\
&= C_{i,j} + \mu_i\ \sum_{l=1}^{k} \gamma_{j+l}\ =\ C_{i,j} + \mu_i\ (\beta_{j+k} - \beta_j)
\end{aligned}
$$

with $\beta_j = \sum_{l=0}^{j} \gamma_l$. This completes the proof. □

This means that the Poisson model satisfies the assumptions for the BF method. Henceforth, we could use the BF estimator for the determination of claims reserves in the Poisson model. Here, we choose a different route. There are different methods for estimating parameters $(\mu_i)_i$ and $(\gamma_j)_j$. One possibility is to use the maximum likelihood (ML) estimators. The likelihood function on the set of observations

$$
\mathcal{D}_I = \{X_{i,j};\ i + j \leq I, 0 \leq j \leq J\}
$$

is given by

$$
L_{\mathcal{D}_I}(\mu_0, \ldots, \mu_I, \gamma_0, \ldots, \gamma_J) = \prod_{i+j \leq I} \left(\exp\left(-\mu_i \gamma_j\right) \frac{(\mu_i\ \gamma_j)^{X_{i,j}}}{X_{i,j}!} \right)
$$

We maximize the log-likelihood function by setting to zero its $I + J + 2$ partial derivatives w.r.t. the unknown parameters μ_i and γ_j. Thus, we obtain on $\mathcal{D}_I$ the ML estimators from

$$
\sum_{j=0}^{I-i} \widehat{\mu}_i\ \widehat{\gamma}_j = \sum_{j=0}^{I-i} X_{i,j}\ =\ C_{i,I-i} \tag{2.16}
$$

$$
\sum_{i=0}^{I-j} \widehat{\mu}_i\ \widehat{\gamma}_j = \sum_{i=0}^{I-j} X_{i,j} \tag{2.17}
$$

for all $i \in \{0, \ldots, I\}$ and $j \in \{0, \ldots, J\}$ under the constraint that $\sum_{j=0}^{J} \widehat{\gamma}_j = 1$. If this system of equations has a unique solution, it gives us the ML estimates $\widehat{\mu}_i$ and $\widehat{\gamma}_j$ for μ_i and γ_j, respectively.

ESTIMATOR 2.14 (Poisson ML estimator) *The ML estimators in the Poisson Model 2.12 for $E[X_{i,j}]$ and $E\left[C_{i,J}\middle|\mathcal{D}_I\right]$ are given by*

$$
\begin{aligned}
\widehat{X_{i,j}}^{\text{Poi}} &= \widehat{E}[X_{i,j}]\ =\ \widehat{\mu}_i\ \widehat{\gamma}_j \\
\widehat{C_{i,J}}^{\text{Poi}} &= \widehat{E}\left[C_{i,J}\middle|\mathcal{D}_I\right]\ =\ C_{i,I-i} + \sum_{j=I-i+1}^{J} \widehat{X_{i,j}}^{\text{Poi}}
\end{aligned}
$$

for $i+j>I$.

Observe that

$$\widehat{C_{i,J}}^{\text{Poi}} = C_{i,I-i} + \left(1 - \sum_{j=0}^{I-i} \widehat{\gamma}_j\right) \widehat{\mu}_i = \widehat{\mu}_i \tag{2.18}$$

hence the Poisson ML estimator has the same form as the BF Estimator 2.10. However, here we will use the ML estimates for μ_i and γ_j that depend on the data $\mathcal{D}_I$.

Example 2.15 (Poisson ML estimator)

We revisit the example given in Table 2.2 (see Example 2.7). Table 2.5 shows the data $\mathcal{D}_I$, that is, the incremental claims $X_{i,j} = C_{i,j} - C_{i,j-1} \geq 0$ for $i+j \leq I$. Solving the system of equations (2.16)–(2.17) gives the ML estimators (see Table 2.6) and the corresponding estimates $\widehat{C_{i,J}}^{\text{Poi}} - C_{i,I-i}$ for the reserves.

Remark The estimated reserves are the same as in the CL model for cumulative data. We prove that this is not just a coincidence for this data set but holds true in general (see Lemma 2.16 below).

Moreover, note that the system of equations (2.16)–(2.17) cannot always be solved easily. In the present case it can be solved easily (see Corollary 2.18) but more general systems of equations can only be solved numerically. For more details on this subject we refer to Chapter 6. □

2.4 POISSON DERIVATION OF THE CL ALGORITHM

In this section we show that the Poisson model (Section 2.3) leads to the CL estimates for the reserves. We assume throughout this section that there is a positive solution to (2.16)–(2.17).

LEMMA 2.16 *The CL Estimator 2.4 and the ML Estimator 2.14 in the Poisson Model 2.12 lead to the same reserve estimates, i.e.* $\widehat{C_{i,J}}^{\text{CL}} = \widehat{C_{i,J}}^{\text{Poi}}$.

In fact, the Poisson ML model/estimator defined in Section 2.3 gives the reserves from the CL algorithm (see formula (2.20)). Moreover, the ML estimators lead to estimators for the age-to-age factors f_j which are the same as in the distribution-free CL model. Therefore, as already mentioned above, we have found two different stochastic motivations for the CL algorithm.

Proof of Lemma 2.16 The Poisson Estimator 2.14 is given by, $i>0$,

$$\widehat{C_{i,J}}^{\text{Poi}} = \widehat{E}\left[C_{i,J} | \mathcal{D}_I\right] = \widehat{\mu}_i \sum_{j=I-i+1}^{J} \widehat{\gamma}_j + C_{i,I-i} = \widehat{\mu}_i \sum_{j=0}^{J} \widehat{\gamma}_j$$

Table 2.5 Observed historical incremental claims $X_{i,j}$

	0	1	2	3	4	5	6	7	8	9
0	5 946 975	3 721 237	895 717	207 760	206 704	62 124	65 813	14 850	11 130	15 813
1	6 346 756	3 246 406	723 222	151 797	67 824	36 603	52 752	11 186	11 646	
2	6 269 090	2 976 223	847 053	262 768	152 703	65 444	53 545	8924		
3	5 863 015	2 683 224	722 532	190 653	132 976	88 340	43 329			
4	5 778 885	2 745 229	653 894	273 395	230 288	105 224				
5	6 184 793	2 828 338	572 765	244 899	104 957					
6	5 600 184	2 893 207	563 114	225 517						
7	5 288 066	2 440 103	528 043							
8	5 290 793	2 357 936								
9	5 675 568									

Table 2.6 Estimated $\widehat{\mu}_i$, $\widehat{\gamma}_j$, incremental claims $\widehat{X_{i,j}}^{\text{Poi}}$ and Poisson reserves

	0	1	2	3	4	5	6	7	8	9	$\widehat{\mu}_i$		Poisson reserves
0											11 148 124		
1										15 126	10 663 318		15 126
2									11 133	15 124	10 662 008		26 257
3								10 506	10 190	13 842	9 758 606		34 538
4							50 361	10 628	10 308	14 004	9 872 218		85 302
5						69 291	51 484	10 865	10 538	14 316	10 092 247		156 494
6					137 754	65 693	48 810	10 301	9991	13 572	9 568 143		286 121
7				188 846	125 332	59 769	44 409	9372	9090	12 348	8 705 378		449 167
8			594 767	188 555	125 139	59 677	44 341	9358	9076	12 329	8 691 972		1 043 242
9		2 795 422	658 707	208 825	138 592	66 093	49 107	10 364	10 052	13 655	9 626 383		3 950 815
$\widehat{\gamma}_j$	58.96%	29.04%	6.84%	2.17%	1.44%	0.69%	0.51%	0.11%	0.10%	0.14%		Total	6 047 061

where in the last step we have used (2.16). Using (2.16) once more we find that

$$\widehat{C_{i,J}}^{\text{Poi}} = \widehat{E}\left[C_{i,J}|\mathcal{D}_I\right] = C_{i,I-i}\,\frac{\sum_{j=0}^{J}\widehat{\gamma}_j}{\sum_{j=0}^{I-i}\widehat{\gamma}_j} \tag{2.19}$$

This last formula can be rewritten, introducing additional factors

$$\widehat{C_{i,J}}^{\text{Poi}} = C_{i,I-i}\,\frac{\sum_{j=0}^{J}\widehat{\gamma}_j}{\sum_{j=0}^{I-i}\widehat{\gamma}_j} = C_{i,I-i}\,\frac{\sum_{j=0}^{I-i+1}\widehat{\gamma}_j}{\sum_{j=0}^{I-i}\widehat{\gamma}_j}\cdots\frac{\sum_{j=0}^{J}\widehat{\gamma}_j}{\sum_{j=0}^{J-1}\widehat{\gamma}_j} \tag{2.20}$$

If we use Lemma 2.17 below, we see that on $\mathcal{D}_I$ we have

$$\sum_{i=0}^{I-j} C_{i,j} = \sum_{i=0}^{I-j}\widehat{\mu}_i\,\sum_{k=0}^{j}\widehat{\gamma}_k \tag{2.21}$$

Moreover, using (2.17), we have

$$\sum_{i=0}^{I-j} C_{i,j-1} = \sum_{i=0}^{I-j}\left(C_{i,j}-X_{i,j}\right) = \sum_{i=0}^{I-j}\widehat{\mu}_i\,\sum_{k=0}^{j-1}\widehat{\gamma}_k \tag{2.22}$$

But (2.21)–(2.22) immediately imply that for $j \le J$

$$\frac{\sum_{k=0}^{j}\widehat{\gamma}_k}{\sum_{k=0}^{j-1}\widehat{\gamma}_k} = \frac{\sum_{i=0}^{I-j} C_{i,j}}{\sum_{i=0}^{I-j} C_{i,j-1}} = \widehat{f}_{j-1}$$

Hence, from (2.20), we obtain

$$\begin{aligned}\widehat{C_{i,J}}^{\text{Poi}} &= C_{i,I-i}\,\frac{\sum_{k=0}^{I-(I-i+1)} C_{k,I-i+1}}{\sum_{k=0}^{I-(I-i+1)} C_{k,I-i}}\cdots\frac{\sum_{k=0}^{I-J} C_{k,J}}{\sum_{k=0}^{I-J} C_{k,J-1}}\\ &= C_{i,I-i}\,\widehat{f}_{I-i}\cdots\widehat{f}_{J-1} = \widehat{C_{i,J}}^{\text{CL}}\end{aligned} \tag{2.23}$$

which is the CL estimate (2.4). This completes the proof of Lemma 2.16. □

Hence, it remains to prove the following lemma. The proof of the lemma explains how the set $[0, I-j]\times[0, j]$ is related to $[0, I-j+1]\times[0, j-1]$. This means that, in view of (2.16)–(2.17), we add one accident year, namely $I-j+1$, but we also subtract one development year, namely j.

LEMMA 2.17 *Under Model Assumptions 2.12 on $\mathcal{D}_I$ we have that*

$$\sum_{i=0}^{I-j} C_{i,j} = \sum_{i=0}^{I-j}\widehat{\mu}_i\,\sum_{k=0}^{j}\widehat{\gamma}_k \tag{2.24}$$

Proof We prove this by induction. Using (2.16) for $i=0$ and $I=J$ we get

$$C_{0,J} = \sum_{j=0}^{J} X_{0,j} = \widehat{\mu}_0\,\sum_{j=0}^{J}\widehat{\gamma}_j$$

which is the starting point of our induction ($j=J=I$ in (2.24)).

Induction step $j \to j-1$. Using (2.16)–(2.17) and the induction assumption in the second step we get (using the geometric argument mentioned before the lemma)

$$\sum_{i=0}^{I-(j-1)} C_{i,j-1} = \sum_{i=0}^{I-j} C_{i,j} - \sum_{i=0}^{I-j} X_{i,j} + \sum_{k=0}^{j-1} X_{I-j+1,k}$$
$$= \sum_{i=0}^{I-j} \widehat{\mu}_i \sum_{k=0}^{j} \widehat{\gamma}_k - \widehat{\gamma}_j \sum_{i=0}^{I-j} \widehat{\mu}_i + \widehat{\mu}_{I-j+1} \sum_{k=0}^{j-1} \widehat{\gamma}_k$$

Hence, we find that

$$\sum_{i=0}^{I-(j-1)} C_{i,j-1} = \sum_{i=0}^{I-j} \widehat{\mu}_i \sum_{k=0}^{j-1} \widehat{\gamma}_k + \widehat{\mu}_{I-j+1} \sum_{k=0}^{j-1} \widehat{\gamma}_k = \sum_{i=0}^{I-(j-1)} \widehat{\mu}_i \sum_{k=0}^{j-1} \widehat{\gamma}_k$$

which proves the claim (2.24). □

COROLLARY 2.18 *Under Model Assumptions 2.12 we have (see also* (2.14)*)*

$$\sum_{k=0}^{j} \widehat{\gamma}_k = \widehat{\beta}_j^{(\mathrm{CL})} = \prod_{k=j}^{J-1} \frac{1}{\widehat{f}_k}$$

for all $0 \leq j \leq J$ *(the empty product is equal to* 1*).*

Proof From (2.19) and (2.23) we obtain for all $i \geq 0$

$$C_{i,I-i} \frac{\sum_{j=0}^{J} \widehat{\gamma}_j}{\sum_{j=0}^{I-i} \widehat{\gamma}_j} = \widehat{C_{i,J}}^{\mathrm{Poi}} = \widehat{C_{i,J}}^{\mathrm{CL}} = C_{i,I-i} \, \widehat{f}_{I-i} \cdots \widehat{f}_{J-1}$$

Since $\sum_{j=0}^{J} \widehat{\gamma}_j = 1$ is normalized, we get

$$1 = \sum_{j=0}^{I-i} \widehat{\gamma}_j \prod_{j=I-i}^{J-1} \widehat{f}_j = \sum_{j=0}^{I-i} \widehat{\gamma}_j \left(\widehat{\beta}_{I-i}^{(\mathrm{CL})}\right)^{-1}$$

which proves the claim. □

Remarks 2.19

- Corollary 2.18 says that the distribution-free CL method and the Poisson model lead to the same development/cashflow pattern $\left(\widehat{\beta}_j^{(\mathrm{CL})}\right)_j$ (and hence to the same BF reserve if we use this development pattern for the estimate of $(\beta_j)_j$). Henceforth, if we use the development pattern $\left(\widehat{\beta}_j^{(\mathrm{CL})}\right)_j$ for the BF method, the BF method and the Poisson model only differ in the choice of the expected ultimate claim μ_i, since with (2.18) we obtain that

$$\widehat{C_{i,J}}^{\mathrm{Poi}} = C_{i,I-i} + \left(1 - \widehat{\beta}_{I-i}^{(\mathrm{CL})}\right) \widehat{\mu}_i$$

  where $\widehat{\mu}_i$ is the ML estimate given in (2.16)–(2.17). This needs to be compared to (2.15).

- Observe that we have to solve a system of linear equations (2.16)–(2.17) to obtain the ML estimates $\widehat{\mu}_i$ and $\widehat{\gamma}_j$. This solution can easily be obtained with the help of the CL factors $\widehat{f}_k$ (see Corollary 2.18), namely

$$\widehat{\gamma}_j = \widehat{\beta}_j^{(\mathrm{CL})} - \widehat{\beta}_{j-1}^{(\mathrm{CL})} = \prod_{k=j}^{J-1} \frac{1}{\widehat{f}_k} \left(1 - \frac{1}{\widehat{f}_{j-1}}\right)$$

and

$$\widehat{\mu}_i = \sum_{j=0}^{I-i} X_{i,j} \Bigg/ \sum_{j=0}^{I-i} \widehat{\gamma}_j = C_{i,I-i} / \widehat{\beta}_{I-i}^{(\mathrm{CL})} = \widehat{C}_{i,J}^{\mathrm{CL}}$$

In Chapter 6 we will see other ML methods and GLM models where the solution of the equations is more complicated, and where one applies numerical methods to find solutions.

- Note that the distribution-free CL model can, in some sense, be applied to more general data sets than the Poisson ML method. The Poisson model (strictly) applies only if all incremental claims $X_{i,j}$ are positive since the Poisson distribution relates to non-negative natural numbers. The distribution-free CL model also applies for negative increments, as long as cumulative claims stay positive.

3 Chain-Ladder Models

3.1 MEAN SQUARE ERROR OF PREDICTION

In the previous chapter we have (only) given an estimate for the mean/expected ultimate claim. Of course, we would also like to know how good this estimate predicts the outcomes of random variables. In order to analyse such questions we need to introduce stochastic models. This means that we could have omitted stochastic models in Chapter 2 and could have viewed the reserving techniques as simple deterministic algorithms for estimating reserves. As soon as we want to quantify the accuracy of these estimates we need an appropriate stochastic framework. This was the reason for introducing stochastic models from the beginning.

Assume that we have a non-life insurance company with, for example, total claims reserves of 6 047 061 and a profit-and-loss statement similar to that shown in Table 3.1. Hence, we have an earning statement that is only slightly positive (+60 000). If we decrease the claims reserves by 1%, the income before taxes is just twice the original value, namely +120 000. Henceforth, only a slight decrease of the claims reserves may have an enormous effect on the earning statement due to the large volume that is behind the reserves. Therefore, it is very important to know the uncertainties in the estimates for the claims reserves.

Table 3.1 Earning statement

		Earning statement at 31 December
(a)	Premium earned	4 020 000
(b)	Claims incurred current accident year	−3 340 000
(c)	Loss experience prior accident years	−40 000
(d)	Underwriting and other expenses	−1 090 000
(e)	Investment income	510 000
	Income before taxes	60 000

To measure the quality of the estimated claims reserves (the predicted outstanding claims liabilities, respectively) we consider second moments. This means that we calculate the so-called mean square error of prediction (MSEP) that we will now define.

Assume that we have a random variable X and a set of observations $\mathcal{D}$. Then we assume that $\widehat{X}$ is a $\mathcal{D}$-measurable estimator for $E[X|\mathcal{D}]$ and a $\mathcal{D}$-measurable predictor for X, respectively.

DEFINITION 3.1 (conditional MSEP) *The conditional MSEP of the predictor $\widehat{X}$ for X is defined by*

$$\mathrm{msep}_{X|\mathcal{D}}(\widehat{X}) = E\left[\left(\widehat{X} - X\right)^2 \middle| \mathcal{D}\right]$$

For a $\mathcal{D}$-measurable estimator/predictor $\widehat{X}$ we have

$$\mathrm{msep}_{X|\mathcal{D}}(\widehat{X}) = \mathrm{Var}\,(X|\,\mathcal{D}) + \left(\widehat{X} - E\,[X|\mathcal{D}]\right)^2 \tag{3.1}$$

The first term on the right-hand side of (3.1) is the so-called conditional process variance (stochastic error), which describes the variation within the stochastic model (this is the pure randomness that cannot be eliminated). The second term on the right-hand side of (3.1) is the parameter estimation error, which reflects the uncertainty in the estimation of the parameters and the (conditional) expectation, respectively. In general, this estimation error becomes smaller the more observations we have, but keep in mind that in many practical situations it does not completely disappear, since we try to predict future expected behaviour based on past information. Even a slight change in the model over time causes lots of problems and questions about how past observations can be transformed to give information for future behaviour. That is, this transformation adds an additional source of uncertainty, which is further discussed in Section 3.4.

In order to find the parameter estimation error, we need to explicitly calculate the last term in (3.1). However, this can only be done if $E\,[X|\mathcal{D}]$ is known, but of course this term is generally not known (we estimate it by $\widehat{X}$); therefore, the derivation of an estimate for the parameter estimation error is quite sophisticated. One way to assess the quality of $\widehat{X}$ is to study its possible fluctuations around $E\,[X|\mathcal{D}]$.

- **Case 1** Assume that X is independent of $\mathcal{D}$. This is the case, for example, where we have i.i.d. experiments and we want to estimate their average outcome. In that case we have

  $$E\,[X|\mathcal{D}] = E[X] \quad \text{and} \quad \mathrm{Var}\,(X|\,\mathcal{D}) = \mathrm{Var}\,(X)$$

  If we consider the unconditional MSEP for the estimator/predictor $\widehat{X}$, we obtain

  $$\mathrm{msep}_X(\widehat{X}) = E\left[\mathrm{msep}_{X|\mathcal{D}}(\widehat{X})\right] = \mathrm{Var}\,(X) + E\left[\left(\widehat{X} - E\,[X]\right)^2\right]$$

  and, if $\widehat{X}$ is an unbiased estimator for $E[X]$, that is, $E[\widehat{X}] = E[X]$, we have

  $$\mathrm{msep}_X(\widehat{X}) = \mathrm{Var}\,(X) + \mathrm{Var}(\widehat{X})$$

  Hence, the parameter estimation error is estimated by the variance of $\widehat{X}$ (the average parameter estimation error).

  Example

  Assume that X and $X_1, \ldots, X_n$ are i.i.d. with mean μ and variance $\sigma^2 < \infty$. Then, for the estimator $\widehat{X} = 1/n\ \sum_{i=1}^n X_i$ we have

  $$\mathrm{msep}_{X|\mathcal{D}}(\widehat{X}) = \sigma^2 + \left(\frac{1}{n}\sum_{i=1}^n X_i - \mu\right)^2$$

  By the strong law of large numbers we know that the last term disappears a.s. for $n \to \infty$. In order to determine this term for finite n, one needs to explicitly calculate the distance between $1/n \sum_{i=1}^{n} X_i$ and μ. However, since in general μ is not known, we can only give an estimate for that distance. If we calculate the unconditional MSEP, we obtain

$$\mathrm{msep}_X(\widehat{X}) = \sigma^2 + \frac{\sigma^2}{n}$$

Henceforth, we can say that the deviation of $1/n \sum_{i=1}^{n} X_i$ around μ is in the average of order $\sigma/\sqrt{n}$. But unfortunately this does not tell us anything about the parameter estimation error for a specific realization of $1/n \sum_{i=1}^{n} X_i$. We will further discuss this issue below.

- **Case 2** Assume that X is not independent of the observations $\mathcal{D}$. Below we present several time series examples in which we do not assume independence between different observations. One example is the distribution-free version of the CL method, which models the time series through link ratios.

  In all these cases the situation becomes more complicated. Observe that the unconditional MSEP is given by

$$\begin{aligned}
\mathrm{msep}_X(\widehat{X}) &= E\left[\mathrm{msep}_{X|\mathcal{D}}(\widehat{X})\right] \\
&= E\left[\mathrm{Var}(X|\mathcal{D})\right] + E\left[\left(\widehat{X} - E[X|\mathcal{D}]\right)^2\right] \\
&= \mathrm{Var}(X) - \mathrm{Var}(E[X|\mathcal{D}]) + E\left[\left(\widehat{X} - E[X|\mathcal{D}]\right)^2\right] \\
&= \mathrm{Var}(X) + E\left[\left(\widehat{X} - E[X]\right)^2\right] \\
&\quad - 2\, E\left[\left(\widehat{X} - E[X]\right)\, \left(E[X|\mathcal{D}] - E[X]\right)\right]
\end{aligned}$$

  If the estimator $\widehat{X}$ is unbiased for $E[X]$, we obtain

$$\mathrm{msep}_X(\widehat{X}) = \mathrm{Var}(X) + \mathrm{Var}(\widehat{X}) - 2\,\mathrm{Cov}\left(\widehat{X}, E[X|\mathcal{D}]\right)$$

  This again tells us something about the average estimation error, but it does not tell us anything about the quality of the estimate $\widehat{X}$ for a specific realization.

Remark

In the following we measure the quality of the estimators and predictors for the ultimate claim/outstanding liabilities by means of second moments such as the (conditional) MSEP and the (conditional) coefficient of variation. However, the 'holy grail' of stochastic claims reserving would be to derive the whole predictive distribution of the claims reserves (cf. England and Verrall 2007, p. 221). Unfortunately, in most cases one is not able to calculate the predictive distribution analytically (see Subsections 4.2.3 and 4.3.1 for two exceptions) and one is forced to adopt numerical algorithms such as Bootstrapping methods (see Chapter 7) and Markov Chain Monte Carlo methods (see Section 4.4) to produce a simulated predictive distribution for the claims reserves. Endowed with the simulated predictive distribution, one is not only able to calculate estimates for the first two moments of the claims reserves but can also derive prediction intervals, quantiles (e.g. Value-at-Risk, see McNeil *et al.* 2005) and risk measures such as the expected shortfall. However, in practical application and solvency considerations, estimates for second moments such as the (conditional) MSEP and its components of (conditional) process variance/estimation error as well as the (conditional) coefficient of variation are often sufficient, since then in most cases one fits an analytic overall distribution using these first two moments. In our opinion analytic solutions (also only for second moments) are important because they allow for explicit interpretations in terms of the parameters involved. Moreover, these estimates are very easy to interpret and allow for sensitivity analysis with respect to parameter changes.

3.2 CHAIN-LADDER METHOD

We have already described the CL algorithm and method in Subsections 2.1 and 2.3. In actuarial literature, the CL method is often understood as a purely computational algorithm and leaves the question open as to which probabilistic model leads to that algorithm. An important cornerstone in the development of stochastic models underlying the CL method was made in 1982 by Kremer (1982). He points out that the parameterized model structure underpinning the CL method is identical to that of the linear statistical model involving a log response variable regressing on two non-interactive covariates (two-way analysis of variance).

Hachemeister and Stanard (1975), Kremer (1985) and Mack (1991) point out that the CL estimator of the ultimate claim can be obtained by maximizing a Poisson likelihood (cf. Lemma 2.16); Renshaw (1989) and Renshaw and Verrall (1998) relate the CL technique directly to generalized linear models (see Section 2.3 and Chapter 6 for generalized linear models); and Verrall (1989) gives a state space representation of the CL method and uses the Kalman filter to predict the ultimate claim.

Another important family of models that justify the CL algorithm are the so-called distribution-free CL models considered in Mack (1993), as well as Bayesian models presented in Gisler (2006) and Gisler and Wüthrich (2007) (cf. Section 9.2).

All these models are different from a stochastic point of view – that is, they have different mathematical properties. On the other hand, they have in common that they lead to the same reserves as the CL algorithm, either using maximum likelihood estimators, unbiased moment estimators or Bayesian estimators. In the present chapter we consider the distribution-free CL model for the description of the CL algorithm (see Mack 1993, Mack and Venter 2000 and Verrall and England 2000 for a discussion).

The CL method can be applied to cumulative payments, to claims incurred, etc. It is the method that is most commonly applied in practice because it is very simple, and by using appropriate estimates for the CL factors, one obtains reliable claims reserves. The main deficiencies of the CL method are:

- The homogeneity property needs to be satisfied; for example, there should be no trends in the development factors, otherwise the data has to be transformed or the run-off portfolio has to be subdivided into several subportfolios, such that each subportfolio satisfies the homogeneity property (see also the discussion at the beginning of Chapter 8).
- For estimating old development factors (f_j for large j) there is very little data available, which in practice may be no longer representative for more recent accident years

(i.e. i is large). For example, assume that we have a claims development with $J = 20$ (years) and $I = 2008$. Hence, we estimate with today's information (accident years < 2008) what will happen with claims of accident year 2008 in 20 years.

- The first observations of an accident year are sometimes not very representative for the claims development, which causes problems for more recent accident years. More general, in case there is an outlier on the last accounting diagonal, this outlier is projected right to the ultimate claim, which is not always appropriate. Therefore, for more recent accident years or in the case of a suspicious observation on the last accounting diagonal, sometimes the BF method is preferred (see also discussion in Section 2.2 and Subsection 4.3.2).
- In long-tailed branches/LoB, the difference between the CL method on cumulative payments and claims incurred is often very large. This is mainly due to the fact that the homogeneity property is not fulfilled. Indeed, if we have new phenomena in the data, methods based on claims incurred usually overestimate such effects, whereas estimates on paid data underestimate the effects since we only observe the new behaviour over time. This is usually because: (1) claims adjusters often overestimate new phenomena (which is reflected in the claims incurred figures); (2) in claims paid figures new phenomena are only observed over time (when a claim is settled via payments). In Section 9.1 we discuss a modification of the CL method which reduces the gap between the reserves estimates based on cumulative payments and reserves estimates based on claims incurred.
- There is an extensive list of references on how the CL method should be applied in practice and areas that require further research. We do not further discuss this here but only give two references (Lyons *et al.* 2002; Jones *et al.* 2006) that relate to such questions. Moreover, we should mention that there is also literature on the appropriateness of the CL method for specific data sets (see, e.g., Barnett and Zehnwirth 2000 and Venter 1998). This is also discussed in Chapter 11.

3.2.1 Mack Model (Distribution-Free CL Model)

A first (distribution-free) answer to the question of which stochastic model underlies the CL method was given by Mack (1993), and a first decisive step towards the derivation of estimates for the conditional MSEP was taken by Schnieper (1991), which is discussed in Section 10.2.

In addition to Model 2.1 we define the distribution-free CL model once more, but this time we extend the definition to include the second moments, so that we are also able to give an estimate for the conditional MSEP for the CL estimator (cf. Subsections 3.2.2–3.2.4).

Model Assumptions 3.2 (distribution-free CL model)

- Cumulative claims $C_{i,j}$ of different accident years i are independent.
- $(C_{i,j})_{j\geq 0}$ form a Markov chain. There exist factors $f_0, \ldots, f_{J-1} > 0$ and variance parameters $\sigma_0^2, \ldots, \sigma_{J-1}^2 > 0$ such that for all $0 \leq i \leq I$ and $1 \leq j \leq J$ we have

$$E\left[C_{i,j} \middle| C_{i,j-1}\right] = f_{j-1}\, C_{i,j-1} \tag{3.2}$$

$$\mathrm{Var}\left(C_{i,j} \middle| C_{i,j-1}\right) = \sigma_{j-1}^2\, C_{i,j-1} \tag{3.3}$$

□

Remark In Mack (1993), the Markov chain assumption is replaced by the weaker assumption only on the first two moments of $(C_{i,j})_{j\geq 0}$. The Markov property is not crucial but will simplify the derivations and notations in what follows. Note that we make no assumption on the explicit distribution of $C_{i,j}$ given $C_{i,j-1}$, all that we do are assumptions on the first two moments (and that cumulative claims $C_{i,j-1}$ are positive a.s., otherwise (3.3) does not make sense).

We recall the results from Section 2.1 (see Lemma 2.5):

- The parameters f_j and σ_j^2 are estimated by

$$\begin{aligned}\widehat{f}_j &= \frac{\sum_{i=0}^{I-j-1} C_{i,j+1}}{\sum_{i=0}^{I-j-1} C_{i,j}} = \sum_{i=0}^{I-j-1} \frac{C_{i,j}}{\sum_{k=0}^{I-j-1} C_{k,j}} \frac{C_{i,j+1}}{C_{i,j}} \\ \widehat{\sigma}_j^2 &= \frac{1}{I-j-1} \sum_{i=0}^{I-j-1} C_{i,j} \left(\frac{C_{i,j+1}}{C_{i,j}} - \widehat{f}_j\right)^2\end{aligned} \tag{3.4}$$

- given $\mathcal{B}_j$, $\widehat{f}_j$ is unconditionally and conditionally unbiased for f_j.
- $\widehat{f}_0, \ldots, \widehat{f}_{J-1}$ are uncorrelated.

If we denote the individual development factors by

$$F_{i,j+1} = \frac{C_{i,j+1}}{C_{i,j}} \tag{3.5}$$

then the age-to-age factor estimates $\widehat{f}_j$ are weighted averages of $F_{i,j+1}$, that is,

$$\widehat{f}_j = \sum_{i=0}^{I-j-1} \frac{C_{i,j}}{\sum_{k=0}^{I-j-1} C_{k,j}} F_{i,j+1} \tag{3.6}$$

Note, that $F_{i,j+1}$ are conditionally unbiased estimators for f_j, given $C_{i,j}$. The following lemma motivates the choice of (3.6).

LEMMA 3.3 *Under Model Assumptions 3.2, the estimator $\widehat{f}_j$ is a $\mathcal{B}_{j+1}$-measurable unbiased estimator for f_j, which has minimal conditional variance among all unbiased linear combinations of the unbiased estimators $(F_{i,j+1})_{0\leq i\leq I-j-1}$ for f_j, conditional on $\mathcal{B}_j$, i.e.*

$$\mathrm{Var}\left(\widehat{f}_j \middle| \mathcal{B}_j\right) = \min_{\substack{\alpha_i\in\mathbb{R} \\ \sum_i \alpha_i=1}} \mathrm{Var}\left(\sum_{i=0}^{I-j-1} \alpha_i\, F_{i,j+1} \middle| \mathcal{B}_j\right)$$

The conditional variance of $\widehat{f}_j$ is given by

$$\mathrm{Var}\left(\widehat{f}_j \middle| \mathcal{B}_j\right) = \frac{\sigma_j^2}{\sum_{i=0}^{I-j-1} C_{i,j}}$$

We need the following lemma to prove the statement of Lemma 3.3.

LEMMA 3.4 *Assume that $P_1, \ldots, P_H$ are stochastically independent unbiased estimators for μ with variances $\sigma_1^2, \ldots, \sigma_H^2 > 0$. Then the minimum variance unbiased linear combination of $P_1, \ldots, P_H$ is given by*

$$P = \frac{\sum_{h=1}^{H} \frac{P_h}{\sigma_h^2}}{\sum_{h=1}^{H} \frac{1}{\sigma_h^2}}$$

with

$$\operatorname{Var}(P) = \left(\sum_{h=1}^{H} \frac{1}{\sigma_h^2} \right)^{-1}$$

Proof We define the two H-dimensional vectors $\mathbf{P} = (P_1, \ldots, P_H)'$ and $\boldsymbol{\alpha} = (\alpha_1, \ldots, \alpha_H)'$. Moreover, we denote by V the covariance matrix of $\mathbf{P}$ which in our case is diagonal with entries σ_h^2. Hence we have for $\mathbf{1} = (1, \ldots, 1)' \in \mathbb{R}^H$

$$E[\boldsymbol{\alpha}'\mathbf{P}] = \mu\ \boldsymbol{\alpha}'\mathbf{1} \quad \text{and} \quad \operatorname{Var}(\boldsymbol{\alpha}'\mathbf{P}) = \boldsymbol{\alpha}'V\boldsymbol{\alpha} = \sum_{h=1}^{H} \alpha_h^2 \sigma_h^2$$

This implies that the Lagrangian for the unbiased minimum variance estimator is given by

$$\mathcal{L}(\boldsymbol{\alpha}, \lambda) = \frac{1}{2}\boldsymbol{\alpha}'V\boldsymbol{\alpha} - \lambda(\boldsymbol{\alpha}'\mathbf{1} - 1)$$

Optimization requires that we solve the following system of equations

$$\frac{\partial}{\partial \boldsymbol{\alpha}}\mathcal{L}(\boldsymbol{\alpha}, \lambda) = V\boldsymbol{\alpha} - \lambda\mathbf{1} = \mathbf{0} \quad \text{and} \quad \frac{\partial}{\partial \lambda}\mathcal{L}(\boldsymbol{\alpha}, \lambda) = \boldsymbol{\alpha}'\mathbf{1} - 1 = 0$$

This implies that $\boldsymbol{\alpha}'\mathbf{1} = \mathbf{1}'\boldsymbol{\alpha} = 1$ and $\boldsymbol{\alpha} = \lambda V^{-1}\mathbf{1}$. Solving these equations for $\boldsymbol{\alpha}$ leads to

$$\boldsymbol{\alpha} = (\mathbf{1}'V^{-1}\mathbf{1})^{-1}V^{-1}\mathbf{1}$$

and the variance of $\boldsymbol{\alpha}'\mathbf{P}$ is given by $(\mathbf{1}'V^{-1}\mathbf{1})^{-1}$. So far, we have only used the fact that V is symmetric and positive definite. If we plug in the special structure of V we find

$$\boldsymbol{\alpha} = \left(\sum_{h=1}^{H} \sigma_h^{-2} \right)^{-1} (\sigma_1^{-2}, \ldots, \sigma_H^{-2})'$$

The claim now easily follows from $P = \boldsymbol{\alpha}'\mathbf{P}$. □

Proof of Lemma 3.3 Consider the individual development factors $F_{i,j+1} = C_{i,j+1}/C_{i,j}$. Conditional on $\mathcal{B}_j$, the individual development factors $\left(F_{i,j+1}\right)_{0 \le i \le I-j-1}$ are unbiased and independent estimators for f_j with

$$\operatorname{Var}(F_{i,j+1} | \mathcal{B}_j) = \operatorname{Var}(F_{i,j+1} | C_{i,j}) = \frac{\sigma_j^2}{C_{i,j}}$$

The claim immediately follows from Lemma 3.4 with

$$\mathrm{Var}(\widehat{f}_j|\mathcal{B}_j) = \frac{\sigma_j^2}{\sum_{i=0}^{I-j-1} C_{i,j}}$$

□

LEMMA 3.5 *Under Model Assumptions 3.2 we have*

(a) *given $\mathcal{B}_j$, $\widehat{\sigma}_j^2$ is an unbiased estimator for σ_j^2, i.e.* $E\left[\widehat{\sigma}_j^2 \middle| \mathcal{B}_j\right] = \sigma_j^2$
(b) *$\widehat{\sigma}_j^2$ is (unconditionally) unbiased for σ_j^2, i.e.* $E\left[\widehat{\sigma}_j^2\right] = \sigma_j^2$.

Remark Note that Lemmas 3.3 and 3.5 motivate the choice of the estimators (3.4), that is, in the distribution-free CL framework they give (conditionally) unbiased parameter estimators for f_j and σ_j^2.

Proof Claim (b) easily follows from (a). Hence we only prove claim (a). Consider

$$E\left[\left(\frac{C_{i,j+1}}{C_{i,j}} - \widehat{f}_j\right)^2 \middle| \mathcal{B}_j\right] = E\left[\left(\frac{C_{i,j+1}}{C_{i,j}} - f_j\right)^2 \middle| \mathcal{B}_j\right]$$
$$- 2\, E\left[\left(\frac{C_{i,j+1}}{C_{i,j}} - f_j\right) \left(\widehat{f}_j - f_j\right) \middle| \mathcal{B}_j\right]$$
$$+ E\left[\left(\widehat{f}_j - f_j\right)^2 \middle| \mathcal{B}_j\right]$$

Next, we calculate each of the terms on the right-hand side of the above equality

$$E\left[\left(\frac{C_{i,j+1}}{C_{i,j}} - f_j\right)^2 \middle| \mathcal{B}_j\right] = \mathrm{Var}\left(\frac{C_{i,j+1}}{C_{i,j}} \middle| \mathcal{B}_j\right) = \frac{1}{C_{i,j}}\, \sigma_j^2$$

Using the independence of different accident years, the middle term is

$$E\left[\left(\frac{C_{i,j+1}}{C_{i,j}} - f_j\right) \left(\widehat{f}_j - f_j\right) \middle| \mathcal{B}_j\right] = \mathrm{Cov}\left(\frac{C_{i,j+1}}{C_{i,j}}, \widehat{f}_j \middle| \mathcal{B}_j\right)$$
$$= \frac{C_{i,j}}{\sum_{i=0}^{I-j-1} C_{i,j}}\, \mathrm{Var}\left(\frac{C_{i,j+1}}{C_{i,j}} \middle| \mathcal{B}_j\right)$$
$$= \frac{\sigma_j^2}{\sum_{i=0}^{I-j-1} C_{i,j}}$$

Whereas for the last term we obtain

$$E\left[\left(\widehat{f}_j - f_j\right)^2 \middle| \mathcal{B}_j\right] = \mathrm{Var}\left(\widehat{f}_j \middle| \mathcal{B}_j\right) = \frac{\sigma_j^2}{\sum_{i=0}^{I-j-1} C_{i,j}}$$

Putting all this together gives

$$E\left[\left(\frac{C_{i,j+1}}{C_{i,j}} - \widehat{f}_j\right)^2 \middle| \mathcal{B}_j\right] = \sigma_j^2 \left(\frac{1}{C_{i,j}} - \frac{1}{\sum_{i=0}^{I-j-1} C_{i,j}}\right)$$

Hence, we have

$$E\left[\widehat{\sigma}_j^2 \middle| \mathcal{B}_j\right] = \frac{1}{I-j-1} \sum_{i=0}^{I-j-1} C_{i,j}\, E\left[\left(\frac{C_{i,j+1}}{C_{i,j}} - \widehat{f}_j\right)^2 \middle| \mathcal{B}_j\right] = \sigma_j^2$$

which proves the claim (a). This completes the proof of Lemma 3.5. □

The following equality plays an important role in the derivation of an estimator for the conditional estimation error (cf. Subsection 3.2.3)

$$E\left[\widehat{f}_j^2 \middle| \mathcal{B}_j\right] = \mathrm{Var}\left(\widehat{f}_j \middle| \mathcal{B}_j\right) + f_j^2 = \frac{\sigma_j^2}{\sum_{i=0}^{I-j-1} C_{i,j}} + f_j^2 \tag{3.7}$$

We have already seen how to predict the ultimate claim $C_{i,J}$ in the CL method, given information $\mathcal{D}_I$ (see Estimator 2.4):

$$\widehat{C_{i,J}}^{\mathrm{CL}} = \widehat{E}\left[C_{i,J} \middle| \mathcal{D}_I\right] = C_{i,I-i}\, \widehat{f}_{I-i} \cdots \widehat{f}_{J-1}$$

Our goal now is to derive within the distribution-free CL model an estimate for the conditional MSEP of $\widehat{C_{i,J}}^{\mathrm{CL}}$ for single accident years $i \in \{1, \ldots, I\}$ (see (3.1))

$$\begin{aligned}
\mathrm{msep}_{C_{i,J}|\mathcal{D}_I}\left(\widehat{C_{i,J}}^{\mathrm{CL}}\right) &= E\left[\left(\widehat{C_{i,J}}^{\mathrm{CL}} - C_{i,J}\right)^2 \middle| \mathcal{D}_I\right] \\
&= \mathrm{Var}\left(C_{i,J} \middle| \mathcal{D}_I\right) + \left(\widehat{C_{i,J}}^{\mathrm{CL}} - E\left[C_{i,J}|\mathcal{D}_I\right]\right)^2
\end{aligned} \tag{3.8}$$

and for aggregated accident years we consider

$$\mathrm{msep}_{\sum_i C_{i,J}|\mathcal{D}_I}\left(\sum_{i=1}^{I} \widehat{C_{i,J}}^{\mathrm{CL}}\right) = E\left[\left(\sum_{i=1}^{I} \widehat{C_{i,J}}^{\mathrm{CL}} - \sum_{i=1}^{I} C_{i,J}\right)^2 \middle| \mathcal{D}_I\right]$$

From (3.8) we see that we need to give an estimate for the conditional process variance and for the conditional estimation error (coming from the fact that f_j are estimated by $\widehat{f}_j$).

3.2.2 Conditional Process Variance

We consider the first term on the right-hand side of (3.8), which is the conditional process variance. Assume that $i > 0$,

$$\begin{aligned}
\mathrm{Var}\left(C_{i,J} \middle| \mathcal{D}_I\right) &= \mathrm{Var}\left(C_{i,J} \middle| C_{i,I-i}\right) \\
&= E\left[\mathrm{Var}\left(C_{i,J} \middle| C_{i,J-1}\right) \middle| C_{i,I-i}\right] + \mathrm{Var}\left(E\left[C_{i,J} \middle| C_{i,J-1}\right] \middle| C_{i,I-i}\right) \\
&= \sigma_{J-1}^2\, E\left[C_{i,J-1} \middle| C_{i,I-i}\right] + f_{J-1}^2\, \mathrm{Var}\left(C_{i,J-1} \middle| C_{i,I-i}\right) \\
&= \sigma_{J-1}^2\, C_{i,I-i} \prod_{m=I-i}^{J-2} f_m + f_{J-1}^2\, \mathrm{Var}\left(C_{i,J-1} \middle| C_{i,I-i}\right)
\end{aligned} \tag{3.9}$$

Hence, we obtain a recursive formula for the conditional process variance of a single accident year i. If we iterate this procedure, we find that

$$\begin{aligned}\operatorname{Var}\left(C_{i,J}\middle|\, C_{i,I-i}\right) &= C_{i,I-i} \sum_{j=I-i}^{J-1} \prod_{n=j+1}^{J-1} f_n^2 \, \sigma_j^2 \prod_{m=I-i}^{j-1} f_m \\ &= \sum_{j=I-i}^{J-1} \prod_{n=j+1}^{J-1} f_n^2 \, \sigma_j^2 \, E\left[C_{i,j}\middle|\, C_{i,I-i}\right] \\ &= \left(E\left[C_{i,J}\middle|\, C_{i,I-i}\right]\right)^2 \sum_{j=I-i}^{J-1} \frac{\sigma_j^2/f_j^2}{E\left[C_{i,j}\middle|\, C_{i,I-i}\right]} \end{aligned} \tag{3.10}$$

This gives the following Lemma:

LEMMA 3.6 (process variance for single accident years) *Under Model Assumptions 3.2, the conditional process variance for the ultimate claim of a single accident year* $i \in \{1, \ldots, I\}$ *is given by*

$$\operatorname{Var}\left(C_{i,J}\middle|\, \mathcal{D}_I\right) = \left(E\left[C_{i,J}\middle|\, C_{i,I-i}\right]\right)^2 \sum_{j=I-i}^{J-1} \frac{\sigma_j^2/f_j^2}{E\left[C_{i,j}\middle|\, C_{i,I-i}\right]} \tag{3.11}$$

We estimate the conditional process variance for a single accident year i by

$$\begin{aligned}\widehat{\operatorname{Var}}\left(C_{i,J}\middle|\, \mathcal{D}_I\right) &= \widehat{E}\left[\left(C_{i,J} - E\left[C_{i,J}\middle|\, \mathcal{D}_I\right]\right)^2\middle|\, \mathcal{D}_I\right] \\ &= \left(\widehat{C_{i,J}}^{\mathrm{CL}}\right)^2 \sum_{j=I-i}^{J-1} \frac{\widehat{\sigma}_j^2/\widehat{f}_j^2}{\widehat{C_{i,j}}^{\mathrm{CL}}} \end{aligned} \tag{3.12}$$

The estimator (3.12) for the conditional process variance can be rewritten in a recursive form, see (3.9). For $j \in \{I-i+1, \ldots, J\}$, we obtain

$$\widehat{\operatorname{Var}}\left(C_{i,j}\middle|\, \mathcal{D}_I\right) = \widehat{\operatorname{Var}}\left(C_{i,j-1}\middle|\, \mathcal{D}_I\right) \widehat{f}_{j-1}^2 + \widehat{\sigma}_{j-1}^2 \, \widehat{C_{i,j-1}}^{\mathrm{CL}}$$

where $\widehat{\operatorname{Var}}\left(C_{i,I-i}\middle|\, \mathcal{D}_I\right) = 0$ and $\widehat{C_{i,I-i}}^{\mathrm{CL}} = C_{i,I-i}$.

Since different accident years are independent, it holds that

$$\operatorname{Var}\left(\sum_{i=1}^{I} C_{i,J}\middle|\, \mathcal{D}_I\right) = \sum_{i=1}^{I} \operatorname{Var}\left(C_{i,J}\middle|\, \mathcal{D}_I\right)$$

Therefore, we estimate the conditional process variance for aggregated accident years by

$$\widehat{\operatorname{Var}}\left(\sum_{i=1}^{I} C_{i,J}\middle|\, \mathcal{D}_I\right) = \sum_{i=1}^{I} \widehat{\operatorname{Var}}\left(C_{i,J}\middle|\, \mathcal{D}_I\right)$$

Example 3.7 (distribution-free CL method, conditional process variance)

We come back to our example in Table 2.2 (see Example 2.7). Since we do not have enough data (i.e. we do not have $I > J$), we are not able to estimate the last variance parameter σ_{J-1}^2 with the estimator $\widehat{\sigma}_{J-1}^2$ (cf. (3.4)). There is an extensive literature on the estimation of tail factors and variance estimates. We do not further discuss this here, but we simply choose the extrapolation used by Mack (1993): take

$$\widehat{\sigma}_{J-1}^2 = \min\left\{\widehat{\sigma}_{J-2}^4/\widehat{\sigma}_{J-3}^2;\ \widehat{\sigma}_{J-3}^2;\ \widehat{\sigma}_{J-2}^2\right\} \tag{3.13}$$

as an estimate for σ_{J-1}^2. This estimate is motivated by the observation that $\sigma_0, \ldots, \sigma_{J-2}$ is usually a decreasing series (cf. Table 3.2). This gives the estimated conditional process standard deviations shown in Table 3.3.

Table 3.2 Observed individual CL factors $F_{i,j+1}$, estimated CL factors $\widehat{f}_j$ and estimated standard deviations $\widehat{\sigma}_j$

	0	1	2	3	4	5	6	7	8
0	1.6257	1.0926	1.0197	1.0192	1.0057	1.0060	1.0013	1.0010	1.0014
1	1.5115	1.0754	1.0147	1.0065	1.0035	1.0050	1.0011	1.0011	
2	1.4747	1.0916	1.0260	1.0147	1.0062	1.0051	1.0008		
3	1.4577	1.0845	1.0206	1.0141	1.0092	1.0045			
4	1.4750	1.0767	1.0298	1.0244	1.0109				
5	1.4573	1.0635	1.0255	1.0107					
6	1.5166	1.0663	1.0249						
7	1.4614	1.0683							
8	1.4457								
9									
$\widehat{f}_j$	1.4925	1.0778	1.0229	1.0148	1.0070	1.0051	1.0011	1.0010	1.0014
$\widehat{\sigma}_j$	135.253	33.803	15.760	19.847	9.336	2.001	0.823	0.219	0.059

Table 3.3 CL reserves and estimated conditional process standard deviations

i	$C_{i,I-i}$	$\widehat{C_{i,J}}^{CL}$	CL reserves	$\widehat{\mathrm{Var}}\left(C_{i,J}\vert\mathcal{D}_I\right)^{1/2}$	$\mathrm{Vco}_i(\%)$
0	11 148 124	11 148 124	0		
1	10 648 192	10 663 318	15 126	191	1.3
2	10 635 751	10 662 008	26 257	742	2.8
3	9 724 068	9 758 606	34 538	2669	7.7
4	9 786 916	9 872 218	85 302	6832	8.0
5	9 935 753	10 092 247	156 494	30 478	19.5
6	9 282 022	9 568 143	286 121	68 212	23.8
7	8 256 211	8 705 378	449 167	80 077	17.8
8	7 648 729	8 691 971	1 043 242	126 960	12.2
9	5 675 568	9 626 383	3 950 815	389 783	9.9
Total			6 047 061	424 379	7.0

The estimated conditional variational coefficient for accident year i relative to the estimated CL reserves is defined as

$$\mathrm{Vco}_i = \widehat{\mathrm{Vco}}\left(C_{i,J} - C_{i,I-i}\middle| \mathcal{D}_I\right) = \frac{\widehat{\mathrm{Var}}\left(C_{i,J}\middle| \mathcal{D}_I\right)^{1/2}}{\widehat{C_{i,J}}^{\mathrm{CL}} - C_{i,I-i}}$$

If we take this estimated variational coefficient as a measure of the uncertainty, we see that the uncertainty of the total CL reserves is about 7%. Note that this is the pure process uncertainty that comes from the fact that we predict the random variables. □

3.2.3 Estimation Error for Single Accident Years

Next we need to derive an estimate for the conditional parameter estimation error, that is, we want to get an estimate for the accuracy of our CL factor estimates $\widehat{f}_j$. The parameter error for a single accident year in the CL estimate is given by (see (3.8), (2.2) and (2.5))

$$\begin{aligned}\left(\widehat{C_{i,J}}^{\mathrm{CL}} - E\left[C_{i,J}\middle| \mathcal{D}_I\right]\right)^2 &= C_{i,I-i}^2 \left(\widehat{f}_{I-i} \cdots \widehat{f}_{J-1} - f_{I-i} \cdots f_{J-1}\right)^2 \\ &= C_{i,I-i}^2 \left(\prod_{j=I-i}^{J-1} \widehat{f}_j^2 + \prod_{j=I-i}^{J-1} f_j^2 - 2 \prod_{j=I-i}^{J-1} \widehat{f}_j\, f_j\right) \end{aligned} \tag{3.14}$$

Hence, we would like to calculate (3.14). Observe that the realizations of the estimators $\widehat{f}_{I-i}, \ldots, \widehat{f}_{J-1}$ are known at time I, but the 'true' CL factors $f_{I-i}, \ldots, f_{J-1}$ are unknown (otherwise we would not estimate them). Henceforth, (3.14) cannot be calculated directly. In order to determine the conditional estimation error we will analyse the extent to which the possible CL factor estimators $\widehat{f}_j$ fluctuate around the true values f_j. The methods involve Bayesian or resampling techniques that will answer such questions as: Which other values could $\widehat{f}_j$ also have taken? There are different techniques to use for resampling: non-parametric bootstrap methods; parametric bootstrap methods; Monte Carlo simulations; or closed analytical calculations. Although in this chapter we will consider closed analytical calculations and bounds, we will nevertheless use the terminology 'resampling'. The non-parametric and parametric bootstrap techniques, as well as the Bayesian approach, are discussed in Chapter 7 and Section 9.2, respectively.

There are various approaches for resampling these values $\widehat{f}_j$, both conditional ones and unconditional ones – see Buchwalder *et al.* (2006b). For the explanation of these approaches we fix accident year $i \in \{1, \ldots, I\}$. Then we see from the right-hand side of (3.14) that the main difficulty in determining the volatility in the estimates comes from the calculation of the squares of the estimated CL factors. Note that the last term in (3.14) can be calculated as an average due to the unbiasedness and the uncorrelatedness of the CL factor estimators.

Therefore, we focus for the moment on these squares, that is, we need to resample the following product of squared estimates

$$\widehat{f}_{I-i}^2 \cdots \widehat{f}_{J-1}^2$$

The treatment of the last term in (3.14) is then straightforward.

To be able to distinguish the following three different resampling approaches, we define

$$\mathcal{D}_{I,i}^{\mathrm{O}} = \left\{C_{k,j} \in \mathcal{D}_I;\ j > I - i\right\} \subseteq \mathcal{D}_I$$

the upper right corner of the observations $\mathcal{D}_I$ with respect to development year $j = I - i + 1$ (Figure 3.1).

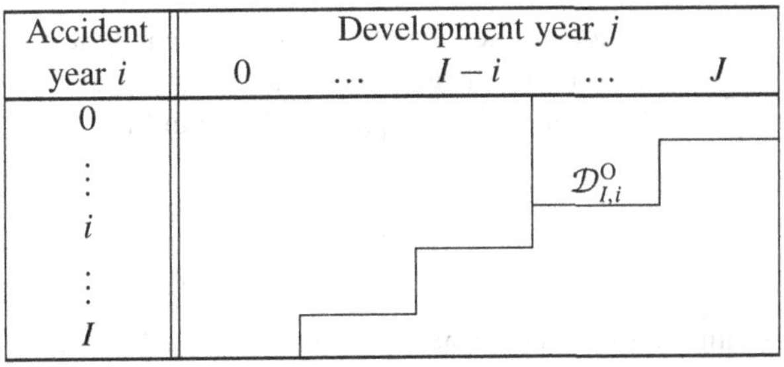

Figure 3.1 The upper right corner $D^{O}_{I,i}$

For the following explanations observe that $\widehat{f}_j$ is $\mathcal{B}_{j+1}$-measurable.

- *Approach 1 (unconditional resampling in* $\mathcal{D}^{O}_{I,i}$*)*
  In this approach one calculates the expectation

$$E\left[\widehat{f}^2_{I-i} \cdots \widehat{f}^2_{J-1} \middle| \mathcal{B}_{I-i}\right] \tag{3.15}$$

  This is the complete averaging over the multidimensional distribution after time $I-i$. Since $\mathcal{D}^{O}_{I,i} \cap \mathcal{B}_{I-i} = \emptyset$, the value (3.15) does not depend on the observations in $\mathcal{D}^{O}_{I,i}$. This means that the observed realizations in the upper corner $\mathcal{D}^{O}_{I,i}$ have no influence on the estimation of the parameter error. Therefore we call this the 'unconditional resampling' approach since it gives the average/expected estimation error, independent of the observations in $\mathcal{D}^{O}_{I,i}$.
- *Approach 2 (partial conditional resampling in* $\mathcal{D}^{O}_{I,i}$*)*
  In this approach one calculates the value

$$\widehat{f}^2_{I-i} \cdots \widehat{f}^2_{J-2}\, E\left[\widehat{f}^2_{J-1} \middle| \mathcal{B}_{J-1}\right] \tag{3.16}$$

  In this version the averaging is done only partially. Note that $\mathcal{D}^{O}_{I,i} \cap \mathcal{B}_{J-1} \neq \emptyset$, that is, (3.16) depends on the observations in $\mathcal{D}^{O}_{I,i}$. If one decouples the resampling problem in a smart way, one can even choose the position $j \in \{I-i, \ldots, J-1\}$ at which the partial resampling is done (see (3.33)–(3.34)).
- *Approach 3 (conditional resampling in* $\mathcal{D}^{O}_{I,i}$*)*
  Calculate the value

$$E\left[\widehat{f}^2_{I-i} \middle| \mathcal{B}_{I-i}\right] E\left[\widehat{f}^2_{I-i+1} \middle| \mathcal{B}_{I-i+1}\right] \cdots E\left[\widehat{f}^2_{J-1} \middle| \mathcal{B}_{J-1}\right] \tag{3.17}$$

  Unlike approach (3.16), averaging is now done at every position $j \in \{I-i, \ldots, J-1\}$ on the conditional structure. Since $\mathcal{D}^{O}_{I,i} \cap \mathcal{B}_j \neq \emptyset$ if $j > I-i$, the observed realizations in $\mathcal{D}^{O}_{I,i}$ have a direct influence on the estimate and (3.17) depends on the observations in $\mathcal{D}^{O}_{I,i}$ (they serve as a fixed volume measure, see below). In contrast to (3.15), averaging is only done over the conditional distributions and not over the multidimensional distribution after $I-i$. Therefore, this approach is referred to as the conditional version. From a numerical point of view it is important to note that Approach 3 allows for a multiplicative structure of the measure of volatility (see Figure 3.2).

We now formalize these three approaches. Approaches 1–3 mean that we consider different probability measures for the conditional and unconditional resampling. Observe that the estimated CL factors $\widehat{f}_j$ are functions of $(C_{k,j+1})_{k=0,\dots,I-j-1}$ and $(C_{k,j})_{k=0,\dots,I-j-1}$, hence

$$\widehat{f}_j = \widehat{f}_j\big((C_{k,j+1})_{k=0,\dots,I-j-1}; (C_{k,j})_{k=0,\dots,I-j-1}\big) = \frac{\sum_{k=0}^{I-j-1} C_{k,j+1}}{\sum_{k=0}^{I-j-1} C_{k,j}}$$

In the conditional resampling the denominator serves as a fixed volume measure, whereas in the unconditional resampling the denominator is also resampled.

Since our time series $(C_{k,j})_{j\geq 0}$ is a Markov chain, we can write its probability distribution (using stochastic kernels $K_j^{(k)}$) as:

$$\begin{aligned} dP_k(x_0,\dots,x_J) &= K_0^{(k)}(dx_0)\; K_1^{(k)}(x_0, dx_1)\; K_2^{(k)}(x_0, x_1, dx_2)\cdots \\ &\quad K_J^{(k)}(x_0,\dots,x_{J-1}, dx_J) \\ &= K_0^{(k)}(dx_0)\; K_1^{(k)}(x_0, dx_1)\; K_2^{(k)}(x_1, dx_2)\cdots\; K_J^{(k)}(x_{J-1}, dx_J) \end{aligned}$$

In Approach 1, we consider a complete resampling on $\mathcal{D}_{I,i}^{\text{O}}$; that is, given $\mathcal{B}_{I-i}$, we look at the measures

$$\begin{aligned} dP\big((x_{k,j})_{k,j}\,|\,\mathcal{B}_{I-i}\big) &= \prod_{k<i} dP_k\big(x_{k,I-i+1},\dots,x_{k,I-k}\big|\,C_{k,I-i}\big) \\ &= \prod_{k<i} K_{I-i+1}^{(k)}\big(C_{k,I-i}, dx_{k,I-i+1}\big)\cdots K_{I-k}^{(k)}\big(x_{k,I-k-1}, dx_{k,I-k}\big) \end{aligned}$$

for the resampling of the estimated CL factors, $x_{k,I-i} = C_{k,I-i}$ for $k<i$,

$$\prod_{j=I-i}^{J-1} \widehat{f}_j = \prod_{j=I-i}^{J-1} \widehat{f}_j\big((x_{k,j+1})_{k=0,\dots,I-j-1}; (x_{k,j})_{k=0,\dots,I-j-1}\big) = \prod_{j=I-i}^{J-1} \frac{\sum_{k=0}^{I-j-1} x_{k,j+1}}{\sum_{k=0}^{I-j-1} x_{k,j}}$$

This means that the whole time series is resampled and that the resampled values $x_{k,j}$ serve as a volume measure for resampling $x_{k,j+1}$.

In Approach 3, we always keep the set of actual observations $C_{k,j}$ fixed and only resample the next step in the time series; that is, given $\mathcal{D}_I$, we consider the following probability measures (see also Figure 3.2)

$$dP^*_{\mathcal{D}_I}\big((x_{k,j})_{k+j\leq I}\big) = \prod_{k=0}^{I-1} K_1^{(k)}\big(C_{k,0}, dx_{k,1}\big)\;\cdots\; K_{I-k}^{(k)}\big(C_{k,I-k-1}, dx_{k,I-k}\big) \tag{3.18}$$

for the resampling of

$$\prod_{j=I-i}^{J-1} \widehat{f}_j = \prod_{j=I-i}^{J-1} \widehat{f}_j\big((x_{k,j+1})_{k=0,\dots,I-j-1}; (C_{k,j})_{k=0,\dots,I-j-1}\big) = \prod_{j=I-i}^{J-1} \frac{\sum_{k=0}^{I-j-1} x_{k,j+1}}{\sum_{k=0}^{I-j-1} C_{k,j}}$$

Hence in this context $C_{k,j}$ serves as a fixed volume measure for the resampled values of $x_{k,j+1}$. In Approach 1 this volume measure is also resampled, whereas in Approach 3 it is kept fixed.

Observation The question of the approach that should be chosen is not a mathematical one and has led to extensive discussions in the actuarial community (see Buchwalder *et al.* 2006b; Mack *et al.* 2006; Gisler 2006; and Venter 2006). As the approach that should be used depends on the circumstances of a specific practical problem and questions that need to be answered, it is no longer a mathematical problem. An alternative way to solve the problem would be Approach 4 (below) using Bayesian techniques. There, the question is solved by the choice of an appropriate model.

- *Approach 4 (Bayesian approach)* To quantify the uncertainties in the choice of the CL factors, we set up a Bayesian framework for the parameters. The detailed discussion is found in Section 9.2.

Approach 1 (Unconditional Resampling)

In the unconditional approach we have (due to the uncorrelatedness and unbiasedness of the CL factors; cf. Lemma 2.5)

$$
\begin{aligned}
E&\left[\left(\widehat{C}_{i,J}^{\text{CL}} - E\left[C_{i,J}\middle|\mathcal{D}_I\right]\right)^2\middle|\mathcal{B}_{I-i}\right]\\
&= C_{i,I-i}^2\, E\left[\prod_{j=I-i}^{J-1}\widehat{f}_j^2 + \prod_{j=I-i}^{J-1} f_j^2 - 2\prod_{j=I-i}^{J-1}\widehat{f}_j\, f_j\middle|\mathcal{B}_{I-i}\right]\\
&= C_{i,I-i}^2\left(E\left[\prod_{j=I-i}^{J-1}\widehat{f}_j^2\middle|\mathcal{B}_{I-i}\right] - \prod_{j=I-i}^{J-1} f_j^2\right)
\end{aligned}
\tag{3.19}
$$

Hence, to give an estimate for the estimation error (in the unconditional version), we need to calculate the expectation in the last term of (3.19) as described in Approach 1. This would be easy, if the estimators of the CL factors $\widehat{f}_j$ were independent. But they are **only** uncorrelated – see Lemma 2.5 and the following lemma (for a similar statement see also Mack *et al.* 2006):

LEMMA 3.8 *Under Model Assumptions 3.2 the squares of two successive CL estimators* $\widehat{f}_{j-1}$ *and* $\widehat{f}_j$, *given* $\mathcal{B}_{j-1}$, *are negatively correlated, i.e.*

$$
\mathrm{Cov}\left(\widehat{f}_{j-1}^2, \widehat{f}_j^2\middle|\mathcal{B}_{j-1}\right) < 0
$$

for $1 \le j \le J-1$.

Proof Assume that $1 \le j \le J-1$ and observe that $\widehat{f}_{j-1}$ is B_j-measurable. We define for $K \ge 0$

$$
S_j^{[K]} = \sum_{i=0}^{K} C_{i,j} \tag{3.20}
$$

Hence, using (3.7), we have

$$
\begin{aligned}
\mathrm{Cov}\left(\widehat{f}^2_{j-1}, \widehat{f}^2_j \middle| \mathcal{B}_{j-1}\right) &= E\left[\mathrm{Cov}\left(\widehat{f}^2_{j-1}, \widehat{f}^2_j \middle| \mathcal{B}_j\right) \middle| \mathcal{B}_{j-1}\right] \\
&\quad + \mathrm{Cov}\left(E\left[\widehat{f}^2_{j-1} \middle| \mathcal{B}_j\right], E\left[\widehat{f}^2_j \middle| \mathcal{B}_j\right] \middle| \mathcal{B}_{j-1}\right) \\
&= \mathrm{Cov}\left(\widehat{f}^2_{j-1}, \frac{\sigma_j^2}{S_j^{[I-j-1]}} + f_j^2 \middle| \mathcal{B}_{j-1}\right) \\
&= \frac{\sigma_j^2}{\left(S_{j-1}^{[I-j]}\right)^2} \mathrm{Cov}\left(\left(\sum_{i=0}^{I-j} C_{i,j}\right)^2, \frac{1}{S_j^{[I-j-1]}} \middle| \mathcal{B}_{j-1}\right)
\end{aligned}
$$

Moreover, using

$$
\left(\sum_{i=0}^{I-j} C_{i,j}\right)^2 = \left(S_j^{[I-j-1]}\right)^2 + 2\, S_j^{[I-j-1]}\, C_{I-j,j} + C_{I-j,j}^2
$$

the independence of different accident years and $E\left[C_{I-j,j} \middle| \mathcal{B}_{j-1}\right] = f_{j-1}\, C_{I-j,j-1}$ leads to

$$
\begin{aligned}
\mathrm{Cov}\left(\widehat{f}^2_{j-1}, \widehat{f}^2_j \middle| \mathcal{B}_{j-1}\right) = \frac{\sigma_j^2}{\left(S_{j-1}^{[I-j]}\right)^2} \Bigg[&\mathrm{Cov}\left(\left(S_j^{[I-j-1]}\right)^2, \frac{1}{S_j^{[I-j-1]}} \middle| \mathcal{B}_{j-1}\right) \\
&+ 2\, f_{j-1}\, C_{I-j,j-1}\, \mathrm{Cov}\left(S_j^{[I-j-1]}, \frac{1}{S_j^{[I-j-1]}} \middle| \mathcal{B}_{j-1}\right) \Bigg]
\end{aligned} \tag{3.21}
$$

Finally, we need to calculate both covariance terms on the right-hand side of (3.21). We set $S_j = S_j^{[I-j-1]}$, then using Jensen's inequality we obtain for $\alpha = 1, 2$

$$
\begin{aligned}
\mathrm{Cov}\left(S_j^\alpha, \frac{1}{S_j} \middle| \mathcal{B}_{j-1}\right) &= E\left[S_j^{\alpha-1} \middle| \mathcal{B}_{j-1}\right] - E\left[S_j^\alpha \middle| \mathcal{B}_{j-1}\right]\, E\left[S_j^{-1} \middle| \mathcal{B}_{j-1}\right] \\
&< E\left[S_j^{\alpha-1} \middle| \mathcal{B}_{j-1}\right] - E\left[S_j \middle| \mathcal{B}_{j-1}\right]^\alpha\, E\left[S_j \middle| \mathcal{B}_{j-1}\right]^{-1} = 0
\end{aligned}
$$

Jensen's inequality is strict because we have assumed strictly positive variances $\sigma_{j-1}^2 > 0$, which implies that $S_j^{[I-j-1]}$ is not deterministic at time $j-1$. This completes the proof of Lemma 3.8. □

Lemma 3.8 implies that the term

$$
E\left[\prod_{j=I-i}^{J-1} \widehat{f}_j^2 \middle| \mathcal{B}_{I-i}\right]
$$

cannot easily be calculated. Hence from this point of view Approach 1 is not a promising route for finding a closed formula for the estimation error. In Section 3.3, however, we show how upper and lower bounds can be derived.

Approach 3 (Conditional Resampling)

In Approach 3 we resample the observed CL factors $\widehat{f}_j$ on the conditional structure. To better understand this resampling, we impose stronger model assumptions by introducing a time series model. Such time series models for the CL method can be found in several papers in the literature – see, for example, Murphy (1994), Barnett and Zehnwirth (2000), or Buchwalder *et al.* (2006b).

Model Assumptions 3.9 (time series model)

- Cumulative claims $C_{i,j}$ of different accident years i are independent.
- There exist constants $f_j > 0$, $\sigma_j > 0$ and random variables $\varepsilon_{i,j+1}$ such that for all $i \in \{0, \ldots, I\}$ and $j \in \{0, \ldots, J-1\}$ we have

$$C_{i,j+1} = f_j \, C_{i,j} + \sigma_j \sqrt{C_{i,j}} \, \varepsilon_{i,j+1} \tag{3.22}$$

where conditionally, given $\mathcal{B}_0$, $\varepsilon_{i,j+1}$ are independent with $E\left[\varepsilon_{i,j+1} \middle| \mathcal{B}_0\right] = 0$, $E\left[\varepsilon_{i,j+1}^2 \middle| \mathcal{B}_0\right] = 1$ and $P\left[C_{i,j+1} > 0 \middle| \mathcal{B}_0\right] = 1$ for all $i \in \{0, \ldots, I\}$ and $j \in \{0, \ldots, J-1\}$.

□

Remarks 3.10

- The time series model defines an autoregressive process. It is particularly useful for the derivation of the estimation error and provides a mechanism for generating sets of 'other possible' observations.
- The random variables $\varepsilon_{i,j+1}$ are defined conditionally, given $\mathcal{B}_0$, in order to ensure that the cumulative claims $C_{i,j+1}$ stay positive, $P[\cdot|\mathcal{B}_0]$–a.s. This implies that all the derivations are done under the conditional probability measure $P[\cdot|\mathcal{B}_0]$; in order to not overload the notation this conditional probability measure is abbreviated by P and all the subsequent statements are done under this conditional measure. Note that the distribution-free CL model (Model Assumptions 3.2) also makes an assumption about the positivity of cumulative claims in order to get a meaningful variance condition.
- It is easy to show that Model Assumptions 3.9 imply Model Assumptions 3.2 of the distribution-free CL model.
- The definition of the time series model in Buchwalder *et al.* (2006b) is slightly different. The difference lies in the fact that here we assume a.s. the positivity of $C_{i,j}$. This could also be done with the help of subsequent conditional assumptions

$$P\left[C_{i,j+1} > 0 \middle| C_{i,j}\right] = 1$$

for all i and j.

In the following we use Approach 3, that is, we use conditional resampling in the time series model. We therefore resample the observations for $\widehat{f}_{I-i}, \ldots, \widehat{f}_{J-1}$, given the upper triangle $\mathcal{D}_I$. Thereby we take into account the possibility that, given $\mathcal{D}_I$, the observations for $\widehat{f}_j$ could have been different from the observed values. To account for this source of uncertainty we proceed as follows. Given $\mathcal{D}_I$, we generate a set of 'new' observations $\widetilde{C}_{i,j+1}$ for $i \in \{0, \ldots, I\}$ and $j \in \{0, \ldots, J-1\}$ using the formula

$$\widetilde{C}_{i,j+1} = f_j \, C_{i,j} + \sigma_j \sqrt{C_{i,j}} \, \widetilde{\varepsilon}_{i,j+1} \tag{3.23}$$

where $\sigma_j > 0$ and $\widetilde{\varepsilon}_{i,j+1}$, $\varepsilon_{i,j+1}$ are independent and identically distributed copies, given $\mathcal{B}_0$ (cf. Model Assumptions 3.9). This means that $C_{i,j}$ acts as a fixed volume measure and we resample $\widetilde{C}_{i,j+1} \stackrel{(d)}{=} C_{i,j+1}$, given $\mathcal{B}_j$. In the language of stochastic kernels, this is equivalent to considering the distributions $K_{j+1}^{(i)}\left(C_{i,j}, dx_{j+1}\right)$ for every step j to $j+1$ in the time series (see (3.18)).

Remark We have chosen a different notation ($\widetilde{C}_{i,j+1}$ vs $C_{i,j+1}$) to clearly illustrate that we resample on the conditional structure, that is, $\widetilde{C}_{i,j+1}$ are random variables and $C_{i,j}$ are (deterministic) volumes, given $\mathcal{D}_I$.

In the spirit of Approach 3 (cf. (3.17)) we resample the observations for $\widehat{f}_j$ by only resampling the observations of development year $j+1$. Together with the resampling assumption (3.23), this leads to the following resampled representation for the estimates of the development factors

$$\widehat{f}_j = \frac{\sum_{i=0}^{I-j-1} \widetilde{C}_{i,j+1}}{\sum_{i=0}^{I-j-1} C_{i,j}} = f_j + \frac{\sigma_j}{S_j^{[I-j-1]}} \sum_{i=0}^{I-j-1} \sqrt{C_{i,j}}\, \widetilde{\varepsilon}_{i,j+1} \tag{3.24}$$

where (once again)

$$S_j^{[I-j-1]} = \sum_{i=0}^{I-j-1} C_{i,j} \tag{3.25}$$

Remark Note that in (3.24) and the following derivation we use the previous notation $\widehat{f}_j$ for the resampled estimates of the development factors f_j to avoid an overloaded notation. This immediately becomes clear when we introduce the measure for the conditional resampling.

As in (3.18) we denote the probability measure of these resampled CL estimates by $P^*_{\mathcal{D}_I}$. The resampled estimates of the development factors $\widehat{f}_j$ have, given $\mathcal{B}_j$, the same distribution as the original estimated CL factors. Unlike the observations $\left\{C_{i,j};\ i+j \le I\right\}$, the observations $\left\{\widetilde{C}_{i,j};\ i+j \le I\right\}$ and the resampled estimates $\widehat{f}_j$ are random variables, given $\mathcal{D}_I$. Furthermore, random variables $\widetilde{\varepsilon}_{i,j}$ are independent, given $\mathcal{B}_0 \subset \mathcal{D}_I$. This and (3.24) show that

(1) the resampled estimates $\widehat{f}_0, \ldots, \widehat{f}_{J-1}$ are independent w.r.t. $P^*_{\mathcal{D}_I}$,
(2) $E^*_{\mathcal{D}_I}\left[\widehat{f}_j\right] = f_j$ for $0 \le j \le J-1$ and
(3) $E^*_{\mathcal{D}_I}\left[\left(\widehat{f}_j\right)^2\right] = f_j^2 + \sigma_j^2 / S_j^{[I-j-1]}$ for $0 \le j \le J-1$.

Therefore, in Approach 3, the conditional estimation error is estimated by (using properties (1)–(3) above)

$$\begin{aligned} & C_{i,I-i}^2\, E^*_{\mathcal{D}_I}\left[\left(\widehat{f}_{I-i} \cdots \widehat{f}_{J-1} - f_{I-i} \cdots f_{J-1}\right)^2\right] \\ & = C_{i,I-i}^2\, \mathrm{Var}_{P^*_{\mathcal{D}_I}}\left(\widehat{f}_{I-i} \cdots \widehat{f}_{J-1}\right) \end{aligned}$$

$$= C_{i,I-i}^2 \left(\prod_{j=I-i}^{J-1} E_{\mathcal{D}_I}^* \left[\left(\widehat{f}_j \right)^2 \right] - \prod_{j=I-i}^{J-1} f_j^2 \right)$$

$$= C_{i,I-i}^2 \left(\prod_{j=I-i}^{J-1} \left(f_j^2 + \frac{\sigma_j^2}{S_j^{[I-j-1]}} \right) - \prod_{j=I-i}^{J-1} f_j^2 \right) \tag{3.26}$$

Observe that this calculation is exact; the estimation has been done using Approach 3 for the conditional estimation error, that is, the estimate was obtained under the conditional probability measure $P_{\mathcal{D}_I}^*$.

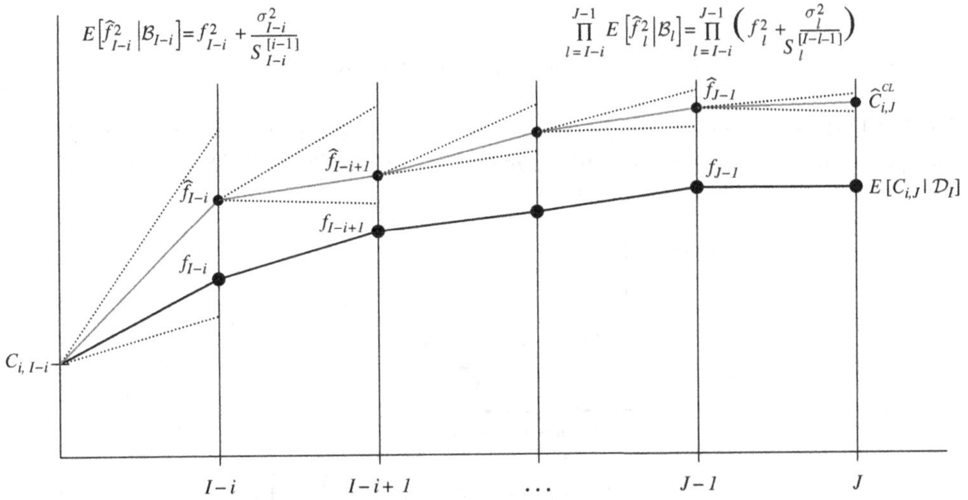

Figure 3.2 Conditional resampling in $\mathcal{D}_{I,i}^O$ (Approach 3)

Figure 3.2 illustrates the conditional resampling approach under measure $P_{\mathcal{D}_I}^*$. It shows the 'true' but unknown CL factors $f_{I-i}, \ldots, f_{J-1}$ that lead to $E[C_{i,J}|\mathcal{D}_I]$ as well as the observed estimates $\widehat{f}_{I-i}, \ldots, \widehat{f}_{J-1}$ that lead to $\widehat{C_{i,J}}^{CL}$. Given the observations $\mathcal{D}_I$, these estimates are successively resampled, as illustrated by the dotted lines. This gives other possible realizations for $\widehat{f}_j$, given $\mathcal{D}_I$ as fixed volume measures.

Next, replacing the parameters $\sigma_{I-i}^2, \ldots, \sigma_{J-1}^2$ and $f_{I-i}, \ldots, f_{J-1}$ with their estimates, we obtain the following estimator for the conditional estimation error for accident year $i \in \{1, \ldots, I\}$

$$\widehat{\mathrm{Var}}\left(\widehat{C_{i,J}}^{CL} \middle| \mathcal{D}_I \right) = \widehat{E}_{\mathcal{D}_I}^* \left[\left(\widehat{C_{i,J}}^{CL} - E\left[C_{i,J} \middle| \mathcal{D}_I \right] \right)^2 \right]$$

$$= C_{i,I-i}^2 \left(\prod_{j=I-i}^{J-1} \left(\widehat{f}_j^2 + \frac{\widehat{\sigma}_j^2}{S_j^{[I-j-1]}} \right) - \prod_{j=I-i}^{J-1} \widehat{f}_j^2 \right) \tag{3.27}$$

This estimator can be written in a recursive form. We obtain for $j \in \{I-i+1, \ldots, J\}$

$$\begin{aligned}
\widehat{\mathrm{Var}}\left(\widehat{C_{i,j}}^{\mathrm{CL}} \Big| \mathcal{D}_I \right) &= \widehat{\mathrm{Var}}\left(\widehat{C_{i,j-1}}^{\mathrm{CL}} \Big| \mathcal{D}_I \right) \widehat{f}_{j-1}^2 \\
&\quad + C_{i,I-i}^2 \frac{\widehat{\sigma}_{j-1}^2}{S_{j-1}^{[I-j-1]}} \prod_{l=I-i}^{j-2} \left(\widehat{f}_l^2 + \frac{\widehat{\sigma}_l^2}{S_l^{[I-l-1]}} \right) \\
&= \widehat{\mathrm{Var}}\left(\widehat{C_{i,j-1}}^{\mathrm{CL}} \Big| \mathcal{D}_I \right) \left(\widehat{f}_{j-1}^2 + \frac{\widehat{\sigma}_{j-1}^2}{S_{j-1}^{[I-j-1]}} \right) \\
&\quad + C_{i,I-i}^2 \frac{\widehat{\sigma}_{j-1}^2}{S_{j-1}^{[I-j-1]}} \prod_{l=I-i}^{j-2} \widehat{f}_l^2
\end{aligned} \tag{3.28}$$

where $\widehat{\mathrm{Var}}\left(\widehat{C_{i,I-i}}^{\mathrm{CL}} \Big| \mathcal{D}_I \right) = 0$ and the empty product is equal to 1.

ESTIMATOR 3.11 (MSEP for single accident years, conditional version) *Under Model Assumptions 3.9 we have the following estimator for the conditional MSEP of the ultimate claim for a single accident year $i \in \{1, \ldots, I\}$*

$$\begin{aligned}
\widehat{\mathrm{msep}}_{C_{i,J}|\mathcal{D}_I}\left(\widehat{C_{i,J}}^{\mathrm{CL}} \right) &= \widehat{E}\left[\left(\widehat{C_{i,J}}^{\mathrm{CL}} - C_{i,J} \right)^2 \Big| \mathcal{D}_I \right] \\
&= \underbrace{\left(\widehat{C_{i,J}}^{\mathrm{CL}} \right)^2 \sum_{j=I-i}^{J-1} \frac{\widehat{\sigma}_j^2 / \widehat{f}_j^2}{\widehat{C_{i,j}}^{\mathrm{CL}}}}_{\text{conditional process variance}} \\
&\quad + \underbrace{C_{i,I-i}^2 \left(\prod_{j=I-i}^{J-1} \left(\widehat{f}_j^2 + \frac{\widehat{\sigma}_j^2}{S_j^{[I-j-1]}} \right) - \prod_{j=I-i}^{J-1} \widehat{f}_j^2 \right)}_{\text{conditional estimation error}}
\end{aligned} \tag{3.29}$$

We can rewrite (3.29) as follows

$$\widehat{\mathrm{msep}}_{C_{i,J}|\mathcal{D}_I}\left(\widehat{C_{i,J}}^{\mathrm{CL}} \right) = \left(\widehat{C_{i,J}}^{\mathrm{CL}} \right)^2 \left(\sum_{j=I-i}^{J-1} \frac{\widehat{\sigma}_j^2 / \widehat{f}_j^2}{\widehat{C_{i,j}}^{\mathrm{CL}}} + \prod_{j=I-i}^{J-1} \left(\frac{\widehat{\sigma}_j^2 / \widehat{f}_j^2}{S_j^{[I-j-1]}} + 1 \right) - 1 \right) \tag{3.30}$$

We could also do a linear approximation to the estimation error:

$$C_{i,I-i}^2 \left(\prod_{j=I-i}^{J-1} \left(\widehat{f}_j^2 + \frac{\widehat{\sigma}_j^2}{S_j^{[I-j-1]}} \right) - \prod_{j=I-i}^{J-1} \widehat{f}_j^2 \right) \approx C_{i,I-i}^2 \prod_{j=I-i}^{J-1} \widehat{f}_j^2 \sum_{j=I-i}^{J-1} \frac{\widehat{\sigma}_j^2 / \widehat{f}_j^2}{S_j^{[I-j-1]}} \tag{3.31}$$

Observe that in fact the right-hand side of (3.31) is a lower bound for the left-hand side. This immediately gives the following estimator:

ESTIMATOR 3.12 (MSEP for single accident years) *Under Model Assumptions 3.9 we have the following estimator for the conditional MSEP of the ultimate claim for a single accident year* $i \in \{1, \ldots, I\}$

$$\widehat{\mathrm{msep}}_{C_{i,J}|\mathcal{D}_I}\left(\widehat{C_{i,J}}^{CL}\right) = \left(\widehat{C_{i,J}}^{CL}\right)^2 \sum_{j=I-i}^{J-1} \frac{\widehat{\sigma}_j^2}{\widehat{f}_j^2} \left(\frac{1}{\widehat{C_{i,j}}^{CL}} + \frac{1}{S_j^{[I-j-1]}}\right) \tag{3.32}$$

The Mack approach

Mack (1993) gives a different approach for the estimation of the parameter estimation error. Introduce for $j \in \{I-i, \ldots, J-1\}$

$$T_j = \widehat{f}_{I-i} \cdots \widehat{f}_{j-1} \left(f_j - \widehat{f}_j\right) f_{j+1} \cdots f_{J-1} \tag{3.33}$$

Observe that

$$\left(\widehat{f}_{I-i} \cdots \widehat{f}_{J-1} - f_{I-i} \cdots f_{J-1}\right)^2 = \left(\sum_{j=I-i}^{J-1} T_j\right)^2 \tag{3.34}$$

This implies that (see also (3.14))

$$\left(\widehat{C_{i,J}}^{CL} - E\left[C_{i,J} \middle| \mathcal{D}_I\right]\right)^2 = C_{i,I-i}^2 \left(\sum_{j=I-i}^{J-1} T_j^2 + 2 \sum_{I-i \le j < k \le J-1} T_j\, T_k\right)$$

Each term in the summations on the right-hand side of the equality above is now estimated by a slightly modified version of Approach 2. Note that $E[T_k | \mathcal{B}_k] = 0$ and that T_j is $\mathcal{B}_k$-measurable for $j < k$. Hence $T_j\, T_k$ is estimated by

$$E\left[T_j\, T_k \middle| \mathcal{B}_k\right] = T_j\, E[T_k | \mathcal{B}_k] = 0$$

and T_j^2 is estimated by

$$\begin{aligned} E\left[T_j^2 \middle| \mathcal{B}_j\right] &= \widehat{f}_{I-i}^2 \cdots \widehat{f}_{j-1}^2\, E\left[\left(f_j - \widehat{f}_j\right)^2 \middle| \mathcal{B}_j\right] f_{j+1}^2 \cdots f_{J-1}^2 \\ &= \widehat{f}_{I-i}^2 \cdots \widehat{f}_{j-1}^2\, \mathrm{Var}\left(\widehat{f}_j \middle| \mathcal{B}_j\right) f_{j+1}^2 \cdots f_{J-1}^2 \\ &= \widehat{f}_{I-i}^2 \cdots \widehat{f}_{j-1}^2\, \frac{\sigma_j^2}{S_j^{[I-j-1]}}\, f_{j+1}^2 \cdots f_{J-1}^2 \end{aligned}$$

Hence, an estimate for (3.14) is given by

$$C_{i,I-i}^2 \sum_{j=I-i}^{J-1} \widehat{f}_{I-i}^2 \cdots \widehat{f}_{j-1}^2\, \frac{\sigma_j^2}{S_j^{[I-j-1]}}\, f_{j+1}^2 \cdots f_{J-1}^2 \tag{3.35}$$

If we now replace the unknown parameters σ_j^2 and f_j by their estimates $\widehat{\sigma}_j^2$ and $\widehat{f}_j$ we obtain estimate (3.31) for the conditional estimation error. Using estimate (3.12) for the conditional process variance, we exactly obtain the estimate $\widehat{\mathrm{msep}}_{C_{i,J}|\mathcal{D}_I}\left(\widehat{C_{i,J}}^{\mathrm{CL}}\right)$ for the conditional MSEP presented in Estimator 3.12.

Remarks 3.13

- We see that the Mack estimate for the conditional estimation error can also be obtained by a linear approximation from below to the estimate coming from Approach 3 (see (3.31)).
- The difference comes from the fact that Mack (1993) decouples the estimation error in an appropriate way (with the help of the terms T_j) and then applies a partial conditional resampling to each of the terms in the decoupling.
- The Time Series Model 3.9 makes slightly stronger assumptions than the weighted average development (WAD) factor model studied in Murphy (1993), Model IV. To obtain the crucial recursive formula for the conditional estimation error (Theorem 3 in Appendix C of Murphy 1994), Murphy assumes independence of the estimators $\widehat{f}_j$ of the CL factors f_j. However, this assumption is inconsistent with Model Assumptions 3.2 since the CL factors indeed are uncorrelated (see Lemma 2.5(c)) but the squares of two successive CL estimators are negatively correlated, as has been shown in Lemma 3.8. The point is that by his assumptions Murphy gets a multiplicative structure for the measure of volatility. In Approach 3 we get the multiplicative structure by the choice of conditional resampling (probability measure $P^*_{\mathcal{D}_I}$) for the measure of the (conditional) volatility of the CL estimator (see discussion in Section 3.2.3), but without assuming that the estimated CL factors are independent. Since the derivation of both estimators lead to a multiplicative structure, it turns out that the recursive estimator (3.28) for the conditional estimation error is equal to the estimator presented in Murphy's Theorem 3 (see also Appendix B in Barnett and Zehnwirth 2000).

Example 3.7, revisited

We come back to our Example 3.7 and calculate the error estimates. From Tables 3.4 and 3.5 we see that the differences in the estimates of the conditional estimation error coming from the conditional approach and from Mack's formula are negligible. In all examples we have looked at, we came to this conclusion. □

Table 3.4 CL reserves and error terms according to Estimator 3.11

i	$\widehat{C_{i,J}}^{\mathrm{CL}}$	CL reserves	$\widehat{\mathrm{Var}}\left(C_{i,J}\mid\mathcal{D}_I\right)^{1/2}$		$\widehat{\mathrm{Var}}\left(\widehat{C_{i,J}}^{\mathrm{CL}}\mid\mathcal{D}_I\right)^{1/2}$		$\widehat{\mathrm{msep}}_{C_{i,J}\mid\mathcal{D}_I}\left(\widehat{C_{i,J}}^{\mathrm{CL}}\right)^{1/2}$	
0	11 148 124							
1	10 663 318	15 126	191	1.3%	187	1.2%	267	1.8%
2	10 662 008	26 257	742	2.8%	535	2.0%	914	3.5%
3	9 758 606	34 538	2669	7.7%	1493	4.3%	3058	8.9%
4	9 872 218	85 302	6832	8.0%	3392	4.0%	7628	8.9%
5	10 092 247	156 494	30 478	19.5%	13 517	8.6%	33 341	21.3%
6	9 568 143	286 121	68 212	23.8%	27 286	9.5%	73 467	25.7%
7	8 705 378	449 167	80 077	17.8%	29 675	6.6%	85 398	19.0%
8	8 691 971	1 043 242	126 960	12.2%	43 903	4.2%	134 337	12.9%
9	9 626 383	3 950 815	389 783	9.9%	129 770	3.3%	410 817	10.4%

Table 3.5 CL reserves and error terms according to Estimator 3.12

i	$\widehat{C_{i,J}}^{CL}$	CL reserves	$\widehat{\mathrm{Var}}\left(C_{i,J}\vert\mathcal{D}_I\right)^{1/2}$		$\widehat{\mathrm{Var}}\left(\widehat{C_{i,J}}^{CL}\vert\mathcal{D}_I\right)^{1/2}$		$\widehat{\mathrm{msep}}_{C_{i,J}\vert\mathcal{D}_I}\left(\widehat{C_{i,J}}^{CL}\right)^{1/2}$	
0	11 148 124							
1	10 663 318	15 126	191	1.3%	187	1.2%	267	1.8%
2	10 662 008	26 257	742	2.8%	535	2.0%	914	3.5%
3	9 758 606	34 538	2669	7.7%	1493	4.3%	3058	8.9%
4	9 872 218	85 302	6832	8.0%	3392	4.0%	7628	8.9%
5	10 092 247	156 494	30 478	19.5%	13 517	8.6%	33 341	21.3%
6	9 568 143	286 121	68 212	23.8%	27 286	9.5%	73 467	25.7%
7	8 705 378	449 167	80 077	17.8%	29 675	6.6%	85 398	19.0%
8	8 691 971	1 043 242	126 960	12.2%	43 903	4.2%	134 337	12.9%
9	9 626 383	3 950 815	389 783	9.9%	129 769	3.3%	410 817	10.4%

3.2.4 Conditional MSEP, Aggregated Accident Years

Consider two different accident years $i < k$. From the model assumptions we know that the ultimate losses $C_{i,J}$ and $C_{k,J}$ are independent. Nevertheless, we have to be careful if we aggregate $\widehat{C_{i,J}}^{CL}$ and $\widehat{C_{k,J}}^{CL}$. The estimators are no longer independent since they use the same observations for estimating the age-to-age factors f_j. We have

$$\begin{aligned}\mathrm{msep}_{C_{i,J}+C_{k,J}|\mathcal{D}_I}\left(\widehat{C_{i,J}}^{CL}+\widehat{C_{k,J}}^{CL}\right) &= E\left[\left(\widehat{C_{i,J}}^{CL}+\widehat{C_{k,J}}^{CL}-(C_{i,J}+C_{k,J})\right)^2\middle|\mathcal{D}_I\right]\\ &= \mathrm{Var}\left(C_{i,J}+C_{k,J}\middle|\mathcal{D}_I\right)\\ &\quad+\left(\widehat{C_{i,J}}^{CL}+\widehat{C_{k,J}}^{CL}-E\left[C_{i,J}+C_{k,J}\middle|\mathcal{D}_I\right]\right)^2\end{aligned}$$

Using the independence of the different accident years, we obtain, for the first term,

$$\mathrm{Var}\left(C_{i,J}+C_{k,J}\middle|\mathcal{D}_I\right)=\mathrm{Var}\left(C_{i,J}\middle|\mathcal{D}_I\right)+\mathrm{Var}\left(C_{k,J}\middle|\mathcal{D}_I\right)$$

whereas, for the second term, we get

$$\begin{aligned}&\left(\widehat{C_{i,J}}^{CL}+\widehat{C_{k,J}}^{CL}-E\left[C_{i,J}+C_{k,J}\middle|\mathcal{D}_I\right]\right)^2\\ &\quad=\left(\widehat{C_{i,J}}^{CL}-E\left[C_{i,J}\middle|\mathcal{D}_I\right]\right)^2+\left(\widehat{C_{k,J}}^{CL}-E\left[C_{k,J}\middle|\mathcal{D}_I\right]\right)^2\\ &\quad\quad+2\left(\widehat{C_{i,J}}^{CL}-E\left[C_{i,J}\middle|\mathcal{D}_I\right]\right)\left(\widehat{C_{k,J}}^{CL}-E\left[C_{k,J}\middle|\mathcal{D}_I\right]\right)\end{aligned}$$

Hence, we have the following decomposition for the conditional MSEP of the sum of two accident years:

$$\begin{aligned}&E\left[\left(\widehat{C_{i,J}}^{CL}+\widehat{C_{k,J}}^{CL}-(C_{i,J}+C_{k,J})\right)^2\middle|\mathcal{D}_I\right]\\ &\quad=E\left[\left(\widehat{C_{i,J}}^{CL}-C_{i,J}\right)^2\middle|\mathcal{D}_I\right]+E\left[\left(\widehat{C_{k,J}}^{CL}-C_{k,J}\right)^2\middle|\mathcal{D}_I\right]\\ &\quad\quad+2\left(\widehat{C_{i,J}}^{CL}-E\left[C_{i,J}\middle|\mathcal{D}_I\right]\right)\left(\widehat{C_{k,J}}^{CL}-E\left[C_{k,J}\middle|\mathcal{D}_I\right]\right)\end{aligned}$$

Thus,

$$\begin{aligned}
&\mathrm{msep}_{C_{i,J}+C_{k,J}|\mathcal{D}_I}\left(\widehat{C_{i,J}}^{\mathrm{CL}}+\widehat{C_{k,J}}^{\mathrm{CL}}\right)\\
&=\mathrm{msep}_{C_{i,J}|\mathcal{D}_I}\left(\widehat{C_{i,J}}^{\mathrm{CL}}\right)+\mathrm{msep}_{C_{k,J}|\mathcal{D}_I}\left(\widehat{C_{k,J}}^{\mathrm{CL}}\right)\\
&\quad+2\left(\widehat{C_{i,J}}^{\mathrm{CL}}-E\left[C_{i,J}\middle|\mathcal{D}_I\right]\right)\left(\widehat{C_{k,J}}^{\mathrm{CL}}-E\left[C_{k,J}\middle|\mathcal{D}_I\right]\right)
\end{aligned}\tag{3.36}$$

In addition to the conditional MSEP for single accident years, we obtain cross-products that have the following form

$$\begin{aligned}
&\left(\widehat{C_{i,J}}^{\mathrm{CL}}-E\left[C_{i,J}\middle|\mathcal{D}_I\right]\right)\left(\widehat{C_{k,J}}^{\mathrm{CL}}-E\left[C_{k,J}\middle|\mathcal{D}_I\right]\right)\\
&=C_{i,I-i}\left(\widehat{f}_{I-i}\cdots\widehat{f}_{J-1}-f_{I-i}\cdots f_{J-1}\right)\\
&\quad\times\ C_{k,I-k}\left(\widehat{f}_{I-k}\cdots\widehat{f}_{J-1}-f_{I-k}\cdots f_{J-1}\right)
\end{aligned}$$

Now we could have the same discussion on resampling as above. Here, we simply use Approach 3 for resampling, that is, we choose the probability measure $P^*_{\mathcal{D}_I}$. We can then explicitly calculate these cross-products. As in (3.26), we obtain as an estimate for the cross-products

$$\begin{aligned}
&C_{i,I-i}\,C_{k,I-k}\,E^*_{\mathcal{D}_I}\left[\left(\prod_{j=I-i}^{J-1}\widehat{f}_j-\prod_{j=I-i}^{J-1}f_j\right)\left(\prod_{j=I-k}^{J-1}\widehat{f}_j-\prod_{j=I-k}^{J-1}f_j\right)\right]\\
&=C_{i,I-i}\,C_{k,I-k}\,\mathrm{Cov}_{P^*_{\mathcal{D}_I}}\left(\widehat{f}_{I-i}\cdots\widehat{f}_{J-1},\widehat{f}_{I-k}\cdots\widehat{f}_{J-1}\right)\\
&=C_{i,I-i}\,C_{k,I-k}\,f_{I-k}\cdots f_{I-i-1}\,\mathrm{Var}_{P^*_{\mathcal{D}_I}}\left(\widehat{f}_{I-i}\cdots\widehat{f}_{J-1}\right)\\
&=C_{i,I-i}\,C_{k,I-k}\,f_{I-k}\cdots f_{I-i-1}\left(\prod_{j=I-i}^{J-1}E^*_{\mathcal{D}_I}\left[\left(\widehat{f}_j\right)^2\right]-\prod_{j=I-i}^{J-1}f_j^2\right)\\
&=C_{i,I-i}\,E\left[C_{k,I-i}\middle|\mathcal{D}_I\right]\left(\prod_{j=I-i}^{J-1}\left(f_j^2+\frac{\sigma_j^2}{S_j^{[I-j-1]}}\right)-\prod_{j=I-i}^{J-1}f_j^2\right)
\end{aligned}$$

Now the estimation of the covariance term is straightforward from the estimate for a single accident year.

ESTIMATOR 3.14 (MSEP aggregated accident years, conditional version) *Under Model Assumptions 3.9 we have the following estimator for the conditional MSEP of the ultimate claim for aggregated accident years*

$$\begin{aligned}
&\widehat{\mathrm{msep}}_{\sum_i C_{i,J}|\mathcal{D}_I}\left(\sum_{i=1}^{I}\widehat{C_{i,J}}^{\mathrm{CL}}\right)=\widehat{E}\left[\left(\sum_{i=1}^{I}\widehat{C_{i,J}}^{\mathrm{CL}}-\sum_{i=1}^{I}C_{i,J}\right)^2\middle|\mathcal{D}_I\right]\\
&=\sum_{i=1}^{I}\widehat{\mathrm{msep}}_{C_{i,J}|\mathcal{D}_I}\left(\widehat{C_{i,J}}^{\mathrm{CL}}\right)\\
&\quad+2\sum_{1\le i<k\le I}C_{i,I-i}\,\widehat{C_{k,I-i}}^{\mathrm{CL}}\left(\prod_{j=I-i}^{J-1}\left(\widehat{f}_j^2+\frac{\widehat{\sigma}_j^2}{S_j^{[I-j-1]}}\right)-\prod_{j=I-i}^{J-1}\widehat{f}_j^2\right)
\end{aligned}\tag{3.37}$$

Remarks 3.15

- The estimates of the covariance terms from the result above (i.e. the second term on the right-hand side of (3.37)) can be rewritten as

$$2 \sum_{1\le i<k\le I} \frac{\widehat{C_{k,I-i}}^{\mathrm{CL}}}{C_{i,I-i}} \widehat{\mathrm{Var}}\left(\widehat{C_{i,J}}^{\mathrm{CL}} \middle| \mathcal{D}_I\right)$$

  where $\widehat{\mathrm{Var}}\left(\widehat{C_{i,J}}^{\mathrm{CL}} \middle| \mathcal{D}_I\right)$ is the conditional estimation error for single accident year i (see (3.27)). This representation may be helpful in the implementation since it leads to matrix multiplications.
- We can again do a linear approximation to the conditional estimation error (for aggregated accident years) and then find the estimator (3.38) for the conditional MSEP presented in Mack (1993).

ESTIMATOR 3.16 (MSEP aggregated accident years, Mack formula) *Under Model Assumptions 3.9 we have the following estimator for the conditional MSEP of the ultimate claim for aggregated accident years*

$$\widehat{\mathrm{msep}}_{\sum_i C_{i,J}|\mathcal{D}_I}\left(\sum_{i=1}^{I} \widehat{C_{i,J}}^{\mathrm{CL}}\right) = \sum_{i=1}^{I} \widehat{\mathrm{msep}}_{C_{i,J}|\mathcal{D}_I}\left(\widehat{C_{i,J}}^{\mathrm{CL}}\right)$$
$$+2 \sum_{1\le i<k\le I} \widehat{C_{i,J}}^{\mathrm{CL}}\, \widehat{C_{k,J}}^{\mathrm{CL}} \sum_{j=I-i}^{J-1} \frac{\widehat{\sigma}_j^2/\widehat{f}_j^2}{S_j^{[I-j-1]}} \tag{3.38}$$

Example 3.7, revisited

We complete Example 3.7 by applying the results of this subsection to estimate the conditional MSEP for the aggregate ultimate claims estimate over all accident years. Numerical values are reported in Table 3.6. □

Table 3.6 CL reserves and error terms (Estimator 3.14)

i	$\widehat{C_{i,J}}^{\mathrm{CL}}$	CL reserves	$\widehat{\mathrm{Var}}(C_{i,J}\|\mathcal{D}_I)^{1/2}$		$\widehat{\mathrm{Var}}\left(\widehat{C_{i,J}}^{\mathrm{CL}}\|\mathcal{D}_I\right)^{1/2}$		$\widehat{\mathrm{msep}}_{C_{i,J}\|\mathcal{D}_I}\left(\widehat{C_{i,J}}^{\mathrm{CL}}\right)^{1/2}$	
0	11 148 124							
1	10 663 318	15 126	191	1.3%	187	1.2%	267	1.8%
2	10 662 008	26 257	742	2.8%	535	2.0%	914	3.5%
3	9 758 606	34 538	2669	7.7%	1493	4.3%	3058	8.9%
4	9 872 218	85 302	6832	8.0%	3392	4.0%	7628	8.9%
5	10 092 247	156 494	30 478	19.5%	13 517	8.6%	33 341	21.3%
6	9 568 143	286 121	68 212	23.8%	27 286	9.5%	73 467	25.7%
7	8 705 378	449 167	80 077	17.8%	29 675	6.6%	85 398	19.0%
8	8 691 971	1 043 242	126 960	12.2%	43 903	4.2%	134 337	12.9%
9	9 626 383	3 950 815	389 783	9.9%	129 770	3.3%	410 817	10.4%
Cov. term					116 811		116 811	
Total		6 047 061	424 379	7.0%	185 026	3.1%	462 960	7.7%

3.3 BOUNDS IN THE UNCONDITIONAL APPROACH

3.3.1 Results and Interpretation

In this section we revisit the unconditional resampling approach presented in (3.15). Due to the fact that the CL estimators $\widehat{f}_j$ are not independent under P we cannot explicitly calculate the estimation error within the unconditional approach. In this section we provide upper and lower bounds on (3.19) that were derived in Wüthrich *et al.* (2007a).

THEOREM 3.17 (lower bound) *Under Model Assumptions 3.9 we have*

$$C_{i,I-i}^2 E\left[\left(\prod_{j=I-i}^{J-1}\widehat{f}_j-\prod_{j=I-i}^{J-1}f_j\right)^2\middle|\mathcal{B}_{I-i}\right]\geq C_{i,I-i}^2\prod_{j=I-i}^{J-1}f_j^2\sum_{j=I-i}^{J-1}\frac{\sigma_j^2/f_j^2}{E\left[S_j^{[I-j-1]}\middle|\mathcal{B}_{I-i}\right]} \tag{3.39}$$

Henceforth, with the right-hand side of (3.39) we obtain a closed form for the lower bound. The upper bound, given by the right-hand side of (3.40), was conjectured by Mack *et al.* (2006) and proved by the same authors in the special case $(J-1)-(I-i)=1$, that is, in the case of two development factors (see Section 6 of Mack *et al.* 2006). The general case was proved by Wüthrich *et al.* (2007a).

THEOREM 3.18 (upper bound) *Under Model Assumptions 3.9 we have*

$$\begin{aligned}&C_{i,I-i}^2\, E\left[\left(\prod_{j=I-i}^{J-1}\widehat{f}_j-\prod_{j=I-i}^{J-1}f_j\right)^2\middle|\mathcal{B}_{I-i}\right]\\&\leq C_{i,I-i}^2\left(E\left[\prod_{j=I-i}^{J-1}\left(\frac{\sigma_j^2}{S_j^{[I-j-1]}}+f_j^2\right)\middle|\mathcal{B}_{I-i}\right]-\prod_{j=I-i}^{J-1}f_j^2\right)\end{aligned} \tag{3.40}$$

Observe that, in general, this upper bound cannot be calculated explicitly. For a numerical value one needs to apply simulation or bootstrap techniques.

The proofs of Theorems 3.17 and 3.18 are provided in Subsection 3.3.3.

Discussion of the Bounds

We compare Theorems 3.17 and 3.18 to the estimates for the conditional estimation error obtained by Mack (1993) (see (3.35)) and in the conditional resampling approach (see (3.27)).

Mack formula The estimation error coming from Mack's (1993) formula has the following form (see (3.35))

$$EE^{\text{Mack}}=C_{i,I-i}^2\sum_{j=I-i}^{J-1}\prod_{k=I-i}^{j-1}\widehat{f}_k^2\prod_{k=j}^{J-1}f_k^2\,\frac{\sigma_j^2/f_j^2}{S_j^{[I-j-1]}}$$

Let us for the time being replace the estimators $\widehat{f}_k$ by the true CL factors f_k, then the modified Mack estimation error reads as

$$\widetilde{EE}^{\text{Mack}} = C_{i,I-i}^2 \prod_{j=I-i}^{J-1} f_j^2 \sum_{j=I-i}^{J-1} \frac{\sigma_j^2/f_j^2}{S_j^{[I-j-1]}}$$

Conditional approach In the conditional approach the estimation error has the following form (see (3.26))

$$EE^{\text{BBMW}} = C_{i,I-i}^2 \left(\prod_{j=I-i}^{J-1} \left(\frac{\sigma_j^2}{S_j^{[I-j-1]}} + f_j^2 \right) - \prod_{j=I-i}^{J-1} f_j^2 \right)$$

Doing the linear approximation from below, we obtain the following inequality (see also (3.31))

$$\widetilde{EE}^{\text{Mack}} \leq EE^{\text{BBMW}}$$

A comparison to the Unconditional Results For the lower bound we obtain, using Jensen's inequality,

$$\begin{aligned} E\left[EE^{\text{BBMW}} \middle| \mathcal{B}_{I-i}\right] &\geq E\left[\widetilde{EE}^{\text{Mack}} \middle| \mathcal{B}_{I-i}\right] \\ &= C_{i,I-i}^2 \prod_{j=I-i}^{J-1} f_j^2 \sum_{j=I-i}^{J-1} \sigma_j^2/f_j^2 \; E\left[\frac{1}{S_j^{[I-j-1]}} \middle| \mathcal{B}_{I-i}\right] \\ &\geq C_{i,I-i}^2 \prod_{j=I-i}^{J-1} f_j^2 \sum_{j=I-i}^{J-1} \frac{\sigma_j^2/f_j^2}{E\left[S_j^{[I-j-1]} \middle| \mathcal{B}_{I-i}\right]} \end{aligned}$$

This means that the conditional estimation error estimates $\widetilde{EE}^{\text{Mack}}$ and EE^{BBMW} are, in the average, bounded from below by the unconditional lower bound given in Theorem 3.17. On the other hand, we have as averaged upper bound

$$\begin{aligned} E\left[\widetilde{EE}^{\text{Mack}} \middle| \mathcal{B}_{I-i}\right] &\leq E\left[EE^{\text{BBMW}} \middle| \mathcal{B}_{I-i}\right] \\ &= C_{i,I-i}^2 \left(E\left[\prod_{j=I-i}^{J-1} \left(\frac{\sigma_j^2}{S_j^{[I-j-1]}} + f_j^2 \right) \middle| \mathcal{B}_{I-i} \right] - \prod_{j=I-i}^{J-1} f_j^2 \right) \end{aligned} \quad (3.41)$$

This means that if we average EE^{BBMW} (unconditionally) over all possible outcomes, given $\mathcal{B}_{I-i}$, we obtain exactly the upper bound.

Note that the unconditional upper bound (3.41) cannot, in general, be calculated explicitly. Therefore, we choose a simulation-based example to illustrate and examine the bounds.

Example 3.19 (bounds in the unconditional approach)

For the set $\mathcal{B}_0$ we use the observations given in Table 3.7 for the first development period ($I=9$). The true parameters f_j and σ_j are given in Table 3.8 ($J=8$).

Table 3.7 Observations $\mathcal{B}_0$

Accident year i	$C_{i,0}$
0	2 357 848
1	2 352 118
2	2 290 507
3	2 310 608
4	2 443 160
5	2 396 132
6	2 440 832
7	2 359 480
8	2 376 686
9	2 344 014

Table 3.8 True parameters f_j and σ_j

$j=$	0	1	2	3	4	5	6	7
f_j	2.500	1.750	1.450	1.200	1.100	1.080	1.040	1.010
σ_j	150	125	100	90	80	60	40	20

The noise terms $\varepsilon_{i,j}$ are assumed to be uniform i.i.d. on $[-\sqrt{3}, \sqrt{3}]$. For our given set $\mathcal{B}_0$, this model satisfies Model Assumptions 3.9, with $\varepsilon_{i,j}$ as centred normalized error terms. Now, we can generate observations $\mathcal{D}_I$; for example, one realization for $\mathcal{D}_I$ is given in Table 3.9.

We see that the estimated values $\widehat{f}_j$ from our simulation differ from the true values f_j. Moreover, we can explicitly calculate the square root of the 'true' estimation error for this specific realization (since the true CL factors are known).

For simplicity, we do the analysis for one fixed accident year $i=I=9$. Hence the square root of the (conditional) estimation error is given by

$$\left|\widehat{C_{I,J}}^{\mathrm{CL}} - E\left[C_{I,J}\middle|\mathcal{D}_I\right]\right| = C_{I,0}\left|\prod_{j=0}^{J-1}\widehat{f}_j - \prod_{j=0}^{J-1} f_j\right|$$

$$= 2\,344\,014\ |9.2095 - 9.4994| = 679\,680$$

This should be put in relation to the expected claims reserves for accident year $i=I=9$, given $\mathcal{D}_I$, which are given by

$$E\left[C_{I,J}\middle|\mathcal{D}_I\right] - C_{I,0} = C_{I,0}\left(\prod_{j=0}^{J-1} f_j - 1\right) = 19\,922\,830$$

Table 3.9 Observations $\mathcal{D}_9$ and CL factor estimates $\widehat{f}_j$

	0	1	2	3	4	5	6	7	8
0	2 357 848	6 194 657	10 804 432	15 538 279	18 710 626	20 318 904	21 796 320	22 904 680	23 148 411
1	2 352 118	5 615 038	9 905 629	14 448 210	16 932 449	18 774 090	20 076 476	21 013 717	21 193 048
2	2 290 507	5 348 320	9 377 174	13 723 332	16 002 956	17 346 200	19 131 294	19 647 332	
3	2 310 608	6 060 981	10 846 276	15 792 649	18 359 829	19 958 378	21 911 347		
4	2 443 160	5 978 767	10 167 136	14 258 266	16 910 203	18 990 284			
5	2 396 132	5 685 230	10 410 969	15 161 495	17 990 186				
6	2 440 832	5 995 705	10 425 172	15 033 938					
7	2 359 480	5 944 283	10 194 524						
8	2 376 686	5 592 105							
9	2 344 014								
$\widehat{f}_j$	2.458	1.754	1.445	1.180	1.097	1.085	1.042	1.010	

The lower bound for the estimation error (cf. Theorem 3.17) can be calculated explicitly. The exact value and the upper bound of the estimation error can only be determined via simulations. Hence, if we repeat the simulation procedure from above we obtain an empirical distribution from which we can calculate the empirical exact value and the empirical upper bound given in Theorem 3.18. With 30 000 independent simulations, Table 3.10 shows the result for the square root of the estimation error for accident year $i=I=9$.

Table 3.10 Lower bound: closed formula. Empirical values: 30 000 simulations

	Reserves $E\left[C_{I,J}\middle\vert \mathcal{D}_I\right]-C_{I,0}$	$\sqrt{\text{lower bound}}$	Empirical $\sqrt{\text{exact value}}$	Empirical $E\left[\widetilde{EE}^{\text{Mack}}\middle\vert \mathcal{B}_0\right]^{1/2}$	Empirical $\sqrt{\text{upper bound}}$
Accid. year $i=9$	19 922 830	515 318	517 906	515 415	515 471

We observe that the empirical upper bound is very close to the exact lower bound: $515\,471-515\,318=153$; moreover the empirical value of the averaged modified Mack estimation $\widetilde{EE}^{\text{Mack}}$ lies within these two bounds (as expected from the discussions above).

However, we also observe that the empirical exact value of the estimation error is larger than the upper bound. At the first sight, this is surprising because we would expect it to lie within the two bounds. However, the empirical distribution for the exact value

$$C_{I,0}^2\left(\prod_{j=0}^{J-1}\widehat{f}_j-\prod_{j=0}^{J-1}f_j\right)^2$$

has a much larger volatility compared to the empirical distribution of the upper bound

$$C_{I,0}^2\left(\prod_{j=0}^{J-1}\left(\frac{\sigma_j^2}{S_j^{[I-j-1]}}+f_j^2\right)-\prod_{j=0}^{J-1}f_j^2\right)$$

The empirical uncertainty (standard deviations of 30 000 simulations) of the upper bound is given in Table 3.11 and compared with the empirical uncertainty of the exact estimation error. We construct the square roots of the upper and lower confidence bounds with a distance of one empirical standard deviation (average estimation error) to the empirical mean (see Table 3.11).

We see that the uncertainty in the exact value is a lot larger than that in the upper bound. Hence, from this point of view one should prefer the empirical upper bound over

Table 3.11 Lower bound (closed formula), empirical exact value and empirical upper bound (30 000 simulations)

	$\sqrt{\text{lower bound}}$	Empirical $\sqrt{\text{exact value}}$	Empirical $\sqrt{\text{upper bound}}$
Empirical value	515 318	517 906	515 471
Upper confidence bound	515 318	544 927	515 716
Lower confidence bound	515 318	489 396	515 226

the empirical exact value. This means that, here, we have an example where a wrong model (upper bound) gives better results than the true empirical model (empirical exact value) due to the fact that the volatility is much smaller in the upper bound. The reason for this behaviour is that, in the upper bound, one calculates terms for the second moments in a closed form and averages (Monte Carlo) only over terms of the first moment. For the empirical exact value one performs a Monte Carlo simulation for second moments, which has a higher volatility. □

3.3.2 Aggregation of Accident Years

For reasons of completeness we also provide the MSEP bounds for aggregated accident years, and study the conditional MSEP of the estimator

$$\sum_{i=1}^{I} \widehat{C_{i,J}}^{\mathrm{CL}}$$

With (3.36) we find

$$\begin{aligned}
&\operatorname{msep}_{\sum_i C_{i,J}|\mathcal{D}_I}\left(\sum_{i=1}^{I} \widehat{C_{i,J}}^{\mathrm{CL}}\right)\\
&\quad=\sum_{i=1}^{I} \operatorname{msep}_{C_{i,J}|\mathcal{D}_I}\left(\widehat{C_{i,J}}^{\mathrm{CL}}\right)\\
&\qquad+2\sum_{1\le i<k\le I}\left(\widehat{C_{i,J}}^{\mathrm{CL}}-E\left[C_{i,J}\middle|\mathcal{D}_I\right]\right)\left(\widehat{C_{k,J}}^{\mathrm{CL}}-E\left[C_{k,J}\middle|\mathcal{D}_I\right]\right)
\end{aligned} \tag{3.42}$$

In addition to the conditional MSEP for single accident years we obtain covariance terms that come from the fact that we use the same estimates $\widehat{f}_j$ for different accident years. Hence, in addition to the conditional estimation errors for single accident years, we need to estimate

$$\begin{aligned}
&\left(\widehat{C_{i,J}}^{\mathrm{CL}}-E\left[C_{i,J}\middle|\mathcal{D}_I\right]\right)\left(\widehat{C_{k,J}}^{\mathrm{CL}}-E\left[C_{k,J}\middle|\mathcal{D}_I\right]\right)\\
&\quad=C_{i,I-i}\,C_{k,I-k}\left(\prod_{j=I-i}^{J-1}\widehat{f}_j-\prod_{j=I-i}^{J-1}f_j\right)\left(\prod_{j=I-k}^{J-1}\widehat{f}_j-\prod_{j=I-k}^{J-1}f_j\right)
\end{aligned} \tag{3.43}$$

Hence, the estimation error in the unconditional approach of the last term in (3.43) is estimated by $(i<k)$

$$\begin{aligned}
&E\left[\left(\prod_{j=I-i}^{J-1}\widehat{f}_j-\prod_{j=I-i}^{J-1}f_j\right)\left(\prod_{j=I-k}^{J-1}\widehat{f}_j-\prod_{j=I-k}^{J-1}f_j\right)\middle|\mathcal{B}_{I-k}\right]\\
&\quad=\operatorname{Cov}\left(\prod_{j=I-i}^{J-1}\widehat{f}_j,\prod_{j=I-k}^{J-1}\widehat{f}_j\middle|\mathcal{B}_{I-k}\right)
\end{aligned} \tag{3.44}$$

This leads to the following theorem for the covariance terms.

THEOREM 3.20 (covariance terms) *Under Model Assumptions 3.9 we have for $i < k$*

$$\prod_{j=I-k}^{I-i-1} f_j \prod_{j=I-i}^{J-1} f_j^2 \sum_{j=I-i}^{J-1} \frac{\sigma_j^2/f_j^2}{E\left[S_j^{[I-j-1]}\middle|\mathcal{B}_{I-k}\right]} \leq \mathrm{Cov}\left(\prod_{j=I-i}^{J-1} \widehat{f}_j, \prod_{j=I-k}^{J-1} \widehat{f}_j \middle| \mathcal{B}_{I-k}\right)$$

$$\leq \prod_{j=I-k}^{I-i-1} f_j \left(E\left[\prod_{j=I-i}^{J-1}\left(\frac{\sigma_j^2}{S_j^{[I-j-1]}}+f_j^2\right)\middle|\mathcal{B}_{I-k}\right]-\prod_{j=I-i}^{J-1} f_j^2\right) \tag{3.45}$$

3.3.3 Proof of Theorems 3.17, 3.18 and 3.20

First we give the proof of the lower bound given in Theorem 3.17. Observe that we have (cf. (3.25) and (3.7))

$$E\left[\widehat{f}_j^2\middle|\mathcal{B}_j\right]=E\left[\left(\frac{S_{j+1}^{[I-j-1]}}{S_j^{[I-j-1]}}\right)^2\middle|\mathcal{B}_j\right]=\frac{\sigma_j^2}{S_j^{[I-j-1]}}+f_j^2 \tag{3.46}$$

We start with a preparatory lemma which is further generalized in Lemma 3.22 below.

LEMMA 3.21 *Under Model Assumptions 3.9 we have*

$$E\left[\widehat{f}_{j-1}^2\,\widehat{f}_j^2\middle|\mathcal{B}_{j-1}\right]\geq\left(\frac{\sigma_{j-1}^2}{S_{j-1}^{[I-j]}}+f_{j-1}^2\right)f_j^2+\frac{\sigma_j^2\,f_{j-1}}{S_{j-1}^{[I-j-1]}}$$

Proof of Lemma 3.21 With formula (3.46) we see

$$\begin{aligned}
&E\left[\widehat{f}_{j-1}^2\,\widehat{f}_j^2\middle|\mathcal{B}_{j-1}\right]\\
&\quad=E\left[\widehat{f}_{j-1}^2\,E\left[\widehat{f}_j^2\middle|\mathcal{B}_j\right]\middle|\mathcal{B}_{j-1}\right]\\
&\quad=E\left[\widehat{f}_{j-1}^2\left(\frac{\sigma_j^2}{S_j^{[I-j-1]}}+f_j^2\right)\middle|\mathcal{B}_{j-1}\right]\\
&\quad=\left(\frac{\sigma_{j-1}^2}{S_{j-1}^{[I-j]}}+f_{j-1}^2\right)f_j^2+\frac{\sigma_j^2}{\left(S_{j-1}^{[I-j]}\right)^2}\,E\left[\left(S_j^{[I-j]}\right)^2\frac{1}{S_j^{[I-j-1]}}\middle|\mathcal{B}_{j-1}\right]
\end{aligned}$$

Our goal is to bound this last term from below. We have

$$\begin{aligned}
&E\left[\left(S_j^{[I-j]}\right)^2\frac{1}{S_j^{[I-j-1]}}\middle|\mathcal{B}_{j-1}\right]\\
&\quad=E\left[\left(S_j^{[I-j-1]}+C_{I-j,j}\right)^2\frac{1}{S_j^{[I-j-1]}}\middle|\mathcal{B}_{j-1}\right]
\end{aligned}$$

$$
\begin{aligned}
&= E\left[S_j^{[I-j-1]} \middle| \mathcal{B}_{j-1} \right] + 2E\left[C_{I-j,j} \middle| \mathcal{B}_{j-1} \right] + E\left[\frac{C_{I-j,j}^2}{S_j^{[I-j-1]}} \middle| \mathcal{B}_{j-1} \right] \\
&= f_{j-1} \left(S_{j-1}^{[I-j]} + C_{I-j,j-1} \right) + E\left[\frac{C_{I-j,j}^2}{S_j^{[I-j-1]}} \middle| \mathcal{B}_{j-1} \right] \qquad (3.47)
\end{aligned}
$$

Observe that the two terms in the fraction of the last term on the right-hand side of (3.47) correspond to different accident years, and hence are independent. This immediately gives, using Jensen's inequality, that

$$
\begin{aligned}
&E\left[\left(S_j^{[I-j]} \right)^2 \frac{1}{S_j^{[I-j-1]}} \middle| \mathcal{B}_{j-1} \right] \\
&\quad = f_{j-1} \left(S_{j-1}^{[I-j]} + C_{I-j,j-1} \right) + E\left[C_{I-j,j}^2 \middle| \mathcal{B}_{j-1} \right] \, E\left[\frac{1}{S_j^{[I-j-1]}} \middle| \mathcal{B}_{j-1} \right] \\
&\quad \geq f_{j-1} \left(S_{j-1}^{[I-j]} + C_{I-j,j-1} \right) + \frac{E\left[C_{I-j,j} \middle| \mathcal{B}_{j-1} \right]^2}{E\left[S_j^{[I-j-1]} \middle| \mathcal{B}_{j-1} \right]} \\
&\quad = f_{j-1} \left(S_{j-1}^{[I-j]} + C_{I-j,j-1} + \frac{C_{I-j,j-1}^2}{S_{j-1}^{[I-j-1]}} \right) = f_{j-1} \frac{\left(S_{j-1}^{[I-j]} \right)^2}{S_{j-1}^{[I-j-1]}} \qquad (3.48)
\end{aligned}
$$

Bringing all pieces together, we obtain

$$
E\left[\widehat{f}_{j-1}^2 \, \widehat{f}_j^2 \middle| \mathcal{B}_{j-1} \right] \geq \left(\frac{\sigma_{j-1}^2}{S_{j-1}^{[I-j]}} + f_{j-1}^2 \right) f_j^2 + \frac{\sigma_j^2 \, f_{j-1}}{S_{j-1}^{[I-j-1]}}
$$

This completes the proof of Lemma 3.21. □

Inequality (3.48) holds true in a more general setup:

LEMMA 3.22 *Under Model Assumptions 3.9 we have for $r \geq 1$ that*

$$
E\left[\left(S_j^{[I-j]} \right)^2 \frac{1}{S_j^{[I-j-r]}} \middle| \mathcal{B}_{j-1} \right] \geq f_{j-1} \frac{\left(S_{j-1}^{[I-j]} \right)^2}{S_{j-1}^{[I-j-r]}}
$$

Proof of Lemma 3.22 The proof is similar to the calculation in (3.48). □

Proof of Theorem 3.17 We prove the theorem by induction.

(a) Assume that $I - i = J - 2$. Then, using Lemma 3.21, we have

$$
E\left[\left(\prod_{j=J-2}^{J-1} \widehat{f}_j - \prod_{j=J-2}^{J-1} f_j \right)^2 \middle| \mathcal{B}_{J-2} \right] = E\left[\prod_{j=J-2}^{J-1} \widehat{f}_j^2 \middle| \mathcal{B}_{J-2} \right] - \prod_{j=J-2}^{J-1} f_j^2
$$

$$\geq \left(\frac{\sigma_{J-2}^2}{S_{J-2}^{[I-J+1]}} + f_{J-2}^2 \right) f_{J-1}^2 + \frac{\sigma_{J-1}^2 \, f_{J-2}}{S_{J-2}^{[I-J]}} - f_{J-2}^2 \, f_{J-1}^2$$

$$= \frac{\sigma_{J-2}^2 \, f_{J-1}^2}{S_{J-2}^{[I-J+1]}} + \frac{\sigma_{J-1}^2 \, f_{J-2}^2}{f_{J-2} \, S_{J-2}^{[I-J]}}$$

$$= f_{J-1}^2 \, f_{J-2}^2 \left(\frac{\sigma_{J-2}^2 / f_{J-2}^2}{E\left[S_{J-2}^{[I-J+1]} \middle| \mathcal{B}_{J-2} \right]} + \frac{\sigma_{J-1}^2 / f_{J-1}^2}{E\left[S_{J-1}^{[I-J]} \middle| \mathcal{B}_{J-2} \right]} \right)$$

(b) Induction step. Assume that the claim is true for $I-i+1$, then we prove that it is also true for $I-i$. Using the induction step we have

$$E\left[\prod_{j=I-i}^{J-1} \widehat{f}_j^2 \middle| \mathcal{B}_{I-i} \right]$$

$$= E\left[\widehat{f}_{I-i}^2 \, E\left[\prod_{j=I-i+1}^{J-1} \widehat{f}_j^2 \middle| \mathcal{B}_{I-i+1} \right] \middle| \mathcal{B}_{I-i} \right]$$

$$\geq E\left[\widehat{f}_{I-i}^2 \prod_{j=I-i+1}^{J-1} f_j^2 \left(\sum_{j=I-i+1}^{J-1} \frac{\sigma_j^2 / f_j^2}{E\left[S_j^{[I-j-1]} \middle| \mathcal{B}_{I-i+1} \right]} + 1 \right) \middle| \mathcal{B}_{I-i} \right]$$

$$= \prod_{j=I-i+1}^{J-1} f_j^2 \left(E\left[\widehat{f}_{I-i}^2 \middle| \mathcal{B}_{I-i} \right] + \sum_{j=I-i+1}^{J-1} E\left[\widehat{f}_{I-i}^2 \frac{\sigma_j^2 / f_j^2}{E\left[S_j^{[I-j-1]} \middle| \mathcal{B}_{I-i+1} \right]} \middle| \mathcal{B}_{I-i} \right] \right)$$

Observe that

$$E\left[\widehat{f}_{I-i}^2 \middle| \mathcal{B}_{I-i} \right] = \frac{\sigma_{I-i}^2}{S_{I-i}^{[i-1]}} + f_{I-i}^2 = f_{I-i}^2 \left(\frac{\sigma_{I-i}^2 / f_{I-i}^2}{S_{I-i}^{[i-1]}} + 1 \right)$$

and, with Lemma 3.22, we have

$$E\left[\widehat{f}_{I-i}^2 \frac{\sigma_j^2 / f_j^2}{E\left[S_j^{[I-j-1]} \middle| \mathcal{B}_{I-i+1} \right]} \middle| \mathcal{B}_{I-i} \right]$$

$$= \frac{\sigma_j^2 / f_j^2}{\left(S_{I-i}^{[i-1]} \right)^2 \prod_{k=I-i+1}^{j-1} f_k} \, E\left[\left(S_{I-i+1}^{[i-1]} \right)^2 \frac{1}{S_{I-i+1}^{[I-j-1]}} \middle| \mathcal{B}_{I-i} \right]$$

$$\geq \frac{\sigma_j^2 / f_j^2}{\left(S_{I-i}^{[i-1]} \right)^2 \prod_{k=I-i+1}^{j-1} f_k} \left(f_{I-i} \frac{\left(S_{I-i}^{[i-1]} \right)^2}{S_{I-i}^{[I-j-1]}} \right) = f_{I-i}^2 \, \frac{\sigma_j^2 / f_j^2}{E\left[S_j^{[I-j-1]} \middle| \mathcal{B}_{I-i} \right]}$$

Putting all pieces together completes the proof of Theorem 3.17. □

To prove the upper bound we use the Fortuin–Kasteleyn–Ginibre (FKG) inequality (see Fortuin *et al.* 1971) in the form stated in Lemma 3.23. The FKG inequality essentially tells us how to deal with correlated random variables. Choose $n \in \mathbb{N}$, and assume that $Y_1, \ldots, Y_n$ is a sequence of independent random variables.

LEMMA 3.23 (FKG inequality) *Assume that $f(Y_1, \ldots, Y_n)$ and $g(Y_1, \ldots, Y_n)$ are two coordinate-wise non-decreasing real functions. Then we have that*

$$E[f(Y_1, \ldots, Y_n)\, g(Y_1, \ldots, Y_n)] \geq E[f(Y_1, \ldots, Y_n)]\; E[g(Y_1, \ldots, Y_n)]$$

Proof of Theorem 3.18 We prove the theorem by induction.

(a) Assume that $I - i = J - 2$. Then, using Lemma 3.8 (negative correlations), we have

$$\begin{aligned} E\left[\widehat{f}_{J-2}^2\, \widehat{f}_{J-1}^2 \middle| \mathcal{B}_{J-2}\right] &\leq E\left[\widehat{f}_{J-2}^2 \middle| \mathcal{B}_{J-2}\right]\, E\left[\widehat{f}_{J-1}^2 \middle| \mathcal{B}_{J-2}\right] \\ &= \left(\frac{\sigma_{J-2}^2}{S_{J-2}^{[I-J+1]}} + f_{J-2}^2\right) E\left[\frac{\sigma_{J-1}^2}{S_{J-1}^{[I-J]}} + f_{J-1}^2 \middle| \mathcal{B}_{J-2}\right] \\ &= E\left[\left(\frac{\sigma_{J-2}^2}{S_{J-2}^{[I-J+1]}} + f_{J-2}^2\right)\left(\frac{\sigma_{J-1}^2}{S_{J-1}^{[I-J]}} + f_{J-1}^2\right) \middle| \mathcal{B}_{J-2}\right] \end{aligned}$$

This completes the proof for $I - i = J - 2$.

(b) Induction step. Assume that the claim is true for $I - i + 1$. We prove that it is also true for $I - i$. Using the induction step, we have

$$\begin{aligned} & E\left[\prod_{j=I-i}^{J-1} \widehat{f}_j^2 \middle| \mathcal{B}_{I-i}\right] \\ &= E\left[\widehat{f}_{I-i}^2\, E\left[\prod_{j=I-i+1}^{J-1} \widehat{f}_j^2 \middle| \mathcal{B}_{I-i+1}\right] \middle| \mathcal{B}_{I-i}\right] \\ &\leq E\left[\widehat{f}_{I-i}^2\, E\left[\prod_{j=I-i+1}^{J-1} \left(\frac{\sigma_j^2}{S_j^{[I-j-1]}} + f_j^2\right) \middle| \mathcal{B}_{I-i+1}\right] \middle| \mathcal{B}_{I-i}\right] \\ &= \frac{1}{\left(S_{I-i}^{[i-1]}\right)^2}\, E\left[\left(S_{I-i+1}^{[i-1]}\right)^2 E\left[\prod_{j=I-i+1}^{J-1} \left(\frac{\sigma_j^2}{S_j^{[I-j-1]}} + f_j^2\right) \middle| \mathcal{B}_{I-i+1}\right] \middle| \mathcal{B}_{I-i}\right] \end{aligned} \tag{3.49}$$

Next, we apply the FKG inequality to the right-hand side of the inequality above (for the measure $P_{\mathcal{B}_{I-i}} = P[\cdot|\mathcal{B}_{I-i}]$). Notice that under the measure $P_{\mathcal{B}_{I-i}}$ the coordinates of the random vector $\varepsilon = \left(\varepsilon_{k,I-i+1}\right)_{k \in \{0,\ldots,I\}}$ are independent. We define

$$\widetilde{f}(\varepsilon) = S_{I-i+1}^{[i-1]} = f_{I-i}\, S_{I-i}^{[i-1]} + \sigma_{I-i} \sum_{k=0}^{i-1} \sqrt{C_{k,I-i}}\; \varepsilon_{k,I-i+1}$$

Note that, due to our assumption $P\left[C_{i,j}>0 \middle| \mathcal{B}_0\right]=1$ for all $i \in \{0,\ldots,I\}$ and $j \in \{1,\ldots,J\}$, we have: conditional on $\mathcal{B}_{I-i}$, $\widetilde{f}$ is a positive function which is coordinate-wise increasing in $\varepsilon_{k,I-i+1}$, hence the function $f(\varepsilon)=\widetilde{f}(\varepsilon)^2$ is also coordinate-wise increasing.

On the other hand, we define the function

$$g(\varepsilon)=E\left[\prod_{j=I-i+1}^{J-1}\left(\frac{\sigma_j^2}{S_j^{[I-j-1]}}+f_j^2\right)\middle|\mathcal{B}_{I-i+1}\right] \tag{3.50}$$

We now prove that $g(\varepsilon)$ is a coordinate-wise non-increasing function in ε.

We first consider the cumulative claims $C_{m,I-i+k}$ as a function of $\varepsilon_{m,I-i+1}$ (for $k\geq 1$). Observe that $C_{m,I-i+k}$ does not depend on $\varepsilon_{n,l}$, $l\leq I-i+1$, for $m\neq n$.

Define

$$\begin{aligned}
C_{m,I-i+1}\left(\varepsilon_{m,I-i+1}\right)&=f_{I-i}\; C_{m,I-i}+\sigma_{I-i}\,\sqrt{C_{m,I-i}}\;\varepsilon_{m,I-i+1}\\
C_{m,I-i+2}\left(\varepsilon_{m,I-i+1}\right)&=C_{m,I-i+2}\left(C_{m,I-i+1}\left(\varepsilon_{m,I-i+1}\right)\right)\\
C_{m,I-i+k}\left(\varepsilon_{m,I-i+1}\right)&=C_{m,I-i+k}\left(C_{m,I-i+k-1}\left(\varepsilon_{m,I-i+1}\right)\right) \qquad k\geq 3
\end{aligned}$$

This means that we consider the functions ($k\geq 1$)

$$C_{m,I-i+k}\left(\varepsilon_{m,I-i+1}\right)=C_{m,I-i+k}\circ C_{m,I-i+k-1}\circ\ldots\circ C_{m,I-i+1}\left(\varepsilon_{m,I-i+1}\right)$$

Observe that

$$\frac{\partial}{\partial\varepsilon_{m,I-i+1}}\;C_{m,I-i+1}=\sigma_{I-i}\,\sqrt{C_{m,I-i}}>0$$

and for $k\geq 2$ we have

$$\frac{\partial}{\partial\varepsilon_{m,I-i+1}}\;C_{m,I-i+k}=\prod_{l=2}^{k}C'_{m,I-i+l}\left(C_{m,I-i+l-1}\right)\;\sigma_{I-i}\,\sqrt{C_{m,I-i}}$$

Moreover, we have for $l\geq 2$

$$\begin{aligned}
C'_{m,I-i+l}(x)&=\frac{\partial}{\partial x}\;\left(f_{I-i+l-1}\;x+\sigma_{I-i+l-1}\,\sqrt{x}\;\varepsilon_{m,I-i+l}\right)\\
&=f_{I-i+l-1}+\sigma_{I-i+l-1}\,\frac{1}{2\,\sqrt{x}}\;\varepsilon_{m,I-i+l}\\
&=\frac{1}{2\,x}\;\left(f_{I-i+l-1}\;x+\sigma_{I-i+l-1}\,\sqrt{x}\;\varepsilon_{m,I-i+l}\right)+\frac{f_{I-i+l-1}}{2}
\end{aligned}$$

Henceforth, this implies, for $l\geq 2$,

$$\begin{aligned}
C'_{m,I-i+l}\left(C_{m,I-i+l-1}\right)&=\frac{1}{2C_{m,I-i+l-1}}\\
&\quad\times\left(f_{I-i+l-1}\;C_{m,I-i+l-1}+\sigma_{I-i+l-1}\,\sqrt{C_{m,I-i+l-1}}\;\varepsilon_{m,I-i+l}\right)+\frac{f_{I-i+l-1}}{2}\\
&=\frac{C_{m,I-i+l}}{2\;C_{m,I-i+l-1}}+\frac{f_{I-i+l-1}}{2}
\end{aligned}$$

Under Model Assumptions 3.9, we know that $C_{m,I-i+l-1}$ and $C_{m,I-i+l}$ are positive, $P[\cdot|\mathcal{B}_0]$–a.s., and that $f_{I-i+l-1} > 0$. This immediately implies that

$$C'_{m,I-i+l}\left(C_{m,I-i+l-1}\right) > 0, \qquad P[\cdot|\mathcal{B}_0]\text{–a.s.}$$

This proves that $C_{m,I-i+k}$ is a strictly increasing function in $\varepsilon_{m,I-i+1}$ for $k \geq 1$.

Consider now for $j \in \{I-i+1, \ldots, J-1\}$

$$S_j^{[I-j-1]} = \sum_{n=0}^{I-j-1} C_{n,j}$$

Hence, for $m \leq I-j-1$ we have that $S_j^{[I-j-1]}$ is a strictly increasing function of $\varepsilon_{m,I-i+1}$. Moreover, $S_j^{[I-j-1]}$ is independent of $\varepsilon_{m',I-i+1}$ if $m' > I-j-1$. But this immediately shows that

$$\prod_{j=I-i+1}^{J-1} \left(\frac{\sigma_j^2}{S_j^{[I-j-1]}} + f_j^2 \right)$$

is a decreasing function of $\varepsilon_{m,I-i+1}$ for $m \in \{0, \ldots, I\}$. Hence, the function $-g(\varepsilon)$ defined in (3.50) is a coordinate-wise increasing function. This implies that we can apply the FKG inequality to the right-hand side of (3.49), which gives

$$\begin{aligned}
&\frac{1}{\left(S_{I-i}^{[i-1]}\right)^2} E\left[\left(S_{I-i+1}^{[i-1]}\right)^2 E\left[\prod_{j=I-i+1}^{J-1} \left(\frac{\sigma_j^2}{S_j^{[I-j-1]}} + f_j^2 \right) \middle| \mathcal{B}_{I-i+1} \right] \middle| \mathcal{B}_{I-i} \right] \\
&\quad \leq \frac{1}{\left(S_{I-i}^{[i-1]}\right)^2} E\left[\left(S_{I-i+1}^{[i-1]}\right)^2 \middle| \mathcal{B}_{I-i} \right] E\left[\prod_{j=I-i+1}^{J-1} \left(\frac{\sigma_j^2}{S_j^{[I-j-1]}} + f_j^2 \right) \middle| \mathcal{B}_{I-i} \right] \\
&\quad = \left(\frac{\sigma_{I-i}^2}{S_{I-i}^{[i-1]}} + f_{I-i}^2 \right) E\left[\prod_{j=I-i+1}^{J-1} \left(\frac{\sigma_j^2}{S_j^{[I-j-1]}} + f_j^2 \right) \middle| \mathcal{B}_{I-i} \right]
\end{aligned}$$

This completes the proof of Theorem 3.18. □

Proof of Theorem 3.20 Choose $i < k$. Then, we have

$$\begin{aligned}
&\text{Cov}\left(\prod_{j=I-i}^{J-1} \widehat{f}_j, \prod_{j=I-k}^{J-1} \widehat{f}_j \middle| \mathcal{B}_{I-k} \right) \\
&\quad = E\left[\prod_{j=I-k}^{I-i-1} \widehat{f}_j \prod_{j=I-i}^{J-1} \widehat{f}_j^2 \middle| \mathcal{B}_{I-k} \right] - \prod_{j=I-k}^{I-i-1} f_j \prod_{j=I-i}^{J-1} f_j^2 \\
&\quad = E\left[\prod_{j=I-k}^{I-i-1} \widehat{f}_j \, E\left[\prod_{j=I-i}^{J-1} \widehat{f}_j^2 \middle| \mathcal{B}_{I-i} \right] \middle| \mathcal{B}_{I-k} \right] - \prod_{j=I-k}^{I-i-1} f_j \prod_{j=I-i}^{J-1} f_j^2 \qquad (3.51)
\end{aligned}$$

Now, we can apply Theorems 3.17 and 3.18 to find the following lower bound

$$E\left[\prod_{j=I-k}^{I-i-1}\widehat{f}_j \prod_{j=I-i}^{J-1} f_j^2 \left(\sum_{j=I-i}^{J-1} \frac{\sigma_j^2/f_j^2}{E\left[S_j^{[I-j-1]}\middle|\mathcal{B}_{I-i}\right]}+1\right)\middle|\mathcal{B}_{I-k}\right]$$

$$-\prod_{j=I-k}^{I-i-1} f_j \prod_{j=I-i}^{J-1} f_j^2$$

and the upper bound

$$E\left[\prod_{j=I-k}^{I-i-1}\widehat{f}_j\, E\left[\prod_{j=I-i}^{J-1}\left(\frac{\sigma_j^2}{S_j^{[I-j-1]}}+f_j^2\right)\middle|\mathcal{B}_{I-i}\right]\middle|\mathcal{B}_{I-k}\right]-\prod_{j=I-k}^{I-i-1} f_j \prod_{j=I-i}^{J-1} f_j^2$$

The proof of the lower bound now follows similarly from Jensen's inequality as in the proof of Theorem 3.17. The proof of the upper bound follows similarly from the FKG inequality as in the proof of Theorem 3.18. This completes the proof of Theorem 3.20. □

3.4 ANALYSIS OF ERROR TERMS IN THE CL METHOD

In this section we further analyse the conditional MSEP of the CL method. In particular, we consider three different kinds of error terms: (a) conditional process error; (b) conditional parameter prediction error; and (c) conditional parameter estimation error. To analyse these three terms we define a model that is different from the classical CL model. Although it is slightly more complicated than the classical model, it leads to a clear distinction between these error terms. A need for a clear distinction between different error types is motivated by the different sources of uncertainties driving the errors. We believe that in the light of the solvency discussions (see, e.g., SST 2006, Sandström 2005, 2007, Buchwalder *et al.* 2005, 2007, Keller 2007, Bühlmann and Merz 2007 or Wüthrich 2006) we should clearly distinguish between the different risk factors.

In this section we closely follow Wüthrich (2008). For a similar Bayesian approach we also refer to Gisler (2006) and Gisler and Wüthrich (2007) as well as Section 9.2 below.

3.4.1 Classical CL Model

The observed individual development factors were defined by (see also (3.5))

$$F_{i,j}=\frac{C_{i,j}}{C_{i,j-1}}$$

then we have, with Model Assumptions 3.2,

$$E\left[F_{i,j}\middle|C_{i,j-1}\right]=f_{j-1} \qquad \text{and} \qquad \operatorname{Var}\left(F_{i,j}\middle|C_{i,j-1}\right)=\frac{\sigma_{j-1}^2}{C_{i,j-1}}$$

The conditional variational coefficients of the development factors $F_{i,j}$ are given by

$$\text{Vco}\left(F_{i,j}\middle| C_{i,j-1}\right) = \text{Vco}\left(C_{i,j}\middle| C_{i,j-1}\right)$$
$$= \frac{\sigma_{j-1}}{f_{j-1}} C_{i,j-1}^{-1/2} \longrightarrow 0, \qquad \text{as } C_{i,j-1} \to \infty \tag{3.52}$$

Hence, for increasing volume, the conditional variational coefficients of $F_{i,j}$ converge to zero! It is exactly property (3.52) that is crucial in risk management. If we assume that risk is defined through these variational coefficients, it means that the risk completely disappears for very large portfolios (law of large numbers). However, it is well known that this is not the case in practice. There are always some external factors that influence a portfolio and are not diversifiable – for example, if jurisdiction changes, it is not helpful to have a large portfolio. Also the experiences in recent years have shown that we must be very careful with external factors and parameter errors since they cannot be diversified. Therefore, in almost all developments of new solvency guidelines and requirements, a lot of attention is given to these risks.

The goal of the following subsection is to define a CL model that takes this risk class into account.

3.4.2 Enhanced CL Model

The approach in this section modifies (3.52) as follows. We assume that there exist constants $a_0^2, a_1^2, \ldots, a_{J-1}^2 \geq 0$ such that for all $1 \leq j \leq J$ we have

$$\text{Vco}^2\left(F_{i,j}\middle| C_{i,j-1}\right) = \frac{\sigma_{j-1}^2}{f_{j-1}^2} C_{i,j-1}^{-1} + a_{j-1}^2 \tag{3.53}$$

Hence,

$$\text{Vco}^2\left(F_{i,j}\middle| C_{i,j-1}\right) > \lim_{C_{i,j-1}\to\infty} \text{Vco}^2\left(F_{i,j}\middle| C_{i,j-1}\right) = a_{j-1}^2$$

which is now bounded from below by a_{j-1}^2. As a result of the above assumptions, we replace the CL condition on the variance by

$$\text{Var}\left(C_{i,j}\middle| C_{i,j-1}\right) = \sigma_{j-1}^2 C_{i,j-1} + a_{j-1}^2 f_{j-1}^2 C_{i,j-1}^2 \tag{3.54}$$

The additional quadratic term $a_{j-1}^2 f_{j-1}^2 C_{i,j-1}^2$ ensures that the variational coefficient does not disappear when the volume is going to infinity for $a_{j-1} > 0$.

Note that the variance definition in Model Assumptions 3.2 was canonical in the sense that it has guaranteed that the CL algorithm gives CL factor estimators (3.6) that were optimal in the sense of Lemma 3.3. Under (3.54) they are no longer optimal but we obtain a model that is interesting from a solvency point of view.

As before, we define a time series model.

Model Assumptions 3.24 (enhanced time series model)

- Cumulative claims $C_{i,j}$ of different accident years i are independent.
- There exist constants $f_j > 0$, $\sigma_j^2 > 0$, $a_j^2 \geq 0$ and random variables $\varepsilon_{i,j+1}$ such that for all $i \in \{0, \ldots, I\}$ and $j \in \{0, \ldots, J-1\}$ we have

$$C_{i,j+1} = f_j\, C_{i,j} + \left(\sigma_j^2 + a_j^2\, f_j^2\, C_{i,j}\right)^{1/2} \sqrt{C_{i,j}}\, \varepsilon_{i,j+1} \tag{3.55}$$

where conditionally, given $\mathcal{B}_0$, $\varepsilon_{i,j+1}$ are independent with $E\left[\varepsilon_{i,j+1}\middle|\mathcal{B}_0\right]=0$, $E\left[\varepsilon_{i,j+1}^2\middle|\mathcal{B}_0\right]=1$ and $P\left[C_{i,j+1}>0\middle|\mathcal{B}_0\right]=1$ for all $i\in\{0,\ldots,I\}$ and $j\in\{0,\ldots,J-1\}$. □

Remark See Remarks 3.10, especially second bullet point.

LEMMA 3.25 *Model Assumptions 3.24 satisfies Model Assumptions 3.2 with* (3.3) *replaced by* (3.54).

This means that the model satisfies the CL assumptions with modified variance function. For $a_j=0$ we obtain the Time Series Version 3.9.

3.4.3 Interpretation

In this subsection we give an interpretation to the variance function (3.54). Note that, alternatively, we could use a model with latent variables $\Theta_{i,j}$. This is similar to the Bayesian approaches used, for example, in Gisler (2006) (see also Gisler and Wüthrich 2007 and Section 9.2 below) saying that the 'true' CL factors f_j are themselves random variables depending on external/latent factors. We assume that $f_j(\Theta_{i,j})$ denotes a random variable and f_j a deterministic value:

- Conditionally, given $\Theta_{i,j}$, we have

$$E\left[C_{i,j+1}\middle|\Theta_{i,j},C_{i,j}\right]=f_j(\Theta_{i,j})\;C_{i,j} \tag{3.56}$$

$$\mathrm{Var}\left(C_{i,j+1}\middle|\Theta_{i,j},C_{i,j}\right)=\sigma_j^2(\Theta_{i,j})\;C_{i,j} \tag{3.57}$$

- $\Theta_{i,j}$ are independent with

$$\begin{aligned}E\left[f_j(\Theta_{i,j})\middle|C_{i,j}\right]&=f_j\\ \mathrm{Var}\left(f_j(\Theta_{i,j})\middle|C_{i,j}\right)&=a_j^2\;f_j^2\\ E\left[\sigma_j^2(\Theta_{i,j})\middle|C_{i,j}\right]&=\sigma_j^2\end{aligned} \tag{3.58}$$

□

Remark The variables $F_{i,j+1}=C_{i,j+1}/C_{i,j}$ satisfy the Bühlmann–Straub credibility model assumptions (see Bühlmann and Gisler 2005 and Section 4.5).

For the conditional variance we obtain

$$\begin{aligned}\mathrm{Var}\left(C_{i,j+1}\middle|C_{i,j}\right)&=E\left[\mathrm{Var}\left(C_{i,j+1}\middle|\Theta_{i,j},C_{i,j}\right)\middle|C_{i,j}\right]+\mathrm{Var}\left(E\left[C_{i,j+1}\middle|\Theta_{i,j},C_{i,j}\right]\middle|C_{i,j}\right)\\&=\sigma_j^2\;C_{i,j}+a_j^2\;f_j^2\;C_{i,j}^2\end{aligned}$$

Moreover, we see that

$$\mathrm{Vco}\left(f_j(\Theta_{i,j})\middle|C_{i,j}\right)=a_j \tag{3.59}$$

Hence, we introduce the following terminology:

(a) ***Conditional process error/Conditional process variance*** The conditional process error corresponds to the term

$$\sigma_j^2 \; C_{i,j}$$

and reflects the fact that $C_{i,j+1}$ are random variables which have to be predicted. For increasing volume $C_{i,j}$ the variational coefficient of this term declines. This error term could also be called diversifiable process error term.

(b) ***Conditional parameter prediction error*** The conditional parameter prediction error corresponds to the term

$$a_j^2 \; f_j^2 \; C_{i,j}^2$$

and reflects the fact that we have to predict the future development factors $f_j(\Theta_{i,j})$. There is uncertainty about these future development factors and, hence, they may be modelled stochastically (Bayesian point of view). This term could also be called the non-diversifiable process error part (if we consider parameter changes as a part of our underlying stochastic process). Estimators 3.14 and 3.16 for the conditional MSEP do not consider this kind of risk.

(c) ***Conditional parameter estimation error*** There is a third kind of risk, namely the risk that comes from the fact that we have to estimate the true (deterministic) parameters f_j in (3.58) from the data. This error term will be called the conditional parameter estimation error. It is also considered in Estimator 3.14 and Estimator 3.16 (Mack formula). For the derivation of an estimate for this term we will use Approach 3 (p. 45 – conditional resampling approach). This derivation will use the time series definition of the CL method.

3.4.4 CL Estimator in the Enhanced Model

Under Model Assumptions 3.24 we have

$$F_{i,j+1} = f_j + \left(\sigma_j^2 \; C_{i,j}^{-1} + a_j^2 \; f_j^2\right)^{1/2} \; \varepsilon_{i,j+1}$$

with

$$E\left[F_{i,j+1} \middle| C_{i,j}\right] = f_j \quad \text{and} \quad \operatorname{Var}\left(F_{i,j+1} \middle| C_{i,j}\right) = \sigma_j^2 \; C_{i,j}^{-1} + a_j^2 \; f_j^2 \tag{3.60}$$

This immediately gives the following lemma:

LEMMA 3.26 *Under Model Assumptions 3.24 we have, for $i > 0$,*

$$E\left[C_{i,J} \middle| \mathcal{D}_I\right] = E\left[C_{i,J} \middle| C_{i,I-i}\right] = C_{i,I-i} \prod_{j=I-i}^{J-1} f_j$$

Proof See proof of Lemma 2.3. □

Remark As soon as we know the CL factors f_j we can calculate the expected conditional ultimate $C_{i,J}$, given the information $\mathcal{D}_I$. Of course, in general, the CL factors f_j are not known and need to be estimated from the data.

3.4.5 Conditional Process and Parameter Prediction Errors

We now derive the recursive formula for the conditional process and parameter prediction error. Under Model Assumptions 3.24 we have, for the ultimate claim $C_{i,J}$ for accident year $i > 0$,

$$\begin{aligned} \operatorname{Var}\left(C_{i,J} \mid \mathcal{D}_I\right) &= \operatorname{Var}\left(C_{i,J} \mid C_{i,I-i}\right) \\ &= E\left[\operatorname{Var}\left(C_{i,J} \mid C_{i,J-1}\right) \mid C_{i,I-i}\right] + \operatorname{Var}\left(E\left[C_{i,J} \mid C_{i,J-1}\right] \mid C_{i,I-i}\right) \end{aligned} \tag{3.61}$$

Under Model Assumptions 3.24 we obtain, for the first term on the right-hand side of (3.61),

$$\begin{aligned} & E\left[\operatorname{Var}\left(C_{i,J} \mid C_{i,J-1}\right) \mid C_{i,I-i}\right] \\ &= E\left[\sigma_{J-1}^2\, C_{i,J-1} + a_{J-1}^2\, f_{J-1}^2\, C_{i,J-1}^2 \mid C_{i,I-i}\right] \\ &= \sigma_{J-1}^2 \prod_{j=I-i}^{J-2} f_j\, C_{i,I-i} + a_{J-1}^2\, f_{J-1}^2 \left(\operatorname{Var}\left(C_{i,J-1} \mid \mathcal{D}_I\right) + E\left[C_{i,J-1} \mid C_{i,I-i}\right]^2\right) \\ &= C_{i,I-i}^2 \left(\frac{\sigma_{J-1}^2}{C_{i,I-i}} \prod_{j=I-i}^{J-2} f_j + a_{J-1}^2 \prod_{j=I-i}^{J-1} f_j^2\right) + a_{J-1}^2\, f_{J-1}^2 \operatorname{Var}\left(C_{i,J-1} \mid \mathcal{D}_I\right) \end{aligned}$$

For the second term on the right-hand side of (3.61) we have

$$\begin{aligned} \operatorname{Var}\left(E\left[C_{i,J} \mid C_{i,J-1}\right] \mid C_{i,I-i}\right) &= \operatorname{Var}\left(f_{J-1}\, C_{i,J-1} \mid C_{i,I-i}\right) \\ &= f_{J-1}^2 \operatorname{Var}\left(C_{i,J-1} \mid \mathcal{D}_I\right) \end{aligned}$$

This leads to the following recursive formula (compare this to (3.9))

$$\begin{aligned} \operatorname{Var}\left(C_{i,J} \mid \mathcal{D}_I\right) = C_{i,I-i}^2 & \left(\frac{\sigma_{J-1}^2}{C_{i,I-i}} \prod_{j=I-i}^{J-2} f_j + a_{J-1}^2 \prod_{j=I-i}^{J-1} f_j^2\right) \\ & + \left(1 + a_{J-1}^2\right) f_{J-1}^2 \operatorname{Var}\left(C_{i,J-1} \mid \mathcal{D}_I\right) \end{aligned} \tag{3.62}$$

For $a_{J-1}^2 = 0$, formula (3.62) coincides with the formula given in (3.9). This gives the following lemma:

LEMMA 3.27 (process and prediction error for single accident years) *Under Model Assumptions 3.24, the conditional process variance and parameter prediction error of the ultimate claim for a single accident year $i \in \{I - j + 1, \ldots, I\}$ are given by*

$$\begin{aligned} \operatorname{Var}\left(C_{i,J} \mid \mathcal{D}_I\right) &= C_{i,I-i}^2 \left[\sum_{j=I-i}^{J-1} \prod_{n=j+1}^{J-1} \left(1 + a_n^2\right) f_n^2 \left(\frac{\sigma_j^2}{C_{i,I-i}} \prod_{m=I-i}^{j-1} f_m + a_j^2 \prod_{m=I-i}^{j} f_m^2\right)\right] \\ &= E\left[C_{i,J} \mid \mathcal{D}_I\right]^2 \left[\sum_{j=I-i}^{J-1} \left(\frac{\sigma_j^2 / f_j^2}{E\left[C_{i,j} \mid \mathcal{D}_I\right]} + a_j^2\right) \prod_{n=j+1}^{J-1} \left(1 + a_n^2\right)\right] \end{aligned} \tag{3.63}$$

Lemma 3.27 implies that the conditional variational coefficient of the ultimate claim $C_{i,J}$ is given by

$$\operatorname{Vco}\left(C_{i,J} \mid \mathcal{D}_I\right) = \left[\sum_{j=I-i}^{J-1} \left(\frac{\sigma_j^2 / f_j^2}{E\left[C_{i,j} \mid \mathcal{D}_I\right]} + a_j^2\right) \prod_{n=j+1}^{J-1} \left(1 + a_n^2\right)\right]^{1/2}$$

Henceforth we see that the ***conditional parameter prediction error*** of $C_{i,J}$ (the conditional process error disappears for infinitely large volume $C_{i,I-i}$) corresponds to

$$\lim_{C_{i,I-i}\to\infty} \mathrm{Vco}\left(C_{i,J}\middle|\mathcal{D}_I\right) = \left[\sum_{j=I-i}^{J-1} a_j^2 \prod_{n=j+1}^{J-1} (1+a_n^2)\right]^{1/2} \tag{3.64}$$

and the conditional variational coefficient for the ***conditional process error*** of $C_{i,J}$ is given by

$$\left[\sum_{j=I-i}^{J-1} \left(\frac{\sigma_j^2/f_j^2}{E\left[C_{i,j}\middle|\mathcal{D}_I\right]}\right) \prod_{n=j+1}^{J-1} (1+a_n^2)\right]^{1/2}$$

3.4.6 CL Factors and Parameter Estimation Error

The conditional parameter estimation error comes from the fact that we have to estimate the CL factors f_j from the data. This part is now more involved when compared to the classical CL model. The reason is that we need clearly to distinguish between the parameter prediction error and the parameter estimation error. This is not always an easy task and there is not always a clear definition for a distinction.

Implicit Estimation Approach

From Lemma 3.4 we obtain the following lemma:

LEMMA 3.28 *Under Model Assumptions 3.24, the estimator*

$$\widehat{F}_j = \frac{\sum_{i=0}^{I-j-1} \frac{C_{i,j}}{\sigma_j^2 + a_j^2\, f_j^2\, C_{i,j}} F_{i,j+1}}{\sum_{k=0}^{I-j-1} \frac{C_{k,j}}{\sigma_j^2 + a_j^2\, f_j^2\, C_{k,j}}} = \frac{\sum_{i=0}^{I-j-1} \frac{C_{i,j+1}}{\sigma_j^2 + a_j^2\, f_j^2\, C_{i,j}}}{\sum_{k=0}^{I-j-1} \frac{C_{k,j}}{\sigma_j^2 + a_j^2\, f_j^2\, C_{k,j}}} \tag{3.65}$$

is a $\mathcal{B}_{j+1}$-measurable unbiased estimator for f_j, which has minimal conditional variance among all linear unbiased combinations of the unbiased estimators $\left(F_{i,j+1}\right)_{0\le i\le I-j-1}$ for f_j, conditioned on $\mathcal{B}_j$, i.e.

$$\mathrm{Var}\left(\widehat{F}_j|\mathcal{B}_j\right) = \min_{\substack{\alpha_i\in\mathbb{R}\\ \sum_i \alpha_i=1}} \mathrm{Var}\left(\sum_{i=0}^{I-j-1} \alpha_i\, F_{i,j+1}\middle|\mathcal{B}_j\right)$$

The conditional variance is given by

$$\mathrm{Var}\left(\widehat{F}_j\middle|\mathcal{B}_j\right) = \left(\sum_{i=0}^{I-j-1} \frac{C_{i,j}}{\sigma_j^2 + a_j^2\, f_j^2\, C_{i,j}}\right)^{-1} \tag{3.66}$$

Proof From (3.60) we see that $F_{i,j+1}$ is an unbiased estimator for f_j, conditioned on $\mathcal{B}_j$, with

$$E\left[F_{i,j+1}\middle|\mathcal{B}_j\right] = E\left[F_{i,j+1}\middle|C_{i,j}\right] = f_j$$

$$\mathrm{Var}\left(F_{i,j+1}\middle|\mathcal{B}_j\right) = \mathrm{Var}\left(F_{i,j+1}\middle|C_{i,j}\right) = \sigma_j^2\, C_{i,j}^{-1} + a_j^2\, f_j^2$$

The proof now follows from Lemma 3.4. □

Remark For $a_j = 0$ we obtain the classical estimates $\widehat{f}_j$ for the age-to-age factors (2.4). Moreover, observe that for calculating the estimate $\widehat{F}_j$ one needs to know the parameters f_j, a_j and σ_j (see (3.65)). Of course this contradicts the fact that we need to estimate f_j. One way out of this dilemma is to use an estimate for f_j that is not optimal, that is, has a larger variance.

Let us assume (in the implicit estimation approach) that we can calculate (3.65).

ESTIMATOR 3.29 (CL estimator, enhanced time series model)
Under Model Assumptions 3.24 the CL estimator for $E\left[C_{i,j}\middle|\mathcal{D}_I\right]$ is given by

$$\widehat{C_{i,j}}^{(CL,2)} = \widehat{E}\left[C_{i,j}\middle|\mathcal{D}_I\right] = C_{i,I-i}\prod_{l=I-i}^{j-1}\widehat{F}_l$$

for $i+j>I$.

We obtain the following lemma for the estimators in the enhanced model:

LEMMA 3.30 *Under Assumptions 3.24 we have:*

(a) *given $\mathcal{B}_j$, $\widehat{F}_j$ is an unbiased estimator for f_j, i.e. $E\left[\widehat{F}_j\middle|\mathcal{B}_j\right]=f_j$;*

(b) *$\widehat{F}_j$ is (unconditionally) unbiased for f_j, i.e. $E\left[\widehat{F}_j\right]=f_j$;*

(c) $E\left[\widehat{F}_0 \cdots \widehat{F}_j\right]=\prod_{k=0}^{j} E\left[\widehat{F}_k\right]$, *i.e. $\widehat{F}_0,\ldots,\widehat{F}_{J-1}$ are uncorrelated;*

(d) *given $C_{i,I-i}$, $\widehat{C_{i,J}}^{(CL,2)}$ is an unbiased estimator for $E\left[C_{i,J}\middle|\mathcal{D}_I\right]$, i.e. $E\left[\widehat{C_{i,J}}^{(CL,2)}\middle|C_{I-i}\right]=E\left[C_{i,J}\middle|\mathcal{D}_I\right]$ and*

(e) *$\widehat{C_{i,J}}^{(CL,2)}$ is (unconditionally) unbiased for $E\left[C_{i,J}\right]$, i.e. $E\left[\widehat{C_{i,J}}^{(CL,2)}\right]=E\left[C_{i,J}\right]$*

Proof See proof of Lemma 2.5. □

Single Accident Years

In the following we assume that the parameters in (3.65) are known to calculate $\widehat{F}_j$. Our goal is to estimate the conditional MSEP as in the classical CL model

$$\begin{aligned}\operatorname{msep}_{C_{i,J}|\mathcal{D}_I}\left(\widehat{C_{i,J}}^{(CL,2)}\right) &= E\left[\left(C_{i,J}-\widehat{C_{i,J}}^{(CL,2)}\right)^2\middle|\mathcal{D}_I\right]\\ &=\operatorname{Var}\left(C_{i,J}\middle|\mathcal{D}_I\right)+\left(E\left[C_{i,J}\middle|\mathcal{D}_I\right]-\widehat{C_{i,J}}^{(CL,2)}\right)^2\end{aligned}$$

The first term is exactly the conditional process variance and the conditional parameter prediction error obtained in Lemma 3.27, the second term is the conditional parameter estimation error, given by

$$\left(E\left[C_{i,J}\middle|\mathcal{D}_I\right]-\widehat{C_{i,J}}^{(CL,2)}\right)^2 = C_{i,I-i}^2\left(\prod_{j=I-i}^{J-1} f_j - \prod_{j=I-i}^{J-1}\widehat{F}_j\right)^2 \tag{3.67}$$

Observe that

$$\widehat{F}_j = \frac{\sum_{i=0}^{I-j-1} \frac{C_{i,j}}{\sigma_j^2 + a_j^2 f_j^2 C_{i,j}} F_{i,j+1}}{\sum_{i=0}^{I-j-1} \frac{C_{i,j}}{\sigma_j^2 + a_j^2 f_j^2 C_{i,j}}}$$

$$= f_j + \frac{1}{\sum_{i=0}^{I-j-1} \frac{C_{i,j}}{\sigma_j^2 + a_j^2 f_j^2 C_{i,j}}} \sum_{i=0}^{I-j-1} \left(\frac{C_{i,j}}{\sigma_j^2 + a_j^2 f_j^2 C_{i,j}} \right)^{1/2} \varepsilon_{i,j+1} \qquad (3.68)$$

Hence, $\widehat{F}_j$ consists of a constant f_j and a stochastic error term (see also Lemma 3.28). In order to determine the conditional parameter estimation error we now proceed as in Subsection 3.2.3 for Model Assumptions 3.9. This means that we use Approach 3 (conditional resampling in $\mathcal{D}_{I,i}^{\mathrm{O}}$, p. 45) to estimate the fluctuations of the estimators $\widehat{F}_0, \ldots, \widehat{F}_{J-1}$ around the true CL factors $f_0, \ldots, f_{J-1}$, that is, to get an estimate for (3.67).

Therefore, we (conditionally) resample the observations $\widehat{F}_0, \ldots, \widehat{F}_{J-1}$, given $\mathcal{D}_I$, and use the resampled estimates to calculate an estimate for the conditional parameter estimation error.

Remark In the following exposition we use the previous notation $\widehat{F}_j$ for the resampled estimates of the development factors f_j to avoid an overloaded notation. Moreover, for the resampled observations we again use the notation $P^*_{\mathcal{D}_I}$ for the conditional resampling measure (for a more detailed discussion, we refer to Subsection 3.2.3).

Under the conditional measure $P^*_{\mathcal{D}_I}$, the random variables $\widehat{F}_j$ are independent with

$$E^*_{\mathcal{D}_I}\left[\widehat{F}_j\right] = f_j \quad \text{and} \quad E^*_{\mathcal{D}_I}\left[\left(\widehat{F}_j\right)^2\right] = f_j^2 + \left(\sum_{i=0}^{I-j-1} \frac{C_{i,j}}{\sigma_j^2 + a_j^2 f_j^2 C_{i,j}} \right)^{-1}$$

(cf. Subsection 3.2.3, Approach 3). This means that the conditional parameter estimation error (3.67) is estimated by

$$C_{i,I-i}^2 \, E^*_{\mathcal{D}_I}\left[\left(\prod_{j=I-i}^{J-1} f_j - \prod_{j=I-i}^{J-1} \widehat{F}_j \right)^2 \right]$$

$$= C_{i,I-i}^2 \, \mathrm{Var}_{P^*_{\mathcal{D}_I}} \left(\prod_{j=I-i}^{J-1} \widehat{F}_j \right)$$

$$= C_{i,I-i}^2 \left(\prod_{j=I-i}^{J-1} E^*_{\mathcal{D}_I}\left[\left(\widehat{F}_j\right)^2\right] - \prod_{j=I-i}^{J-1} f_j^2 \right)$$

$$= C_{i,I-i}^2 \prod_{j=I-i}^{J-1} f_j^2 \left[\prod_{j=I-i}^{J-1} \left(\left(\sum_{k=0}^{I-j-1} \frac{C_{k,j}}{(\sigma_j^2/f_j^2) + a_j^2 \, C_{k,j}} \right)^{-1} + 1 \right) - 1 \right] \qquad (3.69)$$

Finally, if we do a linear approximation to (3.69), we obtain

$$
\begin{aligned}
C_{i,I-i}^2 E^*_{\mathcal{D}_I}&\left[\left(\prod_{j=I-i}^{J-1} f_j - \prod_{j=I-i}^{J-1}\widehat{F}_j\right)^2\right]\\
&= C_{i,I-i}^2\ \mathrm{Var}_{P^*_{\mathcal{D}_I}}\left(\prod_{j=I-i}^{J-1}\widehat{F}_j\right)\\
&\approx C_{i,I-i}^2 \prod_{j=I-i}^{J-1} f_j^2 \sum_{j=I-i}^{J-1}\left(\sum_{k=0}^{I-j-1}\frac{C_{k,j}}{(\sigma_j^2/f_j^2)+a_j^2\ C_{k,j}}\right)^{-1}
\end{aligned}
\tag{3.70}
$$

For $a_j=0$ this is exactly the conditional parameter estimation error in Model Assumptions 3.2 (cf. (3.31)). For an increasing number of observations (accident years i), this error term goes to zero.

If we use the linear approximation (3.70) and replace the parameters in (3.63) and (3.70) by their estimators (cf. Subsection 3.4.7), we obtain the following estimator for the conditional MSEP (for the time being we assume that σ_j^2 and a_j^2 are known):

ESTIMATOR 3.31 (MSEP for single accident years) *Under Model Assumptions 3.24 we have the following estimator for the conditional MSEP of the ultimate claim for a single accident year* $i\in\{1,\ldots,I\}$

$$
\begin{aligned}
\widehat{\mathrm{msep}}_{C_{i,J}|\mathcal{D}_I}\left(\widehat{C_{i,J}}^{(\mathrm{CL},2)}\right) = \left(\widehat{C_{i,J}}^{(\mathrm{CL},2)}\right)^2 \sum_{j=I-i}^{J-1}&\left[\left(\frac{\sigma_j^2}{\widehat{F}_j^2\ \widehat{C_{i,j}}^{(\mathrm{CL},2)}}+a_j^2\right)\prod_{n=j+1}^{J-1}(1+a_n^2)\right.\\
&\left.+\left(\sum_{k=0}^{I-j-1}\frac{C_{k,j}}{(\sigma_j^2/\widehat{F}_j^2)+a_j^2\ C_{k,j}}\right)^{-1}\right]
\end{aligned}
$$

Aggregated Accident Years

Consider two different accident years $i<k$. From our assumptions we know that the ultimate losses $C_{i,J}$ and $C_{k,J}$ are independent. Nevertheless, we have to be careful when we aggregate $\widehat{C_{i,J}}^{(\mathrm{CL},2)}$ and $\widehat{C_{k,J}}^{(\mathrm{CL},2)}$. The estimators are no longer independent since they use the same observations for estimating the CL factors f_j.

$$
\begin{aligned}
E&\left[\left(\widehat{C_{i,J}}^{(\mathrm{CL},2)}+\widehat{C_{k,J}}^{(\mathrm{CL},2)}-(C_{i,J}+C_{k,J})\right)^2\middle|\mathcal{D}_I\right]\\
&=\mathrm{Var}\left(C_{i,J}+C_{k,J}\middle|\mathcal{D}_I\right)+\left(\widehat{C_{i,J}}^{(\mathrm{CL},2)}+\widehat{C_{k,J}}^{(\mathrm{CL},2)}-E\left[C_{i,J}+C_{k,J}\middle|\mathcal{D}_I\right]\right)^2
\end{aligned}
\tag{3.71}
$$

Using the independence of the different accident years, we obtain for the first term

$$
\mathrm{Var}\left(C_{i,J}+C_{k,J}\middle|\mathcal{D}_I\right)=\mathrm{Var}\left(C_{i,J}\middle|\mathcal{D}_I\right)+\mathrm{Var}\left(C_{k,J}\middle|\mathcal{D}_I\right)
$$

This term is exactly the conditional process and parameter prediction error from Lemma 3.27. For the second term (3.71) we obtain

$$\left(\widehat{C_{i,J}}^{(\mathrm{CL},2)} + \widehat{C_{k,J}}^{(\mathrm{CL},2)} - E\left[C_{i,J} + C_{k,J} \middle| \mathcal{D}_I\right]\right)^2$$

$$= \left(\widehat{C_{i,J}}^{(\mathrm{CL},2)} - E\left[C_{i,J} \middle| \mathcal{D}_I\right]\right)^2 + \left(\widehat{C_{k,J}}^{(\mathrm{CL},2)} - E\left[C_{k,J} \middle| \mathcal{D}_I\right]\right)^2$$

$$+2\left(\widehat{C_{i,J}}^{(\mathrm{CL},2)} - E\left[C_{i,J} \middle| \mathcal{D}_I\right]\right)\left(\widehat{C_{k,J}}^{(\mathrm{CL},2)} - E\left[C_{k,J} \middle| \mathcal{D}_I\right]\right)$$

Hence we have the following decomposition for the conditional MSEP of the sum of two accident years:

$$E\left[\left(\widehat{C_{i,J}}^{(\mathrm{CL},2)} + \widehat{C_{k,J}}^{(\mathrm{CL},2)} - \left(C_{i,J} + C_{k,J}\right)\right)^2 \middle| \mathcal{D}_I\right]$$

$$= E\left[\left(\widehat{C_{i,J}}^{(\mathrm{CL},2)} - C_{i,J}\right)^2 \middle| \mathcal{D}_I\right] + E\left[\left(\widehat{C_{k,J}}^{(\mathrm{CL},2)} - C_{k,J}\right)^2 \middle| \mathcal{D}_I\right]$$

$$+ 2\left(\widehat{C_{i,J}}^{(\mathrm{CL},2)} - E\left[C_{i,J} \middle| \mathcal{D}_I\right]\right)\left(\widehat{C_{k,J}}^{(\mathrm{CL},2)} - E\left[C_{k,J} \middle| \mathcal{D}_I\right]\right)$$

In addition to the conditional MSEP for single accident years (see Estimator 3.31), we obtain covariance terms similar to (3.67):

$$\left(\widehat{C_{i,J}}^{(\mathrm{CL},2)} - E\left[C_{i,J} \middle| \mathcal{D}_I\right]\right)\left(\widehat{C_{k,J}}^{(\mathrm{CL},2)} - E\left[C_{k,J} \middle| \mathcal{D}_I\right]\right)$$

$$= C_{i,I-i} \left(\prod_{j=I-i}^{J-1} \widehat{F}_j - \prod_{j=I-i}^{J-1} f_j\right) C_{k,I-k} \left(\prod_{j=I-k}^{J-1} \widehat{F}_j - \prod_{j=I-k}^{J-1} f_j\right) \tag{3.72}$$

As in (3.69), using Approach 3, we obtain for the covariance term (3.72) the estimate

$$C_{i,I-i}\, C_{k,I-k}\, E^*_{\mathcal{D}_I}\left[\left(\prod_{j=I-i}^{J-1} \widehat{F}_j - \prod_{j=I-i}^{J-1} f_j\right)\left(\prod_{j=I-k}^{J-1} \widehat{F}_j - \prod_{j=I-k}^{J-1} f_j\right)\right]$$

$$= C_{i,I-i}\, C_{k,I-k} \prod_{j=I-k}^{I-i-1} f_j \left(\prod_{j=I-i}^{J-1} E^*_{\mathcal{D}_I}\left[\left(\widehat{F}_j\right)^2\right] - \prod_{j=I-i}^{J-1} f_j^2\right)$$

$$= C_{i,I-i} C_{k,I-k} \prod_{j=I-k}^{I-i-1} f_j \prod_{j=I-i}^{J-1} f_j^2 \left[\prod_{j=I-i}^{J-1} \left(\left(\sum_{m=0}^{I-j-1} \frac{C_{m,j}}{(\sigma_j^2/f_j^2) + a_j^2\, C_{m,j}}\right)^{-1} + 1\right) - 1\right]$$

If we do the same linear approximation as in (3.70), the estimation of the covariance term is straightforward from (3.66).

ESTIMATOR 3.32 (MSEP for aggregated accident years) *Under Model Assumptions 3.24 we have the following estimator for the conditional MSEP of the ultimate claim for aggregated accident years:*

$$\widehat{\mathrm{msep}}_{\sum_i C_{i,J}|\mathcal{D}_I}\left(\sum_{i=1}^{I}\widehat{C_{i,J}}^{(\mathrm{CL},2)}\right)=\sum_{i=1}^{I}\widehat{\mathrm{msep}}_{C_{i,J}|\mathcal{D}_I}\left(\widehat{C_{i,J}}^{(\mathrm{CL},2)}\right)$$
$$+\ 2\sum_{1\le i<k\le I}\widehat{C_{i,J}}^{(\mathrm{CL},2)}\ \widehat{C_{k,J}}^{(\mathrm{CL},2)}\sum_{j=I-i}^{J-1}\left(\sum_{m=0}^{I-j-1}\frac{C_{m,j}}{\left(\sigma_j^2/\widehat{F}_j^{\,2}\right)+a_j^2C_{m,j}}\right)^{-1}$$

Explicit Estimation Approach

A problem with getting the estimate $\widehat{F}_j$ under Approach 3 (see (3.65)) is that in the derivation we have assumed that the parameters of the model are known in order to get the estimate. We could also use a different (unbiased) estimator. We define

$$\widehat{F}_j^{(0)}=\frac{\sum_{i=0}^{I-j-1}C_{i,j}\ F_{i,j+1}}{\sum_{i=0}^{I-j-1}C_{i,j}}=\frac{\sum_{i=0}^{I-j-1}C_{i,j+1}}{\sum_{i=0}^{I-j-1}C_{i,j}}\tag{3.73}$$

$\widehat{F}_j^{(0)}=\widehat{f}_j$ is the classical CL factor estimate in the CL Model 3.2. It is optimal under the variance condition (3.3), but is not optimal under our variance condition (3.53). Observe that

$$\begin{aligned}\mathrm{Var}\left(\widehat{F}_j^{(0)}\middle|\mathcal{B}_j\right)&=\frac{1}{\left(\sum_{i=0}^{I-j-1}C_{i,j}\right)^2}\sum_{i=0}^{I-j-1}\mathrm{Var}\left(C_{i,j+1}\middle|C_{i,j}\right)\\&=\frac{\sum_{i=0}^{I-j-1}\left(\sigma_j^2\ C_{i,j}+a_j^2\ f_j^2\ C_{i,j}^2\right)}{\left(\sum_{i=0}^{I-j-1}C_{i,j}\right)^2}\\&=\frac{\sigma_j^2}{\sum_{i=0}^{I-j-1}C_{i,j}}+\frac{a_j^2\ f_j^2\ \sum_{i=0}^{I-j-1}C_{i,j}^2}{\left(\sum_{i=0}^{I-j-1}C_{i,j}\right)^2}\end{aligned}$$

This immediately gives the following corollary:

COROLLARY 3.33 *Under Model Assumptions 3.24, for* $i\in\{1,\ldots,I\}$,

$$C_{i,I-i}\prod_{j=I-i}^{J-1}\widehat{F}_j^{(0)}$$

defines a conditionally, given $C_{i,I-i}$, *unbiased estimator for* $E\left[C_{i,J}\middle|\mathcal{D}_I\right]$. *The process variance and the parameter prediction error are given in Lemma 3.27.*

For the parameter estimation error of a single accident year in Approach 3 we obtain the estimate

$$C_{i,I-i}^2 \left[\prod_{j=I-i}^{J-1} \left(\frac{\sigma_j^2}{\sum_{k=0}^{I-j-1} C_{k,j}} + \frac{a_j^2 f_j^2 \sum_{k=0}^{I-j-1} C_{k,j}^2}{\left(\sum_{k=0}^{I-j-1} C_{k,j}\right)^2} + f_j^2 \right) - \prod_{j=I-i}^{J-1} f_j^2 \right]$$

This expression is of course larger than the one in (3.69). In practice one should probably apply this explicit estimation approach. It is simpler and often still accurate.

3.4.7 Parameter Estimation

We need to estimate three families of parameters f_j, σ_j and a_j. Under the implicit estimation approach, an estimate of f_j is given in (3.65), which gives only an implicit expression for the estimation of f_j, since the CL factors also appear in the weights of the estimates $\widehat{F}_j$. Therefore, we propose an iterative estimation in the implicit estimation approach. On the other hand, there is no difficulty in applying the explicit estimation approach since the estimates $\widehat{F}_j^{(0)}$ are independent of the parameters f_j, σ_j and a_j.

Estimation of a_j The sequence a_j cannot usually be estimated from the data unless we have a very large portfolio ($C_{i,j} \to \infty$) such that the conditional process error becomes negligible. Hence, a_j can only be obtained if we have data from the whole insurance market. This kind of estimation has been done to determine the parameters for prediction errors in the Swiss Solvency Test (see, e.g., Tables 8.4.3 and 8.4.6 in SST 2006). Unfortunately, the tables only give an overall estimate for the conditional parameter prediction error, not a sequence a_j (e.g. the variational coefficient of the overall error (similar to (3.59)) for motor third party liability claims reserves is 3.5%).

An ad-hoc approach for constructing a_j with the help of (3.64) is as follows. Define for $j = 0, \ldots, J-1$

$$V_j^2 = \sum_{m=j-1}^{J-1} a_m^2 \prod_{n=m+1}^{J-1} (1 + a_n^2)$$

Hence a_{j-1} can be determined recursively from $V_j^2 - V_{j+1}^2$:

$$a_{j-1}^2 = \left(V_j^2 - V_{j+1}^2\right) \prod_{n=j}^{J-1} (1 + a_n^2)^{-1} \tag{3.74}$$

Thus, we can estimate a_{j-1} as soon as we have an estimate for $(V_j)_j$. $(V_j)_j$ corresponds to

$$V_j = \lim_{C_{i,j-1} \to \infty} \mathrm{Vco}\left(C_{i,J} \middle| C_{i,j-1}\right) \tag{3.75}$$

(cf. (3.64)). Hence, we need to estimate the conditional prediction error of $C_{i,J}$, given the observation $C_{i,j-1}$. Since we do not really have a good idea/guess about the conditional variational coefficient in (3.75), we express it in terms of reserves

$$\begin{aligned}\operatorname{Vco}\left(C_{i,J}\middle|\, C_{i,j-1}\right) &= \frac{\operatorname{Var}\left(C_{i,J}\middle|\, C_{i,j-1}\right)^{1/2}}{E\left[C_{i,J}\middle|\, C_{i,j-1}\right]} \\ &= \frac{\operatorname{Var}\left(C_{i,J}-C_{i,j-1}\middle|\, C_{i,j-1}\right)^{1/2}}{E\left[C_{i,J}-C_{i,j-1}\middle|\, C_{i,j-1}\right]}\;\frac{E\left[C_{i,J}-C_{i,j-1}\middle|\, C_{i,j-1}\right]}{E\left[C_{i,J}\middle|\, C_{i,j-1}\right]} \\ &= \operatorname{Vco}\left(C_{i,J}-C_{i,j-1}\middle|\, C_{i,j-1}\right)\;\frac{\prod_{l=j-1}^{J-1} f_l - 1}{\prod_{l=j-1}^{J-1} f_l}\end{aligned}$$

In our examples we assume that the conditional variational coefficient for the conditional prediction error of the reserves $C_{i,J}-C_{i,j-1}$ is a constant equal to r and we set

$$\widehat{V}_j = r\;\frac{\prod_{l=j-1}^{J-1}\widehat{F}_l^{(0)} - 1}{\prod_{l=j-1}^{J-1}\widehat{F}_l^{(0)}}$$

This immediately gives an estimate $\widehat{a}_j$ for the parameter a_j (cf. (3.74)).

Estimation of σ_j σ_j^2 is estimated iteratively from the data. A tedious calculation on the conditional expectation gives

$$\begin{aligned}&\frac{1}{I-j-1}\sum_{i=0}^{I-j-1} C_{i,j}\, E\left[\left(F_{i,j+1}-\widehat{F}_j^{(0)}\right)^2\middle|\,\mathcal{B}_j\right] \\ &\quad = \sigma_j^2 + \frac{a_j^2\, f_j^2}{I-j-1}\left(\sum_{i=0}^{I-j-1} C_{i,j} - \frac{\sum_{i=0}^{I-j-1} C_{i,j}^2}{\sum_{i=0}^{I-j-1} C_{i,j}}\right)\end{aligned}$$

Hence, we get the following iterative formula for the estimation of σ_j^2: For $k \geq 1$,

$$\begin{aligned}\widehat{\sigma_j^2}^{(k)} &= \frac{1}{I-j-1}\sum_{i=0}^{I-j-1} C_{i,j}\left(F_{i,j+1}-\widehat{F}_j^{(0)}\right)^2 \\ &\quad - \frac{\widehat{a}_j^2\left(\widehat{F}_j^{(k-1)}\right)^2}{I-j-1}\left(\sum_{i=0}^{I-j-1} C_{i,j} - \frac{\sum_{i=0}^{I-j-1} C_{i,j}^2}{\sum_{i=0}^{I-j-1} C_{i,j}}\right)\end{aligned}$$

If $\widehat{\sigma_j^2}^{(k)}$ becomes negative, it is set to 0, that is, we only have a conditional parameter prediction error and the conditional process error is equal to zero (in this case, the volume is sufficiently large that the conditional process error disappears).

Estimation of $\widehat{F}_j$ The estimates $\widehat{F}_j$ are then iteratively determined via (3.65). For $k \geq 1$

$$\widehat{F}_j^{(k)} = \frac{\sum_{i=0}^{I-j-1} \frac{C_{i,j+1}}{\widehat{\sigma_j^2}^{(k)} + \widehat{a}_j^2 \left(\widehat{F}_j^{(k-1)}\right)^2 C_{i,j}}}{\sum_{i=0}^{I-j-1} \frac{C_{i,j}}{\widehat{\sigma_j^2}^{(k)} + \widehat{a}_j^2 \left(\widehat{F}_j^{(k-1)}\right)^2 C_{i,j}}}.$$

Remarks 3.34

- In all examples we have looked at, we have observed very fast convergence of $\widehat{\sigma_j^2}^{(k)}$ and $\widehat{F}_j^{(k)}$ in the sense that we have not encountered any changes in the ultimate claims after the third iteration for $\widehat{F}_j$.
- To determine σ_j^2, we could also choose a different unbiased estimator via

$$1 = \frac{1}{I-j-1} \sum_{i=0}^{I-j-1} \frac{C_{i,j}}{\sigma_j^2 + a_j^2 f_j^2 C_{i,j}} E\left[\left(F_{i,j+1} - \widehat{F}_j\right)^2 \middle| \mathcal{B}_j\right] \tag{3.76}$$

  The difficulty with (3.76) is that it again leads to an implicit expression for the estimate $\widehat{\sigma_j^2}$.
- The formula for the MSEP, Estimator 3.32, was derived under the assumption that the underlying model parameters f_j, σ_j and a_j are known. If we replace these parameters by their estimates (as described via the iteration in this section), we obtain additional sources for the estimation errors! However, since calculations get too tedious (or even impossible) we omit further derivations of the MSEP and take Estimator 3.32 as a first approximation.

We close this section with an example.

Example 3.55 (MSEP in the enhanced CL model)

We consider two portfolios: A and B. Both are of a similar type (i.e. contain data of the same line of business) and (in fact) Portfolio B is contained in Portfolio A.

Portfolio A

The analysis of Portfolio A is given in Tables 3.12–3.17.

Under Mack's Model Assumptions 3.2, this leads to the reserves and error estimates given in Table 3.14.

Next, we compare the above results to the estimates under the enhanced CL Model 3.24. Setting $r = 5\%$, we obtain the parameter estimates in Table 3.15.

Remark In practice a_j can only be determined with the help of external know how and market data. Therefore, for example, for solvency purposes, a_j should be determined *a priori* by the regulator. It gives an answer to the question: How good can an actuarial estimate be, at most?

Estimates of the model parameters, reserves and error terms for Portfolio A are then given in Tables 3.16 and 3.17. After three iterations the parameters have already converged sufficiently so that the claims reserves remain stable.

Table 3.12 Observed cumulative claims $C_{i,j}$ in Portfolio A

	0	1	2	3	4	5	6	7	8	9	10
0	111 551	154 622	156 159	156 759	157 583	158 666	160 448	160 552	160 568	160 617	160 621
1	116 163	171 449	175 502	176 533	176 989	177 269	178 488	178 556	178 620	178 621	178 644
2	127 615	189 682	193 823	196 324	198 632	200 299	202 740	203 848	204 168	205 560	205 562
3	147 659	217 342	220 123	222 731	222 916	223 320	223 447	223 566	227 103	227 127	227 276
4	157 495	212 770	219 680	220 978	221 276	223 724	223 743	223 765	223 669	223 601	223 558
5	154 969	213 352	219 201	220 469	222 751	223 958	224 005	224 030	223 975	224 048	224 036
6	152 833	209 969	214 692	220 040	223 467	223 754	223 752	223 593	223 585	223 688	223 697
7	144 223	207 644	212 443	214 108	214 661	214 610	214 564	214 484	214 459	214 459	
8	145 612	209 604	214 161	215 982	217 962	220 783	221 078	221 614	221 616		
9	196 695	282 621	288 676	290 036	292 206	294 531	294 671	294 705			
10	181 381	260 308	266 497	269 130	269 404	269 691	269 720				
11	177 168	263 130	268 848	270 787	271 624	271 688					
12	156 505	230 607	237 102	244 847	245 940						
13	157 839	239 723	261 213	264 755							
14	159 429	233 309	239 800								
15	169 990	246 019									
16	173 377										

Table 3.13 CL parameters in Mack's Model 3.2 for Portfolio A

	0	1	2	3	4	5	6	7	8	9
$\widehat{f}_j$	1.4416	1.0278	1.0112	1.0057	1.0048	1.0025	1.0008	1.0020	1.0010	1.0001
$\widehat{\sigma}_j$	18.3478	8.7551	3.9082	2.2050	2.1491	2.0887	0.8302	2.4751	1.0757	0.1280

Table 3.14 Reserves and conditional MSEP in Model Assumptions 3.2 for Portfolio A

i	CL reserves	$\widehat{\mathrm{msep}}_{C_{i,J}\|\mathcal{D}_I}\left(\widehat{C_{i,J}}^{CL}\right)^{1/2}$		$\widehat{\mathrm{Var}}\left(C_{i,J}\|\mathcal{D}_I\right)^{1/2}$		$\widehat{\mathrm{Var}}\left(\widehat{C_{i,J}}^{CL}\middle\|\mathcal{D}_I\right)^{1/2}$	
7	20	64	322.0%	59	300.4%	23	115.8%
8	231	543	235.2%	510	220.8%	187	80.9%
9	898	1582	176.1%	1468	163.4%	589	65.5%
10	1044	1573	150.7%	1470	140.9%	560	53.7%
11	1731	1957	113.1%	1838	106.2%	674	38.9%
12	2747	2169	79.0%	2055	74.8%	693	25.2%
13	4487	2563	57.1%	2426	54.1%	826	18.4%
14	6803	3169	46.6%	3030	44.5%	928	13.6%
15	14025	5663	40.4%	5443	38.8%	1564	11.2%
16	90 809	10 121	11.1%	9762	10.8%	2669	2.9%
Total	122 795	13 941	11.4%	12 336	10.0%	6495	5.3%

Table 3.15 Estimates $\widehat{a}_j$ and $\widehat{V}_j$ in the enhanced CL Model 3.24

	0	1	2	3	4	5	6	7	8	9	10
$\widehat{F}_j^{(0)} = \widehat{f}_j$	1.4416	1.0278	1.0112	1.0057	1.0048	1.0025	1.0008	1.0020	1.0010	1.0001	
$\widehat{V}_j(\%)$	1.7187	0.2697	0.1379	0.0833	0.0552	0.0316	0.0193	0.0152	0.0052	0.0005	0.0000
$\widehat{a}_j(\%)$	1.6974	0.2317	0.1099	0.0624	0.0453	0.0251	0.0119	0.0143	0.0052	0.0005	0.0000

Table 3.16 Estimated parameters in the enhanced CL Model 3.24 for Portfolio A

	0	1	2	3	4	5	6	7	8	9
$\widehat{F}_j^{(1)}$	1.44152	1.02784	1.01123	1.00572	1.00477	1.00249	1.00082	1.00200	1.00095	1.00009
$\widehat{F}_j^{(2)}$	1.44152	1.02784	1.01123	1.00572	1.00477	1.00249	1.00082	1.00200	1.00095	1.00009
$\widehat{F}_j^{(3)}$	1.44152	1.02784	1.01123	1.00572	1.00477	1.00249	1.00082	1.00200	1.00095	1.00009
$\widehat{\sigma}_j^{(1)}$	15.82901	8.68855	3.87516	2.18642	2.13924	2.08568	0.82851	2.47435	1.07546	0.12802
$\widehat{\sigma}_j^{(2)}$	15.82926	8.68856	3.87516	2.18642	2.13924	2.08568	0.82851	2.47435	1.07546	0.12802
$\widehat{\sigma}_j^{(3)}$	15.82926	8.68856	3.87516	2.18642	2.13924	2.08568	0.82851	2.47435	1.07546	0.12802

Table 3.17 Reserves and conditional MSEP in the enhanced CL Model 3.24 for Portfolio A

i	CL reserves	$\widehat{\mathrm{msep}}_{C_{i,J}\vert\mathcal{D}_I}\left(\widehat{C_{i,J}}^{(\mathrm{CL},2)}\right)^{1/2}$		$\widehat{\mathrm{Var}}\left(C_{i,J}\vert\mathcal{D}_I\right)^{1/2}$		process error$^{1/2}$		param. pred. error$^{1/2}$		$\widehat{\mathrm{Var}}\left(\widehat{C_{i,J}}^{(\mathrm{CL},2)}\middle\vert\mathcal{D}_I\right)^{1/2}$	
7	20	64	321.9%	59	300.4%	59	300.4%	1	5.0%	23	115.8%
8	231	543	235.1%	510	220.8%	510	220.7%	12	5.0%	187	80.9%
9	898	1581	176.0%	1468	163.4%	1467	163.3%	45	5.0%	589	65.5%
10	1044	1573	150.7%	1470	140.8%	1469	140.7%	52	5.0%	560	53.7%
11	1731	1956	113.0%	1836	106.1%	1834	106.0%	87	5.0%	674	38.9%
12	2747	2165	78.8%	2051	74.7%	2046	74.5%	137	5.0%	693	25.2%
13	4489	2556	56.9%	2418	53.9%	2408	53.6%	224	5.0%	826	18.4%
14	6804	3153	46.3%	3013	44.3%	2994	44.0%	340	5.0%	928	13.6%
15	14 024	5627	40.1%	5405	38.5%	5360	38.2%	701	5.0%	1565	11.2%
16	90 796	9244	10.2%	8844	9.7%	7590	8.4%	4540	5.0%	2688	3.0%
Total	122 784	13 298	10.8%	11 598	9.4%	10 640	8.7%	4615	3.8%	6504	5.3%

Comment

The resulting reserves are almost the same under the Mack Model 3.2 and the Enhanced CL Model 3.24. We obtain now both a conditional process error of 10 640 and a conditional parameter prediction error term of 4615. The sum of these two terms, 11 598, has about the same size as the conditional process error in the Mack method, 12 336. This comes from the fact that we use the same data to estimate the parameters. But the error term in the enhanced CL model is now bounded from below by the conditional parameter prediction error, whereas the conditional process error in the Mack model converges to zero for increasing volume.

Portfolio B

We consider now a second portfolio, Portfolio B in Tables 3.18–3.20, which includes similar business as our example given in Table 3.12 (Portfolio A). In fact, Portfolio B is a sub-portfolio of Portfolio A, belonging to the exactly same line of business. For the parameters a_j we choose the same values as in Portfolio A, Table 3.15. Therefore, we expect that the conditional parameter prediction errors are similar to those in Table 3.17.

Comments

- The error terms between Portfolio A and Portfolio B are now directly comparable. The conditional parameter prediction errors relative to the estimated CL reserves are about the same. They slightly differ between Portfolio A and Portfolio B since we choose different development factors $\widehat{F}_j$ and since the relative weights $C_{i,I-i}$ between the accident years differ in both portfolios.
- The conditional process error relative to the estimated CL reserves decreases now from Portfolio B to Portfolio A by a factor of about $\sqrt{2}$, since Portfolio A is about twice the

Table 3.18 Observed cumulative claims $C_{i,j}$ in Portfolio B

	0	1	2	3	4	5	6	7	8	9	10
0	53 095	73 067	74 548	75 076	75 894	76 128	77 904	78 008	78 022	78 071	78 075
1	59 183	87 679	89 303	90 033	90 058	90 303	91 454	91 472	91 482	91 483	91 494
2	64 640	95 734	97 648	99 429	100 462	101 683	103 549	104 642	104 917	105 560	105 560
3	72 150	105 349	106 546	106 919	106 934	107 144	107 170	107 225	107 232	107 232	107 232
4	76 272	105 630	108 406	108 677	108 838	110 140	110 110	110 111	110 155	110 155	110 110
5	75 469	105 987	108 779	109 093	111 366	111 390	111 422	111 448	111 367	111 369	111 369
6	78 835	108 835	111 455	116 231	117 896	118 161	118 157	117 940	117 940	117 972	117 974
7	70 780	98 753	101 347	102 624	102 629	102 587	102 545	102 500	102 474	102 474	
8	73 311	101 911	103 657	104 516	105 297	107 749	107 911	107 949	107 949		
9	102 741	144 167	147 211	147 777	149 506	149 753	149 865	149 899			
10	97 797	143 742	147 683	149 575	149 710	149 857	149 890				
11	98 682	147 042	151 029	151 960	152 645	152 682					
12	86 067	126 032	129 969	131 858	131 972						
13	87 013	131 721	150 062	152 883							
14	83 678	124 048	128 322								
15	90 415	129 970									
16	86 382										

Table 3.19 Estimated parameters in the enhanced CL Model 3.24 for Portfolio B

	0	1	2	3	4	5	6	7	8	9
$\widehat{F}_j^{(1)}$	1.43999	1.03310	1.01168	1.00632	1.00463	1.00415	1.00102	1.00026	1.00088	0.99996
$\widehat{F}_j^{(2)}$	1.43999	1.03310	1.01168	1.00632	1.00463	1.00415	1.00102	1.00026	1.00088	0.99996
$\widehat{F}_j^{(3)}$	1.43999	1.03310	1.01168	1.00632	1.00463	1.00415	1.00102	1.00026	1.00088	0.99996
$\widehat{\sigma}_j^{(1)}$	11.16524	10.86582	3.52827	2.24269	2.35370	2.63740	1.10600	0.30292	0.69058	0.05593
$\widehat{\sigma}_j^{(2)}$	11.16676	10.86582	3.52827	2.24269	2.35370	2.63740	1.10600	0.30292	0.69058	0.05593
$\widehat{\sigma}_j^{(3)}$	11.16676	10.86582	3.52827	2.24269	2.35370	2.63740	1.10600	0.30292	0.69058	0.05593

Table 3.20 Reserves and conditional MSEP in the enhanced CL Model 3.24 for Portfolio B

i	CL reserves	$\widehat{\text{msep}}_{C_{i,J}\mid\mathcal{D}_I}(\widehat{C_{i,J}}^{(\text{CL},2)})^{1/2}$		$\widehat{\text{Var}}\left(C_{i,J}\mid\mathcal{D}_I\right)^{1/2}$		process error$^{1/2}$		param. pred. error$^{1/2}$		$\widehat{\text{Var}}\left(\widehat{C_{i,J}}^{(\text{CL},2)}\mid\mathcal{D}_I\right)^{1/2}$	
7	−4	19	−485.1%	18	−453.9%	18	−453.8%	0	−12.0%	7	−171.1%
8	91	242	265.6%	228	249.8%	228	249.7%	6	6.2%	82	90.5%
9	166	318	191.6%	293	176.4%	292	175.8%	23	13.7%	124	74.7%
10	320	557	174.4%	519	162.5%	518	162.2%	29	9.1%	202	63.3%
11	961	1232	128.3%	1159	120.6%	1158	120.5%	49	5.1%	419	43.7%
12	1445	1453	100.6%	1381	95.6%	1379	95.4%	74	5.1%	452	31.3%
13	2650	1835	69.2%	1734	65.4%	1729	65.3%	130	4.9%	599	22.6%
14	3749	2144	57.2%	2051	54.7%	2043	54.5%	182	4.9%	625	16.7%
15	8224	4726	57.5%	4545	55.3%	4530	55.1%	373	4.5%	1295	15.7%
16	45 878	5885	12.8%	5652	12.3%	5175	11.3%	2273	5.0%	1639	3.6%
Total	63 480	8933	14.1%	7967	12.6%	7623	12.0%	2316	3.6%	4041	6.4%

size of Portfolio B. The conditional parameter estimation error relative to the estimated CL reserves decreases from Portfolio B to Portfolio A since in Portfolio A we have more data to estimate the parameters.

- A more conservative model would be to assume total dependence for the conditional parameter prediction errors between the accident years, that is, then we would not allow for any diversification between the accident years. □

4
Bayesian Models

In the broadest sense, Bayesian methods for claims reserving can be viewed as methods in which one combines expert knowledge or existing prior information with observations resulting in an estimate for the ultimate claim. In the simplest case this prior knowledge/information is given, for example, by a single value like a prior estimate for the ultimate claim or for the average loss ratio (see sections below). However, in a strict sense the prior knowledge/information in Bayesian methods for claims reserving is given by a prior distribution of a random quantity such as the ultimate claim or a risk parameter. The Bayesian inference is then understood to be the process of combining the prior distribution of the random quantity with the observed data given in the upper triangle via Bayes' theorem. In this manner it is sometimes possible to obtain an analytic expression for the posterior distribution of the ultimate claim that reflects the change in the uncertainty due to the observations. The posterior expectation of the ultimate claim is then called the 'Bayesian estimator' for the ultimate claim and it minimizes the quadratic loss in the class of all estimators which are square integrable functions of the observations (see Section 4.3).

In cases where we are not able to explicitly calculate the posterior distribution of the ultimate claim there are various possibilities by which we can proceed. On the one hand, we can use numerical algorithms that generate empirical posterior distributions such as Markov Chain Monte Carlo methods (see Section 4.4). These methods have the advantage that they give distributional answers on any arbitrary distributional model, and not only estimates on the first two moments for specific distributional assumptions. However, it is often difficult to interpret numerical results, since parameter sensitivities are much harder to analyse if we do not have closed forms.

On the other hand, there are linear credibility methods that restrict the search for the best estimator to the smaller class of estimators, which are linear functions of the observations (see Sections 4.5, 4.6 and 4.7). These methods only lead to analytical formulas for the uncertainty estimates in terms of second moments such as the coefficient of variation. In practical applications, this is often sufficient and allows for interpretations on the parameters involved.

We start this chapter with two introductory sections (Sections 4.1 and 4.2) which slowly introduce Bayesian inference.

4.1 BENKTANDER–HOVINEN METHOD AND CAPE–COD MODEL

In preparation for this chapter, we start with two claims reserving methods that are not Bayesian models in the strict sense but lead us towards Bayesian considerations.

4.1.1 Benktander–Hovinen Method

This method goes back to Benktander (1976) and Hovinen (1981). They have, independently, developed a method that leads to the same total estimated loss amount.

Fix accident year $i \geq 1$. Assume that we have a known prior estimate μ_i for $E[C_{i,J}]$ and that the claims development pattern $(\beta_j)_{0\leq j\leq J}$ with $E[C_{i,j}] = \mu_i\ \beta_j$ is known. Since the BF method completely ignores the observations $C_{i,I-i}$ on the last observed diagonal and the CL method completely ignores the prior estimate μ_i at hand, one could consider a credibility mixture of these two methods (see (2.12)–(2.13)): For $c \in [0, 1]$ we define the following credibility mixture

$$u_i(c) = c\ \widehat{C_{i,J}}^{CL} + (1-c)\ \mu_i \tag{4.1}$$

for $1 \leq i \leq I$, where $\widehat{C_{i,J}}^{CL}$ is the CL estimate for the ultimate claim, see Estimator 2.4, and μ_i is the prior (point) estimate for the ultimate claim. The parameter c should increase with the development of $C_{i,j}$ since we obtain better information on $C_{i,J}$ with increasing time j. Benktander (1976) proposed to choose $c = \beta_{I-i}$, which leads to the following estimator:

ESTIMATOR 4.1 (Benktander–Hovinen (BH) estimator) *The BH estimator is given by*

$$\widehat{C_{i,J}}^{BH} = C_{i,I-i} + (1-\beta_{I-i})\ \left(\beta_{I-i}\ \widehat{C_{i,J}}^{CL} + (1-\beta_{I-i})\ \mu_i\right) \tag{4.2}$$

for $1 \leq i \leq I$.

Observe that we could again identify the claims development pattern $(\beta_j)_{0\leq j\leq J}$ with the CL factors $(f_j)_{0\leq j<J}$. This can be done if we use Model Assumptions 2.9 for the BF method, see also (2.11). Henceforth, in the remainder of this section we identify

$$\beta_j = \prod_{k=j}^{J-1} f_k^{-1} \tag{4.3}$$

Since the development pattern β_j is known, we also have (using (4.3)) known CL factors, which implies that we set

$$\widehat{f_j} = f_j$$

for $0 \leq j \leq J-1$. Then, the BH estimator (4.2) can be written in the following form

$$\begin{aligned}\widehat{C_{i,J}}^{BH} &= \beta_{I-i}\ \widehat{C_{i,J}}^{CL} + (1-\beta_{I-i})\ \widehat{C_{i,J}}^{BF} \\ &= C_{i,I-i} + (1-\beta_{I-i})\ \widehat{C_{i,J}}^{BF}\end{aligned} \tag{4.4}$$

(cf. (2.10) and (2.13) and $\widehat{C_{i,J}}^{CL} = C_{i,I-i}/\beta_{I-i}$, see also (4.10) below).

Remarks 4.2

- Equation (4.4) shows that the BH estimator can be seen as an iterated BF estimator using the BF estimate as the new prior estimate (see Estimator 2.10)
- The following lemma shows that the weighting β_{I-i} is not a fix point of our iteration since we have to evaluate the BH estimate at $1-(1-\beta_{I-i})^2$.

LEMMA 4.3 *Under the assumption that the claims development pattern* $(\beta_j)_{0\le j\le J}$ *is known and under identification* (4.3) *we have*

$$\widehat{C_{i,J}}^{\mathrm{BH}} = u_i\left(1-(1-\beta_{I-i})^2\right)$$

for $1 \le i \le I$, *where the function* $u_i(\cdot)$ *is given by* (4.1).

Proof It holds that

$$\begin{aligned}
\widehat{C_{i,J}}^{\mathrm{BH}} &= C_{i,I-i} + (1-\beta_{I-i})\left(\beta_{I-i}\,\widehat{C_{i,J}}^{\mathrm{CL}} + (1-\beta_{I-i})\,\mu_i\right)\\
&= \beta_{I-i}\,\widehat{C_{i,J}}^{\mathrm{CL}} + (\beta_{I-i}-\beta_{I-i}^2)\,\widehat{C_{i,J}}^{\mathrm{CL}} + (1-\beta_{I-i})^2\,\mu_i\\
&= \left(1-(1-\beta_{I-i})^2\right)\widehat{C_{i,J}}^{\mathrm{CL}} + (1-\beta_{I-i})^2\,\mu_i\\
&= u_i\left(1-(1-\beta_{I-i})^2\right)
\end{aligned}$$

This completes the proof of the lemma. □

Example 4.4 (BH method)

We revisit the data set given in Examples 2.7 and 2.11. Assume that β_j is known (we choose them equal to $\widehat{\beta}_j^{(\mathrm{CL})}$, see Example 2.11). Then we obtain the results given in Table 4.1. We see that the BH reserves are between the CL reserves and the BF reserves. They are closer to the CL reserves because β_{I-i} is larger than 50% for all accident years $i \in \{1,\ldots,I\}$. □

Table 4.1 Claims reserves from the BH method

						Claims reserves		
i	$C_{i,I-i}$	μ_i	β_{I-i}(%)	$\widehat{C_{i,J}}^{\mathrm{CL}}$	$\widehat{C_{i,J}}^{\mathrm{BH}}$	CL	BH	BF
0	11 148 124	11 653 101	100.0	11 148 124	11 148 124			
1	10 648 192	11 367 306	99.9	10 663 318	10 663 319	15 126	15 127	16 124
2	10 635 751	10 962 965	99.8	10 662 008	10 662 010	26 257	26 259	26 998
3	9 724 068	10 616 762	99.6	9 758 606	9 758 617	34 538	34 549	37 575
4	9 786 916	11 044 881	99.1	9 872 218	9 872 305	85 302	85 389	95 434
5	9 935 753	11 480 700	98.4	10 092 247	10 092 581	156 494	156 828	178 024
6	9 282 022	11 413 572	97.0	9 568 143	9 569 793	286 121	287 771	341 305
7	8 256 211	11 126 527	94.8	8 705 378	8 711 824	449 167	455 612	574 089
8	7 648 729	10 986 548	88.0	8 691 971	8 725 026	1 043 242	1 076 297	1 318 646
9	5 675 568	11 618 437	59.0	9 626 383	9 961 926	3 950 815	4 286 358	4 768 384
Total						6 047 061	6 424 190	7 356 580

The next theorem, due to Mack (2000), says that if we further iterate the BF method, we arrive at the CL reserve.

THEOREM 4.5 *Under the assumption that the claims development pattern* $(\beta_j)_{0\le j\le J}$ *is known and under identification* (4.3) *as well as* $\beta_{I-i}>0$, *we have that*

$$\lim_{m\to\infty}\widehat{C}^{(m)}=\widehat{C_{i,J}}^{\mathrm{CL}}$$

where $\widehat{C}^{(0)}=\mu_i$ *and*

$$\widehat{C}^{(m+1)}=C_{i,I-i}+(1-\beta_{I-i})\;\widehat{C}^{(m)}$$

for $m\ge 0$.

Proof For $m\ge 1$ we claim that

$$\widehat{C}^{(m)}=\left(1-(1-\beta_{I-i})^m\right)\,\widehat{C_{i,J}}^{\mathrm{CL}}+(1-\beta_{I-i})^m\;\mu_i \tag{4.5}$$

The claim is true for $m=1$ (BF estimator) and for $m=2$ (BH estimator, see Lemma 4.3). Hence we prove the claim by induction. Induction step $m\to m+1$:

$$\begin{aligned}\widehat{C}^{(m+1)}&=C_{i,I-i}+(1-\beta_{I-i})\;\widehat{C}^{(m)}\\&=C_{i,I-i}+(1-\beta_{I-i})\;\left(\left(1-(1-\beta_{I-i})^m\right)\,\widehat{C_{i,J}}^{\mathrm{CL}}+(1-\beta_{I-i})^m\;\mu_i\right)\\&=\beta_{I-i}\widehat{C_{i,J}}^{\mathrm{CL}}+\left((1-\beta_{I-i})-(1-\beta_{I-i})^{m+1}\right)\widehat{C_{i,J}}^{\mathrm{CL}}+(1-\beta_{I-i})^{m+1}\mu_i\end{aligned}$$

which proves (4.5). But from (4.5) and $\beta_{I-i}>0$ the claim of the theorem immediately follows. □

Example 4.4, revisited
In view of Theorem 4.5 we have Table 4.2.

Table 4.2 Iteration of the BF/BH method (see Theorem 4.5)

i	$\widehat{C}^{(1)}=\widehat{C_{i,J}}^{\mathrm{BF}}$	$\widehat{C}^{(2)}=\widehat{C_{i,J}}^{\mathrm{BH}}$	$\widehat{C}^{(3)}$	$\widehat{C}^{(4)}$	$\widehat{C}^{(5)}$	...	$\widehat{C}^{(\infty)}=\widehat{C_{i,J}}^{\mathrm{CL}}$
0	11 148 124	11 148 124	11 148 124	11 148 124	11 148 124	...	11 148 124
1	10 664 316	10 663 319	10 663 318	10 663 318	10 663 318		10 663 318
2	10 662 749	10 662 010	10 662 008	10 662 008	10 662 008		10 662 008
3	9 761 643	9 758 617	9 758 606	9 758 606	9 758 606		9 758 606
4	9 882 350	9 872 305	9 872 218	9 872 218	9 872 218	...	9 872 218
5	10 113 777	10 092 581	10 092 252	10 092 247	10 092 247		10 092 247
6	9 623 328	9 569 793	9 568 192	9 568 144	9 568 143		9 568 143
7	8 830 301	8 711 824	8 705 711	8 705 395	8 705 379		8 705 378
8	8 967 375	8 725 026	8 695 938	8 692 447	8 692 028		8 691 971
9	10 443 953	9 961 926	9 764 095	9 682 902	9 649 579	...	9 626 383

4.1.2 Cape–Cod Model

One main deficiency in the CL model is that the ultimate claim completely depends on the last observation on the diagonal (see CL Estimator 2.4). If this last observation is an outlier, this outlier is projected to the ultimate claim (using the estimated age-to-age factors $\widehat{f}_j$). Moreover, often in long-tailed lines of business (like liability insurance) the first observations are not representative. One possibility to smoothen outliers on the last observed diagonal is to combine BF and CL methods as, for instance, in the BH method. Another possibility is to make such diagonal observations more robust. This is done in the Cape–Cod method, which goes back to Bühlmann (1983).

Model Assumptions 4.6 (Cape–Cod method)

- Cumulative claims $C_{i,j}$ of different accident years i are independent.
- There exist parameters $\Pi_0, \ldots, \Pi_I > 0$, $\kappa > 0$, and a claims development pattern $(\beta_j)_{0\le j\le J}$ with $\beta_J = 1$ such that

$$E[C_{i,j}] = \kappa\ \Pi_i\ \beta_j$$

for all $i = 0, \ldots, I$. □

Observe that the Cape–Cod model assumptions coincide with Model Assumptions 2.9, with $\mu_i = \kappa\ \Pi_i$. Thus, one can see that under these Cape–Cod model assumptions, Π_i can be interpreted as the premium received for accident year i and κ reflects the average loss ratio. We assume that κ is independent of the accident year i, that is, the premium level w.r.t. κ is the same for all accident years. Under identification (4.3), we can estimate for each accident year the loss ratio κ using the CL estimate for the ultimate claim; hence we consider

$$\widehat{\kappa}_i = \frac{\widehat{C_{i,J}}^{\mathrm{CL}}}{\Pi_i} = \frac{C_{i,I-i}}{\prod_{j=I-i}^{J-1} f_j^{-1}\ \Pi_i} = \frac{C_{i,I-i}}{\beta_{I-i}\ \Pi_i}$$

This is an unbiased estimator for κ, since

$$E\left[\widehat{\kappa}_i\right] = \frac{1}{\Pi_i}\ E\left[\widehat{C_{i,J}}^{\mathrm{CL}}\right] = \frac{1}{\Pi_i\ \beta_{I-i}}\ E\left[C_{i,I-i}\right] = \frac{1}{\Pi_i}\ E\left[C_{i,J}\right] = \kappa$$

The 'robusted' overall loss ratio is then estimated by (weighted average)

$$\widehat{\kappa}^{\mathrm{CC}} = \sum_{i=0}^{I} \frac{\beta_{I-i}\ \Pi_i}{\sum_{k=0}^{I} \beta_{I-k}\ \Pi_k}\ \widehat{\kappa}_i = \frac{\sum_{i=0}^{I} C_{i,I-i}}{\sum_{i=0}^{I} \beta_{I-i}\ \Pi_i} \tag{4.6}$$

Observe that $\widehat{\kappa}^{\mathrm{CC}}$ is an unbiased estimator for κ.

A 'robusted' value for $C_{i,I-i}$ is then given by $(i > 0)$

$$\widehat{C_{i,I-i}}^{\mathrm{CC}} = \widehat{\kappa}^{\mathrm{CC}}\ \Pi_i\ \beta_{I-i}$$

This leads to the Cape–Cod estimator:

ESTIMATOR 4.7 (Cape–Cod estimator) *The Cape–Cod estimator is given by*

$$\widehat{C_{i,J}}^{\mathrm{CC}} = C_{i,I-i} - \widehat{C_{i,I-i}}^{\mathrm{CC}} + \prod_{j=I-i}^{J-1} f_j \, \widehat{C_{i,I-i}}^{\mathrm{CC}} \tag{4.7}$$

for $1 \le i \le I$.

We obtain the following result:

LEMMA 4.8 *Under Model Assumptions 4.6 and under identification* (4.3), *the estimator* $\widehat{C_{i,J}}^{\mathrm{CC}} - C_{i,I-i}$ *is unbiased for* $E\left[C_{i,J} - C_{i,I-i}\right] = \kappa \, \Pi_i \, (1 - \beta_{I-i})$.

Proof Observe that

$$E\left[\widehat{C_{i,I-i}}^{\mathrm{CC}}\right] = E\left[\widehat{\kappa}^{\mathrm{CC}}\right] \Pi_i \, \beta_{I-i} = \kappa \, \Pi_i \, \beta_{I-i} = E\left[C_{i,I-i}\right]$$

Moreover, we have from (4.3) that

$$\widehat{C_{i,J}}^{\mathrm{CC}} - C_{i,I-i} = \widehat{C_{i,I-i}}^{\mathrm{CC}} \left(\prod_{j=I-i}^{J-1} f_j - 1 \right) = \widehat{\kappa}^{\mathrm{CC}} \, \Pi_i \, (1 - \beta_{I-i}) \tag{4.8}$$

This completes the proof. □

Remarks 4.9

- In the Cape-Cod method the CL iteration is applied to the 'robusted' diagonal value $\widehat{C_{i,I-i}}^{\mathrm{CC}}$, but, in order to calculate the ultimate claim, one still needs to add the difference between the original diagonal observation $C_{i,I-i}$ and the 'robusted' diagonal value.
  If we modify the Cap-Code estimator we obtain (see also (4.8))

  $$\widehat{C_{i,J}}^{\mathrm{CC}} = C_{i,I-i} + (1 - \beta_{I-i}) \, \widehat{\kappa}^{\mathrm{CC}} \, \Pi_i$$

  which is a BF-type estimator with modified *a priori* estimate $\widehat{\kappa}^{\mathrm{CC}} \, \Pi_i$.
- Observe that

  $$\mathrm{Var}\left(\widehat{\kappa}_i\right) = \frac{1}{\Pi_i^2 \, \beta_{I-i}^2} \, \mathrm{Var}\left(C_{i,I-i}\right)$$

  According to the choice of the variance function of $C_{i,j}$ this may also suggest that robustness can be incorporated in another way (with smaller variance), see Lemma 3.4.

Example 4.10 (Cape-Cod method)

We revisit the data set given in Examples 2.7, 2.11 and 4.4.

In Table 4.3, we present the 'robusted' diagonal values $\widehat{C_{i,I-i}}^{\mathrm{CC}}$ along with the Cape–Cod estimates for the ultimate claims $\widehat{C_{i,J}}^{\mathrm{CC}}$. Notice that the Cape–Cod estimates $\widehat{C_{i,J}}^{\mathrm{CC}}$ are

Table 4.3 Claims reserves from the Cape–Cod method

i	Π_i	$\widehat{\kappa}_i$ (%)	$\widehat{C_{i,I-i}}^{CC}$	$\widehat{C_{i,J}}^{CC}$		Claims reserves Cape–Cod	CL	BF
0	15 473 558	72.0	10 411 192	11 148 124		0	0	0
1	14 882 436	71.7	9 999 259	10 662 396		14 204	15 126	16 124
2	14 456 039	73.8	9 702 614	10 659 704		23 953	26 257	26 998
3	14 054 917	69.4	9 423 208	9 757 538		33 469	34 538	37 575
4	14 525 373	68.0	9 688 771	9 871 362		84 446	85 302	95 434
5	15 025 923	67.2	9 953 237	10 092 522		156 769	156 494	178 024
6	14 832 965	64.5	9 681 735	9 580 464		298 442	286 121	341 305
7	14 550 359	59.8	9 284 898	8 761 342		505 131	449 167	574 089
8	14 461 781	60.1	8 562 549	8 816 611		1 167 882	1 043 242	1 318 646
9	15 210 363	63.3	6 033 871	9 875 801		4 200 233	3 950 815	4 768 384
	$\widehat{\kappa}^{CC}$	67.3			Total	6 484 530	6 047 061	7 356 580

smaller than the corresponding BF estimates $\widehat{C_{i,J}}^{BF}$ owing to the fact that the prior estimates μ_i used for the BF method are rather pessimistic. The loss ratios μ_i/Π_i in the BF method are all above 75%, whereas the Cape–Cod method gives loss ratios $\widehat{\kappa}_i$, which are all below 75% (see Figure 4.1). However, as Figure 4.1 shows, we have to be careful with the assumption of constant individual loss ratios κ_i. The figure suggests that we might have to consider underwriting cycles. In soft markets, loss ratios are rather low (so we are able to charge higher premiums). If there is a keen competition we expect low profit margins. If possible, we should adjust our premiums with underwriting cycle information. For this reason one finds in practice modified versions of the Cape–Cod method, for example, smoothing of the last observed diagonal is only done over neighbouring values. □

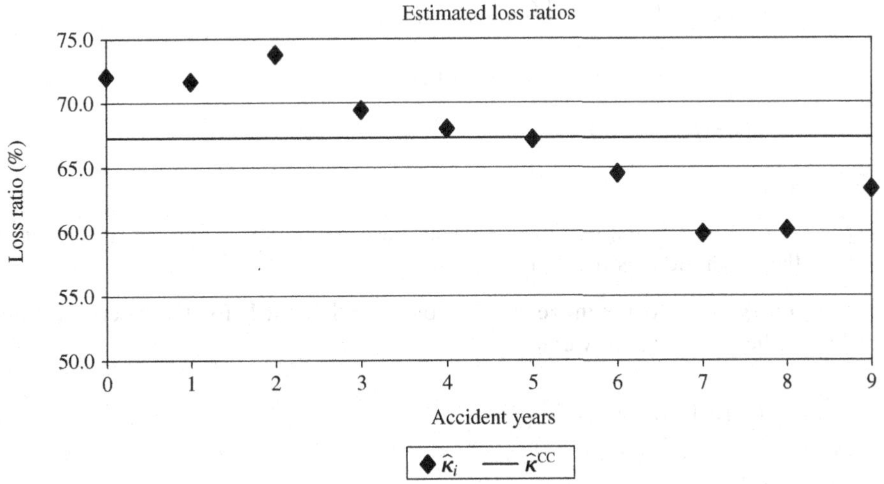

Figure 4.1 Estimated individual loss ratios $\widehat{\kappa}_i$ and estimated Cap–Code overall loss ratio $\widehat{\kappa}^{CC}$

4.2 CREDIBLE CLAIMS RESERVING METHODS

In the subsections of this section we investigate the question: What are the optimal mixtures between CL and BF estimates?, and formulate optimality criteria. Note that, so far, the credibility mixture was done rather ad hoc, for example, in the BH method we have simply said that the credibility into the observation should increase with increasing development.

4.2.1 Minimizing Quadratic Loss Functions

We choose $i > 0$ and define the outstanding claims for accident year i by (see also (1.17))

$$R_i = R_{i,I-i} = C_{i,J} - C_{i,I-i}$$

If $C_{i,j}$ denote cumulative claims, then R_i are exactly the outstanding loss liabilities at time I. Under the assumption that the development pattern and the CL factors are known (and identified by (4.3) under Model Assumptions 2.9) the CL reserve and the BF reserve are given by

$$\widehat{R}_i^{\mathrm{CL}} = \widehat{C_{i,J}}^{\mathrm{CL}} - C_{i,I-i} = C_{i,I-i} \left(\prod_{j=I-i}^{J-1} f_j - 1 \right)$$

$$\widehat{R}_i^{\mathrm{BF}} = \widehat{C_{i,J}}^{\mathrm{BF}} - C_{i,I-i} = (1 - \beta_{I-i})\ \mu_i$$

If we mix the CL and BF methods we obtain for the credibility mixture ($c \in [0, 1]$)

$$c\ \widehat{C_{i,J}}^{\mathrm{CL}} + (1 - c)\ \widehat{C_{i,J}}^{\mathrm{BF}}$$

and the following representations for the reserves

$$\begin{aligned}
\widehat{R}_i(c) &= c\ \widehat{R}_i^{\mathrm{CL}} + (1 - c)\ \widehat{R}_i^{\mathrm{BF}} \\
&= \widehat{C_{i,J}}^{\mathrm{BF}} - C_{i,I-i} + c \left(\widehat{C_{i,J}}^{\mathrm{CL}} - \widehat{C_{i,J}}^{\mathrm{BF}} \right) \\
&= (1 - \beta_{I-i}) \left(c\ \widehat{C_{i,J}}^{\mathrm{CL}} + (1 - c)\ \mu_i \right) \\
&= (1 - \beta_{I-i})\ u_i(c)
\end{aligned}$$

(see also (4.4)).

Main Question Which is the optimal c? In our case optimality is defined in the sense of minimizing the quadratic loss function.

Henceforth, our goal is to minimize the (unconditional) MSEP for the reserve estimates $\widehat{R}_i(c)$ (that predicts the random variable R_i)

$$\mathrm{msep}_{R_i}(\widehat{R}_i(c)) = E\left[\left(R_i - \widehat{R}_i(c) \right)^2 \right] \tag{4.9}$$

see also Section 3.1.

In order to do this minimization we need a proper definition of a stochastic model.

Model Assumptions 4.11

- Cumulative claims $C_{i,j}$ of different accident years i are independent.
- There exists a sequence $(\beta_j)_{0\le j\le J}$ with $\beta_J = 1$ such that we have for all $j \in \{0, \ldots, J\}$

$$E\left[C_{i,j}\right] = \beta_j \; E\left[C_{i,J}\right]$$

- There exist random variables $U_1, \ldots, U_I$, which are unbiased estimators for $E[C_{i,J}]$, that is, $E[U_i] = E[C_{i,J}]$, and assume that U_i is independent of $C_{i,I-i}$ and $C_{i,J}$. □

Remarks 4.12

- Model Assumptions 4.11 coincide with Model Assumptions 2.9 if we assume that $U_i = \mu_i > 0$ is deterministic. That is, here we no longer assume that we have a known deterministic value for the *a priori* expected mean, but rather an estimator (random variable U_i) that is an unbiased estimator for the mean. This reflects that there is also some uncertainty in choosing the 'true' mean $E[C_{i,J}]$ (expert opinion).
- Observe that we do not assume that the CL model is satisfied! The CL model satisfies Model Assumptions 4.11 but not necessarily vice versa. We assume that f_j is identified by β_j via (4.3), and that the CL and BF estimators are given by

$$\widehat{C_{i,J}}^{CL} = \frac{C_{i,I-i}}{\beta_{I-i}} \quad \text{and} \quad \widehat{C_{i,J}}^{BF} = C_{i,I-i} + (1-\beta_{I-i})\; U_i \tag{4.10}$$

Henceforth, the credibility weighted reserves are given by

$$\widehat{R}_i(c) = (1-\beta_{I-i}) \left(c\; \widehat{C_{i,J}}^{CL} + (1-c)\; U_i \right) \tag{4.11}$$

Under these model assumptions and definitions we want to minimize the unconditional MSEP

$$\text{msep}_{R_i}\left(\widehat{R}_i(c)\right) = E\left[\left(R_i - \widehat{R}_i(c)\right)^2\right] \tag{4.12}$$

- Observe also that, if we assumed that the CL model is satisfied, we could not directly compare this situation to the MSEP calculation in Chapter 3. For the derivation of a MSEP formula for the CL method we have always assumed that the CL factors f_j are not known. If they were known, the MSEP of the CL reserves would simply be given by (see (3.8))

$$\begin{aligned}
\text{msep}_{C_{i,J}}\left(\widehat{C_{i,J}}^{CL}\right) &= E\left[E\left[\left(C_{i,J} - \widehat{C_{i,J}}^{CL}\right)^2 \middle| \mathcal{D}_I\right]\right] \\
&= E\left[\text{msep}_{C_{i,J}|\mathcal{D}_I}\left(\widehat{C_{i,J}}^{CL}\right)\right] \\
&= E\left[\text{Var}\left(C_{i,J} \middle| \mathcal{D}_I\right)\right] \\
&= \text{Var}\left(C_{i,J}\right) - \text{Var}\left(E\left[C_{i,J} \middle| \mathcal{D}_I\right]\right) \\
&= \text{Var}\left(C_{i,J}\right) - \text{Var}\left(C_{i,I-i}\right) \prod_{j=I-i}^{J-1} f_j^2
\end{aligned}$$

That is, we only obtain a process variance term from the unconditional MSEP.

If we calculate (4.11) under Model Assumptions 4.11 and (4.10), it holds that $E\left[\widehat{R}_i(c)\right] = E[R_i]$ and

$$\begin{aligned} \text{msep}_{R_i}\left(\widehat{R}_i(c)\right) &= \text{Var}\,(R_i) + E\left[\left(E[R_i] - \widehat{R}_i(c)\right)^2\right] \\ &\quad + 2\,E\left[\left(R_i - E[R_i]\right)\,\left(E[R_i] - \widehat{R}_i(c)\right)\right] \\ &= \text{Var}\,(R_i) + \text{Var}\left(\widehat{R}_i(c)\right) - 2\,\text{Cov}\left(R_i, \widehat{R}_i(c)\right) \end{aligned}$$

We have the following theorem by Mack (2000).

THEOREM 4.13 *Under Model Assumptions 4.11 and* (4.10) *the optimal credibility factor c_i^*, which minimizes the (unconditional) MSEP* (4.12)*, is given by*

$$c_i^* = \frac{\beta_{I-i}}{1-\beta_{I-i}} \, \frac{\text{Cov}(C_{i,I-i}, R_i) + \beta_{I-i}\,(1-\beta_{I-i})\,\text{Var}(U_i)}{\text{Var}(C_{i,I-i}) + \beta_{I-i}^2\,\text{Var}(U_i)}$$

Proof We have that

$$\begin{aligned} E\left[\left(\widehat{R}_i(c_i) - R_i\right)^2\right] &= c_i^2\, E\left[\left(\widehat{R}_i^{\text{CL}} - \widehat{R}_i^{\text{BF}}\right)^2\right] + E\left[\left(R_i - \widehat{R}_i^{\text{BF}}\right)^2\right] \\ &\quad - 2\, c_i\, E\left[\left(\widehat{R}_i^{\text{CL}} - \widehat{R}_i^{\text{BF}}\right)\left(R_i - \widehat{R}_i^{\text{BF}}\right)\right] \end{aligned}$$

Hence, the optimal c_i is given by

$$\begin{aligned} c_i^* &= \frac{E\left[\left(\widehat{R}_i^{\text{CL}} - \widehat{R}_i^{\text{BF}}\right)\left(R_i - \widehat{R}_i^{\text{BF}}\right)\right]}{E\left[\left(\widehat{R}_i^{\text{CL}} - \widehat{R}_i^{\text{BF}}\right)^2\right]} \\ &= \frac{E\left[\left((1/\beta_{I-i} - 1)\, C_{i,I-i} - (1-\beta_{I-i})\, U_i\right)\left(R_i - (1-\beta_{I-i})\, U_i\right)\right]}{E\left[\left((1/\beta_{I-i} - 1)\, C_{i,I-i} - (1-\beta_{I-i})\, U_i\right)^2\right]} \\ &= \frac{\beta_{I-i}}{1-\beta_{I-i}} \, \frac{E\left[\left(C_{i,I-i} - \beta_{I-i}\, U_i\right)\left(R_i - (1-\beta_{I-i})\, U_i\right)\right]}{E\left[\left(C_{i,I-i} - \beta_{I-i}\, U_i\right)^2\right]} \end{aligned}$$

Since $E[\beta_{I-i}\, U_i] = E[C_{i,I-i}]$ and $E[U_i] = E[C_{i,J}]$ we obtain

$$\begin{aligned} c_i^* &= \frac{\beta_{I-i}}{1-\beta_{I-i}} \, \frac{\text{Cov}(C_{i,I-i} - \beta_{I-i}\, U_i, R_i - (1-\beta_{I-i})\, U_i)}{\text{Var}(C_{i,I-i} - \beta_{I-i}\, U_i)} \\ &= \frac{\beta_{I-i}}{1-\beta_{I-i}} \, \frac{\text{Cov}(C_{i,I-i}, R_i) + \beta_{I-i}\,(1-\beta_{I-i})\,\text{Var}(U_i)}{\text{Var}(C_{i,I-i}) + \beta_{I-i}^2\,\text{Var}(U_i)} \end{aligned}$$

This completes the proof. □

We would like to mention once more that we have not considered the estimation errors in the claims development pattern β_j and f_j. In this sense Theorem 4.13 is a statement giving optimal credibility weights taking account of the process variance and the uncertainty in the prior estimate U_i (which itself is described by a distribution).

Remark To explicitly calculate c_i^* in Theorem 4.13 we need to specify an explicit stochastic model. This is done in the next subsection.

4.2.2 Distributional Examples to Credible Claims Reserving

To construct the BH estimate we have used a credibility weighting between the BF method and the CL method. Theorem 4.13 gave an expression for the best weighted average (relative to the quadratic loss function). We now specify an explicit stochastic model in order to apply Theorem 4.13.

Model Assumptions 4.14 (Mack (2000))

- Cumulative claims $C_{i,j}$ of different accident years i are independent.
- There exists a sequence $(\beta_j)_{0\leq j\leq J}$ with $\beta_J = 1$ and a function $\alpha^2(\cdot)$ such that we have

$$E\left[C_{i,j}\middle| C_{i,J}\right] = \beta_j\ C_{i,J}$$
$$\mathrm{Var}\left(C_{i,j}\middle| C_{i,J}\right) = \beta_j\ (1-\beta_j)\ \alpha^2(C_{i,J})$$

for all $i = 0, \ldots, I$ and $j = 0, \ldots, J$. □

Remarks 4.15

- This model is different in spirit from the CL Model 3.2. In the CL model we have a 'forward' iteration, that is, we have a Markov chain and successive cumulative claims are linked through a link ratio. In the model above we have rather a 'backward' consideration, conditioning on the ultimate claim $C_{i,J}$ we determine intermediate cumulative claims states, that is, this is simply a refined stochastic definition of the development pattern. In fact, our goal is then to learn more about the distribution of the ultimate claim $C_{i,J}$ when we have an observation $C_{i,I-i}$ (via Bayes' theorem).
- This model can be viewed as a Bayesian approach, which determines the ultimate claim $C_{i,J}$. This will be further discussed below.
- Observe that this model satisfies Model Assumptions 2.9 with $\mu_i = E\left[C_{i,J}\right]$. Moreover, $C_{i,j}$ satisfies the assumptions given in Model Assumptions 4.11. The CL model is in general not satisfied (see also Subsection 4.2.3 below, e.g. formula (4.23)).
- Observe that the variance condition is such that it converges to zero for $\beta_j \to 1$; that is, if the expected outstanding claims are low, the uncertainty is also low.

In view of Theorem 4.13 we have the following corollary (use definitions (4.11) and (4.10)):

COROLLARY 4.16 *Under Model Assumptions 4.14, the assumption that U_i is an unbiased estimator for $E[C_{i,J}]$ and independent of $C_{i,I-i}$ as well as $C_{i,J}$, the optimal credibility factor c_i^* which minimizes the unconditional MSEP* (4.12) *is given by*

$$c_i^* = \frac{\beta_{I-i}}{\beta_{I-i}+t_i} \qquad \text{with} \qquad t_i = \frac{E\left[\alpha^2(C_{i,J})\right]}{\mathrm{Var}(U_i)+\mathrm{Var}(C_{i,J})-E\left[\alpha^2(C_{i,J})\right]}$$

for $i \in \{1, \ldots, I\}$.

Proof From Theorem 4.13 we have

$$c_i^* = \frac{\beta_{I-i}}{1-\beta_{I-i}} \frac{\mathrm{Cov}(C_{i,I-i}, C_{i,J} - C_{i,I-i}) + \beta_{I-i}\,(1-\beta_{I-i})\,\mathrm{Var}(U_i)}{\mathrm{Var}(C_{i,I-i}) + \beta_{I-i}^2\,\mathrm{Var}(U_i)}$$

Now, we need to calculate the terms on the right-hand side of the above equation. We obtain

$$\begin{aligned}\mathrm{Var}(C_{i,I-i}) &= E\left[\mathrm{Var}(C_{i,I-i}|C_{i,J})\right] + \mathrm{Var}\left(E[C_{i,I-i}|C_{i,J}]\right)\\ &= \beta_{I-i}\,(1-\beta_{I-i})\,E\left[\alpha^2(C_{i,J})\right] + \beta_{I-i}^2\,\mathrm{Var}\left(C_{i,J}\right)\end{aligned}$$

and

$$\mathrm{Cov}(C_{i,I-i}, C_{i,J} - C_{i,I-i}) = \mathrm{Cov}(C_{i,I-i}, C_{i,J}) - \mathrm{Var}(C_{i,I-i})$$

Henceforth, we need to calculate

$$\begin{aligned}\mathrm{Cov}(C_{i,I-i}, C_{i,J}) &= E\left[\mathrm{Cov}(C_{i,I-i}, C_{i,J}|C_{i,J})\right] + \mathrm{Cov}\left(E[C_{i,I-i}|C_{i,J}], E[C_{i,J}|C_{i,J}]\right)\\ &= 0 + \mathrm{Cov}\left(\beta_{I-i}\,C_{i,J}, C_{i,J}\right) = \beta_{I-i}\,\mathrm{Var}(C_{i,J})\end{aligned}$$

This implies that

$$\mathrm{Cov}(C_{i,I-i}, C_{i,J} - C_{i,I-i}) = \beta_{I-i}\,\mathrm{Var}(C_{i,J}) - \mathrm{Var}(C_{i,I-i})$$

Thus, we obtain

$$\begin{aligned}c_i^* &= \frac{\beta_{I-i}}{1-\beta_{I-i}} \frac{\beta_{I-i}\,\mathrm{Var}(C_{i,J}) - \mathrm{Var}(C_{i,I-i}) + \beta_{I-i}\,(1-\beta_{I-i})\,\mathrm{Var}(U_i)}{\mathrm{Var}(C_{i,I-i}) + \beta_{I-i}^2\,\mathrm{Var}(U_i)}\\ &= \frac{\mathrm{Var}(C_{i,J}) - E\left[\alpha^2(C_{i,J})\right] + \mathrm{Var}(U_i)}{(\beta_{I-i}^{-1} - 1)\;E\left[\alpha^2(C_{i,J})\right] + \mathrm{Var}(C_{i,J}) + \mathrm{Var}(U_i)}\\ &= \frac{\mathrm{Var}(C_{i,J}) - E\left[\alpha^2(C_{i,J})\right] + \mathrm{Var}(U_i)}{\beta_{I-i}^{-1}\,E\left[\alpha^2(C_{i,J})\right] + \mathrm{Var}(C_{i,J}) - E\left[\alpha^2(C_{i,J})\right] + \mathrm{Var}(U_i)}\end{aligned}$$

This completes the proof of the corollary. □

Moreover, we have the corollary:

COROLLARY 4.17 *Under Model Assumptions 4.14, the assumption that U_i is an unbiased estimator for $E[C_{i,J}]$ and independent of $C_{i,I-i}$ as well as $C_{i,J}$, we find the following MSEPs (see also* (4.11)–(4.12)*):*

$$\mathrm{msep}_{R_i}\left(\widehat{R}_i(c)\right) = E\left[\alpha^2(C_{i,J})\right]\;\left(\frac{c^2}{\beta_{I-i}} + \frac{1}{1-\beta_{I-i}} + \frac{(1-c)^2}{t_i}\right)\;(1-\beta_{I-i})^2$$

$$\mathrm{msep}_{R_i}\left(\widehat{R}_i(0)\right) = E\left[\alpha^2(C_{i,J})\right] \left(\frac{1}{1-\beta_{I-i}} + \frac{1}{t_i}\right) (1-\beta_{I-i})^2$$

$$\mathrm{msep}_{R_i}\left(\widehat{R}_i(1)\right) = E\left[\alpha^2(C_{i,J})\right] \left(\frac{1}{\beta_{I-i}} + \frac{1}{1-\beta_{I-i}}\right) (1-\beta_{I-i})^2$$

$$\mathrm{msep}_{R_i}\left(\widehat{R}_i(c_i^*)\right) = E\left[\alpha^2(C_{i,J})\right] \left(\frac{1}{\beta_{I-i}+t_i} + \frac{1}{1-\beta_{I-i}}\right) (1-\beta_{I-i})^2$$

for $i \in \{1, \ldots, I\}$.

Proof Exercise. □

Remarks 4.18

- The reserve $\widehat{R}_i(0)$ corresponds to the BF reserve $\widehat{R}_i^{\mathrm{BF}}$ and $\widehat{R}_i(1)$ corresponds to the CL reserve $\widehat{R}_i^{\mathrm{CL}}$. However, $\mathrm{msep}_{R_i}\left(\widehat{R}_i(1)\right)$ and $\mathrm{msep}_{R_i}\left(\widehat{R}_i^{\mathrm{CL}}\right)$ from Chapter 3 are not comparable since (a) we use a completely different model, which leads to different process error and prediction error terms; (b) in Corollary 4.17 we do not investigate the estimation error coming from the fact that we have to estimate f_j and β_j from the data.
- From Corollary 4.17 we see that the BF estimate in Model 4.14 is better (in terms of the MSEP) than the CL estimate as long as

$$t_i > \beta_{I-i} \tag{4.13}$$

  That is, for years with small loss experience β_{I-i} one should take the BF estimate, whereas for previous years one should take the CL estimate. Similar estimates can be derived for the BH estimate.

Example 4.19 (Model Assumptions 4.14)

The following is an easy distributional example satisfying Model Assumptions 4.14. Assume that, conditionally given $C_{i,J}$, $C_{i,j}/C_{i,J}$ has a Beta $\left(\alpha_i\beta_j, \alpha_i(1-\beta_j)\right)$-distribution. Hence

$$E\left[C_{i,j}\middle| C_{i,J}\right] = C_{i,J}\, E\left[\frac{C_{i,j}}{C_{i,J}}\middle| C_{i,J}\right] = \beta_j\, C_{i,J}$$

$$\mathrm{Var}\left(C_{i,j}\middle| C_{i,J}\right) = C_{i,J}^2\, \mathrm{Var}\left(\frac{C_{i,j}}{C_{i,J}}\middle| C_{i,J}\right) = \beta_j\,(1-\beta_j)\,\frac{C_{i,J}^2}{1+\alpha_i}$$

for all $i = 0, \ldots, I$ and $j = 0, \ldots, J$. See appendix, Subsection A.2.5, for the definition of the Beta distribution and its moments.

We revisit the data set given in Examples 2.7, 2.11 and 4.4. Observe that

$$E\left[\alpha^2(C_{i,J})\right] = \frac{1}{1+\alpha_i}\, E\left[C_{i,J}^2\right] = \frac{E\left[C_{i,J}\right]^2}{1+\alpha_i}\, \left(\mathrm{Vco}^2\left(C_{i,J}\right) + 1\right)$$

As already mentioned, we assume that the claims development pattern $(\beta_j)_{0\le j\le J}$ is known. This means that in our estimates no estimation error results from the claims development parameters. We only have the process variance and the uncertainty in the estimation of the ultimate claim U_i. This corresponds to a prediction error term in the language of Section 3.4. We assume that an actuary is able to predict the true value for the *a priori* estimate with an error of 5%, that is,

$$\text{Vco}(U_i) = 5\% \tag{4.14}$$

Moreover, we assume that

$$\text{Vco}\left(C_{i,J}\right) = \left(\text{Vco}^2(U_i) + r^2\right)^{1/2} \tag{4.15}$$

where we set $r = 6\%$, which corresponds to the pure process error. These values correspond to pure expert choices. This leads with $\alpha_i = 600$ to the results in Table 4.4. The prediction errors are given in Table 4.5. We already see from the choices of our parameters α_i, r and $\text{Vco}(U_i)$ that it is rather difficult to apply this method in practice, since we have not

Table 4.4 Claims reserves from Model 4.14

							Claims reserves		
i	α_i	$\text{Vco}(U_i)$ (%)	r (%)	$\text{Vco}(C_{i,J})$ (%)	t_i (%)	c_i^* (%)	CL	BF	$\widehat{R}_i(c_i^*)$
0	600	5.0	6.0	7.8	24.2	80.5	0	0	0
1	600	5.0	6.0	7.8	24.2	80.5	15 126	16 124	15 320
2	600	5.0	6.0	7.8	24.2	80.5	26 257	26 998	26 401
3	600	5.0	6.0	7.8	24.2	80.5	34 538	37 575	35 131
4	600	5.0	6.0	7.8	24.2	80.4	85 302	95 434	87 288
5	600	5.0	6.0	7.8	24.2	80.3	156 494	178 024	160 738
6	600	5.0	6.0	7.8	24.2	80.1	286 121	341 305	297 128
7	600	5.0	6.0	7.8	24.2	79.7	449 167	574 089	474 538
8	600	5.0	6.0	7.8	24.2	78.5	1 043 242	1 318 646	1 102 588
9	600	5.0	6.0	7.8	24.2	70.9	3 950 815	4 768 384	4 188 531
Total							6 047 061	7 356 580	6 387 663

Table 4.5 MSEP according to Corollary 4.17

i	$E[U_i]$	$E[\alpha^2(C_{i,J})]^{1/2}$	$\text{msep}^{1/2}(\widehat{R}_i(1))$	$\text{msep}^{1/2}(\widehat{R}_i(0))$	$\text{msep}^{1/2}(\widehat{R}_i(c_i^*))$
0	11 653 101	476 788			
1	11 367 306	465 094	17 529	17 568	17 527
2	10 962 965	448 551	22 287	22 373	22 282
3	10 616 762	434 386	25 888	26 031	25 879
4	11 044 881	451 902	42 189	42 751	42 153
5	11 480 700	469 734	58 952	60 340	58 862
6	11 413 572	466 987	81 990	85 604	81 745
7	11 126 527	455 243	106 183	113 911	105 626
8	10 986 548	449 515	166 013	190 514	163 852
9	11 618 437	475 369	396 616	500 223	372 199
Total			457 811	560 159	435 814

estimated these parameters from the data available. That is, we did a smart prior choice using expert opinion only. But one could also argue that the choice of the parameters was rather artificial and one should use the observations to get more reasonable estimates.

Observe that these results for the MSEP (Figure 4.2) cannot be compared to the MSEP obtained in the CL method (see Chapter 3). We do not know whether the model assumptions in this example imply the CL model assumptions. Moreover, we do not investigate the uncertainties in the parameter estimates, and the choice of the parameters was rather artificial, motivated by expert opinions only. □

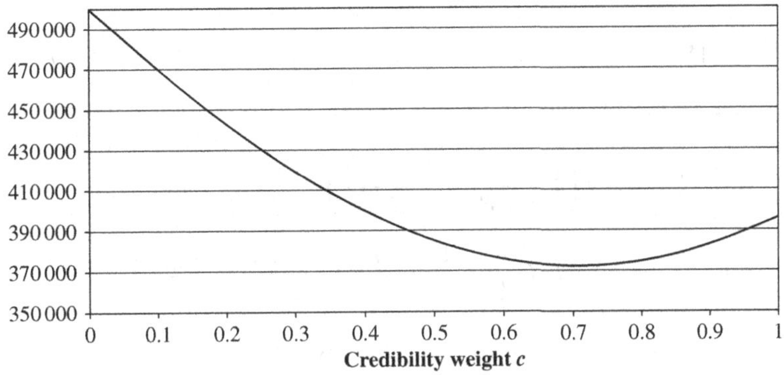

Figure 4.2 $\mathrm{msep}_{R_i}(\widehat{R}_i(c))^{1/2}$ as a function of $c \in [0, 1]$ for accident year $i = 9$

4.2.3 Log-Normal/Log-Normal Model

In this subsection we give a second example for Model Assumptions 4.14. Since we would like to discuss this in a more extended framework we put this second example into a new subsection.

We make distributional assumptions on $C_{i,J}$ and $C_{i,j}|C_{i,J}$ which are consistent with Model Assumptions 4.14 and, hence, would allow for the application of Corollary 4.16. However, in this section we give a different approach. In Corollary 4.16 we have specified a second distribution U_i for a prior estimate $E[U_i] = E[C_{i,J}]$ which then led to Corollary 4.16.

Here, we do not use a distribution for the prior estimate, but we explicitly specify the distribution of $C_{i,J}$ (expert choice). The distributional assumptions will be such that we can determine the exact distribution of $C_{i,J}|C_{i,j}$ according to Bayes' theorem (posterior distribution, Bayesian inference). It turns out that the best estimate for $E\left[C_{i,J}\middle| C_{i,I-i}\right]$ is a credibility mixture between the observation $C_{i,I-i}$ and the prior mean $E[C_{i,J}]$. Gogol (1993) proposed the following model.

Model Assumptions 4.20 (Log-normal/Log-normal model)

- Cumulative claims $C_{i,j}$ of different accident years i are independent.
- $C_{i,J}$ is Log-normally distributed with parameters $\mu^{(i)}$ and σ_i^2 for $i = 0, \ldots, I$.
- Conditionally, given $C_{i,J}$, $C_{i,j}$ has a Log-normal distribution with parameters $\nu_j = \nu_j(C_{i,J})$ and $\tau_j^2 = \tau_j^2(C_{i,J})$ for $i = 0, \ldots, I$ and $j = 0, \ldots, J$. □

Remark In the appendix, Subsection A.2.3, we provide the definition of the Log-normal distribution and its first two moments. $\mu^{(i)}$ and σ_i^2 denote the parameters of the Log-normal distribution of $C_{i,J}$. The prior mean of $C_{i,J}$ is given by

$$\mu_i = E[C_{i,J}] = \exp\left\{\mu^{(i)} + \frac{1}{2}\sigma_i^2\right\} \tag{4.16}$$

If $(C_{i,j})_{0\le j\le J}$ also satisfy Model Assumptions 4.14, we have that

$$E\left[C_{i,j} \middle| C_{i,J}\right] = \exp\left\{\nu_j + \frac{1}{2}\tau_j^2\right\} \stackrel{!}{=} \beta_j\, C_{i,J}$$

$$\mathrm{Var}\left(C_{i,j} \middle| C_{i,J}\right) = \exp\{2\,\nu_j + \tau_j^2\}\ (\exp\{\tau_j^2\} - 1) \stackrel{!}{=} \beta_j\,(1-\beta_j)\ \alpha^2(C_{i,J})$$

This implies that we have to choose

$$\tau_j^2 = \tau_j^2(C_{i,J}) = \log\left(1 + \frac{1-\beta_j}{\beta_j}\ \frac{\alpha^2(C_{i,J})}{C_{i,J}^2}\right) \tag{4.17}$$

$$\nu_j = \nu_j(C_{i,J}) = \log(\beta_j\, C_{i,J}) - \frac{1}{2}\ \log\left(1 + \frac{1-\beta_j}{\beta_j}\ \frac{\alpha^2(C_{i,J})}{C_{i,J}^2}\right) \tag{4.18}$$

The joint distribution $f_{C_{i,j},C_{i,J}}(\cdot,\cdot)$ of $(C_{i,j}, C_{i,J})$ is given by

$$\begin{aligned} f_{C_{i,j},C_{i,J}}(x,y) &= f_{C_{i,j}|C_{i,J}}(x|y)\ f_{C_{i,J}}(y) \\ &= \frac{1}{(2\pi)^{1/2}\tau_j(y)}\frac{1}{x}\exp\left\{-\frac{1}{2}\left(\frac{\log(x)-\nu_j(y)}{\tau_j(y)}\right)^2\right\} \\ &\quad \times \frac{1}{(2\pi)^{1/2}\sigma_i}\frac{1}{y}\exp\left\{-\frac{1}{2}\left(\frac{\log(y)-\mu^{(i)}}{\sigma_i}\right)^2\right\} \\ &= \frac{1}{2\pi\ \sigma_i\ \tau_j(y)}\frac{1}{xy}\exp\left\{-\frac{1}{2}\left(\frac{\log(x)-\nu_j(y)}{\tau_j(y)}\right)^2 - \frac{1}{2}\left(\frac{\log(y)-\mu^{(i)}}{\sigma_i}\right)^2\right\} \end{aligned} \tag{4.19}$$

LEMMA 4.21 *The Model Assumptions 4.20 combined with Model Assumptions 4.14 with $\alpha^2(c) = a^2c^2$ for some $a \in \mathbb{R}$ imply the following equalities:*

$$\tau_j^2(c) = \tau_j^2 = \log\left(1 + \frac{1-\beta_j}{\beta_j}\ a^2\right) \tag{4.20}$$

$$\nu_j(c) = \log(c) + \log(\beta_j) - \frac{1}{2}\tau_j^2 \tag{4.21}$$

Moreover, the conditional distribution of $C_{i,J}$, given $C_{i,j}$, is again a Log-normal distribution with updated parameters

$$\mu_{\text{post}(i,j)} = \left(1 - \frac{\tau_j^2}{\sigma_i^2 + \tau_j^2}\right) \left(\frac{1}{2}\tau_j^2 + \log\left(\frac{C_{i,j}}{\beta_j}\right)\right) + \frac{\tau_j^2}{\sigma_i^2 + \tau_j^2}\ \mu^{(i)}$$

$$\sigma^2_{\text{post}(i,j)} = \frac{\tau_j^2}{\sigma_i^2 + \tau_j^2}\ \sigma_i^2$$

Remarks 4.22

- The model above demonstrates a useful Bayesian and credibility result. In this example of 'conjugated' distributions we can calculate the posterior distribution of the ultimate claim $C_{i,J}$, given the information $C_{i,j}$, analytically (for an explicit discussion on Bayesian inference and credibility we refer to Sections 4.3 and 9.2 and Bühlmann and Gisler 2005).
- The conditional distribution of $C_{i,J}$ changes according to the observations $C_{i,I-i}$ made. In that sense, the posterior distribution $C_{i,J}|C_{i,I-i}$ is the 'best estimate' distribution, given observation $C_{i,I-i}$. Note that we are able to calculate the posterior distribution in an analytical form. This not only allows the posterior expected values to be calculated but also other key figures such as the posterior Value-at-Risk (see, e.g., McNeil *et al.* 2005), etc.
- We see that the parameter $\mu^{(i)}$ has to be updated by choosing a credibility weighted average of the prior parameter $\mu^{(i)}$ and the transformed observation $\frac{1}{2}\tau_j^2 + \log(C_{i,j}/\beta_j)$, where the credibility weights are given by

$$\alpha_{i,j} = \frac{\sigma_i^2}{\sigma_i^2 + \tau_j^2} \qquad \text{and} \qquad 1 - \alpha_{i,j} = \frac{\tau_i^2}{\sigma_i^2 + \tau_j^2} \tag{4.22}$$

This implies that the prior mean of the ultimate claim $C_{i,J}$ is updated from

$$E[C_{i,J}] = \exp\{\mu^{(i)} + \frac{1}{2}\sigma_i^2\}$$

to the posterior mean of the ultimate claim $C_{i,J}$ given by

$$\begin{aligned} E[C_{i,J}|C_{i,j}] &= \exp\left\{\mu_{\text{post}(i,j)} + \frac{1}{2}\sigma^2_{\text{post}(i,j)}\right\} \\ &= \exp\left\{(1-\alpha_{i,j}) \left(\mu^{(i)} + \frac{1}{2}\sigma_i^2\right) + \alpha_{i,j} \left(\log\left(\frac{C_{i,j}}{\beta_j}\right) + \frac{1}{2}\tau_j^2\right)\right\} \\ &= \exp\left\{(1-\alpha_{i,j}) \left(\mu^{(i)} + \frac{1}{2}\sigma_i^2\right) + \alpha_{i,j} \left(-\log(\beta_j) + \frac{1}{2}\tau_j^2\right)\right\} C_{i,j}^{\sigma_i^2/(\sigma_i^2+\tau_j^2)} \end{aligned} \tag{4.23}$$

see also (4.24).
- Observe that this model, in general, does not satisfy the CL assumptions (cf. last expression in (4.23)), as has already been mentioned in Remarks 4.15.

- Also note that in the current derivation we only consider one observation $C_{i,j}$. We could also consider the whole sequence of observations $C_{i,0}, \ldots, C_{i,j}$, then the posterior distribution of $C_{i,J}$ is Log-normally distributed with mean

$$\mu^*_{\text{post}(i,j)} = \frac{\sum_{k=0}^{j}[\log(C_{i,k}) - \log(\beta_k) + \frac{1}{2}\tau_k^2]/\tau_k^2 + \mu^{(i)}/\sigma_i^2}{\sum_{k=0}^{j}(1/\tau_k^2) + (1/\sigma_i^2)}$$

$$= \alpha^*_{i,j}\ \frac{1}{\sum_{k=0}^{j}(1/\tau_k^2)} \sum_{k=0}^{j} \frac{\log(C_{i,k}) - \log(\beta_k) + \frac{1}{2}\tau_k^2}{\tau_k^2} + \left(1 - \alpha^*_{i,j}\right) \mu^{(i)}$$

where

$$\alpha^*_{i,j} = \frac{\sum_{k=0}^{j}(1/\tau_k^2)}{\sum_{k=0}^{j}(1/\tau_k^2) + (1/\sigma_i^2)}$$

and variance parameter

$$\sigma^{2,*}_{\text{post}(i,j)} = \left[\sum_{k=0}^{j} \frac{1}{\tau_k^2} + \frac{1}{\sigma_i^2}\right]^{-1}$$

Observe that this is again a credibility weighted average between the prior estimate $\mu^{(i)}$ and the observations $C_{i,0}, \ldots, C_{i,j}$. The credibility weights are given by $\alpha^*_{i,j}$. Moreover, this model does not have the Markov property, which is in contrast to our CL assumptions.

Proof of Lemma 4.21 Equations (4.20)–(4.21) easily follow from (4.17)–(4.18). Hence, we only need to calculate the conditional distribution of $C_{i,J}$, given $C_{i,j}$. From (4.19) and (4.21) we see that the joint density of $(C_{i,j}, C_{i,J})$ is given by

$$f_{C_{i,j},C_{i,J}}(x, y) = \frac{1}{2\pi\ \sigma_i\ \tau_j}\ \frac{1}{x\ y}$$

$$\times \exp\left\{-\frac{1}{2}\left(\frac{\log(x) - \log(y) - \log(\beta_j) + \frac{1}{2}\tau_j^2}{\tau_j}\right)^2 - \frac{1}{2}\left(\frac{\log(y) - \mu^{(i)}}{\sigma_i}\right)^2\right\}$$

Now, we have that

$$\left(\frac{z-c}{\tau}\right)^2 + \left(\frac{z-\mu}{\sigma}\right)^2 = \frac{\left(z - [(\sigma^2 c + \tau^2 \mu)/(\sigma^2 + \tau^2)]\right)^2}{(\sigma^2\tau^2)/(\sigma^2 + \tau^2)} + \frac{(\mu - c)^2}{\sigma^2 + \tau^2}$$

This implies that the joint distribution is given by

$$f_{C_{i,j},C_{i,J}}(x, y) = \frac{1}{2\pi\sigma_i\tau_j xy}\ \exp\left\{-\frac{1}{2}\left(\frac{\left(\log(y) - [(\sigma_i^2 c(x) + \tau_j^2\mu^{(i)})/(\sigma_i^2 + \tau_j^2)]\right)^2}{\sigma_i^2\tau_j^2/(\sigma_i^2 + \tau_j^2)}\right.\right.$$

$$\left.\left. + \frac{\left(\mu^{(i)} - c(x)\right)^2}{\sigma_i^2 + \tau_j^2}\right)\right\}$$

where

$$c(x) = \log(x) - \log(\beta_j) + \frac{1}{2}\tau_j^2$$

From this we see that

$$f_{C_{i,J}|C_{i,j}}(y|x) = \frac{f_{C_{i,j},C_{i,J}}(x,y)}{f_{C_{i,j}}(x)} = \frac{f_{C_{i,j},C_{i,J}}(x,y)}{\int f_{C_{i,j},C_{i,J}}(x,y)dy}$$

is the density of a Log-normal distribution with parameters

$$\mu_{\text{post}(i,j)} = \frac{\sigma_i^2 \; c(C_{i,j}) + \tau_j^2 \; \mu^{(i)}}{\sigma_i^2 + \tau_j^2} \quad \text{and} \quad \sigma^2_{\text{post}(i,j)} = \frac{\sigma_i^2 \; \tau_j^2}{\sigma_i^2 + \tau_j^2}$$

Finally, we rewrite $\mu_{\text{post}(i,j)}$ as

$$\mu_{\text{post}(i,j)} = \frac{\sigma_i^2 \; (\log(C_{i,j}) - \log(\beta_j) + \frac{1}{2}\tau_j^2) + \tau_j^2 \; \mu^{(i)}}{\sigma_i^2 + \tau_j^2}$$

This completes the proof of Lemma 4.21. □

ESTIMATOR 4.23 (Log-normal/Log-normal model, Gogol (1993)) *Under the assumptions of Lemma 4.21 we have the following estimator for the ultimate claim* $E\left[C_{i,J}\middle| C_{i,I-i}\right]$

$$\begin{aligned}\widehat{C_{i,J}}^{\text{Go}} &= E\left[C_{i,J}\middle| C_{i,I-i}\right] \\ &= \exp\left\{\frac{\tau_{I-i}^2}{\sigma_i^2 + \tau_{I-i}^2} \; \mu^{(i)} + \frac{\sigma_i^2}{\sigma_i^2 + \tau_{I-i}^2} \; \log\left(\frac{C_{i,I-i}}{\beta_{I-i}}\right) + \frac{\sigma_i^2 \; \tau_{I-i}^2}{\sigma_i^2 + \tau_{I-i}^2}\right\}\end{aligned}$$

for $1 \le i \le I$.

Observe that we only condition on the last observation $C_{i,I-i}$; see also Remarks 4.22 on the Markov property.

Remark Alternatively, we could consider

$$\widehat{C_{i,J}}^{\text{Go},2} = C_{i,I-i} + (1 - \beta_{I-i}) \; \widehat{C_{i,J}}^{\text{Go}}$$

From a practical point of view $\widehat{C_{i,J}}^{\text{Go},2}$ is more useful if we have an outlier on the diagonal. However, both estimators are not easily obtained in practice, since there are too many parameters that are difficult to estimate.

Example 4.24 (Model Gogol (1993), Assumptions of Lemma 4.21)

We revisit the data set given in Example 2.7. We choose the same parameters as in Example 4.19 (see Table 4.4). That is, we set $\text{Vco}(C_{i,J})$ equal to the value obtained in (4.15). In formula (4.15) this variational coefficient was decomposed into process error and parameter uncertainty; here we only use the overall uncertainty. Moreover, we choose $a^2 = 1/(1+\alpha_i)$ with $\alpha_i = 600$. Using (4.20), (4.16) and

$$\sigma_i^2 = \log\left(\text{Vco}^2(C_{i,J}) + 1\right)$$

(cf. appendix, Table A.6) leads to Table 4.6. The credibility weights and estimates for the ultimate claims are summarized in Table 4.7 (see also Figure 4.3).

Table 4.6 Parameter choice for the Log-normal/Log-normal model

i	$\mu_i = E[C_{i,J}]$	$\text{Vco}(C_{i,J})$	$\mu^{(i)}$	σ_i	β_{I-i}	a^2	τ_{I-i}
0	11 653 101	7.8%	16.27	7.80%	100.0%	0.17%	0.0%
1	11 367 306	7.8%	16.24	7.80%	99.9%	0.17%	0.2%
2	10 962 965	7.8%	16.21	7.80%	99.8%	0.17%	0.2%
3	10 616 762	7.8%	16.17	7.80%	99.6%	0.17%	0.2%
4	11 044 881	7.8%	16.21	7.80%	99.1%	0.17%	0.4%
5	11 480 700	7.8%	16.25	7.80%	98.4%	0.17%	0.5%
6	11 413 572	7.8%	16.25	7.80%	97.0%	0.17%	0.7%
7	11 126 527	7.8%	16.22	7.80%	94.8%	0.17%	1.0%
8	10 986 548	7.8%	16.21	7.80%	88.0%	0.17%	1.5%
9	11 618 437	7.8%	16.27	7.80%	59.0%	0.17%	3.4%

Table 4.7 Claims reserves in model of Lemma 4.21

						Claims reserves		
i	$C_{i,I-i}$	$1-\alpha_{i,I-i}$	$\mu_{\text{post}(i,I-i)}$	$\sigma_{\text{post}(i,I-i)}$	$\widehat{C_{i,J}}^{\text{Go}}$	Go	CL	BF
0	11 148 124	0.0%	16.23	0.00%	11 148 124			
1	10 648 192	0.0%	16.18	0.15%	10 663 595	15 403	15 126	16 124
2	10 635 751	0.1%	16.18	0.20%	10 662 230	26 479	26 257	26 998
3	9 724 068	0.1%	16.09	0.24%	9 759 434	35 365	34 538	37 575
4	9 786 916	0.2%	16.11	0.38%	9 874 925	88 009	85 302	95 434
5	9 935 753	0.4%	16.13	0.51%	10 097 962	162 209	156 494	178 024
6	9 282 022	0.8%	16.08	0.71%	9 582 510	300 487	286 121	341 305
7	8 256 211	1.5%	15.98	0.94%	8 737 154	480 942	449 167	574 089
8	7 648 729	3.6%	15.99	1.48%	8 766 487	1 117 758	1 043 242	1 318 646
9	5 675 568	16.0%	16.11	3.12%	9 925 132	4 249 564	3 950 815	4 768 384
Total						6 476 218	6 047 061	7 356 580

□

Properties of the estimator $\widehat{C_{i,J}}^{\text{Go}}$ Using (4.22), (4.16) and $\widehat{C_{i,J}}^{\text{CL}} = C_{i,I-i}/\beta_{I-i}$ we obtain the following representation for Estimator 4.23:

$$\begin{aligned}\widehat{C_{i,J}}^{\text{Go}} &= \exp\left\{(1-\alpha_{i,I-i})\,\mu^{(i)} + \alpha_{i,I-i}\,\log\left(\frac{C_{i,I-i}}{\beta_{I-i}}\right) + \alpha_{i,I-i}\,\tau_{I-i}^2\right\} \\ &= \mu_i^{1-\alpha_{i,I-i}}\,\exp\left\{\log\left(\widehat{C_{i,J}}^{\text{CL}}\right) + \frac{1}{2}\tau_{I-i}^2\right\}^{\alpha_{i,I-i}} \end{aligned} \tag{4.24}$$

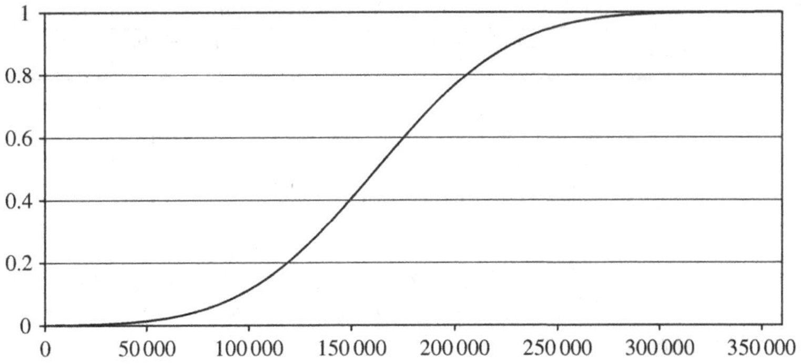

Figure 4.3 Log-normal/Log-normal case: posterior distribution of $C_{i,J} - C_{i,I-i}$, given $C_{i,I-i}$, for $i=5$

Hence, we obtain a weighted average between the prior estimate $\mu^{(i)}$ and the CL estimate $\widehat{C_{i,J}}^{\text{CL}}$ on the log-scale. This leads (together with the bias correction) to multiplicative credibility formula. In Example 4.24 and Table 4.7 we see that the weights $1-\alpha_{i,I-i}$ given to the prior mean $\mu^{(i)}$ are rather low.
Note that in this model we can calculate the whole posterior distribution, see Lemma 4.21. Of course, this also allows for an analytic expression for the MSEP:
For the conditional MSEP we have

$$
\begin{aligned}
\text{msep}_{C_{i,J}|C_{i,I-i}}\left(\widehat{C_{i,J}}^{\text{Go}}\right) &= \text{Var}(C_{i,J}|C_{i,I-i})\\
&= \exp\left\{2\,\mu_{\text{post}(i,I-i)} + \sigma^2_{\text{post}(i,I-i)}\right\}\left(\exp\left\{\sigma^2_{\text{post}(i,I-i)}\right\} - 1\right)\\
&= \left(E\left[C_{i,J}\middle| C_{i,I-i}\right]\right)^2\left(\exp\left\{\sigma^2_{\text{post}(i,I-i)}\right\} - 1\right)\\
&= \left(\widehat{C_{i,J}}^{\text{Go}}\right)^2\left(\exp\left\{\sigma^2_{\text{post}(i,I-i)}\right\} - 1\right)
\end{aligned}
$$

This holds under the assumption that the parameters β_j, $\mu^{(i)}$, σ_i and a^2 are known. Thus, it is not directly comparable to the conditional MSEP obtained from the CL model, since we have no canonical model for the estimation of these parameters and, hence, we cannot quantify the estimation error coming from the parameter estimates.

If we want to compare this MSEP to those obtained in Corollary 4.17 we need to calculate the unconditional version:

$$
\begin{aligned}
\text{msep}_{C_{i,J}}\left(\widehat{C_{i,J}}^{\text{Go}}\right) &= E\left[\left(C_{i,J} - \widehat{C_{i,J}}^{\text{Go}}\right)^2\right]\\
&= E\left[\text{Var}(C_{i,J}|C_{i,I-i})\right]\\
&= E\left[\left(\widehat{C_{i,J}}^{\text{Go}}\right)^2\right]\left(\exp\left\{\sigma^2_{\text{post}(i,I-i)}\right\} - 1\right)
\end{aligned}
$$

This requires the use of the distribution of $\widehat{C_{i,J}}^{\text{CL}} = C_{i,I-i}/\beta_{I-i}$ (cf. (4.24)). We obtain

$$
f_{C_{i,I-i}}(x) = \int_{\mathbb{R}_+} f_{C_{i,I-i},C_{i,J}}(x, y)\; dy
$$

$$= \underbrace{\int_{\mathbb{R}_+} \frac{1}{\sqrt{2\pi}\left(\sigma_i\, \tau_{I-i}/\sqrt{\sigma_i^2+\tau_{I-i}^2}\right)} \frac{1}{y} \exp\left\{-\frac{1}{2} \frac{\left(\log(y) - \left[\left(\sigma_i^2 c(x) + \tau_{I-i}^2 \mu^{(i)}\right)/\left(\sigma_i^2+\tau_{I-i}^2\right)\right]\right)^2}{\left(\sigma_i^2\, \tau_{I-i}^2/\sigma_i^2+\tau_{I-i}^2\right)}\right\} dy}_{=1}$$

$$\times \frac{1}{\sqrt{2\pi\left(\sigma_i^2+\tau_{I-i}^2\right)}} \frac{1}{x} \exp\left\{-\frac{1}{2} \frac{\left(\log(x/\beta_{I-i}) + \frac{1}{2}\tau_{I-i}^2 - \mu^{(i)}\right)^2}{\sigma_i^2+\tau_{I-i}^2}\right\}$$

This shows that the estimator $\widehat{C_{i,J}}^{\mathrm{CL}} = C_{i,I-i}/\beta_{I-i}$ is Log-normally distributed with parameters $\mu^{(i)} - \frac{1}{2}\tau_{I-i}^2$ and $\sigma_i^2 + \tau_{I-i}^2$. Moreover, the multiplicative reproductiveness of the Log-normal distribution implies that for $\gamma > 0$

$$\left(\widehat{C_{i,J}}^{\mathrm{CL}}\right)^{\gamma} \overset{(d)}{\sim} \mathcal{LN}\left(\gamma\, \mu^{(i)} - \gamma\, \tau_{I-i}^2/2,\ \gamma^2\left(\sigma_i^2+\tau_{I-i}^2\right)\right) \tag{4.25}$$

Using (4.24) and (4.16) we get

$$\begin{aligned}
&\mathrm{msep}_{C_{i,J}}\left(\widehat{C_{i,J}}^{\mathrm{Go}}\right)\\
&= E\left[\left(\widehat{C_{i,J}}^{\mathrm{Go}}\right)^2\right]\left(\exp\left\{\sigma^2_{\mathrm{post}(i,I-i)}\right\} - 1\right)\\
&= \mu_i^{2(1-\alpha_{i,I-i})} \exp\left\{\alpha_{i,I-i}\, \tau_{I-i}^2\right\}\\
&\quad \times \left(\exp\left\{\sigma^2_{\mathrm{post}(i,I-i)}\right\} - 1\right) E\left[\left(\widehat{C_{i,J}}^{\mathrm{CL}}\right)^{2\alpha_{i,I-i}}\right]\\
&= \exp\left\{2\mu^{(i)} + (1-\alpha_{i,I-i})\, \sigma_i^2 + \alpha_{i,I-i}\, \tau_{I-i}^2\right\}\\
&\quad \times \exp\left\{-\alpha_{i,I-i}\, \tau_{I-i}^2 + 2\, \alpha_{i,I-i}^2\left(\sigma_i^2+\tau_{I-i}^2\right)\right\}\left(\exp\left\{\sigma^2_{\mathrm{post}(i,I-i)}\right\} - 1\right)
\end{aligned}$$

Observe that

$$\alpha_{i,I-i}\left(\sigma_i^2+\tau_{I-i}^2\right) = \sigma_i^2$$

(cf. (4.22)). This immediately implies the following corollary:

COROLLARY 4.25 *Under the assumptions of Lemma 4.21 we have*

$$\mathrm{msep}_{C_{i,J}}\left(\widehat{C_{i,J}}^{\mathrm{Go}}\right) = \exp\left\{2\, \mu^{(i)} + (1+\alpha_{i,I-i})\, \sigma_i^2\right\}\left(\exp\left\{\sigma^2_{\mathrm{post}(i,I-i)}\right\} - 1\right)$$

for all $1 \le i \le I$.

Remarks 4.26

Note that in this example we can not only calculate the MSEP, but we are able to explicitly calculate the posterior distributions. The entire posterior distribution of $C_{i,J}$, given $C_{i,I-i}$, is again Log-normal with updated parameters (see Lemma 4.21). Moreover, formulas (4.24) and (4.25) provide the explicit distribution for the ultimate claim predictor $\widehat{C_{i,J}}^{\text{Go}}$. Hence, in this specific example we are also able to provide, for example, Value-at-Risk estimators, etc. (always under the assumption that the model parameters $\mu^{(i)}$, σ_i^2, a and β_j are known).

Example 4.24, revisited

The MSEP estimates in Example 4.24 are provided in Table 4.8 and compared to Table 4.5.

Table 4.8 MSEP under the assumptions of Lemma 4.21 and Model 4.14

i	$\text{msep}^{1/2}_{C_{i,J}\mid C_{i,I-i}}\left(\widehat{C_{i,J}}^{\text{Go}}\right)$	$\text{msep}^{1/2}_{C_{i,J}}\left(\widehat{C_{i,J}}^{\text{Go}}\right)$	$\text{msep}^{1/2}_{R_i}(\widehat{R}_i(c_i^*))$
0			
1	16 391	18 832	17 527
2	21 602	23 940	22 282
3	23 714	27 804	25 879
4	37 561	45 276	42 153
5	51 584	63 200	58 862
6	68 339	87 704	81 745
7	82 516	118 195	105 626
8	129 667	174 906	163 852
9	309 586	388 179	372 199
Total	359 869	457 739	435 814

Moreover, the posterior distribution of $C_{i,J} - C_{i,I-i}$, given $C_{i,I-i}$, for $i = 5$ is plotted in Figure 4.3. Hence we can easily calculate such risk measures as Value-at-Risk and Expected Shortfall (see, e.g., McNeil *et al.* 2005).

4.3 EXACT BAYESIAN MODELS

In this section we further investigate the findings from the previous section (the relation between prior and posterior distributions). We start with a general introduction on Bayesian theory and then give explicit models and examples in the claims of reserving context.

Bayesian methods for claims reserving are methods in which one combines prior information or expert knowledge with observations in the upper triangle $\mathcal{D}_I$. Available prior information and expert knowledge are incorporated through a prior distribution of an underlying quantity such as the ultimate claim (see Subsections 4.2.3 and 4.3.1) or a risk parameter (see Subsection 4.3.2) which needs to be modelled by the actuary. This distribution is then connected with the likelihood function via Bayes' theorem. If we use a smart choice for the distribution of observations and the prior distribution, such as the exponential dispersion family (EDF) and its associate conjugates (see Subsection 4.3.2), we are able to derive an analytic expression for the posterior distribution of the underlying quantity such as the ultimate claim. This means that we can, for example, compute the posterior expectation $E\left[C_{i,J}|\mathcal{D}_I\right]$ of the ultimate claim $C_{i,J}$, which is called the 'Bayesian estimator' for the ultimate claim $C_{i,J}$, given the observations $\mathcal{D}_I$. The Bayesian method is called exact since the Bayesian estimator $E\left[C_{i,J}|\mathcal{D}_I\right]$ is optimal in the sense that it minimizes the squared loss function (MSEP) in the class $L^2_{C_{i,J}}(\mathcal{D}_I)$ of all estimators for $C_{i,J}$ that are square integrable functions of the observations in $\mathcal{D}_I$, that is,

$$E\left[C_{i,J}|\mathcal{D}_I\right] = \underset{Y \in L^2_{C_{i,J}}(\mathcal{D}_I)}{\operatorname{argmin}}\, E\left[\left(C_{i,J} - Y\right)^2 \middle| \mathcal{D}_I\right]$$

For its conditional MSEP we have

$$\mathrm{msep}_{C_{i,J}|\mathcal{D}_I}\left(E\left[C_{i,J}|\mathcal{D}_I\right]\right)=\mathrm{Var}(C_{i,J}|\mathcal{D}_I)$$

Of course, if there are unknown parameters in the underlying probabilistic model, we cannot explicitly calculate $E\left[C_{i,J}|\mathcal{D}_I\right]$ in all cases. These parameters need to be estimated by $\mathcal{D}_I$-measurable estimators. Hence, we obtain a $\mathcal{D}_I$-measurable estimator $\widehat{E}\left[C_{i,J}|\mathcal{D}_I\right]$ for $E\left[C_{i,J}|\mathcal{D}_I\right]$ (and predictor for $C_{i,J}|\mathcal{D}_I$, resp.) which implies for the conditional MSEP

$$\mathrm{msep}_{C_{i,J}|\mathcal{D}_I}\left(\widehat{E}\left[C_{i,J}|\mathcal{D}_I\right]\right)=\mathrm{Var}(C_{i,J}|\mathcal{D}_I)+\left(\widehat{E}\left[C_{i,J}|\mathcal{D}_I\right]-E\left[C_{i,J}|\mathcal{D}_I\right]\right)^2$$

and now we are in a situation similar to the CL model, see (3.8). In a full Bayesian approach one should also model the unknown model parameters through Bayesian estimators minimizing a desired loss function (either explicitly or numerically).

We close this introduction with some remarks:

Remarks 4.27

- For pricing and tariffication of insurance contracts, Bayesian ideas and techniques are well investigated and widely used in practice. For the claims reserving problem Bayesian methods are less used although we believe that they are very useful for answering practical questions and for integrating expert opinion and external information (this has also been mentioned in de Alba 2002, for instance).
- In the literature exact Bayesian models have been studied, for example, in a series of papers by Verrall (1990, 2000, 2004), de Alba (2002, 2006), de Alba and Corzo (2006), England and Verrall (2007), Gogol (1993), Haastrup and Arjas (1996), Verrall and England (2006), Ntzoufras and Dellaportas (2002) and the corresponding implementation by Scollnik (2002). Many of these results refer to explicit choices of distributions, for example, the (Log-) Normal-Normal or Poisson–Gamma cases. Below, we give an approach which suits rather general distributions (see Subsection 4.3.2) and allows for an explicit calculation of the posterior distributions. In cases where a posterior distribution cannot be calculated analytically, one often applies Markov Chain Monte Carlo (MCMC) methods to obtain correlated samples from the posterior distribution of interest. These samples can then be used in estimation of quantities such as the maximum *a posteriori* estimator or minimum mean-square estimator (Bayesian estimator), Value-at-Risk, etc. We give a brief introduction to MCMC methods in Section 4.4.

4.3.1 Overdispersed Poisson Model with Gamma Prior Distribution

We will start with an explicit distributional example and will then give a more general framework in the next subsection. We introduce a latent variable Θ_i. Conditioning on Θ_i, we will make distributional assumptions on the cumulative claims $C_{i,j}$ and incremental claims $X_{i,j}$. Θ_i describes the risk characteristics of accident year i (e.g. whether it is a 'good' or a 'bad' year). $C_{i,J}$ is then a random variable with parameters that depend on Θ_i. In the spirit of the previous chapters Θ_i reflects the prediction uncertainties.

We start with the overdispersed Poisson model. This model differs from Model Assumptions 2.12 in that the variance is not equal to the mean. The model was introduced for claims reserving in a Bayesian context by Verrall (1990, 2000, 2004) and Renshaw and Verrall (1998). Furthermore, the overdispersed Poisson model is also used in a generalized linear model context (see McCullagh and Nelder 1989, England and Verrall 2002, 2007 and references therein, and Chapter 6). The overdispersed Poisson model can be generalized to the exponential dispersion family, which we study in Subsection 4.3.2.

We start with the overdispersed Poisson model with Gamma prior distribution (see also Verrall 2000 and 2004).

Model Assumptions 4.28 (overdispersed Poisson–Gamma model)

There exist random variables Θ_i and $Z_{i,j}$ as well as constants $\phi_i > 0$ and $\gamma_0, \ldots, \gamma_J > 0$ with $\sum_{j=0}^{J} \gamma_j = 1$ such that for all $i \in \{0, \ldots, I\}$ and $j \in \{0, \ldots, J\}$ we have

- conditionally, given Θ_i, the $Z_{i,j}$ are independent and Poisson distributed, and the incremental variables $X_{i,j} = \phi_i \, Z_{i,j}$ satisfy

$$E\left[X_{i,j} \middle| \Theta_i\right] = \Theta_i \, \gamma_j \qquad \text{and} \qquad \operatorname{Var}\left(X_{i,j} \middle| \Theta_i\right) = \phi_i \, \Theta_i \, \gamma_j \tag{4.26}$$

- The pairs $\left(\Theta_i, (X_{i,0}, \ldots, X_{i,J})\right)$ $(i = 0, \ldots, I)$ are independent and Θ_i is Gamma distributed with shape parameter a_i and scale parameter b_i. □

Remarks 4.29

- See appendix, Sections A.1.2 and A.2.4, for the definitions of Poisson and Gamma distributions.
- The pamameter ϕ_i denotes overdispersion, see (4.26). For $\phi_i = 1$ we obtain the Poisson distribution and in general we obtain a model where the variance scales linearly with the mean having slope ϕ_i.
- Observe, given Θ_i, that the expectation and variance of $Z_{i,j}$ satisfy

$$E\left[Z_{i,j} \middle| \Theta_i\right] = \operatorname{Var}\left(Z_{i,j} \middle| \Theta_i\right) = \frac{\Theta_i \, \gamma_j}{\phi_i} \tag{4.27}$$

  The prior expectation of the increments $X_{i,j}$ is given by

$$E\left[X_{i,j}\right] = E\left[E\left[X_{i,j} \middle| \Theta_i\right]\right] = \gamma_j \, E[\Theta_i] = \gamma_j \, \frac{a_i}{b_i} \tag{4.28}$$

- For the cumulative ultimate claim $C_{i,J}$ we obtain

$$C_{i,J} = \phi_i \sum_{j=0}^{J} Z_{i,j}$$

  This implies that conditionally, given Θ_i,

$$\frac{C_{i,J}}{\phi_i} \overset{(d)}{\sim} \text{Poisson}(\Theta_i / \phi_i), \qquad \text{and} \qquad E\left[C_{i,J} \middle| \Theta_i\right] = \Theta_i$$

  which means that Θ_i plays the role of the (unknown) expected ultimate claim amount for accident year i. The chosen Bayesian approach tells us how we should combine the prior expectation $E[C_{i,J}] = a_i / b_i$ and the observed information $\mathcal{D}_I$.

- This model is sometimes problematic in practical applications. It assumes that we have no negative increments $X_{i,j}$. If we count the number of reported claims this may hold true. However, if $X_{i,j}$ denotes, for example, incremental payments we may have negative values in the observations. For instance, in motor hull insurance in late development periods the insurance company often receives more money (via subrogation and repayments of deductibles) than it spends.
- We have assumed that the claims development pattern γ_j is known.
- Observe that in the overdispersed Poisson model as above, in general, $C_{i,j}$ is not a natural number. Henceforth, if we work with claims counts with dispersion $\phi_i \neq 1$, there is not really a natural interpretation for this model.

LEMMA 4.30 *Under Model Assumptions 4.28 the posterior distribution of Θ_i, given $(X_{i,0}, \ldots, X_{i,j})$, is a Gamma distribution with updated parameters*

$$a_{i,j}^{\text{post}} = a_i + \frac{C_{i,j}}{\phi_i}$$

$$b_{i,j}^{\text{post}} = b_i + \sum_{k=0}^{j} \frac{\gamma_k}{\phi_i} = b_i + \frac{\beta_j}{\phi_i}$$

where $\beta_j = \sum_{k=0}^{j} \gamma_k$.

Proof Using (4.27) we obtain for the conditional density of $(X_{i,0}, \ldots, X_{i,j})$, given Θ_i, that

$$f_{X_{i,0},\ldots,X_{i,j}|\Theta_i}(x_0, \ldots, x_j|\theta) = \prod_{k=0}^{j} \exp\left\{-\theta\, \frac{\gamma_k}{\phi_i}\right\} \frac{(\theta\, \gamma_k/\phi_i)^{x_k/\phi_i}}{x_k/\phi_i!}$$

Hence the joint distribution of Θ_i and $(X_{i,0}, \ldots, X_{i,j})$ is given by

$$\begin{aligned} f_{\Theta_i, X_{i,0},\ldots,X_{i,j}}(\theta, x_0, \ldots, x_j) &= f_{X_{i,0},\ldots,X_{i,j}|\Theta_i}(x_0, \ldots, x_j|\theta)\, f_{\Theta_i}(\theta) \\ &= \prod_{k=0}^{j} \exp\left\{-\theta\, \frac{\gamma_k}{\phi_i}\right\} \frac{(\theta\, \gamma_k/\phi_i)^{x_k/\phi_i}}{x_k/\phi_i!} \frac{b_i^{a_i}}{\Gamma(a_i)} \theta^{a_i-1} \exp(-b_i\theta) \end{aligned}$$

This shows that the posterior distribution of Θ_i, given $(X_{i,0}, \ldots, X_{i,j})$, is again a Gamma distribution with updated parameters

$$a_{i,j}^{\text{post}} = a_i + \frac{C_{i,j}}{\phi_i} \quad \text{and} \quad b_{i,j}^{\text{post}} = b_i + \sum_{k=0}^{j} \frac{\gamma_k}{\phi_i}$$

This completes the proof of the lemma. □

Remarks 4.31

- Since accident years are independent, it suffices to consider the observations $(X_{i,0}, \ldots, X_{i,j})$ of accident year i for the calculation of the posterior distribution of Θ_i. That is, at the current stage that accident years are not really linked, however they are coupled through the fact that they all have the same claims development pattern γ_j.

- We assume that *a priori* all accident years are equal (Θ_i are i.i.d.). After we have a set of observations $\mathcal{D}_I$, we obtain posterior risk characteristics which differ according to the observations.
- Model 4.28 belongs to the well-known class of exponential dispersion models with associated conjugates (see, e.g., Subsection 2.5.1 in Bühlmann and Gisler 2005, and Subsection 4.3.2).
- Using Lemma 4.30 we obtain for the posterior expectation

$$E[\Theta_i|\mathcal{D}_I] = \frac{a_{i,I-i}^{\text{post}}}{b_{i,I-i}^{\text{post}}} = \frac{a_i + C_{i,I-i}/\phi_i}{b_i + \beta_{I-i}/\phi_i}$$
$$= \frac{b_i}{b_i + \beta_{I-i}/\phi_i} \frac{a_i}{b_i} + \left(1 - \frac{b_i}{b_i + \beta_{I-i}/\phi_i}\right) \frac{C_{i,I-i}}{\beta_{I-i}} \tag{4.29}$$

which is a credibility weighted average between the prior expectation $E[\Theta_i] = a_i/b_i$ and the observation $C_{i,I-i}/\beta_{I-i}$ (see next section and Bühlmann and Gisler 2005 for more detailed discussions).
- In fact we can also specify the posterior distribution of $(C_{i,J} - C_{i,I-i})/\phi_i$, given $\mathcal{D}_I$. It holds for $k \in \{0, 1, \ldots\}$ that

$$P\left[(C_{i,J} - C_{i,I-i})/\phi_i = k \middle| \mathcal{D}_I\right]$$
$$= \int_{\mathbb{R}_+} \exp\left(-(1-\beta_{I-i})\frac{\theta}{\phi_i}\right) \frac{\left((1-\beta_{I-i})\,\frac{\theta}{\phi_i}\right)^k}{k!} \frac{(b_{i,I-i}^{\text{post}})^{a_{i,I-i}^{\text{post}}}}{\Gamma(a_{i,I-i}^{\text{post}})} \theta^{a_{i,I-i}^{\text{post}}-1} \exp\left(-b_{i,I-i}^{\text{post}}\theta\right) d\theta$$
$$= \frac{\left(b_{i,I-i}^{\text{post}}\right)^{a_{i,I-i}^{\text{post}}} \left((1-\beta_{I-i})/\phi_i\right)^k}{\Gamma\left(a_{i,I-i}^{\text{post}}\right)\, k!} \underbrace{\int_{\mathbb{R}_+} \theta^{k+a_{i,I-i}^{\text{post}}-1} \exp\left(-\left(b_{i,I-i}^{\text{post}} + (1-\beta_{I-i})/\phi_i\right)\theta\right) d\theta}_{\propto \text{ density of } \Gamma\left(k+a_{i,I-i}^{\text{post}},\, b_{i,I-i}^{\text{post}} + (1-\beta_{I-i})/\phi_i\right)}$$
$$= \frac{\left(b_{i,I-i}^{\text{post}}\right)^{a_{i,I-i}^{\text{post}}} \left((1-\beta_{I-i})/\phi_i\right)^k}{\Gamma\left(a_{i,I-i}^{\text{post}}\right)\, k!} \frac{\Gamma\left(k+a_{i,I-i}^{\text{post}}\right)}{\left(b_{i,I-i}^{\text{post}} + (1-\beta_{I-i})/\phi_i\right)^{k+a_{i,I-i}^{\text{post}}}}$$
$$= \frac{\Gamma\left(k+a_{i,I-i}^{\text{post}}\right)}{k!\,\Gamma\left(a_{i,I-i}^{\text{post}}\right)} \left(\frac{b_{i,I-i}^{\text{post}}}{b_{i,I-i}^{\text{post}} + (1-\beta_{I-i})/\phi_i}\right)^{a_{i,I-i}^{\text{post}}} \left(\frac{(1-\beta_{I-i})/\phi_i}{b_{i,I-i}^{\text{post}} + (1-\beta_{I-i})/\phi_i}\right)^k$$
$$= \binom{k + a_{i,I-i}^{\text{post}} - 1}{k} \left(\frac{b_{i,I-i}^{\text{post}}}{b_{i,I-i}^{\text{post}} + (1-\beta_{I-i})/\phi_i}\right)^{a_{i,I-i}^{\text{post}}} \left(\frac{(1-\beta_{I-i})/\phi_i}{b_{i,I-i}^{\text{post}} + (1-\beta_{I-i})/\phi_i}\right)^k \tag{4.30}$$

which is a Negative-Binomial distribution with parameters $r = a_{i,I-i}^{\text{post}}$ and $p = b_{i,I-i}^{\text{post}} / \left(b_{i,I-i}^{\text{post}} + (1-\beta_{I-i})/\phi_i\right)$ (see appendix, Section A.1.3).

The important consequence about this derivation is that we can explicitly calculate the conditional distribution of the outstanding liabilities, given $C_{i,I-i}$. This is similar as in the Log-normal/Log-normal model of Gogol (see Remarks 4.26). As a consequence we are not only able to provide estimates for the MSEP but we could, for instance, also calculate Value-at-Risk estimates and other quantities that are of interest from a risk management point of view (always under the assumption that the model parameters γ_j, ϕ_i, a_i and b_i are known).

Hence we recall that in this model we can calculate analytically the posterior distribution of Θ_i, given the observations $\mathcal{D}_I$. This allows for the estimation of the posterior risk characteristic $\Theta_i|\mathcal{D}_I$, for example, using the Bayesian estimator (4.29) (mimimum mean-square estimator) or using the maximum *a posteriori* estimator (MLE of posterior distribution). In addition this model allows for an explicit analytical representation of the ulimate claims distribution of $C_{i,J}$, given $\mathcal{D}_I$, which allows for instance for the quantification of risk measures such as Value-at-Risk.

Using the conditional independence of $X_{i,j}$, given Θ_i, and (4.26), we obtain

$$\begin{aligned} E\left[C_{i,J}\middle|\mathcal{D}_I\right] &= E\left[E\left[C_{i,J}\middle|\Theta_i, \mathcal{D}_I\right]\middle|\mathcal{D}_I\right] \\ &= C_{i,I-i} + E\left[E\left[\sum_{j=I-i+1}^{J} X_{i,j}\middle|\Theta_i\right]\middle|\mathcal{D}_I\right] \\ &= C_{i,I-i} + (1-\beta_{I-i})\, E\left[\Theta_i\middle|\mathcal{D}_I\right] \end{aligned} \tag{4.31}$$

Together with (4.29), this motivates the following estimator:

ESTIMATOR 4.32 (Poisson–Gamma model) *Under Model Assumptions 4.28 we have the following estimator for the ultimate claim* $E\left[C_{i,J}\middle|\mathcal{D}_I\right]$

$$\widehat{C_{i,J}}^{\text{PoiGa}} = C_{i,I-i} + (1-\beta_{I-i}) \left[\frac{b_i}{b_i + (\beta_{I-i}/\phi_i)}\, \frac{a_i}{b_i} + \left(1 - \frac{b_i}{b_i + (\beta_{I-i}/\phi_i)}\right) \frac{C_{i,I-i}}{\beta_{I-i}}\right] \tag{4.32}$$

for $1 \le i \le I$.

Example 4.33 (Poisson–Gamma model)

We revisit the data set given in Example 2.7. For the prior parameters we make the same numerical choices as in Example 4.19 (see Table 4.4). Since Θ_i is Gamma distributed with shape parameter a_i and scale parameter b_i we have

$$\begin{aligned} E[\Theta_i] &= \frac{a_i}{b_i} \\ \text{Vco}(\Theta_i) &= a_i^{-1/2} \end{aligned}$$

and, using (4.26), we obtain

$$\begin{aligned} \text{Var}\left(C_{i,J}\right) &= E\left[\text{Var}\left(C_{i,J}\middle|\Theta_i\right)\right] + \text{Var}\left(E\left[C_{i,J}\middle|\Theta_i\right]\right) \\ &= \phi_i\, E[\Theta_i] + \text{Var}\left(\Theta_i\right) \\ &= \frac{a_i}{b_i}\, \left(\phi_i + b_i^{-1}\right) \end{aligned}$$

Using the prior values as in Example 4.19 and the variational coefficients from Table 4.4 we obtain Table 4.9.

Table 4.9 Parameter choice for the Poisson–Gamma model

i	$E[\Theta_i]$	$\text{Vco}(\Theta_i)$ (%)	$\text{Vco}(C_{i,J})$ (%)	a_i	b_i (%)	ϕ_i
0	11 653 101	5.00	7.8	400	0.00343	41 951
1	11 367 306	5.00	7.8	400	0.00352	40 922
2	10 962 965	5.00	7.8	400	0.00365	39 467
3	10 616 762	5.00	7.8	400	0.00377	38 220
4	11 044 881	5.00	7.8	400	0.00362	39 762
5	11 480 700	5.00	7.8	400	0.00348	41 331
6	11 413 572	5.00	7.8	400	0.00350	41 089
7	11 126 527	5.00	7.8	400	0.00360	40 055
8	10 986 548	5.00	7.8	400	0.00364	39 552
9	11 618 437	5.00	7.8	400	0.00344	41 826

We define the credibility weights $\alpha_{i,I-i}$ by (see (4.29))

$$\alpha_{i,I-i} = \frac{\beta_{I-i}/\phi_i}{b_i + \beta_{I-i}/\phi_i}$$

This is the credibility weight given to the observation $C_{i,I-i}/\beta_{I-i}$ (cf. (4.29)). The credibility weights and estimates for the ultimates are provided in Table 4.10 (see also Figure 4.4).

Observe that the credibility weight can be reformulated as follows

$$\alpha_{i,I-i} = \frac{\beta_{I-i}}{\beta_{I-i} + \phi_i \, b_i} = \frac{\beta_{I-i}}{\beta_{I-i} + \frac{E\left[\text{Var}\left(X_{i,I-i} \middle| \Theta_i\right)\right]}{\gamma_{I-i} \, \text{Var}(\Theta_i)}} \tag{4.33}$$

The term $E\left[\text{Var}\left(X_{i,I-i} \middle| \Theta_i\right)\right]/\gamma_{I-i}\,\text{Var}(\Theta_i)$ is the so-called credibility coefficient (see also Remark 4.40). □

Table 4.10 Claims reserves in the Poisson–Gamma model

						Claims reserves		
i	$C_{i,I-i}$	$\beta_{i,I-i}$(%)	$\alpha_{i,I-i}$(%)	$\frac{a^{\text{post}}_{i,I-i}}{b^{\text{post}}_{i,I-i}}$	$\widehat{C_{i,J}}^{\text{PoiGa}}$	PoiGa	CL	BF
0	11 148 124	100.0	41.0	11 446 143	11 148 124	0	0	0
1	10 648 192	99.9	40.9	11 079 028	10 663 907	15 715	15 126	16 124
2	10 635 751	99.8	40.9	10 839 802	10 662 446	26 695	26 257	26 998
3	9 724 068	99.6	40.9	10 265 794	9 760 401	36 333	34 538	37 575
4	9 786 916	99.1	40.8	10 566 741	9 878 219	91 303	85 302	95 434
5	9 935 753	98.4	40.6	10 916 902	10 105 034	169 281	156 494	178 024
6	9 282 022	97.0	40.3	10 670 762	9 601 115	319 093	286 121	341 305
7	8 256 211	94.8	39.7	10 165 120	8 780 696	524 484	449 167	574 089
8	7 648 729	88.0	37.9	10 116 206	8 862 913	1 214 184	1 043 242	1 318 646
9	5 675 568	59.0	29.0	11 039 755	10 206 452	4 530 884	3 950 815	4 768 384
Total						6 927 973	6 047 061	7 356 580

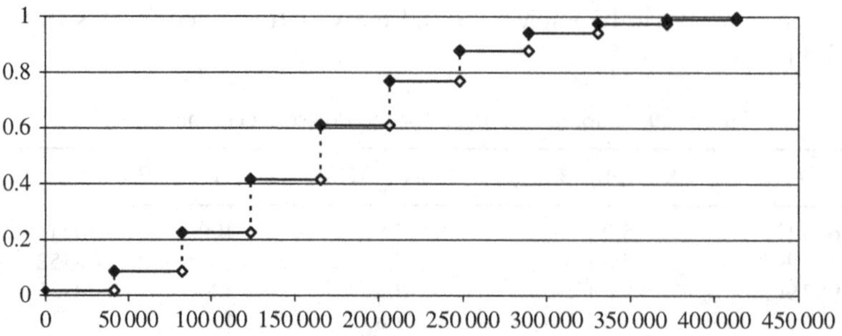

Figure 4.4 Poisson–Gamma case: posterior distribution of $C_{i,J} - C_{i,I-i}$, given $C_{i,I-i}$, for $i=5$

The conditional MSEP is given by

$$\begin{aligned}\mathrm{msep}_{C_{i,J}|\mathcal{D}_I}\left(\widehat{C_{i,J}}^{\mathrm{PoiGa}}\right) &= E\left[\left(C_{i,J} - \widehat{C_{i,J}}^{\mathrm{PoiGa}}\right)^2 \middle| \mathcal{D}_I\right] \\ &= E\left[\left(\sum_{j=I-i+1}^{J} X_{i,j} - (1-\beta_{I-i})\ E[\Theta_i|\,\mathcal{D}_I]\right)^2 \middle| \mathcal{D}_I\right] \\ &= E\left[\left(\sum_{j=I-i+1}^{J} (X_{i,j} - \gamma_j\ E[\Theta_i|\,\mathcal{D}_I])\right)^2 \middle| \mathcal{D}_I\right]\end{aligned}$$

(cf. (4.31)–(4.32)). Since, for the Bayesian estimator it holds that for $j > I-i$,

$$E[X_{i,j}|\,\mathcal{D}_I] = E[E[X_{i,j}|\,\Theta_i, \mathcal{D}_I]|\,\mathcal{D}_I] = E[E[X_{i,j}|\,\Theta_i]|\,\mathcal{D}_I] = \gamma_j\ E[\Theta_i|\,\mathcal{D}_I] \tag{4.34}$$

we have, of course,

$$\mathrm{msep}_{C_{i,J}|\mathcal{D}_I}\left(\widehat{C_{i,J}}^{\mathrm{PoiGa}}\right) = \mathrm{Var}\left(\sum_{j=I-i+1}^{J} X_{i,j} \middle| \mathcal{D}_I\right)$$

This last expression can be calculated. We do the complete calculation, but we could also argue with the help of the Negative-Binomial distribution. Using the conditional independence of $X_{i,j}$, given Θ_i, and (4.26) we obtain

$$\begin{aligned}&\mathrm{Var}\left(\sum_{j=I-i+1}^{J} X_{i,j} \middle| \mathcal{D}_I\right) \\ &\quad = E\left[\mathrm{Var}\left(\sum_{j=I-i+1}^{J} X_{i,j} \middle| \Theta_i\right) \middle| \mathcal{D}_I\right] + \mathrm{Var}\left(E\left[\sum_{j=I-i+1}^{J} X_{i,j} \middle| \Theta_i\right] \middle| \mathcal{D}_I\right) \\ &\quad = E\left[\sum_{j=I-i+1}^{J} \phi_i\ \Theta_i\ \gamma_j \middle| \mathcal{D}_I\right] + \mathrm{Var}\left(\sum_{j=I-i+1}^{J} \Theta_i\ \gamma_j \middle| \mathcal{D}_I\right) \\ &\quad = \phi_i\ (1-\beta_{I-i})\ E[\Theta_i|\,\mathcal{D}_I] + (1-\beta_{I-i})^2\ \mathrm{Var}(\Theta_i|\,\mathcal{D}_I)\end{aligned} \tag{4.35}$$

With Lemma 4.30 this leads to the following corollary:

COROLLARY 4.34 *Under Model Assumptions 4.28 the conditional MSEP of a single accident year $i \in \{1, \ldots, I\}$ is given by*

$$\mathrm{msep}_{C_{i,J}|\mathcal{D}_I}\left(\widehat{C_{i,J}}^{\mathrm{PoiGa}}\right) = \phi_i\ (1-\beta_{I-i})\ \frac{a_{i,I-i}^{\mathrm{post}}}{b_{i,I-i}^{\mathrm{post}}} + (1-\beta_{I-i})^2\ \frac{a_{i,I-i}^{\mathrm{post}}}{\left(b_{i,I-i}^{\mathrm{post}}\right)^2}$$

Remark Observe that we have assumed that the parameters a_i, b_i, ϕ_i and γ_j are known. If these need to be estimated we obtain an additional term in the MSEP calculation which corresponds to the parameter estimation error.

The unconditional MSEP can then easily be calculated. We have

$$\begin{aligned}\mathrm{msep}_{C_{i,J}}\left(\widehat{C_{i,J}}^{\mathrm{PoiGa}}\right) &= E\left[\mathrm{msep}_{C_{i,J}|\mathcal{D}_I}\left(\widehat{C_{i,J}}^{\mathrm{PoiGa}}\right)\right] \\ &= \phi_i\ (1-\beta_{I-i})\ \frac{E\left[a_{i,I-i}^{\mathrm{post}}\right]}{b_{i,I-i}^{\mathrm{post}}} + (1-\beta_{I-i})^2\ \frac{E\left[a_{i,I-i}^{\mathrm{post}}\right]}{\left(b_{i,I-i}^{\mathrm{post}}\right)^2}\end{aligned} \tag{4.36}$$

and using $E[C_{i,I-i}] = \beta_{I-i}\ (a_i/b_i)$ (cf. (4.28)) we obtain

$$\mathrm{msep}_{C_{i,J}}\left(\widehat{C_{i,J}}^{\mathrm{PoiGa}}\right) = \phi_i\ (1-\beta_{I-i})\ \frac{a_i}{b_i}\ \frac{1+\phi_i\ b_i}{\phi_i\ b_i + \beta_{I-i}}$$

Example 4.33, revisited

We obtain Table 4.11 for the conditional and unconditional prediction errors (based on the usual data set).

Table 4.11 MSEP in the Poisson–Gamma model, the Log-normal/Log-normal model and in Model 4.14

	$\mathrm{msep}^{1/2}_{C_{i,J}\vert C_{i,I-i}}(\cdot)$		$\mathrm{msep}^{1/2}_{C_{i,J}}(\cdot)$		
i	$\widehat{C_{i,J}}^{\mathrm{PoiGa}}$	$\widehat{C_{i,J}}^{\mathrm{Go}}$	$\widehat{C_{i,J}}^{\mathrm{PoiGa}}$	$\widehat{C_{i,J}}^{\mathrm{Go}}$	$\widehat{R}_i(c_i^*)$
0					
1	25 367	16 391	25 695	18 832	17 527
2	32 475	21 602	32 659	23 940	22 282
3	37 292	23 714	37 924	27 804	25 879
4	60 359	37 561	61 710	45 276	42 153
5	83 912	51 584	86052	63 200	58 862
6	115 212	68 339	119 155	87 704	81 745
7	146 500	82 516	153 272	113 195	105 626
8	224 738	129 667	234 207	174 906	163 852
9	477 318	309 586	489 668	388 179	372 199
Total	571 707	359 869	588 809	457 739	435 814

We have already seen in Table 4.10 that the Poisson–Gamma reserves are closer to the BF reserves (this stands in contrast with the other methods presented in this chapter). Table 4.11

shows that the prediction error is substantially larger in the Poisson–Gamma model than in the other models (comparable to the estimation error in $\widehat{R}_i(0)$ in Table 4.5). This suggests that in the present case the Poisson–Gamma method is not appropriate (at least the choice of parameters, see also Subsection 4.4).

Moreover, we can calculate the posterior distribution of $C_{i,J} - C_{i,I-i}$, given $\mathcal{D}_I$ (see (4.30)). For accident year $i=5$ we obtain the Negative-Binomial distribution plotted in Figure 4.4. Hence the whole posterior distribution is given which allows for further analysis of the conditionally expected ultimate claim and the corresponding risk measures. This distribution needs to be compared to its analogon in the Log-normal/Log-normal model plotted in Figure 4.3. □

4.3.2 Exponential Dispersion Family with its Associated Conjugates

In the above subsection we have seen that in the Poisson–Gamma model, the posterior distribution of Θ_i is again a Gamma distribution with updated parameters. This indicates that with a smart choice of distributions we are able to calculate the posterior distribution analytically. We generalize the Poisson–Gamma model to the exponential dispersion family (EDF), and look for its associated conjugates. These are standard models in Bayesian inference (for literature we refer to Bernardo and Smith 1994). Similar ideas have been applied for tariffication and pricing (see Bühlmann and Gisler 2005, Chapter 2), whereas we transfer these ideas to the claims reserving context (see also Wüthrich 2007).

Model Assumptions 4.35 (exponential dispersion model)

- There exists a claims development pattern $(\beta_j)_{0\le j\le J}$ with $\beta_J=1$, $\gamma_0=\beta_0>0$ and $\gamma_j=\beta_j-\beta_{j-1}>0$ for $j\in\{1,\ldots,J\}$.
- Conditionally, given Θ_i, the $X_{i,j}$ $(0\le j\le J)$ are independent with

$$\frac{X_{i,j}}{\gamma_j\,\mu_i} \overset{(d)}{\sim} dF_{i,j}^{(\Theta_i)}(x) = a\left(x, \frac{\sigma^2}{w_{i,j}}\right)\ \exp\left\{\frac{x\,\Theta_i - b(\Theta_i)}{\sigma^2/w_{i,j}}\right\} d\nu(x) \tag{4.37}$$

  where ν is a suitable σ-finite measure on $\mathbb{R}$, $b(\cdot)$ is some real-valued twice-differentiable function of Θ_i, $\mu_i>0$, σ^2 and $w_{i,j}>0$ are some real-valued constants, and $F_{i,j}^{(\Theta_i)}$ is a probability distribution on $\mathbb{R}$.
- The random vectors $\left(\Theta_i, (X_{i,0},\ldots,X_{i,J})\right)$ $(i=0,\ldots,I)$ are independent and $\Theta_0,\ldots,\Theta_I$ are real-valued random variables with densities (w.r.t. the Lebesgue measure)

$$u_{\mu,\tau^2}(\theta) = d(\mu,\tau^2)\ \exp\left\{\frac{\mu\theta - b(\theta)}{\tau^2}\right\} \tag{4.38}$$

  with $\mu\equiv 1$ and $\tau^2>0$. □

Remarks 4.36

- In the following the measure ν is given by the Lebesgue measure or by the counting measure.
- A distribution of the type (4.37) is said to be belong to the exponential dispersion family (EDF). The class of EDF covers a large class of families of distributions, for example, the

families of the Poisson, Bernoulli, Gamma, Normal and Inverse-Gaussian distributions (cf. Bühlmann and Gisler 2005, Section 2.5).

- The second assumption implies that the scaled sizes $Y_{i,j} = X_{i,j}/(\gamma_j\ \mu_i)$ have, given Θ_i, a distribution $F_{i,j}^{(\Theta_i)}$ which belongs to the EDF. *A priori* they are all the same, which is described by the fact that Θ_i are i.i.d. that is μ and τ^2 do not depend on i.
- For the time being we assume that all parameters of the underlying distributions are known, and $w_{i,j}$ is a known volume measure which will be further specified below.
- For the moment we could also concentrate on a single accident year i, that is, we only need the Model Assumptions 4.35 for a fixed accident year i. That is, at this point the accident years are not linked, they are only linked through the fact that they have the same claims development pattern γ_j.
- A pair of distributions given by (4.37) and (4.38) is said to be an EDF with associated conjugates. Prominent examples are (see Bühlmann-Gisler 2005, Section 2.5): Poisson–Gamma case (see also Verrall 2000 and 2004, and Subsection 4.3.1), Binomial–Beta case, Gamma–Gamma case or Normal–Normal case.
- The ideas in this chapter also carry forward to other examples such as the Generalized Inverse-Gaussian distribution (for Θ_i), see, for example, Lambrigger *et al.* (2007).
- The EDF also plays an important role in Generalized Linear Models, see Chapter 6.1.

We have the following lemma:

LEMMA 4.37 (associated conjugate) *Under Model Assumptions 4.35 the conditional distribution of* Θ_i*, given* $X_{i,0}, \ldots, X_{i,j}$*, has density* $u_{\mu^{(i)}_{\text{post},j}, \tau^2_{\text{post},j}}(\cdot)$ *with posterior parameters*

$$\tau^2_{\text{post},j} = \sigma^2 \left[\frac{\sigma^2}{\tau^2} + \sum_{k=0}^{j} w_{i,k} \right]^{-1}$$

$$\mu^{(i)}_{\text{post},j} = \frac{\tau^2_{\text{post},j}}{\sigma^2} \left[\frac{\sigma^2}{\tau^2}\ 1 + \sum_{k=0}^{j} w_{i,k}\ \bar{Y}_i^{(j)} \right]$$

where

$$\bar{Y}_i^{(j)} = \sum_{k=0}^{j} \frac{w_{i,k}}{\sum_{l=0}^{j} w_{i,l}}\ \frac{X_{i,k}}{\gamma_k\ \mu_i}$$

Proof Define $Y_{i,j} = X_{i,j}/(\gamma_j\ \mu_i)$. The joint distribution of $(\Theta_i, Y_{i,0}, \ldots, Y_{i,j})$ is given by

$$\begin{aligned} f_{\Theta_i, Y_{i,0}, \ldots, Y_{i,j}}(\theta, y_0, \ldots, y_j) &= f_{Y_{i,0}, \ldots, Y_{i,j}|\Theta_i}(y_0, \ldots, y_j|\theta)\ u_{1,\tau^2}(\theta) \\ &= d(1, \tau^2)\ \exp\left\{ \frac{\theta - b(\theta)}{\tau^2} \right\} \prod_{k=0}^{j} a\left(y_k, \frac{\sigma^2}{w_{i,k}} \right)\ \exp\left\{ \frac{y_k\ \theta - b(\theta)}{\sigma^2/w_{i,k}} \right\} \end{aligned}$$

Hence, the conditional distribution of Θ_i, given $X_{i,0}, \ldots, X_{i,j}$, is proportional to

$$\exp\left\{ \theta \left[\frac{1}{\tau^2} + \sum_{k=0}^{j} \frac{w_{i,k}}{\sigma^2}\ \frac{X_{i,k}}{\gamma_k\ \mu_i} \right] - b(\theta) \left[\frac{1}{\tau^2} + \sum_{k=0}^{j} \frac{w_{i,k}}{\sigma^2} \right] \right\}$$

This completes the proof of the lemma. □

Remarks 4.38

- Lemma 4.37 states that the distribution defined by density (4.38) is a conjugate family of distributions to the distribution given by (4.37). This means that the posterior distribution of Θ_i, given $X_{i,0}, \ldots, X_{i,j}$, is again of the type (4.38) with updated parameters $\tau^2_{\text{post},j}$ and $\mu^{(i)}_{\text{post},j}$. Note that $\tau^2_{\text{post},j}$ also depends on i, we have skipped that index to not overload the notation.
- From Lemma 4.37 we can calculate the distribution of $(Y_{i,I-i+1}, \ldots, Y_{i,J})$, given $\mathcal{D}_I$. First we remark that different accident years are independent, hence we can restrict ourselves to the observations $Y_{i,0}, \ldots, Y_{i,I-i}$, then the posterior distribution is given by

$$\int \prod_{j=I-i+1}^{J} F^{(\theta)}_{i,j}(y_j)\; u_{\mu^{(i)}_{\text{post},I-i}, \tau^2_{\text{post},I-i}}(\theta)\; d\theta \tag{4.39}$$

In the Poisson–Gamma case this is a Negative-Binomial distribution. Observe that for the EDF with its associated conjugates we can determine the explicit distributions, not only estimates for the first two moments (see also Remarks 4.26 and 4.31). However, often the integral in (4.39) cannot be calculated explicitly, which means that these distributions need to be evaluated numerically. This can be done, for instance, using a simple Monte Carlo algorithm (as it is proposed, for example, in Shevchenko and Wüthrich 2006, Section 6) or one can apply more sophisticated methods like Markov Chain Monte Carlo methods as described in Section 4.4. From (4.39) we can then calculate risk measures like Value-at-Risk (see also McNeil *et al.* 2005).

THEOREM 4.39 *Under Model Assumptions 4.35 we have for* $i, j \geq 0$

(1) *The conditional moments of the standardized observations* $X_{i,j}/(\gamma_j\, \mu_i)$ *are given by*

$$\mu(\Theta_i) \stackrel{def.}{=} E\left[\left.\frac{X_{i,j}}{\gamma_j\, \mu_i}\right| \Theta_i\right] = b'(\Theta_i) \tag{4.40}$$

$$\operatorname{Var}\left(\left.\frac{X_{i,j}}{\gamma_j\, \mu_i}\right| \Theta_i\right) = \frac{\sigma^2\, b''(\Theta_i)}{w_{i,j}} \tag{4.41}$$

(2) *If* $\exp\left\{\left(\mu_i\, \theta - b(\theta)\right)/\tau^2\right\}$ *disappears on the boundary of* Θ_i *for all* μ_i, τ^2, *then*

$$E\left[X_{i,j}\right] = \gamma_j\, \mu_i E\left[\mu(\Theta_i)\right] \;=\; \gamma_j\, \mu_i$$

$$E\left[\mu(\Theta_i) \middle| X_{i,0}, \ldots, X_{i,j}\right] = \alpha_{i,j}\; \bar{Y}_i^{(j)} + (1-\alpha_{i,j})\; 1$$

where

$$\alpha_{i,j} = \frac{\sum_{k=0}^{j} w_{i,k}}{\sum_{k=0}^{j} w_{i,k} + \sigma^2/\tau^2}$$

Proof See Lemma 6.6 below, Theorem 2.20 in Bühlmann and Gisler (2005) or Bernardo and Smith (1994). □

Remarks 4.40

- In Model Assumptions 4.35 and in Theorem 4.39 we study the standardized version for the observations $X_{i,j}$. If μ_i is equal for all i, the standardization is not necessary. If they are not equal (different prior means μ_i), the standardized version allows comparisons between the accident years.
- Theorem 4.39 says that the posterior mean of $\mu(\Theta_i)$, given the observations $X_{i,0}, \ldots, X_{i,j}$, is a credibility weighted average between the prior mean $E[\mu(\Theta_i)] = 1$ and the weighted average $\bar{Y}_i^{(j)}$ of the standardized observations. The larger the individual variation σ^2 the smaller the credibility weight $\alpha_{i,j}$ given to the observations; the larger the collective variability τ^2 the larger the credibility weight $\alpha_{i,j}$ given to the observations. For a detailed discussion on the credibility coefficient

$$\kappa = \frac{\sigma^2}{\tau^2}$$

we refer to Bühlmann and Gisler (2005).

ESTIMATOR 4.41 *Under Model Assumptions 4.35 we have the following estimators for the increments $E\left[X_{i,I-i+k} \middle| \mathcal{D}_I\right]$ and the ultimate claims $E\left[C_{i,J} \middle| \mathcal{D}_I\right]$*

$$\widehat{X_{i,I-i+k}}^{\text{EDF}} = \gamma_{I-i+k}\ \mu_i\ \widetilde{\mu(\Theta_i)}$$
$$\widehat{C_{i,J}}^{\text{EDF}} = C_{i,I-i} + (1-\beta_{I-i})\ \mu_i\ \widetilde{\mu(\Theta_i)}$$

for $1 \le i \le I$ and $k \in \{1, \ldots, i\}$, where

$$\widetilde{\mu(\Theta_i)} = E\left[\mu(\Theta_i) \middle| \mathcal{D}_I\right] = \alpha_{i,I-i}\ \bar{Y}_i^{(I-i)} + (1-\alpha_{i,I-i})\ 1$$

We have the following theorem:

THEOREM 4.42 (Bayesian estimator) *Under Model Assumptions 4.35 the estimators $\widetilde{\mu(\Theta_i)}$, $\widehat{X_{i,j+k}}^{\text{EDF}}$ and $\widehat{C_{i,J}}^{\text{EDF}}$ are $\mathcal{D}_I$-measurable and minimize the conditional MSEPs $\text{msep}_{\mu(\Theta_i)|\mathcal{D}_I}(\cdot)$, $\text{msep}_{X_{i,j+k}|\mathcal{D}_I}(\cdot)$ and $\text{msep}_{C_{i,J}|\mathcal{D}_I}(\cdot)$, respectively, for $1 \le i \le I$. This means that these estimators are Bayesian w.r.t. the conditional probability measure, conditioned on $\mathcal{D}_I$, and minimize the quadratic loss function, i.e. the $L^2(P(\cdot|\mathcal{D}_I))$-norm.*

Proof The $\mathcal{D}_I$-measurability is obvious. But then the claim for $\widetilde{\mu(\Theta_i)}$ is also clear, since the conditional expectation minimizes the MSEP, given $\mathcal{D}_I$ (see Theorem 2.5 in Bühlmann and Gisler 2005). Due to our independence assumptions we have

$$E\left[X_{i,I-i+k}|\mathcal{D}_I\right] = E\left[E\left[X_{i,I-i+k}|\Theta_i\right]|\mathcal{D}_I\right] = \gamma_{I-i+k}\ \mu_i\ \widetilde{\mu(\Theta_i)}$$
$$E\left[C_{i,J}|\mathcal{D}_I\right] = C_{i,I-i} + (1-\beta_{I-i})\ \mu_i\ \widetilde{\mu(\Theta_i)} \tag{4.42}$$

which completes the proof of the theorem. □

Explicit Choice of Weights $w_{i,j}$

W.l.o.g. we may and will assume that

$$m_b = E\left[b''(\Theta_i)\right] = 1 \tag{4.43}$$

Otherwise if m_b is not equal to 1 we simply multiply σ^2 and τ^2 by m_b, which in our context of EDF with associated conjugates leads to the same model with $b(\theta)$ replaced by $b_{(1)}(\theta) = m_b\, b(\theta/m_b)$. This rescaled model has then

$$\operatorname{Var}\left(\frac{X_{i,j}}{\gamma_j\,\mu_i}\middle|\,\Theta_i\right) = \frac{m_b\,\sigma^2\, b''_{(1)}(\Theta_i)}{w_{i,j}}, \quad \text{with} \quad E\left[b''_{(1)}(\Theta_i)\right] = 1$$

$$\operatorname{Var}\left(b'_{(1)}(\Theta_i)\right) = m_b\,\tau^2$$

Since both σ^2 and τ^2 are multiplied by m_b, the credibility weights $\alpha_{i,j}$ do not change under this transformation. Hence we assume (4.43) for the rest of this work.

Above we have not specified the weights $w_{i,j}$. In Mack (1990) there is a discussion on choosing appropriate weights (Assumption ($A4^{\alpha}$) in Mack 1990). In fact we could choose a (deterministic) design matrix $\omega_{i,j}$ which gives a whole family of models. We do not further discuss this here. We make a canonical choice that is favoured in many applications. The reason why it is often favoured is that it has the nice consequence that we obtain a natural mixture between the CL estimate/model and the BF estimate/model.

Model Assumptions 4.43

In addition to Model Assumptions 4.35 and (4.43) we assume that there exists $\delta \geq 0$ with $w_{i,j} = \gamma_j\,\mu_i^{\delta}$ for all $i = 0, \ldots, I$ and $j = 0, \ldots, J$ and that $\exp\left\{\left(\mu_0\,\theta - b(\theta)\right)/\tau^2\right\}$ disappears on the boundary of Θ_i for all choices μ_0 and τ^2. □

Under Model Assumptions 4.43 we have $\sum_{k=0}^{j} w_{i,k} = \beta_j\,\mu_i^{\delta}$. This immediately implies:

COROLLARY 4.44 *Under Model Assumptions 4.43 we have*

$$\widetilde{\mu(\Theta_i)} = \alpha_{i,I-i}\,\frac{C_{i,I-i}}{\beta_{I-i}\,\mu_i} + (1-\alpha_{i,I-i})\;1 \tag{4.44}$$

where

$$\alpha_{i,I-i} = \frac{\beta_{I-i}}{\beta_{I-i} + \sigma^2/\mu_i^{\delta}\,\tau^{-2}} \tag{4.45}$$

This motivates the following estimator:

ESTIMATOR 4.45 *Under Model Assumptions 4.43 we have the following estimator for the ultimate claims* $E\left[C_{i,J}\middle|\,\mathcal{D}_I\right]$

$$\widehat{C_{i,J}}^{\text{EDF}} = C_{i,I-i} + (1-\beta_{I-i})\left[\alpha_{i,I-i}\,\frac{C_{i,I-i}}{\beta_{I-i}} + (1-\alpha_{i,I-i})\,\mu_i\right]$$

for $1 \leq i \leq I$ *and* $\alpha_{i,I-i}$ *given by* (4.45).

Remark Compare the weight $\alpha_{i,I-i}$ from (4.45) to $\alpha_{i,I-i}$ from (4.33). In the notation of (4.33) we have

$$\kappa_i = \phi_i \; b_i = \frac{E\left[\mathrm{Var}\left(X_{i,I-i}\middle|\,\Theta_i\right)\right]}{\gamma_{I-i}\;\mathrm{Var}(\Theta_i)}$$

and in the notation of (4.45) we have (see also (4.47)–(4.48))

$$\kappa_i = \frac{\sigma^2/\mu_i^\delta}{\tau^2} = \frac{E\left[\mathrm{Var}\left(X_{i,I-i}/\mu_i\middle|\,\Theta_i\right)\right]}{\gamma_{I-i}\;\mathrm{Var}\big(\mu(\Theta_i)\big)} \tag{4.46}$$

This shows that the estimators $\widehat{C_{i,J}}^{\text{PoiGa}}$ and $\widehat{C_{i,J}}^{\text{EDF}}$ give the same estimated reserve (the Poisson–Gamma model is an example for the EDF with associated conjugates).

Example 4.46 (EDF with associated conjugates)

We revisit the data set given in Example 2.7. For the prior distribution we use the same numerical values for the parameters as in Example 4.19 (see Table 4.4):

Observe that the credibility weights $\alpha_{i,I-i}$ do not depend on the choice of $\delta \geq 0$ for given $\mathrm{Vco}(C_{i,J})$. Namely, using the conditional independence of the increments $X_{i,j}$, given Θ_i, and (4.40), (4.41) as well as (4.43) leads to

$$\begin{aligned}
\mathrm{Var}(C_{i,J}) &= E\left[\mathrm{Var}\left(\sum_{j=0}^{J} X_{i,j}\middle|\,\Theta_i\right)\right] + \mathrm{Var}\left(E\left[\sum_{j=0}^{J} X_{i,j}\middle|\,\Theta_i\right]\right)\\
&= E\left[\sum_{j=0}^{J} \gamma_j^2\;\mu_i^2\;\mathrm{Var}\left(\frac{X_{i,j}}{\gamma_j\;\mu_i}\middle|\,\Theta_i\right)\right] + \mathrm{Var}\left(\sum_{j=0}^{J} \gamma_j\;\mu_i\;E\left[\frac{X_{i,j}}{\gamma_j\;\mu_i}\middle|\,\Theta_i\right]\right)\\
&= \sum_{j=0}^{J} \gamma_j^2\;\mu_i^2\;\frac{\sigma^2}{\omega_{i,j}} + \mu_i^2\;\mathrm{Var}\big(b'(\Theta_i)\big)\\
&= \frac{\mu_i^2}{\mu_i^\delta}\;\sigma^2 + \mu_i^2\;\tau^2
\end{aligned}$$

Hence, we have for the variational coefficient

$$\mathrm{Vco}^2(C_{i,J}) = \frac{\sigma^2}{\mu_i^\delta} + \tau^2 \tag{4.47}$$

For the credibility weight as a function of the variational coefficient, this implies,

$$\alpha_{i,I-i} = \frac{\beta_{I-i}}{\beta_{I-i} + (\sigma^2/\mu_i^\delta)\;\tau^{-2}} = \frac{\beta_{I-i}}{\beta_{I-i} + (\mathrm{Vco}^2(C_{i,J})/\tau^2) - 1} \tag{4.48}$$

For simplicity we have chosen $\delta = 0$ in Table 4.12, which implies for our parameter choices $\tau = 5\%$ and $\sigma = 6\%$ that $\mathrm{Vco}(C_{i,J}) = 7.8\%$ (see also Table 4.9). Moreover, the credibility coefficient κ_i is constant in i.

Table 4.12 Claims reserves under the EDF with associated conjugates

i	τ (%)	σ (%)	κ	$\alpha_{i,I-i}$ (%)	$\widetilde{\mu(\Theta_i)}$	Reserves EDF
0	5.00	6.00	1.4400	41.0	0.9822	0
1	5.00	6.00	1.4400	40.9	0.9746	15 715
2	5.00	6.00	1.4400	40.9	0.9888	26 695
3	5.00	6.00	1.4400	40.9	0.9669	36 333
4	5.00	6.00	1.4400	40.8	0.9567	91 303
5	5.00	6.00	1.4400	40.6	0.9509	169 281
6	5.00	6.00	1.4400	40.3	0.9349	319 093
7	5.00	6.00	1.4400	39.7	0.9136	524 484
8	5.00	6.00	1.4400	37.9	0.9208	1 214 184
9	5.00	6.00	1.4400	29.0	0.9502	4 530 884
Total						6 927 973

The claims reserves in Table 4.10 (Poisson–Gamma case) and Table 4.12 (EDF with associated conjugates) are the same.

Moreover, we see that the Bayesian estimate $\widetilde{\mu(\Theta_i)}$ is below 1 for all accident years i (see Table 4.12). This suggests (once more) that the choices of the prior estimates μ_i for the ultimate claims were too conservative. □

Conclusion 1 Corollary 4.44 implies that the estimator $\widehat{C_{i,J}}^{\text{EDF}}$ gives the optimal mixture between the BF and the CL estimates in the EDF with associated conjugates. Assume that β_j and f_j are related by (4.3) and set $\widehat{C_{i,J}}^{\text{CL}} = C_{i,I-i}/\beta_{I-i}$. Then we obtain

$$\begin{aligned}
\widehat{C_{i,J}}^{\text{EDF}} &= C_{i,I-i} + (1-\beta_{I-i}) \left[\alpha_{i,I-i} \frac{C_{i,I-i}}{\beta_{I-i}} + (1-\alpha_{i,I-i})\, \mu_i\right] \\
&= C_{i,I-i} + (1-\beta_{I-i}) \left[\alpha_{i,I-i} \widehat{C_{i,J}}^{\text{CL}} + (1-\alpha_{i,I-i})\, \mu_i\right] \\
&= C_{i,I-i} + (1-\beta_{I-i})\, u_i\left(\alpha_{i,I-i}\right)
\end{aligned} \tag{4.49}$$

where $u_i(\cdot)$ is the function defined in (4.1). Hence, we have the natural credibility mixture

$$\widehat{C_{i,J}}^{\text{EDF}} = \alpha_{i,I-i}\, \widehat{C_{i,J}}^{\text{CL}} + (1-\alpha_{i,I-i})\, \widehat{C_{i,J}}^{\text{BF}}$$

between the CL estimate and the BF estimate. Moreover, it minimizes the conditional MSEP in the EDF with associated conjugates. Observe that

$$\alpha_{i,I-i} = \frac{\beta_{I-i}}{\beta_{I-i} + \kappa_i}$$

where the credibility coefficient was defined in (4.46). If we choose $\kappa_i = 0$ we obtain the CL estimate and if we choose $\kappa_i = \infty$ we obtain the BF reserve.

Conclusion 2 Using (4.42) we find for all $I-i \le j < J-1$ that

$$
\begin{aligned}
E\left[C_{i,j+1} | C_{i,0}, \ldots, C_{i,I-i}\right] &= C_{i,I-i} + E\left[\sum_{k=I-i+1}^{j+1} X_{i,k} \middle| C_{i,0}, \ldots, C_{i,I-i}\right] \\
&= C_{i,I-i} + \sum_{k=I-i+1}^{j+1} \gamma_k \, \mu_i \, \widetilde{\mu(\Theta_i)} \\
&= \left(1 + \frac{\beta_{j+1} - \beta_{I-i}}{\beta_{I-i}} \, \alpha_{i,I-i}\right) C_{i,I-i} \\
&\quad + (\beta_{j+1} - \beta_{I-i}) \, (1 - \alpha_{i,I-i}) \, \mu_i
\end{aligned}
\tag{4.50}
$$

In the second step we have explicitly used the fact that we have an exact Bayesian estimator. Formula (4.50) does not hold true in the Bühlmann–Straub model (see Section 4.5 below); it suggests that the EDF with associated conjugates gives a credibility mixture between the CL model and the BF model. If we choose the credibility coefficient $\kappa_i = 0$ and assume (4.3), then we have $\alpha_{i,I-i} = 1$ and obtain

$$
E\left[C_{i,j+1} | C_{i,0}, \ldots, C_{i,j}\right] = \left(1 + \frac{\beta_{j+1} - \beta_j}{\beta_j}\right) C_{i,j} = f_j \, C_{i,j}
$$

This is exactly the CL assumption (2.1). If we choose $\kappa_i = \infty$, then $\alpha_{i,I-i} = 0$ and

$$
E\left[C_{i,J} | C_{i,0}, \ldots, C_{i,I-i}\right] = C_{i,I-i} + (1 - \beta_{I-i}) \, \mu_i
$$

which is in line with Model Assumptions 2.8 that we have used to motivate the BF estimate $\widehat{C_{i,J}}^{BF}$.

Hence, the model that we have found is a mixture model between CL and BF. Moreover, observe that (4.50) can also be understood as a linear regression model with intercept

$$
(\beta_{j+1} - \beta_{I-i}) \, (1 - \alpha_{i,I-i}) \, \mu_i
$$

and slope

$$
1 + \frac{\beta_{j+1} - \beta_{I-i}}{\beta_{I-i}} \, \alpha_{i,I-i}
$$

This means that this model can cope with the main criticism of the CL model that many real data show that one should introduce an intercept in the CL model (see Barnett and Zehnwirth 1998).

Under Model Assumptions 4.43 we obtain for the conditional MSEP

$$
\mathrm{msep}_{\mu(\Theta_i)|\mathcal{D}_I}\left(\widetilde{\mu(\Theta_i)}\right) = E\left[\left(\widetilde{\mu(\Theta_i)} - \mu(\Theta_i)\right)^2 \middle| \mathcal{D}_I\right] = \mathrm{Var}(\mu(\Theta_i)|\mathcal{D}_I)
$$

and hence we have for the unconditional MSEP

$$
\mathrm{msep}_{\mu(\Theta_i)}\left(\widetilde{\mu(\Theta_i)}\right) = E\left[\mathrm{Var}(\mu(\Theta_i)|\mathcal{D}_I)\right]
$$

If we plug in the estimator (4.44), we obtain

$$\begin{aligned}
\text{msep}_{\mu(\Theta_i)}\left(\widetilde{\mu(\Theta_i)}\right) &= E\left[\left(\alpha_{i,I-i}\,\frac{C_{i,I-i}}{\beta_{I-i}\,\mu_i} + (1-\alpha_{i,I-i})\,1 - \mu(\Theta_i)\right)^2\right] \\
&= E\left[\left(\alpha_{i,I-i}\,\left(\frac{C_{i,I-i}}{\beta_{I-i}\,\mu_i} - \mu(\Theta_i)\right) - (1-\alpha_{i,I-i})\,(\mu(\Theta_i)-1)\right)^2\right] \\
&= (\alpha_{i,I-i})^2\; E\left[\text{Var}\left(\left.\frac{C_{i,I-i}}{\beta_{I-i}\,\mu_i}\right|\Theta_i\right)\right] + (1-\alpha_{i,I-i})^2\;\text{Var}(\mu(\Theta_i)) \\
&= (\alpha_{i,I-i})^2\;\frac{\sigma^2}{\beta_{I-i}\,\mu_i^\delta} + (1-\alpha_{i,I-i})^2\;\tau^2 \\
&= (1-\alpha_{i,I-i})\;\tau^2
\end{aligned}$$

where, in the last step, we have used

$$\tau^2\;(1-\alpha_{i,I-i}) = \alpha_{i,I-i}\;\frac{\sigma^2}{\mu_i^\delta\;\beta_{I-i}}$$

(cf. (4.45)). From this we derive the unconditional MSEP for the estimate of $C_{i,J}$:

$$\begin{aligned}
\text{msep}_{C_{i,J}}\left(\widehat{C_{i,J}}^{\text{EDF}}\right) &= E\left[\left((1-\beta_{I-i})\;\mu_i\;\widetilde{\mu(\Theta_i)} - (C_{i,J}-C_{i,I-i})\right)^2\right] \\
&= \mu_i^2\;E\left[\left((1-\beta_{I-i})\left(\widetilde{\mu(\Theta_i)} - \mu(\Theta_i) + \mu(\Theta_i)\right) - \frac{C_{i,J}-C_{i,I-i}}{\mu_i}\right)^2\right] \\
&= \mu_i^2\;(1-\beta_{I-i})^2\;\text{msep}_{\mu(\Theta_i)}\left(\widetilde{\mu(\Theta_i)}\right) + \sum_{k=I-i+1}^{J} E\left[\text{Var}\left(X_{i,k}\middle|\,\Theta_i\right)\right] \\
&= \mu_i^2\;\left[(1-\beta_{I-i})^2\;(1-\alpha_{i,I-i})\;\tau^2 + (1-\beta_{I-i})\;\sigma^2/\mu_i^\delta\right]
\end{aligned}\tag{4.51}$$

Moreover, if we set $\delta = 0$, we get

$$\text{msep}_{C_{i,J}}\left(\widehat{C_{i,J}}^{\text{EDF}}\right) = \sigma^2\;(1-\beta_{I-i})\;\mu_i^2\;\frac{1+\frac{\sigma^2}{\tau^2}}{\beta_{i-i}+\frac{\sigma^2}{\tau}}$$

This is the same value as for the Poisson–Gamma case, see after (4.36) and Table 4.11. For the conditional MSEP for the estimate of $C_{i,J}$, one needs to calculate

$$\text{Var}\big(\mu(\Theta_i)|\mathcal{D}_I\big) = \text{Var}\big(b'(\Theta_i)|\mathcal{D}_I\big)$$

where Θ_i, given $\mathcal{D}_I$, has the posterior distribution $u_{\mu^{(i)}_{\text{post},j},\tau^2_{\text{post},j}}(\cdot)$ given in Lemma 4.37. We omit further calculation of the conditional MSEP.

Remarks on Parameter Estimation

So far we have always assumed that μ_i, γ_j, σ^2 and τ^2 are known. Under these assumptions we have calculated the Bayesian estimator which was optimal in the sense that it minimized the (conditional) MSEP (for given parameters). If the parameters are not known, the problem becomes substantially more difficult and in general one loses the optimality results.

If the parameters μ_i, γ_j, σ^2 and τ^2 are unknown one can follow different approaches. Either one uses 'plug-in' estimates for these parameters or one also uses a Bayesian approach. The second approach would be consistent in the sense that one applies a full Bayesian approach to all unknown model parameters (see also Section 4.4). However, in such a full Bayesian approach there is, in general, no analytical solution to the problem and one needs to completely rely on numerical solutions such as the Markov Chain Monte Carlo (MCMC) method (see Section 4.4). The disadvantage of numerical methods is often that it is more difficult to give an interpretation to the results in terms of the parameters and to study parameter sensitivities. For the time being we will omit such numerical solutions and provide plug-in estimators for the unknown model parameters.

Estimation of γ_j There is no canonical way how the plug-in estimate for the claims development pattern should be constructed. In practice one often chooses the CL estimate $\widehat{\beta}_j^{(CL)}$ provided in (2.14) and then sets

$$\widehat{\gamma}_j^{(CL)} = \widehat{\beta}_j^{(CL)} - \widehat{\beta}_{j-1}^{(CL)} \tag{4.52}$$

At the current stage we cannot say anything about the optimality of these estimators. However, observe that for the Poisson–Gamma model this estimator is natural in the sense that it coincides with the MLE estimator provided in the Poisson model (see Corollary 2.18). For more on this topic we refer to Section 4.4.

Estimation of μ_i Usually one takes a plan value, a budget value or the value used for the premium calculation (as in the BF method).

Estimation of σ^2 and τ^2 For known γ_j and μ_i one can give unbiased estimators for these variance parameters. We postpone the formulation of these estimates at this stage, because in Section 4.5 we will see that the EDF with its associated conjugates satisfies the assumptions of the Bühlmann–Straub model and, hence, we can take the same estimators as in the Bühlmann–Straub model (these are provided in the parameter estimation section on p. 151).

4.4 MARKOV CHAIN MONTE CARLO METHODS

In Model Assumptions 4.28 and 4.35 we have assumed that the claims development pattern γ_j is known. Of course, in general this is not the case and in practice one usually uses estimate (4.52) for the claims development pattern. In Verrall (2004), for example, this is called a 'plug-in' estimate (which leads to the CL and BF mixture). However, in a full Bayesian approach one should also estimate this parameter in a Bayesian way (since usually it is not known). This means that we should also give a prior distribution to the claims development pattern γ_j. Then, in general, one no longer obtains analytic forms for posterior distributions if one introduces a prior distribution for the claims development pattern. That is, one only obtains analytic forms for the posterior up to normalization and generally one cannot obtain samples from such a posterior distribution via simple simulation methods. Therefore, one uses more eloborated numerical algorithms to answer the questions of interest.

On the other hand, we have chosen specific families of distributions – for example, the EDF with its associate conjugates – in order to obtain closed forms for posterior distributions.

For general distributions $F_{i,j}^{(\Theta_i)}$ and u_{μ,τ^2} (see Model Assumptions 4.35) one cannot calculate the posterior distribution of Θ_i, given $\mathcal{D}_I$, in a closed form. In such cases we have two possibilities:

(1) approximate the quantities of interest using appropriate methods (this is, for instance, done in Section 4.5); or
(2) use computational power and simulate from the distributions, so that one obtains numerical solutions and answers.

The current state of the art in statistical approaches to sampling from the posterior distribution fall into two categories: the first is known as Markov Chain Monte Carlo (MCMC) methods and the second is Importance Sampling. The main focus of this chapter will be on MCMC methods. MCMC methods provide a flexible framework within which complex problems can be answered. There are various different MCMC methods, such as the Metropolis–Hastings algorithm, Gibbs samplers, or ABC algorithms. For references see Metropolis *et al.* (1953), Hastings (1970), Gilks *et al.* (1996), Peters and Sisson (2006), Beaumont *et al.* (2002), Marjoram *et al.* (2003), Chip and Greenberg (1995) and Kirkpatrick *et al.* (1983). In claims reserving MCMC algorithms have been used in many applications, see Ntzoufras and Dellaportas (2002) and the implementation by Scollnik (2001, 2002) as well as the papers by de Alba (2002, 2006), Verrall (2004) or England and Verrall (2007).

Let us briefly describe the Metropolis–Hastings (MH) algorithm. Assume that conditionally, given Θ, $\mathbf{Y}=(Y_1,\ldots,Y_n)$ has likelihood function $f(\mathbf{Y}|\Theta)$, and Θ has prior density u_Θ. Then using Bayes' rule the posterior of Θ, conditioned on $\mathbf{Y}$, is given by

$$u(\Theta|\mathbf{Y})=\frac{f(\mathbf{Y}|\Theta)\;u_\Theta(\Theta)}{\int_\Theta f(\mathbf{Y}|\Theta)\;u_\Theta(\Theta)\;d\Theta} \tag{4.53}$$

For the EDF with associated conjugates this posterior of Θ, given $\mathbf{Y}$, can explicitly be calculated. However, in general, the normalizing constant takes a complicated form and can only be calculated numerically. An efficient way to simulate from the posterior $u(\Theta|\mathbf{Y})$ is to construct reversible ergodic Markov chains $(\Theta_t)_{t\in\mathbb{N}_0}$ which have the posterior distribution $u(\Theta|\mathbf{Y})$ as its stationary distribution.

Under the general framework established by Metropolis *et al.* (1953) and Hastings (1970), the transition from one state to the next is determined via a time and state homogeneous transition kernel $K(\Theta_t|\Theta_{t-1})$ going from Θ_{t-1} to Θ_t which satisfies the detailed balance condition

$$u(\Theta_{t-1}|\mathbf{Y})\;K(\Theta_t|\Theta_{t-1})=u(\Theta_t|\mathbf{Y})\;K(\Theta_{t-1}|\Theta_t)$$

The transition kernel K contains in its definition a proposal distribution $q(\Theta_t|\Theta_{t-1})$ and an acceptance probability α, which determines whether the proposed value is accepted or rejected (see formula (1.4) in Gilks *et al.* 1996).

$$K(\Theta_t|\Theta_{t-1})=q(\Theta_t|\Theta_{t-1})\alpha(\Theta_{t-1},\Theta_t)+\left[1-\int\alpha(\Theta_{t-1},z)q(z|\Theta_{t-1})\;dz\right]1_{\Theta_t=\Theta_{t-1}}$$

Then the MH algorithm goes as follows (see Gilks *et al.* 1996, Subsection 1.3.3)

1. Initialize Θ_0 and set $t=0$.
2. (a) Sample Θ^* from $q(\cdot|\Theta_t)$.
   (b) Set

$$\alpha(\Theta_t, \Theta^*) = \min\left\{1, \frac{u(\Theta^*|\mathbf{Y})\ q(\Theta_t|\Theta^*)}{u(\Theta_t|\mathbf{Y})\ q(\Theta^*|\Theta_t)}\right\}$$

   (c) Sample $U \overset{(d)}{\sim} \mathcal{U}(0, 1)$.
   (d) If $U \leq \alpha(\Theta_t, \Theta^*)$ then set $\Theta_{t+1} = \Theta^*$, otherwise $\Theta_{t+1} = \Theta_t$.
3. Increment t and go back to step 2.

Remarkably, the proposal distribution $q(\cdot|\cdot)$ can have any form (under some mild regularity restrictions) and the stationary distribution will always have the form $u(\cdot|\mathbf{Y})$. Moreover, the normalizing constant in (4.53) does not need to be known to apply this algorithm, it cancels in the fraction of the acceptance probability. Hence, one needs to find smart proposal distributions $q(\cdot|\cdot)$ which lead to a fast convergence to the stationary state. Then one samples from this algorithm until it has sufficiently converged to the stationary state in order to obtain (dependent) observations $\Theta_t, \Theta_{t+1}, \ldots$ which are approximately $u(\cdot|\mathbf{Y})$ distributed for large t.

For illustrative purposes we apply the MCMC method to one specific model, namely the overdispersed Poisson model (which was also considered in Verrall 2004). We have the following assumptions.

Model Assumptions 4.47 (Bayesian overdispersed Poisson model)

There exists a positive random vector $\Theta = (\mu_0, \ldots, \mu_I, \gamma_0, \ldots, \gamma_J, \phi_0, \ldots, \phi_I)$ such that for all $i \in \{0, \ldots, I\}$ and $j \in \{0, \ldots, J\}$ we have

- conditionally, given Θ, the $X_{i,j}/\phi_i$ are independent and Poisson distributed with mean $\mu_i\ \gamma_j/\phi_i$.
- Θ has density u_Θ. □

Remarks 4.48

- Note that for this multiplicative model, that is,

$$E\left[\left.\frac{X_{i,j}}{\phi_i}\right|\Theta\right] = \mu_i\ \frac{\gamma_j}{\phi_i}$$

  we need to impose a normalization condition in order to get well-defined parameters. In Model 4.28 we have assumed that $\sum_j \gamma_j = 1$; in the MCMC framework it is often easier to impose the normalization $\mu_0 = 1$, that is μ_0 takes a deterministic value. However, the resulting answers will be exactly the same for this normalization condition (see also Section 6.2).
- Note that Model 4.28 is a special case of Model 4.47, namely the parameters $\gamma_0, \ldots, \gamma_J, \phi_0, \ldots, \phi_I$ are assumed to be deterministic and $\mu_0, \ldots, \mu_I$ are assumed to be independent Gamma distributed in Model 4.28.
- This Bayesian model allows us to choose any dependence structure between the parameters, that is, in the choice of the prior distribution u_Θ.

As before, we can calculate the joint likelihood function of $\{X_{i,j}, 0 \leq i+j \leq I\}$ and Θ, which is given by

$$f\left((x_{i,j})_{0\leq i+j\leq I}, \theta\right) = \prod_{0\leq i+j\leq I} \exp\left(\frac{-\mu_i\,\gamma_j}{\phi_i}\right) \frac{(\mu_i\,\gamma_j/\phi_i)^{x_{i,j}/\phi_i}}{(x_{i,j}/\phi_i)!}\; u_\Theta(\theta)$$

The posterior distribution of Θ, given the observations $\mathcal{D}_I$, is then proportional to

$$u(\Theta|\mathcal{D}_I) \propto \prod_{0\leq i+j\leq I} \exp\left(\frac{-\mu_i\,\gamma_j}{\phi_i}\right) \frac{(\mu_i\,\gamma_j/\phi_i)^{X_{i,j}/\phi_i}}{(X_{i,j}/\phi_i)!}\; u_\Theta(\Theta)$$

Hence, in order to apply the MH algorithm we need to choose a smart proposal function $q(\Theta_t|\Theta_{t-1})$ that leads to a fast convergence to the stationary state, and we need to evaluate the acceptance probability α given by

$$\alpha(\Theta_t, \Theta^*) = \min\left\{1, \frac{\prod_{0\leq i+j\leq I} \exp\left(\frac{-\mu_i^*\,\gamma_j^*}{\phi_i^*}\right) \frac{\left(\mu_i^*\,\gamma_j^*/\phi_i^*\right)^{X_{i,j}/\phi_i^*}}{(X_{i,j}/\phi_i^*)!}\; u_\Theta(\Theta^*)\; q(\Theta_t|\Theta^*)}{\prod_{0\leq i+j\leq I} \exp\left(\frac{-\mu_i^{(t)}\,\gamma_j^{(t)}}{\phi_i^{(t)}}\right) \frac{\left(\mu_i^{(t)}\gamma_j^{(t)}/\phi_i^{(t)}\right)^{X_{i,j}/\phi_i^{(t)}}}{(X_{i,j}/\phi_i^{(t)})!}\; u_\Theta(\Theta_t)\; q(\Theta^*|\Theta_t)}\right\}$$

where $\Theta_t = (\mu_0^{(t)}, \ldots, \mu_I^{(t)}, \gamma_0^{(t)}, \ldots, \gamma_J^{(t)}, \phi_0^{(t)}, \ldots, \phi_I^{(t)})$ is the tth state in the Markov chain $(\Theta_t)_{t\in\mathbb{N}_0}$ and

$$\Theta^* = (\mu_0^*, \ldots, \mu_I^*, \gamma_0^*, \ldots, \gamma_J^*, \phi_0^*, \ldots, \phi_I^*)$$

is the sample from $\Theta^* \overset{(d)}{\sim} q(\cdot|\Theta_t)$.

For an explicit application, we have to specify the prior distribution u_Θ and the proposal function $q(\cdot|\cdot)$. Moreover, since Θ is a multidimensional parameter vector, there are different ways of updating the Markov chain, for example, we can update all coordinates at once (as described above) or we can use a single-component updating procedure (as described in Gilks *et al.* 1996 and Scollnik 2001).

We consider different examples.

Example 4.49 (uniform priors for exposures)

In our first example, we assume that the parameters $\gamma_0, \ldots, \gamma_J$ and $\phi_0, \ldots, \phi_I$ are known. This is then a similar situation as in the Poisson–Gamma Example 4.33. We choose the same data set as in Example 4.33 and Example 2.15. For the γ_j pattern we use the scaled MLE estimators from Example 2.15, that is we choose $\gamma_j = \widehat{\gamma}_j\,\widehat{\mu}_0$, which corresponds to the MLE estimators from Example 2.15 if we impose the normalizing constraint $\mu_0 = 1$ (see Table 2.5). For the dispersion we simply choose $\phi_i = 40\,000$ for all $i = 0, \ldots, I$ (see Table 4.9).

Then we need to specify the prior distribution of $(\mu_0, \ldots, \mu_I)$. We choose independent uniform distributions on appropriate intervals. We have already chosen the intervals according to the location of the MLE estimates from Example 2.15, given by $\widehat{\mu}_i/\widehat{\mu}_0$. Hence, we assume that $\Theta = (\mu_0, \ldots, \mu_I)$ has prior distribution

$$u_\Theta(\Theta) = u_\Theta(\mu_0, \ldots, \mu_I) = \prod_{i=0}^{I} u_{\mu_i}(\mu_i)$$

with

$$u_{\mu_i} \stackrel{(d)}{=} \mathcal{U}(a_i, b_i)$$

where $b_i = a_i + 0.25$, $a_0 = a_1 = a_2 = 0.85$, $a_3 = a_4 = a_5 = 0.80$ and $a_6 = \ldots = a_9 = 0.75$. Finally, we need to choose the proposal distribution. We assume that $q(\cdot|\Theta_t) = u_\Theta(\cdot)$. Note that this leads to a simple acceptance probability which only contains the likelihood of the Poisson distribution, and all the other terms cancel out:

$$\alpha(\Theta_t, \Theta^*) = \min\left\{1, \frac{\prod_{0\le i+j\le I} \exp\left(\frac{-\mu_i^* \gamma_j}{\phi_i}\right) \frac{\left(\mu_i^* \gamma_j/\phi_i\right)^{X_{i,j}/\phi_i}}{(X_{i,j}/\phi_i)!}}{\prod_{0\le i+j\le I} \exp\left(\frac{-\mu_i^{(t)} \gamma_j}{\phi_i}\right) \frac{\left(\mu_i^{(t)} \gamma_j/\phi_i\right)^{X_{i,j}/\phi_i}}{(X_{i,j}/\phi_i)!}}\right\} \tag{4.54}$$

Hence we can determine the posterior $u(\Theta|\mathcal{D}_I)$ using the MH algorithm. This leads to the following numerical solutions (we have used 10 000 simulations after subracting the burn-in costs). For illustrative purposes we show the stationary sequence $(\mu_1^{(t)})_t$ and $(\mu_5^{(t)})_t$ in Figure 4.5.

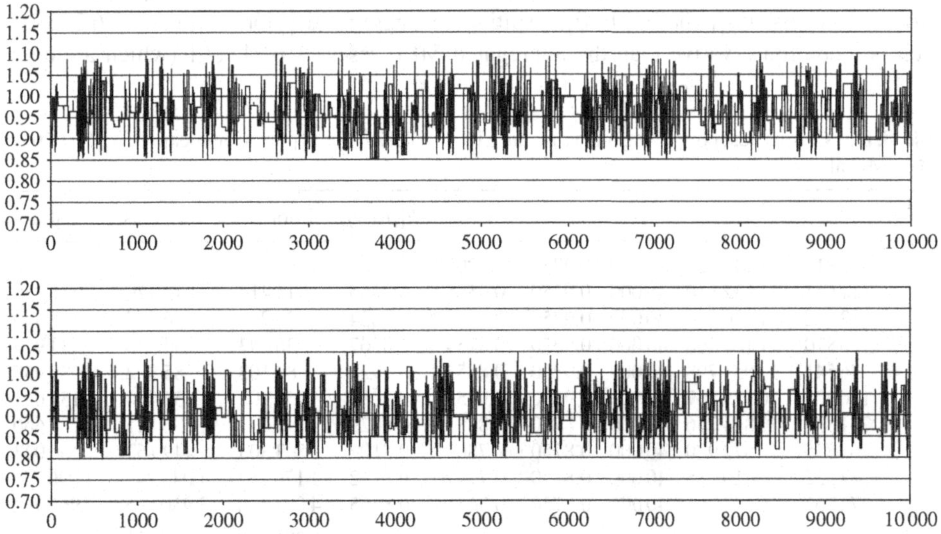

Figure 4.5 Stationary sequence $(\mu_1^{(t)})_t$ and $(\mu_5^{(t)})_t$ generated by the MCMC algorithm (4.54)

The marginal (posterior) distributions of μ_1 and μ_5, conditioned on $\mathcal{D}_I$, are then shown in Figure 4.6.

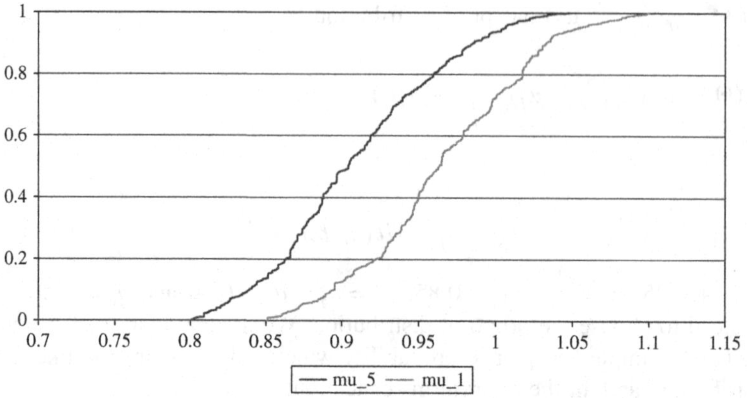

Figure 4.6 Marginals μ_1 and μ_5, given $\mathcal{D}_I$, generated by the MCMC algorithm with acceptance probability (4.54)

The (empirical) claims reserves and the conditional MSEP of accident year $i \in \{1, \ldots, I\}$ are then easily calculated using (4.34) and (4.35) ($\beta_j = \sum_{k=0}^{j} \gamma_k$), which leads to

$$E\left[C_{i,J} - C_{i,I-i} \middle| \mathcal{D}_I\right] = (\beta_J - \beta_{I-i})\ E[\mu_i | \mathcal{D}_I]$$

and

$$\mathrm{Var}\left(C_{i,J} \middle| \mathcal{D}_I\right) = \phi_i\ (\beta_J - \beta_{I-i})\ E[\mu_i | \mathcal{D}_I] + (\beta_J - \beta_{I-i})^2\ \mathrm{Var}(\mu_i | \mathcal{D}_I)$$

In Table 4.13 we see that the choice of the prior distribution and prior mean $E[\mu_i]$ is slightly more conservative than the MLE $\widehat{\mu}_i$ resulting in aggregated prior reserves of 6 296 910, which is more conservative than the aggregated MLE reserves 6 047 061 (which are equal

Table 4.13 Claims reserves using prior mean $E[\mu_i]$, MLE $\widehat{\mu}_i$ and posterior mean $E[\mu_i|\mathcal{D}_I]$ (from the MCMC algorithm)

i	γ_{I-i}	β_{I-i}	ϕ_i	$E[\mu_i]$	MLE $\widehat{\mu}_i$	$E[\mu_i\|\mathcal{D}_I]$	Prior res.	MLE res.	Post. res.
0	15 813	11 148 124	40 000	0.9750	1.0000	0.9966			
1	11 641	11 132 310	40 000	0.9750	0.9565	0.9655	15 418	15 126	15 269
2	12 002	11 120 670	40 000	0.9750	0.9564	0.9634	26 768	26 257	26 449
3	56 870	11 108 668	40 000	0.9250	0.8754	0.8867	36 497	34 538	34 984
4	76 541	11 051 798	40 000	0.9250	0.8855	0.8924	89 102	85 302	85 958
5	160 501	10 975 257	40 000	0.9250	0.9053	0.9083	159 902	156 494	157 023
6	241 836	10 814 756	40 000	0.8750	0.8583	0.8629	291 697	286 121	287 660
7	762 835	10 572 920	40 000	0.8750	0.7809	0.8102	503 303	449 167	466 043
8	3 237 322	9 810 085	40 000	0.8750	0.7797	0.8152	1 170 784	1 043 242	1 090 743
9	6 572 763	6 572 763	40 000	0.8750	0.8635	0.8665	4 003 440	3 950 815	3 964 762
Total							6 296 910	6 047 061	6 128 890

to the aggregated CL reserves, see Lemma 2.16). The posterior mean $E[\mu_i|\mathcal{D}_I]$ then leads to reserves that are between those from the prior mean and the MLE reserves.

The estimates for the conditional MSEP are given in Table 4.14. These values should be compared to the first column in Table 4.11.

Table 4.14 Conditional MSEP from the MCMC algorithm

i	$\mathrm{Var}(\mu_i|\mathcal{D}_I)^{1/2}$	Cond. msep$^{1/2}$
0	0.053184	
1	0.053212	24 728
2	0.055874	32 562
3	0.048409	37 457
4	0.051998	58 851
5	0.054255	79 805
6	0.051884	108 653
7	0.042378	138 694
8	0.044584	217 229
9	0.061083	486 515
Total		572 568

End of proof.

Example 4.50 (Gamma priors for exposures)

In our second example, we assume that the parameters $\gamma_0, \ldots, \gamma_J$ and $\phi_0, \ldots, \phi_I$ are known, and that the priors μ_i are independent Gamma distributions with parameters a_i and b_i. This then corresponds to the Poisson–Gamma case, where we can explicitly calculate the marginal (posterior) distribution of μ_i, given $\mathcal{D}_I$. It is given by the Gamma distribution with parameters (see Lemma 4.30)

$$a_{i,I-i}^{\text{post}} = a_i + \frac{C_{i,I-i}}{\phi_i}$$

$$b_{i,I-i}^{\text{post}} = b_i + \frac{\beta_{I-i}}{\phi_i}$$

We choose the same data set as in Example 4.33 and Example 2.15. For the γ_j pattern we use the MLE estimators from Example 2.15 and for the dispersion we simply choose $\phi_i = 40\,000$ (see Table 4.9). The Gamma priors are given in Table 4.15.

For the proposals we also choose Gamma distributions as for the priors. In order to obtain good fast convergence results, we choose the location of the mean of the distributions close to the MLE $\widehat{\mu}_i$ estimates (see Table 2.5). The parameters are given in Table 4.16.

Now, we are able to compare the numerical MCMC results to the analytical solutions provided by Lemma 4.30. In Figure 4.7 we compare (for illustrative purposes) the analytical posterior and the numerical MCMC posterior of μ_5, given $\mathcal{D}_I$. The figure shows the cumulative distribution functions as well as the Q–Q plot. The figures show that the MCMC algorithm has properly run since the analytical and the empirical result coincide (10 000 simulations after subracting burn-in costs). □

Table 4.15 Prior distributions

i	a_i	b_i	$E[\mu_i]$	$\text{Vco}(\mu_i)$ (%)
0	400	3.59E-05	11 150 000	5.0
1	400	3.64E-05	11 000 000	5.0
2	400	3.81E-05	10 500 000	5.0
3	400	4.10E-05	9 750 000	5.0
4	400	4.44E-05	9 000 000	5.0
5	400	4.00E-05	10 000 000	5.0
6	400	4.21E-05	9 500 000	5.0
7	400	4.57E-05	8 750 000	5.0
8	400	4.57E-05	8 750 000	5.0
9	400	4.21E-05	9 500 000	5.0

Table 4.16 Proposal distributions

i	a	b	E	Vco (%)
0	200	1.79E-05	11 148 124	7.1
1	200	1.88E-05	10 663 318	7.1
2	200	1.88E-05	10 662 008	7.1
3	200	2.05E-05	9 758 606	7.1
4	200	2.03E-05	9 872 218	7.1
5	200	1.98E-05	10 092 247	7.1
6	200	2.09E-05	9 568 143	7.1
7	200	2.30E-05	8 705 378	7.1
8	200	2.30E-05	8 691 971	7.1
9	200	2.08E-05	9 626 383	7.1

Example 4.51 (full Bayesian approach)

We revisit the data set given in the Poisson–Gamma Example 4.33 (see also Example 2.7). This time we choose appropriate prior distributions for all the parameters ϕ_i, γ_j and μ_i.

We assume that ϕ_i does not depend on i, that is $\phi = \phi_0 = \cdots = \phi_I$, P–a.s. Moreover, we use the initialization $\mu_0 = 1$ and we choose independent prior parameters, that is,

$$u_\Theta(\Theta) = u_\Theta(\mu_1, \ldots, \mu_I, \gamma_0, \ldots, \gamma_J, \phi) = \prod_{i=1}^{I} u_{\mu_i}(\mu_i) \prod_{j=0}^{J} u_{\gamma_j}(\gamma_j)\ u_\phi(\phi)$$

with

$$u_{\mu_i} \stackrel{(d)}{=} \mathcal{U}(a_i, b_i)$$

$$u_{\gamma_j} \stackrel{(d)}{=} \Gamma(c_j, d_j)$$

$$u_\phi \stackrel{(d)}{=} \Gamma(\varphi_1, \varphi_2)$$

for $i = 1, \ldots, I$ and $j = 0, \ldots, J$. The constants a_i, b_i are given in Example 4.4 and for appropriate parameters c_j and d_j, see Table 4.17. Moreover, we use the parameters $\varphi_1 = 400$ and $\varphi_2 = 0.01$ for u_ϕ (i.e. expected value $E[\phi] = 40\,000$ and coefficient of variation $\text{Vco}(\phi) = 5.0\%$).

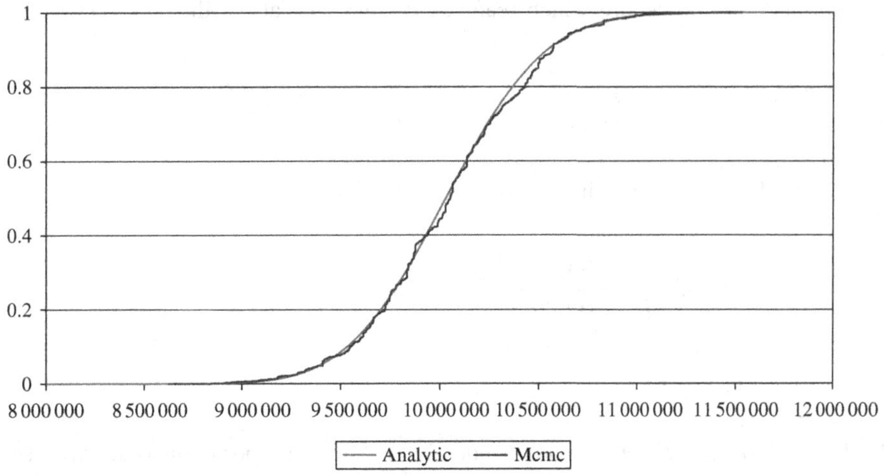

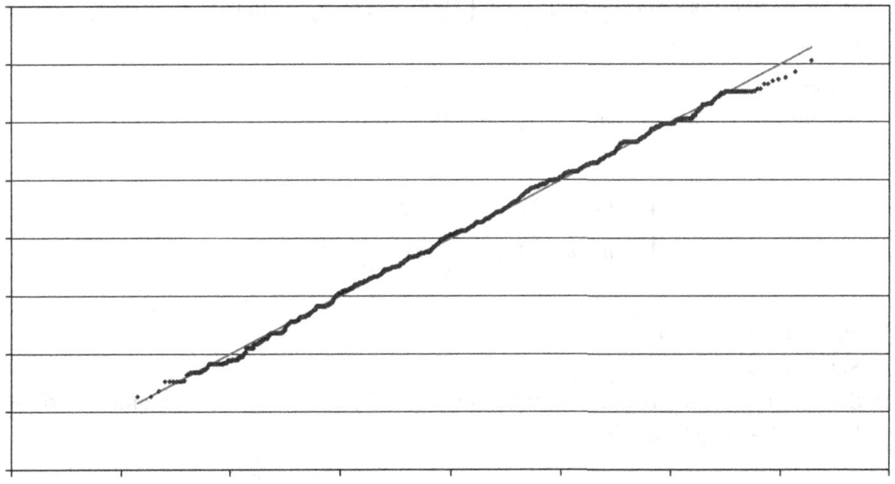

Figure 4.7 Cumulative distributions and Q–Q plot of the analytical and the MCMC posterior distribution of μ_5, given $\mathcal{D}_I$

Table 4.17 Prior distributions

j	c_j	d_j	$E[\gamma_j]$	$\text{Vco}(\gamma_j)$ (%)
0	400	6.15E-05	6 500 000	5.0
1	400	1.25E-04	3 200 000	5.0
2	400	5.33E-04	750 000	5.0
3	400	1.60E-03	250 000	5.0
4	400	2.50E-03	160 000	5.0
5	400	5.33E-03	75 000	5.0
6	400	7.27E-03	55 000	5.0
7	400	3.33E-02	12 000	5.0
8	400	3.33E-02	12 000	5.0
9	400	2.67E-02	15 000	5.0

Then, we can either use the MH algorithm as described above, or we can use a single-component updating procedure which reads as follows (see also Gilks *et al.* 1996, Figure 1.2 on p. 11):

1. Initialize $\Theta_0 = \left(\mu_1^{(0)}, \ldots, \mu_I^{(0)}, \gamma_0^{(0)}, \ldots, \gamma_J^{(0)}, \phi^{(0)}\right)$ and set $t = 0$.
2. (a) For $i = 1, \ldots, I$ sample independently μ_i^* from $\mathcal{U}(a_i, b_i)$.
   Set $\Theta^* = \left(\mu_1^*, \ldots, \mu_I^*, \gamma_0^{(t)}, \ldots, \gamma_J^{(t)}, \phi^{(t)}\right)$.
   Accept this choice Θ^* with acceptance probability

$$\alpha(\Theta_t, \Theta^*) = \min\left\{1, \frac{u(\Theta^*|\mathcal{D}_I)}{u(\Theta_t|\mathcal{D}_I)}\right\}$$

   otherwise $\Theta_{t+1} = \Theta_t$.
   Set $\Theta_t = \Theta_{t+1}$.

   (b) For $j = 0, \ldots, J$ sample independently γ_j^* from proposal distribution $q_j(\cdot|\gamma_j^{(t)})$ given by the Gamma distribution $\Gamma\left(1000, 1000/\gamma_j^{(t)}\right)$, that is $E[\gamma_j^*|\gamma_j^{(t)}] = \gamma_j^{(t)}$ and $\text{Vco}(\gamma_j^*|\gamma_j^{(t)}) = 3.2\%$.
   Set $\Theta^* = \left(\mu_1^{(t)}, \ldots, \mu_I^{(t)}, \gamma_0^*, \ldots, \gamma_J^*, \phi^{(t)}\right)$.
   Accept this choice Θ^* with acceptance probability

$$\alpha(\Theta_t, \Theta^*) = \min\left\{1, \frac{u(\Theta^*|\mathcal{D}_I)\ \prod_{j=0}^J q_j(\gamma_j^{(t)}|\gamma^*)}{u(\Theta_t|\mathcal{D}_I)\ \prod_{j=0}^J q_j(\gamma_j^*|\gamma_j^{(t)})}\right\}$$

   otherwise $\Theta_{t+1} = \Theta_t$.
   Set $\Theta_t = \Theta_{t+1}$.

   (c) Sample ϕ^* from proposal distribution $q(\cdot|\phi^{(t)})$ given by the Gamma distribution $\Gamma\left(300, 300/\phi^{(t)}\right)$, that is

$$E[\phi^*|\phi^{(t)}] = \phi^{(t)} \quad \text{and} \quad \text{Vco}(\phi^*|\phi^{(t)}) = 5.8\%$$

   Set $\Theta^* = \left(\mu_1^{(t)}, \ldots, \mu_I^{(t)}, \gamma_0^{(t)}, \ldots, \gamma_J^{(t)}, \phi^*\right)$.
   Accept this choice Θ^* with acceptance probability

$$\alpha(\Theta_t, \Theta^*) = \min\left\{1, \frac{u(\Theta^*|\mathcal{D}_I)\ q(\phi^{(t)}|\phi^*)}{u(\Theta_t|\mathcal{D}_I)\ q(\phi^*|\phi^{(t)})}\right\}$$

   otherwise $\Theta_{t+1} = \Theta_t$.
3. Increment t and go back to step 2.

This leads to the following stationary distributions, for illustrative purposes we only show selected variables (see Figures 4.8 and 4.9).

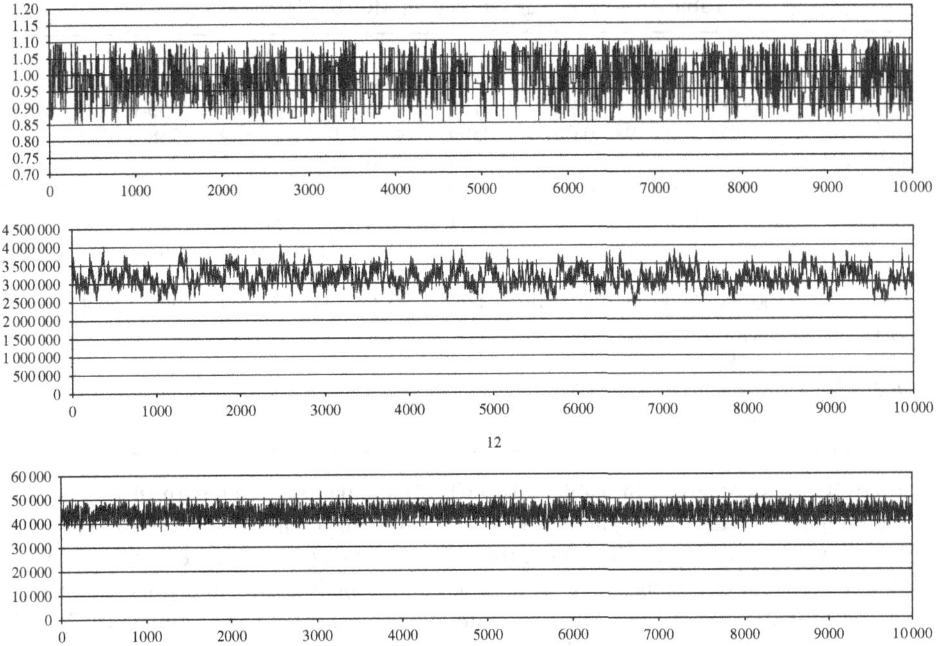

Figure 4.8 Stationary sequence $(\mu_2^{(t)})_t$, $(\gamma_1^{(t)})_t$ and $(\phi^{(t)})_t$ generated by the MCMC algorithm

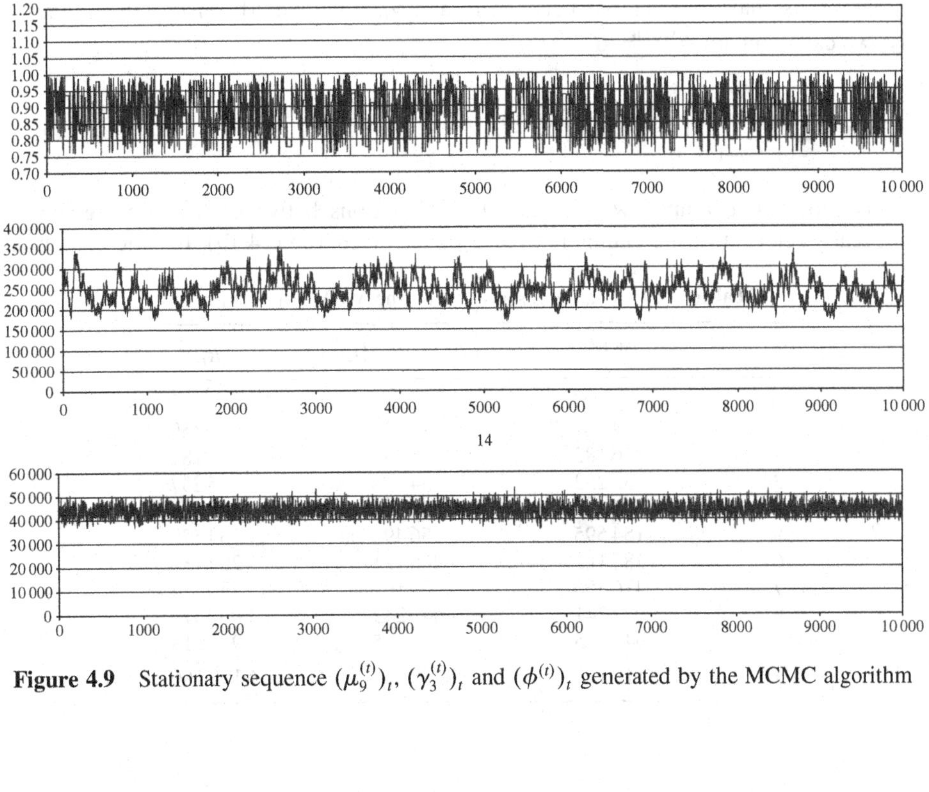

Figure 4.9 Stationary sequence $(\mu_9^{(t)})_t$, $(\gamma_3^{(t)})_t$ and $(\phi^{(t)})_t$ generated by the MCMC algorithm

Table 4.18 Summary statistic of MCMC algorithm

	0	1	2	3	4	5	6	7	8	9
$E[\mu_i \mid \mathcal{D}_I]$	1.0000	0.9829	0.9824	0.9159	0.9195	0.9350	0.8806	0.8355	0.8342	0.8855
$\text{sdev}(\mu_i \mid \mathcal{D}_I)$	0.0000	0.0598	0.0613	0.0599	0.0603	0.0598	0.0589	0.0538	0.0553	0.0658
$\text{Vco}(\mu_i \mid \mathcal{D}_I)(\%)$		6.1	6.2	6.5	6.6	6.4	6.7	6.4	6.6	7.4
$E[\mu_i]$	1.0000	0.9750	0.9750	0.9250	0.9250	0.9250	0.8750	0.8750	0.8750	0.8750
$E[\gamma_j \mid \mathcal{D}_I]$	6 372 012	3 140 522	745 219	246 394	158 478	72 722	54 109	11 843	11 838	14 813
$\text{sdev}(\gamma_j \mid \mathcal{D}_I)$	399 952	269 012	84 306	31 300	21 093	9 190	6 092	1 362	1 456	1 746
$\text{Vco}(\gamma_j \mid \mathcal{D}_I)(\%)$	6.3	8.6	11.3	12.7	13.3	12.6	11.3	11.5	12.3	11.8
$E[\gamma_j]$	6 500 000	3 200 000	750 000	250 000	160 000	75 000	55 000	12 000	12 000	15 000
$E[\phi \mid \mathcal{D}_I]$	43 895									
$\text{sdev}(\phi \mid \mathcal{D}_I)$	2 680									
$\text{Vco}(\phi \mid \mathcal{D}_I)(\%)$	6.1									
$E[\phi]$	40 000									

The key figures are given in Table 4.18 (10 000 simulations after burn-in costs). Note that the summary statistics in Table 4.18 are one-dimensional considerations. However, posterior distributions become dependent through the data $\mathcal{D}_I$, that is, we need to consider joint distributions for obtaining moments such as conditionally expected claims reserves and MSEP. For example, we obtain for the correlation $\text{Corr}(\gamma_0, \gamma_1 \mid \mathcal{D}_I)$ the estimate 0.12.

Now, we calculate the reserves, which are given by

$$\widehat{R}^{\text{MCMC}} = E\left[\sum_{i=1}^{I} \sum_{j=I-i+1}^{J} X_{i,j} \,\middle|\, \mathcal{D}_I \right] = \sum_{i=1}^{I} \sum_{j=I-i+1}^{J} E\left[\mu_i \gamma_j \mid \mathcal{D}_I \right]$$

Note that we also have correlations between μ_i and γ_j. If we would consider them independently, we can compare $\widehat{R}^{\text{MCMC}}$ to

$$\widetilde{R} = \sum_{i=1}^{I} \sum_{j=I-i+1}^{J} E[\mu_i \mid \mathcal{D}_I] \; E\left[\gamma_j \mid \mathcal{D}_I \right]$$

In this particular example, we see that the correlations between μ_i and γ_j, given $\mathcal{D}_I$, are not really relevant in the claims reserve estimates (see Table 4.19). For the conditional

Table 4.19 Claims reserves using the MCMC algorithm

i	$\widehat{R}_i^{\text{MCMC}}$	CL/Poisson MLE	$\widetilde{R}_i$
0			
1	14 561	15 126	14 559
2	26 182	26 257	26 181
3	35 252	34 538	35 257
4	85 149	85 302	85 150
5	154 595	156 494	154 577
6	285 183	286 121	285 132
7	476 356	449 167	476 414
8	1 097 241	1 043 242	1 097 376
9	3 944 595	3 950 815	3 945 519
Total	6 119 116	6 047 061	6 120 166

distribution of the expected outstanding loss liabilities R, given $\mathcal{D}_I$, that is

$$R=\sum_{i=1}^{I}\sum_{j=I-i+1}^{J}\mu_i\,\gamma_j$$

we obtain the posterior distribution provided in Figure 4.10. Note that this posterior distribution now not only allows for calculation of the MSEP, but it allows for calculation of any moment, quantile or risk measure.

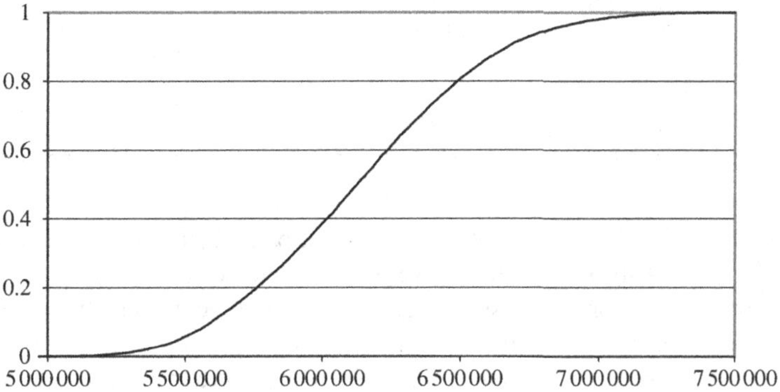

Figure 4.10 Posterior distribution of R, given $\mathcal{D}_I$

The conditional MSEP is then calculated as follows

$$\begin{aligned}
&\mathrm{msep}_{\sum_{i,j}X_{i,j}|\mathcal{D}_I}\left(\widehat{R}^{\mathrm{MCMC}}\right)\\
&=E\left[\left(\sum_{i=1}^{I}\sum_{j=I-i+1}^{J}X_{i,j}-\widehat{R}^{\mathrm{MCMC}}\right)^2\middle|\mathcal{D}_I\right]\\
&=\mathrm{Var}\left(\sum_{i=1}^{I}\sum_{j=I-i+1}^{J}X_{i,j}\middle|\mathcal{D}_I\right)\\
&=E\left[\mathrm{Var}\left(\sum_{i=1}^{I}\sum_{j=I-i+1}^{J}X_{i,j}\middle|\Theta\right)\middle|\mathcal{D}_I\right]+\mathrm{Var}\left(E\left[\sum_{i=1}^{I}\sum_{j=I-i+1}^{J}X_{i,j}\middle|\Theta\right]\middle|\mathcal{D}_I\right)\\
&=\sum_{i=1}^{I}\sum_{j=I-i+1}^{J}E\left[\phi\,\mu_i\,\gamma_j\middle|\mathcal{D}_I\right]+\mathrm{Var}\left(\sum_{i=1}^{I}\sum_{j=I-i+1}^{J}\mu_i\,\gamma_j\middle|\mathcal{D}_I\right)
\end{aligned}\tag{4.55}$$

The first term on the right-hand side of (4.55) again corresponds to the process variance and the second term to the parameter uncertainty. Note that for the calculation of the process variance we average over the possible outcomes of the parameters. The full Bayesian approach (Table 4.20) should be compared to the example where we assume that the dispersion ϕ and the payout pattern γ_j are known (Table 4.14). Of course, we obtain now a larger MSEP because we have additional uncertainty in the unknown parameters ϕ and γ_j.

Table 4.20 Conditional MSEP in the full Bayesian approach

i	$\widehat{R}_i^{\mathrm{MCMC}}$	Process std dev.	Parameter error$^{1/2}$	Cond. msep$^{1/2}$
0				
1	14 561	25 285	1941	25 359
2	26 182	33 903	2786	34 017
3	35 252	39 339	3284	39 476
4	85 149	61 140	8223	61 691
5	154 595	82 380	14 246	83 603
6	285 183	111 894	28 713	115 519
7	476 356	144 602	43 692	151 058
8	1 097 241	219 482	103 329	242 589
9	3 944 595	416 119	381 330	564 418
Correlation term			99 573	99 573
Total	6 119 116	518 284	411 133	661 550

Note that the posterior distribution of the dispersion parameter ϕ reacts very sensitive on the choice of the prior distribution. Below we give three different choices (see Table 4.21). We observe that if the prior has a small variational coefficient then, the posterior mean of the dispersion ϕ stays close to the prior mean. This indicates that the volatility in the observations for the dispersion is rather high. Such a picture may have several reasons, maybe the variational coefficient in the dispersion is high, but it could also indicate that choosing a constant dispersion for all accident years is not the correct model. In that case we should model the dispersion individually for different cells, columns or rows. On the other hand, one always needs carefully consider the question about overparametrization.

Table 4.21 Posterior distribution of the dispersion for different choices of the prior

	Version 1	Version 2	Version 3
φ_1	400	400	20
φ_2	0.0100	0.0267	0.0013
$E[\phi]$	40 000	15 000	15 000
$\mathrm{Vco}(\phi)$	5.0%	5.0%	22.4%
$E[\phi \mid \mathcal{D}_I]$	43 895	17 080	44 027
$\mathrm{Vco}(\phi \mid \mathcal{D}_I)$	6.1%	5.9%	17.0%

One should also notice that if we choose a rather high variational coefficient for the prior distribution, then the posterior mean of the dispersion is between 40 000 and 50 000. □

Remarks 4.52

- Though the MH algorithm is simple in nature and easily implemented, it hides the fact that if one does not choose the proposal distribution carefully then the algorithm only gives a very slow convergence to the stationary distribution. Hence, there have been several studies regarding the optimal scaling of proposal distributions to ensure optimal convergence rates, minimizing in practice the length of the Markov Chain that must be simulated to ensure accurate estimates using samples from the chain (burn-in costs).

Robert and Casella (2004), Gelman *et al.* (1997) and Roberts and Rosenthal (2001) have published theoretical results for optimal scaling problems in MH algorithms with Gaussian proposals. For d-dimensional target distributions with i.i.d. components, the asymptotic acceptance rate optimizing the efficiency of the process is 0.234, independent of the target density. Therefore, standard deviations of proposals are often chosen such to ensure that the acceptance probability is roughly close to 0.234. This number is the acceptance probability obtained for asymptotically optimal acceptance rates for MH algorithms when applied to multidimensional target distributions with scaling terms possibly depending on the dimension. To obtain this acceptance rate, one is required to perform some tuning of the proposal variance prior to final simulations. This tuning can be time consuming.

- Note that in the acceptance probability all terms disappear that come from a uniform distribution with fixed parameters if there is no conflict of domains.
- The Gibbs sampler is a special case where the acceptance probability is 1 and the proposal is the full conditional distribution of the parameter of interest.
- In our examples we have assumed independence between the different parameter distributions. Note, that we could impose any dependence structure between the parameters, which then easily gives a model with dependent risk factors. Moreover, we have only studied a one-dimensional reserving problem (one single claims development triangle). Using MCMC methods we can easily study families of dependent portfolios (multivariate problems).
- There is specialized software for implementing MCMC methods. The most commonly used are the BUGS and WinBUGS software packages that can be freely downloaded, see Spiegelhalter *et al.* (1995) and Scollnik (2001).

4.5 BÜHLMANN–STRAUB CREDIBILITY MODEL

In Subsection 4.3.2 we have seen an exact Bayesian approach to the claims reserving problem. The Bayesian estimator

$$\widetilde{\mu(\Theta_i)} = E\left[\mu(\Theta_i) \,|\, X_{i,0}, \ldots, X_{i,I-i}\right]$$

is the best estimator for $\mu(\Theta_i)$ in the class of all estimators which are square integrable functions of the observations $X_{i,0}, \ldots, X_{i,I-i}$. The crucial point in the calculation was that – from the EDF with its associated conjugates – we were able to explicitly calculate the posterior distribution of $\mu(\Theta_i)$. Moreover, the parameters of the posterior distribution and the Bayesian estimator were linear in the observations. However, in most of the Bayesian models we are not in the situation where we are able to calculate the posterior distribution, and therefore the Bayesian estimator cannot be expressed in a closed analytical form. This means, in general, that the Bayesian estimator does not meet the practical requirements of simplicity and intuitiveness and can only be calculated by numerical procedures such as Markov Chain Monte Carlo (MCMC) methods, see Section 4.4.

If we want to obtain analytical solution, we may also derive the Bayesian estimator, where we restrict the class of possible estimators to a smaller class, in which estimators are linear functions of the observations $X_{i,0}, \ldots, X_{i,I-i}$. In other words, we try to get an estimator that minimizes the quadratic loss function among all estimators that are linear combinations of the observations $X_{i,0}, \ldots, X_{i,I-i}$. The result will be an estimator that is practical and intuitive. This approach is well known in actuarial science as linear credibility theory, and since 'best' is also to be understood in the Bayesian sense, credibility estimators are linear Bayesian estimators (see Bühlmann and Gisler 2005).

In the claims reserving context credibility theory was used, for example, by De Vylder (1982), Neuhaus (1992), Mack (2000) and Gisler and Wüthrich (2007) in the Bühlmann and Straub context (see also Section 9.2).

In the following we always assume that the incremental loss development pattern $(\gamma_j)_{j=0,\ldots,J}$, given by

$$\gamma_0 = \beta_0 > 0 \quad \text{and} \quad \gamma_j = \beta_j - \beta_{j-1} > 0 \quad \text{for } j = 1, \ldots, J \tag{4.56}$$

is known.

We have the following assumptions:

Model Assumptions 4.53 (Bühlmann–Straub model, see Bühlmann and Gisler 2005)

- Conditionally, given Θ_i, the increments $X_{i,0}, \ldots, X_{i,J}$ are independent with

$$E\left[\left.\frac{X_{i,j}}{\gamma_j}\right|\Theta_i\right] = \mu(\Theta_i) \tag{4.57}$$

$$\mathrm{Var}\left(\left.\frac{X_{i,j}}{\gamma_j}\right|\Theta_i\right) = \frac{\sigma^2(\Theta_i)}{\gamma_j} \tag{4.58}$$

  for all $i = 0, \ldots, I$ and $j = 0, \ldots, J$.
- The pairs $(\Theta_i, \boldsymbol{X}_i)$ $(i = 0, \ldots, I)$ are independent, and the $\Theta_0, \ldots, \Theta_I$ are independent and identically distributed $(\boldsymbol{X}_i = (X_{i,0}, \ldots, X_{i,J})')$. □

For the cumulative claim amounts we obtain

$$E\left[C_{i,j}|\Theta_i\right] = \beta_j\ \mu(\Theta_i)$$
$$\mathrm{Var}\left(C_{i,j}|\Theta_i\right) = \beta_j\ \sigma^2(\Theta_i)$$

The latter equation shows that this model is different from Model Assumptions 4.14. The term $(1-\beta_j)\ \alpha^2(C_{i,J})$ is replaced by $\sigma^2(\Theta_i)$. On the other hand, the Bühlmann–Straub model is very much in the spirit of the EDF with its associated conjugates. However, we do not specify an explicit prior distribution for Θ_i, nor do we make an explicit choice for the distribution of the observations $X_{i,j}$, only the first two moments are determined. This is sufficient because we optimize the first two moments as linear functions of the observations. Again the parameter Θ_i plays the role of the underlying risk characteristics of accident year i, that is, it tells us whether we have a good or bad accident year. For a more detailed explanation in the framework of tariffication and pricing we refer to Bühlmann and Gisler (2005).

In the linear credibility theory one looks for an estimate $\widehat{\mu(\Theta_i)}$ of $\mu(\Theta_i)$ that minimizes the quadratic loss function among all estimators which are linear in the observations $X_{i,j}$ (see also Bühlmann and Gisler 2005, Definition 3.8). That is, one has to solve the optimization problem

$$\widehat{\mu(\Theta_i)}^{\text{cred}} = \mathrm{argmin}_{\widetilde{\mu} \in L(\mathbf{X},1)} E\left[\left(\mu(\Theta_i) - \widetilde{\mu}\right)^2\right] \tag{4.59}$$

where

$$L(\mathbf{X},1)=\left\{\widetilde{\mu};\ \widetilde{\mu}=a_{i,0}+\sum_{i=0}^{I}\sum_{j=0}^{I-i}a_{i,j}\ X_{i,j}\quad \text{with } a_{i,j}\in\mathbb{R}\right\} \tag{4.60}$$

Remarks 4.54

- Observe that the credibility estimator $\widehat{\mu(\Theta_i)}^{\text{cred}}$ is linear in the observations $X_{i,j}$ by definition. We could also allow for general real-valued, square integrable functions of the observations $X_{i,j}$. In that case we simply obtain the Bayesian estimator, since the conditional posterior expectation minimizes the quadratic loss function among all estimators which are a square integrable function of the observations.
- Credibility estimators can also be constructed using Hilbert space theory. Indeed (4.59) asks for a minimization in the L^2-sense, which corresponds to orthogonal projections in Hilbert spaces. For more on this topic we refer to Bühlmann and Gisler (2005).

We define the structural parameters

$$\begin{aligned}\mu_0 &= E\left[\mu(\Theta_i)\right]\\ \sigma^2 &= E\left[\sigma^2(\Theta_i)\right]\\ \tau^2 &= \operatorname{Var}\left(\mu(\Theta_i)\right)\end{aligned}$$

THEOREM 4.55 (inhomogeneous Bühlmann–Straub estimator) *Under Model Assumptions 4.53 the optimal linear inhomogeneous estimator of $\mu(\Theta_i)$, conditional on the observations $\mathcal{D}_I$, is given by*

$$\widehat{\mu(\Theta_i)}^{\text{cred}}=\alpha_i\ Y_i+(1-\alpha_i)\ \mu_0 \tag{4.61}$$

for $1\le i\le I$, where

$$\begin{aligned}\alpha_i &= \frac{\beta_{I-i}}{\beta_{I-i}+\sigma^2/\tau^2}\\ Y_i &= \sum_{j=0}^{I-i}\frac{\gamma_j}{\beta_{I-i}}\ \frac{X_{i,j}}{\gamma_j}=\frac{C_{i,I-i}}{\beta_{I-i}}\end{aligned} \tag{4.62}$$

In credibility theory the prior mean μ_0 can also be estimated from the data. This leads to the homogeneous credibility estimator.

THEOREM 4.56 (homogeneous Bühlmann–Straub estimator) *Under Model Assumptions 4.53 the optimal linear homogeneous estimator of $\mu(\Theta_i)$, conditional on the observations $\mathcal{D}_I$, is given by*

$$\widehat{\mu(\Theta_i)}^{\text{hom}}=\alpha_i\ Y_i+(1-\alpha_i)\ \widehat{\mu}_0 \tag{4.63}$$

for $1 \le i \le I$, where α_i and Y_i are given in Theorem 4.55 and

$$\widehat{\mu}_0 = \sum_{i=0}^{I} \frac{\alpha_i}{\alpha_\bullet} Y_i, \qquad \textit{with} \qquad \alpha_\bullet = \sum_{i=0}^{I} \alpha_i \tag{4.64}$$

Proof of Theorem 4.55 and Theorem 4.56 We refer to Theorems 4.2 and 4.4 in Bühlmann and Gisler (2005). □

Remarks 4.57

- If the prior mean μ_0 is known we choose the inhomogeneous credibility estimator $\widehat{\mu(\Theta_i)}^{\text{cred}}$ from Theorem 4.55. This estimator minimizes the quadratic loss function given in (4.59) among all estimators defined in (4.60).
- If the prior mean μ_0 is unknown, we estimate its value from the data. This is done by switching to the homogeneous credibility estimator $\widehat{\mu(\Theta_i)}^{\text{hom}}$ given in Theorem 4.56. The important point is that we have to change the set of possible estimators given in (4.60). The new set is defined as

$$L_e(\mathbf{X}) = \left\{ \widetilde{\mu}\,;\ \widetilde{\mu} = \sum_{i=0}^{I}\sum_{j=0}^{I-i} a_{i,j}\, X_{i,j} \text{ with } a_{i,j} \in \mathbb{R},\ E[\widetilde{\mu}] = \mu_0 \right\}$$

The homogeneous credibility estimator minimizes the quadratic loss function among all estimators from the set $L_e(\mathbf{X})$, that is,

$$\widehat{\mu(\Theta_i)}^{\text{hom}} = \operatorname{argmin}_{\widetilde{\mu} \in L_e(\mathbf{X})} E\left[(\mu(\Theta_i) - \widetilde{\mu})^2 \right]$$

- The credibility estimators (4.61) and (4.63) are weighted averages of Y_i, which in turn is a weighted average of the individual observations of accident year i, and the prior mean μ_0 and its estimator $\widehat{\mu}_0$, respectively. Observe that the weighted average Y_i only depends on the observations of accident year i. This is a consequence of the independence assumption between the accident years. However, the estimator $\widehat{\mu}_0$ uses the observations of all accident years since the prior mean μ_0 holds for all accident years. The credibility weight $\alpha_i \in [0, 1]$ for the weighted average of the individual observations Y_i becomes small when the expected fluctuations within the accidents years, σ^2, are large and becomes large if the fluctuations between the accident years, τ^2, are large.
- The estimator (4.61) is exactly the same as the one from the EDF with associated conjugates (Corollary 4.44) if we assume that all prior means μ_i are equal and $\delta = 0$.
- Since the inhomogeneous estimator $\widehat{\mu(\Theta_i)}^{\text{cred}}$ contains a constant, it is automatically an unbiased estimator for the prior mean μ_0. In contrast to $\widehat{\mu(\Theta_i)}^{\text{cred}}$, the homogeneous estimator $\widehat{\mu(\Theta_i)}^{\text{hom}}$ is unbiased for μ_0 by definition.
- The weights γ_j in the model assumptions could be replaced by weights $\gamma_{i,j}$, in which case the Bühlmann–Straub result still holds true. Indeed, one could choose a design matrix $\gamma_{i,j} = \Gamma_i(j)$ to apply the Bühlmann–Straub model (see Taylor 2000 and Mack 1990) and the variance condition is then replaced by

$$\operatorname{Var}\left(\frac{X_{i,j}}{\gamma_{j,i}} \middle| \Theta_i \right) = \frac{\sigma^2(\Theta_i)}{V_i\, \gamma_{j,i}^{\delta}}$$

where $V_i > 0$ is an appropriate measure for the volume and $\delta > 0$. $\delta = 1$ is the model favoured by Mack (1990), whereas De Vylder (1982) has chosen $\delta = 2$. For $\delta = 0$ we obtain a condition which is independent of j (credibility model of Bühlmann, see Bühlmann and Gisler 2005).

Different a priori *means* μ_i. If $X_{i,j}/\gamma_j$ has different *a priori* means μ_i for different accident years i, we modify the Bühlmann–Straub assumptions (4.57)–(4.58) according to

$$E\left[\frac{X_{i,j}}{\gamma_j\ \mu_i}\middle|\Theta_i\right] = \mu(\Theta_i) \tag{4.65}$$

$$\text{Var}\left(\frac{X_{i,j}}{\gamma_j\ \mu_i}\middle|\Theta_i\right) = \frac{\sigma^2(\Theta_i)}{\gamma_j\ \mu_i^\delta} \tag{4.66}$$

for an appropriate choice $\delta \geq 0$. In this case we have $E[\mu(\Theta_i)] = 1$ and the inhomogeneous and homogeneous credibility estimator are given by

$$\widehat{\mu(\Theta_i)}^{\text{cred}} = \alpha_i\ Y_i + (1-\alpha_i)\ 1$$

and

$$\widehat{\mu(\Theta_i)}^{\text{hom}} = \alpha_i\ Y_i + (1-\alpha_i)\ \widehat{\mu}_0$$

respectively, where

$$Y_i = \frac{C_{i,I-i}}{\mu_i\ \beta_{I-i}}, \qquad \alpha_i = \frac{\beta_{I-i}}{\beta_{I-i} + \kappa_i} \qquad \text{with} \quad \kappa_i = \frac{\sigma^2}{\mu_i^\delta\ \tau^2}$$

Observe that this now gives exactly the same estimator as in the EDF with its associated conjugates (see Corollary 4.44).

As a consequence, we obtain the following estimators:

ESTIMATOR 4.58 (Bühlmann–Straub credibility reserving estimator) *In the Bühlmann–Straub Model 4.53 with generalized assumptions* (4.65)–(4.66), *we have the following estimators*

$$\widehat{C_{i,J}}^{\text{cred}} = \widehat{E}\left[C_{i,J}\middle|\mathcal{D}_I\right] = C_{i,I-i} + (1-\beta_{I-i})\ \mu_i\ \widehat{\mu(\Theta_i)}^{\text{cred}}$$

$$\widehat{C_{i,J}}^{\text{hom}} = \widehat{E}\left[C_{i,J}\middle|\mathcal{D}_I\right] = C_{i,I-i} + (1-\beta_{I-i})\ \mu_i\ \widehat{\mu(\Theta_i)}^{\text{hom}}$$

for $1 \leq i \leq I$.

We obtain for the quadratic losses of the credibility estimators:

LEMMA 4.59 *In the Bühlmann–Straub Model 4.53, the quadratic losses for the credibility estimators are given by*

$$E\left[\left(\widehat{\mu(\Theta_i)}^{\text{cred}} - \mu(\Theta_i)\right)^2\right] = \tau^2\ (1-\alpha_i)$$

$$E\left[\left(\widehat{\mu(\Theta_i)}^{\text{hom}} - \mu(\Theta_i)\right)^2\right] = \tau^2\ (1-\alpha_i)\ \left(1+\frac{1-\alpha_i}{\alpha_\bullet}\right)$$

for $1 \le i \le I$.

Proof We refer to Theorems 4.3 and 4.6 in Bühlmann and Gisler (2005). □

This leads to the following MSEP of the inhomogeneous and homogeneous credibility reserving estimators:

COROLLARY 4.60 *In the Bühlmann–Straub Model 4.53 with generalized assumptions* (4.65)–(4.66)*, the MSEP of the inhomogeneous and homogeneous credibility reserving estimators are given by*

$$\text{msep}_{C_{i,J}}\left(\widehat{C_{i,J}}^{\text{cred}}\right) = \mu_i^2\ \left[(1-\beta_{I-i})\ \sigma^2/\mu_i^\delta + (1-\beta_{I-i})^2\ \tau^2\ (1-\alpha_i)\right]$$

and

$$\text{msep}_{C_{i,J}}\left(\widehat{C_{i,J}}^{\text{hom}}\right) = \text{msep}_{C_{i,J}}\left(\widehat{C_{i,J}}^{\text{cred}}\right) + \mu_i^2\ (1-\beta_{I-i})^2\ \tau^2\ \frac{(1-\alpha_i)^2}{\alpha_\bullet}$$

respectively, for $1 \le i \le I$.

Remarks 4.61

- The first term on the right-hand side of the above equations again stands for the process error, whereas the second terms stand for the parameter/prediction errors (how well can an actuary predict the mean?). Note that we assume that the incremental loss development pattern $(\gamma_j)_{j=0,\ldots,J}$ is known, and hence we do not consider the estimation error in the claims development pattern.
- Observe that the MSEP formula for the credibility estimator coincides with the one for the EDF, see (4.51).

Proof of Corollary 4.60 We rewrite the MSEP as follows

$$\text{msep}_{C_{i,J}}\left(\widehat{C_{i,J}}^{\text{cred}}\right) = E\left[\left((1-\beta_{I-i})\ \mu_i\ \widehat{\mu(\Theta_i)}^{\text{cred}} - (C_{i,J} - C_{i,I-i})\right)^2\right] \tag{4.67}$$

Conditionally on $\Theta = (\Theta_0, \ldots, \Theta_I)$, the increments $X_{i,j}$ are independent. But this immediately implies that the expression in (4.67) is equal to

$$E\left[E\left[(1-\beta_{I-i})^2\ \mu_i^2\ \left(\widehat{\mu(\Theta_i)}^{\text{cred}}-\mu(\Theta_i)\right)^2\middle|\Theta\right]\right]$$
$$+E\left[E\left[\left((1-\beta_{I-i})\ \mu_i\ \mu(\Theta_i)-(C_{i,J}-C_{i,I-i})\right)^2\middle|\Theta\right]\right]$$
$$=(1-\beta_{I-i})^2\ \mu_i^2\ \text{msep}_{\mu(\Theta_i)}\left(\widehat{\mu(\Theta_i)}^{\text{cred}}\right)+E\left[\text{Var}\left(C_{i,J}-C_{i,I-i}\middle|\Theta\right)\right]$$

But then the claim follows from Lemma 4.59 and

$$\text{Var}\left(C_{i,J}-C_{i,I-i}\middle|\Theta\right)=(1-\beta_{I-i})\ \mu_i^{2-\delta}\ \sigma^2(\Theta_i)$$

□

Parameter Estimation

So far, in our examples, the choice of the variance parameters was rather artificial. In this subsection we provide estimators for σ^2 and τ^2 under Model Assumptions 4.53. In practical applications it is often convenient to eliminate/truncate outliers for the estimation of σ^2 and τ^2, since the estimators below are not very robust.

Before we start with the parameter estimation we mention that in this section essentially the same remarks apply as those made on p. 130.

We need to estimate γ_j, σ^2 and τ^2. For the weights γ_j we proceed as in (4.52), that is, we use an 'ad hoc' or 'plug-in' estimate. At first, the claims development pattern β_j is estimated from (2.14), and the incremental loss development pattern γ_j is then obtained by (4.56).

We define

$$s_i^2=\frac{1}{I-i}\sum_{j=0}^{I-i}\gamma_j\ \left(\frac{X_{i,j}}{\gamma_j}-Y_i\right)^2$$

Then, s_i^2 is an unbiased estimator for σ^2 (see Bühlmann and Gisler 2005, (4.22)). Hence, σ^2 is estimated by the following unbiased estimator

$$\widehat{\sigma^2}=\frac{1}{I}\sum_{i=0}^{I-1}s_i^2 \tag{4.68}$$

For the estimation of τ^2 we define

$$T=\sum_{i=0}^{I}\frac{\beta_{I-i}}{\sum_k\beta_{I-k}}\ \left(Y_i-\overline{Y}\right)^2 \tag{4.69}$$

where

$$\overline{Y}=\frac{\sum_i\beta_{I-i}\ Y_i}{\sum_i\beta_{I-i}}=\frac{\sum_i C_{i,I-i}}{\sum_i\beta_{I-i}} \tag{4.70}$$

Then an unbiased estimator for τ^2 is given by (see Bühlmann and Gisler 2005, (4.26))

$$\widehat{\tau^2}=c\ \left\{T-\frac{I\ \sigma^2}{\sum_i\beta_{I-i}}\right\} \tag{4.71}$$

with

$$c = \left(\sum_{i=0}^{I} \frac{\beta_{I-i}}{\sum_k \beta_{I-k}} \left(1 - \frac{\beta_{I-i}}{\sum_k \beta_{I-k}} \right) \right)^{-1}$$

If $\widehat{\tau^2}$ is negative, it is set equal to zero.

When we work with different μ_i's, we have to slightly change the estimators (see Bühlmann and Gisler 2005, Section 4.8).

Example 4.62 (Bühlmann–Straub model, equal μ_i)

We revisit the data given in Example 2.7. Recall that we have set $\mathrm{Vco}(\mu(\Theta_i)) = 5\%$ and $\mathrm{Vco}(C_{i,J}) = 7.8\%$, using external know-how only (see Tables 4.9 and 4.4).

For this example we assume that all prior expectations μ_i are equal and we use the homogeneous credibility estimator. We have the following observations, where the incremental claims development pattern γ_j is estimated via the CL method (see Tables 4.22 and 4.23).

We obtain the following estimators:

$$c = 1.11316$$

$$\overline{Y} = 9\,911\,975$$

$$\widehat{\sigma} = 337\,289$$

$$\widehat{\tau} = 734\,887$$

$$\widehat{\mu}_0 = 9\,885\,584$$

Combining these estimates with $\widehat{\kappa} = \widehat{\sigma^2}/\widehat{\tau^2} = 21.1\%$, $\widehat{\mathrm{Vco}}(\mu(\Theta_i)) = \widehat{\tau}/\widehat{\mu}_0 = 7.4\%$ and $\widehat{\mathrm{Vco}}(C_{i,J}) = \left(\widehat{\sigma^2} + \widehat{\tau^2}\right)^{1/2} / \widehat{\mu}_0 = 8.2\%$ leads to the claims reserve estimates in Table 4.24.

We see that the estimates are close to those from the CL method, and this comes from the fact that the credibility weights are relatively large. Since $\widehat{\kappa}$ is rather small compared to $\widehat{\beta}_{I-i}$ we obtain credibility weights that are all greater than 70%. For credibility weights equal to 1 we simply obtain the CL estimate.

For the MSEP we obtain the values in Table 4.25. □

Example 4.63 (Bühlmann–Straub model, varying μ_i)

We continue in Example 4.62 but assume different prior means for different accident years. In particular, we use the prior means given in Table 4.6. We apply the scaled model (4.65)–(4.66) for $\delta = 0, 1, 2$ and present the reserve values in Table 4.26.

We see that the estimates for different δ's do not differ too much. However, they differ from the estimates for the equal μ_i case (see Table 4.24).

The estimated variational coefficient for $\delta = 0, 1, 2$ is

$$\widehat{\mathrm{Vco}}(\mu(\Theta_i)) \approx 6.8\%$$

It describes the accuracy of the estimate of the 'true' expected mean.

Moreover, we see (once more) that the prior estimate μ_i seems to be rather pessimistic, since $\widehat{\mu}_0$ is substantially smaller than 1 (for all δ). Table 4.27 shows the MSEP. □

Table 4.22 Observed historical cumulative claims $C_{i,j}$ and estimated CL factors $\widehat{f}_j$ (see Table 2.2)

	0	1	2	3	4	5	6	7	8	9
0	5 946 975	9 668 212	10 563 929	10 771 690	10 978 394	11 040 518	11 106 331	11 121 181	11 132 310	11 148 124
1	6 346 756	9 593 162	10 316 383	10 468 180	10 536 004	10 572 608	10 625 360	10 636 546	10 648 192	
2	6 269 090	9 245 313	10 092 366	10 355 134	10 507 837	10 573 282	10 626 827	10 635 751		
3	5 863 015	8 546 239	9 268 771	9 459 424	9 592 399	9 680 740	9 724 068			
4	5 778 885	8 524 114	9 178 009	9 451 404	9 681 692	9 786 916				
5	6 184 793	9 013 132	9 585 897	9 830 796	9 935 753					
6	5 600 184	8 493 391	9 056 505	9 282 022						
7	5 288 066	7 728 169	8 256 211							
8	5 290 793	7 648 729								
9	5 675 568									
$\widehat{f}_j$	1.4925	1.0778	1.0229	1.0148	1.0070	1.0051	1.0011	1.0010	1.0014	

Table 4.23 Observed scaled incremental claims $X_{i,j}/\gamma_j$ and estimated incremental claims development pattern $\widehat{\gamma}_j$

	0	1	2	3	4	5	6	7	8	9
0	10 086 719	12 814 544	13 090 078	9 577 303	14 357 308	9 048 371	12 901 245	13 793 367	10 658 637	11 148 124
1	10 764 791	11 179 404	10 569 215	6 997 504	4 710 946	5 331 290	10 340 861	10 390 677	11 152 804	
2	10 633 061	10 248 997	12 378 890	12 113 052	10 606 498	9 531 934	10 496 344	8 289 406		
3	9 944 313	9 240 019	10 559 131	8 788 679	9 236 259	12 866 767	8 493 606			
4	9 801 620	9 453 540	9 556 060	12 602 942	15 995 382	15 325 912				
5	10 490 085	9 739 738	8 370 426	11 289 335	7 290 128					
6	9 498 524	9 963 120	8 229 388	10 395 847						
7	8 969 136	8 402 801	7 716 853							
8	8 973 762	8 119 848								
9	9 626 383									
$\gamma_j(\%)$	59.0	29.0	6.8	2.2	1.4	0.7	0.5	0.1	0.1	0.1

Table 4.24 Claims reserves in the homogeneous Bühlmann–Straub model (equal μ_i)

i	α_i (%)	$\widehat{C_{i,J}}^{hom}$	Claims reserves CL	Claims reserves hom. cred.
0	82.6	11 148 124		
1	82.6	10 663 125	15 126	14 934
2	82.6	10 661 675	26 257	25 924
3	82.5	9 758 685	34 538	34 616
4	82.5	9 872 238	85 302	85 322
5	82.4	10 091 682	156 494	155 929
6	82.2	9 569 836	286 121	287 814
7	81.8	8 716 445	449 167	460 234
8	80.7	8 719 642	1 043 242	1 070 913
9	73.7	9 654 386	3 950 815	3 978 818
Total			6 047 061	6 114 503

Table 4.25 MSEP in the Bühlmann–Straub model (equal μ_i)

i	$\text{msep}^{1/2}_{C_{i,J}}\left(\widehat{C_{i,J}}^{cred}\right)$	$\text{msep}^{1/2}_{C_{i,J}}\left(\widehat{C_{i,J}}^{hom}\right)$
0		
1	12 711	12 711
2	16 755	16 755
3	20 095	20 096
4	31 465	31 467
5	42 272	42 278
6	59 060	59 076
7	78 301	78 339
8	123 114	123 259
9	265 775	267 229
Total	314 699	315 998

4.6 MULTIDIMENSIONAL CREDIBILITY MODELS

In Section 4.5 we assumed that the incremental claims had the following form

$$E\left[X_{i,j}|\Theta_i\right] = \mu(\Theta_i)\ \gamma_j$$

The constant γ_j denotes the claims ratio/development in period j. If we rewrite this in vector form we obtain

$$E\left[\mathbf{X}_i|\Theta_i\right] = \mu(\Theta_i)\ \gamma$$

where $\mathbf{X}_i = \left(X_{i,0}, \ldots, X_{i,J}\right)'$ and $\gamma = (\gamma_0, \ldots, \gamma_J)'$.

We see that the stochastic terms $\mu(\Theta_i)$ can only act as a scalar. If we would like to have more flexibility, we can replace $\mu(\Theta_i)$ by a vector. This then leads to a generalization of the classical one-dimensional Bühlmann–Straub model.

Table 4.26 Claims reserves in the homogeneous Bühlmann–Straub model (varying μ_i)

	Credibility weights α_i (%)			Reserves CL	Credibility reserves		
i	$\delta=0$	$\delta=1$	$\delta=2$		$\delta=0$	$\delta=1$	$\delta=2$
0	80.2	80.6	81.1				
1	80.1	80.2	80.3	15 126	14 943	14 944	14 944
2	80.1	79.6	79.1	26 257	25 766	25 753	25 740
3	80.1	79.1	78.0	34 538	34 253	34 238	34 222
4	80.0	79.7	79.3	85 302	85 056	85 051	85 046
5	79.9	80.2	80.4	156 494	156 562	156 561	156 559
6	79.7	79.8	80.0	286 121	289 078	289 056	289 035
7	79.3	79.0	78.8	449 167	460 871	461 021	461 180
8	78.1	77.6	77.0	1 043 242	1 069 227	1 069 815	1 070 427
9	70.4	71.0	71.5	3 950 815	4 024 687	4 023 270	4 021 903
Total				6 047 061	6 160 443	6 159 709	6 159 056
$\widehat{\mu_0}$	0.8810	0.8809	0.8809				

Table 4.27 MSEP in the Bühlmann–Straub model (varying μ_i)

	$\text{msep}^{1/2}_{C_{i,J}}\left(\widehat{C_{i,J}}^{\text{hom}}\right)$		
i	$\delta=0$	$\delta=1$	$\delta=2$
1	12 835	12 771	12 711
2	16 317	16 532	16 755
3	18 952	19 511	20 094
4	30 871	31 161	31 464
5	43 110	42 682	42 272
6	59 876	59 456	59 059
7	77 383	77 819	78 282
8	120 119	121 536	123 008
9	273 931	269 926	266 054
Total	320 377	317 540	314 889

4.6.1 Hachemeister Regression Model

The following model is a well-known multidimensional credibility model (Hachemeister 1975):

Model Assumptions 4.64 (Hachemeister regression model)

- There exist p-dimensional design vectors $\gamma_j(i) = (\gamma_{j,1}(i), \ldots, \gamma_{j,p}(i))'$ and random vectors $\mu(\Theta_i) = (\mu_1(\Theta_i), \ldots, \mu_p(\Theta_i))'$ ($p \leq J+1$) such that

$$
\begin{aligned}
E\left[X_{i,j} | \Theta_i\right] &= \gamma_j(i)' \, \mu(\Theta_i) \\
\mathrm{Cov}\left(X_{i,j}, X_{i,k} | \Theta_i\right) &= \Sigma_{j,k,i}(\Theta_i)
\end{aligned}
$$

for all $i \in \{0, \ldots, I\}$ and $j, k \in \{0, \ldots, J\}$.

- The $(J+1) \times p$ matrix $\Gamma_i = \left(\gamma_0(i)', \ldots, \gamma_J(i)'\right)'$ has rank p, and the components $\mu_1(\Theta_i), \ldots, \mu_p(\Theta_i)$ of $\mu(\Theta_i)$ are linearly independent.
- The pairs $(\Theta_i, \mathbf{X}_i)$ $(i = 0, \ldots, I)$ are independent, and the $\Theta_0, \ldots, \Theta_I$ are independent and identically distributed. □

Remarks 4.65

- We are now in the credibility regression case, see Bühlmann and Gisler (2005), Section 8.3, where $\mu(\Theta_i) = \left(\mu_1(\Theta_i), \ldots, \mu_p(\Theta_i)\right)'$ is a p-dimensional vector, which we would like to estimate.
- Γ_i is a known $(J+1) \times p$ design matrix.

We define the following parameters

$$\begin{aligned}
\mu &= E\left[\mu(\Theta_i)\right] \\
S_{j,k,i} &= E\left[\Sigma_{j,k,i}(\Theta_i)\right] \\
T &= \mathrm{Cov}\left(\mu(\Theta_i), \mu(\Theta_i)\right) \\
S_i &= \left(S_{j,k,i}\right)_{j,k=0,\ldots,J}
\end{aligned}$$

for $i \in \{0, \ldots, I\}$ and $j, k \in \{0, \ldots, J\}$. Hence, T is a $p \times p$ covariance matrix for the variability between the different accident years and S_i is a $(J+1) \times (J+1)$ matrix that describes the variability within accident year i. An important special case for S_i is given by

$$S_i = \sigma^2\, W_i^{-1} = \sigma^2\, \mathrm{diag}\left(w_{i,0}^{-1}, \ldots, w_{i,J}^{-1}\right) \tag{4.72}$$

for appropriate weights $w_{i,j} > 0$ and a scalar $\sigma^2 > 0$.

We assume that S_i has full rank.

THEOREM 4.66 (Hachemeister estimator) *Under Model Assumptions 4.64 and the assumption that all inverse matrices exist, the optimal linear inhomogeneous estimator for* $\mu(\Theta_i)$ *is given by*

$$\widehat{\mu(\Theta_i)}^{\text{cred}} = A_i\, \mathbf{B}_i + (1 - A_i)\, \mu \tag{4.73}$$

with

$$\begin{aligned}
A_i &= T\left(T + \left(\Gamma_i^{[I-i]'}\left(S_i^{[I-i]}\right)^{-1}\Gamma_i^{[I-i]}\right)^{-1}\right)^{-1} \\
\mathbf{B}_i &= \left(\Gamma_i^{[I-i]'}\left(S_i^{[I-i]}\right)^{-1}\Gamma_i^{[I-i]}\right)^{-1}\Gamma_i^{[I-i]'}\left(S_i^{[I-i]}\right)^{-1}\mathbf{X}_i^{[I-i]}
\end{aligned} \tag{4.74}$$

where

$$\Gamma_i^{[I-i]} = \left(\gamma_0(i)', \ldots, \gamma_{I-i}(i)'\right)'$$

$$S_i^{[I-i]} = (S_{j,k,i})_{j,k=0,\dots,\ I-i}$$
$$\mathbf{X}_i^{[I-i]} = (X_{i,0}, \dots, X_{i,I-i})'$$

for $1 \le i \le I$ *and* $p \le I-i+1$. *The quadratic loss matrix for the credibility estimator is given by*

$$E\left[\left(\widehat{\mu(\Theta_i)}^{\text{cred}} - \mu(\Theta_i)\right)\left(\widehat{\mu(\Theta_i)}^{\text{cred}} - \mu(\Theta_i)\right)'\right] = (1 - A_i)\ T \tag{4.75}$$

Proof See Theorem 8.7 in Bühlmann and Gisler (2005). □

We have the following corollary:

COROLLARY 4.67 (standard regression) *Under Model Assumption 4.64 with* S_i *given by* (4.72), *we have*

$$A_i = T\left(T + \sigma^2\left(\Gamma_i^{[I-i]'} W_i^{[I-i]} \Gamma_i^{[I-i]}\right)^{-1}\right)^{-1}$$
$$\mathbf{B}_i = \left(\Gamma_i^{[I-i]'} W_i^{[I-i]} \Gamma_i^{[I-i]}\right)^{-1} \Gamma_i^{[I-i]'} W_i^{[I-i]}\ \mathbf{X}_i^{[I-i]}$$

for $1 \le i \le I$ *with* $p \le I-i+1$ *and* $W_i^{[I-i]} = \text{diag}(w_{i,0}, \dots, w_{i,I-i})$.

This leads to the following reserve estimator:

ESTIMATOR 4.68 (Hachemeister credibility reserve estimator) *In the Hachemeister Regression Model 4.64 the estimator is given by*

$$\widehat{C_{i,J}}^{\text{cred}} = C_{i,I-i} + \sum_{j=I-i+1}^{J} \gamma_j(i)'\ \widehat{\mu(\Theta_i)}^{\text{cred}}$$

for $1 \le i \le I$ *with* $p \le I-i+1$.

Remarks 4.69

- Both covariance matrices T and S_i are positive definite. This immediately follows from the linear independence of the components $\mu_1(\Theta_i), \dots, \mu_p(\Theta_i)$ of $\mu(\Theta_i)$ and the full rank assumption for S_i, respectively. Moreover, the positive definiteness of $S_i = S_i^{[J]}$ implies the positive definiteness of all submatrices $S_i^{[0]}, \dots, S_i^{[J-1]}$ because there is an appropriate column vector $\mathbf{a} \in \mathbb{R}^{j+1}$ and a scalar $x \in \mathbb{R}$ for a fixed $j \in \{0, \dots, J-1\}$ so that it holds

$$(\mathbf{y}', 0)\ S_i^{[j+1]} \begin{pmatrix}\mathbf{y}\\0\end{pmatrix} = (\mathbf{y}', 0)\begin{pmatrix}S_i^{[j]} & \mathbf{a}\\ \mathbf{a}' & x\end{pmatrix}\begin{pmatrix}\mathbf{y}\\0\end{pmatrix} = \mathbf{y}'\ S_i^{[j]}\ \mathbf{y}$$

  for all column vectors $\mathbf{y} \in \mathbb{R}^{j+1}$. This means the positive definiteness of $S_i^{[j+1]}$ implies the positive definiteness of $S_i^{[j]}$ for all $j \in \{0, \dots, J-1\}$. An important special case which implies full rank (i.e. positive definiteness) for S_i is given by (4.72).

- If μ is not known, then (4.73) can be replaced by the homogeneous credibility estimator for $\mu(\Theta_i)$ using

$$\widehat{\mu} = \left(\sum_{i=0}^{I} A_i\right)^{-1} \sum_{i=0}^{I} A_i \mathbf{B}_i$$

In that case the right-hand side of (4.75) needs to be replaced by

$$(1 - A_i)\, T \left(1 + \left(\sum_{i=0}^{I} A_i'\right)^{-1} (1 - A_i')\right)$$

- (4.74) gives the formula for the data compression (see also Theorem 8.6 in Bühlmann and Gisler 2005). We already see from this that for $p > 1$ we have some difficulties with considering the youngest years since the dimension of μ is larger than the available number of observations if $p > I - i + 1$.

  Observe that

$$E\left[\mathbf{B}_i \middle| \Theta_i\right] = \mu(\Theta_i)$$

$$s_i = E\left[\left(\mathbf{B}_i - \mu(\Theta_i)\right)\left(\mathbf{B}_i - \mu(\Theta_i)\right)'\right] = \left(\Gamma_i^{[I-i]'} \left(S_i^{[I-i]}\right)^{-1} \Gamma_i^{[I-i]}\right)^{-1}$$

- ***Choices of the design matrix*** Γ_i There are various possibilities in the choice of design matrix Γ_i. One possibility used is the so-called Hoerl curve (see De Jong and Zehnwirth 1983 and Zehnwirth 1998), that means set $p = 3$ and

$$\gamma_j(i) = \left(1, \log(j+1), j\right)' \tag{4.76}$$

- ***Parameter estimation*** It is not straightforward to get good parameter estimates in this model for $p > 1$. If we assume that the covariance matrix $\left(\Sigma_{j,k,i}(\Theta_i)\right)_{j,k=0,\ldots,J}$ is diagonal with mean S_i given by (4.72), we can estimate S_i with the help of the one-dimensional Bühlmann–Straub model (see the parameter estimation section on p. 151). An unbiased estimator for the covariance matrix T is given by

$$\widehat{T} = \frac{1}{I-p} \sum_{i=0}^{I-p} E\left[\left(\mathbf{B}_i - \overline{\mathbf{B}}\right)\left(\mathbf{B}_i - \overline{\mathbf{B}}\right)'\right] - \frac{1}{I-p+1} \sum_{i=0}^{I-p} s_i$$

with

$$\overline{\mathbf{B}} = \frac{1}{I-p+1} \sum_{i=0}^{I-p} \mathbf{B}_i$$

- ***Examples*** In the examples we have looked at it was rather difficult to obtain reasonable estimates for the claims reserves due to a number of reasons: (1) there is no obvious choice for a good design matrix Γ_i; in our examples the Hoerl curve has not behaved well. (2) Estimation of the structural parameters S_i and T is always difficult. Moreover, they are not robust against outliers. (3) Slight perturbations of the data had a significant effect on the resulting reserves. For these reasons we do not give a real data example; that is, the Hachemeister model is very interesting from a theoretical point of view, but from a practical point of view it is rather difficult to apply it to real data.

4.6.2 Other Credibility Models

In the Bühlmann–Straub credibility model we had a deterministic cashflow pattern γ_j and have estimated the exposure $\mu(\Theta_i)$ of the accident years. We could also exchange the role of these two parameters.

Model Assumptions 4.70

There exist scalars μ_i $(i=0, \ldots, I)$ such that

- conditionally on Θ_i, we have for all $j \in \{0, \ldots, J\}$

$$E\left[X_{i,j}|\Theta_i\right] = \gamma_j(\Theta_i)\ \mu_i$$

- the pairs $(\Theta_i, \mathbf{X}_i)$ $(i=0, \ldots, I)$ are independent, and the $\Theta_0, \ldots, \Theta_I$ are independent and identically distributed. □

Remarks 4.71

- Now the whole vector $\gamma(\Theta_i) = \left(\gamma_0(\Theta_i), \ldots, \gamma_J(\Theta_i)\right)'$ is a random draw with

$$E\left[\gamma_j(\Theta_i)\right] = \gamma_j$$
$$\mathrm{Cov}\left(\gamma_j(\Theta_i), \gamma_k(\Theta_i)\right) = T_{j,k}$$
$$\mathrm{Cov}\left(X_{i,j}, X_{i,k}\middle|\, \Theta_i\right) = \Sigma_{j,k,i}(\Theta_i)$$

  This means that in this model we study uncertainties in the cashflow pattern.
- The difficulty in this model is that we have observations $X_{i,0}, \ldots, X_{i,I-i}$ for $\gamma_0(\Theta_i), \ldots, \gamma_{I-i}(\Theta_i)$ and we need to estimate $\gamma_{I-i+1}(\Theta_i), \ldots, \gamma_J(\Theta_i)$. Hence, we have to carefully put additional structure into our model that tells how the information in the upper triangle $\mathcal{D}_I$ is transported to the lower (unknown) triangle. From this it is clear that a crucial role is played by the covariance structure, which is used to project past observations to the future.
- It is difficult to give nice formulas for general covariance structures. Special cases were studied by Jewell (1976) and Hesselager and Witting (1988). Hesselager and Witting assume that the vectors

$$\gamma(\Theta_i) = \left(\gamma_0(\Theta_i), \ldots, \gamma_J(\Theta_i)\right)'$$

  are i.i.d. Dirichlet distributed with parameters $a_0, \ldots, a_J$. Define $a = \sum_{j=0}^{J} a_j$. We have (see Hesselager-Witting 1988, formula (3))

$$E\left[\gamma_j(\Theta_i)\right] = \gamma_j \;=\; \frac{a_j}{a}$$
$$\mathrm{Cov}\left(\gamma_j(\Theta_i), \gamma_k(\Theta_i)\right) = T_{j,k} \;=\; \frac{1}{1+a}\ \left(1_{j=k}\ \gamma_j - \gamma_j\ \gamma_k\right)$$

  If we then choose a specific form for the covariance structure $\Sigma_{j,k,i}(\Theta_i)$, we can work out a credibility formula for the expected ultimate claim.

Of course there is a large variety of other credibility models such as, for example, hierarchical credibility models (see Hesselager 1991), but we do not further discuss them here.

4.7 KALMAN FILTER

Kalman filters can (in some sense) be used as an enhancement of the credibility models presented above. We will treat only the one-dimensional case since, as we already have seen in the multivariate credibility context, it becomes difficult to go to real applications in higher dimensions.

In the present context we consider evolutionary credibility models. If we take, for example, the Bühlmann–Straub model, then it is assumed that the Θ_i $(i=0,\ldots,I)$ are independent and identically distributed (see Model Assumptions 4.53). Going back to Example 4.62, we obtain the following picture for the observations $Y_0,\ldots,Y_I$ and the estimate $\widehat{\mu}_0$ for the prior mean μ_0 (cf. (4.62) and (4.64), respectively): see Figure 4.11.

From Figure 4.11 it is not obvious that $\Theta=(\Theta_0,\Theta_1,\ldots)$ is a process of independent and identically distributed random variables. We could also have underwriting cycles that would suggest that neighbouring Θ_i's are dependent. Hence, we may assume that $\Theta=(\Theta_0,\Theta_1,\ldots)$ is a stochastic process of random variables which are not necessarily independent and identically distributed. For the Kalman filter one assumes that $\Theta=(\Theta_0,\Theta_1,\ldots)$ is a general stochastic process.

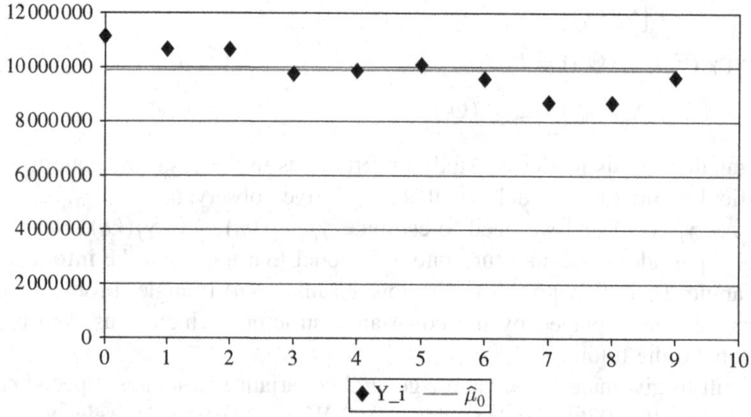

Figure 4.11 Observations Y_i, estimate $\widehat{\mu_0}$

Model Assumptions 4.72

- $\Theta=(\Theta_0,\Theta_1,\ldots)$ is a stochastic process.
- Conditionally on Θ, the increments $X_{i,j}$ are independent for all i, j with

$$E\left[\left.\frac{X_{i,j}}{\gamma_j}\right|\Theta\right]=\mu(\Theta_i) \tag{4.77}$$

$$\mathrm{Cov}\left(\left.\frac{X_{i,j}}{\gamma_j},\frac{X_{k,l}}{\gamma_l}\right|\Theta\right)=1_{\{i=k,j=l\}}\,\frac{\sigma^2(\Theta_i)}{\gamma_j} \tag{4.78}$$

- $\left(\mu(\Theta_i)\right)_{i\geq 0}$ is a martingale. □

Remarks 4.73

- Assumption (4.78) can be relaxed in the sense that we only need conditional uncorrelatedness on average Θ. Assumption (4.78) implies that we obtain an updating procedure that is recursive.
- The martingale assumption implies that we have uncorrelated centered increments $\mu(\Theta_{i+1}) - \mu(\Theta_i)$ (see also (1.4)),

$$E\left[\mu(\Theta_{i+1}) | \mu(\Theta_0), \ldots, \mu(\Theta_i)\right] = \mu(\Theta_i)$$

In Hilbert space language this reads as follows: The orthogonal projection of the random variable $\mu(\Theta_{i+1})$ onto the subspace of all square integrable functions of $\mu(\Theta_0), \ldots, \mu(\Theta_i)$ is simply $\mu(\Theta_i)$, that is, the process $\left(\mu(\Theta_i)\right)_{i\geq 0}$ has centred orthogonal increments. This last assumption could be generalized to linear transformations (see Corollary 9.5 in Bühlmann and Gisler 2005).

We introduce the following notation (motivated by the usual terminology from state space models; see, e.g., Abraham and Ledolter 1983).

$$\mathbf{Y}_i = \left(\frac{X_{i,0}}{\gamma_0}, \ldots, \frac{X_{i,I-i}}{\gamma_{I-i}}\right)$$

$$\mu_{i|i-1} = \operatorname{argmin}_{\widetilde{\mu}\in L(\mathbf{Y}_0,\ldots,\mathbf{Y}_{i-1},1)} E\left[\left(\mu(\Theta_i) - \widetilde{\mu}\right)^2\right]$$

$$\mu_{i|i} = \operatorname{argmin}_{\widetilde{\mu}\in L(\mathbf{Y}_0,\ldots,\mathbf{Y}_{i},1)} E\left[\left(\mu(\Theta_i) - \widetilde{\mu}\right)^2\right]$$

(cf. (4.60)). $\mu_{i|i-1}$ is the best linear forecast for $\mu(\Theta_i)$ based on the information $\mathbf{Y}_0, \ldots, \mathbf{Y}_{i-1}$, whereas $\mu_{i|i}$ is the best linear forecast for $\mu(\Theta_i)$ which is additionally based on $\mathbf{Y}_i$. Hence, there are two updating procedures:

(1) updating from $\mu_{i|i-1}$ to $\mu_{i|i}$ on the basis of the newest observation $\mathbf{Y}_i$ and
(2) updating from $\mu_{i|i}$ to $\mu_{i+1|i}$ due to the parameter movement from $\mu(\Theta_i)$ to $\mu(\Theta_{i+1})$.

We define the following structural parameters:

$$\sigma^2 = E\left[\sigma^2(\Theta_i)\right]$$

$$\delta_i^2 = \operatorname{Var}\left(\mu(\Theta_i) - \mu(\Theta_{i-1})\right)$$

$$q_{i|i-1} = E\left[\left(\mu_{i,i-1} - \mu(\Theta_i)\right)^2\right]$$

$$q_{i|i} = E\left[\left(\mu_{i,i} - \mu(\Theta_i)\right)^2\right]$$

THEOREM 4.74 (Kalman filter recursion formula, Theorem 9.6 in Büllmann and Gisler 2005) *Under Model Assumptions 4.72 we have*

(1) *Anchoring* $(i=0)$

$$\mu_{0|-1} = \mu_0 = E\left[\mu(\Theta_0)\right] \quad \textit{and} \quad q_{0|-1} = \tau_0^2 = \operatorname{Var}\left(\mu(\Theta_0)\right)$$

(2) *Recursion* ($i \geq 0$)

(a) *Observation update:*

$$\mu_{i|i} = \alpha_i \; Y_i + (1-\alpha_i) \; \mu_{i|i-1}$$
$$q_{i|i} = (1-\alpha_i) \; q_{i|i-1}$$

with

$$\alpha_i = \frac{\beta_{I-i}}{\beta_{I-i} + \sigma^2 / q_{i|i-1}}$$
$$Y_i = \sum_{j=0}^{I-i} \frac{\gamma_j}{\beta_{I-i}} \frac{X_{i,j}}{\gamma_j} = \frac{C_{i,I-i}}{\beta_{I-i}} \tag{4.79}$$

(b) *Parameter update:*

$$\mu_{i+1|i} = \mu_{i|i} \quad \text{and} \quad q_{i+1|i} = q_{i|i} + \delta^2_{i+1}$$

Proof For the proof we refer to Theorem 9.6 in Bühlmann and Gisler (2005). □

This leads to the following reserve estimator:

ESTIMATOR 4.75 (Kalman filter reserve estimator) *Under Model Assumptions 4.72 the estimator for the ultimate claim* $C_{i,J}$, *conditioned on* $\mathcal{D}_I$, *is given by*

$$\widehat{C_{i,J}}^{\text{Ka}} = \widehat{E}\left[C_{i,J} \middle| \mathcal{D}_I\right] = C_{i,I-i} + (1-\beta_{I-i}) \; \mu_{i|i}$$

for $1 \leq i \leq I$.

Remarks 4.76

- In practice we face two difficulties: (1) We need to estimate all the parameters. (2) We need 'good' estimates for the starting values μ_0 and τ_0^2 for the iteration.
- Parameter estimation: For the estimation of σ^2 we choose $\widehat{\sigma^2}$ as in the Bühlmann–Straub model (see (4.68)). The estimation of δ_i^2 is less straightforward; in fact we define a special case of Model Assumptions 4.72.
- Instead of plug-in estimates for the parameters we could also use a full Bayesian approach modelling all unknown parameters with prior distributions. This approach then needs to be solved numerically.

Model Assumptions 4.77 (Gerber and Jones (1975))

- Model Assumptions 4.72 hold.
- There exists a sequence $(\epsilon_i)_{i\geq 1}$ of independent random variables with $E[\epsilon_i]=0$ and $\mathrm{Var}(\epsilon_i)=\delta^2$ such that

$$\mu(\Theta_i)=\mu(\Theta_{i-1})+\epsilon_i$$

  for all $i\geq 1$.
- $\mu(\Theta_0)$ and ϵ_i are independent for all $i\geq 1$. □

Remark In this model holds, $\delta_i^2=\mathrm{Var}\big(\mu(\Theta_i)-\mu(\Theta_{i-1})\big)=\mathrm{Var}(\epsilon_i)=\delta^2$.

Let us first calculate the variances and covariances of Y_i defined in (4.79).

$$\begin{aligned}\mathrm{Var}(Y_i)&=\mathrm{Var}\big(E\,[Y_i|\,\Theta]\big)+E\big[\mathrm{Var}\,(Y_i|\,\Theta)\big]\\&=\mathrm{Var}\big(\mu(\Theta_i)\big)+E\left[\sum_{j=0}^{I-i}\frac{\gamma_j^2}{\beta_{I-i}^2}\,\mathrm{Var}\left(\frac{X_{i,j}}{\gamma_j}\middle|\,\Theta\right)\right]\\&=\mathrm{Var}\big(\mu(\Theta_0)\big)+i\;\delta^2+\frac{1}{\beta_{I-i}}\;\sigma^2\end{aligned}$$

For $i>l$,

$$\begin{aligned}\mathrm{Cov}(Y_i,Y_l)&=\mathrm{Cov}\big(E\,[Y_i|\,\Theta]\,,E\,[Y_l|\,\Theta]\big)+E\big[\mathrm{Cov}\,(Y_i,Y_l|\,\Theta)\big]\\&=\mathrm{Cov}\big(\mu(\Theta_i),\mu(\Theta_l)\big)\\&=\mathrm{Cov}\left(\mu(\Theta_l)+\sum_{k=l+1}^{i}\epsilon_k,\mu(\Theta_l)\right)\\&=\mathrm{Var}\big(\mu(\Theta_0)\big)+l\;\delta^2\end{aligned}$$

We define $\overline{Y}$ as in (4.70) with $\beta_\bullet=\sum_{i=0}^{I}\beta_{I-i}$. Hence,

$$\begin{aligned}\sum_{i=0}^{I}\frac{\beta_{I-i}}{\beta_\bullet}\;E\left[\left(Y_i-\overline{Y}\right)^2\right]&=\sum_{i=0}^{I}\frac{\beta_{I-i}}{\beta_\bullet}\;\mathrm{Var}\left(Y_i-\frac{\sum_{k=0}^{I}\beta_{I-k}\;Y_k}{\beta_\bullet}\right)\\&=\sum_{i=0}^{I}\frac{\beta_{I-i}}{\beta_\bullet}\;\mathrm{Var}(Y_i)-\sum_{k,i=0}^{I}\frac{\beta_{I-k}\,\beta_{I-i}}{\beta_\bullet^2}\;\mathrm{Cov}(Y_k,Y_i)\\&=\frac{(I+1)\;\sigma^2}{\beta_\bullet}+\delta^2\;\sum_{i=0}^{I}\left(i\;\frac{\beta_{I-i}}{\beta_\bullet}-\sum_{k=0}^{I}\min\{i,k\}\;\frac{\beta_{I-k}\,\beta_{I-i}}{\beta_\bullet^2}\right)\\&=\frac{(I+1)\;\sigma^2}{\beta_\bullet}+\delta^2\;\sum_{i=0}^{I}\sum_{k=0}^{i-1}(i-k)\;\frac{\beta_{I-k}\,\beta_{I-i}}{\beta_\bullet^2}\end{aligned}$$

This motivates the following unbiased estimator for δ^2 (see also (4.69)):

$$\widehat{\delta^2} = \left(\sum_{i=0}^{I} \sum_{k=0}^{i-1} (i-k) \frac{\beta_{I-k}\, \beta_{I-i}}{\beta_\bullet^2} \right)^{-1} \left(\sum_{i=0}^{I} \frac{\beta_{I-i}}{\beta_\bullet} \left(Y_i - \overline{Y}\right)^2 - \frac{(I+1)\, \sigma^2}{\beta_\bullet} \right)$$
$$= c^* \left(T - \frac{(I+1)\, \sigma^2}{\beta_\bullet} \right) \tag{4.80}$$

with

$$c^* = \left(\sum_{i,k=0}^{I} \max\{i-k, 0\} \frac{\beta_{I-i}\, \beta_{I-k}}{\beta_\bullet^2} \right)^{-1}$$

Observe that expression (4.80) is similar to the estimator of τ^2 in the Bühlmann–Straub model (4.71). The difference lies in the constant.

Example 4.78 (Kalman filter)

We revisit Example 4.62 under the Gerber and Jones (1975) model (Model Assumptions 4.77), and obtain the following parameter estimates:

$$c^* = 0.62943$$
$$\overline{Y} = 9\,911\,975$$
$$\widehat{\sigma} = 337\,289$$
$$\widehat{\delta} = 545\,637$$

We start the iteration (Table 4.28) with the estimates

$$\widehat{\mu}_0 = 9\,885\,584 \qquad \text{and} \qquad \widehat{\tau}_0 = \widehat{\delta} = 545\,637$$

(see also (4.64)).

Table 4.28 Iteration in the Kalman filter

i	$\mu_{i\|i-1}$	$q_{i\|i-1}^{1/2}$	α_i (%)	Y_i	$\mu_{i\|i}$	$q_{i\|i}^{1/2}$	$\mu_{i+1\|i}$	$q_{i+1\|i}^{1/2}$
0	9 885 584	545 637	72.4	11 148 123	10 799 066	286 899	10 799 066	616 466
1	10 799 066	616 466	76.9	10 663 316	10 694 625	296 057	10 694 625	620 781
2	10 694 625	620 781	77.2	10 662 005	10 669 454	296 651	10 669 454	621 064
3	10 669 454	621 064	77.2	9 758 602	9 966 628	296 805	9 966 628	621 138
4	9 966 628	621 138	77.1	9 872 213	9 893 857	297 401	9 893 857	621 423
5	9 893 857	621 423	77.0	10 092 241	10 046 550	298 230	10 046 550	621 820
6	10 046 550	621 820	76.7	9 568 136	9 679 468	299 967	9 679 468	622 655
7	9 679 468	622 655	76.4	8 705 370	8 935 539	302 670	8 935 539	623 962
8	8 935 539	623 962	75.1	8 691 961	8 752 681	311 533	8 752 681	628 309
9	8 752 681	628 309	67.2	9 626 366	9 339 528	360 009	9 339 528	653 702

Table 4.29 CL reserves, homogeneous Bühlmann–Straub and Kalman filter reserves

		Claims reserves		
i	$\widehat{C_{i,J}}^{Ka}$	CL	hom. cred.	Kalman
0	11 148 123	0	0	0
1	10 663 360	15 126	14 934	15 170
2	10 662 023	26 257	25 924	26 275
3	9 759 339	34 538	34 616	35 274
4	9 872 400	85 302	85 322	85 489
5	10 091 532	156 494	155 929	155 785
6	9 571 465	286 121	287 814	289 450
7	8 717 246	449 167	460 234	461 042
8	8 699 249	1 043 242	1 070 913	1 050 529
9	9 508 643	3 950 815	3 978 818	3 833 085
Total		6 047 061	6 114 503	5 952 100

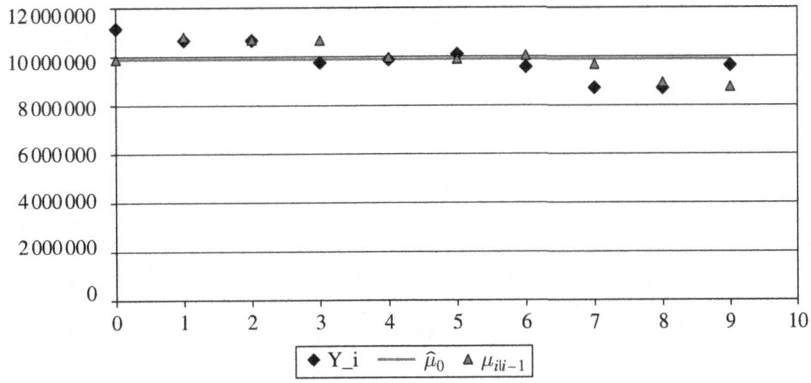

Figure 4.12 Observations Y_i, estimate $\widehat{\mu_0}$ and estimates $\mu_{i|i-1}$

In this example, the credibility weights in Table 4.28 are smaller compared to the Bühlmann–Straub model (see Table 4.24). However, they are still fairly high, which means that the prior value $\mu_{i|i-1}$ will move closely with the observations Y_{i-1}. Hence, we are now able to model dependent time-series, where the prior value incorporates the past observed loss ratios; see Figure 4.12 and Tables 4.28 and 4.29. □

5 Distributional Models

Many of the models we have considered in the previous chapters were so-called distribution-free models, that is, we have not specified explicit probability distributions (e.g. in the CL methods in Chapter 3 or in the credibility estimates in Sections 4.5–4.7) but we have specified the estimators using methods of moments. For the Bayesian models in Subsection 4.3.2 we considered the EDF with associated conjugates to enable us to calculate the interesting quantities in a closed form using posterior moments. In this chapter we present some models that depend on explicit choices of probability distributions (for incremental or cumulative claims).

In that sense this chapter has three purposes: (1) it gives explicit distributional models for simulations, (2) it does some preparatory work for Chapter 6 on generalized linear models (GLM) and (3) it gives some recreation before we go to the GLM approaches.

However, we would like to stress item (1). Explicit distributional models make it possible to use simulations. So far, we have only used simulations in Section 4.4 on MCMC methods. In most distributional models, analytical calculations do not go beyond second moments. Henceforth, when one is interested in higher moments, quantiles or risk measures for example, one needs to apply numerical algorithms using explicit distributional assumptions.

On the other hand, we would also like to mention that practitioners are often satisfied by second moments. Usually, they have 'a good feeling/experience' about reasonable ranges for variational coefficients. Then, they fit a distribution (like Gamma or Log-normal distribution) to the overall reserves using the method of moments. This approach may not seem consistent from a mathematical point of view, however, it often leads to very reasonable results.

5.1 LOG-NORMAL MODEL FOR CUMULATIVE CLAIMS

In this section we consider a model that was first considered by Hertig (1985) and described in Taylor (2000), Section 7.3 and De Jong (2006). The model considers cumulative claims and Log-normal distributions; it is assumed that the individual CL factors $F_{i,j} = C_{i,j}/C_{i,j-1}$ are Log-normally distributed. We derive different unbiased and biased estimators, depending on whether the variance parameter σ^2 is known or unknown.

Model Assumptions 5.1 (Log-normal model, cumulative claims)

- The individual development factors $F_{i,j} = C_{i,j}/C_{i,j-1}$ are Log-normally distributed with deterministic parameters ξ_j and σ_j^2, that is,

$$\eta_{i,j} = \log(F_{i,j}) \overset{(d)}{\sim} \mathcal{N}(\xi_j, \sigma_j^2) \tag{5.1}$$

  for all $i \in \{0, \ldots, I\}$ and $j \in \{0, \ldots, J\}$. We set $C_{i,-1} = 1$.
- $\eta_{i,j}$ are independent for $i \in \{0, \ldots, I\}$ and $j \in \{0, \ldots, J\}$. □

Remark See appendix, Sections A.2.2 and A.2.3, for the definition of the Normal distribution $\mathcal{N}(\mu, \sigma^2)$ and the Log-normal distribution $\mathcal{LN}(\mu, \sigma^2)$, respectively.

If $\left(F_{i,j}\right)_{0\le j\le J}$ satisfies Model Assumptions 5.1 we have

$$E\left[F_{i,j}\right] = \exp\{\xi_j + \frac{1}{2}\sigma_j^2\}$$
$$\mathrm{Var}\left(F_{i,j}\right) = \exp\{2\xi_j + \sigma_j^2\}\ \left(\exp\{\sigma_j^2\} - 1\right)$$

LEMMA 5.2 *Under Model Assumptions 5.1, the CL assumption* (3.2) *is satisfied with CL factor* $f_{j-1} = \exp\left\{\xi_j + \frac{1}{2}\sigma_j^2\right\}$.

Proof Model Assumptions 5.1 imply

$$E\left[C_{i,j}\middle| C_{i,j-1}\right] = C_{i,j-1}\ E\left[F_{i,j}\middle| C_{i,j-1}\right] = C_{i,j-1}\ \exp\left\{\xi_j + \frac{1}{2}\sigma_j^2\right\}$$ □

However, the variance function is different from the one in distribution-free CL Model 3.2, namely

$$\mathrm{Var}\left(C_{i,j}\middle| C_{i,j-1}\right) = C_{i,j-1}^2\ \mathrm{Var}\left(F_{i,j}\middle| C_{i,j-1}\right)$$
$$= C_{i,j-1}^2\ \exp\{2\xi_j + \sigma_j^2\}\ \left(\exp\{\sigma_j^2\} - 1\right)$$

Hence Model Assumptions 5.1 imply a CL link-ratio model with CL factors $f_{j-1} = \exp\left\{\xi_j + \sigma_j^2/2\right\}$ but with a different variance function compared to Model 3.2. Moreover, observe that the distribution of the individual development factors $F_{i,j}$ does not depend on $C_{i,j-1}$, this has direct consequences in the calculations of the MSEP.

Parameter Estimation

We estimate the parameters ξ_j and σ_j^2 as follows

$$\widehat{\xi}_j = \frac{1}{I-j+1} \sum_{i=0}^{I-j} \log\left(\frac{C_{i,j}}{C_{i,j-1}}\right) \tag{5.2}$$

$$\widehat{\sigma_j^2} = \frac{1}{I-j} \sum_{i=0}^{I-j} \left(\log\left(\frac{C_{i,j}}{C_{i,j-1}}\right) - \widehat{\xi}_j\right)^2 \tag{5.3}$$

For these estimators we have the following lemma.

LEMMA 5.3 *Under Model Assumptions 5.1 we have*

$$\widehat{\xi}_j \stackrel{(d)}{\sim} \mathcal{N}\left(\xi_j, \frac{\sigma_j^2}{I-j+1}\right) \tag{5.4}$$

$$\frac{I-j}{\sigma_j^2}\,\widehat{\sigma_j^2} \stackrel{(d)}{\sim} \chi^2_{I-j} \tag{5.5}$$

where χ^2_{I-j} is the χ^2-distribution with $I-j$ degrees of freedom. Moreover, $\widehat{\xi}_j$ and $\widehat{\sigma_j^2}$ are stochastically independent.

Proof The first part, formula (5.4), easily follows from Model Assumptions 5.1. The other part is a special case of the well-known Theorem of Cochran. See Hogg and Craig (1995), pp. 214–216 for a simple proof of this special case. □

Remark The χ^2-distribution with n degrees of freedom ($n \in \mathbb{N}$) is the Gamma distribution $\Gamma(\gamma, c)$ with $\gamma = n/2$ and $c = \frac{1}{2}$. For the definition of the Gamma distribution see appendix, Subsection A.2.4.

First, we consider the random variables on the Log-scale (additive model). We define

$$Z_{i,j} = \log(C_{i,j}) \tag{5.6}$$

Observe that

$$Z_{i,J} = Z_{i,I-i} + \sum_{j=I-i+1}^{J} \log\left(\frac{C_{i,j}}{C_{i,j-1}}\right) = Z_{i,I-i} + \sum_{j=I-i+1}^{J} \eta_{i,j} \tag{5.7}$$

Hence, we obtain, with (5.1) and (5.4)

$$E\left[Z_{i,J}\middle|\mathcal{D}_I\right] = Z_{i,I-i} + \sum_{j=I-i+1}^{J} \xi_j$$

which is estimated by

$$\widehat{Z_{i,J}} = \widehat{E}\left[Z_{i,J}\middle|\mathcal{D}_I\right] = Z_{i,I-i} + \sum_{j=I-i+1}^{J} \widehat{\xi}_j \tag{5.8}$$

LEMMA 5.4 *Under Model Assumptions 5.1 we have*

(a) *given $Z_{i,I-i}$, $\widehat{Z_{i,J}}$ is an unbiased estimator for $E\left[Z_{i,J}\middle|\mathcal{D}_I\right] = E\left[Z_{i,J}\middle|Z_{i,I-i}\right]$,*
(b) *$\widehat{Z_{i,J}}$ is (unconditionally) unbiased for $E\left[Z_{i,J}\right]$,*
(c) *the conditional MSEP is given by*

$$\text{msep}_{Z_{i,J}|\mathcal{D}_I}\left(\widehat{Z_{i,J}}\right) = \sum_{j=I-i+1}^{J} \sigma_j^2 + \left(\sum_{j=I-i+1}^{J} \left(\widehat{\xi}_j - \xi_j\right)\right)^2 \quad \textit{and}$$

(d) *the unconditional MSEP is given by*

$$\mathrm{msep}_{Z_{i,J}}\left(\widehat{Z_{i,J}}\right)=\mathrm{msep}_{Z_{i,J}|Z_{i,I-i}}\left(\widehat{Z_{i,J}}\right)=\sum_{j=I-i+1}^{J}\sigma_j^2\left(1+\frac{1}{I-j+1}\right)$$

Proof (a) Using (5.1) and (5.4), we have

$$E\left[\widehat{Z_{i,J}}-Z_{i,J}\middle|Z_{i,I-i}\right]=E\left[\sum_{j=I-i+1}^{J}\widehat{\xi_j}\right]-E\left[\sum_{j=I-i+1}^{J}\eta_{i,j}\right]=0 \tag{5.9}$$

(b) This follows immediately from (a).
(c) Using the Model Assumptions 5.1 we have for the conditional MSEP

$$\begin{aligned}
\mathrm{msep}_{Z_{i,J}|\mathcal{D}_I}\left(\widehat{Z_{i,J}}\right)&=E\left[\left(\widehat{Z_{i,J}}-Z_{i,J}\right)^2\middle|\mathcal{D}_I\right]\\
&=E\left[\left(\sum_{j=I-i+1}^{J}\widehat{\xi_j}-\sum_{j=I-i+1}^{J}\eta_{i,j}\right)^2\middle|\mathcal{D}_I\right]\\
&=\mathrm{Var}\left(\sum_{j=I-i+1}^{J}\eta_{i,j}\right)+\left(\sum_{j=I-i+1}^{J}\left(\widehat{\xi_j}-\xi_j\right)\right)^2\\
&=\sum_{j=I-i+1}^{J}\sigma_j^2+\left(\sum_{j=I-i+1}^{J}\left(\widehat{\xi_j}-\xi_j\right)\right)^2
\end{aligned}$$

(d) Observe that $\widehat{Z_{i,J}}-Z_{i,J}$ is independent of $Z_{i,I-i}$. Using Lemma 5.3, this implies that

$$\begin{aligned}
\mathrm{msep}_{Z_{i,J}|Z_{i,I-i}}\left(\widehat{Z_{i,J}}\right)=\mathrm{msep}_{Z_{i,J}}\left(\widehat{Z_{i,J}}\right)&=E\left[\mathrm{msep}_{Z_{i,J}|\mathcal{D}_I}\left(\widehat{Z_{i,J}}\right)\right]\\
&=\mathrm{Var}\left(\sum_{j=I-i+1}^{J}\eta_{i,j}\right)+\mathrm{Var}\left(\sum_{j=I-i+1}^{J}\widehat{\xi_j}\right)\\
&=\sum_{j=I-i+1}^{J}\sigma_j^2\left(1+\frac{1}{I-j+1}\right)
\end{aligned} \tag{5.10}$$

This completes the proof. □

Remark Observe that $Z_{i,I-i}=\log(C_{i,I-i})$ cancels out in this (additive) model (cf. (5.9)–(5.10)). This is different from the multiplicative models like the CL model 3.2.

5.1.1 Known variances σ_j^2

In this subsection we assume that the variances $\sigma_0^2,\ldots,\sigma_J^2$ are known. Note,

$$E\left[C_{i,J}\middle|C_{i,I-i}\right]=E\left[\exp\{Z_{i,J}\}\middle|C_{i,I-i}\right]$$
$$=\exp\{Z_{i,I-i}\}\exp\left\{\sum_{j=I-i+1}^{J}\xi_j+\sum_{j=I-i+1}^{J}\sigma_j^2/2\right\}$$
$$=C_{i,I-i}\exp\left\{\sum_{j=I-i+1}^{J}\xi_j+\frac{1}{2}\sum_{j=I-i+1}^{J}\sigma_j^2\right\} \tag{5.11}$$

and

$$E\left[\exp\left\{\widehat{Z_{i,J}}\right\}\middle|C_{i,I-i}\right]=\exp\{Z_{i,I-i}\}\,E\left[\exp\left\{\sum_{j=I-i+1}^{J}\widehat{\xi_j}\right\}\right]$$
$$=C_{i,I-i}\exp\left\{\sum_{j=I-i+1}^{J}\xi_j+\frac{1}{2}\sum_{j=I-i+1}^{J}\frac{\sigma_j^2}{I-j+1}\right\} \tag{5.12}$$

Note, that due to the different conditional variances of $Z_{i,J}$ and $\widehat{Z_{i,J}}$ we obtain different conditional expected values for the Log-normal distribution. Thus, the next estimator is straightforward from (5.11) and (5.12).

ESTIMATOR 5.5 (unbiased estimator, σ_j^2 known) *Under Model Assumptions 5.1 we define the following estimator*

$$\widehat{C_{i,J}}^{LN}=\widehat{E}\left[C_{i,J}\middle|\mathcal{D}_I\right]=\exp\left\{\widehat{Z_{i,J}}+\frac{1}{2}\sum_{j=I-i+1}^{J}\sigma_j^2\left(1-\frac{1}{I-j+1}\right)\right\} \tag{5.13}$$

for $i=1,\ldots,I$.

For this estimator we have the following result:

LEMMA 5.6 (unbiasedness, σ_j^2 known) *Under Model Assumptions 5.1 we have*

(a) *given* $C_{i,I-i}$, $\widehat{C_{i,J}}^{LN}$ *is unbiased for* $E\left[C_{i,J}\middle|C_{i,I-i}\right]=E\left[C_{i,J}\middle|\mathcal{D}_I\right]$,
(b) $\widehat{C_{i,J}}^{LN}$ *is unconditionally unbiased for* $E\left[C_{i,J}\right]$ *and*
(c) *the MSEP is given by*

$$\mathrm{msep}_{C_{i,J}|C_{i,I-i}}\left(\widehat{C_{i,J}}^{LN}\right)=E\left[C_{i,J}\middle|C_{i,I-i}\right]^2$$
$$\times\left(\exp\left\{\sum_{j=I-i+1}^{J}\sigma_j^2\right\}+\exp\left\{\sum_{j=I-i+1}^{J}\frac{\sigma_j^2}{I-j+1}\right\}-2\right)$$

Remarks 5.7

- Observe that in Lemma 5.6 we calculate the unconditional approach to the parameter estimation error (Approach 1 on p. 45). The conditional MSEP is given by

$$\mathrm{msep}_{C_{i,J}|\mathcal{D}_I}\left(\widehat{C_{i,J}}^{\mathrm{LN}}\right) = E\left[\left(C_{i,J} - \widehat{C_{i,J}}^{\mathrm{LN}}\right)^2 \middle| \mathcal{D}_I\right]$$
$$= C_{i,I-i}^2 \operatorname{Var}\left(\exp\left\{\sum_{j=I-i+1}^{J} \eta_{i,j}\right\}\right) + \left(E\left[C_{i,J}\middle| C_{i,I-i}\right] - \widehat{C_{i,J}}^{\mathrm{LN}}\right)^2 \tag{5.14}$$

In this particular model, we can explicitly calculate the conditional expectation of the second term on the right-hand side of (5.14), given $\mathcal{B}_{I-i}$. This then corresponds to Approach 1 (unconditional resampling), but it also corresponds to Approach 3 (conditional resampling) since in that particular example the volume measure does not depend on any realization.

- Hence, Lemma 5.6 states

$$\mathrm{msep}_{C_{i,J}|C_{i,I-i}}\left(\widehat{C_{i,J}}^{\mathrm{LN}}\right) = E\left[C_{i,J}\middle| C_{i,I-i}\right]^2$$
$$\times\left(\exp\left\{\sum_{j=I-i+1}^{J} \sigma_j^2\right\} - 1 + \exp\left\{\sum_{j=I-i+1}^{J} \frac{\sigma_j^2}{I-j+1}\right\} - 1\right)$$

which consist of the process variance that corresponds to the term

$$\exp\left\{\sum_{j=I-i+1}^{J} \sigma_j^2\right\} - 1$$

and of the parameter estimation error that corresponds to the term

$$\exp\left\{\sum_{j=I-i+1}^{J} \frac{\sigma_j^2}{I-j+1}\right\} - 1 \tag{5.15}$$

Proof of Lemma 5.6 (a) We have

$$E\left[\widehat{C_{i,J}}^{\mathrm{LN}}\middle| C_{i,I-i}\right] = E\left[\exp\left\{\widehat{Z_{i,J}}\right\}\middle| C_{i,I-i}\right]\exp\left\{\frac{1}{2}\sum_{j=I-i+1}^{J}\left(\sigma_j^2 - \frac{\sigma_j^2}{I-j+1}\right)\right\}$$
$$= E\left[C_{i,J}\middle| C_{i,I-i}\right] = E\left[C_{i,J}\middle| \mathcal{D}_I\right]$$

(b) This follows immediately from (a).
(c) Using the uncorrelatedness

$$E\left[C_{i,J}\,\widehat{C_{i,J}}^{\mathrm{LN}}\middle| C_{i,I-i}\right] = E\left[C_{i,J}\middle| C_{i,I-i}\right]\, E\left[\widehat{C_{i,J}}^{\mathrm{LN}}\middle| C_{i,I-i}\right]$$

and unbiasedness we obtain for the conditional MSEP

$$\mathrm{msep}_{C_{i,J}|C_{i,I-i}}\left(\widehat{C_{i,J}}^{\mathrm{LN}}\right) = E\left[\left(C_{i,J} - \widehat{C_{i,J}}^{\mathrm{LN}}\right)^2 \middle| C_{i,I-i}\right]$$
$$= \operatorname{Var}\left(C_{i,J} - \widehat{C_{i,J}}^{\mathrm{LN}}\middle| C_{i,I-i}\right)$$

$$
\begin{aligned}
&= \operatorname{Var}\left(C_{i,J} \middle| C_{i,I-i}\right) + \operatorname{Var}\left(\widehat{C_{i,J}}^{\mathrm{LN}} \middle| C_{i,I-i}\right) \\
&= C_{i,I-i}^2 \operatorname{Var}\left(\exp\left\{\sum_{j=I-i+1}^{J} \eta_{i,j}\right\}\right) \\
&\quad + C_{i,I-i}^2 \exp\left\{\sum_{j=I-i+1}^{J} \sigma_j^2\left(1-\frac{1}{I-j+1}\right)\right\} \\
&\quad \times \operatorname{Var}\left(\exp\left\{\sum_{j=I-i+1}^{J} \widehat{\xi}_j\right\}\right)
\end{aligned} \tag{5.16}
$$

This implies that

$$
\begin{aligned}
&E\left[\left(\widehat{C_{i,J}}^{\mathrm{LN}} - C_{i,J}\right)^2 \middle| C_{i,I-i}\right] \\
&= C_{i,I-i}^2 \exp\left\{\sum_{j=I-i+1}^{J} \left(2\,\xi_j + \sigma_j^2\right)\right\} \left[\exp\left(\sum_{j=I-i+1}^{J} \sigma_j^2\right)\right. \\
&\quad \left. + \exp\left(\sum_{j=I-i+1}^{J} \frac{\sigma_j^2}{I-j+1}\right) - 2\right]
\end{aligned}
$$

Using (5.11) completes the proof. □

Aggregation of Accident Years

The MSEP for aggregated claims is estimated by

$$
\begin{aligned}
\widehat{\mathrm{msep}}_{\sum_i C_{i,J}|\cdot}\left(\sum_{i=1}^{I} \widehat{C_{i,J}}^{\mathrm{LN}}\right) &= \sum_{i=1}^{I} \mathrm{msep}_{C_{i,J}|C_{i,I-i}}\left(\widehat{C_{i,J}}^{\mathrm{LN}}\right) + 2 \sum_{1\le i<k\le I} E\left[C_{i,J}\middle| C_{i,I-i}\right] \\
&\quad \times E\left[C_{k,J}\middle| C_{k,I-k}\right] \left(\exp\left\{\sum_{j=I-i+1}^{J} \frac{\sigma_j^2}{I-j+1}\right\} - 1\right)
\end{aligned} \tag{5.17}
$$

The last term in (5.17) comes (as in Subsection 3.2.4) from the fact that we use the same estimators $\widehat{\xi}_j$ for different accident years. Observe that we have written '$\cdot$' in the condition of $\widehat{\mathrm{msep}}_{\sum_i C_{i,J}|\cdot}\left(\sum_{i=1}^{I} \widehat{C_{i,J}}^{\mathrm{LN}}\right)$. This illustrates that we condition on the latest diagonal for the volume measure $C_{i,I-i}$, but, on the other hand, $C_{i,I-i}$ is considered to be a random variable in the estimator of ξ_{I-i}.

Example 5.8 (Log-normal model, σ_j known)

We revisit the data set given in Example 3.7 and compare the results to Table 3.6. This implies the results in Table 5.2 (we assume that σ_j^2 is known an given by $\widehat{\sigma_j^2}$ from Table 5.1).

In Table 5.2 we obtain a typical result. Often the estimates from the CL method (see Table 3.6) and the estimates from the Log-normal model for cumulative claims (see Table 5.2) are very close.

Table 5.1 Observed $\eta_{i,j}$ and estimated parameters $\widehat{\xi}_j$ and $\widehat{\sigma}_j$

	0	1	2	3	4	5	6	7	8	9
0		0.4860	0.0886	0.0195	0.0190	0.0056	0.0059	0.0013	0.0010	0.0014
1		0.4131	0.0727	0.0146	0.0065	0.0035	0.0050	0.0011	0.0011	
2		0.3885	0.0877	0.0257	0.0146	0.0062	0.0051	0.0008		
3		0.3768	0.0812	0.0204	0.0140	0.0092	0.0045			
4		0.3887	0.0739	0.0294	0.0241	0.0108				
5		0.3766	0.0616	0.0252	0.0106					
6		0.4165	0.0642	0.0246						
7		0.3794	0.0661							
8		0.3686								
9										
$\widehat{\xi}_j$		0.3993	0.0745	0.0228	0.0148	0.0071	0.0051	0.0011	0.0010	0.0014
$\widehat{\sigma}_j^2$		0.0364	0.0104	0.0049	0.0062	0.0029	0.0006	0.0002	0.0001	0.0001

Table 5.2 Claims reserves and prediction errors

i	$C_{i,I-i}$	CL reserves	LN reserves	Process std dev.	Estimation error$^{1/2}$	$\widehat{\mathrm{msep}}^{1/2}_{C_{i,J}\mid C_{i,I-i}}\left(\widehat{C_{i,J}}^{\mathrm{LN}}\right)$
0	11 148 124					
1	10 648 192	15 126	15 126	709	709	1002
2	10 635 751	26 257	26 268	1002	868	1326
3	9 724 068	34 538	34 511	2599	1613	3059
4	9 786 916	85 302	85 046	6606	3442	7449
5	9 935 753	156 494	157 374	30 249	13 648	33 185
6	9 282 022	286 121	287 692	65 803	27 423	71 288
7	8 256 211	449 167	451 948	73 574	29 728	79 353
8	7 648 729	1 043 242	1 042 996	116 745	43 703	124 657
9	5 675 568	3 950 815	3 945 346	373 209	126 296	394 000
Cov. term					117 052	117 052
Total		6 047 061	6 046 308	404 505	182 755	443 874

In Taylor (2000), there is a different approach for the backward transformation $\widehat{Z_{i,J}}$ to $\widehat{C_{i,J}}$.

ESTIMATOR 5.9 (central predictor, σ_j^2 known) *Under Model Assumptions 5.1 we define the following estimator*

$$\widehat{C_{i,J}}^{\mathrm{cp}} = \widehat{E}\left[C_{i,J}\middle|\mathcal{D}_I\right] = \exp\left\{\widehat{Z_{i,J}} + \frac{1}{2}\sum_{j=I-i+1}^{J}\sigma_j^2\left(1+\frac{1}{I-j+1}\right)\right\}$$

$$= \widehat{C_{i,J}}^{\mathrm{LN}} \exp\left\{\sum_{j=I-i+1}^{J}\frac{\sigma_j^2}{I-j+1}\right\} > \widehat{C_{i,J}}^{\mathrm{LN}} \tag{5.18}$$

for $i=1,\ldots,I$, *where* $\widehat{C_{i,J}}^{\mathrm{LN}}$ *is defined in* (5.13).

LEMMA 5.10 (central predictor, σ_j^2 known) *Under Model Assumptions 5.1 we have*

(a) $\widehat{C_{i,J}}^{\text{cp}}$ *satisfies*

$$E\left[\left.\frac{C_{i,J}}{\widehat{C_{i,J}}^{\text{cp}}}\right| C_{i,I-i}\right] = 1 \tag{5.19}$$

(b) *the MSEP is given by*

$$\begin{aligned}\text{msep}_{C_{i,J}|C_{i,I-i}}\left(\widehat{C_{i,J}}^{\text{cp}}\right) &= E\left[C_{i,J}|C_{i,I-i}\right]^2 \left(\exp\left\{\sum_{j=I-i+1}^{J} \frac{3\,\sigma_j^2}{I-j+1}\right\}\right. \\ &\qquad \left. + \exp\left\{\sum_{j=I-i+1}^{J} \sigma_j^2\right\} - 2\,\exp\left\{\sum_{j=I-i+1}^{J} \frac{\sigma_j^2}{I-j+1}\right\}\right) \\ &> \text{msep}_{C_{i,J}|C_{i,I-i}}\left(\widehat{C_{i,J}}^{\text{LN}}\right)\end{aligned}$$

Remark Our expression for the MSEP is different from the expression in Taylor (2000), (7.35). This comes from the fact that in Taylor the following approximation is used:

$$\begin{aligned}\text{msep}_{C_{i,J}|C_{i,I-i}}\left(\widehat{C_{i,J}}^{\text{cp}}\right) &= E\left[\left.\left(\widehat{C_{i,J}}^{\text{cp}}\right)^2 \left(\frac{C_{i,J}}{\widehat{C_{i,J}}^{\text{cp}}} - 1\right)^2 \right| C_{i,I-i}\right] \\ &\approx C_{i,I-i}^2\, \exp\left\{\sum_{j=I-i+1}^{J} (2\,\xi_j + \sigma_j^2)\right\} \text{Var}\left(\left.\frac{C_{i,J}}{\widehat{C_{i,J}}^{\text{cp}}}\right| C_{i,I-i}\right)\end{aligned}$$

Proof of Lemma 5.10 (a) Using (5.6)–(5.8), (5.13) and (5.18) and we obtain

$$\begin{aligned}&E\left[\left.\frac{C_{i,J}}{\widehat{C_{i,J}}^{\text{cp}}}\right| C_{i,I-i}\right] \\ &= E\left[\exp\left\{\sum_{j=I-i+1}^{J} \eta_{i,j} - \sum_{j=I-i+1}^{J} \widehat{\xi}_i - \frac{1}{2} \sum_{j=I-i+1}^{J} \sigma_j^2 \left(1 + \frac{1}{I-j+1}\right)\right\}\right] \\ &= \exp\left\{-\frac{1}{2} \sum_{j=I-i+1}^{J} \sigma_j^2 \left(1 + \frac{1}{I-j+1}\right)\right\} \prod_{j=I-i+1}^{J} E\left[\exp(\eta_{i,j})\right] \prod_{j=I-i+1}^{J} E\left[\exp(-\widehat{\xi}_{i,j})\right]\end{aligned}$$

Using

$$E\left[\exp(\eta_{i,j})\right] = \exp\{\xi_j + \sigma_j^2/2\}$$

and

$$E\left[\exp(-\widehat{\xi}_{i,j})\right] = \exp\left\{-\xi_j + \frac{1}{2}\frac{\sigma_j^2}{I-j+1}\right\}$$

(cf. (5.1) and (5.4)) gives the claim.

(b) The derivation for an estimate of the MSEP is more delicate since $\widehat{C_{i,J}}^{\text{cp}}$ is not an unbiased estimator. We have (cf. (5.16))

$$
\begin{aligned}
\operatorname{msep}_{C_{i,J}|C_{i,I-i}}\left(\widehat{C_{i,J}}^{\text{cp}}\right) &= E\left[\left(\widehat{C_{i,J}}^{\text{cp}} - C_{i,J}\right)^2 \middle| C_{i,I-i}\right] \\
&= C_{i,I-i}^2 \operatorname{Var}\left(\exp\left\{\sum_{j=I-i+1}^{J} \eta_{i,j}\right\}\right) \\
&\quad + E\left[\left(E\left[C_{i,J}\middle| C_{i,I-i}\right] - \widehat{C_{i,J}}^{\text{cp}}\right)^2 \middle| C_{i,I-i}\right]
\end{aligned} \tag{5.20}
$$

For the expected value we have

$$
E\left[\widehat{C_{i,J}}^{\text{cp}}\middle| C_{i,I-i}\right] = E\left[C_{i,J}\middle| C_{i,I-i}\right] \exp\left\{\sum_{j=I-i+1}^{J} \frac{\sigma_j^2}{I-j+1}\right\}
$$

Thus, the last term on the right-hand side of (5.20) is equal to

$$
E\left[C_{i,J}\middle| C_{i,I-i}\right]^2 \left(1 - \exp\left\{\sum_{j=I-i+1}^{J} \frac{\sigma_j^2}{I-j+1}\right\}\right)^2 + \operatorname{Var}\left(\widehat{C_{i,J}}^{\text{cp}}\middle| C_{i,I-i}\right)
$$

Using (5.18) and (5.16), this leads to

$$
\begin{aligned}
\operatorname{msep}_{C_{i,J}|C_{i,I-i}}\left(\widehat{C_{i,J}}^{\text{cp}}\right) &= C_{i,I-i}^2 \operatorname{Var}\left(\exp\left\{\sum_{j=I-i+1}^{J} \eta_{i,j}\right\}\right) \\
&\quad + E\left[C_{i,J}\middle| C_{i,I-i}\right]^2 \left(1 - \exp\left\{\sum_{j=I-i+1}^{J} \frac{\sigma_j^2}{I-j+1}\right\}\right)^2 \\
&\quad + \exp\left\{2 \sum_{j=I-i+1}^{J} \frac{\sigma_j^2}{I-j+1}\right\} \operatorname{Var}\left(\widehat{C_{i,J}}^{\text{LN}}\middle| C_{i,I-i}\right) \\
&> \operatorname{Var}\left(C_{i,J}\middle| C_{i,I-i}\right) + \operatorname{Var}\left(\widehat{C_{i,J}}^{\text{LN}}\middle| C_{i,I-i}\right) \\
&= \operatorname{msep}_{C_{i,J}|C_{i,I-i}}\left(\widehat{C_{i,J}}^{\text{LN}}\right)
\end{aligned} \tag{5.21}
$$

This completes the proof. □

Example 5.8 (revisited) If we compare the Log-normal estimate $\widehat{C_{i,J}}^{\text{LN}}$ and the central predictor $\widehat{C_{i,J}}^{\text{cp}}$ we obtain the following results for the reserves (see Table 5.3). This shows that in many practical applications the correction term coming from the variance of the estimators $\widehat{\xi}_j$ is negligible.

Table 5.3 Claims reserves and prediction errors

	Claims reserves from		$\widehat{\text{msep}}^{1/2}_{C_{i,J}\mid C_{i,I-i}}$	
i	$\widehat{C_{i,J}}^{\text{LN}}$	$\widehat{C_{i,J}}^{\text{cp}}$	$\widehat{C_{i,J}}^{\text{LN}}$	$\widehat{C_{i,J}}^{\text{cp}}$
0				
1	15 126	15 126	1002	1002
2	26 268	26 268	1326	1326
3	34 511	34 511	3059	3059
4	85 046	85 048	7449	7449
5	157 374	157 393	33 185	33 185
6	287 692	287 771	71 288	71 289
7	451 948	452 050	79 353	79 354
8	1 042 996	1 043 216	124 657	124 661
9	3 945 346	3 947 004	394 000	394 078
Total	6 046 308	6 048 386		

5.1.2 Unknown Variances

In general, the variances σ_j^2 need also be estimated from the data (see (5.5)). Assume that W has a χ^2-distribution with p degrees of freedom. That is, W is $\Gamma(p/2, 1/2)$ distributed and the moment generating function of W is given by

$$E\left[\exp\{t\ W\}\right] = (1-2t)^{-p/2} \quad \text{for } t < 1/2 \tag{5.22}$$

(see the appendix, Subsection A.2.4 for the definition of the Gamma distribution). This implies for $t\sigma_j^2/(I-j) < 1/2$

$$E\left[\exp\left\{t\ \widehat{\sigma_j^2}\right\}\right] = \left(1 - \frac{2\ t\ \sigma_j^2}{I-j}\right)^{-(I-j)/2} \tag{5.23}$$

(cf. Lemma 5.3b). Therefore, we choose t such that

$$\left(1 - \frac{2\ t\ \sigma_j^2}{I-j}\right)^{-(I-j)/2} = \exp\left\{\frac{1}{2}\ \sigma_j^2\ \left(1 - \frac{1}{I-j+1}\right)\right\}$$

This leads to

$$t = \frac{I-j}{2\ \sigma_j^2}\left(1 - \exp\left\{-\frac{\sigma_j^2}{I-j}\ \left(1 - \frac{1}{I-j+1}\right)\right\}\right)$$

We define (cf. (5.13) and pay attention to the fact that we cancel a factor 1/2)

$$\begin{aligned} t_j(\sigma_j^2) &= \frac{I-j}{\sigma_j^2}\left(1 - \exp\left\{\frac{-\sigma_j^2}{I-j}\ \left(1 - \frac{1}{I-j+1}\right)\right\}\right) \\ &= \frac{I-j}{\sigma_j^2}\left(1 - \exp\left\{\frac{-\sigma_j^2}{I-j+1}\right\}\right) \end{aligned} \tag{5.24}$$

ESTIMATOR 5.11 (**σ_j^2 unknown**) *Under the Model Assumptions 5.1 we define the following estimator*

$$\widehat{C_{i,J}}^{\mathrm{LN}\sigma,1} = \widehat{E}\left[C_{i,J} \mid \mathcal{D}_I\right] = \exp\left\{\widehat{Z_{i,J}} + \frac{1}{2}\sum_{j=I-i+1}^{J} t_j(\sigma_j^2)\,\widehat{\sigma_j^2}\right\} \tag{5.25}$$

for $i = 1, \ldots, I$.

For Estimator 5.11 we have the following result:

LEMMA 5.12 (**σ_j^2 unknown**) *Under Model Assumptions 5.1 and the assumption that $t_j(\sigma_j^2) < 1$ is known for all $0 \le j \le J$, we have*

(a) *given $C_{i,I-i}$, $\widehat{C_{i,J}}^{\mathrm{LN}\sigma,1}$ is an unbiased for $E\left[C_{i,J} \mid C_{i,I-i}\right] = E\left[C_{i,J} \mid \mathcal{D}_I\right]$ and*
(b) *$\widehat{C_{i,J}}^{\mathrm{LN}\sigma,1}$ is unconditionally unbiased for $E\left[C_{i,J}\right]$.*

Proof (a) The proof follows from the independence of $\widehat{\xi_j}$ and $\widehat{\sigma_j^2}$ (cf. Lemma 5.3) and from the choice of $t_j(\sigma_j^2)$ (cf. (5.23)–(5.24)). We have

$$\begin{aligned}
&E\left[\widehat{C_{i,J}}^{\mathrm{LN}\sigma,1} \middle| C_{i,I-i}\right] \\
&= E\left[\exp\left\{\widehat{Z_{i,J}}\right\} \middle| C_{i,I-i}\right] E\left[\exp\left\{\frac{1}{2}\sum_{j=I-i+1}^{J} t_j(\sigma_j^2)\,\widehat{\sigma_j^2}\right\} \middle| C_{i,I-i}\right] \\
&= E\left[\exp\left\{\widehat{Z_{i,J}}\right\} \middle| C_{i,I-i}\right] \prod_{j=I-i+1}^{J} E\left[\exp\left\{\frac{1}{2}\, t_j(\sigma_j^2)\,\widehat{\sigma_j^2}\right\}\right] \\
&= E\left[\exp\left\{\widehat{Z_{i,J}}\right\} \middle| C_{i,I-i}\right] \prod_{j=I-i+1}^{J} \exp\left\{\frac{1}{2}\,\sigma_j^2\left(1 - \frac{1}{I-j+1}\right)\right\}
\end{aligned} \tag{5.26}$$

Using (5.11)–(5.12), this leads to

$$E\left[\widehat{C_{i,J}}^{\mathrm{LN}\sigma,1} \middle| C_{i,I-i}\right] = E\left[C_{i,J} \mid C_{i,I-i}\right]$$

(b) This follows immediately from (a).

This finishes the proof. □

Remark Observe that this estimator does not really solve the problem. The estimator $\widehat{C_{i,J}}^{\mathrm{LN}\sigma,1}$ cannot explicitly be calculated from the data, because it still depends on the unknown parameters σ_j^2 via $t_j(\sigma_j^2)$. We could obtain an estimator by replacing σ_j^2 by $\widehat{\sigma_j^2}$, but this estimator is no longer unbiased.

Therefore one often uses the following estimator.

ESTIMATOR 5.13 (**σ_j^2 unknown**) *Under Model Assumptions 5.1 we define the following estimator*

$$\widehat{C_{i,J}}^{\mathrm{LN}\sigma,2} = \widehat{E}\left[C_{i,J} \middle| \mathcal{D}_I\right] = \exp\left\{\widehat{Z_{i,J}} + \frac{1}{2} \sum_{j=I-i+1}^{J} \widehat{\sigma_j^2} \left(1 - \frac{1}{I-j+1}\right)\right\} \tag{5.27}$$

for $i = 1, \ldots, I$.

Hence, we have, using the independence of $\widehat{\xi}_j$ and $\widehat{\sigma_j^2}$ and (5.11)–(5.12),

$$\begin{aligned}
E\left[\widehat{C_{i,J}}^{\mathrm{LN}\sigma,2} \middle| C_{i,I-i}\right] &= C_{i,I-i} \exp\left\{\sum_{j=I-i+1}^{J} \xi_j + \frac{1}{2} \sum_{j=I-i+1}^{J} \frac{\sigma_j^2}{I-j+1}\right\} \\
&\quad \times E\left[\exp\left\{\frac{1}{2} \sum_{j=I-i+1}^{J} \widehat{\sigma_j^2}\left(1 - \frac{1}{I-j+1}\right)\right\} \middle| C_{i,I-i}\right] \\
&= E\left[C_{i,J} \middle| C_{i,I-i}\right] \\
&\quad \times E\left[\exp\left\{\frac{1}{2} \sum_{j=I-i+1}^{J} \left(\widehat{\sigma_j^2} - \sigma_j^2\right)\left(1 - \frac{1}{I-j+1}\right)\right\}\right]
\end{aligned}$$

Using (5.23) and $\lim_{n\to\infty}(1 + x/n)^n = e^x$, we have

$$\begin{aligned}
&\lim_{I\to\infty} E\left[\exp\left\{\frac{1}{2}\left(\widehat{\sigma_j^2} - \sigma_j^2\right)\left(1 - \frac{1}{I-j+1}\right)\right\}\right] \\
&= \lim_{I\to\infty}\left[\left(1 - \frac{\sigma_j^2}{I-j+1}\right)^{-(I-j)/2} \exp\left\{-\frac{\sigma_j^2\,(I-j)}{2\,(I-j+1)}\right\}\right] \\
&= \exp\left(\sigma_j^2/2\right)\ \exp\left(-\sigma_j^2/2\right) = 1
\end{aligned}$$

This immediately gives the approximation

$$E\left[\widehat{C_{i,J}}^{\mathrm{LN}\sigma,2} \middle| C_{i,I-i}\right] \approx E\left[C_{i,J} \middle| C_{i,I-i}\right] \tag{5.28}$$

which means that we have an asymptotically (conditionally) unbiased predictor for the ultimate claim $C_{i,J}$ if $I \to \infty$.

Remark Finney (1941) used a different method for an unbiased backward transformation (see also Verrall 1991). Define the function

$$g_m(t) = \sum_{k=0}^{\infty} \frac{m^k\ (m+2k)}{m\ (m+2)\cdots(m+2k)}\ \frac{t^k}{k!}$$

Now we set

$$m = m(j) = I - j \qquad \text{and} \qquad t = \frac{1}{2}\left(1 - \frac{1}{I-j+1}\right)\widehat{\sigma_j^2}$$

Then, one can show that, conditional on $C_{i,I-i}$,

$$\widehat{C_{i,J}}^{\mathrm{LN}\sigma,3} = \exp\left\{\widehat{Z_{i,J}}\right\}\, g_{I-j}(t)$$

is an unbiased estimator for $E\left[C_{i,J}\middle| C_{i,I-i}\right] = E\left[C_{i,J}\middle| \mathcal{D}_I\right]$. The nice thing about Finney's choice is that one can give an unbiased estimator for the estimation error (see Verrall 1991)

$$\operatorname{Var}\left(\widehat{C_{i,J}}^{\mathrm{LN}\sigma,3}\middle| C_{i,I-i}\right)$$

In the sequel, we concentrate on the estimator $\widehat{C_{i,J}}^{\mathrm{LN}\sigma,1}$.

LEMMA 5.14 (unbiased estimator, σ_j^2 unknown, $t_j(\sigma_j^2)$ known) *Under Model Assumptions 5.1 and the assumption that $t_j(\sigma_j^2) < 1$ is known for all j we have that the MSEP of $\widehat{C_{i,J}}^{\mathrm{LN}\sigma,1}$, given $C_{i,I-i}$, is given by*

$$\begin{aligned}\mathrm{msep}_{C_{i,J}|C_{i,I-i}}\left(\widehat{C_{i,J}}^{\mathrm{LN}\sigma,1}\right) = {} & E\left[C_{i,J}\middle| C_{i,I-i}\right]^2 \\ & \times\left(\exp\left\{\sum_{j=I-i+1}^{J}\sigma_j^2\left(\frac{2}{I-j+1}-1\right)\right.\right. \\ & \left.\left. -\frac{I-j}{2}\log\left(1-\frac{2\,t_j(\sigma_j^2)\,\sigma_j^2}{I-j}\right)\right\}+\exp\left\{\sum_{j=I-i+1}^{J}\sigma_j^2\right\}-2\right)\end{aligned}$$

Compare this to Lemma 5.6. Observe that the estimation error has now changed from (see (5.15))

$$\exp\left\{\sum_{j=I-i+1}^{J}\frac{\sigma_j^2}{I-j+1}\right\}-1$$

to

$$\exp\left\{\sum_{j=I-i+1}^{J}\sigma_j^2\left(\frac{2}{I-j+1}-1\right)-\frac{I-j}{2}\log\left(1-\frac{2\,t_j(\sigma_j^2)\,\sigma_j^2}{I-j}\right)\right\}-1$$

Henceforth, we have a larger estimation error. This comes from the fact that in the estimates of σ_j^2 there are also some uncertainties.

Proof of Lemma 5.14 Observe that we have

$$\begin{aligned}
\text{msep}_{C_{i,J}|C_{i,I-i}}\left(\widehat{C_{i,J}}^{\text{LN}\sigma,1}\right) &= E\left[\left(C_{i,J} - \widehat{C_{i,J}}^{\text{LN}\sigma,1}\right)^2 \middle| C_{i,I-i}\right] \\
&= C_{i,I-i}^2 \operatorname{Var}\left(\exp\left\{\sum_{j=I-i+1}^{J} \eta_{i,j}\right\}\right) \\
&\quad + E\left[\left(E\left[C_{i,J}\middle| C_{i,I-i}\right] - \widehat{C_{i,J}}^{\text{LN}\sigma,1}\right)^2 \middle| C_{i,I-i}\right] \\
&= C_{i,I-i}^2 \operatorname{Var}\left(\exp\left\{\sum_{j=I-i+1}^{J} \eta_{i,j}\right\}\right) + \operatorname{Var}\left(\widehat{C_{i,J}}^{\text{LN}\sigma,1} \middle| C_{i,I-i}\right)
\end{aligned}$$

There remains to calculate the last term in the equality above:

$$\operatorname{Var}\left(\widehat{C_{i,J}}^{\text{LN}\sigma,1} \middle| C_{i,I-i}\right) = \operatorname{Var}\left(\exp\left\{\widehat{Z_{i,J}} + \frac{1}{2}\sum_{j=I-i+1}^{J} t_j(\sigma_j^2)\, \widehat{\sigma_j^2}\right\} \middle| C_{i,I-i}\right)$$

This last term is equal to

$$\begin{aligned}
&E\left[\exp\left\{2\,\widehat{Z_{i,J}} + \sum_{j=I-i+1}^{J} t_j(\sigma_j^2)\, \widehat{\sigma_j^2}\right\} \middle| C_{i,I-i}\right] \\
&\qquad - E\left[\exp\left\{\widehat{Z_{i,J}} + \frac{1}{2}\sum_{j=I-i+1}^{J} t_j(\sigma_j^2)\, \widehat{\sigma_j^2}\right\} \middle| C_{i,I-i}\right]^2
\end{aligned}$$

Using the independencies and the distributional properties of $\widehat{\xi}_j$ and $\widehat{\sigma}_j^2$, we can decouple and calculate all terms (cf. (5.21) and (5.26)). This completes the proof of Lemma 5.14. □

Table 5.4 Claims reserves and prediction errors

	Claims reserves from		$\widehat{\text{msep}}^{1/2}_{C_{i,J},C_{i,I-i}}$	
i	$\widehat{C_{i,J}}^{\text{LN}\sigma,1}$	$\widehat{C_{i,J}}^{\text{LN}\sigma,2}$	$\widehat{C_{i,J}}^{\text{LN}\sigma,1}$	$\widehat{C_{i,J}}^{\text{LN}}$
0				
1	15 126	15 126	1002	1002
2	26 268	26 268	1326	1326
3	34 511	34 511	3059	3059
4	85 046	85 046	7449	7449
5	157 374	157 374	33 185	33 185
6	287 692	287 692	71 288	71 288
7	451 948	451 948	79 353	79 353
8	1 042 996	1 042 996	124 658	124 657
9	3 945 346	3 945 346	394 010	394 000
Total	6 046 308.0	6 046 308.3		

Example 5.8 (revisited) If we compare the Log-normal estimates $\widehat{C_{i,J}}^{\mathrm{LN}\sigma,1}$ and $\widehat{C_{i,J}}^{\mathrm{LN}\sigma,2}$ we obtain the results in Table 5.4 for the estimated claims reserves (we set $t_j(\sigma_j^2) = t_j(\widehat{\sigma_j^2})$).

We see that the estimated claims reserves are almost the same for $\widehat{C_{i,J}}^{\mathrm{LN}\sigma,1}$ and $\widehat{C_{i,J}}^{\mathrm{LN}\sigma,2}$, that is, the bias correction for the σ_j^2 terms (with the function $t_j(\widehat{\sigma_j^2})$) has only a marginal influence on the overall result.

Moreover, observe also that the MSEP of the estimates $\widehat{C_{i,J}}^{\mathrm{LN}\sigma,1}$ (unknown σ_j^2's) and the MSEP of the estimates $\widehat{C_{i,J}}^{\mathrm{LN}}$ (known σ_j^2's) are almost the same. Overall this means, that the estimation uncertainty in the parameters σ_j^2 are almost negligible. This is comparable to the analysis of higher order terms in MSEP for the CL model.

5.2 INCREMENTAL CLAIMS

In this section we consider models for the incremental claims $X_{i,j}$ (incremental payments, change of claims incurred or number of reported claims in period j for accident year i). Most of them are described in England and Verrall (2002), and we will meet many of these examples again in Chapter 6 on generalized linear models (GLMs). Therefore, we will give a short overview on these distributional models.

5.2.1 (Overdispersed) Poisson Model

We have already seen a first model for incremental claims in Section 2.3 in Model 2.12. We have assumed that there exist parameters $\mu_0, \ldots, \mu_I > 0$ and $\gamma_0, \ldots, \gamma_J > 0$ such that $X_{i,j}$ are independent Poisson distributed with

$$x_{i,j} = E[X_{i,j}] = \mu_i \; \gamma_j \tag{5.29}$$

for all $0 \le i \le I$ and $0 \le j \le J$, and $\sum_{j=0}^{J} \gamma_j = 1$ (see Model Assumptions 2.12). Then, the variance satisfies

$$\mathrm{Var}(X_{i,j}) = \mu_i \; \gamma_j = x_{i,j} \tag{5.30}$$

That is, the variance lies on the same linear scale as the expectation (i.e. linear variance function). The parameters were estimated by the ML method, and the estimator for the ultimate claim was given in Estimator 2.14. For an explicit example we refer to Example 2.15. We also recall that this model gives the CL reserves (similar to the link ratio model presented in Chapter 3), see Lemma 2.16.

The Poisson model can be generalized with the help of an additional dispersion parameter ϕ. This leads to the overdispersed Poisson model. That is, for $\phi > 0$ we assume

$$E[X_{i,j}] = x_{i,j} \quad \text{and} \quad \mathrm{Var}(X_{i,j}) = \phi \; x_{i,j}$$

We met an example of the overdispersed Poisson model in the first bullet of Model Assumptions 4.28, in Subsection 4.3.1. Moreover, the overdispersed Poisson model fits into the framework of the EDF (see Subsection 4.3.2). It is important to note that the dispersion parameter ϕ cancels if one estimates the parameters using MLE as long as it is constant. Henceforth, the Poisson model, the overdispersed Poisson model and the distribution-free CL model lead to the same claims reserves. However, there will be substantial differences if one calculates the (conditional) MSEP in these models. The MSEP in the overdispersed Poisson model using MLE is considered in Chapter 6, and an example is provided in Example 6.16 (overdispersed Poisson model). Crucial in the derivation of the Poisson model was the assumption of the multiplicative structure (5.29) for the expected value.

5.2.2 Negative-Binomial model

The Negative-Binomial model can be expressed for both incremental claims and cumulative claims. The Negative-Binomial distribution is obtained from the Poisson distribution by assuming that the Poisson parameter follows a Gamma distribution (see also (4.30)). This model was derived in Verrall (2000).

Assume that $X_{i,j}$ satisfies the Poisson Model Assumptions 2.12 with (5.29). Hence, for all $0 \le j \le J$ we have

$$E\left[C_{i,j}\right] = \mu_i\, \beta_j, \qquad \text{with} \quad \beta_j = \sum_{k=0}^{j} \gamma_k$$

This implies that we can rewrite (5.29). Define $f_{j-1} = \beta_j / \beta_{j-1}$ (see also (2.11) and the subsequent discussion). Henceforth, for $1 \le j \le J$ we obtain

$$E[X_{i,j}] = \frac{E\left[C_{i,j-1}\right]}{\beta_{j-1}}\, \gamma_j \; = \; E\left[C_{i,j-1}\right](f_{j-1} - 1)$$

$$E[C_{i,j}] = E\left[C_{i,j-1}\right] \frac{\beta_j}{\beta_{j-1}} \; = \; E\left[C_{i,j-1}\right] f_{j-1}$$

where f_j are CL factors for expected values. Observe that the CL algorithm is applied to the (deterministic) expected claims. This is in the spirit of the deterministic CL understanding. Hence we have

$$X_{i,j} \stackrel{(d)}{\sim} \text{Poisson}\left(E\left[C_{i,j-1}\right] \left(\frac{\beta_j}{\beta_{j-1}} - 1 \right) \right)$$

Our aim is to get a stochastic understanding for this model. In a first step, we use a Bayesian approach and replace the true mean $E\left[C_{i,j-1}\right]$ by a random variable $\Theta_{i,j-1}$ that follows a Gamma distribution

$$\Theta_{i,j-1} \stackrel{(d)}{\sim} \Gamma\left(c_{i,j-1}, 1\right) \tag{5.31}$$

(see appendix, Subsection A.2.4 for the definition of the Gamma distribution). From this it follows that $X_{i,j}$ has a Negative-Binomial distribution (cf. (4.30)) with

$$\begin{aligned} x_{i,j} &= E\left[X_{i,j}\right] = E\left[E\left[X_{i,j} \middle| \Theta_{i,j-1}\right]\right] \\ &= E\left[\Theta_{i,j-1}\right]\, (f_{j-1} - 1) = c_{i,j-1}\, \left(f_{j-1} - 1\right) \end{aligned}$$

and

$$\begin{aligned}\operatorname{Var}\left(X_{i,j}\right) &= E\left[\operatorname{Var}\left(X_{i,j}|\Theta_{i,j-1}\right)\right] + \operatorname{Var}\left(E\left[X_{i,j}\middle|\,\Theta_{i,j-1}\right]\right)\\ &= E\left[\Theta_{i,j-1}\right]\ (f_{j-1}-1) + \operatorname{Var}\left(\Theta_{i,j-1}\right)\ (f_{j-1}-1)^2\\ &= c_{i,j-1}\ \left(f_{j-1}-1\right)\ f_{j-1} = x_{i,j}\ f_{j-1} \end{aligned} \tag{5.32}$$

Hence, this model can also be understood (for fixed deterministic $c_{i,j-1}$) as an overdispersed Poisson model with dispersion parameter f_{j-1} (see also Sections 5.2.1 and 6.3).

In a second step, we replace the deterministic $c_{i,j-1}$ by a time series understanding – that is, we assume that the distribution of $X_{i,j}$ depends on $\{C_{i,j-1}=c_{i,j-1}\}$. Then, the time series model reads as follows:

Model Assumptions 5.15 (Negative-Binomial model, Verrall (2000))

- Claims of different accident years i are independent.
- There exist factors $f_0, \ldots, f_{J-1} \geq 1$ such that for all $0 \leq i \leq I$ and $1 \leq j \leq J$ we have, conditional on $C_{0,i}, \ldots, C_{i,j-1}$, the increment $X_{i,j}$ has a Negative-Binomial distribution with

$$\begin{aligned} E\left[X_{i,j}\middle|\,C_{i,0},\ldots,C_{i,j-1}\right] &= C_{i,j-1}\ \left(f_{j-1}-1\right)\\ \operatorname{Var}\left(X_{i,j}\middle|\,C_{i,0},\ldots,C_{i,j-1}\right) &= C_{i,j-1}\ \left(f_{j-1}-1\right)\ f_{j-1}\end{aligned}$$

□

Remarks 5.16

- See appendix, Subsection A.1.3, for the definition of the Negative-Binomial distribution.
- The Negative-Binomial model satisfies the CL Assumptions 3.2

$$\begin{aligned} E\left[C_{i,j}\middle|\,C_{i,0},\ldots,C_{i,j-1}\right] &= E\left[X_{i,j}+C_{i,j-1}\middle|\,C_{i,0},\ldots,C_{i,j-1}\right]\\ &= f_{j-1}\ C_{i,j-1}\end{aligned}$$

with variance function

$$\begin{aligned} \operatorname{Var}\left(C_{i,j}\middle|\,C_{i,0},\ldots,C_{i,j-1}\right) &= \operatorname{Var}\left(X_{i,j}+C_{i,j-1}\middle|\,C_{i,0},\ldots,C_{i,j-1}\right)\\ &= C_{i,j-1}\ \left(f_{j-1}-1\right)\ f_{j-1}\end{aligned}$$

This implies that we can immediately apply the CL theory with variance parameter $\sigma_{j-1}^2 = \left(f_{j-1}-1\right)\ f_{j-1}$.
- Observe that we must assume that $f_j > 1$ (increasing payout pattern), otherwise the variance function does not make sense. Observe that in practical examples, $f_j > 1$ is not always the case, for example, for claims incurred data we often observe that $f_j < 1$ if, for instance, claims adjusters overestimate the average claim. Also for cumulative payments one sometimes observes CL factors smaller than one which is often mainly due to subrogation and deductibles.
- England and Verrall (2002), cf. Section 2.5, propose an approximation for the discrete Negative-Binomial distribution for the increments $X_{i,j}$ by the Gaussian distribution with mean $C_{i,j-1}\ \left(f_{j-1}-1\right)$ and variance $\phi_{i,j-1}\ C_{i,j-1}$. In this way they avoid the problems of

having negative values for $X_{i,j}$. Note that this is in the spirit of the Time Series Model 3.9 if we assume that $\varepsilon_{i,j}$ has a standard Gaussian distribution. However, the England and Verrall normal approach still hides the difficulty that cumulative claims $C_{i,j}$ can become negative (since Gaussian distribution is not bounded from below) and in that case one cannot develop the time series any further (see also Remarks 3.10). Note that the MLE for f_j in the Gaussian model is exactly the same as the minimum variance unbiased estimator in the distribution-free CL model, see (3.4). Note also that here we use a distributional assumption for parameter estimation, whereas in (3.4) we only need assumptions on the first two moments.

- Hence, we can now either use GLM theory (see Chapter 6) or the distribution-free approach to derive further key figures in this model.

5.2.3 Log-Normal Model for Incremental Claims

Unlike in Model Assumptions 5.1, we now assume that the incremental claims $X_{i,j}$ have a Log-normal distribution. This model has been introduced by Kremer (1982) and has been used by many other actuaries.

Model Assumptions 5.17 (Log-normal model for incremental sizes)

There exist parameters $m_{i,j}$ and σ^2 such that the incremental claims $X_{i,j}$ are independent Log-normally distributed with

$$\log(X_{i,j}) \overset{(d)}{\sim} \mathcal{N}\left(m_{i,j}, \sigma^2\right)$$

for all $0 \le i \le I$ and $0 \le j \le J$. □

Remark For the definition of the Log-normal distribution we refer to the appendix, Subsection A.2.3.

We have

$$x_{i,j} = E\left[X_{i,j}\right] = \exp\left\{m_{i,j} + \frac{1}{2}\sigma^2\right\}$$

and

$$\mathrm{Var}\left(X_{i,j}\right) = x_{i,j}^2 \left(\exp\left\{\sigma^2\right\} - 1\right) \tag{5.33}$$

That is, we now have a quadratic variance function. Thus, in a generalized linear setup this can also be understood as a Gamma model (see also Section 6.3).

One can show that the transformed data $\log(X_{i,j})$ have an additive structure (cf. Kremer (1982)). Without going into details, we need to assume an additional structure for $m_{i,j}$. Often one assumes

$$m_{i,j} = c + a_i + b_j$$

with $\sum_{j=0}^{J} \exp\{b_j\} = 1$. The parameters can then be estimated with the help of the ML method (analogously as in the Poisson case in Section 2.3). Moreover, we have

$$x_{i,j} = \exp\{c + \tfrac{1}{2}\sigma^2\} \exp\{a_i\} \exp\{b_j\} = \mu_i \ \gamma_j$$

with $\mu_i = \exp\{c + \sigma^2/2\} \exp\{a_i\}$ and $\gamma_j = \exp\{b_j\}$. Hence as in the Poisson Model 2.12 and in the Negative-Binomial model (5.31)–(5.32) we obtain a multiplicative model for the mean. This time, we have a different variance function and dispersion $(\exp\{\sigma^2\} - 1)$.

5.2.4 Gamma Model

In (5.33) we have seen that in the Log-normal model we arrive at a variance function that corresponds to a Gamma situation. Mack (1991) has directly defined the Gamma model in his derivation for a quadratic variance function.

Model Assumptions 5.18 (Gamma model)

There exist deterministic numbers $r_{i,j}$ and independent Gamma distributed random variables $X_{i,j}^{(k)}$ with mean $m_{i,j}$ and variational coefficient $\nu^{-1/2}$ such that for all $0 \le i \le I$ and $0 \le j \le J$ we have

$$X_{i,j} = \sum_{k=0}^{r_{i,j}} X_{i,j}^{(k)}$$

□

Remark For the definition of the Gamma distribution we refer to the appendix, Subsection A.2.4.

If $X_{i,j}^{(k)}$ has a Gamma distribution with parameters $a_{i,j}$ and $b_{i,j}$, $X_{i,j}^{(k)} \overset{(d)}{\sim} \Gamma(a_{i,j}, b_{i,j})$, then its mean is given by

$$m_{i,j} = E\left[X_{i,j}^{(k)}\right] = \frac{a_{i,j}}{b_{i,j}}$$

and the variance is given by

$$\operatorname{Var}\left(X_{i,j}^{(k)}\right) = \frac{a_{i,j}}{b_{i,j}^2}$$

This implies that

$$\nu^{-1/2} = \operatorname{Vco}\left(X_{i,j}^{(k)}\right) = a_{i,j}^{-1/2}$$

and $X_{i,j}^{(k)} \overset{(d)}{\sim} \Gamma(\nu, \nu/m_{i,j})$. Therefore, Model Assumptions 5.18 imply that

$$X_{i,j} \overset{(d)}{\sim} \Gamma\left(\nu \ r_{i,j}, \frac{\nu}{m_{i,j}}\right)$$

with

$$x_{i,j} = E\left[X_{i,j}\right] = r_{i,j}\ m_{i,j}$$

and the variance is given by

$$\operatorname{Var}\left(X_{i,j}\right) = r_{i,j}\ \nu^{-1}\ m_{i,j}^2 = x_{i,j}^2\ r_{i,j}^{-1}\ \nu^{-1} \tag{5.34}$$

Thus, we find a quadratic variance function. In the following, we assume that we have a multiplicative structure for $E\left[X_{i,j}\right]$.

Model Assumptions 5.19 (Gamma model, multiplicative structure)

In addition to Model Assumptions 5.18 we assume that there exist parameters $\mu_0, \ldots, \mu_I > 0$ and $\gamma_0, \ldots, \gamma_J > 0$ such that $\sum_{j=0}^{J} \gamma_j = 1$ and

$$x_{i,j} = E[X_{i,j}] = r_{i,j}\ m_{i,j} = \mu_i\ \gamma_j \tag{5.35}$$

□

Hence the likelihood function is given by

$$L_{\mathcal{D}_I}(\mu_0, \ldots, \mu_I, \gamma_0, \ldots, \gamma_J) = \prod_{i+j\le I} \frac{\left(\nu r_{i,j}/\mu_i \gamma_j\right)^{\nu r_{i,j}}}{\Gamma(\nu r_{i,j})}\ X_{i,j}^{\nu r_{i,j}-1} \exp\left\{-\frac{\nu r_{i,j}}{\mu_i \gamma_j}\ X_{i,j}\right\} \tag{5.36}$$

We maximize this function of $\mathcal{D}_I = \{X_{i,j};\ i+j \le I, j \le J\}$ by setting its $I+J+2$ partial derivatives w.r.t. the unknown parameters μ_i and γ_j equal to zero. Thus, we obtain on $\mathcal{D}_I$ the estimates

$$\widehat{\mu}_i = \sum_{j=0}^{I-i} r_{i,j}\ \frac{X_{i,j}}{\widehat{\gamma}_j} \Big/ \sum_{j=0}^{I-i} r_{i,j} \tag{5.37}$$

$$\widehat{\gamma}_j = \sum_{i=0}^{I-j} r_{i,j}\ \frac{X_{i,j}}{\widehat{\mu}_i} \Big/ \sum_{i=0}^{I-j} r_{i,j} \tag{5.38}$$

for all $i \in \{0, \ldots, I\}$ and all $j \in \{0, \ldots, J\}$ under the constraint that $\sum \widehat{\gamma}_j = 1$. These estimates are weighted averages of the observations, where the weights are given by $r_{i,j}$.

ESTIMATOR 5.20 (Gamma ML estimator) *The ML estimator in the Gamma Model 5.19 is given by*

$$\widehat{X_{i,j}}^{\text{Ga}} = \widehat{E}[X_{i,j}] = \widehat{\mu}_i\ \widehat{\gamma}_j$$

$$\widehat{C_{i,J}}^{\text{Ga}} = \widehat{E}[C_{i,J}|\mathcal{D}_I] = C_{i,I-i} + \sum_{j=I-i+1}^{J} \widehat{X_{i,j}}^{\text{Ga}}$$

for $i+j>I$.

Remarks 5.21

- To estimate the parameters μ_i and γ_j of this model we need the additional information $r_{i,j}$, $i+j\le I$. If $X_{i,j}^{(k)}$ denote individual claims payments, then $r_{i,j}$ corresponds to the number of individual claims payments. These are not always easily available from the IT systems. In this spirit $r_{i,j}$ acts as a volume measure.
- One could also try to estimate the average payment $m_{i,j}$ for $i+j>I$ in a multiplicative structure (see Mack 1991, p. 100). However then, in addition, one would have to estimate the number of future payments, $r_{i,j}$ for $i+j>I$, which involves an additional modelling part.
- In Chapter 6.1 we consider an other setup for the Gamma model, namely (see (6.4)–(6.5))

$$E\left[X_{i,j}\right]=x_{i,j},$$
$$\mathrm{Var}\left(X_{i,j}\right)=\phi_{i,j}/w_{i,j}\; x_{i,j}^2$$

  The model parameters are then estimated in the generalized linear model (GLM) framework (with the EDF), which allows for other interpretations of the volume measures $w_{i,j}$.

5.2.5 Tweedie's Compound Poisson Model

In the previous sections we have presented the Poisson model, which has a linear variance function, and the Gamma model, which has a quadratic variance function. Tweedie's compound Poisson model closes the gap between the Poisson model and Gamma model with respect to the variance function. Tweedie's compound Poisson model has been studied in Wüthrich (2003) in a claims reserving context.

Model Assumptions 5.22 (Tweedie's compound Poisson model)

- There exist random variables $R_{i,j}$ and $X_{i,j}^{(k)}$ such that the independent incremental payments are given by

$$X_{i,j}=\sum_{k=0}^{R_{i,j}} X_{i,j}^{(k)}$$

  for all $0\le i\le I$ and $0\le j\le J$.
- $R_{i,j}$ are independent Poisson distributed with mean $\lambda_{i,j}w_i>0$ and the single payments $X_{i,j}^{(k)}$ are independent Gamma distributed with mean $m_{i,j}>0$ and variational coefficient $\nu^{-1/2}>0$.
- $R_{i,j}$ and $X_{i,j}^{(1)}, X_{i,j}^{(2)}, \ldots$ are independent for all $0\le i\le I$ and $0\le j\le J$. □

Remarks 5.23

- w_i denotes a weight function for accident year i. There are several different possibilities from which to choose appropriate weights w_i – for example, total number of policies in year i, total number of claims incurred in year i, etc. If one chooses the total number of claims incurred, one needs first to estimate the expected number of IBNyR claims.

- $R_{i,j}$ denotes the number of payments. Often one does not have this information and therefore it is sometimes convenient to define $R_{i,j}$ as the number of claims with accident year i that have at least one payment in period j.
- It can easily be seen that, conditional on $R_{i,j}$, we have the Gamma Model 5.18.

We define the normalized incremental payments by

$$Y_{i,j} = \frac{X_{i,j}}{w_i}$$

The joint distribution of $R_{i,j}$ and $Y_{i,j}$ is given by the following formulas (we skip the indices i, j for the moment): for any $\phi > 0$ and $r > 0$, $y > 0$

$$\begin{aligned} f_{R,Y}(r, y; \lambda, m, \nu)dy &= P[y < Y < y + dy | R = r] \; P[R = r] \\ &= \frac{(\nu/m)^{\nu r}}{\Gamma(\nu r)} (wy)^{\nu r-1} \exp\left\{-\frac{\nu}{m} yw\right\} \frac{(w\lambda)^r}{r!} \exp\{-w\lambda\} \; w \, dy \\ &= \left(\lambda \left(\frac{\nu}{m}\right)^{\nu} y^{\nu} w^{\nu+1}\right)^r \frac{1}{r!\Gamma(\nu r) y} \exp\left\{\frac{w}{\phi}\left(-\frac{\nu\phi}{m} y - \lambda\phi\right)\right\} dy \end{aligned}$$

(cf. (5.36)). Now we reparameterize as follows

$$\begin{aligned} p &= (\nu+2)/(\nu+1) \in (1, 2) \\ \mu &= \lambda \; m \\ \phi &= \lambda^{1-p} \; m^{2-p}/(2-p) \end{aligned}$$

Hence, we obtain $\nu = (2-p)/(p-1)$ and

$$\begin{aligned} f_{R,Y}(r, y; \lambda, m, \nu)dy &= \left(\frac{y^{\nu} \; (w/\phi)^{\nu+1}}{(p-1)^{\nu} \; (2-p)}\right)^r \frac{1}{r! \; \Gamma(\nu r) \; y} \\ &\quad \times \exp\left\{\frac{w}{\phi}\left(y \, \frac{\mu^{1-p}}{1-p} - \frac{\mu^{2-p}}{2-p}\right)\right\} dy \end{aligned} \tag{5.39}$$

Therefore, the density of Y on $y > 0$ is given by

$$\begin{aligned} f_Y(y; \lambda, m, \nu) &= \sum_{r \geq 1} f_{R,Y}(r, y; \lambda, m, \nu) \\ &= c\left(y; \frac{w}{\phi}, p\right) \exp\left\{\frac{w}{\phi}\left(y \, \frac{\mu^{1-p}}{1-p} - \frac{\mu^{2-p}}{2-p}\right)\right\} \\ &= c\left(y; \frac{w}{\phi}, p\right) \exp\left\{\frac{w}{\phi}\left(y \, \theta - \kappa_p(\theta)\right)\right\} \end{aligned} \tag{5.40}$$

where

$$\theta = \theta(\mu) \; = \; \frac{\mu^{1-p}}{1-p} < 0 \tag{5.41}$$

$$\kappa_p(\theta) = \frac{1}{2-p}\left((1-p)\,\theta\right)^{\frac{2-p}{1-p}} \tag{5.42}$$

$$c(y; \frac{w}{\phi}, p) = \sum_{r \geq 1}\left(\frac{y^\nu\,(w/\phi)^{\nu+1}}{(p-1)^\nu(2-p)}\right)^r \frac{1}{r!\;\Gamma(\nu r)\;y} \tag{5.43}$$

We have just proved the following lemma:

LEMMA 5.24 *Under Model Assumptions 5.22, the distribution of $Y_{i,j}$ belongs to the EDF with parameters p, $\theta_{i,j}$, $\phi_{i,j}/w_i$, and $\kappa_p(\cdot)$ given by (5.42). That is, $Y_{i,j}$ has density of the form* $(y > 0)$

$$f_Y\left(y; \theta_{i,j}, \frac{\phi_{i,j}}{w_i}, p\right) = c\left(y; \frac{w_i}{\phi_{i,j}}, p\right)\;\exp\left\{\frac{w_i}{\phi_{i,j}}(y\;\theta_{i,j} - \kappa_p\left(\theta_{i,j}\right))\right\} \tag{5.44}$$

Remarks 5.25

- If the density of $Y_{i,j}$ is given by (5.44) then we write

$$Y_{i,j} \overset{(d)}{\sim} \mathrm{ED}^{(p)}\left(\mu_{i,j}, \frac{\phi_{i,j}}{w_i}\right)$$

- Observe that we have met the EDF already in the Exponential Dispersion Model 4.35. Here, the function $b(\cdot)$ has the special form $\kappa_p(\cdot)$.
- See Theorem 4.39 and Lemma 6.6 below,

$$E\left[Y_{i,j}\right] = \kappa_p'(\theta_{i,j}) \;=\; \mu_{i,j} \tag{5.45}$$

$$\mathrm{Var}\left(Y_{i,j}\right) = \frac{\phi_{i,j}}{w_i}\;\kappa_p''(\theta_{i,j}) \;=\; \frac{\phi_{i,j}}{w_i}\;\mu_{i,j}^p \tag{5.46}$$

  Hence, if we define the variance function

$$V_p(\mu) = \mu^p$$

  we immediately see that Tweedie's compound Poisson model satisfies

$$x_{i,j} = E\left[X_{i,j}\right] = w_i\;\mu_{i,j}$$

  and

$$\mathrm{Var}\left(X_{i,j}\right) = \frac{\phi_{i,j}}{w_i^{p-1}}\;V_p(x_{i,j}) \qquad \text{with } p \in (1,2)$$

  Therefore this model closes the gap between the Poisson Model 2.12 and the Gamma Model 5.18.
- In practical applications such as MLE and MCMC methods it is sometimes necessary to evaluate the constant given in (5.43). In these calculations one often faces the difficulties

about stopping the summation of the infinite sum (since succeeding terms do not substantially contribute to the summation). For more on this topic we refer to the remark on p. 196. Moreover, one often has numerical instabilities for real data due to under- and overflows, etc. In such cases one often needs to study the terms on the Log-scale where terms possibly cancel.

Model Assumptions 5.26 (constant dispersion)

In addition to the Model Assumptions 5.22 we assume that the dispersion is constant, that is, $\phi_{i,j} = \phi$ for all $0 \le i \le I$ and $0 \le j \le J$, and that the mean has the multiplicative structure

$$\mu_{i,j} = \mu_i \, \gamma_j$$

□

Remark Theoretically, we could also model the dispersion $\phi_{i,j}$. This means, we could assume that the dispersion is not constant. On the one hand, data often indicates that dispersion is not constant. However, on the other hand, one often observes that modelling with non-constant dispersion does not lead to appropriate results. This comes from the fact that the model often becomes overparametrized when one is also modelling a non-constant dispersion parameter.

***p* known**

Assume $p \in (1, 2)$ is known. In that case it is not necessary to know $R_{i,j}$. The likelihood function is given by (see (5.40))

$$L_{\mathcal{D}_I}(\mu_0, \ldots, \mu_I, \gamma_0, \ldots, \gamma_J) = \prod_{i+j \le I} c\left(\frac{X_{i,j}}{w_i}; \frac{w_i}{\phi}, p\right) \exp\left\{\frac{w_i}{\phi}\left(\frac{X_{i,j}}{w_i}\,\theta_{i,j} - \kappa_p(\theta_{i,j})\right)\right\} \tag{5.47}$$

with

$$\theta_{i,j} = \frac{(\mu_i \gamma_j)^{1-p}}{1-p} \quad \text{and} \quad \kappa_p(\theta_{i,j}) = \frac{(\mu_i \gamma_j)^{2-p}}{2-p} \tag{5.48}$$

We maximize the likelihood function (5.47) by setting its $I + J + 2$ partial derivatives w.r.t. μ_i and γ_j equal to zero, under the constraint $\sum_j \widehat{\gamma}_j^{(0)} = 1$. This leads to the following estimators for μ_i and γ_j:

$$\widehat{\mu}_i^{(0)} = \sum_{j=0}^{I-i} \frac{X_{i,j}}{w_i} \left(\widehat{\gamma}_j^{(0)}\right)^{1-p} \Big/ \sum_{j=0}^{I-i} \left(\widehat{\gamma}_j^{(0)}\right)^{2-p} \tag{5.49}$$

$$\widehat{\gamma}_j^{(0)} = \sum_{i=0}^{I-j} X_{i,j} \left(\widehat{\mu}_i^{(0)}\right)^{1-p} \Big/ \sum_{i=0}^{I-j} w_i \left(\widehat{\mu}_i^{(0)}\right)^{2-p} \tag{5.50}$$

Observe that the dispersion ϕ cancels, that is, for the estimation of the claims reserves, we do not need to know the dispersion parameter. However, ϕ becomes important as soon as we estimate prediction errors (see Chapter 6.1).

Example 5.27 (Tweedie, p known)

We revisit the data set given in Examples 2.7 and 2.11. In Example 2.15 we have already calculated the Poisson estimator for the expected reserves (using the MLE method). The same calculation for Tweedie's compound Poisson model gives, for different p's, the claims reserves in Table 5.5. □

Table 5.5 Reserves from Tweedie's compound Poisson model for different p's

i	Poisson ($p=1$)	$p=1.2$	$p=1.5$
1	15 126	14 682	13 708
2	26 257	26 205	26 241
3	34 538	34 367	34 379
4	85 302	86 425	90 719
5	156 494	154 805	151 687
6	286 121	285 176	282 882
7	449 167	446 156	439 621
8	1 043 242	1 038 347	1 029 197
9	3 950 815	3 945 268	3 934 434
Total	6 047 061	6 031 431	6 002 866

$R_{i,j}$ known, p unknown

If p is unknown, we need the additional information $R_{i,j}$ to estimate p (and ϕ) from the data. The likelihood function of the observations $\widetilde{\mathcal{D}}_I = \{X_{i,j}, R_{i,j};\ i+j \le I\}$ is given by (see (5.39))

$$
\begin{aligned}
&L_{\widetilde{\mathcal{D}}_I}(\mu_0, \ldots, \mu_I, \gamma_0, \ldots, \gamma_J, \phi, p) \\
&= \prod_{i+j\le I} \frac{1}{R_{i,j}!\Gamma(\nu R_{i,j})(X_{i,j}/w_i)} \left(\frac{(X_{i,j}/w_i)^{\nu} (w_i/\phi)^{\nu+1}}{(p-1)^{\nu}(2-p)} \right)^{R_{i,j}} \\
&\quad \times \exp\left\{ \frac{w_i}{\phi} \left(\frac{X_{i,j}}{w_i}\theta_{i,j} - \kappa_p(\theta_{i,j}) \right) \right\}
\end{aligned}
\tag{5.51}
$$

where $\theta_{i,j}$ as well as $\kappa_p(\theta_{i,j})$ satisfy (5.48).

We choose an iterative procedure:

1. Choose a reasonable initialization $p^{(0)}$.
2. For $k \ge 1$ use MLE to estimate $\widehat{\mu}_i^{(k)}$ and $\widehat{\gamma}_j^{(k)}$ from

$$
L_{\widetilde{\mathcal{D}}_I}(\mu_0, \ldots, \mu_I, \gamma_0, \ldots, \gamma_J, \phi, p^{(k-1)})
$$

   with $\sum_j \widehat{\gamma}_j^{(k)} = 1$. The MLE are given by (5.49)–(5.50) with p replaced by $p^{(k-1)}$. Observe that ϕ and $R_{i,j}$ are not needed for the ML optimization.
3. For the estimation of $p^{(k)}$, $k \ge 1$, we consider the profile likelihood of $p^{(k)}$. Consider

$$
L_{\widetilde{\mathcal{D}}_I}(\widehat{\mu}_0^{(k)}, \ldots, \widehat{\mu}_I^{(k)}, \widehat{\gamma}_0^{(k)}, \ldots, \widehat{\gamma}_J^{(k)}, \phi, p^{(k)})
\tag{5.52}
$$

Hence the MLE for ϕ (given $p^{(k)}$) is given by

$$\phi^{(k)} = \frac{-\sum_{i+j\le I} w_i \left((X_{i,j}/w_i)\, \theta_{i,j}^{(k)} - \kappa_{p^{(k)}}\left(\theta_{i,j}^{(k)}\right) \right)}{\left(1+\nu^{(k)}\right) \sum_{i+j\le I} R_{i,j}}$$

(cf. (5.51)), with

$$\theta_{i,j}^{(k)} = \frac{\left(\widehat{\mu}_i^{(k)}\ \widehat{\gamma}_j^{(k)}\right)^{1-p^{(k)}}}{1-p^{(k)}}, \qquad \kappa_{p^{(k)}}(\theta_{i,j}^{(k)}) = \frac{\left(\widehat{\mu}_i^{(k)}\ \widehat{\gamma}_j^{(k)}\right)^{2-p^{(k)}}}{2-p^{(k)}}$$

and

$$\nu^{(k)} = \frac{2-p^{(k)}}{p^{(k)}-1}$$

If we plug $\phi^{(k)}$ into the likelihood function (5.52) we obtain the profile likelihood function $L_{\widetilde{\mathcal{D}}_I}(p^{(k)})$ of $p^{(k)}$. Thus, the profile log-likelihood function of $p^{(k)}$ is given by

$$\begin{aligned}\log L_{\widetilde{\mathcal{D}}_I}(p^{(k)}) &= \log L_{\widetilde{\mathcal{D}}_I}\left(\widehat{\mu}_0^{(k)}, \ldots, \widehat{\mu}_I^{(k)}, \widehat{\gamma}_0^{(k)}, \ldots, \widehat{\gamma}_J^{(k)}, \phi^{(k)}, p^{(k)}\right) \\ &= \widetilde{\widetilde{c}} + (1+\nu^{(k)}) \sum_{i+j\le I} R_{i,j} \left(\log\left(\frac{w_i}{\phi^{(k)}}\right) - 1 \right) \\ &\quad + \sum_{i+j\le I} R_{i,j} \log\left(\frac{1}{2-p^{(k)}} \left(\frac{X_{i,j}/w_i}{p^{(k)}-1} \right)^{\nu^{(k)}} \right) - \sum_{i+j\le I} \log\Gamma\left(\nu^{(k)}\, R_{i,j}\right)\end{aligned} \tag{5.53}$$

Observe that ϕ is replaced by $\phi^{(k)}$ which is now a function of $p^{(k)}$. Hence we maximize this profile likelihood function for given $\widetilde{\mathcal{D}}_I, \widehat{\mu}_0^{(k)}, \ldots, \widehat{\mu}_I^{(k)}, \widehat{\gamma}_0^{(k)}, \ldots, \widehat{\gamma}_J^{(k)}$ and obtain an estimate for $p^{(k)}$. This optimization is usually done using an appropriate numerical algorithm (like the Newton–Raphson algorithm) or an appropriate software package.

4. Steps 2 and 3 are iterated until parameters have sufficiently converged.

Remarks 5.28

- Observe that for unknown p we use the additional information $R_{i,j}$.
- The parameters $(\mu_0, \ldots, \mu_I, \gamma_0, \ldots, \gamma_J)$ and the parameters (ϕ, p) are orthogonal in the sense that the Fisher information matrix is zero in the off-diagonal (see, e.g., Jørgensen and de Souza 1994, p. 76, or Smyth and Jørgensen 2002, p. 150). This implies that the algorithm described above for the parameter estimation is very efficient with typically fast convergence. Moreover, estimated standard errors of $(\mu_0, \ldots, \mu_I, \gamma_0, \ldots, \gamma_J)$, which are of most interest, do not require adjustments by standard errors of (ϕ, p), since these are orthogonal.
- Observe that, by the choice of p, we make an explicit model choice. Hence, within the family of Tweedie's compound Poisson model, we can not only study estimation

errors, but also model errors. Model errors are only purely treated in the literature in, for example, Barnett and Zehnwirth (1998), Venter (1998), Cairns (2000) or Gigante and Sigalotti (2005). We believe that, in the light of Solvency 2, this is a main issue in claims reserving.

Example 5.29 (Tweedie's compound Poisson model)

In order to apply the Gamma Model 5.19 and Tweedie's compound Poisson Model 5.26, we need additional information about the number of payments $r_{i,j}$. Therefore, we do not choose the data set given in Example 2.7. We choose a new data set where we have this additional information. This new data set is also such that not every accident year has the same volume w_i. In this data set the volume w_i is given by the number of reported claims and we assume that the number of IBNyR claims with reporting delay of more than two years is almost zero (for the kind of business under consideration) – see Tables 5.6 and 5.7.

p **known** We then calculate the MLE for the Poisson model (see (2.16)–(2.17)), Tweedie's compound Poisson model with $p = 1.5$ (see (5.49)–(5.50) for $p = 1.5$) and the Gamma model (see (5.37)–(5.38)) and obtain the results shown in Table 5.8.

For the claims reserves we obtain Table 5.9.

Note that the analysis of Gamma model (5.37)–(5.38) requires the knowledge of $r_{i,j}$. If these are not known we can still apply Gamma model (5.49)–(5.50), which leads to the total reserves of 1 386 034 (vs 1 449 959).

p **unknown** The same analysis is performed for unknown p, that is, we estimate p with the help of the profile log-likelihood function (5.53) see also Figure 5.1. We observe a very fast convergence of $p^{(k)}$ and $\widehat{\mu}_i^{(k)}$ and $\widehat{\gamma}_j^{(k)}$ (see Table 5.10).

Tables 5.10 and 5.11 show the iteration and the final claims reserves under p optimization. □

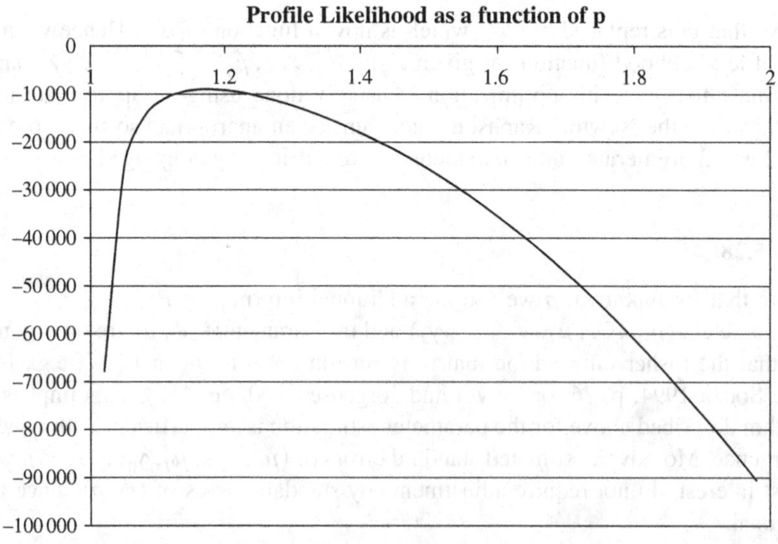

Figure 5.1 Profile log-likelihood function (5.53)

Table 5.6 Observed incremental payments $X_{i,j}$ and volume w_i

$X_{i,j}$	0	1	2	3	4	5	6	7	8	9	10	w_i
0	17 841 110	7 442 433	895 413	407 744	207 130	61 569	15 978	24 924	1236	15 643	321	112 953
1	19 519 117	6 656 520	941 458	155 395	69 458	37 769	53 832	111 391	42 263	25 833		110 364
2	19 991 172	6 327 483	1 100 177	279 649	162 654	70 000	56 878	9881	19 656			105 400
3	19 305 646	5 889 791	793 020	309 042	145 921	97 465	27 523	61 920				102 067
4	18 291 478	5 793 282	689 444	288 626	342 524	110 585	115 843					99 124
5	18 832 520	5 741 214	581 798	248 563	106 875	94 212						101 460
6	17 152 710	5 908 286	524 806	230 456	346 904							94 753
7	16 615 059	5 111 177	553 277	252 877								92 326
8	16 835 453	5 001 897	489 356									89 545

Table 5.7 Observed number of payments $r_{i,j}$

$r_{i,j}$	0	1	2	3	4	5	6	7	8	9	10
0	6 229	3500	425	134	51	24	13	12	6	4	1
1	6395	3342	402	108	31	14	12	5	6	5	
2	6406	2940	401	98	42	18	5	3	3		
3	6148	2898	301	92	41	23	12	10			
4	5952	2699	304	94	49	22	7				
5	5924	2692	300	91	32	23					
6	5545	2754	292	77	35						
7	5520	2459	267	81							
8	5390	2224	223								

Table 5.8 Estimated parameters in the Poisson model, Tweedie's compound Poisson model with $p = 1.5$ and the Gamma model

	Poisson model	Tweedie's model	Gamma model (5.37)–(5.38)
$\widehat{\mu}_0 w_0$	26 913 503	27 092 616	27 725 168
$\widehat{\mu}_1 w_1$	27 613 366	27 521 254	27 817 990
$\widehat{\mu}_2 w_2$	28 039 193	27 775 062	28 147 487
$\widehat{\mu}_3 w_3$	26 671 319	26 483 260	26 562 467
$\widehat{\mu}_4 w_4$	25 720 313	27 640 803	25 553 524
$\widehat{\mu}_5 w_5$	25 745 316	24 792 613	25 642 991
$\widehat{\mu}_6 w_6$	24 367 306	24 928 728	24 354 141
$\widehat{\mu}_7 w_7$	22 895 102	22 548 844	22 801 872
$\widehat{\mu}_8 w_8$	22 929 478	22 201 300	22 845 603
$\widehat{\gamma}_0\%$	71.19	71.20	71.06
$\widehat{\gamma}_1\%$	23.33	23.35	23.38
$\widehat{\gamma}_2\%$	2.84	2.84	2.90
$\widehat{\gamma}_3\%$	1.04	1.04	1.05
$\widehat{\gamma}_4\%$	0.75	0.74	0.79
$\widehat{\gamma}_5\%$	0.29	0.29	0.33
$\widehat{\gamma}_6\%$	0.20	0.20	0.18
$\widehat{\gamma}_7\%$	0.19	0.19	0.15
$\widehat{\gamma}_8\%$	0.08	0.08	0.09
$\widehat{\gamma}_9\%$	0.08	0.08	0.08
$\widehat{\gamma}_{10}\%$	0.00	0.00	0.00

Table 5.9 Claims reserves in the Poisson model, Tweedie's compound Poisson model with $p = 1.5$ and the Gamma model

	Claims reserves		
i	Poisson model	Tweedie's $p = 1.5$	Gamma model (5.37)–(5.38)
0			
1	330	326	319
2	21 663	21 374	22 026
3	41 007	40 572	43 541
4	88 546	95 291	81 303
5	140 150	133 848	127 058
6	204 157	207 179	200 050
7	362 724	353 407	367 652
8	602 784	579 269	608 010
Total	1 461 359	1 431 266	1 449 959

Remark In numerical applications such as the MLE and MCMC methods, the evaluation of the constant given in (5.43) often causes some difficulties. Set $w = 1$. Then the difficulty in the determination of the variable $c(y; \phi, p)$ is the infinite sum given by

$$c(y; \phi, p) = \sum_{r \geq 1} \left(\frac{(1/\phi)^{\nu+1} y^{\nu}}{(p-1)^{\nu}(2-p)} \right)^r \frac{1}{r! \Gamma(r\nu) y} = \frac{1}{y} \sum_{r \geq 1} W_r$$

Tweedie (1984) identified this summation as Wright's (1933) generalized Bessel function. Hence, it is known that this form of Bessel function cannot be expressed in terms of more

Table 5.10 Iteration of Tweedie's compound Poisson model with $p^{(k)}$, $k=0,1,2,3$

	Iteration			
	$k=0$	$k=1$	$k=2$	$k=3$
$p^{(k)}$	1.5000000	1.1742644	1.1741136	
$\widehat{\mu_0}^{(k)}$		239.86	240.63	240.63
$\widehat{\mu_1}^{(k)}$		249.37	249.78	249.78
$\widehat{\mu_2}^{(k)}$		263.52	266.12	266.12
$\widehat{\mu_3}^{(k)}$		259.47	260.68	260.68
$\widehat{\mu_4}^{(k)}$		278.85	262.24	262.23
$\widehat{\mu_5}^{(k)}$		244.36	251.35	251.35
$\widehat{\mu_6}^{(k)}$		263.09	258.09	258.09
$\widehat{\mu_7}^{(k)}$		244.23	246.87	246.87
$\widehat{\mu_8}^{(k)}$		247.93	253.94	253.95
$\widehat{\gamma_0}^{(k)}\%$		71.20	71.19	71.19
$\widehat{\gamma_1}^{(k)}\%$		23.35	23.34	23.34
$\widehat{\gamma_2}^{(k)}\%$		2.84	2.84	2.84
$\widehat{\gamma_3}^{(k)}\%$		1.04	1.04	1.04
$\widehat{\gamma_4}^{(k)}\%$		0.74	0.74	0.74
$\widehat{\gamma_5}^{(k)}\%$		0.29	0.29	0.29
$\widehat{\gamma_6}^{(k)}\%$		0.20	0.20	0.20
$\widehat{\gamma_7}^{(k)}\%$		0.19	0.19	0.19
$\widehat{\gamma_8}^{(k)}\%$		0.08	0.08	0.08
$\widehat{\gamma_9}^{(k)}\%$		0.08	0.08	0.08
$\widehat{\gamma_{10}}^{(k)}\%$		0.00	0.00	0.00

Table 5.11 Claims reserves in Tweedie's compound Poisson model for unknown p

	Claims reserves			
	Poisson	Tweedie's compound Poisson model		
p	1	1.5	1.1742644	1.1741136
0				
1	330	326	326	326
2	21 663	21 374	21 565	21 565
3	41 007	40 572	40 716	40 716
4	88 546	95 291	89 279	89 278
5	140 150	133 848	138 336	138 338
6	204 157	207 179	204 270	204 269
7	362 724	353 407	360 114	360 117
8	602 784	579 269	596 683	596 690
Total	1 461 359	1 431 266	1 451 290	1 451 299

common Bessel functions. The approach we propose to perform the calculations is aimed at selecting only the terms in the infinite sums that contribute most to the series. To do this we utilize the approach of Dunn and Smyth (2005), which directly sums the infinite series, only including terms that significantly contribute to the summation. We have

$$\log(W_r) = r\log(z) - \log\Gamma(r+1) - \log\Gamma(\nu r)$$

where

$$z = \frac{(1/\phi)^{\nu+1} y^{\nu}}{(p-1)^{\nu}(2-p)}$$

Next we replace the Gamma functions using Stirling's approximation and the approximation νr by $\nu r + 1$ and we get

$$\log(W_r) \approx r\{\log(z) + (1+\nu) - \nu\log(\nu) - (1+\nu)\log(r)\}$$
$$- \log(2\pi) - \frac{1}{2}\log(\nu) - \log(r)$$

which is, as stated in Dunn and Smyth (2005), also a reasonable approximation for small r. Now taking the partial derivative w.r.t. r gives,

$$\frac{\partial \log(W_r)}{\partial r} \approx \log(z) - \frac{1}{r} - \log(r) - \nu\log(\nu r)$$
$$\approx \log(z) - \log(r) - \nu\log(\nu r)$$

hence the sequence W_r is unimodal in r. Now we solve for $\partial W_r/\partial r = 0$ in order to find the (approximative) maximum of W_r. Hence, we get that the approximate maximum lies close to

$$R_0 = R_0(\phi, p) = \frac{y^{2-p}}{(2-p)\phi}$$

As stated in Dunn and Smyth (2005), this gives a surprisingly accurate approximation to the true maximum of W_r, $r \in \mathbb{N}$.

Our aim is now to find $R_L < R_0 < R_U$ such that following approximation is sufficiently accuarte for finding the maximum likelihood estimators

$$c(y; \phi, p) \approx \widetilde{c}(y; \phi, p) = \frac{1}{y}\sum_{r=R_L}^{R_U} W_r$$

The fact that $(\partial\log(W_r))/\partial r$ is monotonic and decreasing implies that $\log(W_r)$ is strictly convex in r and hence the terms in W_r decay at a faster rate than geometrically on either side of R_0. Hence, following Dunn and Smyth (2005), we find the bounds

$$c(y; \phi, p) - \widetilde{c}(y; \phi, p) < W_{R_L-1}\frac{1-q_L^{R_L-1}}{1-q_L} + W_{R_U+1}\frac{1}{1-q_U}$$

with

$$q_L = \exp\left(\frac{\partial \log(W_r)}{\partial r}\right)\Bigg|_{r=R_L-1}$$

$$q_U = \exp\left(\frac{\partial \log(W_r)}{\partial r}\right)\Bigg|_{r=R_U+1}$$

Note that Dunn and Smyth (2005) point out that these bounds are typically too conservative since the decay is much faster than geometrically and hence too many non-important terms are considered. Hence they propose to use $R_L < R_0$ and $R_U > R_0$ such that these are the first integers either side of the maximum R_0 for the given parameters ϕ and p.

Hence one is now ready to computationally implement the likelihood function in the IT system using the approximation $\widetilde{c}(y;\, \phi, p)$ for $c(y;\, \phi, p)$.

5.2.6 Wright's model

Wright (1990) has considered a model similar to Tweedie's compound Poisson model, and has used the following model assumptions:

Model Assumptions 5.30 (Wright 1990)

- There exist random variables $R_{i,j}$ and $X_{i,j}^{(k)}$ such that the independent incremental claims are given by

$$X_{i,j} = \sum_{k=0}^{R_{i,j}} X_{i,j}^{(k)}$$

  for all $0 \le i \le I$ and $0 \le j \le J$.
- $R_{i,j}$ are independent Poisson distributed with mean $e_i a_j \kappa_i j^{A_i} \exp\{-b_i j\} > 0$, and the single claim amounts $X_{i,j}^{(k)}$ are independent with mean $m_{i,j} = \exp\{\delta(i+j)\} k j^{\lambda}$ and variational coefficient $\nu^{1/2}$. □

Remarks 5.31

- For the $R_{i,j}$ we have: e_i is a known measure of exposure and a_j is a known adjustment. The parameters κ_i, A_i and b_i need to be estimated.
- For the single claim amounts $X_{i,j}^{(k)}$ we have that k and λ need to be estimated and $\exp\{\delta\ (i+j)\}$ stands for the claims inflation.

One then obtains

$$E\left[X_{i,j}\right] = e_i a_j \kappa_i j^{A_i} \exp\{-b_i j\} \exp\{\delta(i+j)\} k j^{\lambda}$$

$$\mathrm{Var}\left(X_{i,j}\right) = (1+\nu) \exp\{\delta(i+j)\} k j^{\lambda}\ E\left[X_{i,j}\right]$$

This model can then be put into the generalized linear model (GLM) framework and one obtains a structure which is close to the Hoerl curve (see Wright 1990, Renshaw 1994, Zehnwirth 1998 and England and Verrall 2002, Section 4.3).

6 Generalized Linear Models

In Chapters 2, 4 and 5 we have met several models for incremental claims which have a generalized linear model (GLM) basis (e.g. Poisson model, overdispersed Poisson model, Gamma model and Tweedie's compound Poisson model). These models belong to the EDF and the parameters were estimated with maximum likelihood estimators (MLEs) or Bayesian methods. In this chapter we give a systematic GLM approach to EDF models that gives numerical methods for MLE of the parameters. In fact it would also have been possible to present this chapter at an earlier stage of the book to emphasize its importance. That is, GLM methods play an important role in claims reserving, because they provide the basis for finding, for example, MSEP estimates in several problems with MLE.

Renshaw (1995) and Renshaw and Verrall (1998) were the first who implemented the standard GLM techniques for the derivation of estimates for incremental data in a claims reserving context. A good overview on the use of GLM techniques in claims reserving can be found in England and Verrall (2002, 2007). For the theoretical background of GLM theory we refer to McCullagh and Nelder (1989), Fahrmeir and Tutz (2001) and Wood (2006). For an extensive discussion of EDF models see Jørgensen (1997).

6.1 MAXIMUM LIKELIHOOD ESTIMATORS

Before we consider the claims reserving problem, we give a short introduction to point estimation via MLE. For a detailed discussion we refer to Lehmann (1983), Chapter 6.

Assume that $X_1, \ldots, X_n$ are i.i.d. with density $f_\theta(\cdot)$, where θ is the unknown parameter of the distribution that we would like to estimate. We denote the true value of θ by θ_0. Then, under appropriate assumptions (see Theorem 6.2.1 in Lehmann 1983) we have

$$P_{\theta_0}\left[\prod_{k=1}^{n} f_{\theta_0}(X_k) > \prod_{k=1}^{n} f_\theta(X_k)\right] \to 1, \qquad \text{as } n \to \infty \tag{6.1}$$

for any fixed $\theta \neq \theta_0$. That is, the density of $X_1, \ldots, X_n$ at the true value θ_0 exceeds the density at any other fixed value θ for large sample sizes n. Henceforth, we determine/estimate the value of θ_0 by maximizing the density for given observations $X_1, \ldots, X_n$, that is,

$$\widehat{\theta}_n^{\text{MLE}} = \arg\max_\theta \prod_{k=1}^{n} f_\theta(X_k) \tag{6.2}$$

If this value $\widehat{\theta}_n^{\text{MLE}}$ exists and is unique then it is called maximum likelihood estimator (MLE) for θ.

Example 6.1

Assume that $X_1, \ldots, X_n$ are i.i.d. normally distributed with unknown mean θ and variance 1. Henceforth, we have

$$\begin{aligned}\widehat{\theta}_n^{\mathrm{MLE}} &= \arg\max_{\theta} \prod_{k=1}^{n} \frac{1}{\sqrt{2\pi}} \exp\{-\tfrac{1}{2}(X_k-\theta)^2\}\\ &= \arg\max_{\theta} \log\left(\prod_{k=1}^{n} \frac{1}{\sqrt{2\pi}} \exp\{-\tfrac{1}{2}(X_k-\theta)^2\}\right)\\ &= \arg\max_{\theta} \sum_{k=1}^{n} -\tfrac{1}{2}(X_k-\theta)^2\end{aligned}$$

This immediately implies that

$$\widehat{\theta}_n^{\mathrm{MLE}} = \frac{1}{n}\sum_{k=1}^{n} X_k$$

□

The next theorem gives properties of the MLE. For precise assumptions and a proof we refer to Lehmann (1983), Theorem 6.2.3.

THEOREM 6.2 *Assume that $X_1, \ldots, X_n$ are i.i.d. with density $f_\theta(\cdot)$. Under mild conditions we have the following convergence in distribution*

$$n^{1/2}\left(\widehat{\theta}_n^{\mathrm{MLE}} - \theta\right) \xrightarrow{(d)} \mathcal{N}\left(0, \frac{1}{H(\theta)}\right), \quad \text{as } n \to \infty$$

with

$$H(\theta) = -E_\theta\left[\frac{\partial^2}{\partial\theta^2}\log f_\theta(X)\right] = E_\theta\left[\left(\frac{\partial}{\partial\theta}\log f_\theta(X)\right)^2\right]$$

Remarks 6.3

- $H(\theta)$ is called information or Fisher information that X contains about the parameter θ.
- The asymptotic result in Theorem 6.2 justifies the estimators and estimation errors that we construct in the following. It essentially says that MLEs are asymptotically unbiased with asymptotic variance (estimation error) given by the inverse Fisher information. Thus, we will use the Fisher information to approximate the estimation error. Be aware of the fact that all the statements only hold in an asymptotic sense, that is, we have neither unbiasedness nor exact calculations for second moments. The remaining question (which we will not answer) is whether we are already in the asymptotic regime.
- The mild conditions can be found in Lehmann (1983), Section 6.2. Though they are mild, they are often difficult to be proved. The EDF defined in (4.37) satisfies the mild conditions of Theorem 6.2 (see Example 6.2.5 in Lehmann 1983).

In the multivariate parameter case, that is, $X_1, \ldots, X_n$ are i.i.d. with density $f_\theta(\cdot)$ and parameter $\theta = (\theta_1, \ldots, \theta_p)$, we define the Fisher information matrix by $H(\theta) = \left(H(\theta)_{r,s}\right)_{r,s=1,\ldots,p}$ with

$$H(\theta)_{r,s} = -E_\theta\left[\frac{\partial^2}{\partial\theta_r\,\partial\theta_s}\log f_\theta(X)\right] = E_\theta\left[\frac{\partial}{\partial\theta_r}\log f_\theta(X)\,\frac{\partial}{\partial\theta_s}\log f_\theta(X)\right] \tag{6.3}$$

Then $n^{1/2}\left(\widehat{\theta}_n^{\mathrm{MLE}} - \theta\right)$ is asymptotically multivariate normal with mean vector zero and covariance matrix $H(\theta)^{-1}$.

6.2 GENERALIZED LINEAR MODELS FRAMEWORK

In this section we sketch the structure needed to apply the GLM theory for claims reserving. The incremental models in Chapter 5 were of the following structure:

1. ***Random component.*** The random components $X_{i,j}$, $0 \le i \le I$ and $0 \le j \le J$, satisfy

$$E\left[X_{i,j}\right] = x_{i,j} \tag{6.4}$$

$$\mathrm{Var}\left(X_{i,j}\right) = \frac{\phi_{i,j}}{w_{i,j}}\, V(x_{i,j}) \tag{6.5}$$

where $\phi_{i,j} > 0$ is the dispersion parameter, $V(\cdot)$ is an appropriate variance function and $w_{i,j} > 0$ are known weights or volume measures.

At this stage the model has $(I+1)(J+1)$ unknown parameters $x_{i,j}$ for the means of $X_{i,j}$. We have observations in the upper triangle $\mathcal{D}_I$ for estimating $x_{i,j}$ with $i + j \le I$, and we would like to predict the lower triangle $\mathcal{D}_I^c$. This means that we need additional structure that transports the information from the upper to the lower triangle. In other words, we need to reduce the dimension of unknown parameters. This is precisely done by the next component.

2. ***Systematic component.*** Assume that $x_{i,j}$ $(0 \le i \le I,\ 0 \le j \le J)$ can be specified by a small number of unknown parameters $\boldsymbol{b} = (b_1, \ldots, b_p)'$ which produce a linear predictor $\boldsymbol{\eta} = (\eta_{i,j})_{\{0\le i\le I, 0\le j\le J\}}$:

$$\eta_{i,j} = \Gamma_{i,j}\,\boldsymbol{b} \tag{6.6}$$

for appropriate (deterministic) $(1 \times p)$-design matrices $\Gamma_{i,j}$ (model matrices, covariates).

3. ***Response and link function.*** The link between the random components and the systematic components is given by a response function $h(\cdot)$:

$$x_{i,j} = h(\eta_{i,j}) \tag{6.7}$$

If the inverse $g = h^{-1}$ of the response function h exists, then

$$g(x_{i,j}) = \eta_{i,j} = \Gamma_{i,j}\,\boldsymbol{b} \tag{6.8}$$

and g is called the link function.

Now, we specify the additional structure for the means of $X_{i,j}$. Assume that we have a multiplicative structure

$$x_{i,j} = \mu_i \, \gamma_j \tag{6.9}$$

with μ_i standing for the exposure of accident year i (e.g. expected claims load, expected number of claims, total number of policies, etc.) and γ_j defining an expected claims/reporting/cashflow pattern over the different development periods j. The multiplicative structure (6.9) exactly defines how the information from the upper triangle is transported to the lower triangle. It reduces the dimension of unknown parameters from $(I+1)(J+1)$ to $I+J+2$.

For the multiplicative structure, it is straightforward to choose the log-link

$$g(\cdot) = h^{-1}(\cdot) = \log(\cdot) \tag{6.10}$$

as the link function. Then we have

$$\eta_{i,j} = \log(x_{i,j}) = \log(\mu_i) + \log(\gamma_j) \tag{6.11}$$

Of course, (6.9) shows that μ_i and γ_j can only be determined up to a constant factor, that is, $\widetilde{\mu}_i = c\mu_i$ and $\widetilde{\gamma}_j = \gamma_j / c$ would give the same estimate for $x_{i,j}$ for any $c > 0$. Therefore, in Chapter 2, we have assumed that $(\gamma_j)_{0 \le j \le J}$ is a claims development pattern, i.e. sums up to 1. In this chapter it is easier to choose a different constraint/scaling. We set $\mu_0 = 1$, hence $\log(\mu_0) = 0$ and

$$\eta_{0,j} = \log(\gamma_j) \tag{6.12}$$

(cf. (6.11)). This leads to

$$\boldsymbol{b} = \big(\log(\mu_1), \ldots, \log(\mu_I), \log(\gamma_0), \ldots, \log(\gamma_J)\big)' \tag{6.13}$$

and

$$\Gamma_{0,j} = (0, \ldots, 0, 0, 0, \ldots, 0, e_{I+j+1}, 0, \ldots, 0) \tag{6.14}$$

$$\Gamma_{i,j} = (0, \ldots, 0, e_i, 0, \ldots, 0, e_{I+j+1}, 0, \ldots, 0) \tag{6.15}$$

for $1 \le i \le I$ and $0 \le j \le J$, where the entries $e_i = 1$ and $e_{I+j+1} = 1$ are on the ith and the $(I+j+1)$st position, respectively. We obtain

$$\eta_{i,j} = \Gamma_{i,j} \, \boldsymbol{b}$$

Hence, we have reduced the dimension from $(I+1)(J+1)$ unknown parameters $x_{i,j}$ to $p = I+J+1$ unknown parameters μ_i and γ_j.

These parameters $\boldsymbol{b}$ are then estimated with the MLE method. This is further investigated in the next sections, after having introduced the distributional model for the incremental claims $X_{i,j}$.

6.3 EXPONENTIAL DISPERSION FAMILY

We assume that the distributions of the incremental claims $X_{i,j}$ belong to the EDF. We have met this family before, for example, in Model Assumptions 4.35 and Lemma 5.24.

Model Assumptions 6.4

- Increments $X_{i,j}$ of different accident years i and/or different development years j are independent.
- The increments $X_{i,j}$ have densities (w.r.t. to the counting or Lebesgue measure)

$$f(x; \theta_{i,j}, \phi_{i,j}, w_{i,j}) = a\left(x, \frac{\phi_{i,j}}{w_{i,j}}\right) \exp\left\{\frac{x\,\theta_{i,j} - b(\theta_{i,j})}{\phi_{i,j}/w_{i,j}}\right\} \tag{6.16}$$

where $b(\cdot)$ is a real-valued twice-differentiable function of the so-called natural parameter $\theta_{i,j}$ such that $(b')^{-1}(\cdot)$ exists, $\phi_{i,j} > 0$ is the dispersion parameter, $w_{i,j} > 0$ is some known constant (exposure weight) and $a(\cdot, \cdot)$ is the appropriate real-valued normalizing function. □

Remarks 6.5

- A distribution of type (6.16) is called EDF. Each member of the EDF is characterized by the specific form of the real-valued functions $a(\cdot, \cdot)$ and $b(\cdot)$. The EDF contains the following examples: Poisson, overdispersed Poisson, Bernoulli, Binomial, Negative-Binomial, Gamma, Tweedie's compound Poisson model (i.e. compound Poisson distribution with independent Gamma distributed severities), Gaussian, Inverse-Gaussian distribution (see, e.g., McCullagh and Nelder (1989), Table 2.1, p. 30).
- A specific GLM model is fully characterized by the following three components:
  - the type of the EDF distribution for the random component $X_{i,j}$,
  - the response function h or the link function g for the link between the random component $X_{i,j}$ and the systematic component $\eta_{i,j}$ and
  - the design matrix $\Gamma_{i,j}$.

  In this formulation, the special case of the classical linear model is defined by a Gaussian distribution and the identity function $g(x) = x$ for the link between the random component $X_{i,j}$ and the systematic component $\eta_{i,j} = \Gamma_{i,j}\, \boldsymbol{b}$:

$$E[X_{i,j}] = \Gamma_{i,j}\, \boldsymbol{b},$$
$$X_{i,j} = \Gamma_{i,j}\, \boldsymbol{b} + \varepsilon_{i,j}$$

  where $\varepsilon_{i,j} \overset{(d)}{\sim} \mathcal{N}(0, \sigma^2)$.
- Compared to the classical linear model, the GLM allows for two extensions:
  (i) the distribution of the random component $X_{i,j}$ may come from an EDF distribution different to the Gaussian distribution, and
  (ii) the link function g may become any strictly monotone, differentiable function other than the identity function.

The price we have to pay for these extensions is that there are, in general, no direct methods but only iterative procedures to calculate the parameter estimates (cf. Subsection 6.4.2). A further consequence is that most results about properties of the estimators only hold in an asymptotic sense (cf. Remarks 6.15).

- The choice of a suitable response or link function h and g, respectively, depends on the specific EDF. For each EDF, there exists a so-called canonical link function. The canonical link function g relates the natural parameter $\theta_{i,j}$ directly to the linear predictor (systematic component) $\eta_{i,j}$,

$$\eta_{i,j} = g(x_{i,j}) = \theta_{i,j}$$

Since $x_{i,j} = b'(\theta_{i,j})$, see (6.17) below, this means that $g\big(b'(\theta_{i,j})\big) = \theta_{i,j}$ and the canonical link function is given by $g = (b')^{-1}$. Thus, using the canonical link function we have the linear model $\theta_{i,j} = \Gamma_{i,j}\, \boldsymbol{b}$ for the natural parameter. Therefore, canonical link functions lead to GLMs with convenient mathematical and statistical properties and some calculations become easier. However, this should not be the main reason for choosing them. In general, there is no *a priori* reason why the systematic effects should be additive on the scale given by the canonical link function. Sometimes a non-canonical link function is more appropriate. Such a situation is given by the multiplicative model (6.9), where it is natural to use the log-link $g(x_{i,j}) = \log(x_{i,j})$ as link function (see (6.11)). Multiplicative models are standard in insurance practice and, usually, are a reasonable choice in insurance rating and reserving context. For example, most models for claims counts based on an independence assumption in cross-classified data lead to multiplicative models. However, observe that the log-link is the canonical link function only for the Poisson distribution.

- Sometimes the assumption that the true density of the response variable belongs to a specific EDF is too idealistic. In this case quasi-likelihood models are suitable extensions of the original class of GLMs. In quasi-likelihood models the EDF assumption is dropped and no full distribution assumptions are necessary. In quasi-likelihood models only the mean and the variance functions are to be specified (see, e.g., Fahrmeir and Tutz 2001, Section 2.3).

LEMMA 6.6 *Under Model Assumptions 6.4 we have the following identities*

$$E\left[X_{i,j}\right] = x_{i,j} = b'(\theta_{i,j}) \tag{6.17}$$

$$\operatorname{Var}\left(X_{i,j}\right) = \frac{\phi_{i,j}}{w_{i,j}}\, b''(\theta_{i,j}) \tag{6.18}$$

Remark Due to formulas (6.17)–(6.18), one often introduces a variance function V in terms of the mean $x_{i,j}$

$$V(x_{i,j}) = b''\left((b')^{-1}\left(x_{i,j}\right)\right) \tag{6.19}$$

We have already seen the following variance functions (within the EDF)

$$\begin{aligned} &V(x_{i,j}) = x_{i,j} && \text{Poisson model (5.30)} \\ &V(x_{i,j}) = x_{i,j}^2 && \text{Gamma model (5.34)} \\ &V(x_{i,j}) = x_{i,j}^p && p \in (1,2) \quad \text{Tweedie's compound Poisson model (5.46)} \end{aligned} \tag{6.20}$$

Other examples are

$$\begin{aligned} &V(x_{i,j}) = 1 && \text{Gaussian model} \\ &V(x_{i,j}) = x_{i,j}^3 && \text{Inverse-Gaussian model} \end{aligned}$$

To prove Lemma 6.6 we define the log-likelihood function of $f(x;\, \theta_{i,j}, \phi_{i,j}, w_{i,j})$

$$l(x;\, \theta_{i,j}, \phi_{i,j}, w_{i,j}) = \log f(x;\, \theta_{i,j}, \phi_{i,j}, w_{i,j}) \tag{6.21}$$

Proof Lemma 6.6 W.l.o.g. we assume that $f(x;\, \theta_{i,j}, \phi_{i,j}, w_{i,j})$ is a density w.r.t. to the Lebesgue measure. Observe that

$$\begin{aligned} 0 &= \frac{\partial}{\partial \theta_{i,j}} 1 \\ &= \frac{\partial}{\partial \theta_{i,j}} \int_x f(x;\, \theta_{i,j}, \phi_{i,j}, w_{i,j})\, dx \\ &= \int_x \frac{\partial l(x;\, \theta_{i,j}, \phi_{i,j}, w_{i,j})}{\partial \theta_{i,j}} f(x;\, \theta_{i,j}, \phi_{i,j}, w_{i,j})\, dx \\ &= E\left[\frac{\partial l(X_{i,j};\, \theta_{i,j}, \phi_{i,j}, w_{i,j})}{\partial \theta_{i,j}}\right] \\ &= \frac{w_{i,j}}{\phi_{i,j}} \left(E\left[X_{i,j}\right] - b'(\theta_{i,j})\right) \end{aligned}$$

This proves (6.17). Analogously, using (6.17), we obtain

$$\begin{aligned} 0 &= \frac{\partial^2}{\partial \theta_{i,j}^2} 1 \\ &= \frac{\partial^2}{\partial \theta_{i,j}^2} \int_x f(x;\, \theta_{i,j}, \phi_{i,j}, w_{i,j})\, dx \\ &= E\left[\frac{\partial^2 l(X_{i,j};\, \theta_{i,j}, \phi_{i,j}, w_{i,j})}{\partial \theta_{i,j}^2}\right] + E\left[\left(\frac{\partial l(X_{i,j};\, \theta_{i,j}, \phi_{i,j}, w_{i,j})}{\partial \theta_{i,j}}\right)^2\right] \\ &= \frac{w_{i,j}}{\phi_{i,j}} \left(-b''(\theta_{i,j}) + \frac{w_{i,j}}{\phi_{i,j}}\, E\left[\left(X_{i,j} - b'(\theta_{i,j})\right)^2\right]\right) \\ &= \frac{w_{i,j}}{\phi_{i,j}} \left(-b''(\theta_{i,j}) + \frac{w_{i,j}}{\phi_{i,j}}\, \mathrm{Var}\left(X_{i,j}\right)\right) \end{aligned} \tag{6.22}$$

This finishes the proof of Lemma 6.6. □

Remark In the proof of Lemma 6.6 we have used the fact that it is permissible to exchange the order of differentiation and integration if the distribution belongs to the EDF (see, e.g., Witting 1985, p. 152 or Pfanzagl 1994, p. 24).

Note that (6.22) allows for direct calculation of the (one-dimensional) Fisher information for $\theta_{i,j}$ within EDF. As will be seen below, we will have a multivariate parameter Fisher information matrix corresponding to the log-link function that is chosen (see Section 6.4).

6.4 PARAMETER ESTIMATION IN THE EDF

In this section we restrict ourselves to the multiplicative model (6.9), that is

$$x_{i,j} = \mu_i \; \gamma_j$$

hence we have reduced the number of $(I+1)(J+1)$ unknown parameters $x_{i,j}$ to $I+J+1$ unknown parameters μ_i and γ_j (with an appropriate normalization condition). This implies that we need at least $I+J+1$ observations $X_{i,j}$ for the estimation of the parameters. Then, for the response function $x_{i,j} = h(\eta_{i,j}) = \exp(\eta_{i,j})$ (i.e., log-link function $g(x_{i,j}) = \log(x_{i,j})$), the parameter vector $\boldsymbol{b}$ (cf. (6.13)) and the design matrix $\Gamma_{i,j}$ (cf. (6.14)–(6.15)), the mean $x_{i,j} = E[X_{i,j}]$ is given by

$$x_{i,j} = \exp\left(\eta_{i,j}\right) = \exp\left(\Gamma_{i,j}\; \boldsymbol{b}\right) = \exp\{\log(\mu_i) + \log(\gamma_j)\} = \mu_i \; \gamma_j$$

for $i = 0, \ldots, I$ and $j = 0, \ldots, J$.

Often it is appropriate to express the log-likelihood function (6.21) in terms of its mean, that is, one replaces $\theta_{i,j}$ by $x_{i,j} = b'(\theta_{i,j})$ (cf. (6.17)), and identifies

$$l(x;\, x_{i,j}, \phi_{i,j}, w_{i,j}) \quad \Leftrightarrow \quad l(x;\, \theta_{i,j}, \phi_{i,j}, w_{i,j})$$

From the context it will always be clear which form of the log-likelihood function is used.

6.4.1 MLE for the EDF

As mentioned at the end of Section 6.2, now we use MLE on the set of observations $\mathcal{D}_I = \{X_{i,j};\; i+j \le I\}$ to estimate the unknown parameter vector $\boldsymbol{b}$. That is, we maximize the function

$$\begin{aligned} l_{\mathcal{D}_I}(\boldsymbol{b}) &= \log \prod_{i+j\le I} f\left(X_{i,j};\, (b')^{-1}(x_{i,j}), \phi_{i,j}, w_{i,j}\right) \\ &= \sum_{i+j\le I} l(X_{i,j};\, x_{i,j}, \phi_{i,j}, w_{i,j}) \\ &= \sum_{i+j\le I} l(X_{i,j};\, \mu_i\gamma_j, \phi_{i,j}, w_{i,j}) \end{aligned} \tag{6.23}$$

We maximize the log-likelihood $l_{\mathcal{D}_I}(\boldsymbol{b})$ by setting the $I+J+1$ partial derivatives w.r.t. the unknown parameters μ_i and γ_j equal to zero. Thus, we obtain estimates $\widehat{\mu_i}$ and $\widehat{\gamma_j}$ and hence

$$\widehat{\boldsymbol{b}} = \left(\log(\widehat{\mu_1}), \ldots, \log(\widehat{\mu_I}), \log(\widehat{\gamma_0}), \ldots, \log(\widehat{\gamma_J})\right)' \tag{6.24}$$

with $\widehat{\log(\mu_i)} = \log(\widehat{\mu}_i)$ and $\widehat{\log(\gamma_j)} = \log(\widehat{\gamma}_j)$. From this we derive an estimator for the mean $x_{i,j}$ as follows

$$\widehat{x_{i,j}} = \exp\left\{\widehat{\eta_{i,j}}\right\} = \exp\left\{\Gamma_{i,j}\, \widehat{\boldsymbol{b}}\right\} = \exp\left\{\widehat{\log(\mu_i)} + \widehat{\log(\gamma_j)}\right\} = \widehat{\mu}_i\, \widehat{\gamma}_j \tag{6.25}$$

ESTIMATOR 6.7 (MLE for EDF) *The MLE in the EDF Model 6.4 is given by*

$$\widehat{X_{i,j}}^{\text{EDF}} = \widehat{x_{i,j}} = \widehat{E}\left[X_{i,j} \middle| \mathcal{D}_I\right] = \widehat{\mu}_i\, \widehat{\gamma}_j$$

$$\widehat{C_{i,J}}^{\text{EDF}} = \widehat{E}\left[C_{i,J} \middle| \mathcal{D}_I\right] = C_{i,I-i} + \sum_{j=I-i+1}^{J} \widehat{X_{i,j}}^{\text{EDF}}$$

for $i + j > I$.

Remarks 6.8

- This is exactly what we have found in Section 5.2.
- Observe that sometimes it is appropriate to scale $X_{i,j}$ by some volume measure which gives a different scaling in μ_i.
- We remark that for the estimate $\widehat{x_{i,j}}$ we do not need an explicit choice for $\phi_{i,j}$ and $w_{i,j}$ whenever $\phi_{i,j}/w_{i,j}$ is constant in i and j (see (6.30)). We have only used an explicit choice in Tweedie's compound Poisson model to estimate the unknown power p of the variance function (see Subsection 5.2.5).
- We have already seen that we obtain a system of equations for $\widehat{\mu}_i$ and $\widehat{\gamma}_j$ which we have to solve (see, e.g., Poisson model (2.16)–(2.17), Gamma model (5.37)–(5.38) and Tweedie's compound Poisson model (5.49)–(5.50)). Standard GLM software often uses a variant of the Newton–Raphson algorithm (also known as Fisher's scoring method or iteratively weighted least-squares (IWLS)) to solve these equations (see also McCullagh and Nelder 1989, Fahrmeir and Tutz 2001 or Wood 2006). We describe the method below, since it is used to justify the MSEP estimates.
- We could now do a goodness of fit analysis involving deviance and residuals. For a detailed analysis on this topic we refer to McCullagh and Nelder (1989), Fahrmeir and Tutz (2001) and England and Verrall (2001).
- Examples: we have already seen the MLE in the Poisson case (2.16)–(2.17) and for Tweedie's compound Poisson model (5.49)–(5.50). For the Gamma model with $w_{i,j} = w_i$ and $\phi_{i,j} = \phi$, we obtain the following estimates

$$\widehat{\mu}_i = \frac{1}{I - i + 1} \sum_{j=0}^{I-i} X_{i,j}\, \widehat{\gamma}_j^{-1} \tag{6.26}$$

$$\widehat{\gamma}_j = \sum\nolimits_{i=0}^{I-j} w_i\, X_{i,j}\, \widehat{\mu}_i^{-1} \Big/ \sum\nolimits_{i=0}^{I-j} w_i \tag{6.27}$$

with $\sum_j \widehat{\gamma}_j = 1$. If we compare this to the Gamma model (5.37)–(5.38), we see that the number of payments $r_{i,j}$ is now replaced by the volume measure w_i.

6.4.2 Fisher's Scoring Method

In this subsection we present an iterative algorithm (known as Fisher's scoring method or iteratively weighted least-squares (IWLS)) which can be used for the calculation of the MLE for the parameter vector $\boldsymbol{b} = (b_1, \ldots, b_{I+J+1})'$, that is, for finding the roots of the maximization problem.

Recall that $\eta_{i,j} = \Gamma_{i,j}\, \boldsymbol{b}$, $x_{i,j} = h(\eta_{i,j})$ and $\theta_{i,j} = (b')^{-1}(x_{i,j})$. We have the following lemma.

LEMMA 6.9 *Under Model Assumptions 6.4 the log-likelihood function given by*

$$l(x;\, \theta_{i,j}, \phi_{i,j}, w_{i,j}) = \log a\left(x, \frac{\phi_{i,j}}{w_{i,j}}\right) + \frac{x\, \theta_{i,j} - b(\theta_{i,j})}{\phi_{i,j}/w_{i,j}} \tag{6.28}$$

satisfies for $k = 1, \ldots, I + J + 1$ the following equalities

$$\frac{\partial}{\partial b_k} l(x;\, \theta_{i,j}, \phi_{i,j}, w_{i,j}) = W(x_{i,j})\, \left(x - x_{i,j}\right)\, \frac{\partial \eta_{i,j}}{\partial x_{i,j}}\, \Gamma_{i,j}^{(k)}$$

where $\Gamma_{i,j}^{(k)}$ is the kth coordinate of the design matrix $\Gamma_{i,j}$ (cf. (6.14)–(6.15)*) and*

$$W(x_{i,j}) = \frac{w_{i,j}}{\phi_{i,j}}\, \frac{1}{V(x_{i,j})}\, \left(\frac{\partial \eta_{i,j}}{\partial x_{i,j}}\right)^{-2} \tag{6.29}$$

where $V(x_{i,j})$ is the variance function given by (6.19).

Proof By the chain rule we have

$$\frac{\partial}{\partial b_k} l(x;\, \theta_{i,j}, \phi_{i,j}, w_{i,j}) = \frac{\partial l(x;\, \theta_{i,j}, \phi_{i,j}, w_{i,j})}{\partial \theta_{i,j}}\, \frac{\partial \theta_{i,j}}{\partial x_{i,j}}\, \frac{\partial x_{i,j}}{\partial \eta_{i,j}}\, \frac{\partial \eta_{i,j}}{\partial b_k}$$

Next we calculate the single terms in the equation above. Using Lemma 6.6 we derive

$$\frac{\partial l(x;\, \theta_{i,j}, \phi_{i,j}, w_{i,j})}{\partial \theta_{i,j}} = \frac{w_{i,j}}{\phi_{i,j}}\left(x - b'(\theta_{i,j})\right) = \frac{w_{i,j}}{\phi_{i,j}}\left(x - x_{i,j}\right)$$

$$\frac{\partial x_{i,j}}{\partial \theta_{i,j}} = b''(\theta_{i,j}) = V(x_{i,j}) \quad \text{and}$$

$$\frac{\partial \eta_{i,j}}{\partial b_k} = \Gamma_{i,j}^{(k)}$$

Henceforth, we obtain

$$\begin{aligned}\frac{\partial}{\partial b_k} l(x;\, \theta_{i,j}, \phi_{i,j}, w_{i,j}) &= \frac{w_{i,j}}{\phi_{i,j}}\, \left(x - x_{i,j}\right)\, \frac{1}{V(x_{i,j})}\, \frac{\partial x_{i,j}}{\partial \eta_{i,j}}\, \Gamma_{i,j}^{(k)} \\ &= W(x_{i,j})\, \left(x - x_{i,j}\right)\, \frac{\partial \eta_{i,j}}{\partial x_{i,j}}\, \Gamma_{i,j}^{(k)}\end{aligned}$$

This completes the proof of the lemma. □

Since the MLE $\widehat{\boldsymbol{b}}$ maximizes the log-likelihood function $l_{\mathcal{D}_I}(\boldsymbol{b})$ (given in (6.23)) we know that the partial derivatives of $l_{\mathcal{D}_I}(\boldsymbol{b})$ w.r.t. the parameters b_k disappear for every $k=1,\ldots,I+J+1$ at $\widehat{\boldsymbol{b}}$. Using Lemma 6.9, this implies that the MLE $\widehat{\boldsymbol{b}}$ satisfies

$$\frac{\partial}{\partial b_k}\sum_{i+j\le I} l(X_{i,j};\theta_{i,j},\phi_{i,j},w_{i,j})\bigg|_{\widehat{b}} = \sum_{i+j\le I} W(x_{i,j})\,(X_{i,j}-x_{i,j})\,\frac{\partial\eta_{i,j}}{\partial x_{i,j}}\Gamma_{i,j}^{(k)}\bigg|_{\widehat{b}} = 0 \tag{6.30}$$

for every $k=1,\ldots,I+J+1$. Thus, we have found the MLE $\widehat{\boldsymbol{b}}$ for $\boldsymbol{b}$ based on the observations $\mathcal{D}_I$ if the so-called score function

$$\begin{aligned}\mathbf{u}=\mathbf{u}(\boldsymbol{b}) &= \left(\frac{\partial}{\partial b_k}\sum_{i+j\le I} l(X_{i,j};\theta_{i,j},\phi_{i,j},w_{i,j})\right)_{k=1,\ldots,I+J+1}\\ &= \left(\sum_{i+j\le I} W(x_{i,j})\;(X_{i,j}-x_{i,j})\;\frac{\partial\eta_{i,j}}{\partial x_{i,j}}\;\Gamma_{i,j}^{(k)}\right)_{k=1,\ldots,I+J+1}\end{aligned} \tag{6.31}$$

is equal to the null vector and the Hessian matrix of $l(\,\cdot\,;\theta_{i,j},\phi_{i,j},w_{i,j})$ on $\mathcal{D}_I$

$$\mathbf{W}=\mathbf{W}(\boldsymbol{b}) = \left(\sum_{i+j\le I}\frac{\partial^2}{\partial b_k\,\partial b_l} l(X_{i,j};\theta_{i,j},\phi_{i,j},w_{i,j})\right)_{k,l=1,\ldots,I+J+1} \tag{6.32}$$

is negative definite.

We define $N=|\mathcal{D}_I|$ to be the number of observations. In the following we consider the Hessian matrix $\mathbf{W}$ as a function of the random variables $X_{i,j}$ and define the Fisher information matrix by

$$\begin{aligned}H=H^{(N)}(\boldsymbol{b}) &= -E\big[\mathbf{W}(\boldsymbol{b})\big]\\ &= \left(-E\left[\sum_{i+j\le I}\frac{\partial^2}{\partial b_k\,\partial b_l} l(X_{i,j};\theta_{i,j},\phi_{i,j},w_{i,j})\right]\right)_{k,l=1,\ldots,I+J+1}\end{aligned} \tag{6.33}$$

Remarks 6.10

- Observe that, due to the summation over $i+j\le I$, the number of observations N is already contained in $H^{(N)}$.
- The matrices $-\mathbf{W}$ and $H=-E[\mathbf{W}]$ are often called observed and expected Fisher information matrix, respectively (see, e.g., Fahrmeir and Tutz 2001).

LEMMA 6.11 *Under Model Assumptions 6.4 the Fisher information matrix* $H=H^{(N)}=\left(H_{k,l}\right)_{k,l=1,\ldots,I+J+1}$ *satisfies*

$$H_{k,l}=H_{k,l}(\boldsymbol{b}) = \sum_{i+j\le I} W(x_{i,j})\;\Gamma_{i,j}^{(k)}\;\Gamma_{i,j}^{(l)}$$

Proof of Lemma 6.11 Observe that we have

$$H_{k,l}(\boldsymbol{b}) = -E\left[\frac{\partial}{\partial b_l} u_k(\boldsymbol{b})\right]$$

Moreover, using $x_{i,j} = h(\Gamma_{i,j}\ \boldsymbol{b})$, $\eta_{i,j} = \Gamma_{i,j}\ \boldsymbol{b}$ and Lemma 6.9 we have

$$\begin{aligned}\frac{\partial}{\partial b_l} u_k(\boldsymbol{b}) &= \frac{\partial}{\partial b_l} \sum_{i+j\le I} W(x_{i,j})\ (X_{i,j} - x_{i,j})\ \frac{\partial \eta_{i,j}}{\partial x_{i,j}}\ \Gamma_{i,j}^{(k)} \\ &= \sum_{i+j\le I} \left(\frac{\partial}{\partial b_l}(X_{i,j} - x_{i,j})\right)\ W(x_{i,j})\ \frac{\partial \eta_{i,j}}{\partial x_{i,j}}\ \Gamma_{i,j}^{(k)} \\ &\quad + \sum_{i+j\le I} (X_{i,j} - x_{i,j})\ \frac{\partial}{\partial b_l}\left(W(x_{i,j})\ \frac{\partial \eta_{i,j}}{\partial x_{i,j}}\ \Gamma_{i,j}^{(k)}\right)\end{aligned} \tag{6.34}$$

For the first term on the right-hand side of (6.34) we have

$$\begin{aligned}&\sum_{i+j\le I} \left(\frac{\partial}{\partial b_l}(X_{i,j} - x_{i,j})\right)\ W(x_{i,j}) \frac{\partial \eta_{i,j}}{\partial x_{i,j}} \Gamma_{i,j}^{(k)} \\ &\qquad = -\sum_{i+j\le I} \left(\frac{\partial}{\partial b_l} x_{i,j}\right)\ W(x_{i,j}) \frac{\partial \eta_{i,j}}{\partial x_{i,j}}\ \Gamma_{i,j}^{(k)} \\ &\qquad = -\sum_{i+j\le I} W(x_{i,j})\ \Gamma_{i,j}^{(k)}\ \Gamma_{i,j}^{(l)}\end{aligned}$$

The second term on the right-hand side of (6.34) disappears if we take the expected value over $X_{i,j}$ (since the expected value is equal to $x_{i,j}$). This completes the proof of the lemma. □

Consider now a vector $\mathbf{b}^* = (b_1^*, \ldots, b_{I+J+1}^*)' \in \mathbb{R}^{I+J+1}$. Assume that the inverse of the Fisher information matrix $H = H(\mathbf{b}^*)$ exists. Hence we have, with $\eta_{i,j} = \eta_{i,j}(\mathbf{b}^*) = \Gamma_{i,j}\ \mathbf{b}^*$, $x_{i,j} = x_{i,j}(\mathbf{b}^*)$ (cf. (6.6)–(6.7)) and Lemma 6.11 the following equalities

$$\begin{aligned}(H\mathbf{b}^*)_k = \sum_{l=1}^{I+J+1} H_{k,l}\ b_l^* &= \sum_{l=1}^{I+J+1} \sum_{i+j\le I} W(x_{i,j})\, \Gamma_{i,j}^{(k)}\, \Gamma_{i,j}^{(l)}\ b_l^* \\ &= \sum_{i+j\le I} W(x_{i,j})\, \Gamma_{i,j}^{(k)}\ \eta_{i,j}(\mathbf{b}^*)\end{aligned}$$

for $k = 1, \ldots, I+J-1$. Consider an adjustment to $\mathbf{b}^*$, that is, we define

$$\delta\mathbf{b}^* = H^{-1}\mathbf{u}(\mathbf{b}^*) \tag{6.35}$$

where $\mathbf{u}$ is the score function (cf. (6.31)).

This implies that the new estimate $\mathbf{b}^* + \delta\mathbf{b}^*$ satisfies

$$(H(\mathbf{b}^* + \delta\mathbf{b}^*))_k = (H\mathbf{b}^*)_k + (H\delta\mathbf{b}^*)_k = (H\mathbf{b}^*)_k + u_k(\mathbf{b}^*)$$

$$= \sum_{i+j\le I} W(x_{i,j})\, \Gamma_{i,j}^{(k)} \left[\eta_{i,j} + (X_{i,j} - x_{i,j})\, \frac{\partial \eta_{i,j}}{\partial x_{i,j}}\right]$$

$$= \sum_{i+j\le I} W(x_{i,j})\, \Gamma_{i,j}^{(k)} \left[g(x_{i,j}) + g'(x_{i,j})\, \left(X_{i,j} - x_{i,j}\right)\right] \tag{6.36}$$

for $k = 1, \ldots, I + J - 1$. The last expression is simply a weighted linearized form of the link function, that is,

$$g(X_{i,j}) \approx g(x_{i,j}) + g'\left(x_{i,j}\right)\, \left(X_{i,j} - x_{i,j}\right)$$

Observe that the last term $u_k(\mathbf{b}^*)$ on the right-hand side of (6.36) disappears if $\mathbf{b}^*$ is equal to the MLE $\widehat{\boldsymbol{b}}$ of $\boldsymbol{b}$ for the observations $\mathcal{D}_I$. This means that given the data $\mathcal{D}_I$, we are looking for the roots of $u_k(\mathbf{b}^*)$ that satisfy $H(\mathbf{b}^* + \delta\mathbf{b}^*) = H(\mathbf{b}^*)$.

On the one hand this can be done with the help of the Newton–Raphson algorithm where the $(m+1)$st estimate $\widehat{\boldsymbol{b}}^{(m+1)}$ for $\boldsymbol{b}$ is defined by the first-order Taylor series expansion of $\mathbf{u}\left(\widehat{\boldsymbol{b}}^{(m+1)}\right)$ around $\widehat{\boldsymbol{b}}^{(m)}$, that is, solve

$$\mathbf{u}\left(\widehat{\boldsymbol{b}}^{(m)}\right) + \mathbf{W}\left(\widehat{\boldsymbol{b}}^{(m)}\right)\left(\widehat{\boldsymbol{b}}^{(m+1)} - \widehat{\boldsymbol{b}}^{(m)}\right) = \mathbf{0} \tag{6.37}$$

On the other hand, Fisher's scoring method is then a variant of the Newton–Raphson algorithm where the (possible indefinite) Hessian matrix $\mathbf{W}(\boldsymbol{b})$ is replaced by the Fisher information matrix $H(\boldsymbol{b})$ (which is minus the expected value of the Hessian matrix $\mathbf{W}(\boldsymbol{b})$), that is,

$$\mathbf{u}\left(\widehat{\boldsymbol{b}}^{(m)}\right) - H\left(\widehat{\boldsymbol{b}}^{(m)}\right)\left(\widehat{\boldsymbol{b}}^{(m+1)} - \widehat{\boldsymbol{b}}^{(m)}\right) = \mathbf{0} \tag{6.38}$$

The use of the Fisher information matrix $H(\boldsymbol{b})$ has the advantages that $H(\boldsymbol{b})$ is easier to evaluate than the Hessian matrix $\mathbf{W}(\boldsymbol{b})$ and that it is always positive semi-definite.

Using $H\left(\widehat{\boldsymbol{b}}^{(m)}\right)^{-1}$ and starting with an initial value $\widehat{\boldsymbol{b}}^{(0)}$ in (6.38) leads to the iteration rule (this is adding the adjustment (6.35))

$$\widehat{\boldsymbol{b}}^{(m+1)} = \widehat{\boldsymbol{b}}^{(m)} + H\left(\widehat{\boldsymbol{b}}^{(m)}\right)^{-1} \mathbf{u}\left(\widehat{\boldsymbol{b}}^{(m)}\right) = \widehat{\boldsymbol{b}}^{(m)} + \delta\, \widehat{\boldsymbol{b}}^{(m)} \tag{6.39}$$

for $m = 0, 1, 2, \ldots$. The Fisher's scoring method iterates (6.39) until changes are sufficiently small. This means that the iterations are stopped if some termination criterion is reached, for example, if

$$\frac{\left\|\widehat{\boldsymbol{b}}^{(m+1)} - \widehat{\boldsymbol{b}}^{(m)}\right\|}{\left\|\widehat{\boldsymbol{b}}^{(m)}\right\|} \le \varepsilon$$

for some pre-chosen small number $\varepsilon > 0$. This means that we stop the iteration as soon as changes in the estimates are sufficiently small, which implies that we are close to the roots of $\mathbf{u}(\cdot)$.

If we plug (6.39) into (6.36) and multiply both sides of (6.36) by $H\left(\widehat{\boldsymbol{b}}^{(m)}\right)^{-1}$ we obtain

$$\widehat{\boldsymbol{b}}^{(m+1)} = H\left(\widehat{\boldsymbol{b}}^{(m)}\right)^{-1} \left(\sum_{i+j\le I} W\left(x_{i,j}^{(m)}\right) \Gamma_{i,j}^{(k)} \, z^{(m)} \right)_{k=1,\ldots,I+J+1} \tag{6.40}$$

for $m = 0, 1, 2, \ldots$, where

$$z^{(m)} = z^{(m)}(X_{i,j}) = g\left(x_{i,j}^{(m)}\right) + g'\left(x_{i,j}^{(m)}\right) \left(X_{i,j} - x_{i,j}^{(m)}\right)$$

and

$$x_{i,j}^{(m)} = h\left(\widehat{\eta_{i,j}}^{(m)}\right) = h\left(\Gamma_{i,j}\, \widehat{\boldsymbol{b}}^{(m)}\right)$$

Hence $z^{(m)}$ is just the linearized form of the link function applied to the data

$$g(X_{i,j}) \approx Z_{i,j} = g(x_{i,j}) + g'\left(x_{i,j}\right)\left(X_{i,j} - x_{i,j}\right) \tag{6.41}$$

Moreover, (6.40) gives a second form of the updating algorithm which is known as the Fisher's scoring update. Iterate (6.40) until changes in $\widehat{\boldsymbol{b}}^{(m)}$ are sufficiently small.

Observe that the MLE $\widehat{\boldsymbol{b}}$ of $\boldsymbol{b}$ for $\mathcal{D}_I$ satisfies the identity

$$\widehat{\boldsymbol{b}} = H(\widehat{\boldsymbol{b}})^{-1} \left(\sum_{i+j\le I} W(\widehat{x_{i,j}})\, \Gamma_{i,j}^{(k)}\, \widehat{\eta_{i,j}} \right)_{k=1,\ldots,I+J+1} \tag{6.42}$$

Remarks 6.12

- Unlike in classical linear models in the GLM framework we have to solve a nonlinear system of equations to calculate the MLE $\widehat{\boldsymbol{b}}$ of $\boldsymbol{b}$ (cf. (6.30)). This nonlinear system of equations can, in most problems, only be solved by iterative procedures like the Fisher scoring method (iteratively weighted least-squares (IWLS)) described above, which is a variant of the Newton–Raphson algorithm. Note that for the canonical link function the expected value and the actual value of the Hessian matrix $\mathbf{W}$ coincide, so that Fisher's scoring method and the Newton–Raphson method reduce to the same algorithm (cf. (6.37)–(6.38)).
- Note that the parameters $\phi_{i,j}/w_{i,j}$ cancel in (6.39) and (6.40) if $\phi_{i,j}/w_{i,j}$ is constant in i and j.

6.4.3 Mean Square Error of Prediction

In this subsection we give an estimate for the (conditional) MSEP

$$\begin{aligned} \mathrm{msep}_{\sum_i C_{i,J}|\mathcal{D}_I}\left(\sum_{i=1}^{I} \widehat{C_{i,J}}^{\mathrm{EDF}} \right) &= E\left[\left(\sum_{i=1}^{I} \widehat{C_{i,J}}^{\mathrm{EDF}} - \sum_{i=1}^{I} C_{i,J} \right)^2 \middle| \mathcal{D}_I \right] \\ &= E\left[\left(\sum_{i+j>I} \widehat{X_{i,j}}^{\mathrm{EDF}} - \sum_{i+j>I} X_{i,j} \right)^2 \middle| \mathcal{D}_I \right] \end{aligned} \tag{6.43}$$

This is done using the multivariate parameter version of the asymptotic result given in Theorem 6.2.

For the $\mathcal{D}_I$-measurable estimator $\sum_{i+j>I} \widehat{X_{i,j}}^{\text{EDF}}$ the last term can be decomposed as usual in the two parts (conditional) process variance and (conditional) estimation error

$$
\begin{aligned}
&\text{msep}_{\sum_i C_{i,J}|\mathcal{D}_I}\left(\sum_{i=1}^{I} \widehat{C_{i,J}}^{\text{EDF}}\right) \\
&= \text{Var}\left(\sum_{i+j>I} X_{i,j}\,\middle|\,\mathcal{D}_I\right) + \left(\sum_{i+j>I}\left(\widehat{X_{i,j}}^{\text{EDF}} - E\left[X_{i,j}\middle|\mathcal{D}_I\right]\right)\right)^2 \\
&= \text{Var}\left(\sum_{i+j>I} X_{i,j}\right) + \left(\sum_{i+j>I}\left(\widehat{X_{i,j}}^{\text{EDF}} - E\left[X_{i,j}\right]\right)\right)^2
\end{aligned}
$$

where we have used that $X_{i,j}$ and $\mathcal{D}_I$ are independent for $i+j>I$. Using the independence of the single cells again and Lemma 6.6 we obtain

$$
\begin{aligned}
&\text{msep}_{\sum_i C_{i,J}|\mathcal{D}_I}\left(\sum_{i=1}^{I} \widehat{C_{i,J}}^{\text{EDF}}\right) \\
&= \sum_{i+j>I} \text{Var}\left(X_{i,j}\right) + \left(\sum_{i+j>I}\left(\widehat{X_{i,j}}^{\text{EDF}} - E\left[X_{i,j}\right]\right)\right)^2 \\
&= \sum_{i+j>I} \frac{\phi_{i,j}}{w_{i,j}}\, V(x_{i,j}) + \left(\sum_{i+j>I}\left(\widehat{X_{i,j}}^{\text{EDF}} - E\left[X_{i,j}\right]\right)\right)^2 \qquad (6.44)
\end{aligned}
$$

The first term can easily be estimated (for given variance function $V(x_{i,j})$ and parameters $\phi_{i,j}$ and $w_{i,j}$). The difficulty is again to find a sound estimate for the (conditional) estimation error (i.e. the second term). The unconditional MSEP is given by

$$
\begin{aligned}
&\text{msep}_{\sum_i C_{i,J}}\left(\sum_{i=1}^{I} \widehat{C_{i,J}}^{\text{EDF}}\right) \\
&= E\left[\text{msep}_{\sum_i C_{i,J}|\mathcal{D}_I}\left(\sum_{i=1}^{I} \widehat{C_{i,J}}^{\text{EDF}}\right)\right] \\
&= \sum_{i+j>I} \frac{\phi_{i,j}}{w_{i,j}}\, V(x_{i,j}) + E\left[\left(\sum_{i+j>I}\left(\widehat{X_{i,j}}^{\text{EDF}} - E\left[X_{i,j}\right]\right)\right)^2\right] \qquad (6.45)
\end{aligned}
$$

The difficulty now is the estimation of the last term (estimation error)

$$
\begin{aligned}
&E\left[\left(\sum_{i+j>I}\left(\widehat{X_{i,j}}^{\text{EDF}} - E\left[X_{i,j}\right]\right)\right)^2\right] \\
&= \sum_{i+j>I,\, m+n>I} E\left[\left(\widehat{X_{i,j}}^{\text{EDF}} - E\left[X_{i,j}\right]\right)\left(\widehat{X_{m,n}}^{\text{EDF}} - E\left[X_{m,n}\right]\right)\right] \qquad (6.46)
\end{aligned}
$$

Observe that $\widehat{X_{i,j}}^{\text{EDF}}$ is in general not an unbiased estimator for $E\left[X_{i,j}\right]$ (see also Remarks 6.15). This means that the terms in (6.46) may have an additional bias. However, this bias is (often) of negligible order so that the terms in (6.46) are simply approximated by the following covariances. The quadratic terms in (6.46) are approximated by

$$\begin{aligned}
\operatorname{Var}\left(\widehat{X_{i,j}}^{\text{EDF}}\right) &= \operatorname{Var}\left(\exp\{\widehat{\eta_{i,j}}\}\right) \\
&= \exp\{2\eta_{i,j}\} \operatorname{Var}\left(\exp\{\widehat{\eta_{i,j}} - \eta_{i,j}\}\right) \\
&\approx \exp\{2\eta_{i,j}\} \operatorname{Var}\left(\widehat{\eta_{i,j}}\right) \\
&= x_{i,j}^2\ \Gamma_{i,j}\ \operatorname{Cov}\left(\widehat{\boldsymbol{b}}, \widehat{\boldsymbol{b}}\right)\ \Gamma_{i,j}'
\end{aligned} \tag{6.47}$$

where we have used $\widehat{x_{i,j}} = \exp(\widehat{\eta_{i,j}})$, $\widehat{\eta_{i,j}} = \Gamma_{i,j}\ \widehat{\boldsymbol{b}}$ and the linearization $\exp(z) \approx 1 + z$ for $z \approx 0$. Analogously, the cross-terms in (6.46) are approximated by

$$\begin{aligned}
\operatorname{Cov}\left(\widehat{X_{i,j}}^{\text{EDF}}, \widehat{X_{m,n}}^{\text{EDF}}\right) &\approx \exp\{\eta_{i,j} + \eta_{n,m}\} \operatorname{Cov}\left(\widehat{\eta_{i,j}}, \widehat{\eta_{m,n}}\right) \\
&= x_{i,j}\ x_{n,m}\ \Gamma_{i,j}\ \operatorname{Cov}\left(\widehat{\boldsymbol{b}}, \widehat{\boldsymbol{b}}\right)\ \Gamma_{m,n}'
\end{aligned} \tag{6.48}$$

Thus, we need to calculate the covariance matrix of $\widehat{\boldsymbol{b}}$. Assume that $X_{i,j}$ belongs to the EDF with given variance function $V(x_{i,j})$ and parameter $\boldsymbol{b}$ and define the random variable

$$\mathbf{B} = H(\boldsymbol{b})^{-1} \left(\sum_{i+j \le I} W(x_{i,j})\ \Gamma_{i,j}^{(k)}\ Z_{i,j} \right)_{k=1,\ldots,I+J+1} \tag{6.49}$$

(cf. (6.42)), where

$$Z_{i,j} = Z_{i,j}(\boldsymbol{b}) = g(x_{i,j}) + g'\left(x_{i,j}\right)\ \left(X_{i,j} - x_{i,j}\right) \tag{6.50}$$

(cf. (6.41)), and $x_{i,j} = x_{i,j}(\boldsymbol{b}) = h(\Gamma_{i,j}\ \boldsymbol{b})$.

LEMMA 6.13 *Under Model Assumptions 6.4 the covariance matrix of* **B** *is given as follows*

$$\operatorname{Cov}(\mathbf{B}, \mathbf{B}) = H(\boldsymbol{b})^{-1}$$

Proof Since the single cells are independent the covariance between $Z_{i,j}$ and $Z_{n,m}$ is zero if the coordinates do not coincide. Thus, we only have to consider

$$\operatorname{Var}\left(Z_{i,j}\right) = \left(\frac{\partial \eta_{i,j}}{\partial x_{i,j}}\right)^2 \operatorname{Var}\left(X_{i,j}\right) = W(x_{i,j})^{-1}$$

where we have used that $g'(x_{i,j}) = \partial\eta_{i,j}/\partial x_{i,j}$, (6.29) and Lemma 6.6. This and Lemma 6.11 imply that

$$\mathrm{Cov}\left(\left(\sum_{i+j\le I} W(x_{i,j})\Gamma_{i,j}^{(k)}\, Z_{i,j}\right)_k, \left(\sum_{i+j\le I} W(x_{i,j})\Gamma_{i,j}^{(l)}\, Z_{i,j}\right)_l\right)$$

$$= \left(\sum_{i+j\le I} W(x_{i,j})\; \Gamma_{i,j}^{(k)}\; \mathrm{Var}(Z_{i,j})\; \Gamma_{i,j}^{(l)}\; W(x_{i,j})\right)_{k,l}$$

$$= \left(\sum_{i+j\le I} W(x_{i,j})\; \Gamma_{i,j}^{(k)}\; \Gamma_{i,j}^{(l)}\right)_{k,l}$$

$$= \left(H_{k,l}\right)_{k,l} = H(\boldsymbol{b})$$

Thus, we obtain

$$\mathrm{Cov}\,(\mathbf{B}, \mathbf{B}) = H(\boldsymbol{b})^{-1}\; H(\boldsymbol{b})\; H(\boldsymbol{b})^{-1} = H(\boldsymbol{b})^{-1}$$

□

Observe that for the MLE $\widehat{\boldsymbol{b}}$ of $\boldsymbol{b}$ for $\mathcal{D}_I$ we have (cf. (6.42))

$$\widehat{\boldsymbol{b}} = H(\widehat{\boldsymbol{b}})^{-1} \left(\sum_{i+j\le I} W(\widehat{x_{i,j}})\; \Gamma_{i,j}^{(k)}\; \widehat{\eta_{i,j}}\right)_{k=1,\dots,I+J+1}$$

$$= H(\widehat{\boldsymbol{b}})^{-1} \left(\sum_{i+j\le I} W(\widehat{x_{i,j}})\; \Gamma_{i,j}^{(k)}\; Z_{i,j}(\widehat{\boldsymbol{b}})\right)_{k=1,\dots,I+J+1} \tag{6.51}$$

where in the second step we have used that $g(x_{i,j}) = \eta_{i,j}$ and the fact that the sum coming from $g'\big(x_{i,j}(\mathbf{b}^*)\big)\ \big(X_{i,j} - x_{i,j}(\mathbf{b}^*)\big)$ in (6.50) disappears if $\mathbf{b}^*$ is the MLE $\widehat{\boldsymbol{b}}$ of $\boldsymbol{b}$ for $\mathcal{D}_I$ (see (6.30)).

If we replace the estimated parameters $\widehat{\boldsymbol{b}}$ by its true values $\boldsymbol{b}$ on the right-hand side of (6.51) we obtain the random variable $\mathbf{B}$ (cf. (6.49)). This justifies that we estimate the covariance matrix of the MLE $\widehat{\boldsymbol{b}}$ by

$$\widehat{\mathrm{Cov}}\left(\widehat{\boldsymbol{b}}, \widehat{\boldsymbol{b}}\right) = H(\widehat{\boldsymbol{b}})^{-1} = \left(\left(\sum_{i+j\le I} W(\widehat{x_{i,j}})\; \Gamma_{i,j}^{(k)}\; \Gamma_{i,j}^{(l)}\right)_{k,l=1,\dots I+J+1}\right)^{-1} \tag{6.52}$$

This means that the term (6.46) can be estimated via the Fisher information matrix $H(\widehat{\boldsymbol{b}})$ which is a standard output in all GLM software packages.

We are now ready for the MSEP estimate:

ESTIMATOR 6.14 (MSEP for GLM) *The MSEP of the ultimate claim predictor $\sum_i \widehat{C_{i,J}}^{\mathrm{EDF}}$ in the EDF Model 6.4 is estimated by*

$$\widehat{\mathrm{msep}}_{\sum_i C_{i,J}}\left(\sum_{i=1}^{I} \widehat{C_{i,J}}^{\mathrm{EDF}}\right) = \sum_{i+j>I} \frac{\phi_{i,j}}{w_{i,j}}\; V(\widehat{x_{i,j}})$$

$$+ \sum_{i+j>I,\, n+m>I} \widehat{x_{i,j}}\; \widehat{x_{n,m}}\; \Gamma_{i,j}\; H(\widehat{\boldsymbol{b}})^{-1}\; \Gamma_{n,m}' \tag{6.53}$$

where $H(\widehat{\boldsymbol{b}})^{-1}$ is given by (6.52).

Remarks 6.15

- Lemma 6.13 gives an exact calculation for the covariance matrix of the random vector **B**. The covariance matrix is given by the inverse of the Fisher information matrix that is then used for the estimation of the covariance matrix of $\widehat{\boldsymbol{b}}$. This procedure can be viewed as rather heuristic. On the other hand, we could argue via the asymptotic arguments described in Theorem 6.2. That is, for the number of observations N going to infinity (in an appropriate way), we have

$$\frac{\widehat{\boldsymbol{b}}-\boldsymbol{b}}{H^{(N)}(\boldsymbol{b})^{-1/2}} \stackrel{(d)}{\to} N(\mathbf{0}, \mathrm{I}) \tag{6.54}$$

  where I is the identity matrix.
- MLE estimates may be biased. This bias is usually ignored in practice because it is often of negligible order w.r.t. to the estimation error. That is, we assume that (6.54) has sufficiently converged (see Example 6.16). For bias corrections we refer to Cordeiro and McCullagh (1991).
- If we choose a multiplicative structure with link function g given by the logarithm $\eta_{i,j} = \log(x_{i,j})$, then

$$\frac{\partial \eta_{i,j}}{\partial x_{i,j}} = x_{i,j}^{-1}$$

  which implies

$$W(x_{i,j}) = \frac{w_{i,j}}{\phi_{i,j}} \frac{x_{i,j}^2}{V(x_{i,j})} \tag{6.55}$$

  (cf. (6.29)).
- For the estimation of $\phi_{i,j}/w_{i,j}$ we assume that it is constant (after appropriate scaling). It can then be estimated with the help of the Pearson residuals (see McCullagh and Nelder 1989). As in England and Verrall (1999) we choose the Pearson residuals given by

$$R_{i,j}^{(\mathrm{P})}(x_{i,j}) = \frac{X_{i,j} - x_{i,j}}{V(x_{i,j})^{1/2}} \tag{6.56}$$

  Observe that

$$E\left[\left(R_{i,j}^{(\mathrm{P})}(x_{i,j})\right)^2\right] = \frac{\phi_{i,j}}{w_{i,j}}$$

  (cf. Lemma 6.6). If we assume that $\phi_{i,j}/w_{i,j} = \phi$ for all i, j then we set

$$\widehat{R}_{i,j}^{(\mathrm{P})} = \frac{X_{i,j} - \widehat{x_{i,j}}}{V(\widehat{x_{i,j}})^{1/2}} \tag{6.57}$$

  and we estimate ϕ by

$$\widehat{\phi_{\mathrm{P}}} = \frac{\sum_{i+j\le I}\left(\widehat{R}_{i,j}^{(\mathrm{P})}\right)^2}{N-p} \tag{6.58}$$

where

$$N = \text{number of observations } X_{i,j} \text{ in } \mathcal{D}_I$$

$$p = \text{number of estimated parameters } b_k = I + J + 1$$

Note that if one needs to find a refined dispersion modelling one often assumes that the dispersion is a function of the development periods (see, e.g., England and Verrall 2002, Section 7.4).

Example 6.16 (GLM method (overdispersed Poisson case))

We revisit the data set given in Examples 2.7 and 2.11. In Example 2.15 we have already calculated the Poisson estimator for the expected claims reserves (using the MLE method). In the following we assume that the dispersion $\phi = \phi_{i,j}/w_{i,j}$ is constant in i and j (which implies that the MLE for the Poisson model and the overdispersed Poisson model are equal). Using the Fisher's scoring algorithm (see (6.39)) for the variance function $V(x_{i,j}) = x_{i,j}$ (cf. (6.20)) we obtain the result shown in Table 6.1.

Of course the reserves for the linear variance function $V(x_{i,j}) = x_{i,j}$ are the same as those obtained in the Poisson Example 2.15 and in the CL Example 2.7. However, here we have a different scaling in the parameters μ_i and γ_j compared to the Poisson MLE estimator, see (6.12), where we set $\mu_0 = 1$ vs $\sum_j \gamma_j = 1$ in Example 2.15.

This should also be compared to the Bayesian results from the MCMC algorithm given in Tables 4.18 and 4.19. Then, we estimate the MSEP of the overdispersed Poisson GLM reserving method. We therefore need to estimate the dispersion parameter ϕ and the Fisher information matrix $H(\widehat{\boldsymbol{b}})$. $H(\widehat{\boldsymbol{b}})$ has already been calculated and used for the estimation of the expected claims reserves, hence there remains to estimate the dispersion ϕ. If we use Pearson's residuals we obtain (see (6.58))

$$\widehat{\phi_{\mathrm{P}}} = 14\,714 \tag{6.59}$$

Hence with (6.53) we obtain the result shown in Table 6.2. We see that the overall MSEP is of comparable size in the two methods. However, there is a substantial difference in allocating this error to process variance and estimation error. If we compare the results with the MCMC modelling (Table 4.20) we see that the main difference in the MSEP comes from the estimation of the dispersion of ϕ. On the other hand, we have already seen the difficulty giving an appropriate estimate to the dispersion (see, e.g., Table 4.21), which may have various reasons. □

Remarks 6.17

- We remark once more that originally the CL method was just an algorithm for calculating claims reserves. Probabilistic models that justify the CL reserves were only derived later. The distribution free CL model from Chapter 3 is one model, the overdispersed Poisson model from this chapter is another model. They both have in common that the best estimate for the outstanding loss liabilities is equal to the CL reserves. By studying higher moments like MSEP we see that indeed these are very different models, see Table 6.2.
- In Example 6.16 we have chosen a constant dispersion ϕ which seems very restrictive. Theoretically, one could also model the dispersion individually for different cells (i, j).

Table 6.1 Estimated $\widehat{\mu}_i$, $\widehat{\gamma}_j$, incremental claims $\widehat{X_{i,j}}^{\text{EDF}}$ and overdispersed Poisson reserves (i.e. variance function $V(x_{i,j}) = x_{i,j}$) with constant dispersion

	0	1	2	3	4	5	6	7	8	9	μ_i	Poisson reserves
0											1.000	
1										15 126	0.957	15 126
2									11 133	15 124	0.956	26 257
3								10 506	10 190	13 842	0.875	34 538
4							50 361	10 628	10 308	14 004	0.886	85 302
5						69 291	51 484	10 865	10 538	14 316	0.905	156 494
6					137 754	65 693	48 810	10 301	9 991	13 572	0.858	286 121
7				188 846	125 332	59 769	44 409	9 372	9 090	12 348	0.781	449 167
8			594 767	188 555	125 139	59 677	44 341	9 358	9 076	12 329	0.780	1 043 242
9		2 795 421	658 706	208 825	138 592	66 093	49 107	10 364	10 052	13 655	0.863	3 950 815
γ_j	6 572 763	3 237 322	762 835	241 836	160 501	76 541	56 870	12 002	11 641	15 813		6 047 061

Table 6.2 Comparison of the overdispersed Poisson GLM method and the CL method as presented in Chapter 3

	Reserves	Process std dev.	Estimation error$^{1/2}$	msep$^{1/2}$
GLM (Poisson) estimator	6 047 061	298 290	309 563	429 891
CL estimator	6 047 061	424 379	185 026	462 960

Data often indicates that this could be appropriate, but, on the other hand, we also need to be very careful that our model does not become overparametrized. That is, we have the typical trade-off situation between goodness of fit and good predictions (or model uncertainty vs parameter uncertainty).

Example 6.18 (GLM method (Gamma case))

We choose the same data set as for Example 6.16, but this time, we assume that we have a quadratic variance function $V(x_{i,j}) = x_{i,j}^2$. We obtain the result shown in Table 6.3.

If we use Pearson's residuals we obtain (see (6.58)) the following estimate for the dispersion ϕ in the Gamma case

$$\widehat{\phi_{\mathrm{P}}} = 0.045$$

Hence with (6.53) we obtain the results shown in Table 6.4.

We see that the Gamma model has a substantially larger MSEP. This suggests that the Gamma GLM assumption $V(x_{i,j}) = x_{i,j}^2$ does not fit to this data set. In principle, we can now choose every power p of $x_{i,j}$ as variance function $V(x_{i,j})$ and ask for an optimal power. Tweedie's compound Poisson model (see Subsection 5.2.5) deals with exactly this question. □

Example 6.19 (Tweedie's compound Poisson model revisited)

We revisit Example 5.29 for the calculation of the MSEP in Tweedie's compound Poisson model (see Table 6.5).

Remarks 6.20

- $p = 1$ corresponds to the overdispersed Poisson model, that is, the reserves must be equal to the reserves of the CL method (see Lemma 2.16). $p = 2$ corresponds to the Gamma GLM model, observe that this model is different from the Gamma model used in Subsection 5.2.4. In Subsection 5.2.4 we use the additional information $r_{i,j}$ in order to estimate the parameters. In the Gamma GLM model, we assume that $X_{i,j}$ belongs to the EDF with quadratic variance function, then all parameters can be estimated for ϕ constant without using $r_{i,j}$, that is, we use different weights w_i.
- Value $p = 1.1741136$ in Example 6.19 corresponds to the profile likelihood estimate obtained in Tweedie's compound Poisson model with unknown p. This means that with the help of the information $r_{i,j}$ one estimates $\lim_{k\to\infty} p^{(k)} = p = 1.1741136$ (see Subsection 5.2.5).

Concluding Remarks on EDF

For Tweedie's compound Poisson model we consider a whole family of models (that are parametrized via the variance function $V(x) = x^p$, $p \in (1, 2)$). At this stage, we can introduce the notion of model uncertainty (among Tweedie's compound Poisson models for different p's). In the light of Solvency 2, the discussion about model uncertainty is absolutely necessary. However, this topic is only poorly treated in the literature (see, e.g., Gigante and Sigalotti (2005) and Cairns (2000)).

We immediately have questions like: (1) For which p are the estimated reserves minimal or maximal? (2) For which p do we have minimal estimation error? (3) May a change in p double the estimated reserves? etc.

Table 6.3 Estimated $\widehat{\mu}_i$, $\widehat{\gamma}_j$, incremental claims $\widehat{X_{i,j}}^{EDF}$ and Gamma reserves (i.e. variance function $V(x_{i,j}) = x_{i,j}^2$

	0	1	2	3	4	5	6	7	8	9	μ_i	Gamma reserves
0											1.000	
1										12 020	0.760	12 020
2									11 909	14 239	0.900	26 148
3								11 181	11 237	13 437	0.850	35 855
4							64 598	13 841	13 910	16 632	1.052	108 981
5						62 601	49 679	10 644	10 697	12 791	0.809	146 413
6					131 132	62 729	49 780	10 666	10 719	12 817	0.811	277 844
7				178 718	114 700	54 869	43 543	9 329	9 376	11 211	0.709	421 745
8			578 289	182 007	116 811	55 879	44 344	9 501	9 549	11 417	0.722	1 007 796
9		2 778 441	649 449	204 403	131 185	62 755	49 801	10 670	10 724	12 822	0.811	3 910 250
γ_j	6 999 546	3 426 587	800 951	252 086	161 787	77 394	61 418	13 159	13 225	15 813		5 947 052

Table 6.4 Comparison of the Gamma GLM method, the Poisson GLM method and the CL method as presented in Chapter 3

	Reserves	Process std dev.	Estimation error$^{1/2}$	msep$^{1/2}$
GLM (Gamma) estimator	5 947 052	624 808	926 367	1 117 381
GLM with $V(x_{i,j}) = x_{i,j}^{1.5}$	6 002 866	374 027	449 212	584 541
GLM with $V(x_{i,j}) = x_{i,j}^{1.2}$	6 031 431	309 932	331 732	453 987
GLM (Poisson) estimator	6 047 061	298 290	309 563	429 891
CL estimator	6 047 061	424 379	185 026	462 960

Table 6.5 Comparison of Tweedie's estimates and the CL method as presented in Chapter 3

	Reserves	Process std dev.	Estimation error$^{1/2}$	msep$^{1/2}$	Dispersion $\widehat{\phi_P}$
$p=2$	1 386 034	177 004	231 032	291 044	21 914
$p=1.5$	1 431 266	180 700	159 628	241 109	23 472
$p=1.1742644$	1 451 290	204 840	181 269	273 528	29 711
$p=1.1741136$	1 451 299	204 860	181 293	273 559	29 716
$p=1$	1 461 359	234 960	220 300	322 085	37 777
CL	1 461 359	222 224	165 251	276 932	

6.5 OTHER GLM MODELS

Recall that we have assumed a multiplicative model $x_{i,j}=\mu_i\,\gamma_j$ in the previous section. This has led to a substantial reduction of parameters from $(I+1)(J+1)$ to $I+J+1$. The linear predictor with log-link function was then given by $\eta_{i,j}=\log(x_{i,j})=\log(\mu_i)+\log(\gamma_j)$.

There are various other approaches to model the mean $x_{i,j}$. To even further reduce the number of parameters one could fit a curve that depends only on very few parameters, see, for example, Clark (2003). Another possibility is to choose the Hoerl curve, which we met previously in (4.76):

$$\eta_{i,j}=\log(x_{i,j})=d+a_i+b_i\ \log(j)+c_i\ j$$

Now, the 'development pattern' γ_j is given and we need to estimate the exposure μ_i in terms of a_i, b_i and c_i. Note that, there is the difficulty that for the youngest accident years we do not have enough data to fit the parameters. The interested reader can find more on this topic in Zehnwirth (1998) and Taylor (2000), Chapter 8.

Wright (1990) extends the Hoerl curve allowing for a possible claims inflation. For general models with parameters in three directions we refer to De Vylder and Goovaerts (1979) and Barnett and Zehnwirth (1998).

$$\eta_{i,j}=a_i+\sum_{k=0}^{j}b_k+\sum_{k=0}^{i+j-1}c_k$$

6.6 BORNHUETTER–FERGUSON METHOD, REVISITED

In this section we derive an estimate for the MSEP of the BF method as it is usually used in practice. Recall that we have defined the model for the BF method in Model Assumptions 2.8, namely it was defined by

$$E[C_{i,j+k}|C_{i,0},\ldots,C_{i,j}]=C_{i,j}+\left(\beta_{j+k}-\beta_j\right)\ \mu_i$$

This has led to the BF estimator for the ultimate claim $C_{i,J}$, which was given by (see Estimator 2.10)

$$\widehat{C_{i,J}}^{\mathrm{BF}}=\widehat{E}\left[C_{i,J}\middle|\mathcal{D}_I\right]=C_{i,I-i}+\left(1-\widehat{\beta}_{I-i}\right)\ \widehat{\mu}_i$$

where $\widehat{\beta}_{I-i}$ is an appropriate estimate for the claims development pattern β_{I-i} and $\widehat{\mu}_i$ is a prior estimate for the expected ultimate claim $E[C_{i,J}]$.

The claims development pattern β_j was then estimated using the CL link ratio estimators (see (2.14))

$$\widehat{\beta}_j^{(\mathrm{CL})} = \widehat{\beta}_j = \prod_{k=j}^{J-1} \frac{1}{\widehat{f}_k} \tag{6.60}$$

where $\widehat{f}_k$ are the CL factor estimators given in (2.4). This is the usual approach used in practice (see also Mack 2006, bottom of p. 142). At this stage we denote $\widehat{\beta}_j^{(\mathrm{CL})}$ as 'plug in' or 'ad-hoc' estimates for β_j because they are not really justified by a unified stochastic model. The main criticism to this 'ad-hoc' approach is that the use of the CL link ratios $\widehat{f}_k$ contradicts the basic idea of independence between $C_{i,I-i}$ and $\widehat{C_{i,J}}^{\mathrm{BF}} - C_{i,I-i}$, which is fundamental to the BF method (see Mack 2006). Therefore, Mack (2006) constructs different estimators for the claims development pattern β_j which follow the spirit of the BF method.

We do not follow this route here, but we follow Alai *et al.* (2007) who use the (overdispersed) Poisson model motivation for the use of $\widehat{f}_k$ (see Corollary 2.18). That is, we define a stochastic model that perfectly motivates the choice (6.60) for the use in the BF method, that is, in that spirit the choice (6.60) usually used in practice is no longer an ad-hoc choice but fits into the stochastic model. In the following we explain this in careful detail.

Model Assumptions 6.21

- The increments $X_{i,j}$ are independent and belong to the EDF with an overdispersed Poisson distribution with: there exist positive parameters $\gamma_0, \ldots, \gamma_J, \mu_0, \ldots, \mu_I$ and $\phi > 0$ such that

$$E\left[X_{i,j}\right] = x_{i,j} = \gamma_j \, \mu_i,$$
$$\mathrm{Var}\left(X_{i,j}\right) = \phi \, x_{i,j}$$

  and $\sum_{j=0}^{J} \gamma_j = 1$ (normalizing condition).
- $\widehat{\mu}_i$, $i = 0, \ldots, I$, are independent and unbiased prior estimates for $\mu_i = E\left[C_{i,J}\right]$.
- $X_{i,j}$ and $\widehat{\mu}_k$ are independent for all i, j, k. □

Remarks 6.22

- Hence $X_{i,j}$ belongs to the EDF (see Model Assumptions 6.4) with $b(\theta) = \exp\{\theta\}$ and variance function $V(x) = x$.
- Under Model Assumptions 6.21 we have that the BF Model Assumptions 2.8 are fulfilled with $\beta_j = \sum_{k=0}^{j} \gamma_k$. Hence, this overdispersed Poisson model is one that can be used to explain the BF method (see also Lemma 2.13).
- The MLEs $\widehat{\gamma}_j^{(\mathrm{MLE})}$ and $\widehat{\mu}_i^{(\mathrm{MLE})}$ for γ_j and μ_i, respectively, under the normalizing condition $\sum_j \widehat{\gamma}_j^{(\mathrm{MLE})} = 1$ are given by the solution of (2.16)–(2.17) (see also Remarks 6.8).
- $\widehat{\mu}_k$ is a prior estimatefor the expected ultimate claim μ_k. As described on p. 23 it is assumed that this estimate is done prior to the observation of the data. Henceforth, it is an exogenous estimate that is based only on external data and expert opinion. We assume that it is independent of the data $X_{i,j}$. Moreover, in order to obtain a meaningful model,

we assume that it is unbiased for the expected ultimate claim (observe that $\widehat{\mu}_k$ plays the role of U_k in Model Assumptions 4.11). In this sense, we apply a 'pure' BF method. If we modify the prior estimates $\widehat{\mu}_k$ with the help of the observations $\mathcal{D}_I$ we obtain, for example, the BH method (see Section 4.1).

If we now use these MLEs $\widehat{\gamma}_j^{(\text{MLE})}$ from (2.16)–(2.17) for the estimation of the claims development pattern γ_j, we obtain the following BF estimator

$$\widehat{\widehat{C_{i,J}}}^{\text{BF}} = C_{i,I-i} + \left(1 - \sum_{j=0}^{I-i} \widehat{\gamma}_j^{(\text{MLE})}\right) \widehat{\mu}_i \tag{6.61}$$

Moreover, Corollary 2.18 gives that

$$\sum_{k=0}^{j} \widehat{\gamma}_k^{(\text{MLE})} = \widehat{\beta}_j^{(\text{CL})} = \prod_{k=j}^{J-1} \frac{1}{\widehat{f}_k}$$

which implies that

$$\widehat{\widehat{C_{i,J}}}^{\text{BF}} = C_{i,I-i} + \left(1 - \widehat{\beta}_{I-i}^{(\text{CL})}\right) \widehat{\mu}_i \tag{6.62}$$

is perfectly motivated by Model Assumptions 6.21 and the use of MLE estimators for γ_j. This is exactly the BF estimator as it is usually used in practice (see also (2.15)). Henceforth, in this understanding we do not motivate the use of the estimator $\widehat{\beta}_{I-i}^{(\text{CL})}$ by link ratios but rather by the MLEs in the overdispersed Poisson model. Just 'by coincidence', that is Corollary 2.18, link ratios are used to calculate the MLEs.

Remarks 6.23

- Note that if we replace the prior estimate $\widehat{\mu}_i$ by the MLE $\widehat{\mu}_i^{(\text{MLE})}$ we obtain the estimator

$$\widehat{C_{i,J}}^{\text{EDF}} = C_{i,I-i} + \left(1 - \sum_{j=0}^{I-i} \widehat{\gamma}_j^{(\text{MLE})}\right) \widehat{\mu}_i^{(\text{MLE})} \tag{6.63}$$

  given in Estimator 6.7 for the variance function $V(x) = x$.
- The BF estimator (6.61) is also similar to the estimator of the univariate additive model (i.e. only one subportfolio), which can also be interpreted as a GLM model (see (8.44)–(8.45) below). If we compare the BF estimator (6.61) in the representation (see (2.16)–(2.17))

$$\widehat{\widehat{C_{i,J}}}^{\text{BF}} = C_{i,I-i} + \sum_{j=I-i+1}^{J} \frac{\sum_{k=0}^{I-j} X_{k,j}}{\sum_{k=0}^{I-j} \widehat{\mu}_k^{(\text{MLE})}} \widehat{\mu}_i \tag{6.64}$$

  with estimator (8.50) of the univariate additive method we see that the (deterministic) volume measures V_i are now replaced by the MLEs $\widehat{\mu}_k^{(\text{MLE})}$ and prior estimates $\widehat{\mu}_i$ for the expected ultimate claims.

6.6.1 MSEP in the BF Method, Single Accident Year

Our goal is to estimate the conditional MSEP given by

$$\mathrm{msep}_{C_{i,J}|\mathcal{D}_I}\left(\widehat{C_{i,J}}^{\mathrm{BF}}\right) = E\left[\left(C_{i,J} - \widehat{C_{i,J}}^{\mathrm{BF}}\right)^2 \middle| \mathcal{D}_I\right]$$

$$= E\left[\left(\sum_{j=I-i+1}^{J} X_{i,j} - \left(1 - \widehat{\beta}_{I-i}^{(\mathrm{CL})}\right)\widehat{\mu}_i\right)^2 \middle| \mathcal{D}_I\right]$$

Now, we need to decouple this last term. Note that the $X_{i,j}$'s are independent (and hence future incremental claims are independent from $\mathcal{D}_I$). This implies

$$E\left[\left(\sum_{j=I-i+1}^{J} X_{i,j} - \left(1 - \widehat{\beta}_{I-i}^{(\mathrm{CL})}\right)\widehat{\mu}_i\right)^2 \middle| \mathcal{D}_I\right]$$

$$= \sum_{j=I-i+1}^{J} \mathrm{Var}\left(X_{i,j}\right) + E\left[\left(\sum_{j=I-i+1}^{J} E\left[X_{i,j}\right] - \left(1 - \widehat{\beta}_{I-i}^{(\mathrm{CL})}\right)\widehat{\mu}_i\right)^2 \middle| \mathcal{D}_I\right]$$

$$+ 2E\left[\left(\sum_{j=I-i+1}^{J}\left(X_{i,j} - E\left[X_{i,j}\right]\right)\right)\left(\sum_{j=I-i+1}^{J} E\left[X_{i,j}\right] - \left(1 - \widehat{\beta}_{I-i}^{(\mathrm{CL})}\right)\widehat{\mu}_i\right) \middle| \mathcal{D}_I\right]$$

Note that $\widehat{\mu}_i$ is independent of $X_{j,k}$ for all j, k, that $\widehat{\beta}_{I-i}^{(\mathrm{CL})}$ is $\mathcal{D}_I$-measurable and that $E\left[\widehat{\mu}_i\right] = \mu_i$. Therefore the last term in the above equality disappears and we get

$$\mathrm{msep}_{C_{i,J}|\mathcal{D}_I}\left(\widehat{C_{i,J}}^{\mathrm{BF}}\right) = \sum_{j=I-i+1}^{J} \mathrm{Var}\left(X_{i,j}\right) + \left(1 - \widehat{\beta}_{I-i}^{(\mathrm{CL})}\right)^2 \mathrm{Var}\left(\widehat{\mu}_i\right)$$

$$+ \mu_i^2 \left(\sum_{j=I-i+1}^{J} \gamma_j - \sum_{j=I-i+1}^{J} \widehat{\gamma}_j^{(\mathrm{MLE})}\right)^2 \tag{6.65}$$

Henceforth, the three terms on the right-hand side of the above equality need to be estimated in order to get an appropriate estimate for the conditional MSEP in the BF method.

The process variance can easily be estimated using (6.58) and the overdispersed Poisson assumption. An estimator is given by

$$\widehat{\mathrm{Var}}\left(X_{i,j}\right) = \widehat{\phi_P}\, \widehat{\gamma}_j^{(\mathrm{MLE})}\, \widehat{\mu}_i \tag{6.66}$$

The second term contains the uncertainty in the prior estimate of $\widehat{\mu}_i$. This can in general only be determined using external data, market experience and expert opinion (since also $\widehat{\mu}_i$ is determined exogenously). For example, the regulator provides an estimator for the coefficient of variation of $\widehat{\mu}_i$, denoted by $\widehat{\text{Vco}}(\widehat{\mu}_i)$, that quantifies how good the exogenous estimator is. Often a reasonable range for the coefficient of variation is between 5% and 10% (see, e.g., Swiss Solvency Test 2006). Then the second term is estimated by

$$\left(1-\widehat{\beta}_{I-i}^{(\text{CL})}\right)^2 \widehat{\text{Var}}(\widehat{\mu}_i) = \left(1-\widehat{\beta}_{I-i}^{(\text{CL})}\right)^2 \widehat{\mu}_i^2 \, \widehat{\text{Vco}}(\widehat{\mu}_i)^2 \tag{6.67}$$

The last term in (6.65) requires more work. As in the previous sections we study the volatilities of the MLE around the true parameters.

In order to adapt the GLM techniques and the asymptotic normality approximation (with its Fisher information matrix $H(\boldsymbol{b})$) we need to modify the MLE $\widehat{\gamma}_j^{(\text{MLE})}$. Observe that we have assumed the following normalizing condition

$$\sum_{j=0}^{J} \widehat{\gamma}_j^{(\text{MLE})} = 1$$

For Fisher's Scoring method, we have normalized in a different way, namely $\mu_0 = 1$ (see before (6.12)). With this second normalization condition we have obtained MLE estimators (see (6.24))

$$\widehat{\boldsymbol{b}} = \left(\widehat{\log(\mu_1)}^{(\text{GLM})}, \ldots, \widehat{\log(\mu_I)}^{(\text{GLM})}, \widehat{\log(\gamma_0)}^{(\text{GLM})}, \ldots, \widehat{\log(\gamma_J)}^{(\text{GLM})} \right)'$$

Note that for this second normalizing condition we use the superscript GLM. This implies that we obtain a second (unscaled) claims development pattern

$$\widehat{\gamma}_0^{(\text{GLM})}, \ldots, \widehat{\gamma}_J^{(\text{GLM})}$$

with $\widehat{\log(\gamma_j)}^{(\text{GLM})} = \log(\widehat{\gamma}_j^{(\text{GLM})})$ for all $j = 0, \ldots, J$ (see after (6.24)). Moreover, we know that

$$\left(\log(\widehat{\gamma}_0^{(\text{GLM})}), \ldots, \log(\widehat{\gamma}_J^{(\text{GLM})})\right)'$$

is asymptotically normally distributed with variance approximated by the appropriate part of the inverse Fisher information $H^{-1}(\boldsymbol{b})$ (see Lemma 6.13).

Moreover, note that we have

$$\widehat{\gamma}_j^{(\text{MLE})} = \frac{\widehat{\gamma}_j^{(\text{GLM})}}{\sum_{l=0}^{J} \widehat{\gamma}_l^{(\text{GLM})}} \tag{6.68}$$

Neglecting that MLEs have a possible bias term, we estimate the last term on the right-hand side of (6.65), which is

$$\left(\sum_{j=I-i+1}^{J} \gamma_j - \sum_{j=I-i+1}^{J} \widehat{\gamma}_j^{(\text{MLE})} \right)^2$$

by the following expression

$$\begin{aligned}\operatorname{Var}\left(\sum_{j=I-i+1}^{J}\widehat{\gamma}_j^{(\mathrm{MLE})}\right) &= \sum_{j,k=I-i+1}^{J}\operatorname{Cov}\left(\widehat{\gamma}_j^{(\mathrm{MLE})},\widehat{\gamma}_k^{(\mathrm{MLE})}\right)\\ &= \sum_{j,k=I-i+1}^{J}\operatorname{Cov}\left(\frac{\widehat{\gamma}_j^{(\mathrm{GLM})}}{\sum_{l=0}^{J}\widehat{\gamma}_l^{(\mathrm{GLM})}},\frac{\widehat{\gamma}_k^{(\mathrm{GLM})}}{\sum_{l=0}^{J}\widehat{\gamma}_l^{(\mathrm{GLM})}}\right)\\ &= \sum_{j,k=I-i+1}^{J}\operatorname{Cov}\left(\frac{1}{1+\sum_{l\neq j}\frac{\widehat{\gamma}_l^{(\mathrm{GLM})}}{\widehat{\gamma}_j^{(\mathrm{GLM})}}},\frac{1}{1+\sum_{l\neq k}\frac{\widehat{\gamma}_l^{(\mathrm{GLM})}}{\widehat{\gamma}_k^{(\mathrm{GLM})}}}\right)\end{aligned} \tag{6.69}$$

We define

$$\Delta_j=\sum_{l\neq j}\frac{\widehat{\gamma}_l^{(\mathrm{GLM})}}{\widehat{\gamma}_j^{(\mathrm{GLM})}}\qquad\text{and}\qquad\delta_j=E\left[\Delta_j\right] \tag{6.70}$$

Hence we need to calculate

$$\operatorname{Cov}\left(\frac{1}{1+\Delta_j},\frac{1}{1+\Delta_k}\right) \tag{6.71}$$

In our next step we do a Taylor approximation around δ_j. Define the function

$$f(x)=\frac{1}{1+x}\qquad\text{with}\qquad f'(x)=-\frac{1}{(1+x)^2}$$

Hence we have

$$f(x)\approx f(\delta_j)+f'(\delta_j)\,(x-\delta_j)=\frac{1}{1+\delta_j}-\frac{1}{(1+\delta_j)^2}\,(x-\delta_j)$$

This implies, if we consider all the stochastic terms,

$$\begin{aligned}\operatorname{Cov}\left(\frac{1}{1+\Delta_j},\frac{1}{1+\Delta_k}\right) &\approx \frac{1}{(1+\delta_j)^2}\,\frac{1}{(1+\delta_k)^2}\operatorname{Cov}\left(\Delta_j,\Delta_k\right)\\ &= \frac{1}{(1+\delta_j)^2}\,\frac{1}{(1+\delta_k)^2}\sum_{l\neq j}\sum_{m\neq k}\operatorname{Cov}\left(\frac{\widehat{\gamma}_l^{(\mathrm{GLM})}}{\widehat{\gamma}_j^{(\mathrm{GLM})}},\frac{\widehat{\gamma}_m^{(\mathrm{GLM})}}{\widehat{\gamma}_k^{(\mathrm{GLM})}}\right)\end{aligned} \tag{6.72}$$

There remains to calculate these last covariance terms. We proceed as in (6.48), $\exp\{x\}\approx 1+x$ for $x\approx 0$, neglecting a possible bias and expanding around the expected values

$$\operatorname{Cov}\left(\frac{\widehat{\gamma}_l^{(\mathrm{GLM})}}{\widehat{\gamma}_j^{(\mathrm{GLM})}},\frac{\widehat{\gamma}_m^{(\mathrm{GLM})}}{\widehat{\gamma}_k^{(\mathrm{GLM})}}\right)\approx\frac{\gamma_l}{\gamma_j}\,\frac{\gamma_m}{\gamma_k}\operatorname{Cov}\left(\log\left(\frac{\widehat{\gamma}_l^{(\mathrm{GLM})}}{\widehat{\gamma}_j^{(\mathrm{GLM})}}\right),\log\left(\frac{\widehat{\gamma}_m^{(\mathrm{GLM})}}{\widehat{\gamma}_k^{(\mathrm{GLM})}}\right)\right) \tag{6.73}$$

Now, we define the design matrices (see also (6.14))

$$\widetilde{\Gamma}_j=\Gamma_{0,j}=(0,\ldots,0,e_{I+j+1},0,\ldots,0)' \tag{6.74}$$

for $j=0,\dots,J$ which implies that (see (6.24))

$$\log\left(\widehat{\gamma}_j^{(\mathrm{GLM})}\right)=\widetilde{\Gamma}_j\,\widehat{\boldsymbol{b}}$$

Hence

$$\mathrm{Cov}\left(\log\left(\frac{\widehat{\gamma}_l^{(\mathrm{GLM})}}{\widehat{\gamma}_j^{(\mathrm{GLM})}}\right),\log\left(\frac{\widehat{\gamma}_m^{(\mathrm{GLM})}}{\widehat{\gamma}_k^{(\mathrm{GLM})}}\right)\right)=\left(\widetilde{\Gamma}_l-\widetilde{\Gamma}_j\right)\,\mathrm{Cov}\left(\widehat{\boldsymbol{b}},\widehat{\boldsymbol{b}}\right)\,\left(\widetilde{\Gamma}_m-\widetilde{\Gamma}_k\right)' \tag{6.75}$$

Using (6.52) for the estimation of the covariance term we obtain

$$\begin{aligned}\mathrm{Var}\left(\sum_{j=I-i+1}^{J}\widehat{\gamma}_j^{(\mathrm{MLE})}\right)&\approx\sum_{j,k=I-i+1}^{J}\frac{1}{(1+\delta_j)^2}\,\frac{1}{(1+\delta_k)^2}\\&\quad\times\sum_l\sum_m\frac{\gamma_l}{\gamma_j}\,\frac{\gamma_m}{\gamma_k}\,\left(\widetilde{\Gamma}_l-\widetilde{\Gamma}_j\right)\,H(\widehat{\boldsymbol{b}})^{-1}\,\left(\widetilde{\Gamma}_m-\widetilde{\Gamma}_k\right)'\end{aligned} \tag{6.76}$$

Hence we define the estimator

$$\begin{aligned}\widehat{\mathrm{Var}}\left(\sum_{j=I-i+1}^{J}\widehat{\gamma}_j^{(\mathrm{MLE})}\right)&=\sum_{j,k=I-i+1}^{J}\frac{1}{(1+\widehat{\delta}_j)^2}\,\frac{1}{(1+\widehat{\delta}_k)^2}\\&\quad\times\sum_l\sum_m\frac{\widehat{\gamma}_l^{(\mathrm{GLM})}}{\widehat{\gamma}_j^{(\mathrm{GLM})}}\,\frac{\widehat{\gamma}_m^{(\mathrm{GLM})}}{\widehat{\gamma}_k^{(\mathrm{GLM})}}\,\left(\widetilde{\Gamma}_l-\widetilde{\Gamma}_j\right)H(\widehat{\boldsymbol{b}})^{-1}\,\left(\widetilde{\Gamma}_m-\widetilde{\Gamma}_k\right)'\end{aligned} \tag{6.77}$$

where

$$\widehat{\delta}_j=\sum_{l\neq j}\frac{\widehat{\gamma}_l^{(\mathrm{GLM})}}{\widehat{\gamma}_j^{(\mathrm{GLM})}}$$

Note that this procedure/approximation leads to reasonable MSEP estimates. However, we face mathematical difficulties in the case where there is no positive solution in (6.70) to the ML maximization.

ESTIMATOR 6.24 (MSEP for the BF method, single accident year) *Under Model Assumptions 6.21 an estimator for the (conditional) MSEP for a single accident year $i\in\{1,\dots,I\}$ is given by*

$$\begin{aligned}\widehat{\mathrm{msep}}_{C_{i,J}|\mathcal{D}_I}\left(\widehat{\widehat{C_{i,J}}}^{\mathrm{BF}}\right)&=\widehat{\phi}_{\mathrm{P}}\,\left(1-\widehat{\beta}_{I-i}^{(\mathrm{CL})}\right)\,\widehat{\mu}_i+\left(1-\widehat{\beta}_{I-i}^{(\mathrm{CL})}\right)^2\,\widehat{\mu}_i^2\,\widehat{\mathrm{Vco}}\,(\widehat{\mu}_i)^2\\&\quad+\,\widehat{\mu}_i^2\,\widehat{\mathrm{Var}}\left(\sum_{j=I-i+1}^{J}\widehat{\gamma}_j^{(\mathrm{MLE})}\right)\end{aligned}$$

6.6.2 MSEP in the BF Method, Aggregated Accident Years

For aggregated accident years we start by considering two different accident years $i < k$,

$$\mathrm{msep}_{C_{i,J}+C_{k,J}|\mathcal{D}_I}\left(\widehat{\widehat{C_{i,J}}}^{\mathrm{BF}} + \widehat{\widehat{C_{k,J}}}^{\mathrm{BF}}\right) = E\left[\left(C_{i,J} + C_{k,J} - \widehat{\widehat{C_{i,J}}}^{\mathrm{BF}} - \widehat{\widehat{C_{k,J}}}^{\mathrm{BF}}\right)^2 \middle| \mathcal{D}_I\right]$$

By the usual decomposition we find

$$\begin{aligned}\mathrm{msep}_{C_{i,J}+C_{k,J}|\mathcal{D}_I}\left(\widehat{\widehat{C_{i,J}}}^{\mathrm{BF}} + \widehat{\widehat{C_{k,J}}}^{\mathrm{BF}}\right) &= \sum_{l=i,k} \mathrm{msep}_{C_{l,J}|\mathcal{D}_I}\left(\widehat{\widehat{C_{l,J}}}^{\mathrm{BF}}\right) \\ &+ 2\, \mu_i\, \mu_k \left(\sum_{j=I-i+1}^{J} \gamma_j - \sum_{j=I-i+1}^{J} \widehat{\gamma}_j^{(\mathrm{MLE})}\right)\left(\sum_{l=I-k+1}^{J} \gamma_l - \sum_{l=I-k+1}^{J} \widehat{\gamma}_l^{(\mathrm{MLE})}\right)\end{aligned}$$

That is, we need to give an estimate for this last covariance term. Neglecting the possible bias of MLEs we again estimate this term by (see also (6.76))

$$\begin{aligned}&\mathrm{Cov}\left(\sum_{j=I-i+1}^{J} \widehat{\gamma}_j^{(\mathrm{MLE})}, \sum_{l=I-k+1}^{J} \widehat{\gamma}_l^{(\mathrm{MLE})}\right) \\ &= \sum_{j=I-i+1}^{J} \sum_{l=I-k+1}^{J} \mathrm{Cov}\left(\widehat{\gamma}_j^{\mathrm{MLE}}, \widehat{\gamma}_l^{\mathrm{MLE}}\right) \\ &\approx \sum_{j=I-i+1}^{J} \sum_{l=I-k+1}^{J} \frac{1}{(1+\delta_j)^2}\, \frac{1}{(1+\delta_l)^2} \\ &\quad \times \sum_n \sum_m \frac{\gamma_n}{\gamma_j}\, \frac{\gamma_m}{\gamma_l} \left(\widetilde{\Gamma}_n - \widetilde{\Gamma}_j\right) H(\boldsymbol{b})^{-1} \left(\widetilde{\Gamma}_m - \widetilde{\Gamma}_l\right)' \end{aligned} \tag{6.78}$$

This motivates the following estimator for the covariance

$$\begin{aligned}\widehat{\Upsilon}_{i,k} &= \widehat{\mathrm{Cov}}\left(\sum_{j=I-i+1}^{J} \widehat{\gamma}_j^{\mathrm{MLE}}, \sum_{l=I-k+1}^{J} \widehat{\gamma}_l^{\mathrm{MLE}}\right) \\ &= \sum_{j=I-i+1}^{J} \sum_{l=I-k+1}^{J} \frac{1}{(1+\widehat{\delta}_j)^2}\, \frac{1}{(1+\widehat{\delta}_l)^2} \\ &\quad \times \sum_n \sum_m \frac{\widehat{\gamma}_n^{(\mathrm{GLM})}}{\widehat{\gamma}_j^{(\mathrm{GLM})}}\, \frac{\widehat{\gamma}_m^{(\mathrm{GLM})}}{\widehat{\gamma}_l^{(\mathrm{GLM})}} \left(\widetilde{\Gamma}_n - \widetilde{\Gamma}_j\right) H(\widehat{\boldsymbol{b}})^{-1} \left(\widetilde{\Gamma}_m - \widetilde{\Gamma}_l\right)' \end{aligned} \tag{6.79}$$

ESTIMATOR 6.25 (MSEP for the BF method, aggregated accident years) *Under Model Assumptions 6.21 an estimator for the (conditional) MSEP for aggregated accident years is given by*

$$\widehat{\mathrm{msep}}_{\sum_{i=1}^{I} C_{i,J}|\mathcal{D}_I}\left(\sum_{i=1}^{I} \widehat{\widehat{C_{i,J}}}^{\mathrm{BF}}\right) = \sum_{i=1}^{I} \widehat{\mathrm{msep}}_{C_{i,J}|\mathcal{D}_I}\left(\widehat{\widehat{C_{i,J}}}^{\mathrm{BF}}\right) + 2\sum_{1\le i<k\le I} \widehat{\mu}_i\,\widehat{\mu}_k\,\widehat{\Upsilon}_{i,k}$$

Example 6.26 (MSEP in the BF method)

We revisit the data set from Example 2.11 (the cumulative data $C_{i,j}$ is given in Table 2.2). Our goal is to calculate the MSEP Estimator 6.25 to obtain the quality of the BF reserve given in Table 2.4. Note that the estimate of the claims development pattern β_j is either obtained via the CL factor estimators $\widehat{f}_k$ or via the MLEs $\gamma_k^{(\mathrm{MLE})}$ (see Corollary 2.18), but in our case we always use the MLE motivation because this leads to a consistent mathematical model motivating the BF method.

Moreover, we need to estimate the dispersion parameter ϕ. This has already been done in (6.59), namely

$$\widehat{\phi_{\mathrm{P}}} = 14\,714 \tag{6.80}$$

Furthermore, we need to specify the uncertainty in the estimation of the prior value $\widehat{\mu}_i$. Here, we assume that for all $i = 0, \ldots, I$

$$\widehat{\mathrm{Vco}}\,(\widehat{\mu}_i) = 5\% \tag{6.81}$$

This choice is completely analogous to (4.14). Then we obtain the results given in Table 6.6.

Table 6.6 BF reserves: process error$^{1/2}$ (6.66), uncertainty in prior estimate$^{1/2}$ (6.67), parameter estimation β uncertainty$^{1/2}$, total of prior and parameter estimation uncertainty$^{1/2}$ and msep$^{1/2}$

i	BF reserves	Process std dev.	Prior std dev.	Parameter β std dev.	Prior and parameter	msep$^{1/2}$	Vco (%)
0							
1	16 124	15 403	806	15 543	15 564	21 897	135.8
2	26 998	19 931	1 350	17 573	17 624	26 606	98.5
3	37 575	23 514	1 879	18 545	18 640	30 005	79.9
4	95 434	37 473	4 772	24 168	24 635	44 845	47.0
5	178 024	51 181	8 901	29 600	30 910	59 790	33.6
6	341 305	70 866	17 065	35 750	39 614	81 187	23.8
7	574 089	91 909	28 704	41 221	50 231	104 739	18.2
8	1 318 646	139 294	65 932	53 175	84 703	163 025	12.4
9	4 768 384	264 882	238 419	75 853	250 195	364 362	7.6
Total	7 356 580	329 007	249 828	228 252	338 397	471 973	6.4

Note that the total prediction uncertainty msep$^{1/2}$ of 471 973 in the BF method is comparable to the one in the distribution free CL method (462 960 given in Table 3.6). Perhaps the exogenous choice (6.81) is too low, which would increase the prediction uncertainty in the BF method.

If we compare the results to the Poisson GLM method (see Table 6.2) we observe the following: The process error in the BF method is larger than that in the Poisson GLM method. This comes from the fact that the prior estimates $\widehat{\mu}_i$ are rather conservative (we have noticed this throughout these notes). On the other hand, the parameter uncertainties in $\widehat{\mu}_i$ and $\widehat{\beta}_j^{(CL)}$ of 338 397 are only slightly higher than the estimation error of 309 563 in the Poisson GLM method (see Tables 6.6 and 6.2). □

Example 6.27 (MSEP in the BF method, Taylor approximations)

In the derivation of an estimate for the parameter estimation error in the BF method we have used several approximations (see the derivation after formula (6.69)). Using a simulation approach we would like to study how good these approximations are. We assume that the incremental claims $X_{i,j}$ are overdispersed Poisson distributed with parameters γ_j and μ_i given by Table 2.6 and dispersion parameter ϕ given by (6.80). With these assumptions we can generate overdispersed Poisson triangles $\mathcal{D}_I$ from which we can calculate (for each simulation) the estimated payout pattern $\widehat{\beta}_j^{(CL)}$. We have generated 5000 triangles, and hence have obtained an empirical distribution for the payout pattern consisting of 5000 vector observations.

From this empirical distribution we calculate the empirical standard deviation and compare it to the approximation derived in (6.77). The results are given in Table 6.7.

Table 6.7 Comparison of the approximated estimation error (6.77) and the empirical estimation error in $\widehat{\beta}_j^{(CL)}$ from 5000 simulations

i	β_j exact (%)	Estimation error approximation (%)	Average empirical $\widehat{\beta}_j^{(CL)}$ (%)	Estimation error simulation (%)
0				
1	99.86	0.137	99.86	0.139
2	99.75	0.160	99.75	0.164
3	99.65	0.175	99.64	0.179
4	99.14	0.219	99.13	0.221
5	98.45	0.258	98.44	0.260
6	97.01	0.313	97.00	0.315
7	94.84	0.370	94.82	0.372
8	88.00	0.484	87.96	0.485
9	58.96	0.653	58.88	0.645

We observe that the approximation and the empirical value for the estimation error in $\widehat{\beta}_j^{(CL)}$ are close to each other, which justifies that for this choice of parameters the approximation given in (6.77) is good. □

7
Bootstrap Methods

7.1 INTRODUCTION

So far we have concentrated on the estimation and prediction of the (expected) ultimate claims $C_{i,J}$, $i \in \{0, \ldots, I\}$, and MSEPs. This means that we have estimated the first and second moments of the outstanding liabilities and their predictors. However, often one is not able to calculate first and second moments in a closed form; calculating the bias term in the GLM examples is not straightforward. Moreover, one is often interested in the whole probability distribution with applications, for example, to Value-at-Risk considerations or solvency discussions. In most of the cases/models considered above we cannot give a closed analytical expression for the resulting distribution of the claims reserves and their predictors. One way out of this dilemma is to estimate the first two moments (as above) and make distributional assumptions on the total reserves and their predictors. That is, one avoids the difficulties about marginal distributions, dependence structures and aggregation/convolution by simply making an overall choice for the resulting distribution (for an example to this approach we refer to the Swiss Solvency Test 2006).

The bootstrap method is a powerful technique for obtaining information about an aggregate distribution from single samples of data. The bootstrap method has been introduced by Efron (1979), and a general theory on bootstrap methods can be found in Efron and Tibshirani (1993) or Davison and Hinkley (1997). The bootstrap method proposed by Efron (1979) is, by now, considered to be a breakthrough in statistics. Essentially, the bootstrap can be described as 'simulating from an estimated model', which turns out to be tremendously useful in practice. That is, to apply the bootstrap method we introduce as little model structure as necessary to resample observations using the samples of data.

In the actuarial literature, bootstrap methods appear, for example, in Taylor (1987), Kirschner *et al.* (2002), Taylor and McGuire (2005, 2007), England and Verrall (1999, 2007), England (2002), Lowe (1994) or Pinheiro *et al.* (2003). In theory, bootstrap can be applied to all the models that we have seen so far. In the following we demonstrate the bootstrap method for some selected examples.

General Bootstrap Idea

The general idea behind the bootstrap is to make a data resampling. The resampling takes place from the data themselves, that is, one looks for an appropriate structure within the model. With the help of this structure one resamples new data sets from the observed data set.

7.1.1 Efron's Non-parametric Bootstrap

We start with an example. Assume that we have n i.i.d. realizations

$$Z_1, \ldots, Z_n \quad \text{i.i.d.} \overset{(d)}{\sim} F \tag{7.1}$$

where F denotes an unknown distribution. The random variables Z_i may be real-valued or vector-valued. Assume that we want to estimate a parameter $h(F)$ of the distribution F. Parameter $h(F)$ may be, for example, the mean, the variance, the Value-at-Risk or the Expected Shortfall of the random variable Z_1.

Assume that we have a known function g of the data $Z_1, \ldots, Z_n$ which estimates $h(F)$, that is,

$$\widehat{\theta}_n = g(Z_1, \ldots, Z_n)$$

is an estimator for $h(F)$. Our goal is to learn more about the probability distribution of $\widehat{\theta}_n$.

Bootstrap Idea

If we knew the distribution F we could sample new i.i.d. observations from this distribution F. This would give a new value for the estimator $\widehat{\theta}_n$. Repeating this procedure several times would lead to the empirical distribution of $\widehat{\theta}_n$.

Unfortunately, we do not know the data generating mechanism F. Therefore we use the empirical distribution $\widehat{F}_n$ to reproduce observations. The empirical distribution $\widehat{F}_n$ gives weight $1/n$ to every observation Z_i, and from this we generate new data

$$Z_1^*, \ldots, Z_n^* \quad \text{i.i.d.} \overset{(d)}{\sim} \widehat{F}_n \tag{7.2}$$

This simulated new data vector $(Z_1^*, \ldots, Z_n^*)$ is called a bootstrap sample. Then, for the bootstrap sample we can calculate a new value for the estimator $\widehat{\theta}_n$

$$\widehat{\theta}_n^* = g(Z_1^*, \ldots, Z_n^*)$$

and, repeating this idea several times, we get an empirical distribution F_n^* for $\widehat{\theta}_n^*$.

Example 7.1

Assume that $Z_1, \ldots, Z_n$ i.i.d. $\overset{(d)}{\sim} \mathcal{N}(\theta, 1)$. The goal is to estimate the mean θ of the distribution; this means that we want to estimate $h\big(\mathcal{N}(\theta, 1)\big) = E[Z_i] = \theta$. We choose the estimator $\widehat{\theta}_n = g(Z_1, \ldots, Z_n) = \sum_{i=1}^n Z_i/n$. Define for the observations $Z_1, \ldots, Z_n$ the empirical distribution

$$\widehat{F}_n(x) = \frac{1}{n} \sum_{i=1}^{n} 1_{\{x \geq Z_i\}}$$

and draw new observations from this empirical distribution

$$Z_1^*, \ldots, Z_n^* \quad \text{i.i.d.} \overset{(d)}{\sim} \widehat{F}_n$$

Then we calculate the value

$$\widehat{\theta}_n^* = g(Z_1^*, \ldots, Z_n^*) = \frac{1}{n} \sum_{i=1}^{n} Z_i^*$$

and the empirical distribution of $\widehat{\theta}_n^*$ by repeating the resampling from $\widehat{F}_n$ several times. □

Bootstrap Distribution

The bootstrap distribution F_n^* for $\widehat{\theta}_n^*$ is the conditional distribution which is induced by i.i.d. resampling of the data

$$Z_1^*, \ldots, Z_n^* \quad \text{i.i.d.} \overset{(d)}{\sim} \widehat{F}_n$$

given the original data $Z_1, \ldots, Z_n$. The fact that we condition on the data allows us to treat the resampling distribution $\widehat{F}_n$ as a fixed distribution. Henceforth, the distribution F_n^* is a conditional distribution, given the original data $Z_1, \ldots, Z_n$.

Remarks 7.2

- If the empirical distribution $\widehat{F}_n$ is close to the true distribution F, then the bootstrap distribution F_n^* for $\widehat{\theta}_n^*$ is also close to the true distribution of estimator $\widehat{\theta}_n$. Observe that, so far, we have not made a precise statement about 'closeness'.
- Note that this procedure only allows us to reproduce information that is already contained in the observations $Z_1, \ldots, Z_n$, that is, we are not able to generate new information. This means that the whole bootstrap information is contained in or conditioned on $Z_1, \ldots, Z_n$, respectively. Or, in other words, this means that we hope that the observations $Z_1, \ldots, Z_n$ are rich enough to capture the main properties of the model.

DEFINITION 7.3 *The bootstrap is called consistent for $\widehat{\theta}_n$ with sequence $(a_n)_{n\in\mathbb{N}}$ if, for all x,*

$$\lim_{n\to\infty} \left(P\left[a_n\left(\widehat{\theta}_n - h(F)\right) \le x\right] - P_{F_n^*}\left[a_n\left(\widehat{\theta}_n^* - \widehat{\theta}_n\right) \le x\right]\right) \xrightarrow{(P)} 0$$

□

Example 7.1 (revisited)

Observe that due to the central limit theorem we can choose $a_n = n^{1/2}$ for all $n \in \mathbb{N}$ and then we obtain for $h(F) = E[Z_1]$

$$a_n\left(\widehat{\theta}_n - E[Z_1]\right) \xrightarrow{(d)} \mathcal{N}(0, 1) \qquad \text{as } n \to \infty$$

Bootstrap consistency then means that for $n \to \infty$ we have

$$a_n\left(\widehat{\theta}_n^* - \widehat{\theta}_n\right) \xrightarrow{(d)} \mathcal{N}(0, 1) \quad \text{in probability}$$

□

In general, it is difficult to prove consistency. Consistency usually holds when the random variables $Z_1, \ldots, Z_n$ are i.i.d. and if the limiting distribution of $\widehat{\theta}_n$ is Gaussian. Moreover, in that situation we usually have, for $n \to \infty$,

$$\frac{E_{F_n^*}[\widehat{\theta}_n^*] - \widehat{\theta}_n}{E\left[\widehat{\theta}_n\right] - h(F)} \xrightarrow{(P)} 1, \qquad \frac{\mathrm{Var}_{F_n^*}(\widehat{\theta}_n^*)}{\mathrm{Var}\left(\widehat{\theta}_n\right)} \xrightarrow{(P)} 1$$

Construction of Confidence Intervals

Assume that q_α denotes the α-quantile of $a_n(\widehat{\theta}_n - h(F))$ and $\widehat{q}_\alpha$ denotes the α-quantile of $a_n(\widehat{\theta}_n^* - \widehat{\theta}_n)$, given the observations $Z_1, \ldots, Z_n$. Hence the two-sided confidence interval with coverage $1-\alpha$ for the parameter $h(F)$ is given by

$$\left[\widehat{\theta}_n - a_n^{-1}\, q_{\alpha/2}, \widehat{\theta}_n - a_n^{-1}\, q_{1-\alpha/2}\right]$$

and hence, given $Z_1, \ldots, Z_n$, the bootstrap estimated confidence interval is

$$\left[\widehat{\theta}_n - a_n^{-1}\, \widehat{q}_{\alpha/2}, \widehat{\theta}_n - a_n^{-1}\, \widehat{q}_{1-\alpha/2}\right] \tag{7.3}$$

Remark The confidence interval given in (7.3) is not exact. Using different levels of bootstrap (double bootstrap) one can further improve the bootstrap confidence interval.

7.1.2 Parametric Bootstrap

Efron's non-parametric bootstrap can be viewed as simulating from an empirical distribution $\widehat{F}_n$. That is, simulating from a non-parametric model where the observations are i.i.d. with an unknown distribution F. Assume that we have additional information about the class of distribution of Z_i, that is,

$$Z_1, \ldots, Z_n \quad \text{i.i.d.} \overset{(d)}{\sim} F_\theta \tag{7.4}$$

where F_θ denotes a known distribution type with unknown parameter θ.

In order to resample our bootstrap sample, we first estimate the unknown parameter θ by $\widehat{\theta}$ (such as least squares or MLE). The parametric bootstrap then uses the bootstrap distribution

$$Z_1^*, \ldots, Z_n^* \quad \text{i.i.d.} \overset{(d)}{\sim} \widehat{F_\theta} = F_{\widehat{\theta}} \tag{7.5}$$

instead of the empirical distribution (7.2). All the other steps in the bootstrap procedure are then done as in Efron's non-parametric bootstrap method.

Conclusions Efron's bootstrap can essentially be applied to every stochastic claims reserving model that we have considered so far. If we have, in addition, distributional model assumptions we can apply the parametric bootstrap method.

Outline of this Chapter

In the next sections we perform a bootstrap analysis for selected models, that is the Log-normal model for cumulative claims (see Chapter 5), the GLM model for incremental claims (see Chapter 6) and the distribution-free CL model (see Chapter 3). In Section 7.5 we provide mathematical insights into bootstrap structures. Finally, in Section 7.6 we present ideas how the bootstrap method can be used to model unknown dependencies between accident years.

7.2 LOG-NORMAL MODEL FOR CUMULATIVE SIZES

We revisit the model given in Model Assumptions 5.1: we assume that the individual development factors are i.i.d. Log-normally distributed with

$$\eta_{i,j} = \log\left(\frac{C_{i,j}}{C_{i,j-1}}\right) \overset{(d)}{\sim} \mathcal{N}(\xi_j, \sigma_j^2)$$

Our goal is to apply the parametric bootstrap method.

In the above context, $\theta_j = (\xi_j, \sigma_j^2)$ are the unknown parameters of the distribution of $\eta_{i,j}$. Conditionally, given $\mathcal{D}_I$, we are interested in the distribution of

$$h(F) = \sum_{i+j>I} E\left[X_{i,j}\middle|\mathcal{D}_I\right] \tag{7.6}$$

which are the expected open loss liabilities/outstanding claims reserves at time I. Hence, using (5.11), we see that these are given by

$$h(F) = \sum_{i=1}^{I} C_{i,I-i}\left(\exp\left\{\sum_{j=I-i+1}^{J}\xi_j + \frac{1}{2}\sum_{j=I-i+1}^{J}\sigma_j^2\right\} - 1\right)$$

For known parameters this is a constant, given the information $\mathcal{D}_I$. This means that for known parameters there is no uncertainty in the estimate of the conditionally expected open loss liabilities (no parameter estimation error term). Since, in general, the parameters are not known they need to be estimated, and the appropriate estimators were provided by (5.2) and (5.3)

$$\widehat{\xi}_j = \frac{1}{I-j+1}\sum_{i=0}^{I-j}\log\left(\frac{C_{i,j}}{C_{i,j-1}}\right) = \frac{1}{I-j+1}\sum_{i=0}^{I-j}\eta_{i,j} \tag{7.7}$$

$$\widehat{\sigma_j^2} = \frac{1}{I-j}\sum_{i=0}^{I-j}\left(\log\left(\frac{C_{i,j}}{C_{i,j-1}}\right) - \widehat{\xi}_j\right)^2 = \frac{1}{I-j}\sum_{i=0}^{I-j}\left(\eta_{i,j} - \widehat{\xi}_j\right)^2 \tag{7.8}$$

This has led to the following estimator for $h(F)$, given the observations $\mathcal{D}_I$, see (5.27):

$$\begin{aligned} g(\mathcal{D}_I) &= \sum_{i=1}^{I} \widehat{C_{i,J}}^{\mathrm{LN}\sigma,2} - C_{i,I-i} \\ &= \sum_{i=1}^{I} C_{i,I-i}\left(\exp\left\{\sum_{j=I-i+1}^{J}\widehat{\xi}_j + \frac{1}{2}\sum_{j=I-i+1}^{J}\widehat{\sigma_j^2}\left(1 - \frac{1}{I-j+1}\right)\right\} - 1\right) \end{aligned} \tag{7.9}$$

Our goal is to study the distribution of the estimator $g(\mathcal{D}_I)$. Note that we have not proved that $g(\mathcal{D}_I)$ is an unbiased estimator for $h(F)$, we have only made an asymptotic statement, see (5.28). We are going to analyse this now.

Since we have explicit distributional assumptions we would like to apply the parametric bootstrap method. This means that we need to estimate the unknown parameters ξ_j and σ_j^2 from the data $\mathcal{D}_I$ (see (7.7)–(7.8)). Applying the parametric bootstrap method, we then generate new independent observations

$$\eta_{i,j}^* \overset{(d)}{\sim} \mathcal{N}(\widehat{\xi}_j, \widehat{\sigma}_j^2) \tag{7.10}$$

This new bootstrap observations lead to bootstrap estimates for ξ_j and σ_j^2 given by

$$\widehat{\xi}_j^* = \frac{1}{I-j+1} \sum_{i=0}^{I-j} \eta_{i,j}^* \tag{7.11}$$

$$\widehat{\sigma_j^2}^* = \frac{1}{I-j} \sum_{i=0}^{I-j} \left(\eta_{i,j}^* - \widehat{\xi}_j^* \right)^2 \tag{7.12}$$

This then leads to the bootstrap reserves

$$g^*(\mathcal{D}_I) = \sum_{i=1}^{I} C_{i,I-i} \left(\exp\left\{ \sum_{j=I-i+1}^{J} \widehat{\xi}_j^* + \frac{1}{2} \sum_{j=I-i+1}^{J} \widehat{\sigma_j^2}^* \left(1 - \frac{1}{I-j+1} \right) \right\} - 1 \right) \tag{7.13}$$

If we repeat this procedure several times we obtain the conditional empirical distribution of $g^*(\mathcal{D}_I)$, given observations $\mathcal{D}_I$. We are now ready to study the bias of $g^*(\mathcal{D}_I) - g(\mathcal{D}_I)$ as well as the volatility of $g^*(\mathcal{D}_I)$. Note that we have the following decomposition (due to the $\mathcal{D}_I$-measurability of $g(\mathcal{D}_I)$)

$$E^*_{\widehat{\theta}(\mathcal{D}_I)}\left[\left(g^*(\mathcal{D}_I) - g(\mathcal{D}_I) \right)^2 \right] = \mathrm{Var}^*_{\widehat{\theta}(\mathcal{D}_I)}\left(g^*(\mathcal{D}_I) \right) + \left(E^*_{\widehat{\theta}(\mathcal{D}_I)}[g^*(\mathcal{D}_I)] - g(\mathcal{D}_I) \right)^2$$

where $P^*_{\widehat{\theta}(\mathcal{D}_I)}$ denotes the conditional probability distribution obtained from (7.10), conditioned on $\mathcal{D}_I$.

Basically, this means that we assume that the true parameters are given by $\widehat{\xi}_j$ and $\widehat{\sigma_j^2}$. Under these assumptions we analyse the possible fluctuations of other bootstrap/resampled observations $\eta_{i,j}^*$.

Example 5.8 (revisited), parametric bootstrap

We revisit Example 5.8. Observe that we had different estimators according to whether the variance parameters σ_j are known or not known. Moreover, we have chosen different estimators for the bias correction. For the bootstrap example we compare our results to the estimator $\widehat{C_{i,J}}^{\mathrm{LN}\sigma,2}$ from Table 5.4 and to the estimation error from Table 5.2.

Our (parametric) bootstrap results are given in Figure 7.1.

Observe that we obtain a very small bias correction of

$$E^*_{\widehat{\theta}(\mathcal{D}_I)}[g^*(\mathcal{D}_I)] - g(\mathcal{D}_I) = 6\,047\,253 - 6\,046\,308 = 944 \tag{7.14}$$

Mean	6 046 308
Emprical mean (bootstrap)	6 047 253
Std dev. (bootstrap)	183 775
99% VaR (bootstrap)	423 645
99% VaR (normal)	427 524
99% VaR (Log-normal)	439 898

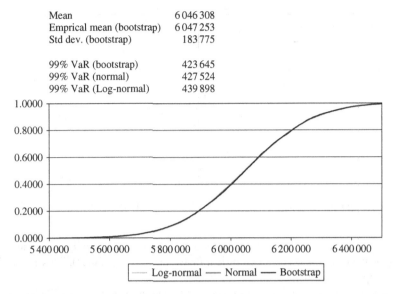

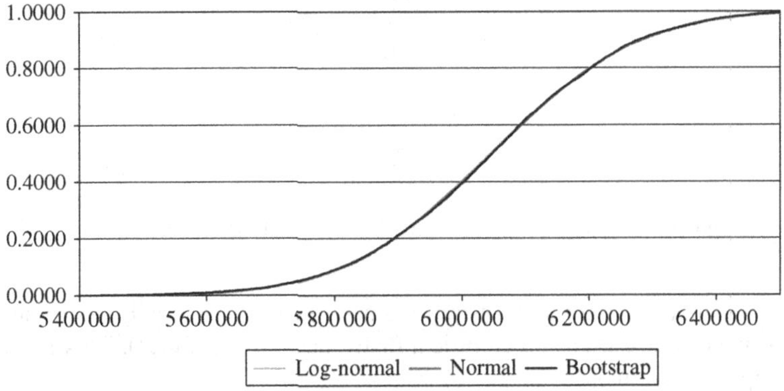

Figure 7.1 Parametric bootstrap distribution for the claims reserves (Log-normal model) compared to the Normal and the Log-normal distribution. The distributional fits are so close that one cannot see any differences on that scale

Of course, this is negligible with respect to the standard deviation of

$$\mathrm{Var}^*_{\widehat{\theta}(\mathcal{D}_I)}\left(g^*(\mathcal{D}_I)\right)^{1/2} = 183\,775$$

This means that the bias correction in $\widehat{C_{i,J}}^{\mathrm{LN}\sigma,2}$ is 'rather good' for this set of parameters. This means that we do not have to work with more elaborate bias corrections like Finney's method (1941), see p. 179. Indeed, the volatility in the $\widehat{\sigma}_j$ parameters are negligible for the estimation of the expected ultimate claims.

Our estimation error is slightly larger than that given in Table 5.2, and comes from the fact that for the derivation of the estimation error in the table we have not taken into account the uncertainties in the estimates of $\widehat{\sigma}_j$.

Moreover, we have compared the bootstrap distribution to closed analytical distributions for the expected reserves that were fitted with the help of the first two moments (Normal and Log-normal approximation for $g(\mathcal{D}_I)$). Observe that the bootstrap 99% Value-at-Risk is only slightly smaller compared to the one coming from the Normal distribution with the same mean and variance.

Notice also that we have (blindly) assumed that the individual development factors $F_{i,j}$ are Log-normally distributed. If we consider the Q–Q plot for the residuals, we obtain Figure 7.2. This Q–Q plot rather suggests that the individual development factors $F_{i,j}$ do not follow a Log-normal distribution. Indeed, with the exception of one outlier $F_{0,1}$, we observe a distribution that has lighter tails than the Log-normal distribution. In our opinion, one should not give too much weight to this outlier because the very first accident year seems to be rather special and there could be a break in the data structure after this year (which cannot be captured by our model). Figure 7.2 tells us that we should rather use Efron's non-parametric bootstrap method. □

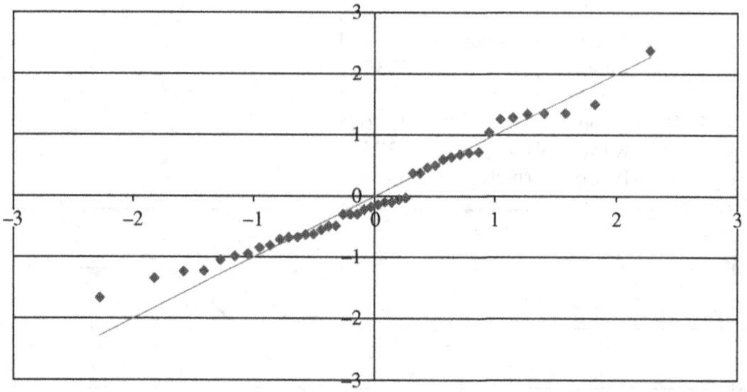

Figure 7.2 Q–Q plot logged residuals against normal distribution

To apply Efron's non-parametric bootstrap we need to find identically distributed observations, so that we can construct the empirical distribution $\widehat{F}_n$, see (7.2). This is usually done finding appropriate residuals.

Hence, Efron's non-parametric bootstrap is obtained as follows: define the residuals

$$D_{i,j} = \frac{\eta_{i,j} - \widehat{\xi}_j}{\widehat{\sigma}_j}$$

Then the set of observations $\{D_{i,j};\ i+j \le I, j \ge 1\}$ defines the bootstrap distribution $\widehat{F}_{\mathcal{D}_I}$. We resample i.i.d. residuals

$$D^*_{i,j} \overset{(d)}{\sim} \widehat{F}_{\mathcal{D}_I}$$

and hence define the bootstrapped observations of $\eta_{i,j}$ by

$$\eta^*_{i,j} = \widehat{\sigma}_j D^*_{i,j} + \widehat{\xi}_j \tag{7.15}$$

Now, we 'hope' that the bootstrap distribution, given the observation $\mathcal{D}_I$, is sufficiently close to the original/true distribution, that is

$$\{\eta^*_{i,j};\ i+j \le I, j \ge 1\} \overset{(d)}{\approx} \{\eta_{i,j};\ i+j \le I, j \ge 1\} \tag{7.16}$$

Hence (7.11)–(7.13) lead to bootstrap observations $g^*(\mathcal{D}_I)$ for $g(\mathcal{D}_I)$ with, hopefully, approximately the same properties as the estimator $g(\mathcal{D}_I)$.

Example 5.8 (revisited), Efron's non-parametric bootstrap

For the non-parametric bootstrap we find (see Figure 7.3)

$$E^*_{\widehat{\theta}(\mathcal{D}_I)}[g^*(\mathcal{D}_I)] - g(\mathcal{D}_I) = 6\,035\,953 - 6\,046\,308 = -10\,355 \tag{7.17}$$

Of course, this is still small with respect to the standard deviation

$$\mathrm{Var}^*_{\widehat{\theta}(\mathcal{D}_I)}(g^*(\mathcal{D}_I))^{1/2} = 154\,286$$

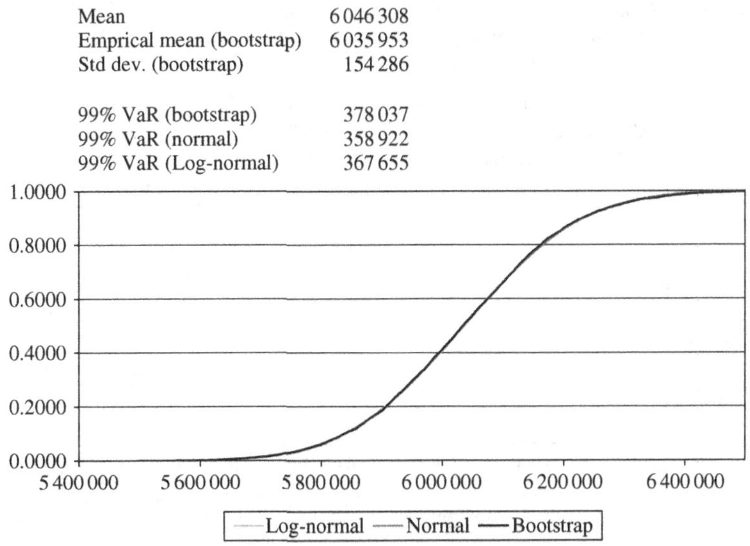

Figure 7.3 Non-parametric bootstrap distribution for the claims reserves compared to the Normal and the Log-normal distribution. The distributional fits are so close that one cannot see any differences on that scale

We see that we obtain a larger (negative) bias. It is clear that we should obtain a different bias correction, since the bias correction in (7.14) was done with respect to a Log-normal distribution. The empirical distribution has lighter tails, hence we obtain an empirical expected value that is too small, see (7.17).

We see (as expected) that the non-parametric bootstrap has lighter tails than the parametric bootstrap with a Log-normal distribution (see Figure 7.2). Moreover, one should note that the variance estimates from the parametric bootstrap and the non-parametric bootstrap are not comparable. For the parametric bootstrap we have chosen $\eta^*_{i,j}$ which have variances $\widehat{\sigma}^2_j$. On the other hand, observe that the variance of the bootstrap distribution $\widehat{F}_{\mathcal{D}_I}$ is equal to $(0.915)^2$. This means that our bootstrap distribution has a variance that is too small (it should be equal to 1 since residuals are usually appropriately scaled, that is, they have mean 0 and variance 1). Therefore, the variance of the bootstrap samples $\eta^*_{i,j}$ (non-parametric version) is *too small*, and hence the parameter estimation error is *underestimated* if we do not adjust the empirical distribution (we will further comment on this in Section 7.5, see also (7.23)).

We have already mentioned that $F_{0,1}$ seems to be special. It could be that this value does not fit into our model due to possible changes in the payout patterns, etc. If we remove this value from the statistics and run the non-parametric bootstrap we obtain a picture that has even lighter tails (see Figure 7.4). □

Remarks 7.4

We emphasize that the bootstrap method is a powerful technique that gives distributional answers if properly applied (and if $\mathcal{D}_I$ is rich enough). This means that the bootstrap method does not only give estimates for the first and second moments, but it estimates an entire distribution. This bootstrap distribution can be used to answer such questions as Value-at-Risk estimates, expected discounted reserves, etc.

Mean	6 046 308
Emprical mean (bootstrap)	5 986 146
Std dev. (bootstrap)	148 209
99% VaR (bootstrap)	365 602
99% VaR (normal)	344 787
99% VaR (Log-normal)	352 911

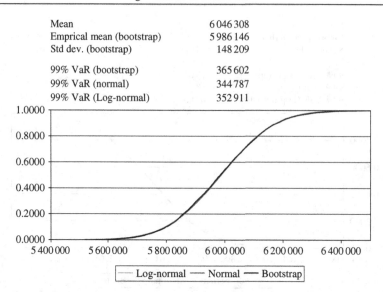

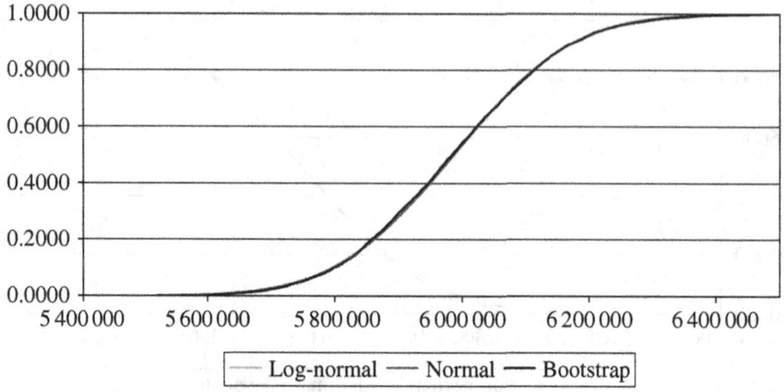

Figure 7.4 Non-parametric bootstrap distribution for the claims reserves compared to the Normal and the Log-normal distribution if we remove $F_{0,1}$ from the data. The distributional fits are so close that one cannot see any differences on that scale

7.3 GENERALIZED LINEAR MODELS

In Chapter 6 we studied EDF models of the following type for incremental claims (see Model Assumptions 6.4):

$$E\left[X_{i,j}\right] = x_{i,j}$$

$$\mathrm{Var}\left(X_{i,j}\right) = \frac{\phi_{i,j}}{w_{i,j}} V(x_{i,j})$$

where $\phi_{i,j}$ is the dispersion, $V(\cdot)$ is an appropriate variance function and the $w_{i,j}$ are known weights. Moreover, we have assumed a multiplicative structure for the expected claims

$$x_{i,j} = \mu_i \, \gamma_j$$

Parameter estimation of μ_i and γ_j was then performed using MLE methods (see Section 6.4). The estimation of the MSEP was a rather tedious approximation using the Fisher information matrix and asymptotic arguments. The main difficulty was to find an estimate for the estimation error (6.46). Here, using bootstrap techniques, we find another estimate.

In order to apply Efron's non-parametric bootstrap method we once again need to find identically distributed residuals that allow for the construction of the empirical distribution $\widehat{F}_n$, see (7.2). Assume that $\phi = \phi_{i,j}/w_{i,j}$ is constant.

In the following outline we follow England and Verrall (2002). For GLM there are several different definitions for residuals (Pearson, deviance, Anscombe residuals, see McCullagh and Nelder 1989). As in England and Verrall (2002, 2007) and Pinheiro *et al.* (2003) we choose the Pearson residuals given by (see (6.56))

$$R_{i,j}^{(P)}(x_{i,j}) = \frac{X_{i,j} - x_{i,j}}{V(x_{i,j})^{1/2}} \tag{7.18}$$

Note that these residuals have mean 0 and variance ϕ. Therefore $R_{i,j}^{(\mathrm{P})}(x_{i,j})$ is a natural object to define the bootstrap distribution. Hence, we set for $i+j \leq I$ (see also (6.25))

$$Z_{i,j} = \frac{X_{i,j} - \widehat{x_{i,j}}}{V(\widehat{x_{i,j}})^{1/2}}$$

These $\{Z_{i,j}, i+j \leq I\}$ define the bootstrap distribution $\widehat{F}_{\mathcal{D}_I}$. Then, we resample i.i.d. residuals

$$Z_{i,j}^* \overset{(d)}{\sim} \widehat{F}_{\mathcal{D}_I}$$

and hence we define the bootstrap observations of $X_{i,j}$ by

$$X_{i,j}^* = \widehat{x_{i,j}} + V(\widehat{x_{i,j}})^{1/2}\, Z_{i,j}^* \tag{7.19}$$

These bootstrap observations $X_{i,j}^*$ now lead to bootstrap claims reserving triangles $\mathcal{D}_I^* = \{X_{i,j}^*;\ i+j \leq I\}$. Using GLM methods, we calculate bootstrap estimates μ_i^*, γ_j^* and $\widehat{x_{i,j}}^*$ from the bootstrap observations $X_{i,j}^*$, $i+j \leq I$. This leads to the bootstrap claims reserves $\widehat{X_{i,j}^*}^{\mathrm{EDF}}$, $i+j > I$ (see Estimator 6.7). Repeating this bootstrap sampling we obtain the bootstrap distribution of the claims reserves, conditioned on $\mathcal{D}_I$.

Example 6.16 (revisited) – Efron's non-parametric bootstrap

We revisit the overdispersed Poisson example, that is, the variance function is given by $V(x_{i,j}) = x_{i,j}$. For this example we bootstrap the total expected claims reserves. We also bootstrap the estimated dispersion parameter ϕ given by (see (6.58))

$$\widehat{\phi}_{\mathrm{P}} = \frac{\sum_{i+j \leq I} Z_{i,j}^2}{N - p} \tag{7.20}$$

where, again,

$$N = \text{number of observations } X_{i,j} \text{ in } \mathcal{D}_I \text{ (i.e. } N = |\mathcal{D}_I|)$$
$$p = \text{number of estimated parameters } b_k \text{ (i.e. } p = I + J + 1)$$

Finally, the standard error from the bootstrap method needs to be scaled appropriately so that it becomes comparable to the analytic model. The reason for this scaling is that the empirical distribution has a variance which is *too small* (we will further comment on this in Section 7.5, see also equation (7.23)). The scaling factor is given by

$$\frac{N}{N - p} \tag{7.21}$$

We see that the parameter uncertainties in the overdispersed Poisson model are substantially larger than those in the Log-normal model (see Figures 7.1 and 7.5). This was already indicated in Table 6.2. On the other hand, as Table 6.2 indicates, we have a process error in the overdispersed Poisson model which is much smaller than that from the distribution-free CL and the Log-normal model. This shows that the error classes are not directly comparable, since the uncertainties partly move into different error classes.

Mean	6 047 061
Emprical mean (bootstrap)	6 041 432
Std dev. (bootstrap)	241 786
Scaled std dev.	298 855
99% VaR (bootstrap)	571 558
99% VaR (normal)	562 477
99% VaR (Log-normal)	583 943

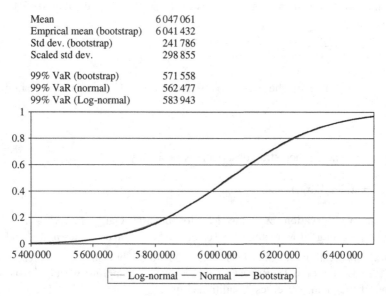

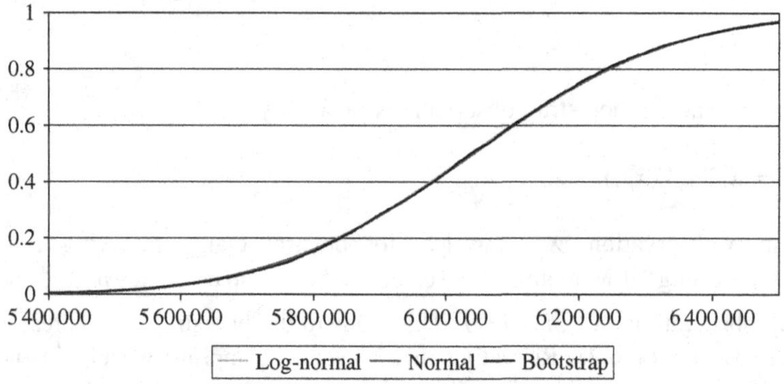

Figure 7.5 Non-parametric bootstrap distribution for the claims reserves (GLM model) compared to the Normal and the Log-normal distribution. The distributional fits are so close that one cannot see any differences on that scale

Let us now compare the bootstrap results to the analytical derivations in Chapter 6. As stated in Remarks 6.15: MLE have a possible bias. Here, the bootstrap mean is smaller than the 'true' mean. However, we see that, in practice, this error is negligible compared to the other uncertainties (for reasonable claims reserving examples and parameter sets). The bootstrap estimation error (scaled standard deviation of 298 855) is very close to the analytical estimation error of 309 563 (see Table 6.2 and Figure 7.5).

The bootstrap analysis for the dispersion parameter ϕ turns out to be very unstable, which indicates that we have to be rather careful when choosing meaningful variance parameters. These findings correspond to those obtained in the MCMC section (see Table 4.21). □

7.4 CHAIN-LADDER METHOD

In Chapter 3 we studied the classical distribution-free CL model. For the derivation of an estimate for the conditional MSEP we used different approaches, conditional and unconditional resampling approaches. We are further analysing them in this section.

To derive the resampling approaches we have defined the Time Series Model 3.9 of the distribution-free CL model. It was given by

$$C_{i,j+1} = f_j \; C_{i,j} + \sigma_j \; \sqrt{C_{i,j}} \; \varepsilon_{i,j+1}$$

We assume that conditionally, given $\mathcal{B}_0$, the $\varepsilon_{i,j}$ are i.i.d. The individual development factors are then given by

$$F_{i,j+1} = \frac{C_{i,j+1}}{C_{i,j}} = f_j + \sigma_j \; C_{i,j}^{-1/2} \; \varepsilon_{i,j+1}$$

For the time being we assume that σ_j is known.

In order to apply the bootstrap method we again need to find appropriate residuals that allow for the construction of the empirical distribution $\widehat{F}_n$, see (7.2), from which the bootstrap observations are constructed. Of course, the obvious candidates are $\varepsilon_{i,j}$.

Consider the following residuals for $i+j \leq I$, $j \geq 1$,

$$\widetilde{\varepsilon}_{i,j} = \frac{F_{i,j} - \widehat{f}_{j-1}}{\sigma_{j-1} \; C_{i,j-1}^{-1/2}} \tag{7.22}$$

where the estimators $\widehat{f}_j$ are given in (3.4). Note that these residuals $\widetilde{\varepsilon}_{i,j}$ are observable for given σ_j, whereas $\varepsilon_{i,j}$ are not observable for unknown f_j. There are two important remarks about these residuals $\widetilde{\varepsilon}_{i,j}$.

Remarks 7.5

- We have that $E\left[\widetilde{\varepsilon}_{i,j} \middle| \mathcal{B}_{j-1}\right] = 0$ and

$$\mathrm{Var}\left(\widetilde{\varepsilon}_{i,j} \middle| \mathcal{B}_{j-1}\right) = 1 - \frac{C_{i,j-1}}{\sum_{i=0}^{I-j} C_{i,j-1}} < 1 \tag{7.23}$$

  This means that we should adjust our observable residuals $\widetilde{\varepsilon}_{i,j}$ in order to obtain the correct order for the estimation error (the empirical distribution has a variance that is too small). This is similar to the findings in Sections 7.2 and 7.3 where we have to adjust the bootstrap variance.
- Observe that (see also (7.32))

$$\sum_{i=0}^{I-j-1} \sqrt{C_{i,j}} \; \widetilde{\varepsilon}_{i,j+1} = 0$$

  This immediately implies that, a.s., the bootstrap distribution of the residuals $\widetilde{\varepsilon}_{i,j+1}$ is not centred, that is, has non-zero mean, a.s.

In the following, we neglect the second remark (since we can explicitly calculate the mean), but we adjust our residuals such that the bootstrap distribution has an adjusted variance function. We define

$$Z_{i,j} = \left(1 - \frac{C_{i,j-1}}{\sum_{i=0}^{I-j} C_{i,j-1}}\right)^{-1/2} \; \frac{F_{i,j} - \widehat{f}_{j-1}}{\widehat{\sigma}_{j-1} \; C_{i,j-1}^{-1/2}} \tag{7.24}$$

where the estimators $\widehat{f}_j$ and $\widehat{\sigma}_j^2$ are given in (3.4). These residuals $\{Z_{i,j},\ i+j \le I\}$, define a bootstrap distribution $\widehat{F}_{\mathcal{D}_I}$. Then, we resample i.i.d. residuals from this bootstrap distribution

$$Z^*_{i,j} \overset{(d)}{\sim} \widehat{F}_{\mathcal{D}_I} \tag{7.25}$$

and hence define the bootstrap observations $F^*_{i,j}$, $i+j \le I$. In contrast to the methods in Sections 7.2 and 7.3 this next step of reproducing bootstrap observations $F^*_{i,j}$ of $F_{i,j}$ is not straightforward. Because we have a time series with dependent increments, we can do both an unconditional and a conditional backtransformation/bootstrapping. This corresponds to Approaches 1 and 3 on p. 45.

Note that the question about backtransformation in a conditional or an unconditional way only appears in the distribution-free CL method of Section 7.3 because this model deals with Markov chains (the link ratio model). If we use the overdispersed Poisson model as an explanation for the CL reserves, we do not have this problem, because that model considers independent increments (see Section 7.3).

7.4.1 Approach 1: Unconditional Estimation Error

For the unconditional approach we produce completely new triangles. For the moment, we fix one accident year i. For the consideration of accident year i we could either produce new triangles in $\mathcal{D}^{\mathrm{O}}_{I,i}$ (as described in Approach 1 on p. 45, or completely resample the triangle $\mathcal{D}_I \setminus \mathcal{B}_0$. We choose the second version since it is easier to implement.

Henceforth, in the unconditional approach the bootstrap individual development factors are produced as follows. We define $C^*_{i,0} = C_{i,0}$ and, for $j \ge 1$, we define

$$C^*_{i,j} = \widehat{f}_{j-1}\ C^*_{i,j-1} + \widehat{\sigma}_{j-1} \sqrt{C^*_{i,j-1}}\ Z^*_{i,j} \tag{7.26}$$

Hence, the unconditional bootstrap individual development factors are given by

$$F^*_{i,j+1} = \frac{C^*_{i,j+1}}{C^*_{i,j}} = \widehat{f}_j + \frac{\widehat{\sigma}_j}{\sqrt{C^*_{i,j}}}\ Z^*_{i,j+1}$$

and the observed bootstrapped development factors are given by

$$\widehat{f}^*_j = \frac{\sum_{i=0}^{I-j-1} C^*_{i,j+1}}{\sum_{i=0}^{I-j-1} C^*_{i,j}} = \sum_{i=0}^{I-j-1} \frac{C^*_{i,j}}{\sum_{k=0}^{I-j-1} C^*_{k,j}}\ F^*_{i,j+1} \tag{7.27}$$

Then, the CL estimate for the ultimate claims $C_{i,J}$ in the unconditional approach are given by

$$\widehat{C_{i,J}}^* = C_{i,I-i} \prod_{j=I-i}^{J-1} \widehat{f}^*_j$$

Example 2.7 (revisited), unconditional approach

We perform the bootstrap analysis for the results obtained in Table 3.6. For a Q–Q plot of the residuals $\widetilde{\varepsilon}_{i,j}$ we refer to Figure 11.3.

The bootstrap algorithm is applied to three different versions:

1. Efron's non-parametric bootstrap for residuals $\widetilde{\varepsilon}_{i,j}$ (see (7.22)).
2. Efron's non-parametric bootstrap for scaled residuals $Z_{i,j}$ (see (7.24)).
3. Parametric bootstrap under the assumption that the residuals have a standard Gaussian distribution, that is $Z^*_{i,j}$ is resampled from $\mathcal{N}(0, 1)$.

Table 7.1 clearly illustrates the difficulty we face in the application of the non-parametric bootstrap. Observe that the bootstrap distributions of $\{\widetilde{\varepsilon}_{i,j};\ i+j \leq I\}$ and $\{Z_{i,j};\ i+j \leq I\}$ have, given $\mathcal{D}_I$, a mean of -0.0007 and -0.0008, respectively. This slight difference implies that the bootstrap mean is about 10 000 below its average. If we apply a parametric bootstrap method with standard Gaussian residuals, then the bootstrap mean almost matches the true mean (we have used 10 000 simulations).

Table 7.1 Three different bootstrap methods applied to the CL model (unconditional approach)

	Non-parametric unscaled $\widetilde{\varepsilon}_{i,j}$	Non-parametric scaled $Z_{i,j}$	Parametric standard Gaussian
True mean	6 047 061	6 047 061	6 047 061
Bootstrap mean	6 037 418	6 036 929	6 048 247
Bootstrap std dev.	159 948	174 988	184 706

For the estimation variances we have a similar picture, we observe that the bootstrap distribution of $\{\widetilde{\varepsilon}_{i,j};\ i+j \leq I\}$ has a standard deviation of 0.915, hence it is substantially *smaller* than 1. As an implication we obtain an estimation error that lies substantially below the according value for the non-parametric bootstrap with scaled residuals and for the parametric bootstrap. Moreover, we observe in Figure 7.6 that the non-parametric bootstrap gives substantially lighter tails compared to the parametric bootstrap. □

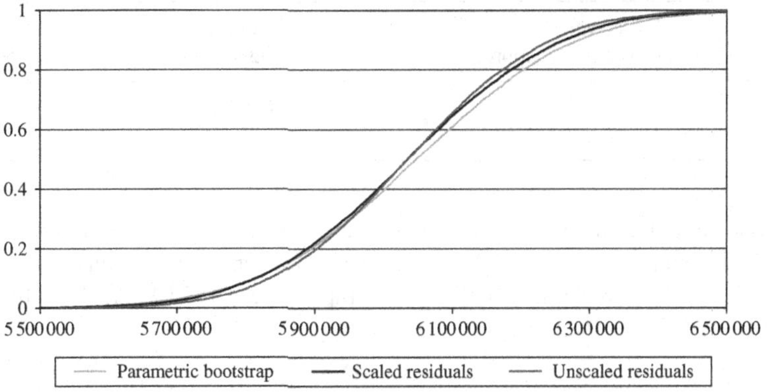

Figure 7.6 The three bootstrap methods (CL model)

7.4.2 Approach 3: Conditional Estimation Error

For the conditional approach, we only produce new observations for the next step in the time series. This means that this approach is always a conditional distribution, given $\mathcal{D}_I$.

Henceforth, in the conditional approach the bootstrap development factors are produced as follows

$$\widehat{f}_j^* = \sum_{i=0}^{I-j-1} \frac{C_{i,j}}{\sum_{k=0}^{I-j-1} C_{k,j}} F_{i,j+1}^* \tag{7.28}$$

with

$$F_{i,j+1}^* = \widehat{f}_j + \frac{\widehat{\sigma}_j}{\sqrt{C_{i,j}}} Z_{i,j+1}^* \tag{7.29}$$

Then, the CL estimate for the ultimate claim $C_{i,J}$ in the conditional approach is given by

$$\widehat{C_{i,J}}^* = C_{i,I-i} \prod_{j=I-i}^{J-1} \widehat{f}_j^*$$

Example 2.7 (revisited), conditional approach

We compare the unconditional estimation error to the conditional estimation error. Since the parametric bootstrap gave the best empirical fit to the true mean, we only consider this version. The results are given in Table 7.2, where we see that (as expected) the unconditional bootstrap gives a lower value for the standard deviation compared to the conditional bootstrap (this is due to the negative correlation of the squares of successive CL factor estimates, see Lemma 3.8). However, the differences are fairly small (or even negligible). This is similar to the findings in Example 3.19 (bounds in the unconditional approach).

Table 7.2 Comparison unconditional bootstrap, conditional bootstrap and exact value from the conditional approach (from Chapter 3, Table 3.6)

	Exact values (conditional approach)	Unconditional bootstrap	Conditional bootstrap
Mean	6 047 061	6 048 247	6 050 768
Std dev.	185 026	184 706	185 319

Finally, one should compare these results to the analytical results (conditional resampling Estimator 3.14) obtained in Table 3.6. The estimation error in the analytical derivation was equal to 185 026. We see that the bootstrap value 185 319 matches the analytical approximation (see Table 7.2). □

7.5 MATHEMATICAL THOUGHTS ABOUT BOOTSTRAPPING METHODS

In this subsection we make some mathematical considerations about the bootstrap. These considerations are rather general, but for illustrative purposes we restrict ourselves to the distribution-free CL model. The more practically oriented reader may also skip this section.

Model Assumptions 7.6 (Gaussian residuals)

- Cumulative claims of different accident years i are independent.
- There exist constants $f_j > 0$, $\sigma_j > 0$ and i.i.d. standard Gaussian random variables $\varepsilon_{i,j+1}$ such that for all $i \in \{0, \ldots, I\}$ and $j \in \{0, \ldots, J-1\}$ we have

$$C_{i,j+1} = f_j \; C_{i,j} + \sigma_j \sqrt{C_{i,j}} \varepsilon_{i,j+1}$$

□

Remark Observe that Model Assumptions 7.6 do not give a well-defined model. Theoretically, it could happen that cumulative claims become negative, and hence the time series cannot be further developed. For the time being we neglect this problem and refer to Remarks 3.10.

General assumptions In the following we assume that σ_j is known.

If the true CL factors f_j are not known, then of course the error factors $\varepsilon_{i,j}$ are not observable. Only the following error terms are observable (see also (7.22))

$$\begin{aligned}\widetilde{\varepsilon}_{i,j+1} &= \frac{C_{i,j+1} - \widehat{f}_j \; C_{i,j}}{\sigma_j \sqrt{C_{i,j}}} = \varepsilon_{i,j+1} + \frac{\left(f_j - \widehat{f}_j\right) \; C_{i,j}}{\sigma_j \sqrt{C_{i,j}}} \\ &= \varepsilon_{i,j+1} - \frac{\sqrt{C_{i,j}}}{\sum_{k=0}^{I-j-1} C_{k,j}} \sum_{k=0}^{I-j-1} \sqrt{C_{k,j}} \; \varepsilon_{k,j+1}\end{aligned} \tag{7.30}$$

Note that these observable error terms $\widetilde{\varepsilon}_{i,j+1}$ are not independent. Our first goal is to find $\mathcal{B}_j$-measurable transformations $A^{(j)}$ such that the transformed observable error terms are i.i.d. (under Model Assumptions 7.6). Observe that this can be done using linear transformations due to the Gaussian assumption, that is, in Gaussian models uncorrelated random variables are independent.

Define the rescaled observable error terms according to

$$\Delta_{i,j+1} = \sqrt{C_{i,j}} \; \widetilde{\varepsilon}_{i,j+1}$$

With (7.30) we find for the rescaled observable error terms

$$\begin{aligned}\Delta_{i,j+1} &= \frac{C_{i,j+1} - \widehat{f}_j \; C_{i,j}}{\sigma_j} \\ &= \sqrt{C_{i,j}} \; \varepsilon_{i,j+1} - \frac{C_{i,j}}{\sum_{k=0}^{I-j-1} C_{k,j}} \sum_{k=0}^{I-j-1} \sqrt{C_{k,j}} \; \varepsilon_{k,j+1}\end{aligned} \tag{7.31}$$

Define the vector $\Delta_{j+1} = \left(\Delta_{0,j+1}, \ldots, \Delta_{I-j-1,j+1}\right)' \in \mathbb{R}^{I-j}$. Equation (7.31) immediately implies that these rescaled observable error terms span a $(I-j-1)$-dimensional hyperplane H in the $(I-j)$-dimensional space $\mathbb{R}^{I-j}$, since

$$(1, \ldots, 1) \; \Delta_{j+1} = \sum_{i=0}^{I-j-1} \Delta_{i,j+1} = 0 \tag{7.32}$$

Thus, we look for a new basis $(\Delta^*_{i,j+1})_{i=1,\dots,I-j-1}$ that spans this $(I-j-1)$-dimensional hyperplane H such that $\Delta^*_{i,j+1}$ and $\Delta^*_{k,j+1}$ are orthogonal for $i \neq k$. In matrix notation this means: find a $\mathcal{B}_j$-measurable matrix $B^{(j)} \in \mathbb{R}^{(I-j)(I-j)}$ with

$$B^{(j)}\ \Delta_{j+1} = \left(0, \Delta^*_{1,j+1}, \dots, \Delta^*_{I-j-1,j+1}\right)' \in \mathbb{R}^{I-j} \tag{7.33}$$

such that for all $i \neq k$

$$\operatorname{Cov}\left(\Delta^*_{i,j+1}, \Delta^*_{k,j+1} \middle| \mathcal{B}_j\right) = 0 \tag{7.34}$$

We define the $\mathcal{B}_j$-measurable matrix as follows

$$B^{(j)} = \begin{pmatrix} 1 & 1 & 1 & 1 & \cdots & 1 & 1 \\ 1 & -\frac{C_{0,j}}{C_{1,j}} & 0 & 0 & \cdots & 0 & 0 \\ 1 & 1 & -\frac{C_{0,j}+C_{1,j}}{C_{2,j}} & 0 & \cdots & 0 & 0 \\ \vdots & & & & & & \vdots \\ 1 & 1 & 1 & 1 & \cdots & -\frac{\sum_{i=0}^{I-j-3} C_{i,j}}{C_{I-j-2,j}} & 0 \\ 1 & 1 & 1 & 1 & \cdots & 1 & -\frac{\sum_{i=0}^{I-j-2} C_{i,j}}{C_{I-j-1,j}} \end{pmatrix} \tag{7.35}$$

LEMMA 7.7 *The matrix $B^{(j)}$ defined in* (7.35) *satisfies* (7.33)–(7.34) *with*

$$\tau^2_{k,j} = \operatorname{Var}\left(\Delta^*_{k,j+1} \middle| \mathcal{B}_j\right) = \sum_{i=0}^{k-1} C_{i,j} \left(1 + \sum_{m=0}^{k-1} \frac{C_{m,j}}{C_{k,j}}\right)$$

Proof of Lemma 7.7 Define the random vector

$$(Y_0, \dots, Y_{I-j-1})' = B^{(j)}\ \Delta_{j+1} \quad \in \mathbb{R}^{I-j}$$

Observe that $Y_0 = 0$, due to (7.32) and (7.35), and for $k \geq 1$ we have

$$\begin{aligned} Y_k = \sum_{i=0}^{I-j-1} B^{(j)}_{k,i}\ \Delta_{i,j+1} &= \sum_{i=0}^{k-1} \Delta_{i,j+1} - \sum_{i=0}^{k-1} \frac{C_{i,j}}{C_{k,j}}\ \Delta_{k,j+1} \\ &= \sum_{i=0}^{k-1} C_{i,j} \left(\frac{\Delta_{i,j+1}}{C_{i,j}} - \frac{\Delta_{k,j+1}}{C_{k,j}}\right) \end{aligned}$$

To prove the lemma we need to calculate, for $k, l \geq 1$, the covariances

$$\begin{aligned}
&\mathrm{Cov}\left(Y_k, Y_l \middle| \mathcal{B}_j\right) \\
&= \sum_{i=0}^{k-1} \sum_{m=0}^{l-1} C_{i,j}\, C_{m,j} \mathrm{Cov}\left(\left(\frac{\Delta_{i,j+1}}{C_{i,j}} - \frac{\Delta_{k,j+1}}{C_{k,j}} \right), \left(\frac{\Delta_{m,j+1}}{C_{m,j}} - \frac{\Delta_{l,j+1}}{C_{l,j}} \right) \middle| \mathcal{B}_j \right) \\
&= \sum_{i=0}^{k-1} \sum_{m=0}^{l-1} C_{i,j} C_{m,j} \mathrm{Cov}\left(\left(\frac{C_{i,j+1}}{\sigma_j C_{i,j}} - \frac{C_{k,j+1}}{\sigma_j C_{k,j}} \right), \left(\frac{C_{m,j+1}}{\sigma_j C_{m,j}} - \frac{C_{l,j+1}}{\sigma_j C_{l,j}} \right) \middle| \mathcal{B}_j \right)
\end{aligned}$$

where in the last step we have used (7.31). For the covariance terms we have

$$\mathrm{Cov}\left(\frac{C_{k,j+1}}{\sigma_j\, C_{k,j}}, \frac{C_{l,j+1}}{\sigma_j\, C_{l,j}} \middle| \mathcal{B}_j \right) = \frac{1}{C_{k,j}}\, 1_{\{k=l\}}$$

This implies for the variances

$$\begin{aligned}
&\mathrm{Var}\left(Y_k \middle| \mathcal{B}_j\right) \\
&= \sum_{i=0}^{k-1} C_{i,j}^2\, \mathrm{Var}\left(\frac{C_{i,j+1}}{\sigma_j\, C_{i,j}} \middle| \mathcal{B}_j \right) + \sum_{i=0}^{k-1} \sum_{m=0}^{k-1} C_{i,j}\, C_{m,j}\, \mathrm{Var}\left(\frac{C_{k,j+1}}{\sigma_j\, C_{k,j}} \middle| \mathcal{B}_j \right) \\
&= \sum_{i=0}^{k-1} C_{i,j} \left(1 + \sum_{m=0}^{k-1} \frac{C_{m,j}}{C_{k,j}} \right) = \tau_{k,j}^2
\end{aligned}$$

and, for $1 \leq l < k \leq I - j - 1$, this implies that

$$\begin{aligned}
&\mathrm{Cov}\left(Y_k, Y_l \middle| \mathcal{B}_j\right) \\
&= \sum_{i=0}^{k-1} \sum_{m=0}^{l-1} C_{i,j}\, C_{m,j}\, \mathrm{Cov}\left(\frac{C_{i,j+1}}{\sigma_j\, C_{i,j}}, \left(\frac{C_{m,j+1}}{\sigma_j\, C_{m,j}} - \frac{C_{l,j+1}}{\sigma_j\, C_{l,j}} \right) \middle| \mathcal{B}_j \right) \\
&= \sum_{i=0}^{l-1} C_{i,j}^2\, \mathrm{Var}\left(\frac{C_{i,j+1}}{\sigma_j\, C_{i,j}} \middle| \mathcal{B}_j \right) - \sum_{m=0}^{l-1} C_{l,j}\, C_{m,j}\, \mathrm{Var}\left(\frac{C_{l,j+1}}{\sigma_j\, C_{l,j}} \middle| \mathcal{B}_j \right) = 0
\end{aligned}$$

This completes the proof of Lemma 7.7 with $\Delta_{i,j+1}^* = Y_i$. □

This immediately gives the next corollary:

COROLLARY 7.8 *We assume Model Assumptions 7.6. For $j \in \{0, \ldots, J-2\}$ we define the $\mathcal{B}_j$-measurable matrix*

$$A^{(j)} = \begin{pmatrix} 1 & & 0 \\ & \tau_{1,j}^{-2} & \\ & & \ddots & \\ 0 & & & \tau_{I-j-1,j}^{-2} \end{pmatrix} B^{(j)}$$

and the random vector

$$\boldsymbol{\delta}_{j+1} = \left(0, \delta_{1,j+1}, \ldots, \delta_{I-j-1,j+1}\right)' = A^{(j)} \, \Delta_{j+1} \quad \in \mathbb{R}^{I-j}$$

The set $\widetilde{\mathcal{D}}_I = \left\{\delta_{i,j};\ 1 \le i \le I,\ 1 \le j \le J-1,\ i+j \le I\right\}$ *gives a family of i.i.d. standard Gaussian distributed random variables.*

Corollary 7.8 implies that we obtain a set $\widetilde{\mathcal{D}}_I$ of i.i.d. bootstrap random variables. Now, we have several different possibilities to generate new data sets from $\widetilde{\mathcal{D}}_I$ with

$$\widetilde{\mathcal{D}}_I^{\Pi} = \left\{\delta_{\Pi(i,j)};\ 1 \le i \le I,\ 1 \le j \le J-1,\ i+j \le I\right\} \stackrel{(d)}{=} \widetilde{\mathcal{D}}_I \tag{7.36}$$

where Π can have the following meanings:

V1. Π denotes resampling with replacement (drawing from an urn with replacement). This is the non-parametric bootstrap.

V2. Since we know that $\delta_{i,j}$ are i.i.d. standard Gaussian, we could generate a new sample $\widetilde{\mathcal{D}}_I^{\Pi}$ by generating (independently of $\widetilde{\mathcal{D}}_I$) new i.i.d. random variables $\delta_{\Pi(i,j)}$ from a standard Gaussian distribution. This is the parametric bootstrap.

V3. $\Pi(\cdot,\cdot)$ could also be a permutation of the coordinates (i, j), the set $\widetilde{\mathcal{D}}_I^{\Pi}$ can then be viewed as resampling without replacement. This is the permutation bootstrap.

Remarks

- Usually, the non-parametric bootstrap method involves resampling with replacement. Since we have the possibility of choosing the same observation twice (with positive probability), distributional equality (7.36) holds true only in an asymptotic sense.
- For V2 and V3 the distributional equality (7.36) holds true in an exact sense. Moreover, for V2 we even have that $\widetilde{\mathcal{D}}_I^{\Pi}$ and $\widetilde{\mathcal{D}}_I$ are independent copies.
- The advantage in applying V2 is that we can generate as many independent copies as we want. The disadvantage is that we have to make stronger assumptions on the distributions.
- The advantage in applying V1 is that one hopes that the observations are rich enough to capture the main distributional properties of the model; for example, that the observations have the correct skewness, curtosis, etc. However, the answer is always conditioned on the observations $\mathcal{D}_I$.

If we denote the bootstrap sample by

$$\left(0, \delta^*_{1,j+1}, \ldots, \delta^*_{I-j-1,j+1}\right) \stackrel{(d)}{=} \left(0, \delta_{1,j+1}, \ldots, \delta_{I-j-1,j+1}\right)$$

we have

$$\left(A^{(j)}\right)^{-1} \left(0, \delta^*_{1,j+1}, \ldots, \delta^*_{I-j-1,j+1}\right)' \stackrel{(d)}{=} \Delta_{j+1} = \left(\Delta_{0,j+1} \ldots \Delta_{I-j-1,j+1}\right)'$$

Hence, the bootstrap algorithm generates new residuals which have the same distribution as the original residuals.

In the preceding subsections we have not used a normalization transformation $B^{(j)}$. Note that for $i \neq k$ we have

$$\mathrm{Cov}\left(\widetilde{\varepsilon}_{i,j+1}, \widetilde{\varepsilon}_{k,j+1} \middle| \mathcal{B}_j\right) = -\frac{\sqrt{C_{i,j}\, C_{k,j}}}{\sum_{k=0}^{I-j-1} C_{k,j}}$$

This last term is sufficiently small if we have enough observations. Therefore, in the bootstrap method (under the assumption that we have high-dimensional observations), the joint distribution of $\delta_{i,j}$ is approximated by the joint distribution of $\widetilde{\varepsilon}_{i,j}$. However, in practical applications one should rescale the residuals such that they have the correct mean and variance (see (7.23)). Otherwise we underestimate, for example, the estimation error, as occurs in all the above examples if we do not rescale the residual distribution.

7.6 SYNCHRONOUS BOOTSTRAPPING OF SEEMINGLY UNRELATED REGRESSIONS

So far, we have avoided discussions about dependencies between accident years or dependencies among accounting year diagonals. This could be considered in a Bayesian approach using MCMC. Taylor and McGuire (2005, 2007) have presented interesting ideas dealing with such questions using bootstrap methods.

The seemingly unrelated regressions (SUR) were introduced by Zellner (1962) and discussed by Srivastava and Giles (1987). In the context of claims reserving, Taylor and McGuire have introduced the SUR bootstrap technique and we will apply this technique to the CL method. Therefore, we use the following framework.

Assume that $\mathbf{Z}_i = \left(Z_i^{(1)}, \ldots, Z_i^{(d)}\right)$ are d-dimensional vector-valued observations and, in analogy to (7.1), that

$$\mathbf{Z}_1, \ldots, \mathbf{Z}_n \quad \text{i.i.d.} \overset{(d)}{\sim} F$$

where F denotes an unknown d-dimensional distribution with unknown dependence structure between the coordinates. Assume that this d-dimensional distribution is characterized by a d-dimensional parameter vector $(\theta^{(1)}, \ldots, \theta^{(d)})$ and that $\theta^{(k)}$ corresponds to the kth marginal $F^{(k)}$ of F. Moreover, assume that we have estimators of $\theta^{(k)}$, given by

$$\widehat{\theta}_n^{(k)} = g_k\left(Z_1^{(k)}, \ldots, Z_n^{(k)}\right)$$

for $k \in \{1, \ldots, d\}$.

One-Dimensional Bootstrap

We could perform a one-dimensional bootstrap for every coordinate $k \in \{1, \ldots, d\}$. Denote by $\widehat{F}_n^{(k)}$ the bootstrap distribution of $Z_1^{(k)}, \ldots, Z_n^{(k)}$. Then, we generate bootstrap data

$$Z_1^{k,*}, \ldots, Z_n^{k,*} \quad \text{i.i.d.} \overset{(d)}{\sim} \widehat{F}_n^{(k)} \tag{7.37}$$

Calculating

$$\widehat{\theta}_n^{k,*} = g_k\left(Z_1^{k,*}, \ldots, Z_n^{k,*}\right)$$

and repeating this idea we get the marginal distributions $F_n^{k,*}$ for $\widehat{\theta}_n^{k,*}$ for $k \in \{1, \ldots, d\}$. However, we do not take into account possible dependencies between the coordinates.

Multidimensional Bootstrap

If we have dependencies within the vectors $\mathbf{Z}_i$, then, of course, we should do a multivariate bootstrap. Denote by $\widehat{F}_n$ the multivariate bootstrap distribution of $\mathbf{Z}_1, \ldots, \mathbf{Z}_n$. Then we generate multivariate bootstrap data

$$\mathbf{Z}_1^*, \ldots, \mathbf{Z}_n^* \quad \text{i.i.d.} \overset{(d)}{\sim} \widehat{F}_n \tag{7.38}$$

We can now calculate

$$\widehat{\theta}_n^{k,*} = g_k\left(Z_1^{k,*}, \ldots, Z_n^{k,*}\right)$$

and repeating this procedure we get the marginal distributions $F_n^{k,*}$ for $\widehat{\theta}_n^{k,*}$ as well as the multivariate distribution F_n^* for $\left(\widehat{\theta}_n^{1,*}, \ldots, \widehat{\theta}_n^{d,*}\right)$. Using this multivariate bootstrap we also capture the (unknown) dependencies between the coordinates.

This multivariate bootstrap can now be applied for two different dependent triangles, but it can also be applied within a triangle to different geometric subsets.

Example 2.7 (revisited)

We apply this multivariate bootstrap technique to a fictitious example. We assume that the individual CL factors $F_{i,1}$ and $F_{i-1,2}$ are dependent, for $i \geq 1$.

We also assume that we have Model Assumptions 3.9, but we drop the independence assumptions between $F_{i,1}$ and $F_{i-1,2}$. Observe that in this case we are no longer in the distribution-free CL model, where we have assumed that accident years are independent. In general, $\widehat{f}_j$, given $\mathcal{B}_j$, is no longer an unbiased estimator for f_j. However, we would like to apply the bootstrap method to this model. This is done for illustrative purposes without having a discussion about model assumptions and their implications.

We distinguish the cases $j \geq 3$ and $j \leq 2$.

On the set $\{j \geq 3\} \cup \{i=0, j=1\}$ we define the scaled residuals $Z_{i,j}$ as in (7.24). For the residuals

$$\left\{Z_{i,j};\ i+j \leq I \text{ and } j \geq 3\right\} \cup \left\{Z_{0,1}\right\}$$

we proceed as above in (7.25).

On the set $\{j \leq 2\} \setminus \{i=0, j=1\}$ we use a bivariate bootstrap for the vectors

$$\left\{\mathbf{Z}_i = \left(Z_{i,1}, Z_{i-1,2}\right);\ i \in \{1, \ldots, I\}\right\}$$

We consider the bootstrap distribution of the bivariate observations $\mathbf{Z}_i$ and generate bivariate bootstrap observations $\mathbf{Z}_i^*$ according to this second bootstrap distribution. This means that we model dependence in the accounting year direction among the first two development periods, see Figure 7.7.

	0	1	2	3	4	5	6	7	8
0	1.6257	1.0926	1.0197	1.0192	1.0057	1.0060	1.0013	1.0010	1.0014
1	1.5115	1.0754	1.0147	1.0065	1.0035	1.0050	1.0011	1.0011	
2	1.4747	1.0916	1.0260	1.0147	1.0062	1.0051	1.0008		
3	1.4577	1.0845	1.0206	1.0141	1.0092	1.0045			
4	1.4750	1.0767	1.0298	1.0244	1.0109				
5	1.4573	1.0635	1.0255	1.0107					
6	1.5166	1.0663	1.0249						
7	1.4614	1.0683							
8	1.4457								
9									
CL factors	1.4925	1.0778	1.0229	1.0148	1.0070	1.0051	1.0011	1.0010	1.0014

Figure 7.7 Dependence modelling for the first two individual development factors $F_{i,1}$ and $F_{i-1,2}$ in accounting years (the table shows the observed individual CL factors $F_{i,j+1}$ and the estimated CL factors $\widehat{f}_j$, see Table 3.2)

If we perform this multivariate bootstrap analysis (unconditional version) we obtain the results given in Table 7.3.

Table 7.3 Comparison univariate and multivariate bootstrap

	One-dimensional bootstrap	Multivariate bootstrap
Mean	6 036 692	6 035 168
Std dev.	174 998	184 368

We see that the dependence modelling effect is negligible for the estimation of the mean. The mean becomes slightly smaller in the multivariate approach, since the empirical distributions of the scaled residuals have negative expected values (which we have not adjusted, see discussion in Section 7.5). However, we see that the estimation error becomes larger due to the fact that we observe positive correlations between $F_{i,1}$ and $F_{i-1,2}$. These correlations are small (about 8%), but already have some influence on the parameter estimation uncertainties. □

8

Multivariate Reserving Methods

In this chapter we consider the claims reserving problem in a multivariate context. The term 'multivariate' can be understood in several different ways. Here, we estimate the claims reserves simultaneously for several correlated claims reserving triangles. These studies are motivated by the fact that, in practice, it is quite natural to subdivide a non-life run-off portfolio into subportfolios such that each satisfies certain homogeneity properties – for example, the CL assumptions or the assumptions of the additive claims reserving method (an explicit definition follows below). In such cases the total reserves are then usually obtained by applying an appropriate method on every individual subportfolio and by simply aggregating the individual claims reserves.

In this chapter we present methods that allow for a simultaneous study of the individual subportfolios. This has the advantage that, from the observations of one portfolio, one may learn about the behaviour of the other portfolios (e.g. subportfolios of small and large claims) and it addresses the problem of dependence between run-off portfolios of different lines of business (e.g. bodily injury claims in auto liability and general liability). Moreover, a simultaneous study allows for a unified approach for estimating the resulting MSEP of the total portfolio.

An alternative idea for calculating aggregated reserves and their uncertainties is to calculate them only on the total aggregated run-off triangle. But one should pay attention to the fact that if the subportfolios satisfy, for example, the CL assumptions, the aggregated run-off triangle does not necessarily satisfy them (see Ajne 1994 and Klemmt 2004). Therefore, in most cases this is not a promising solution to the claims reserving problem on several subportfolios. An additional advantage of multivariate reserving methods is that they resolve the problem of additivity. This means that their estimators of the ultimate claims for the whole portfolio are obtained by summation over the estimators of the ultimate claims for the individual subportfolios.

In the literature multivariate claims reserving methods have been studied by Brehm (2002), Kirschner *et al.* (2002), Braun (2004), Taylor and McGuire (2005, 2007), Schmidt (2006a, b), Pröhl and Schmidt (2005), Mildenhall (2006), Hürlimann (2005), Hess *et al.* (2006) or Merz and Wüthrich (2007b, c, d, 2008). Another type of multivariate claims reserving method is studied in Quarg and Mack (2004) and Merz and Wüthrich (2006), where one combines different sources of information in the same estimate (see Section 9.1).

8.1 GENERAL MULTIVARIATE FRAMEWORK

In the following we assume that the subportfolios consist of $N \geq 1$ run-off triangles of observations of the same size. In these triangles the indices

n,	$1 \le n \le N$,	refer to subportfolios (triangles)
i,	$0 \le i \le I$,	refer to accident years (rows)
j,	$0 \le j \le J$,	refer to development years (columns).

The incremental claims of triangle n for accident year i and development year j are denoted by $X_{i,j}^{(n)}$, and cumulative claims of accident year i up to development year j are given by

$$C_{i,j}^{(n)} = \sum_{k=0}^{j} X_{i,k}^{(n)}$$

As in the univariate models we assume that the last development year is given by J, that is $X_{i,j}^{(n)} = 0$ for all $j > J$, and the last accident year is given by I. Moreover, we make our General Assumption 1.4, that is, we assume that $I = J$.

Figure 8.1 shows the claims data structure for N claims development triangles as described above.

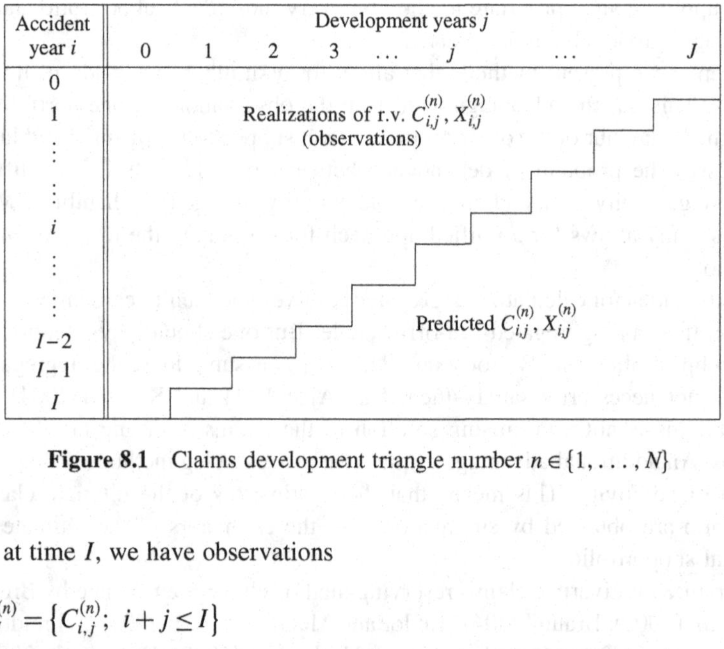

Figure 8.1 Claims development triangle number $n \in \{1, \ldots, N\}$

Usually, at time I, we have observations

$$\mathcal{D}_I^{(n)} = \{C_{i,j}^{(n)};\ i + j \le I\}$$

for all run-off subportfolios $n \in \{1, \ldots, N\}$. This means that at time I (calendar year I) we have a total set of observations over all subportfolios given by

$$\mathcal{D}_I^N = \bigcup_{n=1}^{N} \mathcal{D}_I^{(n)}$$

and we need to predict the random variables in its complement, which is given by

$$\mathcal{D}_I^{N,c} = \{C_{i,j}^{(n)};\ i + j > I,\ 1 \le n \le N,\ i \le I\}$$

For the derivation of the conditional MSEP of multivariate methods it is convenient to write the N subportfolios in vector form. Thus, we define the N-dimensional random vectors of incremental and cumulative claims by

$$\mathbf{X}_{i,j} = \left(X_{i,j}^{(1)}, \ldots, X_{i,j}^{(N)}\right)' \quad \text{and} \quad \mathbf{C}_{i,j} = \left(C_{i,j}^{(1)}, \ldots, C_{i,j}^{(N)}\right)'$$

for $i \in \{0, \ldots, I\}$ and $j \in \{0, \ldots, J\}$. Moreover, we define for $k \in \{0, \ldots, J\}$

$$\mathcal{B}_k^N = \left\{\mathbf{C}_{i,j};\, i+j \le I \text{ and } 0 \le j \le k\right\} \tag{8.1}$$

and the N-dimensional column vector consisting of 1's by

$$\mathbf{1} = (1, \ldots, 1)' \in \mathbb{R}^N$$

The set $\mathcal{B}_k^N$ consists of all N-dimensional random variables of cumulative claims, up to development year k, that are observed at time I.

8.2 MULTIVARIATE CHAIN-LADDER METHOD

Pröhl and Schmidt (2005) and Schmidt (2006b) have studied a multivariate CL method for a portfolio of N correlated run-off triangles based on multivariate age-to-age estimators. However, their study did not go beyond best estimators – that is, they have not derived an estimator for the conditional MSEP for the total ultimate claim predictors.

On the other hand, Braun (2004) has generalized Mack's univariate CL model (see Model Assumptions 3.2) to the multivariate case where he incorporates correlations between different subportfolios. In this setup he derives estimates for the conditional MSEP. This derivation is based on Mack's approach (see Subsection 3.2.3). In a similar setup Merz and Wüthrich (2007b) have given an estimator for the conditional MSEP, but they have used studied the conditional resampling approach (see Approach 3 in Subsection 3.2.3). Both, the Braun (2004) paper and the Merz and Wüthrich (2007b) paper have the disadvantage that the CL factors are estimated in a univariate way – that is, for the estimation of the age-to-age factors they have restricted themselves to the univariate claims development triangles.

Finally, Merz and Wüthrich (2007c) have derived an estimate for the conditional MSEP in the multivariate CL model, where the CL factors are also estimated in a multivariate way. That is, Merz and Wüthrich (2007c) have studied the conditional MSEP for the multivariate age-to-age factor estimates proposed by Pröhl and Schmidt (2005) and Schmidt (2006b). These results are presented in this section.

8.2.1 Multivariate CL Model

Analogous to the univariate case, the central objects of interest in the multivariate CL method are the development factors (link ratios) of the cumulative claims: we define for $n \in \{1, \ldots, N\}$, $i \in \{0, \ldots, I\}$ and $j \in \{1, \ldots, J\}$ the individual development factors for accident year i and development year j by

$$F_{i,j}^{(n)} = \frac{C_{i,j}^{(n)}}{C_{i,j-1}^{(n)}} \quad \text{and} \quad \mathbf{F}_{i,j} = \left(F_{i,j}^{(1)}, \ldots, F_{i,j}^{(N)}\right)'$$

In the following we denote by

$$\mathrm{D}(\mathbf{a}) = \begin{pmatrix} a_1 & & 0 \\ & \ddots & \\ 0 & & a_N \end{pmatrix} \quad \text{and} \quad \mathrm{D}(\mathbf{c})^b = \begin{pmatrix} c_1^b & & 0 \\ & \ddots & \\ 0 & & c_N^b \end{pmatrix}$$

the $N \times N$ diagonal matrices of the N-dimensional vectors $\mathbf{a} = (a_1, \ldots, a_N)' \in \mathbb{R}^N$ and $(c_1^b, \ldots, c_N^b)' \in \mathbb{R}_+^N$, where $b \in \mathbb{R}$ and $\mathbf{c} = (c_1, \ldots, c_N)' \in \mathbb{R}_+^N$. Then, we have

$$\mathbf{C}_{i,j} = \mathrm{D}(\mathbf{C}_{i,j-1})\ \mathbf{F}_{i,j} = \mathrm{D}(\mathbf{F}_{i,j})\ \mathbf{C}_{i,j-1}$$

for all $j = 1, \ldots, J$ and $i = 0, \ldots, I$.

The distribution-free multivariate CL model is then given by the following definition.

Model Assumptions 8.1 (multivariate CL model)

- Cumulative claims $\mathbf{C}_{i,j}$ of different accident years i are independent.
- $(\mathbf{C}_{i,j})_{j \geq 0}$ form an N-dimensional Markov chain. There are N-dimensional deterministic vectors

$$\mathbf{f}_j = \left(f_j^{(1)}, \ldots, f_j^{(N)} \right)'$$

with $f_j^{(n)} > 0$, $n = 1, \ldots, N$, and symmetric positive definite $N \times N$ matrices Σ_j for $j = 0, \ldots, J-1$ such that for all $0 \leq i \leq I$ and $1 \leq j \leq J$ we have

$$E\left[\mathbf{C}_{i,j} \middle| \mathbf{C}_{i,j-1}\right] = \mathrm{D}(\mathbf{f}_{j-1})\ \mathbf{C}_{i,j-1} \tag{8.2}$$

$$\mathrm{Cov}\left(\mathbf{C}_{i,j}, \mathbf{C}_{i,j} \middle| \mathbf{C}_{i,j-1}\right) = \mathrm{D}(\mathbf{C}_{i,j-1})^{1/2}\ \Sigma_{j-1}\ \mathrm{D}(\mathbf{C}_{i,j-1})^{1/2} \tag{8.3}$$

□

Remarks 8.2

- The factors $\mathbf{f}_j$ are called N-dimensional development factors, CL factors, age-to-age factors or link ratios.
- Note that the dependence between different subportfolios is defined through the correlation matrix Σ_{j-1}, which describes the conditional dependence between $C_{i,j}^{(n)}$ and $C_{i,j}^{(m)}$, given by $\mathbf{C}_{i,j-1}$. That is, we have a special type of conditional dependence that directly links the cells in different triangles that have the same coordinates.
- For practical purposes one often wants to introduce dependence in accounting years that corresponds to diagonals in the claims reserving triangles. As with almost all models, this model cannot handle dependencies on diagonals, and this can probably only be done using such numerical methods as bootstrap or MCMC.

LEMMA 8.3 *Under Model Assumptions 8.1 we have for all* $1 \leq i \leq I$

$$E\left[\mathbf{C}_{i,J} \middle| \mathcal{D}_I^N\right] = E\left[\mathbf{C}_{i,J} \middle| \mathbf{C}_{i,I-i}\right] = \prod_{j=I-i}^{J-1} \mathrm{D}(\mathbf{f}_j)\ \mathbf{C}_{i,I-i}$$

Proof The proof is similar to the proof of Lemma 2.3 (univariate CL model). □

This result motivates a recursive algorithm for estimating the conditionally expected ultimate claim and predicting the ultimate claim, respectively, given the observation $\mathcal{D}_I^N$. If the N-dimensional CL factors $\mathbf{f}_j$ are known, the expected outstanding claims liabilities of accident year i for the N correlated run-off triangles based on the information $\mathcal{D}_I^N$ are estimated at time I by

$$E\left[\mathbf{C}_{i,J}\middle|\,\mathcal{D}_I^N\right]-\mathbf{C}_{i,I-i}=\mathrm{D}(\mathbf{f}_{J-1})\cdots\mathrm{D}(\mathbf{f}_{I-i})\;\mathbf{C}_{i,I-i}-\mathbf{C}_{i,I-i}$$

However, in most practical applications we have to estimate the CL factors from the data. Pröhl and Schmidt (2005) and Schmidt (2006b) propose the following multivariate age-to-age factor estimates for $\mathbf{f}_j$, $j=0,\ldots,J-1$,

$$\widehat{\mathbf{f}}_j=\left(\widehat{f}_j^{(1)},\ldots,\widehat{f}_j^{(N)}\right)'=\left(\sum_{i=0}^{I-j-1}\mathrm{D}(\mathbf{C}_{i,j})^{1/2}\Sigma_j^{-1}\mathrm{D}(\mathbf{C}_{i,j})^{1/2}\right)^{-1}$$
$$\times\sum_{i=0}^{I-j-1}\mathrm{D}(\mathbf{C}_{i,j})^{1/2}\Sigma_j^{-1}\mathrm{D}(\mathbf{C}_{i,j})^{1/2}\;\mathbf{F}_{i,j+1} \tag{8.4}$$

Note that the coordinate $\widehat{f}_j^{(n)}$ denotes the age-to-age factor estimate for development year j and run-off triangle $n\in\{1,\ldots,N\}$ based on the information $\mathcal{D}_I^N$. Moreover, this estimator assumes that the covariance matrices Σ_j are known.

We then define the following multivariate CL estimator.

ESTIMATOR 8.4 (multivariate CL estimator) *The multivariate CL estimator for* $E\left[\mathbf{C}_{i,j}\middle|\,\mathcal{D}_I^N\right]$ *is defined by*

$$\widehat{\mathbf{C}_{i,j}}^{CL}=\left(\widehat{C_{i,j}^{(1)}}^{CL},\ldots,\widehat{C_{i,j}^{(N)}}^{CL}\right)'=\widehat{E}\left[\mathbf{C}_{i,j}\middle|\,\mathcal{D}_I^N\right]=\prod_{l=I-i}^{j-1}\mathrm{D}(\widehat{\mathbf{f}}_l)\;\mathbf{C}_{i,I-i}$$

for $i+j>I$.

Remarks 8.5

- In the case $N=1$ (i.e. only one run-off triangle) the age-to-age factor estimates (8.4) coincide with the classical age-to-age factor estimates

$$\widehat{f}_j=\sum_{i=0}^{I-j-1}\frac{C_{i,j}}{\sum_{k=0}^{I-j-1}C_{k,j}}\,F_{i,j+1} \tag{8.5}$$

  which are used in the univariate CL method (see (2.4)).
- In the approaches of Braun (2004) and Merz and Wüthrich (2007b), the estimators for the future cumulative claims of the N correlated run-off triangles are based on the univariate age-to-age factor estimates (8.5) which do not take into account the correlation

structure between the different run-off triangles. In our matrix notation this means that the N-dimensional CL factors $\mathbf{f}_j$ are estimated by the univariate ones

$$\widehat{\mathbf{f}}_j^{(0)} = \left(\sum_{k=0}^{I-j-1} \mathrm{D}(\mathbf{C}_{k,j})\right)^{-1} \sum_{i=0}^{I-j-1} \mathrm{D}(\mathbf{C}_{i,j})\ \mathbf{F}_{i,j+1} \tag{8.6}$$

with coordinates

$$\widehat{f}_j^{(n)(0)} = \sum_{i=0}^{I-j-1} \frac{C_{i,j}^{(n)}}{\sum_{k=0}^{I-j-1} C_{k,j}^{(n)}}\ F_{i,j+1}^{(n)}$$

for $n = 1, \ldots, N$. Note that both $\widehat{\mathbf{f}}_j$ and $\widehat{\mathbf{f}}_j^{(0)}$ give conditionally unbiased estimators for the multivariate CL factors $\mathbf{f}_j$ (this is further described below). However, $\widehat{\mathbf{f}}_j$ is optimal in the sense that it has smaller conditional variance (for a precise definition see Lemma 8.8 below). If the $N \times N$ covariance matrix Σ_j is diagonal then $\widehat{\mathbf{f}}_j$ and $\widehat{\mathbf{f}}_j^{(0)}$ coincide.

- If $\Sigma_0, \ldots, \Sigma_{J-2}$ are diagonal matrices, the following three estimates coincide: (1) the sum of the univariate CL estimates on every individual subportfolio; (2) the multivariate CL estimation proposed by Braun (2004) and Merz and Wüthrich (2007b) based on the age-to-age factor estimators (8.6); and (3) the multivariate CL estimation based on the multivariate age-to-age factor estimates (8.4). However, in other cases it is more reasonable to use multivariate estimates (8.4) (see Lemma 8.8 below) when one has appropriate estimates for the covariance matrices Σ_j.

In Lemma 8.6 we have the following properties (these are analogous to the univariate case, see Lemma 2.5):

LEMMA 8.6 *Under Model Assumptions 8.1 we have:*

(a) *given* $\mathcal{B}_j^N$, $\widehat{\mathbf{f}}_j$ *is an unbiased estimator for* $\mathbf{f}_j$, *i.e.* $E\left[\widehat{\mathbf{f}}_j \middle| \mathcal{B}_j^N\right] = \mathbf{f}_j$;

(b) $\widehat{\mathbf{f}}_j$ *is (unconditionally) unbiased for* $\mathbf{f}_j$, *i.e.* $E\left[\widehat{\mathbf{f}}_j\right] = \mathbf{f}_j$;

(c) $\widehat{\mathbf{f}}_j$ *and* $\widehat{\mathbf{f}}_k$ *are uncorrelated for* $j \neq k$, *i.e.* $E\left[\widehat{\mathbf{f}}_j\, \widehat{\mathbf{f}}_k'\right] = \mathbf{f}_j\, \mathbf{f}_k' = E\left[\widehat{\mathbf{f}}_j\right] E\left[\widehat{\mathbf{f}}_k\right]'$;

(d) *given* $\mathbf{C}_{i,I-i}$, *the estimator* $\widehat{\mathbf{C}_{i,J}}^{\mathrm{CL}}$ *is an unbiased estimator for* $E\left[\mathbf{C}_{i,J} \middle| \mathcal{D}_I^N\right] = E\left[\mathbf{C}_{i,J} \middle| \mathbf{C}_{i,I-i}\right]$, *i.e.* $E\left[\widehat{\mathbf{C}_{i,J}}^{\mathrm{CL}} \middle| \mathbf{C}_{i,I-i}\right] = E\left[\mathbf{C}_{i,J} \middle| \mathcal{D}_I^N\right]$;

(e) $\widehat{\mathbf{C}_{i,J}}^{\mathrm{CL}}$ *is (unconditionally) unbiased for* $E\left[\mathbf{C}_{i,J}\right]$, *i.e.* $E\left[\widehat{\mathbf{C}_{i,J}}^{\mathrm{CL}}\right] = E\left[\mathbf{C}_{i,J}\right]$.

Proof (a) Using $\mathbf{F}_{i,j} = \mathrm{D}(\mathbf{C}_{i,j-1})^{-1}\ \mathbf{C}_{i,j}$ and (8.2) we obtain

$$E\left[\widehat{\mathbf{f}}_j \middle| \mathcal{B}_j^N\right] = \left(\sum_{i=0}^{I-j-1} \mathrm{D}(\mathbf{C}_{i,j})^{1/2} \Sigma_j^{-1} \mathrm{D}(\mathbf{C}_{i,j})^{1/2}\right)^{-1}$$
$$\times \sum_{i=0}^{I-j-1} \mathrm{D}(\mathbf{C}_{i,j})^{1/2} \Sigma_j^{-1} \mathrm{D}(\mathbf{C}_{i,j})^{-1/2}\ E\left[\mathbf{C}_{i,j+1} \middle| \mathcal{B}_j^N\right] = \mathbf{f}_j$$

(b) This follows immediately from (a).
(c) Using (a) and (b) we have for $j<k$

$$E\left[\widehat{\mathbf{f}}_j\, \widehat{\mathbf{f}}_k'\right] = E\left[E\left[\widehat{\mathbf{f}}_j\, \widehat{\mathbf{f}}_k'\middle|\mathcal{B}_k^N\right]\right]$$
$$= E\left[\widehat{\mathbf{f}}_j\, E\left[\widehat{\mathbf{f}}_k'\middle|\mathcal{B}_k^N\right]\right] = E\left[\widehat{\mathbf{f}}_j\right]\, \mathbf{f}_k' = E\left[\widehat{\mathbf{f}}_j\right] E\left[\widehat{\mathbf{f}}_k\right]'$$

(d) Using (a) we obtain

$$E\left[\widehat{\mathbf{C}_{i,J}}^{\mathrm{CL}}\middle|\mathbf{C}_{i,I-i}\right] = E\left[\mathrm{D}(\widehat{\mathbf{f}}_{J-1})\, \mathrm{D}(\widehat{\mathbf{f}}_{J-2})\cdots \mathrm{D}(\widehat{\mathbf{f}}_{I-i})\, \mathbf{C}_{i,I-i}\middle|\mathbf{C}_{i,I-i}\right]$$
$$= E\left[E\left[\mathrm{D}(\widehat{\mathbf{f}}_{J-1})\middle|\mathcal{B}_{J-1}^N\right]\, \mathrm{D}(\widehat{\mathbf{f}}_{J-2})\cdots \mathrm{D}(\widehat{\mathbf{f}}_{I-i})\, \mathbf{C}_{i,I-i}\middle|\mathbf{C}_{i,I-i}\right]$$
$$= \mathrm{D}(\mathbf{f}_{J-1})\, E\left[\widehat{\mathbf{C}_{i,J-1}}^{\mathrm{CL}}\middle|\mathbf{C}_{i,I-i}\right]$$

Iteration of this procedure and Lemma 8.3 leads to

$$E\left[\widehat{\mathbf{C}_{i,J}}^{\mathrm{CL}}\middle|\mathbf{C}_{i,I-i}\right] = \mathrm{D}(\mathbf{f}_{J-1})\cdots \mathrm{D}(\mathbf{f}_{I-i})\, \mathbf{C}_{i,I-i} = E\left[\mathbf{C}_{i,J}\middle|\mathbf{C}_{i,I-i}\right]$$

(e) This follows immediately from (d). □

Remarks 8.7

- Observe that Lemma 8.6(d) shows that we obtain an unbiased estimator $\widehat{\mathbf{C}_{i,J}}^{\mathrm{CL}}$ for the conditionally expected ultimate claim $E\left[\mathbf{C}_{i,J}|\mathcal{D}_I^N\right]$.
- This implies that the estimator for the aggregated ultimate claim of accident year $i\in\{1,\ldots,I\}$

$$\sum_{n=1}^{N} \widehat{C_{i,J}^{(n)}}^{\mathrm{CL}} = \mathbf{1}'\, \widehat{\mathbf{C}_{i,J}}^{\mathrm{CL}} \tag{8.7}$$

is, given $\mathbf{C}_{i,I-i}$, unbiased for $\sum_{n=1}^{N} E\left[C_{i,J}^{(n)}\middle|\mathbf{C}_{i,I-i}\right]$

The following result is the multivariate counterpart of Lemma 3.3.

LEMMA 8.8 *Under Model Assumptions 8.1, the estimator $\widehat{\mathbf{f}}_j$ is a $\mathcal{B}_{j+1}^N$-measurable unbiased estimator for $\mathbf{f}_j$, which minimizes the conditional expected squared loss to $\mathbf{f}_j$ among all N-dimensional unbiased linear combinations of the unbiased estimators $\left(\mathbf{F}_{i,j+1}\right)_{0\le i\le I-j-1}$ for $\mathbf{f}_j$, conditional on $\mathcal{B}_j^N$, i.e.*

$$E\left[(\mathbf{f}_j-\widehat{\mathbf{f}}_j)'(\mathbf{f}_j-\widehat{\mathbf{f}}_j)\middle|\mathcal{B}_j^N\right]$$
$$= \min_{\mathrm{W}_{i,j}\in\mathbb{R}^{N\times N}} E\left[\left(\mathbf{f}_j - \sum_{i=0}^{I-j-1} \mathrm{W}_{i,j}\, \mathbf{F}_{i,j+1}\right)'\left(\mathbf{f}_j - \sum_{i=0}^{I-j-1} \mathrm{W}_{i,j}\, \mathbf{F}_{i,j+1}\right)\middle|\mathcal{B}_j^N\right]$$

Proof The proof is similar to the proof of Lemma 3.4 (univariate CL model). See also Pröhl and Schmidt (2005), Theorem 3.1. □

Our goal now is to derive an estimate for the conditional MSEP of the multivariate CL predictor (8.7) for single accident years $i \in \{1, \ldots, I\}$

$$\begin{aligned}
\mathrm{msep}_{\sum_n C_{i,J}^{(n)}|\mathcal{D}_I^N}\left(\sum_{n=1}^N \widehat{C_{i,J}^{(n)}}^{\mathrm{CL}}\right) &= E\left[\left(\sum_{n=1}^N \widehat{C_{i,J}^{(n)}}^{\mathrm{CL}} - \sum_{n=1}^N C_{i,J}^{(n)}\right)^2 \middle| \mathcal{D}_I^N\right] \\
&= \mathbf{1}' \, E\left[\left(\widehat{\mathbf{C}_{i,J}}^{\mathrm{CL}} - \mathbf{C}_{i,J}\right)\left(\widehat{\mathbf{C}_{i,J}}^{\mathrm{CL}} - \mathbf{C}_{i,J}\right)' \middle| \mathcal{D}_I^N\right] \mathbf{1} \\
&= \mathbf{1}' \, \mathrm{Var}\left(\mathbf{C}_{i,J} \middle| \mathcal{D}_I^N\right) \mathbf{1} \\
&\quad + \mathbf{1}' \left(\widehat{\mathbf{C}_{i,J}}^{\mathrm{CL}} - E\left[\mathbf{C}_{i,J} \middle| \mathcal{D}_I^N\right]\right)\left(\widehat{\mathbf{C}_{i,J}}^{\mathrm{CL}} - E\left[\mathbf{C}_{i,J} \middle| \mathcal{D}_I^N\right]\right)' \mathbf{1}
\end{aligned} \tag{8.8}$$

For aggregated accident years we consider

$$\mathrm{msep}_{\sum_{i,n} C_{i,J}^{(n)}|\mathcal{D}_I^N}\left(\sum_{i,n} \widehat{C_{i,J}^{(n)}}^{\mathrm{CL}}\right) = E\left[\left(\sum_{i,n} \widehat{C_{i,J}^{(n)}}^{\mathrm{CL}} - \sum_{i,n} C_{i,J}^{(n)}\right)^2 \middle| \mathcal{D}_I^N\right]$$

Analogous to the univariate case, we first give an estimate for the process variance and estimation error of a single accident year (cf. Subsections 3.2.2 and 3.2.3 for the univariate case).

8.2.2 Conditional Process Variance

The conditional process variance $\mathbf{1}' \, \mathrm{Var}\left(\mathbf{C}_{i,J} \middle| \mathcal{D}_I^N\right) \mathbf{1}$ originates from the stochastic movement of $\mathbf{C}_{i,J}$. If we identify the empty product by $\prod_{l=k+1}^{k} \mathrm{D}(\mathbf{f}_l) = \mathrm{I}$, where I is the $N \times N$ identity matrix, we obtain the following result:

LEMMA 8.9 (Process variance for single accident years) *Under Model Assumptions 8.1 the conditional process variance for the ultimate claim $\mathbf{C}_{i,J}$ of accident year $i \in \{1, \ldots, I\}$, given the observations $\mathcal{D}_I^N$, is given by*

$$\mathbf{1}' \, \mathrm{Var}\left(\mathbf{C}_{i,J} \middle| \mathcal{D}_I^N\right) \mathbf{1} = \mathbf{1}' \left(\sum_{j=I-i}^{J-1} \prod_{k=j+1}^{J-1} \mathrm{D}(\mathbf{f}_k) \, \Sigma_{i,j}^{\mathbf{C}} \prod_{k=j+1}^{J-1} \mathrm{D}(\mathbf{f}_k)\right) \mathbf{1} \tag{8.9}$$

where

$$\Sigma_{i,j}^{\mathbf{C}} = E\left[\mathrm{D}(\mathbf{C}_{i,j})^{1/2} \, \Sigma_j \, \mathrm{D}(\mathbf{C}_{i,j})^{1/2} \middle| \mathbf{C}_{i,I-i}\right] \tag{8.10}$$

Proof We assume $i \in \{1, \ldots, I\}$. Using the Markov property and the independence of different accident years we have

$$\begin{aligned}
\mathbf{1}' \, \mathrm{Var}\left(\mathbf{C}_{i,J} \middle| \mathcal{D}_I^N\right) \mathbf{1} &= \mathbf{1}' \, \mathrm{Var}\left(\mathbf{C}_{i,J} \middle| \mathbf{C}_{i,I-i}\right) \mathbf{1} \\
&= \mathbf{1}' \, E\left[\mathrm{Var}\left(\mathbf{C}_{i,J} \middle| \mathbf{C}_{i,J-1}\right) \middle| \mathbf{C}_{i,I-i}\right] \mathbf{1} \\
&\quad + \mathbf{1}' \, \mathrm{Var}\left(E\left[\mathbf{C}_{i,J} \middle| \mathbf{C}_{i,J-1}\right] \middle| \mathbf{C}_{i,I-i}\right) \mathbf{1}
\end{aligned} \tag{8.11}$$

For the second term on the right-hand side of (8.11) we obtain, with (8.2),

$$\mathbf{1}'\mathrm{Var}\left(E\left[\mathbf{C}_{i,J}\middle|\mathbf{C}_{i,J-1}\right]\middle|\mathbf{C}_{i,I-i}\right)\,\mathbf{1}=\mathbf{1}'\,\mathrm{D}(\mathbf{f}_{J-1})\,\mathrm{Var}\left(\mathbf{C}_{i,J-1}\middle|\mathbf{C}_{i,I-i}\right)\,\mathrm{D}(\mathbf{f}_{J-1})\,\mathbf{1}$$

Using (8.3) we obtain for the first term on the right-hand side of (8.11)

$$\begin{aligned}&\mathbf{1}'\,E\left[\mathrm{Var}\left(\mathbf{C}_{i,J}\middle|\mathbf{C}_{i,J-1}\right)\middle|\mathbf{C}_{i,I-i}\right]\,\mathbf{1}\\&=\mathbf{1}'\,E\left[\mathrm{D}(\mathbf{C}_{i,J-1})^{1/2}\,\Sigma_{J-1}\,\mathrm{D}(\mathbf{C}_{i,J-1})^{1/2}\middle|\mathbf{C}_{i,I-i}\right]\,\mathbf{1}\end{aligned}$$

Henceforth, we obtain the following recursive formula for the conditional process variance of accident year $i\in\{1,\ldots,I\}$

$$\begin{aligned}&\mathbf{1}'\,\mathrm{Var}\left(\mathbf{C}_{i,J}\middle|\mathcal{D}_I^N\right)\,\mathbf{1}\\&=\mathbf{1}'\left(\Sigma_{i,J-1}^{\mathbf{C}}+\mathrm{D}(\mathbf{f}_{J-1})\,\mathrm{Var}\left(\mathbf{C}_{i,J-1}\middle|\mathcal{D}_I^N\right)\,\mathrm{D}(\mathbf{f}_{J-1})\right)\,\mathbf{1}\end{aligned}\tag{8.12}$$

Iteration of this recursive formula completes the proof of the lemma. □

Remarks 8.10

- Formula (8.12) gives a recursive formula for the conditional process variance of N correlated run-off triangles. This is similar to the univariate CL case.
- For $N=1$, formulas (8.9)–(8.10) reduce to the conditional process variance for single accident years of a individual run-off triangle (cf. Subsection 3.2.2).

If we replace the parameters $\mathbf{f}_k$ and $\Sigma_{i,j}^{\mathbf{C}}$ in (8.9) by their estimates (cf. Subsection 8.2.5, below), we obtain an estimator of the conditional process variance for a single accident year.

8.2.3 Conditional Estimation Error for Single Accident Years

In this subsection we treat the second term

$$\mathbf{1}'\left(\widehat{\mathbf{C}_{i,J}}^{\mathrm{CL}}-E\left[\mathbf{C}_{i,J}\middle|\mathcal{D}_I^N\right]\right)\left(\widehat{\mathbf{C}_{i,J}}^{\mathrm{CL}}-E\left[\mathbf{C}_{i,J}\middle|\mathcal{D}_I^N\right]\right)'\,\mathbf{1}\tag{8.13}$$

on the right-hand side of (8.8). This means that we want to determine the uncertainty in the estimation of the conditional expectation (mean value) $E\left[\mathbf{C}_{i,J}\middle|\mathcal{D}_I^N\right]$ by the estimator $\widehat{\mathbf{C}_{i,J}}^{\mathrm{CL}}$.

Using Lemma 8.3 and Estimator 8.4 we have, for the conditional estimation error of accident year $i>0$, the representation:

$$\begin{aligned}&\mathbf{1}'\left(\widehat{\mathbf{C}_{i,J}}^{\mathrm{CL}}-E\left[\mathbf{C}_{i,J}\middle|\mathcal{D}_I^N\right]\right)\left(\widehat{\mathbf{C}_{i,J}}^{\mathrm{CL}}-E\left[\mathbf{C}_{i,J}\middle|\mathcal{D}_I^N\right]\right)'\mathbf{1}\\&=\mathbf{1}'\left(\prod_{j=I-i}^{J-1}\mathrm{D}(\widehat{\mathbf{f}}_j)-\prod_{j=I-i}^{J-1}\mathrm{D}(\mathbf{f}_j)\right)\mathbf{C}_{i,I-i}\,\mathbf{C}_{i,I-i}'\left(\prod_{j=I-i}^{J-1}\mathrm{D}(\widehat{\mathbf{f}}_j)-\prod_{j=I-i}^{J-1}\mathrm{D}(\mathbf{f}_j)\right)\mathbf{1}\end{aligned}$$

Moreover, since it holds that

$$\mathrm{D}(\mathbf{b})\,\mathbf{a}\,\mathbf{c}'\,\mathrm{D}(\mathbf{d})=\mathrm{D}(\mathbf{a})\,\mathbf{b}\,\mathbf{d}'\,\mathrm{D}(\mathbf{c})\tag{8.14}$$

for arbitrary N-dimensional vectors $\mathbf{a}, \mathbf{b}, \mathbf{c}$ and $\mathbf{d}$, we obtain for the conditional estimation error

$$\mathbf{1}' \left(\widehat{\mathbf{C}_{i,J}}^{\mathrm{CL}} - E\left[\mathbf{C}_{i,J} \middle| \mathcal{D}_I^N\right]\right)\left(\widehat{\mathbf{C}_{i,J}}^{\mathrm{CL}} - E\left[\mathbf{C}_{i,J} \middle| \mathcal{D}_I^N\right]\right)' \mathbf{1}$$
$$= \mathbf{1}' \,\mathrm{D}(\mathbf{C}_{i,I-i}) \left(\widehat{\mathbf{g}}_{i|J} - \mathbf{g}_{i|J}\right)\left(\widehat{\mathbf{g}}_{i|J} - \mathbf{g}_{i|J}\right)' \mathrm{D}(\mathbf{C}_{i,I-i})\, \mathbf{1} \tag{8.15}$$

where the product of the multivariate CL estimators and factors $\widehat{\mathbf{g}}_{i|j}$ and $\mathbf{g}_{i|j}$, respectively, are defined by

$$\widehat{\mathbf{g}}_{i|j} = \mathrm{D}(\widehat{\mathbf{f}}_{I-i}) \cdots \mathrm{D}(\widehat{\mathbf{f}}_{j-1})\, \mathbf{1}$$
$$\mathbf{g}_{i|j} = \mathrm{D}(\mathbf{f}_{I-i}) \cdots \mathrm{D}(\mathbf{f}_{j-1})\, \mathbf{1} \tag{8.16}$$

for $j = I - i + 1, \ldots, J$.

In order to determine the conditional estimation error we proceed as in Chapter 3 for a single run-off triangle. This means that we consider resampling in the multivariate CL model. Analogous to the univariate case, we introduce stronger model assumptions, such as a multivariate CL time series model which is the counterpart of the univariate Time Series Model 3.9. This multivariate time series model is helpful and illustrative to describe the conditional resampling approach (see Approach 3 in Subsection 3.2.3) to estimate the fluctuations of the estimators $\widehat{\mathbf{f}}_0, \ldots, \widehat{\mathbf{f}}_{J-1}$ around the true multivariate CL factors $\mathbf{f}_0, \ldots, \mathbf{f}_{J-1}$.

Model Assumptions 8.11 (multivariate Time Series Model)

- Cumulative claims $\mathbf{C}_{i,j}$ of different accident years i are independent.
- There exist N-dimensional constants

$$\mathbf{f}_j = \left(f_j^{(1)}, \ldots, f_j^{(N)}\right)' \quad \text{and} \quad \boldsymbol{\sigma}_j = \left(\sigma_j^{(1)}, \ldots, \sigma_j^{(N)}\right)'$$

with $f_j^{(n)} > 0$, $\sigma_j^{(n)} > 0$ and N-dimensional random variables

$$\boldsymbol{\varepsilon}_{i,j+1} = \left(\varepsilon_{i,j+1}^{(1)}, \ldots, \varepsilon_{i,j+1}^{(N)}\right)'$$

such that for all $i \in \{0, \ldots, I\}$ and $j \in \{0, \ldots, J-1\}$ we have

$$\mathbf{C}_{i,j+1} = \mathrm{D}(\mathbf{f}_j)\, \mathbf{C}_{i,j} + \mathrm{D}(\mathbf{C}_{i,j})^{1/2}\, \mathrm{D}(\boldsymbol{\varepsilon}_{i,j+1})\, \boldsymbol{\sigma}_j \tag{8.17}$$

Moreover, the random variables $\boldsymbol{\varepsilon}_{i,j+1}$ are independent with $E\left[\boldsymbol{\varepsilon}_{i,j+1}\right] = \mathbf{0}$ and positive definite

$$\mathrm{Cov}\left(\boldsymbol{\varepsilon}_{i,j+1}, \boldsymbol{\varepsilon}_{i,j+1}\right) = E\left[\boldsymbol{\varepsilon}_{i,j+1}\, \boldsymbol{\varepsilon}_{i,j+1}'\right] = \begin{pmatrix} 1 & \rho_j^{(1,2)} & \cdots & \rho_j^{(1,N)} \\ \rho_j^{(2,1)} & 1 & \cdots & \rho_j^{(2,N)} \\ \vdots & \vdots & \ddots & \vdots \\ \rho_j^{(N,1)} & \rho_j^{(N,2)} & \cdots & 1 \end{pmatrix}$$

where $\rho_j^{(n,m)} \in (-1, 1)$ for $n, m \in \{1, \ldots, N\}$ and $n \neq m$. □

Observe that under Model Assumptions 8.11 and using (8.14) we have

$$
\begin{aligned}
&\operatorname{Cov}\left(\mathbf{C}_{i,j}, \mathbf{C}_{i,j} \middle| \mathbf{C}_{i,j-1}\right) \\
&= \mathrm{D}(\mathbf{C}_{i,j-1})^{1/2}\, E\left[\mathrm{D}(\boldsymbol{\varepsilon}_{i,j})\, \boldsymbol{\sigma}_{j-1}\, \boldsymbol{\sigma}'_{j-1}\, \mathrm{D}(\boldsymbol{\varepsilon}_{i,j})\right] \mathrm{D}(\mathbf{C}_{i,j-1})^{1/2} \\
&= \mathrm{D}(\mathbf{C}_{i,j-1})^{1/2}\, \mathrm{D}(\boldsymbol{\sigma}_{j-1})\, E\left[\boldsymbol{\varepsilon}_{i,j}\, \boldsymbol{\varepsilon}'_{i,j}\right] \mathrm{D}(\boldsymbol{\sigma}_{j-1})\, \mathrm{D}(\mathbf{C}_{i,j-1})^{1/2}
\end{aligned}
$$

Remarks 8.12

- Note that we should restrict the distributions of the N-dimensional random variables $\boldsymbol{\varepsilon}_{i,j+1}$ such that the multivariate cumulative claims $\mathbf{C}_{i,j+1}$ stay positive a.s., otherwise we are not able to continue the iteration in the time series. As in Chapter 3 this can be achieved, for example, by defining the distribution of $\boldsymbol{\varepsilon}_{i,j+1}$ conditionally, given $\mathcal{B}_0^N$. To ensure that we do not overload the outline, we consider this, for the time being, as a pure mathematical problem, and do not further discuss this issue here.
- For the special case $N=1$ (i.e. only one run-off triangle) we obtain Time Series model 3.9 from Chapter 3.
- It is easy to show that Time Series Model Assumptions 8.11 imply the Model Assumption 8.1 of the multivariate CL model with

$$
\begin{aligned}
\Sigma_{j-1} &= E\left[\mathrm{D}(\boldsymbol{\varepsilon}_{i,j})\, \boldsymbol{\sigma}_{j-1}\, \boldsymbol{\sigma}'_{j-1}\, \mathrm{D}(\boldsymbol{\varepsilon}_{i,j})\right] \\
&= \mathrm{D}(\boldsymbol{\sigma}_{j-1})\, \operatorname{Cov}\left(\boldsymbol{\varepsilon}_{i,j}, \boldsymbol{\varepsilon}_{i,j}\right) \mathrm{D}(\boldsymbol{\sigma}_{j-1}) \\
&= \begin{pmatrix}
\left(\sigma_{j-1}^{(1)}\right)^2 & \sigma_{j-1}^{(1)}\sigma_{j-1}^{(2)}\rho_{j-1}^{(1,2)} & \cdots & \sigma_{j-1}^{(1)}\sigma_{j-1}^{(N)}\rho_{j-1}^{(1,N)} \\
\sigma_{j-1}^{(2)}\sigma_{j-1}^{(1)}\rho_{j-1}^{(2,1)} & \left(\sigma_{j-1}^{(2)}\right)^2 & \cdots & \sigma_{j-1}^{(2)}\sigma_{j-1}^{(N)}\rho_{j-1}^{(2,N)} \\
\vdots & \vdots & & \vdots \\
\sigma_{j-1}^{(N)}\sigma_{j-1}^{(1)}\rho_{j-1}^{(N,1)} & \sigma_{j-1}^{(N)}\sigma_{j-1}^{(2)}\rho_{j-1}^{(N,2)} & \cdots & \left(\sigma_{j-1}^{(N)}\right)^2
\end{pmatrix}
\end{aligned} \tag{8.18}
$$

- Often correlations between different run-off triangles are attributed to claims inflation. Under this point of view it may seem more reasonable to allow for correlation between the cumulative claims of the same calendar year (diagonals of the claims development triangles). However, this would contradict the CL model assumption of independent accident years. Therefore, calculating prediction errors by allowing calendar year-based correlations within the CL framework is at the moment inadvisable. All calendar year-based dependencies should be removed from the data before calculating the reserves with the CL method. After correcting the data for the calendar year-based correlations, further direct and indirect sources for correlations between different run-off triangles of a portfolio exist (cf. Houltram 2003).

We now describe the conditional resampling approach (Approach 3 in Subsection 3.2.3) in the multivariate setup, that is, we conditionally resample $\widehat{\mathbf{f}}_{I-i}, \ldots, \widehat{\mathbf{f}}_{J-1}$ in the multivariate Time Series Model 8.11, given the triangles $\mathcal{D}_I^N$. Hence, we generate 'new' observations $\widetilde{\mathbf{C}}_{i,j+1}$ for $i \in \{0, \ldots, I\}$ and $j \in \{0, \ldots, J-1\}$ using the approach

$$
\widetilde{\mathbf{C}}_{i,j+1} = \mathrm{D}(\mathbf{f}_j)\, \mathbf{C}_{i,j} + \mathrm{D}(\mathbf{C}_{i,j})^{1/2}\, \mathrm{D}(\widetilde{\boldsymbol{\varepsilon}}_{i,j+1})\, \boldsymbol{\sigma}_j \tag{8.19}
$$

where

$$\widetilde{\boldsymbol{\varepsilon}}_{i,j+1}, \boldsymbol{\varepsilon}_{i,j+1} \text{ are i.i.d. copies, given } \mathcal{B}_0^N \tag{8.20}$$

This means that $\mathbf{C}_{i,j}$ acts as a deterministic volume measure and we resample successively the next observation $\widetilde{\mathbf{C}}_{i,j+1} \stackrel{(d)}{=} \mathbf{C}_{i,j+1}$, given $\mathcal{B}_j^N$.

In the spirit of the conditional resampling approach this leads to the following resampled estimates of the multivariate development factors

$$\begin{aligned}\widehat{\mathbf{f}}_j &= \left(\sum_{i=0}^{I-j-1} \mathrm{D}(\mathbf{C}_{i,j})^{1/2}\Sigma_j^{-1}\mathrm{D}(\mathbf{C}_{i,j})^{1/2}\right)^{-1} \\ &\quad \times \sum_{i=0}^{I-j-1} \mathrm{D}(\mathbf{C}_{i,j})^{1/2}\Sigma_j^{-1}\mathrm{D}(\mathbf{C}_{i,j})^{1/2}\mathrm{D}(\mathbf{C}_{i,j})^{-1}\,\widetilde{\mathbf{C}}_{i,j+1} \\ &= \mathbf{f}_j + \left(\sum_{i=0}^{I-j-1} \mathrm{D}(\mathbf{C}_{i,j})^{1/2}\Sigma_j^{-1}\mathrm{D}(\mathbf{C}_{i,j})^{1/2}\right)^{-1} \sum_{i=0}^{I-j-1} \mathrm{D}(\mathbf{C}_{i,j})^{1/2}\Sigma_j^{-1}\mathrm{D}(\widetilde{\boldsymbol{\varepsilon}}_{i,j+1})\,\boldsymbol{\sigma}_j\end{aligned} \tag{8.21}$$

Remark In (8.21) and the following exposition we use the previous notation $\widehat{\mathbf{f}}_j$ for the resampled estimates of the multivariate development factors $\mathbf{f}_j$ to avoid an overloaded notation.

We define

$$\mathrm{W}_j = \left(\sum_{k=0}^{I-j-1} \mathrm{D}(\mathbf{C}_{k,j})^{1/2}\Sigma_j^{-1}\mathrm{D}(\mathbf{C}_{k,j})^{1/2}\right)^{-1} \tag{8.22}$$

Hence we have

$$\widehat{\mathbf{f}}_j = \mathbf{f}_j + \mathrm{W}_j \sum_{i=0}^{I-j-1} \mathrm{D}(\mathbf{C}_{i,j})^{1/2}\Sigma_j^{-1}\mathrm{D}(\widetilde{\boldsymbol{\varepsilon}}_{i,j+1})\,\boldsymbol{\sigma}_j$$

(see also (3.24)–(3.25)). As in the univariate CL model we denote the conditional probability measure of these resampled multivariate CL estimates by $P^*_{\mathcal{D}_I^N}$. For a more detailed discussion we refer to Subsection 3.2.3. This way we obtain the following lemma for the properties of the resampled multivariate CL estimates:

LEMMA 8.13 *Under the resampling assumptions* (8.19)–(8.20) *we have*

(a) *the estimators* $\widehat{\mathbf{f}}_0, \ldots, \widehat{\mathbf{f}}_{J-1}$ *are independent under the probability measure* $P^*_{\mathcal{D}_I^N}$,

(b) $E^*_{\mathcal{D}_I^N}\left[\widehat{\mathbf{f}}_j\right] = \mathbf{f}_j$ *for* $0 \le j \le J-1$ *and*

(c) $E^*_{\mathcal{D}_I^N}\left[\widehat{f}_j^{(n)}\,\widehat{f}_j^{(m)}\right] = f_j^{(n)}\,f_j^{(m)} + \mathrm{W}_j(n,m)$, *where* $\mathrm{W}_j(n,m)$ *is the entry* (n,m) *of the* $N \times N$ *matrix* W_j.

Proof (a) This follows from (8.21) and the independence of $\widetilde{\boldsymbol{\varepsilon}}_{i,j+1}$ and $\widetilde{\boldsymbol{\varepsilon}}_{i,k+1}$ for $j \neq k$.

(b) This follows from (8.21) and $E^*_{\mathcal{D}_I^N}\left[\widetilde{\boldsymbol{\varepsilon}}_{i,j+1}\right]=\mathbf{0}$.

(c) Using the independence of different accident years we obtain

$$\begin{aligned}
\mathrm{Cov}_{P^*_{\mathcal{D}_I^N}}\left(\widehat{\mathbf{f}}_j,\widehat{\mathbf{f}}_j\right) &= \mathrm{W}_j \sum_{i=0}^{I-j-1} \mathrm{D}(\mathbf{C}_{i,j})^{1/2}\Sigma_j^{-1}\mathrm{Cov}_{P^*_{\mathcal{D}_I^N}}\left(\mathrm{D}(\widetilde{\boldsymbol{\varepsilon}}_{i,j+1})\,\boldsymbol{\sigma}_j, \mathrm{D}(\widetilde{\boldsymbol{\varepsilon}}_{i,j+1})\,\boldsymbol{\sigma}_j\right) \\
&\quad \times \Sigma_j^{-1}\mathrm{D}(\mathbf{C}_{i,j})^{1/2}\mathrm{W}_j \\
&= \mathrm{W}_j\left(\sum_{i=0}^{I-j-1} \mathrm{D}(\mathbf{C}_{i,j})^{1/2}\Sigma_j^{-1}\Sigma_j\Sigma_j^{-1}\mathrm{D}(\mathbf{C}_{i,j})^{1/2}\right)\mathrm{W}_j = \mathrm{W}_j
\end{aligned}$$

Hence

$$\begin{aligned}
E^*_{\mathcal{D}_I^N}\left[\widehat{f}_j^{(n)}\,\widehat{f}_j^{(m)}\right] &= f_j^{(n)}\,f_j^{(m)} + \mathrm{Cov}_{P^*_{\mathcal{D}_I^N}}\left(\widehat{f}_j^{(n)},\widehat{f}_j^{(m)}\right) \\
&= f_j^{(n)}\,f_j^{(m)} + \mathrm{W}_j(n,m)
\end{aligned}$$

where $\mathrm{W}_j(n,m)$ is the entry (n,m) of the $N\times N$ matrix W_j. This completes the proof of Lemma 8.13. □

Using Lemma 8.13 (a)–(c) we obtain the following estimator for the conditional estimation error (8.15) of accident year $i>0$

$$\begin{aligned}
&\mathbf{1}'\,\mathrm{D}(\mathbf{C}_{i,I-i})E^*_{\mathcal{D}_I^N}\left[\left(\widehat{\mathbf{g}}_{i|J}-\mathbf{g}_{i|J}\right)\left(\widehat{\mathbf{g}}_{i|J}-\mathbf{g}_{i|J}\right)'\right]\,\mathrm{D}(\mathbf{C}_{i,I-i})\,\mathbf{1} \\
&\quad = \mathbf{1}'\,\mathrm{D}(\mathbf{C}_{i,I-i})\left(\Delta_{i,J}^{(n,m)}\right)_{1\le n,m\le N}\mathrm{D}(\mathbf{C}_{i,I-i})\,\mathbf{1}
\end{aligned}$$

where the $N\times N$ matrix $\left(\Delta_{i,J}^{(n,m)}\right)_{1\le n,m\le N}$ is defined by

$$\begin{aligned}
\left(\Delta_{i,J}^{(n,m)}\right)_{1\le n,m\le N} &= \mathrm{Var}_{P^*_{\mathcal{D}_I^N}}\left(\widehat{\mathbf{g}}_{i|J}\right) \\
&= E^*_{\mathcal{D}_I^N}\left[\widehat{\mathbf{g}}_{i|J}\,\widehat{\mathbf{g}}'_{i|J}\right] - E^*_{\mathcal{D}_I^N}\left[\widehat{\mathbf{g}}_{i|J}\right]E^*_{\mathcal{D}_I^N}\left[\widehat{\mathbf{g}}'_{i|J}\right] \qquad (8.23)
\end{aligned}$$

The single entries of this matrix are given by

$$\Delta_{i,J}^{(n,m)} = \prod_{j=I-i}^{J-1}\left(f_j^{(n)}\,f_j^{(m)} + \mathrm{W}_j(n,m)\right) - \prod_{j=I-i}^{J-1} f_j^{(n)}\,f_j^{(m)} \qquad (8.24)$$

Remarks 8.14

- Note that (8.24) has the same form as in the one-dimensional case.
- The components $\Delta_{i,J}^{(n,m)}$ of the $N\times N$ matrix $\mathrm{Var}_{P^*_{\mathcal{D}_I^N}}\left(\widehat{\mathbf{g}}_{i|J}\right)$ can be rewritten in a recursive form (see also (3.28))

$$\Delta_{i,j}^{(n,m)} = \Delta_{i,j-1}^{(n,m)}\,f_{j-1}^{(n)}\,f_{j-1}^{(m)} + \prod_{l=I-i}^{j-2}\left(f_l^{(n)}\,f_l^{(m)} + \mathrm{W}_l(n,m)\right)\,\mathrm{W}_{j-1}(n,m)$$

with $\Delta_{i,I-i}^{(n,m)} = 0$ for all $i>0$ and $1\le n,m\le N$.

- If we use the estimates $\widehat{\mathbf{f}}_j^{(0)}$ for the CL factors $\mathbf{f}_j$ (cf. (8.6)), instead of $\widehat{\mathbf{f}}_j$, and disregard the correlation structure between the different subportfolios (cf. Remarks 8.5), the term (8.24) for the estimation error is then given by

$$\Delta_{i,J}^{(n,m)} = \prod_{l=I-i}^{J-1} \left(f_l^{(n)} f_l^{(m)} + \frac{\rho_l^{(n,m)} \sigma_l^{(n)} \sigma_l^{(m)}}{S_l^{[I-l-1](n)} S_l^{[I-l-1](m)}} \sum_{k=0}^{I-l-1} \sqrt{C_{k,l}^{(n)} C_{k,l}^{(m)}} \right) - \prod_{l=I-i}^{J-1} f_l^{(n)} f_l^{(m)} \tag{8.25}$$

with

$$S_l^{[I-l-1](n)} = \sum_{i=0}^{I-l-1} C_{i,l}^{(n)}$$

For a proof we refer to Merz and Wüthrich (2007b). Notice that the estimation error for $\widehat{\mathbf{f}}_j^{(0)}$ is expected to become larger compared to $\widehat{\mathbf{f}}_j$. This is justified by Lemma 8.8 which gives an optimality statement for $\widehat{\mathbf{f}}_j$. However, observe that in Lemma 8.8 the optimization only takes place on the diagonal

$$\left(\mathbf{f}_j - \widehat{\mathbf{f}}_j\right)' \left(\mathbf{f}_j - \widehat{\mathbf{f}}_j\right) = \sum_{n=1}^{N} \left(f_j^{(n)} - \widehat{f}_j^{(n)}\right)^2 \tag{8.26}$$

of the matrix $\left(\mathbf{f}_j - \widehat{\mathbf{f}}_j\right) \left(\mathbf{f}_j - \widehat{\mathbf{f}}_j\right)'$. Formula (8.13) suggests that we should optimize

$$\mathbf{1}' \left(\mathbf{f}_j - \widehat{\mathbf{f}}_j\right) \left(\mathbf{f}_j - \widehat{\mathbf{f}}_j\right)' \mathbf{1} = \left(\sum_{n=1}^{N} f_j^{(n)} - \widehat{f}_j^{(n)} \right)^2 \tag{8.27}$$

which indicates that the conditional estimation error can further be reduced. We omit further (technical) derivations in that direction.
- Note that we have assumed that the covariance matrix Σ_j is known. If Σ_j is not known we obtain additional parameter estimation error terms (which often cannot be estimated in a closed form). Moreover, if we are not able to estimate these covariances in an appropriate form it is more convenient to use $\widehat{\mathbf{f}}_j^{(0)}$ instead of $\widehat{\mathbf{f}}_j$. Therefore we have provided (8.25), see also (8.30) below.
- If we approximate (8.25) linearly from below (as in the univariate case, see (3.31)) we obtain

$$\widetilde{\Delta}_{i,J}^{(n,m)} = \prod_{l=I-i}^{J-1} f_l^{(n)} f_l^{(m)} \sum_{l=I-i}^{J-1} \frac{\rho_l^{(n,m)} \sigma_l^{(n)} / f_l^{(n)} \sigma_l^{(m)} / f_l^{(m)}}{S_l^{[I-l-1](n)} S_l^{[I-l-1](m)}} \sum_{k=0}^{I-l-1} \sqrt{C_{k,l}^{(n)} C_{k,l}^{(m)}}$$

This formula is the conditional estimation error obtained by Braun (2004) and corresponds to the multivariate version of the Mack (1993) formula for the conditional estimation error of a single run-off triangle.

If we replace the parameters in (8.9)–(8.10) and (8.24)–(8.25) by their estimates (see Subsection 8.2.5 for parameter estimates), we obtain the estimator for the conditional MSEP of a single accident year in our multivariate time series framework:

ESTIMATOR 8.15 (MSEP for single accident years, conditional version) *Under Model Assumptions 8.1 we have the following estimator for the conditional MSEP of the ultimate claim for a single accident year* $i \in \{1, \ldots, I\}$

$$\widehat{\mathrm{msep}}_{\sum_n C_{i,J}^{(n)} | \mathcal{D}_I^N}\left(\sum_{n=1}^{N} \widehat{C_{i,J}^{(n)}}^{\mathrm{CL}}\right) = \underbrace{\mathbf{1}'\left(\sum_{j=I-i}^{J-1} \prod_{k=j+1}^{J-1} \mathrm{D}(\widehat{\mathbf{f}}_k)\widehat{\Sigma}_{i,j}^{\mathbf{C}} \prod_{k=j+1}^{J-1} \mathrm{D}(\widehat{\mathbf{f}}_k)\right)\mathbf{1}}_{\text{process variance}}$$

$$+ \underbrace{\mathbf{1}'\,\mathrm{D}(\mathbf{C}_{i,I-i})\left(\widehat{\Delta}_{i,J}^{(n,m)}\right)_{1\le n,m\le N}\mathrm{D}(\mathbf{C}_{i,I-i})\,\mathbf{1}}_{\text{estimation error}} \tag{8.28}$$

with

$$\widehat{\Sigma}_{i,j}^{\mathbf{C}} = \mathrm{D}\left(\widehat{\mathbf{C}_{i,j}}^{\mathrm{CL}}\right)^{1/2} \widehat{\Sigma}_j\, \mathrm{D}\left(\widehat{\mathbf{C}_{i,j}}^{\mathrm{CL}}\right)^{1/2}$$

and

$$\widehat{\Delta}_{i,J}^{(n,m)} = \prod_{l=I-i}^{J-1}\left(\widehat{f}_l^{(n)}\,\widehat{f}_l^{(m)} + \widehat{\mathrm{W}}_l(n,m)\right) - \prod_{l=I-i}^{J-1} \widehat{f}_l^{(n)}\,\widehat{f}_l^{(m)} \tag{8.29}$$

where $\widehat{\mathrm{W}}_l(n,m)$ *is the entry* (n,m) *of the estimate* $\widehat{\mathrm{W}}_l$ *for the* $N \times N$ *matrix* W_l *(see* (8.36) *below), and* $\widehat{\Sigma}_j$ *is an estimate for* Σ_j *(see* (8.35) *below).*

Remarks 8.16

- For $N = 1$, Estimator 8.15 reduces to Estimator 3.11 of the MSEP for single accident years (conditional version) for a individual run-off-triangle.
- If we replace (8.29) by

$$\widehat{\Delta}_{i,J}^{(n,m)} = \prod_{l=I-i}^{J-1}\left(\widehat{f}_l^{(n)}\,\widehat{f}_l^{(m)} + \frac{\widehat{\rho}_l^{(n,m)}\widehat{\sigma}_l^{(n)}\widehat{\sigma}_l^{(m)}}{S_l^{[I-l-1](n)}\,S_l^{[I-l-1](m)}}\right.$$
$$\left.\times\left(\sum_{k=0}^{I-l-1}\sqrt{\widehat{C_{k,l}^{(n)}}^{\mathrm{CL}}\,\widehat{C_{k,l}^{(m)}}^{\mathrm{CL}}}\right)\right) - \prod_{l=I-i}^{J-1}\widehat{f}_l^{(n)}\,\widehat{f}_l^{(m)} \tag{8.30}$$

  then the second term on the right-hand side of formula (8.28) provides the estimator of the conditional estimation error for the use of the age-to-age factor estimates $\widehat{\mathbf{f}}_j^{(0)}$. The linear approximation to (8.30) is then given by

$$\widehat{\widetilde{\Delta}}_{i,J}^{(n,m)} = \prod_{l=I-i}^{J-1} \widehat{f}_l^{(n)} \widehat{f}_l^{(m)} \sum_{l=I-i}^{J-1} \frac{\widehat{\rho}_l^{(n,m)} \widehat{\sigma}_l^{(n)} / \widehat{f}_l^{(n)} \widehat{\sigma}_l^{(m)} / \widehat{f}_l^{(m)}}{S_l^{[I-l-1](n)} S_l^{[I-l-1](m)}} \sum_{k=0}^{I-l-1} \sqrt{\widehat{C_{k,l}^{(n)}}^{\mathrm{CL}} \widehat{C_{k,l}^{(m)}}^{\mathrm{CL}}} \tag{8.31}$$

We mention again, that sometimes it is more convenient to use $\widehat{\mathbf{f}}_j^{(0)}$ because then the estimations of the covariance matrices Σ_j have no influence on best estimates for the ultimate claims. Moreover, as described in (8.26)–(8.27), $\widehat{\mathbf{f}}_j$ is not optimal since it only optimizes over the diagonal.

8.2.4 Conditional MSEP, Aggregated Accident Years

We consider two different accident years $1 \le i < k \le I$. From Model Assumptions 8.1 we know that the ultimate claims $\mathbf{C}_{i,J}$ and $\mathbf{C}_{k,J}$ are independent. However, as in the univariate case we have to be careful if we aggregate the estimators $\widehat{\mathbf{C}}_{i,J}$ and $\widehat{\mathbf{C}}_{k,J}$ since they use the same observations for estimating the CL factors $\mathbf{f}_j$ and therefore are no longer independent. We define by

$$\mathrm{msep}_{\sum_n C_{i,J}^{(n)} + \sum_n C_{k,J}^{(n)} | \mathcal{D}_I^N} \left(\sum_{n=1}^N \widehat{C_{i,J}^{(n)}}^{\mathrm{CL}} + \sum_{n=1}^N \widehat{C_{k,J}^{(n)}}^{\mathrm{CL}} \right)$$

$$= E\left[\left(\sum_{n=1}^N \left(\widehat{C_{i,J}^{(n)}}^{\mathrm{CL}} + \widehat{C_{k,J}^{(n)}}^{\mathrm{CL}} \right) - \sum_{n=1}^N \left(C_{i,J}^{(n)} + C_{k,J}^{(n)} \right) \right)^2 \middle| \mathcal{D}_I^N \right]$$

the conditional MSEP of two aggregated accident years i and k. We have

$$\mathrm{msep}_{\sum_n C_{i,J}^{(n)} + \sum_n C_{k,J}^{(n)} | \mathcal{D}_I^N} \left(\sum_{n=1}^N \widehat{C_{i,J}^{(n)}}^{\mathrm{CL}} + \sum_{n=1}^N \widehat{C_{k,J}^{(n)}}^{\mathrm{CL}} \right)$$

$$= \mathbf{1}' \operatorname{Var}\left(\mathbf{C}_{i,J} + \mathbf{C}_{k,J} \middle| \mathcal{D}_I^N \right) \mathbf{1}$$

$$+ \mathbf{1}' \left(\widehat{\mathbf{C}}_{i,J}^{\mathrm{CL}} + \widehat{\mathbf{C}}_{k,J}^{\mathrm{CL}} - E\left[\mathbf{C}_{i,J} + \mathbf{C}_{k,J} \middle| \mathcal{D}_I^N \right] \right)$$

$$\times \left(\widehat{\mathbf{C}}_{i,J}^{\mathrm{CL}} + \widehat{\mathbf{C}}_{k,J}^{\mathrm{CL}} - E\left[\mathbf{C}_{i,J} + \mathbf{C}_{k,J} \middle| \mathcal{D}_I^N \right] \right)' \mathbf{1}$$

Using the independence of different accident years, the conditional process variance can be decoupled as follows

$$\mathbf{1}' \operatorname{Var}\left(\mathbf{C}_{i,J} + \mathbf{C}_{k,J} \middle| \mathcal{D}_I^N \right) \mathbf{1} = \mathbf{1}' \operatorname{Var}\left(\mathbf{C}_{i,J} \middle| \mathcal{D}_I^N \right) \mathbf{1} + \mathbf{1}' \operatorname{Var}\left(\mathbf{C}_{k,J} \middle| \mathcal{D}_I^N \right) \mathbf{1}$$

For the conditional estimation error we obtain

$$\begin{aligned}
&\mathbf{1}'\left(\widehat{\mathbf{C}_{i,J}}^{\mathrm{CL}}+\widehat{\mathbf{C}_{k,J}}^{\mathrm{CL}}-E\left[\mathbf{C}_{i,J}+\mathbf{C}_{k,J}\middle|\mathcal{D}_I^N\right]\right)\\
&\qquad\times\left(\widehat{\mathbf{C}_{i,J}}^{\mathrm{CL}}+\widehat{\mathbf{C}_{k,J}}^{\mathrm{CL}}-E\left[\mathbf{C}_{i,J}+\mathbf{C}_{k,J}\middle|\mathcal{D}_I^N\right]\right)'\,\mathbf{1}\\
&\quad=\mathbf{1}'\left(\widehat{\mathbf{C}_{i,J}}^{\mathrm{CL}}-E\left[\mathbf{C}_{i,J}\middle|\mathcal{D}_I^N\right]\right)\left(\widehat{\mathbf{C}_{i,J}}^{\mathrm{CL}}-E\left[\mathbf{C}_{i,J}\middle|\mathcal{D}_I^N\right]\right)'\,\mathbf{1}\\
&\qquad+\mathbf{1}'\left(\widehat{\mathbf{C}_{k,J}}^{\mathrm{CL}}-E\left[\mathbf{C}_{k,J}\middle|\mathcal{D}_I^N\right]\right)\left(\widehat{\mathbf{C}_{k,J}}^{\mathrm{CL}}-E\left[\mathbf{C}_{k,J}\middle|\mathcal{D}_I^N\right]\right)'\,\mathbf{1}\\
&\qquad+2\,\mathbf{1}'\left(\widehat{\mathbf{C}_{i,J}}^{\mathrm{CL}}-E\left[\mathbf{C}_{i,J}\middle|\mathcal{D}_I^N\right]\right)\left(\widehat{\mathbf{C}_{k,J}}^{\mathrm{CL}}-E\left[\mathbf{C}_{k,J}\middle|\mathcal{D}_I^N\right]\right)'\,\mathbf{1}
\end{aligned}$$

Hence we have the following decomposition for the conditional MSEP of two aggregated accident years

$$\begin{aligned}
&\mathrm{msep}_{\sum_n C_{i,J}^{(n)}+\sum_n C_{k,J}^{(n)}|\mathcal{D}_I^N}\left(\sum_{n=1}^N\widehat{C_{i,J}^{(n)}}^{\mathrm{CL}}+\sum_{n=1}^N\widehat{C_{k,J}^{(n)}}^{\mathrm{CL}}\right)\\
&\quad=\mathrm{msep}_{\sum_n C_{i,J}^{(n)}|\mathcal{D}_I^N}\left(\sum_{n=1}^N\widehat{C_{i,J}^{(n)}}^{\mathrm{CL}}\right)+\mathrm{msep}_{\sum_n C_{k,J}^{(n)}|\mathcal{D}_I^N}\left(\sum_{n=1}^N\widehat{C_{k,J}^{(n)}}^{\mathrm{CL}}\right)\\
&\qquad+2\,\mathbf{1}'\left(\widehat{\mathbf{C}_{i,J}}^{\mathrm{CL}}-E\left[\mathbf{C}_{i,J}\middle|\mathcal{D}_I^N\right]\right)\left(\widehat{\mathbf{C}_{k,J}}^{\mathrm{CL}}-E\left[\mathbf{C}_{k,J}\middle|\mathcal{D}_I^N\right]\right)'\,\mathbf{1}
\end{aligned}\tag{8.32}$$

This means that, in addition to the conditional MSEP for single accident years, we obtain twice the cross products

$$\begin{aligned}
&\mathbf{1}'\left(\widehat{\mathbf{C}_{i,J}}^{\mathrm{CL}}-E\left[\mathbf{C}_{i,J}\middle|\mathcal{D}_I^N\right]\right)\left(\widehat{\mathbf{C}_{k,J}}^{\mathrm{CL}}-E\left[\mathbf{C}_{k,J}\middle|\mathcal{D}_I^N\right]\right)'\,\mathbf{1}\\
&\quad=\mathbf{1}'\left(\prod_{j=I-i}^{J-1}\mathrm{D}(\widehat{\mathbf{f}}_j)-\prod_{j=I-i}^{J-1}\mathrm{D}(\mathbf{f}_j)\right)\mathbf{C}_{i,I-i}\mathbf{C}'_{k,I-k}\left(\prod_{j=I-k}^{J-1}\mathrm{D}(\widehat{\mathbf{f}}_j)-\prod_{j=I-k}^{J-1}\mathrm{D}(\mathbf{f}_j)\right)\mathbf{1}\\
&\quad=\mathbf{1}'\,\mathrm{D}(\mathbf{C}_{i,I-i})\left(\widehat{\mathbf{g}}_{i|J}-\mathbf{g}_{i|J}\right)\left(\widehat{\mathbf{g}}_{k|J}-\mathbf{g}_{k|J}\right)'\,\mathrm{D}(\mathbf{C}_{k,I-k})\,\mathbf{1}
\end{aligned}\tag{8.33}$$

Using the conditional resampling approach we derive an estimator for the cross products (8.33). As in the case of a single accident year we denote the conditional probability measure of the resampled multivariate CL estimates by $P^*_{\mathcal{D}_I^N}$. Then we can explicitly calculate the cross products (8.33) under the measure $P^*_{\mathcal{D}_I^N}$ and obtain the estimator

$$\begin{aligned}
&\mathbf{1}'\,\mathrm{D}(\mathbf{C}_{i,I-i})\,E^*_{\mathcal{D}_I^N}\left[\left(\widehat{\mathbf{g}}_{i|J}-\mathbf{g}_{i|J}\right)\left(\widehat{\mathbf{g}}_{k|J}-\mathbf{g}_{k|J}\right)'\right]\mathrm{D}(\mathbf{C}_{k,I-k})\,\mathbf{1}\\
&\quad=\mathbf{1}'\,\mathrm{D}(\mathbf{C}_{i,I-i})\left(\Delta_{i,J}^{(n,m)}\right)_{1\le n,m\le N}\mathrm{D}(\mathbf{C}_{k,I-k})\prod_{j=I-k}^{I-i-1}\mathrm{D}(\mathbf{f}_j)\,\mathbf{1}
\end{aligned}\tag{8.34}$$

where $\left(\Delta_{i,J}^{(n,m)}\right)_{1\le n,m\le N}$ is defined in (8.23)–(8.24). Replacing the parameters with their estimators (see Subsection 8.2.5 for estimators) we obtain, from (8.32) and (8.34), the following estimator for the conditional MSEP of aggregated years:

ESTIMATOR 8.17 (MSEP aggregated accident years, conditional version) *Under Model Assumptions 8.1 we have the following estimator for the conditional MSEP of the ultimate claim for aggregated accident years*

$$\widehat{\text{msep}}_{\sum_i \sum_n C_{i,J}^{(n)}|\mathcal{D}_I^N}\left(\sum_{i=1}^{I}\sum_{n=1}^{N}\widehat{C_{i,J}^{(n)}}^{\text{CL}}\right)=\sum_{i=1}^{I}\widehat{\text{msep}}_{\sum_n C_{i,J}^{(n)}|\mathcal{D}_I^N}\left(\sum_{n=1}^{N}\widehat{C_{i,J}^{(n)}}^{\text{CL}}\right)$$
$$+2\sum_{1\le i<k\le I}\mathbf{1}'\,\text{D}(\mathbf{C}_{i,I-i})\left(\widehat{\Delta}_{i,J}^{(n,m)}\right)_{1\le n,m\le N}\text{D}(\mathbf{C}_{k,I-k})\prod_{j=I-k}^{I-i-1}\text{D}(\widehat{\mathbf{f}}_j)\,\mathbf{1}$$

with $\widehat{\Delta}_{i,J}^{(n,m)}$ *given by* (8.29).

8.2.5 Parameter Estimation

In this section we give estimates $\widehat{\mathbf{f}}_j$, $\widehat{\boldsymbol{\sigma}}_j$ and $\widehat{\text{Cov}}\left(\boldsymbol{\varepsilon}_{i,j+1},\boldsymbol{\varepsilon}_{i,j+1}\right)$ of the N-dimensional parameters $\mathbf{f}_j$, $\boldsymbol{\sigma}_j$ and of the $(N\times N)$-dimensional parameters $\text{Cov}\left(\boldsymbol{\varepsilon}_{i,j+1},\boldsymbol{\varepsilon}_{i,j+1}\right)$ for $j=0,\ldots,J-1$. Observe that the age-to-age factor estimates $\widehat{\mathbf{f}}_j$ can only be calculated when the covariance matrices Σ_j are known.

Motivated by (8.18), (8.10) and (8.22) we use these parameter estimates to define the following estimates for Σ_j, $\Sigma_{i,j}^{\mathbf{C}}$ and W_j, respectively:

$$\begin{aligned}\widehat{\Sigma}_j&=\text{D}(\widehat{\boldsymbol{\sigma}}_j)\,\widehat{\text{Cov}}\left(\boldsymbol{\varepsilon}_{i,j+1},\boldsymbol{\varepsilon}_{i,j+1}\right)\,\text{D}(\widehat{\boldsymbol{\sigma}}_j)\\ \widehat{\Sigma}_{i,j}^{\mathbf{C}}&=\text{D}\big(\widehat{\mathbf{C}_{i,j}}^{\text{CL}}\big)^{1/2}\,\widehat{\Sigma}_j\,\text{D}\big(\widehat{\mathbf{C}_{i,j}}^{\text{CL}}\big)^{1/2}\end{aligned}\tag{8.35}$$

and

$$\widehat{\text{W}}_j=\left(\sum_{k=0}^{I-j-1}\text{D}(\mathbf{C}_{k,j})^{1/2}\widehat{\Sigma}_j^{-1}\text{D}(\mathbf{C}_{k,j})^{1/2}\right)^{-1}\tag{8.36}$$

The estimation of the CL factor $\mathbf{f}_j$ is given in (8.4). However, in contrast to the CL method for a single run-off triangle this provides only an implicit expression since the multivariate CL estimators $\widehat{\mathbf{f}}_j$ depend on the parameters $\boldsymbol{\sigma}_j$ and $\text{Cov}\left(\boldsymbol{\varepsilon}_{i,j+1},\boldsymbol{\varepsilon}_{i,j+1}\right)$ (see (8.4) and (8.18)), which, on the other hand, are estimated by means of $\widehat{\mathbf{f}}_j$. Therefore we propose an iterative estimation procedure of these parameters.

Estimation of $\mathbf{f}_j$ As starting values we define $\widehat{\mathbf{f}}_j^{(0)}$ by (8.6). These are the 'best' estimators if we neglect the covariance structure. The coordinates of $\widehat{\mathbf{f}}_j^{(0)}$ are the univariate CL estimators from (8.6). Estimator $\widehat{\mathbf{f}}_j^{(0)}$ is an unbiased optimal estimator for $\mathbf{f}_j$ if the N subportfolios are uncorrelated, but it is not optimal if the subportfolios are correlated (cf. Remarks 8.5 and Lemma 8.8). From $\widehat{\mathbf{f}}_j^{(0)}$ we derive estimates $\widehat{\boldsymbol{\sigma}}_j^{(1)}$ and $\widehat{\text{Cov}}\left(\boldsymbol{\varepsilon}_{i,j+1},\boldsymbol{\varepsilon}_{i,j+1}\right)^{(1)}$ of $\boldsymbol{\sigma}_j$ and $\text{Cov}\left(\boldsymbol{\varepsilon}_{i,j+1},\boldsymbol{\varepsilon}_{i,j+1}\right)$, respectively (see (8.37) and (8.39)–(8.40) below). Then these estimates are used to determine $\widehat{\mathbf{f}}_j^{(1)}$. If we iterate this procedure we obtain for $k\ge 1$

$$\widehat{\mathbf{f}}_j^{(k)} = \left(\widehat{f}_j^{(1)(k)}, \ldots, \widehat{f}_j^{(N)(k)}\right)'$$

$$= \left(\sum_{i=0}^{I-j-1} \mathrm{D}(\mathbf{C}_{i,j})^{1/2} \left(\widehat{\Sigma}_j^{(k)}\right)^{-1} \mathrm{D}(\mathbf{C}_{i,j})^{1/2} \right)^{-1}$$

$$\times \sum_{i=0}^{I-j-1} \mathrm{D}(\mathbf{C}_{i,j})^{1/2} \left(\widehat{\Sigma}_j^{(k)}\right)^{-1} \mathrm{D}(\mathbf{C}_{i,j})^{1/2}\, \mathbf{F}_{i,j+1}$$

with

$$\widehat{\Sigma}_j^{(k)} = \mathrm{D}(\widehat{\boldsymbol{\sigma}}_j^{(k)})\, \widehat{\mathrm{Cov}}\left(\boldsymbol{\varepsilon}_{i,j+1}, \boldsymbol{\varepsilon}_{i,j+1}\right)^{(k)}\, \mathrm{D}(\widehat{\boldsymbol{\sigma}}_j^{(k)})$$

Estimation of $\boldsymbol{\sigma}_j$ The N-dimensional parameters $\boldsymbol{\sigma}_j$ are also estimated iteratively from the data. An unbiased estimator of

$$\boldsymbol{\sigma}_j^2 = \left(\left(\sigma_j^{(1)}\right)^2, \ldots, \left(\sigma_j^{(N)}\right)^2 \right)'$$

is given by

$$\widehat{\boldsymbol{\sigma}_j^2} = \frac{1}{I-j-1} \sum_{i=0}^{I-j-1} \left(\mathrm{D}(\mathbf{F}_{i,j+1}) - \mathrm{D}(\widehat{\mathbf{f}}_j^{(0)})\right)^2 \mathbf{C}_{i,j}$$

for $0 \le j \le J-1$ (see Lemma 8.18 below). This estimator is used as initial value for the iteration which is given by the estimators of $\boldsymbol{\sigma}_j$:

$$\widehat{\boldsymbol{\sigma}}_j^{(k)} = \sqrt{\frac{1}{I-j-1} \sum_{i=0}^{I-j-1} \left(\mathrm{D}(\mathbf{F}_{i,j+1}) - \mathrm{D}(\widehat{\mathbf{f}}_j^{(k-1)})\right)^2 \mathbf{C}_{i,j}} \tag{8.37}$$

for $0 \le j \le J-1$ and $k \ge 1$. Note that $\left(\widehat{\boldsymbol{\sigma}}_j^{(1)}\right)^2 = \widehat{\boldsymbol{\sigma}_j^2}$.

LEMMA 8.18 *Under Model Assumptions 8.11 we have*

(a) *given* $\mathcal{B}_j^N$, $\widehat{\boldsymbol{\sigma}_j^2}$ *is an unbiased estimator for* $\boldsymbol{\sigma}_j^2$, *i.e.* $E\left[\widehat{\boldsymbol{\sigma}_j^2} \middle| \mathcal{B}_j^N\right] = \boldsymbol{\sigma}_j^2$,

(b) $\widehat{\boldsymbol{\sigma}_j^2}$ *is (unconditionally) unbiased for* $\boldsymbol{\sigma}_j^2$, *i.e.* $E\left[\widehat{\boldsymbol{\sigma}_j^2}\right] = \boldsymbol{\sigma}_j^2$.

Proof (b) easily follows from (a). Hence we only prove (a) (this is similar to Lemma 3.5). We consider

$$E\left[\left(\mathrm{D}(\mathbf{F}_{i,j+1}) - \mathrm{D}(\widehat{\mathbf{f}}_j^{(0)})\right)^2 \middle| \mathcal{B}_j^N\right]$$

$$= E\left[\left(\mathrm{D}(\mathbf{F}_{i,j+1}) - \mathrm{D}(\mathbf{f}_j)\right)^2 \middle| \mathcal{B}_j^N\right]$$

$$- 2E\left[\left(\mathrm{D}(\mathbf{F}_{i,j+1}) - \mathrm{D}(\mathbf{f}_j)\right)\left(\mathrm{D}(\widehat{\mathbf{f}}_j^{(0)}) - \mathrm{D}(\mathbf{f}_j)\right) \middle| \mathcal{B}_j^N\right]$$

$$+ E\left[\left(\mathrm{D}(\widehat{\mathbf{f}}_j^{(0)}) - \mathrm{D}(\mathbf{f}_j)\right)^2 \middle| \mathcal{B}_j^N\right]$$

Henceforth, we calculate each of the three terms on the right-hand side of the above equality. We obtain for the first term

$$E\left[\left(\mathrm{D}(\mathbf{F}_{i,j+1})-\mathrm{D}(\mathbf{f}_j)\right)^2\Big|\,\mathcal{B}_j^N\right]=E\left[\left(\mathrm{D}(\mathbf{C}_{i,j})^{-1/2}\,\mathrm{D}(\boldsymbol{\varepsilon}_{i,j+1})\,\mathrm{D}(\boldsymbol{\sigma}_j)\right)^2\Big|\,\mathcal{B}_j^N\right]$$
$$=\mathrm{D}(\mathbf{C}_{i,j})^{-1}\,\mathrm{D}(\boldsymbol{\sigma}_j)^2$$

Using the independence of different accident years we have, for the second term,

$$E\left[\left(\mathrm{D}(\mathbf{F}_{i,j+1})-\mathrm{D}(\mathbf{f}_j)\right)\left(\mathrm{D}(\widehat{\mathbf{f}}_j^{(0)})-\mathrm{D}(\mathbf{f}_j)\right)\Big|\,\mathcal{B}_j^N\right]$$
$$=\left(\sum_{k=0}^{I-j-1}\mathrm{D}(\mathbf{C}_{k,j})\right)^{-1}\mathrm{D}(\mathbf{C}_{i,j})\,E\left[\left(\mathrm{D}(\mathbf{F}_{i,j+1})-\mathrm{D}(\mathbf{f}_j)\right)^2\Big|\,\mathcal{B}_j^N\right]$$
$$=\left(\sum_{k=0}^{I-j-1}\mathrm{D}(\mathbf{C}_{k,j})\right)^{-1}\mathrm{D}(\boldsymbol{\sigma}_j)^2$$

Whereas for the last term, using the independence of different accident years, we obtain

$$E\left[\left(\mathrm{D}(\widehat{\mathbf{f}}_j^{(0)})-\mathrm{D}(\mathbf{f}_j)\right)^2\Big|\,\mathcal{B}_j^N\right]$$
$$=\left(\sum_{k=0}^{I-j-1}\mathrm{D}(\mathbf{C}_{k,j})\right)^{-2}E\left[\left(\sum_{k=0}^{I-j-1}\mathrm{D}(\mathbf{C}_{k,j})^{1/2}\,\mathrm{D}(\boldsymbol{\varepsilon}_{k,j+1})\right)^2\Bigg|\,\mathcal{B}_j^N\right]\mathrm{D}(\boldsymbol{\sigma}_j)^2$$
$$=\left(\sum_{k=0}^{I-j-1}\mathrm{D}(\mathbf{C}_{k,j})\right)^{-1}\mathrm{D}(\boldsymbol{\sigma}_j)^2$$

Putting all pieces together gives

$$E\left[\left(\mathrm{D}(\mathbf{F}_{i,j+1})-\mathrm{D}(\widehat{\mathbf{f}}_j^{(0)})\right)^2\Big|\,\mathcal{B}_j^N\right]=\mathrm{D}(\boldsymbol{\sigma}_j)^2\left(\mathrm{D}(\mathbf{C}_{i,j})^{-1}-\left(\sum_{k=0}^{I-j-1}\mathrm{D}(\mathbf{C}_{k,j})\right)^{-1}\right)$$

Hence we have

$$E\left[\widehat{\boldsymbol{\sigma}_j^2}\,\Big|\,\mathcal{B}_j^N\right]=\frac{1}{I-j-1}\sum_{i=0}^{I-j-1}E\left[\left(\mathrm{D}(\mathbf{F}_{i,j+1})-\mathrm{D}(\widehat{\mathbf{f}}_j^{(0)})\right)^2\Big|\,\mathcal{B}_j^N\right]\mathbf{C}_{i,j}$$
$$=\frac{1}{I-j-1}\,\mathrm{D}(\boldsymbol{\sigma}_j)^2\,\left((I-j)\,\mathbf{1}-\mathbf{1}\right)=\boldsymbol{\sigma}_j^2$$

which proves claim (a). This completes the proof of Lemma 8.18. □

Estimation of $\mathrm{Cov}\left(\boldsymbol{\varepsilon}_{i,j+1}, \boldsymbol{\varepsilon}_{i,j+1}\right)$ The $N \times N$ matrices $\mathrm{Cov}\left(\boldsymbol{\varepsilon}_{i,j+1}, \boldsymbol{\varepsilon}_{i,j+1}\right)$ are estimated iteratively from the data, too. If $\boldsymbol{\sigma}_j$ is known, then the Hadamard product (entrywise product)

$$\widehat{\mathrm{Cov}}\left(\boldsymbol{\varepsilon}_{i,j+1}, \boldsymbol{\varepsilon}_{i,j+1}\right) = \left(\widehat{\rho}_j^{(n,m)}\right)_{1\le n,m\le N} = \widehat{P_{j+1}} \odot Q_{j+1} \tag{8.38}$$

of the two matrices

$$\widehat{P_{j+1}} = \sum_{l=0}^{I-j-1} \mathrm{D}(\boldsymbol{\sigma}_j)^{-1} \mathrm{D}(\mathbf{C}_{l,j})^{1/2} \left(\mathbf{F}_{l,j+1} - \widehat{\mathbf{f}}_j^{(0)}\right) \left(\mathbf{F}_{l,j+1} - \widehat{\mathbf{f}}_j^{(0)}\right)' \mathrm{D}(\mathbf{C}_{l,j})^{1/2} \mathrm{D}(\boldsymbol{\sigma}_j)^{-1}$$

and

$$Q_{j+1} = \left(q_{j+1}^{(n,m)}\right)_{1\le n,m\le N} = \left(\frac{1}{I-j-2+w_{j+1}^{(n,m)}}\right)_{1\le n,m\le N}$$

with

$$w_{j+1}^{(n,m)} = \frac{\left(\sum_{l=0}^{I-j-1} \sqrt{C_{l,j}^{(n)}}\sqrt{C_{l,j}^{(m)}}\right)^2}{\sum_{l=0}^{I-j-1} C_{l,j}^{(n)} \sum_{l=0}^{I-j-1} C_{l,j}^{(m)}}$$

is a positive semi-definite unbiased estimator for the positive definite covariance matrix $\mathrm{Cov}\left(\boldsymbol{\varepsilon}_{i,j+1}, \boldsymbol{\varepsilon}_{i,j+1}\right)$ for $j=0, \ldots, J-1$ (see Lemma 8.19 below).

The estimator (8.38) leads to the initial value of the iteration when we replace the unknown $\boldsymbol{\sigma}_j$ with the estimator $\widehat{\boldsymbol{\sigma}}_j^{(1)}$. Henceforth, the iteration for the estimation of the $(N \times N)$-dimensional parameter $\mathrm{Cov}\left(\boldsymbol{\varepsilon}_{i,j+1}, \boldsymbol{\varepsilon}_{i,j+1}\right)$ is given by

$$\widehat{\mathrm{Cov}}\left(\boldsymbol{\varepsilon}_{i,j+1}, \boldsymbol{\varepsilon}_{i,j+1}\right)^{(k)} = \left(\widehat{\rho}_j^{(n,m)(k)}\right)_{1\le n,m\le N} = \widehat{P_{j+1}}^{(k)} \odot Q_{j+1} \tag{8.39}$$

for $0 \le j \le J-1$ and $k \ge 1$, where

$$\widehat{P_{j+1}}^{(k)} = \sum_{l=0}^{I-j-1} \mathrm{D}(\widehat{\boldsymbol{\sigma}}_j^{(k)})^{-1} \mathrm{D}(\mathbf{C}_{l,j})^{1/2} \left(\mathbf{F}_{l,j+1} - \widehat{\mathbf{f}}_j^{(k-1)}\right)$$
$$\times \left(\mathbf{F}_{l,j+1} - \widehat{\mathbf{f}}_j^{(k-1)}\right)' \mathrm{D}(\mathbf{C}_{l,j})^{1/2} \mathrm{D}(\widehat{\boldsymbol{\sigma}}_j^{(k)})^{-1} \tag{8.40}$$

If $\widehat{\rho}_j^{(n,m)} \notin (-1, 1)$ we proceed as described in Example 8.21, below.

LEMMA 8.19 *Under Model Assumptions 8.11 we have*

(a) *given* $\mathcal{B}_j^N$, $\widehat{\mathrm{Cov}}\left(\boldsymbol{\varepsilon}_{i,j+1}, \boldsymbol{\varepsilon}_{i,j+1}\right)$ *is an unbiased estimator for* $\mathrm{Cov}\left(\boldsymbol{\varepsilon}_{i,j+1}, \boldsymbol{\varepsilon}_{i,j+1}\right)$, *i.e.* $E\left[\widehat{\mathrm{Cov}}\left(\boldsymbol{\varepsilon}_{i,j+1}, \boldsymbol{\varepsilon}_{i,j+1}\right)\middle| \mathcal{B}_j^N\right] = \mathrm{Cov}\left(\boldsymbol{\varepsilon}_{i,j+1}, \boldsymbol{\varepsilon}_{i,j+1}\right)$,

(b) $\widehat{\mathrm{Cov}}\left(\boldsymbol{\varepsilon}_{i,j+1}, \boldsymbol{\varepsilon}_{i,j+1}\right)$ *is (unconditionally) unbiased for* $\mathrm{Cov}\left(\boldsymbol{\varepsilon}_{i,j+1}, \boldsymbol{\varepsilon}_{i,j+1}\right)$, *i.e.* $E\left[\widehat{\mathrm{Cov}}\left(\boldsymbol{\varepsilon}_{i,j+1}, \boldsymbol{\varepsilon}_{i,j+1}\right)\right] = \mathrm{Cov}\left(\boldsymbol{\varepsilon}_{i,j+1}, \boldsymbol{\varepsilon}_{i,j+1}\right)$.

Proof (b) easily follows from (a). Hence we only prove (a) again. We consider component

$$\widehat{\rho}_j^{(n,m)} = q_{j+1}^{(n,m)} \sum_{l=0}^{I-j-1} \frac{\sqrt{C_{l,j}^{(n)}}\sqrt{C_{l,j}^{(m)}}}{\sigma_j^{(n)}\,\sigma_j^{(m)}} \left(\frac{C_{l,j+1}^{(n)}}{C_{l,j}^{(n)}} - \widehat{f}_j^{(n)(0)}\right)\left(\frac{C_{l,j+1}^{(m)}}{C_{l,j}^{(m)}} - \widehat{f}_j^{(m)(0)}\right)$$

of the estimator $\widehat{\mathrm{Cov}}\left(\boldsymbol{\varepsilon}_{i,j+1}, \boldsymbol{\varepsilon}_{i,j+1}\right)$ for $j \in \{0, \ldots, J-1\}$. Using the conditional unbiasedness of the individual CL factors we have

$$f_j^{(n)} = E\left[F_{l,j+1}^{(n)} \middle| \mathcal{B}_j^{(N)}\right] = E\left[\frac{C_{l,j+1}^{(n)}}{C_{l,j}^{(n)}} \middle| \mathcal{B}_j^{(N)}\right] = E\left[\widehat{f}_j^{(n)(0)} \middle| \mathcal{B}_j^{(N)}\right]$$

for $l = 0, \ldots, I-j-1$ and $n = 1, \ldots, N$. This implies

$$\begin{aligned} &E\left[\widehat{\rho}_j^{(n,m)} \middle| \mathcal{B}_j^{(N)}\right] \\ &= q_{j+1}^{(n,m)} \sum_{l=0}^{I-j-1} \frac{\sqrt{C_{l,j}^{(n)} C_{l,j}^{(m)}}}{\sigma_j^{(n)} \sigma_j^{(m)}} \mathrm{Cov}\left(F_{l,j+1}^{(n)} - \widehat{f}_j^{(n)(0)}, F_{l,j+1}^{(m)} - \widehat{f}_j^{(m)(0)} \middle| \mathcal{B}_j^{(N)}\right) \end{aligned}$$

For the covariance term we have

$$\begin{aligned} &\mathrm{Cov}\left(F_{l,j+1}^{(n)} - \widehat{f}_j^{(n)(0)}, F_{l,j+1}^{(m)} - \widehat{f}_j^{(m)(0)} \middle| \mathcal{B}_j^{(N)}\right) \\ &= \mathrm{Cov}\left(F_{l,j+1}^{(n)}, F_{l,j+1}^{(m)} \middle| \mathcal{B}_j^{(N)}\right) - \mathrm{Cov}\left(\widehat{f}_j^{(n)(0)}, F_{l,j+1}^{(m)} \middle| \mathcal{B}_j^{(N)}\right) \\ &\quad - \mathrm{Cov}\left(F_{l,j+1}^{(n)}, \widehat{f}_j^{(m)(0)} \middle| \mathcal{B}_j^{(N)}\right) + \mathrm{Cov}\left(\widehat{f}_j^{(n)(0)}, \widehat{f}_j^{(m)(0)} \middle| \mathcal{B}_j^{(N)}\right) \\ &= \rho_j^{(n,m)} \sigma_j^{(n)} \sigma_j^{(m)} \left(C_{l,j}^{(n)}\, C_{l,j}^{(m)}\right)^{-1/2} \left(1 - \frac{C_{l,j}^{(n)}}{\sum_{i=0}^{I-j-1} C_{i,j}^{(n)}} - \frac{C_{l,j}^{(m)}}{\sum_{i=0}^{I-j-1} C_{i,j}^{(m)}}\right) \\ &\quad + \rho_j^{(n,m)} \sigma_j^{(n)} \sigma_j^{(m)} \frac{\sum_{i=0}^{I-j-1} \sqrt{C_{i,j}^{(n)}\, C_{i,j}^{(m)}}}{\sum_{i=0}^{I-j-1} C_{i,j}^{(n)} \sum_{i=0}^{I-j-1} C_{i,j}^{(m)}} \end{aligned}$$

Hence, we obtain

$$\begin{aligned} E\left[\widehat{\rho}_j^{(n,m)} \middle| \mathcal{B}_j^{(N)}\right] &= q_{j+1}^{(n,m)} \sum_{l=0}^{I-j-1} \rho_j^{(n,m)} \left(1 - \frac{C_{l,j}^{(n)}}{\sum_{i=0}^{I-j-1} C_{i,j}^{(n)}} - \frac{C_{l,j}^{(m)}}{\sum_{i=0}^{I-j-1} C_{i,j}^{(m)}}\right) \\ &\quad + q_{j+1}^{(n,m)}\, \rho_j^{(n,m)} \frac{\left(\sum_{i=0}^{I-j-1} \sqrt{C_{i,j}^{(n)} C_{i,j}^{(m)}}\right)^2}{\sum_{i=0}^{I-j-1} C_{i,j}^{(n)} \sum_{i=0}^{I-j-1} C_{i,j}^{(m)}} \\ &= q_{j+1}^{(n,m)} \rho_j^{(n,m)} \left(I - j - 2 + w_{j+1}^{(n,m)}\right) = \rho_j^{(n,m)} \end{aligned}$$

which completes the proof of claim (a). □

Remarks 8.20

- The initial values $\widehat{\rho}_j^{(n,m)(1)}$ of $\widehat{\mathrm{Cov}}\left(\boldsymbol{\varepsilon}_{i,j+1}, \boldsymbol{\varepsilon}_{i,j+1}\right)^{(1)}$ are the estimators used in the approaches of Braun (2004) and Merz and Wüthrich (2007a) to estimate the correlation coefficients $\rho_j^{(n,m)}$.
- If we have enough data (i.e. $I > J$), we are able to estimate iteratively the parameters $\boldsymbol{\sigma}_{J-1}$ and $\mathrm{Cov}\left(\boldsymbol{\varepsilon}_{i,J}, \boldsymbol{\varepsilon}_{i,J}\right)$ by (8.37) and (8.39)–(8.40), respectively. Otherwise, if $I = J$, we cannot estimate the last variance and covariance terms from the data. In such cases one extrapolates, for $1 \leq n < m \leq N$ and $k \geq 1$, the often exponentially decreasing series

$$\widehat{\sigma}_0^{(n)(k)}, \ldots, \widehat{\sigma}_{J-2}^{(n)(k)}$$

and

$$\left|\widehat{\rho}_0^{(n,m)(k)}\ \widehat{\sigma}_0^{(n)(k)}\ \widehat{\sigma}_0^{(m)(k)}\right|, \ldots, \left|\widehat{\rho}_{J-2}^{(n,m)(k)}\ \widehat{\sigma}_{J-2}^{(n)(k)}\ \widehat{\sigma}_{J-2}^{(m)(k)}\right|$$

by one additional member $\widehat{\sigma}_{J-1}^{(n)(k)}$ and $\widehat{\rho}_{J-1}^{(n,m)(k)}$, respectively. From these estimates we obtain an estimate $\widehat{\mathrm{Cov}}\left(\boldsymbol{\varepsilon}_{i,J}, \boldsymbol{\varepsilon}_{i,J}\right)^{(k)}$ for the covariance matrix $\mathrm{Cov}\left(\boldsymbol{\varepsilon}_{i,J}, \boldsymbol{\varepsilon}_{i,J}\right)$ by

$$\widehat{\mathrm{Cov}}\left(\boldsymbol{\varepsilon}_{i,J}, \boldsymbol{\varepsilon}_{i,J}\right)^{(k)} = \left(\widehat{\rho}_{J-1}^{(n,m)(k)}\right)_{1\leq n,m\leq N}$$

with

$$\widehat{\rho}_{J-1}^{(n,m)(k)} = \frac{\widehat{\varphi}_{J-1}^{(n,m)(k)}}{\widehat{\sigma}_{J-1}^{(n)(k)}\ \widehat{\sigma}_{J-1}^{(m)(k)}}$$

for $1 \leq n < m \leq N$, for the definition of $\widehat{\varphi}_{J-1}^{(n,m)(k)}$ we refer to Example 8.21, below.
- Observe, that the $(N \times N)$-dimensional estimate $\widehat{P_{j+1}}^{(k)}$ is singular when $j \geq I - N + 1$ since in this case the dimension of the linear space generated by any realizations of the $(I - j)$ N-dimensional random vectors

$$\mathrm{D}(\widehat{\boldsymbol{\sigma}}_j^{(k)})^{-1}\mathrm{D}(\mathbf{C}_{l,j})^{1/2}\left(\mathbf{F}_{l,j+1} - \widehat{\mathbf{f}}_j^{(k-1)}\right) \quad \text{with } l \in \{0, \ldots, I - j - 1\} \tag{8.41}$$

is at most $I - j \leq I - (I - N + 1) = N - 1$. Furthermore, the realizations of (8.41) may be linearly dependent for some $j < I - N + 1$ which implies that the corresponding realization of the random matrix $\widehat{P_{j+1}}^{(k)}$ is singular. In practical applications, it is thus important to verify whether the estimates $\widehat{P_{j+1}}^{(k)}$ are invertible or not and to modify those estimates (e.g. by extrapolation as in the example below) that are not invertible.

We close this section with an example. In this example we consider two different liability portfolios. Another popular example for a multivariate approach is to split a given run-off portfolio into two triangles, one containing "small" claims and the other containing "large" claims.

Example 8.21 (MSEP in the multivariate CL model)

We use the data set from Braun (2004). We consider two portfolios A and B (i.e. $N = 2$) which contain data of general liability and auto liability, respectively. The data sets are given in Tables 8.1 and 8.2. The positive correlation between these two lines of business is justified by the fact that both portfolios contain liability business. Hence, certain (external) events may influence both portfolios, and we are able to learn from the observations of one portfolio about the behaviour of the other.

It holds that $I = J = 13$. This means that we do not have sufficient data to apply the estimators (8.37) and (8.39)–(8.40) to derive estimates $\widehat{\sigma}_{12}^{(1)(k)}$, $\widehat{\sigma}_{12}^{(2)(k)}$ and $\widehat{\rho}_{12}^{(1,2)(k)}$ for $\sigma_{12}^{(1)}$, $\sigma_{12}^{(2)}$ and $\rho_{12}^{(1,2)}$, respectively (cf. Remarks 8.20). Therefore, in the following we apply an extrapolation to obtain estimates for these last terms (see also Example 3.7):

$$\widehat{\sigma}_{12}^{(1)(k)} = \min\left\{\widehat{\sigma}_{11}^{(1)(k)}, \widehat{\sigma}_{10}^{(1)(k)}, \left(\widehat{\sigma}_{11}^{(1)(k)}\right)^2 / \widehat{\sigma}_{10}^{(1)(k)}\right\}$$

$$\widehat{\sigma}_{12}^{(2)(k)} = \min\left\{\widehat{\sigma}_{11}^{(2)(k)}, \widehat{\sigma}_{10}^{(2)(k)}, \left(\widehat{\sigma}_{11}^{(2)(k)}\right)^2 / \widehat{\sigma}_{10}^{(2)(k)}\right\}$$

$$\widehat{\rho}_{12}^{(1,2)(k)} = \frac{\widehat{\varphi}_{12}^{(1,2)(k)}}{\widehat{\sigma}_{12}^{(1)(k)}\,\widehat{\sigma}_{12}^{(2)(k)}} > 0$$

with

$$\widehat{\varphi}_{12}^{(1,2)(k)} = \min\left\{\left|\widehat{\rho}_{11}^{(1,2)(k)}\widehat{\sigma}_{11}^{(1)(k)}\widehat{\sigma}_{11}^{(2)(k)}\right|, \left|\widehat{\rho}_{10}^{(1,2)(k)}\widehat{\sigma}_{10}^{(1)(k)}\widehat{\sigma}_{10}^{(2)(k)}\right|, \frac{\left|\widehat{\rho}_{11}^{(1,2)(k)}\widehat{\sigma}_{11}^{(1)(k)}\widehat{\sigma}_{11}^{(2)(k)}\right|^2}{\left|\widehat{\rho}_{10}^{(1,2)(k)}\widehat{\sigma}_{10}^{(1)(k)}\widehat{\sigma}_{10}^{(2)(k)}\right|}\right\}$$

Since (8.39)–(8.40) leads to the estimate $\widehat{\rho}_{11}^{(1,2)} = 1,001 > 1$, which is only based on two observations, we have also extrapolated $\widehat{\rho}_{11}^{(1,2)(k)}$ by

$$\widehat{\rho}_{11}^{(1,2)(k)} = \frac{\widehat{\varphi}_{11}^{(1,2)(k)}}{\widehat{\sigma}_{11}^{(1)(k)}\,\widehat{\sigma}_{11}^{(2)(k)}} > 0$$

with

$$\widehat{\varphi}_{11}^{(1,2)(k)} = \min\left\{\left|\widehat{\rho}_{10}^{(1,2)(k)}\widehat{\sigma}_{10}^{(1)(k)}\widehat{\sigma}_{10}^{(2)(k)}\right|, \left|\widehat{\rho}_{9}^{(1,2)(k)}\widehat{\sigma}_{9}^{(1)(k)}\widehat{\sigma}_{9}^{(2)(k)}\right|, \frac{\left|\widehat{\rho}_{10}^{(1,2)(k)}\widehat{\sigma}_{10}^{(1)(k)}\widehat{\sigma}_{10}^{(2)(k)}\right|^2}{\left|\widehat{\rho}_{9}^{(1,2)(k)}\widehat{\sigma}_{9}^{(1)(k)}\widehat{\sigma}_{9}^{(2)(k)}\right|}\right\}$$

Table 8.3 shows the parameter estimates in the first three iterations $k = 1, 2, 3$. (See also Tables 8.4–8.8.)

Table 8.1 Observed cumulative claims $C_{i,j}^{(1)}$ in Portfolio A

	0	1	2	3	4	5	6	7	8	9	10	11	12	13
0	59 966	163 152	254 512	349 524	433 265	475 778	513 660	520 309	527 978	539 039	537 301	540 873	547 696	549 589
1	49 685	153 344	272 936	383 349	458 791	503 358	532 615	551 437	555 792	556 671	560 844	563 571	562 795	
2	51 914	170 048	319 204	425 029	503 999	544 769	559 475	577 425	588 342	590 985	601 296	602 710		
3	84 937	273 183	407 318	547 288	621 738	687 139	736 304	757 440	758 036	782 084	784 632			
4	98 921	278 329	448 530	561 691	641 332	721 696	742 110	752 434	768 638	768 373				
5	71 708	245 587	416 882	560 958	654 652	726 813	768 358	793 603	811 100					
6	92 350	285 507	466 214	620 030	741 226	827 979	873 526	896 728						
7	95 731	313 144	553 702	755 978	857 859	962 825	1 022 241							
8	97 518	343 218	575 441	769 017	934 103	1 019 303								
9	173 686	459 416	722 336	955 335	1 141 750									
10	139 821	436 958	809 926	1 174 196										
11	154 965	528 080	1 032 684											
12	196 124	772 971												
13	204 325													

Table 8.2 Observed cumulative claims $C_{i,j}^{(2)}$ in Portfolio B

	0	1	2	3	4	5	6	7	8	9	10	11	12	13
0	114 423	247 961	312 982	344 340	371 479	371 102	380 991	385 468	385 152	392 260	391 225	391 328	391 537	391 428
1	152 296	305 175	376 613	418 299	440 308	465 623	473 584	478 427	478 314	479 907	480 755	485 138	483 974	
2	144 325	307 244	413 609	464 041	519 265	527 216	535 450	536 859	538 920	539 589	539 765	540 742		
3	145 904	307 636	387 094	433 736	463 120	478 931	482 529	488 056	485 572	486 034	485 016			
4	170 333	341 501	434 102	470 329	482 201	500 961	504 141	507 679	508 627	507 752				
5	189 643	361 123	446 857	508 083	526 562	540 118	547 641	549 605	549 693					
6	179 022	396 224	497 304	553 487	581 849	611 640	622 884	635 452						
7	205 908	416 047	520 444	565 721	600 609	630 802	648 365							
8	210 951	426 429	525 047	587 893	640 328	663 152								
9	213 426	509 222	649 433	731 692	790 901									
10	249 508	580 010	722 136	844 159										
11	258 425	686 012	915 109											
12	368 762	909 066												
13	394 997													

Table 8.3 Estimates $\widehat{\mathbf{f}}_j^{(k-1)}$, $\widehat{\boldsymbol{\sigma}}_j^{(k)}$ and $\widehat{\rho}_j^{(1,2)(k)}$ for the parameters $\mathbf{f}_j$, $\boldsymbol{\sigma}_j$ and $\rho_j^{(1,2)}$ in the first three iterations $k = 1, 2, 3$

Portfolio A/B	0	1	2	3	4	5	6	7	8	9	10	11	12
$\widehat{\mathbf{f}}_j^{(0)}$	3,23473	1,72048	1,35361	1,17889	1,10650	1,05466	1,02610	1,01448	1,01199	1,00619	1,00454	1,00548	1,00346
	2,22582	1,26945	1,12036	1,06676	1,03542	1,01677	1,00968	1,00006	1,00374	0,99946	1,00387	0,99891	0,99972
$\widehat{\boldsymbol{\sigma}}_j^{(1)}$	132,83	83,83	37,85	26,18	12,01	14,49	7,13	7,21	11,70	6,95	1,63	7,35	1,63
	105,38	24,64	17,94	19,07	12,50	5,55	4,52	2,13	5,14	1,40	3,21	1,37	0,58
$\widehat{\rho}_j^{(1,2)(1)}$	0,24537	0,49513	0,68236	0,44649	0,48686	0,45062	−0,17157	0,80209	0,33660	0,68744	−0,00379	0,00001	0,00000
$\widehat{\mathbf{f}}_j^{(1)}$	3,22696	1,71949	1,35247	1,17885	1,10644	1,05471	1,02612	1,01512	1,01208	1,00642	1,00454	1,00548	1,00346
	2,22236	1,26881	1,12002	1,06652	1,03563	1,01684	1,00970	1,00022	1,00383	0,99943	1,00387	0,99891	0,99972
$\widehat{\boldsymbol{\sigma}}_j^{(2)}$	132,85	83,83	37,86	26,18	12,01	14,49	7,13	7,24	11,70	6,59	1,63	7,35	1,63
	105,39	24,64	17,94	19,07	12,51	5,55	4,52	2,13	5,14	1,40	3,21	1,37	0,58
$\widehat{\rho}_j^{(1,2)(2)}$	0,24754	0,49562	0,68281	0,44666	0,48724	0,45081	−0,17176	0,80563	0,33718	0,68938	−0,00380	0,00001	0,00000
$\widehat{\mathbf{f}}_j^{(2)}$	3,22687	1,71949	1,35247	1,17885	1,10644	1,05471	1,02612	1,01514	1,01208	1,00642	1,00454	1,00548	1,00346
	2,22232	1,26881	1,12002	1,06652	1,03563	1,01684	1,00970	1,00022	1,00383	0,99943	1,00387	0,99891	0,99972
$\widehat{\boldsymbol{\sigma}}_j^{(3)}$	132,85	83,83	37,86	26,18	12,01	14,49	7,13	7,24	11,70	6,59	1,63	7,35	1,63
	105,39	24,64	17,94	19,07	12,51	5,55	4,52	2,13	5,14	1,40	3,21	1,37	0,58
$\widehat{\rho}_j^{(1,2)(3)}$	0,24757	0,49563	0,68281	0,44666	0,48724	0,45081	−0,17176	0,80573	0,33718	0,68939	−0,00380	0,00001	0,00000

Comments

- Table 8.3 contains the resulting parameter estimates in the first three iterations. We observe fast convergence of the two-dimensional estimates $\widehat{\mathbf{f}}_j^{(k-1)}$, $\widehat{\boldsymbol{\sigma}}_j^{(k)}$ and the one-dimensional estimates $\widehat{\rho}_j^{(1,2)(k)}$ $(k = 1, 2, 3)$ in the sense that there are only small changes in the estimates after three iterations.
- Except for development years 6 and 10 we observe positive estimates $\widehat{\rho}_j^{(1,2)(k)}$ for the correlation coefficients. The two negative estimates should not be overstated since the estimates $\widehat{\rho}_6^{(1,2)(k)}$ and $\widehat{\rho}_{10}^{(1,2)(k)}$ are based only on seven and three observations, respectively. Observe that the estimates for the correlation coefficients are quite stable for the first six development years.

Table 8.4 Claims reserves in the multivariate CL method

i	Subportfolio A reserves	Subportfolio B reserves	Portfolio reserves ($k=1$)	Portfolio reserves ($k=2$)	Portfolio reserves ($k=3$)	Portfolio reserves overall calc.
1	1945	−135	1810	1810	1810	1988
2	5394	−740	4655	4655	4655	5117
3	10 616	1211	11 827	11 826	11 826	11 083
4	15 220	992	16 212	16 370	16 371	15 344
5	25 988	3132	29 120	29 408	29 409	28 010
6	42 133	3661	45 793	46 813	46 829	44 553
7	75 959	10 045	86 004	87 222	87 241	81 339
8	135 599	21 567	157 165	158 548	158 569	149 553
9	289 659	54 642	344 301	346 116	346 142	329 840
10	561 237	118 575	679 812	681 699	681 729	644 927
11	1 033 307	254 151	1 287 458	1 287 622	1 287 654	1 230 370
12	1 887 590	565 448	2 453 038	2 450 981	2 451 016	2 331 408
13	2 070 616	1 031 063	3 101 679	3 092 156	3 092 098	3 080 525
Total	6 155 261	2 063 612	8 218 874	8 215 277	8 215 350	7 954 058

Comment

The first two columns of Table 8.4 show for each accident year the reserves for subportfolio A and B estimated by the (univariate) CL method from Chapter 3. Column 'portfolio ($k=1$)' shows the claims reserves for the whole portfolio consisting of the two subportfolios A and B with the multivariate CL method. These values are based on the estimates $\widehat{\mathbf{f}}_j^{(0)}$ and therefore are equal to the sum of the univariate CL reserves of the two subportfolios. Columns 'portfolio ($k=2$)' and 'portfolio ($k=3$)' contain the reserves for the whole portfolio based on the estimates $\widehat{\mathbf{f}}_j^{(1)}$ and $\widehat{\mathbf{f}}_j^{(2)}$, respectively. These estimates lead to a total reserve which is 3500 less than the one based on $\widehat{\mathbf{f}}_j^{(0)}$. The last column shows the claims reserve when first aggregating both run-off triangles to one single triangle and then estimating the reserve with the (univariate) CL method. This calculation is denoted 'overall calculation' and only serves for comparison purposes. As already mentioned, one should note that if two subportfolios satisfy the univariate CL assumptions with different CL factors, then the aggregated portfolio does in general not satisfy the CL assumption. From this point of view, the last column 'overall calculation' is not based on a sound mathematical model.

Table 8.5 Estimated conditional process standard deviations

i	Subportfolio A		Subportfolio B		Portfolio		Portfolio		Portfolio		Portfolio overall calculation	
	$\widehat{\mathrm{Var}}(C_{i,J}^{(1)}\|\mathcal{D}_I)^{1/2}$		$\widehat{\mathrm{Var}}(C_{i,J}^{(2)}\|\mathcal{D}_I)^{1/2}$		$\widehat{\mathrm{Var}}(\mathbf{C}_{i,J}\|\mathcal{D}_I^N)^{1/2}$		$\widehat{\mathrm{Var}}(\mathbf{C}_{i,J}\|\mathcal{D}_I^N)^{1/2}$		$\widehat{\mathrm{Var}}(\mathbf{C}_{i,J}\|\mathcal{D}_I^N)^{1/2}$			
					$(k=1)$		$(k=2)$		$(k=3)$			
1	1224	62,9%	404	−299,8%	1289	71,2%	1289	71,2%	1289	71,2%	2536	127,5%
2	5866	108,7%	1091	−147,5%	5966	128,2%	5966	128,2%	5966	128,2%	7551	147,6%
3	6864	64,7%	2461	203,2%	7290	61,6%	7290	61,6%	7290	61,6%	8453	76,3%
4	8984	59,0%	2708	273,1%	9801	60,5%	9805	59,9%	9805	59,9%	10 435	68,0%
5	14 204	54,7%	4750	151,7%	16 143	55,4%	16 149	54,9%	16 149	54,9%	16 665	59,5%
6	16 613	39,4%	5384	147,1%	19 120	41,8%	19 144	40,9%	19 145	40,9%	19 610	44,0%
7	19 488	25,7%	6577	65,5%	21 910	25,5%	21 937	25,2%	21 937	25,1%	21 971	27,0%
8	25 425	18,7%	8127	37,7%	28 933	18,4%	28 965	18,3%	28 966	18,3%	28 869	19,3%
9	31 823	11,0%	14 609	26,7%	39 281	11,4%	39 321	11,4%	39 322	11,4%	40 512	12,3%
10	49 924	8,9%	24 366	20,5%	63 663	9,4%	63 723	9,3%	63 724	9,3%	62 871	9,7%
11	78 731	7,6%	33 227	13,1%	99 918	7,8%	100 003	7,8%	100 004	7,8%	98 979	8,0%
12	172 409	9,1%	47 888	8,5%	199 543	8,1%	199 605	8,1%	199 608	8,1%	174 416	7,5%
13	261 006	12,6%	117 293	11,4%	316 020	10,2%	316 015	10,2%	316 020	10,2%	304 289	9,9%
Total	330 485	5,4%	134 676	6,5%	396 731	4,8%	396 799	4,8%	396 805	4,8%	375 000	4,7%

Comment

Table 8.5 shows for each accident year the estimates for the conditional process standard deviations and the corresponding estimates for the variational coefficients. The first two columns of Table 8.5 contain the estimated conditional process standard deviations and variational coefficients for the individual subportfolios A and B calculated with estimator (3.12). Column 'portfolio ($k=1$)' shows the estimated conditional process standard deviations for the portfolio consisting of the two subportfolios A and B if we use the multivariate CL method with parameter estimates $\widehat{\mathbf{f}}_j^{(0)}$, $\widehat{\boldsymbol{\sigma}}_j^{(1)}$ and $\widehat{\rho}_j^{(1,2)(1)}$. In contrast, columns 'portfolio ($k=2$)' and 'portfolio ($k=3$)' contain the values based on the parameter estimates $\widehat{\mathbf{f}}_j^{(k-1)}$, $\widehat{\boldsymbol{\sigma}}_j^{(k)}$ and $\widehat{\rho}_j^{(1,2)(k)}$ with $k=2$ and $k=3$, respectively. The last column shows the results for the (non-rigorous) overall calculation. For younger accident years these values are small compared to the other approaches.

Table 8.6 Square roots of estimated conditional estimation errors

i	Subportfolio A		Subportfolio B		Portfolio		Portfolio		Portfolio		Portfolio		Portfolio		Portfolio overall calculation	
	$\widehat{\mathrm{Var}}\left(\widehat{C_{i,J}^{(1)}}^{\mathrm{CL}}\middle\vert\mathcal{D}_I\right)^{1/2}$		$\widehat{\mathrm{Var}}\left(\widehat{C_{i,J}^{(2)}}^{\mathrm{CL}}\middle\vert\mathcal{D}_I\right)^{1/2}$		$\widehat{\mathrm{Var}}\left(\widehat{\mathbf{C}_{i,J}}^{\mathrm{CL}}\middle\vert\mathcal{D}_I^N\right)^{1/2}$		$\widehat{\mathrm{Var}}\left(\widehat{\mathbf{C}_{i,J}}^{\mathrm{CL}}\middle\vert\mathcal{D}_I^N\right)^{1/2}$		$\widehat{\mathrm{Var}}\left(\widehat{\mathbf{C}_{i,J}}^{\mathrm{CL}}\middle\vert\mathcal{D}_I^N\right)^{1/2}$		$\widehat{\mathrm{Var}}\left(\widehat{\mathbf{C}_{i,J}}^{\mathrm{CL}}\middle\vert\mathcal{D}_I^N\right)^{1/2}$		$\widehat{\mathrm{Var}}\left(\widehat{\mathbf{C}_{i,J}}^{\mathrm{CL}}\middle\vert\mathcal{D}_I^N\right)^{1/2}$			
					formula (8.30)		formula (8.31)		$(k=1)$		$(k=2)$		$(k=3)$			
1	1241	63,8%	449	−333,3%	1320	72,9%	1320	72,9%	1320	72,9%	1320	72,9%	1320	72,9%	2677	134,7%
2	4436	82,2%	934	−126,3%	4533	97,4%	4533	97,4%	4533	97,4%	4533	97,4%	4533	97,4%	6119	119,6%
3	5885	55,4%	1556	128,5%	6087	51,5%	6087	51,5%	6087	51,5%	6087	51,5%	6087	51,5%	7055	63,7%
4	6656	43,7%	1708	172,2%	7037	43,4%	7037	43,4%	7032	43,4%	7034	43,0%	7034	43,0%	7834	51,1%
5	8936	34,4%	2606	83,2%	9796	33,6%	9796	33,6%	9791	33,6%	9795	33,3%	9795	33,3%	10 490	37,5%
6	10 570	25,1%	3115	85,1%	11 738	25,6%	11 738	25,6%	11 726	25,6%	11 741	25,1%	11 742	25,1%	12 539	28,1%
7	12 853	16,9%	3570	35,5%	13 991	16,3%	13 991	16,3%	13 978	16,3%	13 996	16,0%	13 996	16,0%	14 328	17,6%
8	15 129	11,2%	4144	19,2%	16 637	10,6%	16 637	10,6%	16 624	10,6%	16 644	10,5%	16 644	10,5%	16 800	11,2%
9	19 823	6,8%	6980	12,8%	22 767	6,6%	22 767	6,6%	22 749	6,6%	22 775	6,6%	22 776	6,6%	23 311	7,1%
10	28 777	5,1%	11 022	9,3%	34 105	5,0%	34 103	5,0%	34 081	5,0%	34 116	5,0%	34 116	5,0%	33 520	5,2%
11	42 542	4,1%	15 669	6,2%	51 417	4,0%	51 413	4,0%	51 355	4,0%	51 385	4,0%	51 386	4,0%	50 394	4,1%
12	87 223	4,6%	23 625	4,2%	99 947	4,1%	99 933	4,1%	99 845	4,1%	99 856	4,1%	99 857	4,1%	87 224	3,7%
13	109 321	5,3%	47 683	4,6%	131 770	4,2%	131 734	4,2%	131 682	4,2%	131 589	4,3%	131 590	4,3%	127 150	4,1%
Total	270 878	4,4%	91 599	4,4%	313 751	3,8%	313 718	3,8%	313 122	3,8%	313 071	3,8%	313 074	3,8%	304 861	3,8%

Comment

Table 8.6 shows for each accident year the square roots of estimated conditional estimation errors. The first two columns contain the estimates for the individual subportfolios A and B calculated by estimator (3.27). The next two columns show the estimation errors if we use the univariate CL factors and formula (8.30) and its linear approximation from below (8.31), respectively, for estimating $\Delta_{i,J}^{(n,m)}$. In contrast to the conditional process standard deviation these estimates do not coincide with the values in column 'portfolio $(k=1)$'. Finally, the multivariate approach leads to a slightly lower result for the conditional estimation error than the (univariate) approaches. This comes from the fact that the multivariate estimators have smaller variance (see Lemma 8.8). Again, the last column only serves for comparison purposes. Observe that the multivariate estimates are only slightly lower than the column 'formula (8.30)' (313 074 vs 313 751) which suggest that in this example we can work with the univariate CL estimators $\widehat{\mathbf{f}}_j^{(0)}$ (which is much easier from a technical point of view).

Table 8.7 Estimated prediction standard errors

i	Subportfolio A		Subportfolio B		Portfolio		Portfolio		Portfolio		Portfolio		Portfolio		Portfolio overall calculation	
	$\widehat{\text{msep}}^{1/2}_{C^{(1)}_{i,J}\mid\mathcal{D}_I}$		$\widehat{\text{msep}}^{1/2}_{C^{(2)}_{i,J}\mid\mathcal{D}_I}$		$\widehat{\text{msep}}^{1/2}_{\text{C}_{i,J}\mid\mathcal{D}^N_I}$		$\widehat{\text{msep}}^{1/2}_{\text{C}_{i,J}\mid\mathcal{D}^N_I}$		$\widehat{\text{msep}}^{1/2}_{\text{C}_{i,J}\mid\mathcal{D}^N_I}$		$\widehat{\text{msep}}^{1/2}_{\text{C}_{i,J}\mid\mathcal{D}^N_I}$		$\widehat{\text{msep}}^{1/2}_{\text{C}_{i,J}\mid\mathcal{D}^N_I}$			
					formula (8.30)		formula (8.31)		$(k=1)$		$(k=2)$		$(k=3)$			
1	1743	89,6%	604	−448,2%	1845	101,9%	1845	101,9%	1845	101,9%	1845	101,9%	1845	101,9%	3688	185,5%
2	7354	136,3%	1436	−194,2%	7493	161,0%	7493	161,0%	7493	161,0%	7493	161,0%	7493	161,0%	9720	190,0%
3	9042	85,2%	2912	240,4%	9497	80,3%	9497	80,3%	9497	80,3%	9497	80,3%	9497	80,3%	11 010	99,3%
4	11 181	73,5%	3202	322,8%	12 066	74,4%	12 066	74,4%	12 063	74,4%	12 067	73,7%	12 067	73,7%	13 049	85,0%
5	16 781	64,6%	5418	173,0%	18 883	64,8%	18 883	64,8%	18 880	64,8%	18 887	64,2%	18 887	64,2%	19 692	70,3%
6	19 691	46,7%	6221	169,9%	22 435	49,0%	22 435	49,0%	22 429	49,0%	22 458	48,0%	22 459	48,0%	23 276	52,2%
7	23 344	30,7%	7483	74,5%	25 996	30,2%	25 996	30,2%	25 989	30,2%	26 021	29,8%	26 022	29,8%	26 230	32,2%
8	29 586	21,8%	9123	42,3%	33 376	21,2%	33 376	21,2%	33 369	21,2%	33 407	21,1%	33 407	21,1%	33 401	22,3%
9	37 492	12,9%	16 191	29,6%	45 402	13,2%	45 401	13,2%	45 393	13,2%	45 441	13,1%	45 442	13,1%	46 739	14,2%
10	57 624	10,3%	26 742	22,6%	72 223	10,6%	72 222	10,6%	72 212	10,6%	72 281	10,6%	72 282	10,6%	71 249	11,0%
11	89 490	8,7%	36 737	14,5%	112 372	8,7%	112 370	8,7%	112 343	8,7%	112 432	8,7%	112 434	8,7%	111 069	9,0%
12	193 217	10,2%	53 399	9,4%	223 175	9,1%	223 169	9,1%	223 129	9,1%	223 189	9,1%	223 192	9,1%	195 010	8,4%
13	282 975	13,7%	126 615	12,3%	342 392	11,0%	342 377	11,0%	342 358	11,0%	342 318	11,1%	342 322	11,1%	329 786	10,7%
Total	427 311	6,9%	162 874	7,9%	505 802	6,2%	505 781	6,2%	505 412	6,1%	505 433	6,2%	505 440	6,2%	483 287	6,1%

Comment

Table 8.7 contains for each accident year the estimated prediction standard errors and the corresponding estimates for the variational coefficients. The first two columns contain the estimates for the individual subportfolios A and B calculated with Estimator 3.11. The next two columns show the estimated prediction standard deviations if we use the univariate CL factors and formula (8.30) and its linear approximation from below (8.31), respectively, for estimating $\Delta^{(n,m)}_{i,J}$. The next columns show the iteration procedure for the calculation of the prediction standard deviations in the multivariate CL method. Again, the last column shows the estimates for the (non-rigorous) overall calculation.

Table 8.8 Estimated prediction standard errors assuming correlation 1, 0 and −1, respectively

i	Portfolio $\widehat{\mathrm{msep}}^{1/2}_{\mathbf{C}_{i,J}\mid\mathcal{D}_I^N}$ correlation = 1	Portfolio $\widehat{\mathrm{msep}}^{1/2}_{\mathbf{C}_{i,J}\mid\mathcal{D}_I^N}$ correlation = 0	Portfolio $\widehat{\mathrm{msep}}^{1/2}_{\mathbf{C}_{i,J}\mid\mathcal{D}_I^N}$ correlation = −1
1	2347	1845	1139
2	8790	7493	5918
3	11 593	9499	6130
4	14 383	11 631	7980
5	22 199	17 634	11 363
6	25 911	20 650	13 470
7	30 827	24 514	15 861
8	38 708	30 960	20 463
9	53 683	40 839	21 301
10	84 366	63 527	30 881
11	126 226	96 737	52 753
12	246 615	200 460	139 818
13	409 590	310 010	156 360
Total	590 186	457 300	264 437

Comment

Table 8.8 contains the results for the estimated prediction standard errors assuming a perfect positive correlation, no correlation and perfect negative correlation between the corresponding conditional MSEP estimates of all columns of the two subportfolios A and B. These values are calculated by

$$\widehat{\mathrm{msep}}_{\mathbf{C}_{i,J}\mid\mathcal{D}_I^N} = \widehat{\mathrm{msep}}_{C_{i,J}^{(1)}\mid\mathcal{D}_I} + \widehat{\mathrm{msep}}_{C_{i,J}^{(2)}\mid\mathcal{D}_I} + 2\,c\;\widehat{\mathrm{msep}}^{1/2}_{C_{i,J}^{(1)}\mid\mathcal{D}_I}\;\widehat{\mathrm{msep}}^{1/2}_{C_{i,J}^{(2)}\mid\mathcal{D}_I} \tag{8.42}$$

with $c = 1$, $c = 0$ and $c = -1$, respectively. We observe that the multivariate estimates 3–7 in Table 8.7 are between those assuming no correlation and a correlation equal to 1 for all accident years. Note that the dependence modelling adds about 10% to the $\mathrm{msep}^{1/2}$, that is, 457 300 (Table 8.8) vs 505 440 (Table 8.7). This means that we observe a substantial increase in uncertainty caused by correlations between different portfolios.

8.3 MULTIVARIATE ADDITIVE LOSS RESERVING METHOD

In this section we present the multivariate additive loss reserving (ALR) method which was proposed by Hess *et al.* (2006) and Schmidt (2006b). The multivariate ALR method is based on incremental claims, and hence is more in the spirit of the (univariate) GLM models. As in the multivariate CL model we will assume that the multivariate ALR model consists of several correlated subportfolios. Within this framework we look for multivariate estimators that respect the correlation structure.

In this section we closely follow Merz and Wüthrich (2007d) and provide a framework for the multivariate ALR method to derive an estimator for the conditional MSEP. The model considered will allow us to combine the multivariate ALR method with the multivariate CL Time Series Model 8.11. This is done in the next section.

8.3.1 Multivariate Additive Loss Reserving Model

In the multivariate ALR method we study normalized incremental claims (individual incremental loss ratios). We define for $i \in \{0, \ldots, I\}$ and $j \in \{1, \ldots, J\}$ the N-dimensional vector of normalized incremental claims for accident year i and development year j by

$$\mathbf{M}_{i,j} = \left(M_{i,j}^{(1)}, \ldots, M_{i,j}^{(N)}\right)' = \mathrm{V}_i^{-1}\, \mathbf{X}_{i,j}$$

with

$$\mathrm{V}_i = \begin{pmatrix} V_i^{(1,1)} & V_i^{(1,2)} & \cdots & V_i^{(1,N)} \\ V_i^{(2,1)} & V_i^{(2,2)} & \cdots & V_i^{(2,N)} \\ \vdots & \vdots & \ddots & \vdots \\ V_i^{(N,1)} & V_i^{(N,2)} & \cdots & V_i^{(N,N)} \end{pmatrix}$$

is a deterministic positive definite symmetric $N \times N$ matrix. The coordinates $M_{i,j}^{(n)}$ of $\mathbf{M}_{i,j}$ $(n = 1, \ldots, N)$ denote the normalized incremental claims for accident year i and development year j of subportfolio n. In the univariate case $N = 1$ we have

$$M_{i,j} = X_{i,j} / V_i$$

where $V_i \in \mathbb{R}$ is an appropriate (deterministic) volume measure. If $X_{i,j}$ denotes incremental claims and V_i is the total premium received for accident year i, then $M_{i,j}$ tells how the total loss ratio is paid over time.

The following multivariate ALR model was studied by Merz and Wüthrich (2007d). It is a time series version of the ALR model in Hess *et al.* (2006) and Schmidt (2006b).

Model Assumptions 8.22 (multivariate ALR time series model)

- Incremental claims $\mathbf{X}_{i,j}$ of different accident years i are independent.
- There exist $(N \times N)$-dimensional deterministic positive definite symmetric matrices $\mathrm{V}_0, \ldots, \mathrm{V}_I$ and N-dimensional constants $(j = 1, \ldots, J)$

$$\mathbf{m}_j = \left(m_j^{(1)}, \ldots, m_j^{(N)}\right)' \quad \text{and} \quad \boldsymbol{\sigma}_{j-1} = \left(\sigma_{j-1}^{(1)}, \ldots, \sigma_{j-1}^{(N)}\right)'$$

with $\sigma_j^{(n)} > 0$ for all $n = 1, \ldots, N$ as well as a N-dimensional random variables

$$\boldsymbol{\varepsilon}_{i,j} = \left(\varepsilon_{i,j}^{(1)}, \ldots, \varepsilon_{i,j}^{(N)}\right)'$$

such that for all $i \in \{0, \ldots, I\}$ and $j \in \{1, \ldots, J\}$ we have

$$\mathbf{X}_{i,j} = \mathrm{V}_i \; \mathbf{m}_j + \mathrm{V}_i^{1/2} \; \mathrm{D}(\boldsymbol{\varepsilon}_{i,j}) \; \boldsymbol{\sigma}_{j-1} \tag{8.43}$$

Moreover, the random variables $\boldsymbol{\varepsilon}_{i,j}$ are independent with $E[\boldsymbol{\varepsilon}_{i,j}] = \mathbf{0}$ and positive definite

$$\mathrm{Cov}(\boldsymbol{\varepsilon}_{i,j}, \boldsymbol{\varepsilon}_{i,j}) = E\left[\boldsymbol{\varepsilon}_{i,j} \; \boldsymbol{\varepsilon}_{i,j}'\right] = \begin{pmatrix} 1 & \rho_{j-1}^{(1,2)} & \cdots & \rho_{j-1}^{(1,N)} \\ \rho_{j-1}^{(2,1)} & 1 & \cdots & \rho_{j-1}^{(2,N)} \\ \vdots & \vdots & \ddots & \vdots \\ \rho_{j-1}^{(N,1)} & \rho_{j-1}^{(N,2)} & \cdots & 1 \end{pmatrix}$$

where $\rho_{j-1}^{(n,m)} \in (-1, 1)$ for $n, m \in \{1, \ldots, N\}$ and $n \neq m$. □

In the univariate case $N = 1$, the ALR model satisfies

$$\frac{X_{i,j}}{V_i} = m_j + V_i^{-1/2} \; \sigma_{j-1} \; \varepsilon_{i,j} \tag{8.44}$$

with

$$E\left[X_{i,j}\right] = V_i \; m_j \qquad \text{and} \qquad \mathrm{Var}\left(X_{i,j}\right) = V_i \; \sigma_{j-1}^2 \tag{8.45}$$

Hence this model can also be interpreted as a GLM model with Gaussian variance function $(p = 0)$, volume V_i and dispersion σ_{j-1}^2 / V_i.

Observe, under Model Assumptions 8.22, that we have

$$\mathrm{Cov}\left(\mathbf{X}_{i,j}, \mathbf{X}_{i,j}\right) = \mathrm{V}_i^{1/2} \; \mathrm{E}\left[\mathrm{D}(\boldsymbol{\varepsilon}_{i,j}) \; \boldsymbol{\sigma}_{j-1} \; \boldsymbol{\sigma}_{j-1}' \; \mathrm{D}(\boldsymbol{\varepsilon}_{i,j})\right] \; \mathrm{V}_i^{1/2} \tag{8.46}$$

Analogous to the multivariate CL Time Series Model 8.11, we obtain for the expected value on the right-hand side of (8.46)

$$
\begin{aligned}
\Sigma_{j-1} &= \mathrm{E}\left[\mathrm{D}(\boldsymbol{\varepsilon}_{i,j})\ \boldsymbol{\sigma}_{j-1}\ \boldsymbol{\sigma}'_{j-1}\mathrm{D}(\boldsymbol{\varepsilon}_{i,j})\right] \\
&= \mathbf{D}(\boldsymbol{\sigma}_{j-1})\ \mathrm{Cov}\left(\boldsymbol{\varepsilon}_{i,j}, \boldsymbol{\varepsilon}_{i,j}\right)\ \mathbf{D}(\boldsymbol{\sigma}_{j-1}) \\
&= \begin{pmatrix}
\left(\sigma_{j-1}^{(1)}\right)^2 & \sigma_{j-1}^{(1)}\sigma_{j-1}^{(2)}\rho_{j-1}^{(1,2)} & \cdots & \sigma_{j-1}^{(1)}\sigma_{j-1}^{(N)}\rho_{j-1}^{(1,N)} \\
\sigma_{j-1}^{(2)}\sigma_{j-1}^{(1)}\rho_{j-1}^{(2,1)} & \left(\sigma_{j-1}^{(2)}\right)^2 & \cdots & \sigma_{j-1}^{(2)}\sigma_{j-1}^{(N)}\rho_{j-1}^{(2,N)} \\
\vdots & \vdots & & \vdots \\
\sigma_{j-1}^{(N)}\sigma_{j-1}^{(1)}\rho_{j-1}^{(N,1)} & \sigma_{j-1}^{(N)}\sigma_{j-1}^{(2)}\rho_{j-1}^{(N,2)} & \cdots & \left(\sigma_{j-1}^{(N)}\right)^2
\end{pmatrix}
\end{aligned} \tag{8.47}
$$

(cf. Remarks 8.12) and we restrict any assumption regarding the correlation between the N subportfolios to each of the corresponding development years j ($j = 1, \ldots, J$) in the N run-off triangles. Matrix Σ_{j-1} reflects the correlation structure between the incremental claims of development year j in the N different subportfolios (see also Remarks 8.2).

Remarks 8.23

- The incremental claims $\mathbf{X}_{i,j}$ and $\mathbf{X}_{k,l}$ are independent for $i \neq k$ or $j \neq l$.
- The N-dimensional expected incremental loss ratios $(\mathbf{m}_j)_{1\le j\le J}$ can be interpreted as a multivariate scaled expected reporting/cashflow pattern over the different development years.
- In most practical applications matrix V_i is chosen to be diagonal in order to represent a volume measure of accident year i, *a priori* known (e.g. premiums, number of contracts, expected number of claims, etc.) or external knowledge from experts, similar portfolios or market statistics.
- Since we assume that V_i is a positive definite symmetric matrix, there is a well-defined positive definite symmetric matrix $\mathrm{V}_i^{1/2}$ (called the square root of V_i) satisfying $\mathrm{V}_i = \mathrm{V}_i^{1/2}\ \mathrm{V}_i^{1/2}$.
- The multivariate ALR Time Series Model 8.22 is a special case of the multivariate ALR model proposed by Hess *et al.* (2006) and Schmidt (2006b) with independent incremental claims $\mathbf{X}_{i,j}$ and positive definite symmetric matrices $\Sigma_j = \mathrm{E}\left[\mathrm{D}(\boldsymbol{\varepsilon}_{i,j+1})\ \boldsymbol{\sigma}_j\ \boldsymbol{\sigma}_j^T\ \mathrm{D}(\boldsymbol{\varepsilon}_{i,j+1})\right]$.

LEMMA 8.24 *Under Model Assumptions 8.22 we have for all* $1 \le i \le I$

$$
E\left[\mathbf{C}_{i,J}\middle|\mathcal{D}_I^N\right] = E\left[\mathbf{C}_{i,J}\middle|\mathbf{C}_{i,I-i}\right] = \mathbf{C}_{i,I-i} + \mathrm{V}_i \sum_{j=I-i+1}^{J} \mathbf{m}_j
$$

Proof Using the independence of the incremental claims we obtain

$$
\begin{aligned}
E\left[\mathbf{C}_{i,J}\middle|\mathcal{D}_I^N\right] &= \mathbf{C}_{i,I-i} + E\left[\sum_{j=I-i+1}^{J} \mathbf{X}_{i,j}\middle|\mathcal{D}_I^N\right] \\
&= \mathbf{C}_{i,I-i} + \sum_{j=I-i+1}^{J} E[\mathbf{X}_{i,j}] \\
&= \mathbf{C}_{i,I-i} + \mathrm{V}_i \sum_{j=I-i+1}^{J} \mathbf{m}_j = E\left[\mathbf{C}_{i,J}\middle|\mathbf{C}_{i,I-i}\right]
\end{aligned}
$$

This completes the proof of the lemma. □

This result motivates an algorithm for estimating the expected ultimate claims given the observation $\mathcal{D}_I^N$. If the N-dimensional expected incremental loss ratios $(\mathbf{m}_j)_{1\le j\le J}$ are known, the expected outstanding claims liabilities of accident year i for the N correlated run-off triangles based on the information $\mathcal{D}_I^N$ are simply determined by

$$E\left[\mathbf{C}_{i,J}\middle|\mathcal{D}_I^N\right]-\mathbf{C}_{i,I-i}=\mathrm{V}_i\sum_{j=I-i+1}^{J}\mathbf{m}_j$$

In most practical applications we have to estimate the ratios $\mathbf{m}_j$ from the data in the upper triangle. Hess *et al.* (2006) and Schmidt (2006b) propose the following multivariate estimates; for $j=1,\ldots,J$ we set

$$\begin{aligned}\widehat{\mathbf{m}}_j&=\left(\widehat{m}_j^{(1)},\ldots,\widehat{m}_j^{(N)}\right)'\\&=\left(\sum_{i=0}^{I-j}\mathrm{V}_i^{1/2}\,\Sigma_{j-1}^{-1}\,\mathrm{V}_i^{1/2}\right)^{-1}\sum_{i=0}^{I-j}\left(\mathrm{V}_i^{1/2}\,\Sigma_{j-1}^{-1}\,\mathrm{V}_i^{1/2}\right)\mathbf{M}_{i,j}\end{aligned}\tag{8.48}$$

The coordinates $\widehat{m}_j^{(n)}$ denotes the estimated incremental loss ratio for development year j and run-off triangle $n\in\{1,\ldots,N\}$ based on the information $\mathcal{D}_I^N$. Note that the covariance structure is incorporated into the estimation of $\mathbf{m}_j$.

ESTIMATOR 8.25 (multivariate ALR estimator) *The multivariate ALR estimator for* $E\left[\mathbf{C}_{i,j}\middle|\mathcal{D}_I^N\right]$ *is, for* $i+j>I$, *given by*

$$\widehat{\mathbf{C}_{i,j}}^{\mathrm{AD}}=\left(\widehat{C_{i,j}^{(1)}}^{\mathrm{AD}},\ldots,\widehat{C_{i,j}^{(N)}}^{\mathrm{AD}}\right)'=\widehat{E}\left[\mathbf{C}_{i,j}\middle|\mathcal{D}_I^N\right]=\mathbf{C}_{i,I-i}+\mathrm{V}_i\sum_{l=I-i+1}^{j}\widehat{\mathbf{m}}_l$$

This means that in the multivariate ALR method we predict the normalized cumulative claims $\mathrm{V}_i^{-1}\,\mathbf{C}_{i,j}$ by the sum of the last observed normalized cumulative claims $\mathrm{V}_i^{-1}\,\mathbf{C}_{i,I-i}$ and the weighted estimated ratios $\widehat{\mathbf{m}}_{I-i+1},\ldots,\widehat{\mathbf{m}}_j$, given the information $\mathcal{D}_I^N$. From Estimator 8.25 we obtain, for the incremental claims $\mathbf{X}_{i,j}$ with $i+j>I$, the predictors

$$\widehat{\mathbf{X}_{i,j}}^{\mathrm{AD}}=\left(\widehat{X_{i,j}^{(1)}}^{\mathrm{AD}},\ldots,\widehat{X_{i,j}^{(N)}}^{\mathrm{AD}}\right)'=\mathrm{V}_i\,\widehat{\mathbf{m}}_j$$

The following remarks are similar to those for the age-to-age factor estimates $\widehat{\mathbf{f}}_j$ in the multivariate CL method (cf. Remarks 8.5):

Remarks 8.26

- In the case $j = J$ (note that we assume $I = J$) we have $\widehat{\mathbf{m}}_J = \mathbf{M}_{0,J}$.
- Estimator (8.48) is a weighted average of the observed individual normalized incremental claims $\mathbf{M}_{i,j}$. In the case $N = 1$ (i.e. only one subportfolio) the estimators (8.48) coincide with the univariate estimated incremental loss ratios

$$\widehat{m}_j = \sum_{i=0}^{I-j} \frac{V_i}{\sum_{k=0}^{I-j} V_k} M_{i,j} \tag{8.49}$$

with deterministic weights V_i which are used in the univariate ALR method (see, e.g., Radtke and Schmidt (2004) and Schmidt (2006a).
- In the case $N = 1$ we obtain from Estimator 8.25 the univariate ALR estimator

$$\widehat{C_{i,J}}^{\mathrm{AD}} = C_{i,I-i} + \sum_{j=I-i+1}^{J} \frac{\sum_{k=0}^{I-j} X_{k,j}}{\sum_{k=0}^{I-j} V_k} V_i, \tag{8.50}$$

which is similar to the BF estimators (6.63) and (6.64) in the GLM Model 6.21 (cf. Remarks 6.23).
- The covariance matrix Σ_{j-1} in estimator (8.48) reflects the correlation structure between the different subportfolios. If we neglect the covariance structure we obtain the following (unbiased) estimator

$$\widehat{\mathbf{m}}_j^{(0)} = \left(\sum_{i=0}^{I-j} \mathrm{V}_i \right)^{-1} \sum_{i=0}^{I-j} \mathrm{V}_i \, \mathbf{M}_{i,j} \tag{8.51}$$

If the volume V_i is a diagonal matrix then the coordinates of (8.51) are given by

$$\widehat{m}_j^{(n)(0)} = \sum_{i=0}^{I-j} \frac{V_i^{(n,n)}}{\sum_{k=0}^{I-j} V_k^{(n,n)}} M_{i,j}^{(n)} \tag{8.52}$$

This means that, in this case, the coordinates of $\widehat{\mathbf{m}}_j^{(0)}$ are given by the estimators of the univariate ALR method.
- Hess *et al.* (2006) and Schmidt (2006b) showed that the multivariate incremental loss ratio estimates (8.48) are optimal estimators of $\mathbf{m}_j$ w.r.t. the criterion of minimal expected squared loss in the case of correlated run-off triangles (see Lemma 8.29 below). However, as in the multivariate CL case, this assumes that the covariance matrix Σ_{j-1} is known. If we do not have reliable estimates for this covariance matrix it is often more appropriate to use the univariate estimators.
- It can easily be seen that $\widehat{\mathbf{m}}_j$ does not depend on the matrix Σ_{j-1} if $j = J$ or if Σ_{j-1} and $\mathrm{V}_0, \ldots, \mathrm{V}_{I-j}$ are diagonal. In this case the N coordinates $\widehat{m}_j^{(1)}, \ldots, \widehat{m}_j^{(N)}$ of (8.48) coincide with the univariate estimators (8.52) for the N subportfolios. This means that if $\Sigma_0, \ldots, \Sigma_{J-2}$ and $\mathrm{V}_0, \ldots, \mathrm{V}_J$ are diagonal matrices, the following estimates coincide: (1) the estimation for the whole portfolio based on the univariate estimators (8.49) for every individual subportfolio, (2) the multivariate prediction based on the estimators (8.51) and (3) the multivariate prediction based on the multivariate estimators (8.48). However, in other cases it is more reasonable to use the multivariate estimators (8.48)

(cf. Lemma 8.29 below), whenever one has appropriate estimates for the covariance matrices Σ_j.

We have the following lemma:

LEMMA 8.27 *Under Model Assumptions 8.22 we have*

(a) *given* $\mathcal{B}_{j-1}^N$, $\widehat{\mathbf{m}}_j$ *is an unbiased estimator for* $\mathbf{m}_j$, *i.e.* $E\left[\widehat{\mathbf{m}}_j \middle| \mathcal{B}_{j-1}^N\right]=\mathbf{m}_j$;
(b) $\widehat{\mathbf{m}}_j$ *is (unconditionally) unbiased for* $\mathbf{m}_j$, *i.e.* $E\left[\widehat{\mathbf{m}}_j\right]=\mathbf{m}_j$;
(c) $\widehat{\mathbf{m}}_j$ *and* $\widehat{\mathbf{m}}_k$ *are independent for* $j \neq k$;
(d) $\mathrm{Var}\left(\widehat{\mathbf{m}}_j\right)=\left(\sum_{l=0}^{I-j} \mathrm{V}_l^{1/2}\, \Sigma_{j-1}^{-1}\, \mathrm{V}_l^{1/2}\right)^{-1}$;
(e) *given* $\mathbf{C}_{i,I-i}$, *the estimator* $\widehat{\mathbf{C}_{i,J}}^{AD}$ *is an unbiased estimator for* $E\left[\mathbf{C}_{i,J}|\mathcal{D}_I^N\right]=E[\mathbf{C}_{i,J}|\mathbf{C}_{i,I-i}]$, *i.e.* $E\left[\widehat{\mathbf{C}_{i,J}}^{AD}\middle|\mathbf{C}_{i,I-i}\right]=E\left[\mathbf{C}_{i,J}|\mathcal{D}_I^N\right]$;
(f) $\widehat{\mathbf{C}_{i,J}}^{AD}$ *is (unconditionally) unbiased for* $E[\mathbf{C}_{i,J}]$, *i.e.* $E\left[\widehat{\mathbf{C}_{i,J}}^{AD}\right]=E[\mathbf{C}_{i,J}]$.

Proof (a) Using the independence of $\mathbf{X}_{i,j}$ and $\mathbf{C}_{i,k}$ with $k \le j-1$ as well as $E\left[\mathbf{M}_{i,j}\middle|\mathcal{B}_{j-1}^N\right]=E\left[\mathbf{M}_{i,j}\right]=\mathrm{V}_i^{-1}\,E\left[\mathbf{X}_{i,j}\right]=\mathbf{m}_j$ we obtain the claim from

$$E\left[\widehat{\mathbf{m}}_j\middle|\mathcal{B}_{j-1}^N\right]=\left(\sum_{i=0}^{I-j}\mathrm{V}_i^{1/2}\,\Sigma_{j-1}^{-1}\,\mathrm{V}_i^{1/2}\right)^{-1}\sum_{i=0}^{I-j}\left(\mathrm{V}_i^{1/2}\,\Sigma_{j-1}^{-1}\mathrm{V}_i^{1/2}\right)E\left[\mathbf{M}_{i,j}\middle|\mathcal{B}_{j-1}^N\right]$$

(b) This follows immediately from (a).
(c) This follows from the independence of the normalized incremental claims $\mathbf{M}_{i,j}=\mathrm{V}_i^{-1}\,\mathbf{X}_{i,j}$ and $\mathbf{M}_{k,l}=\mathrm{V}_k^{-1}\,\mathbf{X}_{k,l}$ for $j \neq l$.
(d) Using (8.46) we obtain

$$\mathrm{Var}\left(\mathbf{M}_{l,j}\right)=\mathrm{V}_l^{-1}\,\mathrm{Var}\left(\mathbf{X}_{l,j}\right)\,\mathrm{V}_l^{-1}=\mathrm{V}_l^{-1/2}\,\Sigma_{j-1}\,\mathrm{V}_l^{-1/2} \tag{8.53}$$

With the independence of the $\mathbf{M}_{l,j}$ this leads to

$$\begin{aligned}\mathrm{Var}\left(\widehat{\mathbf{m}}_j\right)&=\mathrm{A}_j\mathrm{Var}\left(\sum_{l=0}^{I-j}\left(\mathrm{V}_l^{1/2}\Sigma_{j-1}^{-1}\mathrm{V}_l^{1/2}\right)\mathbf{M}_{l,j}\right)\mathrm{A}_j\\&=\mathrm{A}_j\left[\sum_{l=0}^{I-j}\left(\mathrm{V}_l^{1/2}\,\Sigma_{j-1}^{-1}\mathrm{V}_l^{1/2}\right)\mathrm{Var}\left(\mathbf{M}_{l,j}\right)\left(\mathrm{V}_l^{1/2}\,\Sigma_{j-1}^{-1}\,\mathrm{V}_l^{1/2}\right)\right]\mathrm{A}_j\\&=\mathrm{A}_j\left[\sum_{l=0}^{I-j}\mathrm{V}_l^{1/2}\,\Sigma_{j-1}^{-1}\,\mathrm{V}_l^{1/2}\right]\mathrm{A}_j=\mathrm{A}_j\end{aligned}$$

where

$$\mathrm{A}_j=\left(\sum_{l=0}^{I-j}\mathrm{V}_l^{1/2}\,\Sigma_{j-1}^{-1}\,\mathrm{V}_l^{1/2}\right)^{-1} \tag{8.54}$$

(e) Using the independence of $\mathbf{C}_{i,I-i}$ and $\widehat{\mathbf{m}}_l$ for $l > I-i$ and claim (b) we have

$$E\left[\widehat{\mathbf{C}_{i,J}}^{\mathrm{AD}} \middle| \mathbf{C}_{i,I-i}\right] = \mathbf{C}_{i,I-i} + \mathrm{V}_i \sum_{l=I-i+1}^{J} E[\widehat{\mathbf{m}}_l] = \mathbf{C}_{i,I-i} + \mathrm{V}_i \sum_{l=I-i+1}^{J} \mathbf{m}_l$$

(f) This follows immediately from (e). This finishes the proof of the lemma. □

Remarks 8.28

- Observe that Lemma 8.27 (e) shows that we obtain unbiased estimators for the conditionally expected ultimate claims $E\left[\mathbf{C}_{i,J}|\mathcal{D}_I^N\right]$.
- This implies that the estimator for the aggregated ultimate claim of accident year $i \in \{1, \ldots, I\}$

$$\sum_{n=1}^{N} \widehat{C_{i,J}^{(n)}}^{\mathrm{AD}} = \mathbf{1}' \, \widehat{\mathbf{C}_{i,J}}^{\mathrm{AD}}$$

is, given $\mathbf{C}_{i,I-i}$, unbiased for $\sum_{n=1}^{N} E\left[C_{i,J}^{(n)} \middle| \mathbf{C}_{i,I-i}\right]$

The following result is the counterpart of Lemma 8.8 for the multivariate CL method.

LEMMA 8.29 *Under Model Assumptions 8.22, the estimator $\widehat{\mathbf{m}}_j$ is a $\mathcal{B}_j^N$-measurable unbiased estimator for $\mathbf{m}_j$, which minimizes the expected squared loss among all N-dimensional unbiased linear combinations of the unbiased estimators $(\mathbf{M}_{l,j})_{0 \le l \le I-j}$ for $\mathbf{m}_j$, i.e.*

$$\mathrm{E}\left[(\mathbf{m}_j - \widehat{\mathbf{m}}_j)'(\mathbf{m}_j - \widehat{\mathbf{m}}_j)\right]$$

$$= \min_{\mathrm{W}_{l,j} \in \mathbb{R}^{N \times N}} E\left[\left(\mathbf{m}_j - \sum_{l=0}^{I-j} \mathrm{W}_{l,j}\, \mathbf{M}_{l,j}\right)' \left(\mathbf{m}_j - \sum_{l=0}^{I-j} \mathrm{W}_{l,j}\, \mathbf{M}_{l,j}\right)\right]$$

Proof The proof is similar to the proof of Lemma 3.4 (optimality of the age-to-age factor estimates in the univariate CL model), see also Theorem 4.1 in Schmidt (2006b). □

In the following we derive in two steps an estimate for the conditional MSEP of $\sum_{n=1}^{N} \widehat{C_{i,J}^{(n)}}^{\mathrm{AD}} = \mathbf{1}' \, \widehat{\mathbf{C}_{i,J}}^{\mathrm{AD}}$ for single accident years $i \in \{1, \ldots, I\}$:

$$\mathrm{msep}_{\sum_n C_{i,J}^{(n)} | \mathcal{D}_I^N}\left(\sum_{n=1}^{N} \widehat{C_{i,J}^{(n)}}^{\mathrm{AD}}\right)$$

$$= E\left[\left(\sum_{n=1}^{N} \widehat{C_{i,J}^{(n)}}^{\mathrm{AD}} - \sum_{n=1}^{N} C_{i,J}^{(n)}\right)^2 \middle| \mathcal{D}_I^N\right]$$

$$= \mathbf{1}' \, E\left[\left(\widehat{\mathbf{C}_{i,J}}^{\mathrm{AD}} - \mathbf{C}_{i,J}\right)\left(\widehat{\mathbf{C}_{i,J}}^{\mathrm{AD}} - \mathbf{C}_{i,J}\right)' \middle| \mathcal{D}_I^N\right] \mathbf{1}$$

$$= \mathbf{1}' \operatorname{Var}\left(\mathbf{C}_{i,J} \middle| \mathcal{D}_I^N\right) \mathbf{1}$$

$$+ \mathbf{1}' \left(\widehat{\mathbf{C}_{i,J}}^{AD} - E\left[\mathbf{C}_{i,J} \middle| \mathcal{D}_I^N\right]\right) \left(\widehat{\mathbf{C}_{i,J}}^{AD} - E\left[\mathbf{C}_{i,J} \middle| \mathcal{D}_I^N\right]\right)' \mathbf{1} \tag{8.55}$$

and for aggregated accident years

$$\operatorname{msep}_{\sum_{i,n} C_{i,J}^{(n)} | \mathcal{D}_I^N} \left(\sum_{i,n} \widehat{C_{i,J}^{(n)}}^{AD} \right) = E\left[\left(\sum_{i,n} \widehat{C_{i,J}^{(n)}}^{AD} - \sum_{i,n} C_{i,j}^{(n)} \right)^2 \middle| \mathcal{D}_I^N \right]$$

8.3.2 Conditional Process Variance

In this subsection we derive an estimate for the conditional process variance of a single accident year $\mathbf{1}' \operatorname{Var}\left(\mathbf{C}_{i,J} \middle| \mathcal{D}_I^N\right) \mathbf{1}$ which originates from the stochastic movement of the ultimate claim $\mathbf{C}_{i,J}$.

LEMMA 8.30 (process variance for single accident years) *Under Model Assumptions 8.22 the conditional process variance for the ultimate claim $\mathbf{C}_{i,J}$ of accident year $i > 0$, given the observations $\mathcal{D}_I^N$, is given by (see also (8.35))*

$$\mathbf{1}' \operatorname{Var}\left(\mathbf{C}_{i,J} \middle| \mathcal{D}_I^N\right) \mathbf{1} = \mathbf{1}' \,\mathrm{V}_i^{1/2} \sum_{j=I-i+1}^{J} \Sigma_{j-1} \,\mathrm{V}_i^{1/2} \,\mathbf{1} \tag{8.56}$$

Proof Using the independence of the incremental claims $\mathbf{X}_{i,j}$ we have (see also (8.35))

$$\mathbf{1}' \operatorname{Var}\left(\mathbf{C}_{i,J} \middle| \mathcal{D}_I^N\right) \mathbf{1} = \mathbf{1}' \operatorname{Var}\left(\sum_{j=I-i+1}^{J} \mathbf{X}_{i,j} \right) \mathbf{1} = \mathbf{1}' \sum_{j=I-i+1}^{J} \operatorname{Var}\left(\mathbf{X}_{i,j}\right) \mathbf{1}$$

$$= \mathbf{1}' \,\mathrm{V}_i^{1/2} \sum_{j=I-i+1}^{J} \Sigma_{j-1} \,\mathrm{V}_i^{1/2} \,\mathbf{1}$$

for $i > 0$. This completes the proof of the lemma. □

If we replace the parameters Σ_{j-1} in (8.56) by their estimates (cf. Subsection 8.3.5, below), we obtain an estimator of the conditional process variance for a single accident year.

Remark From the proof of (8.56) we obtain the following recursive formula for the conditional process variance of a single accident year

$$\mathbf{1}' \operatorname{Var}\left(\mathbf{C}_{i,J} \middle| \mathcal{D}_I^N\right) \mathbf{1} = \mathbf{1}' \left(\operatorname{Var}\left(\mathbf{C}_{i,J-1} \middle| \mathcal{D}_I^N\right) + \mathrm{V}_i^{1/2} \,\Sigma_{J-1} \,\mathrm{V}_i^{1/2} \right) \mathbf{1}$$

with $\operatorname{Var}\left(\mathbf{C}_{i,I-i} \middle| \mathcal{D}_I^N\right) = \mathbf{0}$.

8.3.3 Conditional Estimation Error for Single Accident Years

Now we estimate the uncertainty in the estimation of the conditional expectation $E\left[\mathbf{C}_{i,J} \middle| \mathcal{D}_I^N\right]$ by the estimator $\widehat{\mathbf{C}_{i,J}}^{AD}$. This means that we derive an estimator for the second term on the right-hand side of (8.55). The conditional estimation error is estimated by its expected value, unconditional resampling, which is in this case equivalent to the conditional resampling because the volumes are deterministic.

$$\mathbf{1}' \, E\Big[\Big(\widehat{\mathbf{C}_{i,J}}^{\mathrm{AD}} - E\left[\mathbf{C}_{i,J}\middle|\mathcal{D}_I^N\right]\Big)\Big(\widehat{\mathbf{C}_{i,J}}^{\mathrm{AD}} - E\left[\mathbf{C}_{i,J}\middle|\mathcal{D}_I^N\right]\Big)'\Big]\mathbf{1}$$

Using the independence of the incremental claims $\mathbf{X}_{i,j}$, the independence of the estimators $\widehat{\mathbf{X}_{i,j}}^{\mathrm{AD}}$ for different development years j, as well as $E\Big[\widehat{\mathbf{X}_{i,j}}^{\mathrm{AD}}\Big] = E\left[\mathbf{X}_{i,j}\right]$ (cf. Lemma 8.27 (c), (f) and (d)), we obtain

$$\begin{aligned}
&\mathbf{1}' \, E\Big[\Big(\widehat{\mathbf{C}_{i,J}}^{\mathrm{AD}} - E\left[\mathbf{C}_{i,J}\middle|\mathcal{D}_I^N\right]\Big)\Big(\widehat{\mathbf{C}_{i,J}}^{\mathrm{AD}} - E\left[\mathbf{C}_{i,J}\middle|\mathcal{D}_I^N\right]\Big)'\Big]\mathbf{1}\\
&\quad = \mathbf{1}' \, \mathrm{Var}\left(\sum_{j=I-i+1}^{J} \widehat{\mathbf{X}_{i,j}}^{\mathrm{AD}}\right) \mathbf{1}\\
&\quad = \mathbf{1}' \, \mathrm{V}_i \sum_{j=I-i+1}^{J} \mathrm{Var}\left(\widehat{\mathbf{m}}_j\right) \mathrm{V}_i \, \mathbf{1}\\
&\quad = \mathbf{1}' \, \mathrm{V}_i \sum_{j=I-i+1}^{J} \left(\sum_{l=0}^{I-j} \mathrm{V}_l^{1/2} \, \Sigma_{j-1}^{-1} \, \mathrm{V}_l^{1/2}\right)^{-1} \mathrm{V}_i \, \mathbf{1}
\end{aligned}$$

On the other hand, using Lemma 8.27 (e), we have

$$\begin{aligned}
&\mathbf{1}' \, E\Big[\Big(\widehat{\mathbf{C}_{i,J}}^{\mathrm{AD}} - E\left[\mathbf{C}_{i,J}\middle|\mathcal{D}_I^N\right]\Big)\Big(\widehat{\mathbf{C}_{i,J}}^{\mathrm{AD}} - E\left[\mathbf{C}_{i,J}\middle|\mathcal{D}_I^N\right]\Big)'\Big]\mathbf{1}\\
&\quad = \mathbf{1}' \, E\left[\mathrm{Var}\left(\widehat{\mathbf{C}_{i,J}}^{\mathrm{AD}}\middle|\mathbf{C}_{i,I-i}\right)\right]\mathbf{1}
\end{aligned}$$

This leads to

$$\mathbf{1}' \, E\left[\mathrm{Var}\left(\widehat{\mathbf{C}_{i,J}}^{\mathrm{AD}}\middle|\mathbf{C}_{i,I-i}\right)\right] \mathbf{1} = \mathbf{1}' \, \mathrm{V}_i \sum_{j=I-i+1}^{J} \left(\sum_{l=0}^{I-j} \mathrm{V}_l^{1/2} \, \Sigma_{j-1}^{-1} \, \mathrm{V}_l^{1/2}\right)^{-1} \mathrm{V}_i \, \mathbf{1} \tag{8.57}$$

Remarks 8.31

- We can rewrite (8.57) in the following recursive form

$$\begin{aligned}
\mathbf{1}' \, \mathrm{E}\left[\mathrm{Var}\left(\widehat{\mathbf{C}_{i,k}}^{\mathrm{AD}}\middle|\mathbf{C}_{i,I-i}\right)\right] \mathbf{1} &= \mathbf{1}' \, E\left[\mathrm{Var}\left(\widehat{\mathbf{C}_{i,k-1}}^{\mathrm{AD}}\middle|\mathbf{C}_{i,I-i}\right)\right] \mathbf{1}\\
&\quad + \mathbf{1}' \, \mathrm{V}_i \left(\sum_{l=0}^{I-k} \mathrm{V}_l^{1/2} \, \Sigma_{k-1}^{-1} \, \mathrm{V}_l^{1/2}\right)^{-1} \mathrm{V}_i \, \mathbf{1}
\end{aligned}$$

  for $k = I-i+1, \ldots, J$ with $\mathrm{Var}\left(\widehat{\mathbf{C}_{i,I-i}}^{\mathrm{AD}}\middle|\mathbf{C}_{i,I-i}\right) = \mathbf{0}$.
- Note that we have derived the estimation error under the assumption that the covariance matrices Σ_j are known. If these are not known, which in general is the case, we obtain an additional parameter estimation term. As in the multivariate CL method we neglect this additional term for the time being.

Replacing the parameters Σ_{j-1} in (8.56) and (8.57) by their estimates (see Subsection 8.3.5), we obtain the following estimator of the conditional MSEP for a single accident year.

ESTIMATOR 8.32 (MSEP for single accident years, conditional version) *Under Model Assumptions 8.22 we have the following estimator for the conditional MSEP of the ultimate claim for a single accident year $i \in \{1, \ldots, I\}$*

$$\widehat{\text{msep}}_{\sum_n C_{i,J}^{(n)}|\mathcal{D}_I^N}\left(\sum_{n=1}^N \widehat{C_{i,J}^{(n)}}^{\text{AD}}\right)$$
$$= \mathbf{1}'\, \text{V}_i^{1/2} \sum_{j=I-i+1}^J \widehat{\Sigma}_{j-1}\, \text{V}_i^{1/2}\, \mathbf{1} + \mathbf{1}'\, \text{V}_i \sum_{j=I-i+1}^J \left(\sum_{l=0}^{I-j} \text{V}_l^{1/2}\, \widehat{\Sigma}_{j-1}^{-1}\, \text{V}_l^{1/2}\right)^{-1} \text{V}_i\, \mathbf{1}$$

Remark For $N = 1$, Estimator 8.32 reduces to the estimator of the conditional MSEP for single accident years in the univariate ALR method

$$\widehat{\text{msep}}_{C_{i,J}|\mathcal{D}_I}\left(\widehat{C_{i,J}}^{\text{AD}}\right) = V_i \sum_{j=I-i+1}^J \widehat{\sigma}_{j-1}^2 + V_i^2 \sum_{j=I-i+1}^J \frac{\widehat{\sigma}_{j-1}^2}{\sum_{l=0}^{I-j} V_l} \tag{8.58}$$

where V_i is a known one-dimensional volume measure for accident year i (cf. Mack 1997, pp. 234–235).

8.3.4 Conditional MSEP, Aggregated Accident Years

In the following we consider the ultimate claims for aggregated accident years. From Model Assumptions 8.22 we know that the ultimate claims $\mathbf{C}_{i,J}$ and $\mathbf{C}_{k,J}$ of two accident years i and k with $1 \leq i < k \leq I$ are independent. However, since the estimators $\widehat{\mathbf{C}_{i,J}}^{\text{AD}}$ and $\widehat{\mathbf{C}_{k,J}}^{\text{AD}}$ use the same observations $\mathcal{D}_I^N$ for estimating the parameters $\mathbf{m}_j$, they are not independent. We consider for $i < k$

$$\text{msep}_{\sum_n C_{i,J}^{(n)}+\sum_n C_{k,J}^{(n)}|\mathcal{D}_I^N}\left(\sum_{n=1}^N \widehat{C_{i,J}^{(n)}}^{\text{AD}} + \sum_{n=1}^N \widehat{C_{k,J}^{(n)}}^{\text{AD}}\right)$$
$$= E\left[\left(\sum_{n=1}^N \left(\widehat{C_{i,J}^{(n)}}^{\text{AD}} + \widehat{C_{k,J}^{(n)}}^{\text{AD}}\right) - \sum_{n=1}^N \left(C_{i,J}^{(n)} + C_{k,J}^{(n)}\right)\right)^2 \middle| \mathcal{D}_I^N\right]$$

the conditional MSEP of two aggregated accident years i and k. As in the corresponding Subsection 8.2.4 for the multivariate CL method, we obtain, for the conditional MSEP of the sum of two accident years, the decomposition into process variance and conditional estimation error

$$\begin{aligned}
&\operatorname{msep}_{\sum_n C_{i,J}^{(n)}+\sum_n C_{k,J}^{(n)}|\mathcal{D}_I^N}\left(\sum_{n=1}^N \widehat{C_{i,J}^{(n)}}^{\mathrm{AD}}+\sum_{n=1}^N \widehat{C_{k,J}^{(n)}}^{\mathrm{AD}}\right)\\
&\quad=\operatorname{msep}_{\sum_n C_{i,J}^{(n)}|\mathcal{D}_I^N}\left(\sum_{n=1}^N \widehat{C_{i,J}^{(n)}}^{\mathrm{AD}}\right)+\operatorname{msep}_{\sum_n C_{k,J}^{(n)}|\mathcal{D}_I^N}\left(\sum_{n=1}^N \widehat{C_{k,J}^{(n)}}^{\mathrm{AD}}\right)\\
&\quad\quad+2\,\mathbf{1}'\left(\widehat{\mathbf{C}_{i,J}}^{\mathrm{AD}}-E\left[\mathbf{C}_{i,J}\middle|\mathcal{D}_I^N\right]\right)\left(\widehat{\mathbf{C}_{k,J}}^{\mathrm{AD}}-E\left[\mathbf{C}_{k,J}\middle|\mathcal{D}_I^N\right]\right)'\,\mathbf{1}
\end{aligned}$$

This shows that we additionally have to derive an estimator for the cross product. We estimate this cross product by its expected value (unconditional approach)

$$\mathbf{1}'\,E\left[\left(\widehat{\mathbf{C}_{i,J}}^{\mathrm{AD}}-E\left[\mathbf{C}_{i,J}\middle|\mathcal{D}_I^N\right]\right)\left(\widehat{\mathbf{C}_{k,J}}^{\mathrm{AD}}-E\left[\mathbf{C}_{k,J}\middle|\mathcal{D}_I^N\right]\right)'\right]\mathbf{1}$$

Again, using the independence of the incremental claims $\mathbf{X}_{i,j}$, the independence of the estimators $\widehat{\mathbf{X}_{i,j}}^{\mathrm{AD}}$ for different development years j, as well as $E\left[\widehat{\mathbf{X}_{i,j}}^{\mathrm{AD}}\right]=E\left[\mathbf{X}_{i,j}\right]$, we have

$$\begin{aligned}
&\mathbf{1}'\,E\left[\left(\widehat{\mathbf{C}_{i,J}}^{\mathrm{AD}}-E\left[\mathbf{C}_{i,J}\middle|\mathcal{D}_I^N\right]\right)\left(\widehat{\mathbf{C}_{k,J}}^{\mathrm{AD}}-E\left[\mathbf{C}_{k,J}\middle|\mathcal{D}_I^N\right]\right)'\right]\mathbf{1}\\
&\quad=\mathbf{1}'\,E\left[\left(\sum_{j=I-i+1}^{J}\left(\widehat{\mathbf{X}_{i,j}}^{\mathrm{AD}}-E\left[\widehat{\mathbf{X}_{i,j}}^{\mathrm{AD}}\right]\right)\right)\left(\sum_{j=I-k+1}^{J}\left(\widehat{\mathbf{X}_{k,j}}^{\mathrm{AD}}-E\left[\widehat{\mathbf{X}_{k,j}}^{\mathrm{AD}}\right]\right)\right)'\right]\mathbf{1}\\
&\quad=\mathbf{1}'\,E\left[\left(\sum_{j=I-i+1}^{J}\left(\widehat{\mathbf{X}_{i,j}}^{\mathrm{AD}}-E\left[\widehat{\mathbf{X}_{i,j}}^{\mathrm{AD}}\right]\right)\right)\left(\sum_{j=I-i+1}^{J}\left(\widehat{\mathbf{X}_{k,j}}^{\mathrm{AD}}-E\left[\widehat{\mathbf{X}_{k,j}}^{\mathrm{AD}}\right]\right)\right)'\right]\mathbf{1}\\
&\quad=\mathbf{1}'\,\mathrm{V}_i\sum_{j=I-i+1}^{J}\operatorname{Var}\left(\widehat{\mathbf{m}}_j\right)\mathrm{V}_k\,\mathbf{1}
\end{aligned}$$

With Lemma 8.27 (d) this leads to

$$\begin{aligned}
&\mathbf{1}'\,E\left[\left(\widehat{\mathbf{C}_{i,J}}^{\mathrm{AD}}-E\left[\mathbf{C}_{i,J}\middle|\mathcal{D}_I^N\right]\right)\left(\widehat{\mathbf{C}_{k,J}}^{\mathrm{AD}}-E\left[\mathbf{C}_{k,J}\middle|\mathcal{D}_I^N\right]\right)'\right]\mathbf{1}\\
&\quad=\mathbf{1}'\,\mathrm{V}_i\sum_{j=I-i+1}^{J}\left(\sum_{l=0}^{I-j}\mathrm{V}_l^{1/2}\,\Sigma_{j-1}^{-1}\,\mathrm{V}_l^{1/2}\right)^{-1}\mathrm{V}_k\,\mathbf{1}
\end{aligned}\tag{8.59}$$

ESTIMATOR 8.33 (MSEP aggregated accident years, conditional version) *Under Model Assumptions 8.22 we have the following estimator for the conditional MSEP of the ultimate claim for aggregated accident years*

$$\begin{aligned}
&\widehat{\operatorname{msep}}_{\sum_i\sum_n C_{i,J}^{(n)}|\mathcal{D}_I^N}\left(\sum_{i=1}^{I}\sum_{n=1}^{N}\widehat{C_{i,J}^{(n)}}^{\mathrm{AD}}\right)=\sum_{i=1}^{I}\widehat{\operatorname{msep}}_{\sum_n C_{i,J}^{(n)}|\mathcal{D}_I^N}\left(\sum_{n=1}^{N}\widehat{C_{i,J}^{(n)}}^{\mathrm{AD}}\right)\\
&\quad+2\sum_{1\le i<k\le I}\mathbf{1}'\,\mathrm{V}_i\sum_{j=I-i+1}^{J}\left(\sum_{l=0}^{I-j}\mathrm{V}_l^{1/2}\,\Sigma_{j-1}^{-1}\,\mathrm{V}_l^{1/2}\right)^{-1}\mathrm{V}_k\,\mathbf{1}
\end{aligned}$$

Remark For $N=1$ Estimator (8.33) reduces to the estimator of the conditional MSEP for aggregated accident years in the univariate ALR method

$$\widehat{\text{msep}}_{\sum_i C_{i,J}|\mathcal{D}_I}\left(\sum_{i=1}^{I}\widehat{C_{i,J}}^{\text{AD}}\right)=\sum_{i=1}^{I}\widehat{\text{msep}}_{C_{i,J}|\mathcal{D}_I}\left(\widehat{C_{i,J}}^{\text{AD}}\right)$$
$$+2\sum_{1\le i<k\le I}V_i\,V_k\sum_{j=I-i+1}^{J}\frac{\widehat{\sigma}_{j-1}^2}{\sum_{l=0}^{I-j}V_l} \tag{8.60}$$

with known one-dimensional volume measure V_i for accident year i (cf. Mack 1997, p. 236).

8.3.5 Parameter Estimation

For the estimation of the reserves and the conditional MSEP we need estimates of the N-dimensional parameters $\mathbf{m}_1,\ldots,\mathbf{m}_J$ and of the $(N\times N)$-dimensional parameters $\Sigma_0,\ldots,\Sigma_{J-1}$.

Estimates of the multivariate incremental loss ratios $\mathbf{m}_j$ are given in (8.48). However, estimator (8.48) is only an implicit estimator of $\mathbf{m}_j$ since it depends on the parameter Σ_{j-1}, which, on the other hand, is estimated by means of $\widehat{\mathbf{m}}_j$. Therefore, as in the multivariate CL method, we propose an iterative estimation of these parameters.

Estimation of $\mathbf{m}_j$ As starting values for the iteration, we define $\widehat{\mathbf{m}}_j^{(0)}$ by (8.51) for $j=1,\ldots,J$. Estimator $\widehat{\mathbf{m}}_j^{(0)}$ is an unbiased estimator for $\mathbf{m}_j$. From $\widehat{\mathbf{m}}_j^{(0)}$ we derive an estimate $\widehat{\Sigma}_{j-1}^{(1)}$ of Σ_{j-1} for $j=1,\ldots,J$ (see estimator (8.62) below). Then this estimate is used to determine $\widehat{\mathbf{m}}_j^{(1)}$ via, $k\ge 1$,

$$\begin{aligned}\widehat{\mathbf{m}}_j^{(k)}&=\left(\widehat{m}_j^{(1)(k)},\ldots,\widehat{m}_j^{(N)(k)}\right)'\\&=\left(\sum_{l=0}^{I-j}\mathrm{V}_l^{1/2}\left(\widehat{\Sigma}_{j-1}^{(k)}\right)^{-1}\mathrm{V}_l^{1/2}\right)^{-1}\sum_{l=0}^{I-j}\left(\mathrm{V}_l^{1/2}\left(\widehat{\Sigma}_{j-1}^{(k)}\right)^{-1}\mathrm{V}_l^{1/2}\right)\mathbf{M}_{l,j}\end{aligned}$$

for $j=1,\ldots,J$. This algorithm is then iterated.

Estimation of Σ_{j-1} The $(N\times N)$-dimensional parameters Σ_{j-1} are estimated iteratively from the data for $j=1,\ldots,J$. A positive semi-definite estimator of the positive definite matrix Σ_{j-1} is given by

$$\widehat{\Sigma}_{j-1}=\frac{1}{I-j}\sum_{i=0}^{I-j}\mathrm{V}_i^{-1/2}\left(\mathbf{X}_{i,j}-\mathrm{V}_i\,\widehat{\mathbf{m}}_j^{(0)}\right)\left(\mathbf{X}_{i,j}-\mathrm{V}_i\,\widehat{\mathbf{m}}_j^{(0)}\right)'\mathrm{V}_i^{-1/2} \tag{8.61}$$

for $j=1,\ldots,J$. If the matrices V_i are all diagonal, the diagonal elements of the random matrix (8.61) are unbiased estimators of the corresponding diagonal elements $\left(\sigma_{j-1}^{(1)}\right)^2,\ldots,\left(\sigma_{j-1}^{(N)}\right)^2$ of Σ_{j-1} (cf. Lemma 8.34 below). However, its non-diagonal elements slightly underestimate the corresponding non-diagonal elements of Σ_{j-1} (cf. Remarks 8.35 below).

This leads to the following iteration for the estimator of Σ_{j-1}:

$$\widehat{\Sigma}_{j-1}^{(k)} = \frac{1}{I-j} \sum_{i=0}^{I-j} \mathrm{V}_i^{-1/2} \left(\mathbf{X}_{i,j} - \mathrm{V}_i\, \widehat{\mathbf{m}}_j^{(k-1)}\right) \left(\mathbf{X}_{i,j} - \mathrm{V}_i\, \widehat{\mathbf{m}}_j^{(k-1)}\right)' \mathrm{V}_i^{-1/2} \tag{8.62}$$

for $j = 1, \ldots, J$ and $k \geq 1$.

LEMMA 8.34 *Under Model Assumptions 8.22 and the additional assumption that the matrices* $\mathrm{V}_0, \ldots, \mathrm{V}_{I-j}$ *are all diagonal, the diagonal elements of estimator* $\widehat{\Sigma}_{j-1}$ *are unbiased estimators of the corresponding diagonal elements of* Σ_{j-1} *for* $j = 1, \ldots, J$.

Proof We denote the nth diagonal element of estimator $\widehat{\Sigma}_{j-1}$ by $\left(\widehat{\sigma}_{j-1}^{(n)}\right)^2$ for $j = 1, \ldots, J$ and $n = 1, \ldots, N$. Since the matrices $\mathrm{V}_0, \ldots, \mathrm{V}_{I-j}$ are all diagonal it holds that

$$\left(\widehat{\sigma}_{j-1}^{(n)}\right)^2 = \frac{1}{I-j} \sum_{i=0}^{I-j} \frac{1}{V_i^{(n,n)}} \left(X_{i,j}^{(n)} - V_i^{(n,n)}\, \widehat{m}_j^{(n)(0)}\right)^2$$

for $j = 1, \ldots, J$ and $n = 1, \ldots, N$. But then the claim follows as in Lemma 3.5. □

Remarks 8.35

- In general, estimator (8.61) is not an unbiased estimator of Σ_{j-1}. However, its lack of unbiasedness is not too important since it has to be inverted and the inverse of an unbiased estimator is generally not unbiased.
- If we have enough data (i.e. $I > J$), we are able to estimate iteratively the parameter Σ_{J-1} by (8.62). Otherwise, we can use the estimates $\widehat{\varphi}_{j-1}^{(n,m)(k)}$ of the elements $\varphi_{j-1}^{(n,m)}$ of Σ_{j-1} for $j \leq J-1$ in iteration $k \geq 1$ (i.e. $\widehat{\varphi}_{j-1}^{(n,m)(k)}$ is an estimate of $\varphi_{j-1}^{(n,m)} = \sigma_{j-1}^{(n)}\, \sigma_{j-1}^{(m)}\, \rho_{j-1}^{(n,m)}$ in iteration $k \geq 1$, cf. (8.47)) to derive estimates $\widehat{\varphi}_{J-1}^{(n,m)(k)}$ of the elements of Σ_{J-1} for all $1 \leq n < m \leq N$. For example, this can be done by extrapolating the usually decreasing series

$$\left|\widehat{\varphi}_0^{(n,m)(k)}\right|, \ldots, \left|\widehat{\varphi}_{J-2}^{(n,m)(k)}\right|$$

by one additional member $\widehat{\varphi}_{J-1}^{(n,m)(k)}$ for $1 \leq n < m \leq N$ and $k \geq 1$.
- Observe, that the $(N \times N)$-dimensional estimate $\widehat{\Sigma}_{j-1}^{(k)}$ is singular when $j \geq I - N + 2$ since, in this case, the dimension of the linear space generated by any realizations of the $(I - j + 1)$ N-dimensional random vectors

$$\mathrm{V}_i^{-1/2} \left(\mathbf{X}_{i,j} - \mathrm{V}_i\, \widehat{\mathbf{m}}_j^{(k-1)}\right) \quad \text{with } i \in \{0, \ldots, I-j\} \tag{8.63}$$

is at most $I - j + 1 \leq I - (I - N + 2) + 1 = N - 1$. Furthermore, the realizations of (8.63) may be linearly dependent for some $j < I - N + 2$, which implies that the corresponding realization of the random matrix $\widehat{\Sigma}_{j-1}^{(k)}$ is singular. Therefore, in practical application it is important to verify whether the estimates $\widehat{\Sigma}_{j-1}^{(k)}$ are invertible or not and to modify those estimates (e.g. by extrapolation as in the example below) that are not invertible.

We close the section with an example.

Example 8.36 (MSEP in the multivariate ALR model)

We illustrate the multivariate ALR method using the same data as in Example 8.21, Tables 8.1 and 8.2. In this example the 2×2 matrices V_i are diagonal and their diagonal elements $V_i^{(1,1)}$ and $V_i^{(2,2)}$ are *a priori* estimates of the ultimate claims in the different accident years i in portfolios A and B, respectively. Table 8.9 shows these *a priori* estimates as well as the corresponding CL estimates $\widehat{C_{i,J}^{(1)}}^{CL}$ and $\widehat{C_{i,J}^{(2)}}^{CL}$ for comparison. We see that *a priori* estimates and CL estimates are close together.

Table 8.9 *A priori* estimates and CL estimates of the ultimate claims

i	Subportfolio A		Subportfolio B	
	$V_i^{(1,1)}$	$\widehat{C_{i,J}^{(1)}}^{CL}$	$V_i^{(2,2)}$	$\widehat{C_{i,J}^{(2)}}^{CL}$
0	510 301	549 589	413 213	391 428
1	632 897	564 740	537 988	483 839
2	658 133	608 104	589 145	540 002
3	723 456	795 248	523 419	486 227
4	709 312	783 593	501 498	508 744
5	845 673	837 088	598 345	552 825
6	904 378	938 861	608 376	639 113
7	1 156 778	1 098 200	698 993	658 410
8	1 214 569	1 154 902	704 129	684 719
9	1 397 123	1 431 409	903 557	845 543
10	1 832 676	1 735 433	947 326	962 734
11	2 156 781	2 065 991	1 134 129	1 169 260
12	2 559 345	2 660 561	1 538 916	1 474 514
13	2 456 991	2 274 941	1 487 234	1 426 060
Total	17 758 413	17 498 658	11 186 268	10 823 418

Since it holds that $I = J = 13$, we do not have sufficient data to derive an estimate of the 2×2 matrix Σ_{12} using (8.62). Therefore, we use the extrapolation

$$\widehat{\varphi}_{12}^{(n,m)} = \min\left\{ \left|\varphi_{10}^{(n,m)}\right|, \frac{\left(\varphi_{11}^{(n,m)}\right)^2}{\left|\varphi_{10}^{(n,m)}\right|} \right\}$$

to derive estimates of its elements $\varphi_{12}^{(n,m)} = \sigma_{12}^{(n)} \sigma_{12}^{(m)} \rho_{12}^{(n,m)}$ for $n, m = 1, 2$ (note $\rho_{12}^{(1,1)} = \rho_{12}^{(2,2)} = 1$). Moreover, since estimator (8.62) would lead to a poorly defined conditioned matrix $\widehat{\Sigma}_{11}$, we have also estimated its elements by

$$\widehat{\varphi}_{11}^{(n,m)} = \min\left\{ \left|\varphi_{9}^{(n,m)}\right|, \frac{\left(\varphi_{10}^{(n,m)}\right)^2}{\left|\varphi_{9}^{(n,m)}\right|} \right\}$$

Table 8.10 shows the estimates for the parameters $\mathbf{m}_j$, $\boldsymbol{\sigma}_j$ and $\rho_j^{(1,2)}$ after three iterations $k = 1, 2, 3$. (see also Table 8.11–8.15.)

Table 8.10 Estimates $\widehat{\mathbf{m}}_j^{(k-1)}$, $\widehat{\boldsymbol{\sigma}}_j^{(k)}$ and $\widehat{\rho}_j^{(1,2)(k)}$ for the parameters $\mathbf{m}_j$, $\boldsymbol{\sigma}_j$ and $\rho_j^{(1,2)}$ in the first three iterations $k=1,2,3$

Portfolio A/B	0	1	2	3	4	5	6	7	8	9	10	11	12	13
$\widehat{\mathbf{m}}_j^{(0)}$		0.19969	0.20638	0.17528	0.12117	0.08466	0.04852	0.02474	0.01403	0.01186	0.00606	0.00428	0.00529	0.00371
		0.32897	0.16129	0.09054	0.05577	0.03166	0.01548	0.00910	0.00006	0.00349	−0.00050	0.00355	−0.00100	−0.00026
$\widehat{\boldsymbol{\sigma}}_j^{(1)}$	31.58	20.03	14.42	18.92	13.64	13.91	5.79	7.15	12.21	6.09	1.84	0.56	0.17	
	27.74	18.19	15.17	16.00	11.74	5.17	4.70	2.05	4.96	1.35	3.00	1.35	0.61	
$\widehat{\rho}_j^{(1,2)(1)}$	−0.02644	0.84865	0.59119	0.37108	0.34004	0.31249	−0.10460	0.75342	0.33212	0.66573	−0.13915	0.14397	0.14895	
$\widehat{\mathbf{m}}_j^{(1)}$		0.19974	0.20640	0.17493	0.12119	0.08452	0.04844	0.02476	0.01441	0.01195	0.00614	0.00428	0.00529	0.00371
		0.32899	0.16172	0.09061	0.05572	0.03170	0.01550	0.00910	0.00017	0.00354	−0.00051	0.00354	−0.00097	−0.00026
$\widehat{\boldsymbol{\sigma}}_j^{(2)}$	31.58	20.03	14.42	18.92	13.64	13.91	5.79	7.15	12.21	6.09	1.84	0.56	0.17	
	27.74	18.20	15.17	16.00	11.74	5.17	4.70	2.05	4.96	1.35	3.00	1.35	0.61	
$\widehat{\rho}_j^{(1,2)(2)}$	−0.02654	0.84893	0.59215	0.37111	0.34034	0.31262	−0.10467	0.75527	0.33235	0.66612	−0.13921	0.14399	0.14894	
$\widehat{\mathbf{m}}_j^{(2)}$		0.19974	0.20640	0.17493	0.12119	0.08452	0.04844	0.02476	0.01441	0.01195	0.00614	0.00428	0.00529	0.00371
		0.32899	0.16172	0.09061	0.05572	0.03170	0.01550	0.00910	0.00017	0.00354	−0.00051	0.00354	−0.00097	−0.00026
$\widehat{\boldsymbol{\sigma}}_j^{(3)}$	31.58	20.03	14.42	18.92	13.64	13.91	5.79	7.16	12.21	6.09	1.84	0.56	0.17	
	27.74	18.20	15.17	16.00	11.74	5.17	4.70	2.05	4.96	1.35	3.00	1.35	0.61	
$\widehat{\rho}_j^{(1,2)(3)}$	−0.02654	0.84893	0.59216	0.37111	0.34034	0.31262	−0.10467	0.75529	0.33235	0.66612	−0.13921	0.14399	0.14894	

Comments

- Table 8.10 contains the resulting parameter estimates in the first three iterations. We observe fast convergence of the two-dimensional estimates $\widehat{\mathbf{m}}_j^{(k-1)}$, $\widehat{\boldsymbol{\sigma}}_j^{(k)}$ and the one-dimensional estimates $\widehat{\rho}_j^{(1,2)(k)}$ $(k=1,2,3)$ in the sense that there are barely any changes in the estimates after three iterations. The first and second coordinate of the estimates $\widehat{\mathbf{m}}_j^{(0)}$ and $\widehat{\boldsymbol{\sigma}}_j^{(1)}$ are the parameter estimates used in the univariate ALR method applied to the individual subportfolios A and B, respectively.
- Except for development years 0, 6 and 10 we observe positive estimates $\widehat{\rho}_j^{(1,2)(k)}$ for the correlation coefficients. The three negative estimates should not be overstated since they are close to zero, this is similar to the multivariate CL case (see Table 8.3).

Table 8.11 Claims reserves in the ALR method

i	Subportfolio A reserves	Subportfolio B reserves	Portfolio reserves			Portfolio reserves overall calc.
			$(k=1)$	$(k=2)$	$(k=3)$	
1	2348	−142	2206	2206	2206	2262
2	5923	−747	5176	5199	5199	5442
3	9608	1193	10 801	10 820	10 820	10 356
4	13 717	893	14 610	14 626	14 626	13 821
5	26 386	3154	29 541	29 656	29 656	28 266
6	40 906	3243	44 149	44 597	44 600	41 604
7	80 946	10 087	91 032	91 565	91 569	84 451
8	143 915	21 058	164 973	165 508	165 512	153 693
9	283 823	55 625	339 448	340 098	340 103	328 700
10	594 362	111 151	705 513	706 181	706 186	659 509
11	1 077 515	235 757	1 313 272	1 314 505	1 314 513	1 246 294
12	1 806 833	568 114	2 374 947	2 379 530	2 379 547	2 325 704
13	2 225 221	1 038 295	3 263 516	3 267 997	3 268 014	3 223 750
Total	6 311 503	2 047 680	8 359 183	8 372 487	8 372 551	8 123 852

Comment

The first two columns of Table 8.11 show for each accident year the reserves for subportfolio A and B estimated by the (univariate) ALR method. Column 'portfolio ($k=1$)' shows the reserves for the whole portfolio consisting of the two subportfolios A and B estimated by the multivariate ALR method. These values are based on the estimates $\widehat{\mathbf{m}}_j^{(0)}$ and therefore coincide with the sum of the reserves for the two individual subportfolios. Columns 'portfolio ($k=2$)' and 'portfolio ($k=3$)' contain the reserves for the whole portfolio based on the estimates $\widehat{\mathbf{m}}_j^{(1)}$ and $\widehat{\mathbf{m}}_j^{(2)}$, respectively. These estimates lead to a total reserve which is about 13 300 higher than the one based on $\widehat{\mathbf{m}}_j^{(0)}$. The last column denoted by 'overall calculation' shows the claims reserve when first aggregating both run-off triangles to one single triangle and then estimating the reserve with the (univariate) ALR method. Since in this approach two run-off triangles with different development patterns were added together (cf. coordinates of estimates $\widehat{\mathbf{m}}_j^{(k)}$ in Table 8.10) this approach is not sensible and leads to a total reserve which is about 235 000–249 000 less than the one obtained by separate calculation of the reserves in subportfolios A and B.

Table 8.12 Estimated conditional process standard deviations

i	Subportfolio A $\widehat{\mathrm{Var}}\left(C_{i,J}^{(1)} \mid \mathcal{D}_I\right)^{1/2}$		Subportfolio B $\widehat{\mathrm{Var}}\left(C_{i,J}^{(2)} \mid \mathcal{D}_I\right)^{1/2}$		Portfolio $\widehat{\mathrm{Var}}\left(\mathbf{C}_{i,J} \mid \mathcal{D}_I^N\right)^{1/2}$ $(k=1)$		$(k=2)$		$(k=3)$		Portfolio overall calculation	
1	133	5,7%	444	−313,1%	483	21,9%	483	21,9%	483	21,9%	2471	109,2%
2	471	7,9%	1134	−151,8%	1289	24,9%	1289	24,8%	1289	24,8%	7865	144,5%
3	1640	17,1%	2418	202,7%	2783	25,8%	2783	25,7%	2783	25,7%	8267	79,8%
4	5381	39,2%	2552	285,9%	6420	43,9%	6421	43,9%	6421	43,9%	9842	71,2%
5	12 669	48,0%	4743	150,3%	14 781	50,0%	14 782	49,8%	14 782	49,8%	16 868	59,7%
6	14 763	36,1%	5043	155,5%	17 227	39,0%	17 233	38,6%	17 234	38,6%	19 046	45,8%
7	17 819	22,0%	6682	66,3%	20 537	22,6%	20 544	22,4%	20 544	22,4%	22 248	26,3%
8	23 840	16,6%	7989	37,9%	27 112	16,4%	27 118	16,4%	27 118	16,4%	28 326	18,4%
9	30 227	10,6%	14 366	25,8%	36 978	10,9%	36 985	10,9%	36 985	10,9%	39 300	12,0%
10	43 067	7,2%	21 419	19,3%	53 848	7,6%	53 854	7,6%	53 854	7,6%	55 208	8,4%
11	51 294	4,8%	28 466	12,1%	67 390	5,1%	67 404	5,1%	67 404	5,1%	71 084	5,7%
12	64 413	3,6%	40 112	7,1%	91 552	3,9%	91 569	3,8%	91 569	3,8%	95 897	4,1%
13	80 204	3,6%	51 955	5,0%	107 567	3,3%	107 580	3,3%	107 580	3,3%	111 084	3,4%
Total	131 444	2,1%	77 162	3,8%	174 596	2,1%	174 624	2,1%	174 624	2,1%	182 644	2,2%

Comment

Table 8.12 shows for each accident year the estimates for the conditional process standard deviations and the corresponding estimates for the variational coefficients. The first two columns contain the values for the individual subportfolios A and B calculated by the univariate ALR method. Column 'portfolio ($k=1$)' shows the estimated conditional process standard deviations for the portfolio consisting of the two subportfolios A and B if we use the multivariate ALR method with parameter estimates $\widehat{\mathbf{m}}_j^{(0)}$, $\widehat{\boldsymbol{\sigma}}_j^{(1)}$ and $\widehat{\rho}_j^{(1,2)(1)}$. By contrast, columns 'portfolio ($k=2$)' and 'portfolio ($k=3$)' contain the values based on the parameter estimates $\widehat{\mathbf{m}}_j^{(k-1)}$, $\widehat{\boldsymbol{\sigma}}_j^{(k)}$ and $\widehat{\rho}_j^{(1,2)(k)}$ with $k=2$ and $k=3$, respectively. The last column shows the results for the unreasonable overall calculation. These estimates are higher than the values calculated by the multivariate method.

Table 8.13 Square roots of estimated conditional estimation errors

i	Subportfolio A $\widehat{\mathrm{Var}}\left(\widehat{C_{i,J}^{(1)}}^{\mathrm{CL}}\middle\vert\mathcal{D}_I\right)^{1/2}$		Subportfolio B $\widehat{\mathrm{Var}}\left(\widehat{C_{i,J}^{(2)}}^{\mathrm{CL}}\middle\vert\mathcal{D}_I\right)^{1/2}$		Portfolio $\widehat{\mathrm{Var}}\left(\widehat{C_{i,J}}^{\mathrm{CL}}\middle\vert\mathcal{D}_I^N\right)^{1/2}$ $(k=1)$		$(k=2)$		$(k=3)$		Portfolio overall calculation	
1	149	6,3%	507	−357,2%	549	24,9%	549	24,9%	549	24,9%	2782	123,0%
2	375	6,3%	985	−131,9%	1103	21,3%	1103	21,2%	1103	21,2%	6461	118,7%
3	1074	11,2%	1538	128,9%	1809	16,7%	1809	16,7%	1809	16,7%	6644	64,2%
4	2916	21,3%	1547	173,3%	3515	24,1%	3515	24,0%	3515	24,0%	7048	51,0%
5	6710	25,4%	2615	82,9%	7810	26,4%	7810	26,3%	7810	26,3%	10 618	37,6%
6	7859	19,2%	2750	84,8%	9087	20,6%	9090	20,4%	9090	20,4%	11 715	28,2%
7	10 490	13,0%	3584	35,5%	11 887	13,1%	11 890	13,0%	11 890	13,0%	14 735	17,4%
8	12 953	9,0%	4000	19,0%	14 510	8,8%	14 513	8,8%	14 513	8,8%	16 871	11,0%
9	16 473	5,8%	6934	12,5%	19 523	5,8%	19 527	5,7%	19 527	5,7%	22 720	6,9%
10	24 583	4,1%	9520	8,6%	28 861	4,1%	28 865	4,1%	28 865	4,1%	31 228	4,7%
11	30 469	2,8%	13 116	5,6%	36 975	2,8%	36 982	2,8%	36 982	2,8%	40 454	3,2%
12	38 904	2,2%	20 318	3,6%	50 834	2,1%	50 843	2,1%	50 843	2,1%	55 743	2,4%
13	42 287	1,9%	23 687	2,3%	54 274	1,7%	54 282	1,7%	54 282	1,7%	58 554	1,8%
Total	172 174	2,7%	74 052	3,6%	207 119	2,5%	207 157	2,5%	207 157	2,5%	246 429	3,0%

Comment

Table 8.13 shows the square roots of estimated conditional estimation errors. The first two columns contain the estimates for the individual subportfolios A and B calculated by the univariate method. Columns 'portfolio ($k=1$)', 'portfolio ($k=2$)' and 'portfolio ($k=3$)' show the estimated conditional estimation errors for the portfolio consisting of the two subportfolios A and B if we use the multivariate ALR method with parameter estimates $\widehat{\mathbf{m}}_j^{(k-1)}$, $\widehat{\boldsymbol{\sigma}}_j^{(k)}$ and $\widehat{\rho}_j^{(1,2)(k)}$. Again, the last column shows the estimates for the overall calculation. These values are high compared to the results obtained by the multivariate method.

Table 8.14 Estimated prediction standard errors

i	Subportfolio A $\widehat{\mathrm{msep}}^{1/2}_{C^{(1)}_{i,J}\mid\mathcal{D}_I}$		Subportfolio B $\widehat{\mathrm{msep}}^{1/2}_{C^{(2)}_{i,J}\mid\mathcal{D}_I}$		Portfolio $\widehat{\mathrm{msep}}^{1/2}_{C_{i,J}\mid\mathcal{D}^N_I}$ $(k=1)$		$(k=2)$		$(k=3)$		Portfolio overall calculation	
1	200	8,5%	674	−475,0%	731	33,1%	731	33,1%	731	33,1%	3721	164,5%
2	602	10,2%	1502	−201,1%	1696	32,8%	1697	32,6%	1697	32,6%	10 179	187,0%
3	1961	20,4%	2866	240,3%	3319	30,7%	3319	30,7%	3319	30,7%	10 606	102,4%
4	6120	44,6%	2984	334,3%	7319	50,1%	7320	50,0%	7320	50,0%	12 105	87,6%
5	14 337	54,3%	5416	171,7%	16 717	56,6%	16 718	56,4%	16 718	56,4%	19 932	70,5%
6	16 724	40,9%	5744	177,1%	19 477	44,1%	19 484	43,7%	19 484	43,7%	22 360	53,7%
7	20 677	25,5%	7583	75,2%	23 729	26,1%	23 737	25,9%	23 737	25,9%	26 685	31,6%
8	27 131	18,9%	8935	42,4%	30 751	18,6%	30 757	18,6%	30 757	18,6%	32 969	21,5%
9	34 424	12,1%	15 952	28,7%	41 815	12,8%	41 823	12,3%	41 823	12,3%	45 395	13,8%
10	49 589	8,3%	23 440	21,1%	61 094	8,7%	61 102	8,7%	61 102	8,7%	63 428	9,6%
11	59 660	5,5%	31 342	13,3%	76 868	5,9%	76 883	5,8%	76 883	5,8%	81 789	6,6%
12	75 250	4,2%	44 965	7,9%	104 718	4,4%	104 737	4,4%	104 738	4,4%	110 922	4,8%
13	90 670	4,1%	57 100	5,5%	120 484	3,7%	120 499	3,7%	120 499	3,7%	125 571	3,9%
Total	216 613	3,4%	106 947	5,2%	270 891	3,2%	270 938	3,2%	270 939	3,2%	306 734	3,8%

Comment

Table 8.14 contains for each accident year the estimated prediction standard errors and the corresponding estimates for the variational coefficients. The first two columns contain the estimates for the individual subportfolios A and B calculated by the univariate ALR method (cf. estimators (8.58) and (8.60)). Columns 'portfolio ($k=1$)', 'portfolio ($k=2$)' and 'portfolio ($k=3$)' show the estimates of the prediction standard errors for the portfolio consisting of the two subportfolios A and B resulting in the multivariate ALR method in the first three iterations. Table 8.14 shows that in this example the prediction standard errors are substantially smaller in the multivariate ALR method than in the multivariate CL method (cf. Example 8.21, Table 8.7).

Table 8.15 Estimated prediction standard errors assuming correlation 1, 0 and −1, respectively

i	Portfolio $\widehat{\mathrm{msep}}^{1/2}_{\mathbf{C}_{i,J}\mid\mathcal{D}_I^N}$	Portfolio $\widehat{\mathrm{msep}}^{1/2}_{\mathbf{C}_{i,J}\mid\mathcal{D}_I^N}$	Portfolio $\widehat{\mathrm{msep}}^{1/2}_{\mathbf{C}_{i,J}\mid\mathcal{D}_I^N}$
	correlation = 1	correlation = 0	correlation = −1
1	874	703	474
2	2104	1618	901
3	4826	3472	905
4	9105	6809	3136
5	19 752	15 325	8921
6	22 469	17 683	10 980
7	28 260	22 024	13 094
8	36 066	28 565	1197
9	50 376	37 940	18 472
10	73 029	54 850	26 149
11	91 003	67 392	28 318
12	120 215	87 661	30 286
13	147 769	107 151	33 570
Total	323 561	241 576	109 666

Comment Table 8.15 shows the results for the estimated prediction standard errors assuming a perfect positive correlation, no correlation and perfect negative correlation between the corresponding individual incremental claims of all columns of the two subportfolios A and B (cf. (8.42)). As in the example of the multivariate CL method (cf. Example 8.21, Tables 8.7 and 8.8) we observe that the estimator in the multivariate ALR method leads to estimates of the prediction standard errors which are between those assuming no correlation and a correlation equal to one for all accident years and all accident years together (cf. estimates 3–5 in Table 8.14). The unreasonable overall calculation yields for the five oldest accident years $i=1$ to $i=5$ results (cf. last column in Table 8.14) which are larger than the corresponding estimates for the portfolio under the assumption of a perfect positive correlation between both run-off triangles. This shows that the overall calculation is not suited to estimate the reserves for several correlated run-off triangles. Moreover, we see that an assumed correlation of 0 or 1 would lead to an estimated prediction standard error that is about 29 500 lower and 52 500 higher, respectively, than the one taking the estimated correlation between the two subportfolios into account, hence we experience substantial differences in higher moments using correlation structures.

8.4 COMBINED MULTIVARIATE CL AND ALR METHOD

In this section we present the combined method that was proposed by Merz and Wüthrich (2008). In this framework the multivariate CL Time Series Model 8.11 and the multivariate ALR Time Series Model 8.22 are combined into one model. The consideration of such a combination of two different models constitutes a first step towards an estimate for the overall MSEP for aggregated subportfolios using different reserving methods for different subportfolios. The use of different reserving methods for different subportfolios is motivated by the fact that, in general, not all subportfolios satisfy the same homogeneity assumptions and/or sometimes we have *a priori* information (e.g. premium, number of contracts, external knowledge from experts, data from similar portfolios, market statistics) for some selected subportfolios which we want to incorporate into our claims reserving analysis.

In these cases the use of the CL method for a subset of subportfolios on the one hand and the use of the ALR method for the complementary subset on the other may be a reasonable approach. From this point of view it is interesting to note that the CL method and the ALR method are very different in some aspects and therefore exploit differing features of the data belonging to the individual subportfolios:

1. The CL method is based on cumulative claims whereas the ALR method is applied to incremental claims (i.e. the ALR method allows modelling negative incremental claims and is therefore also suitable for the use of incurred data, which exhibits negative incremental if claims are overestimated).
2. Unlike the ALR method, the CL method regresses on past observations in the upper triangle and does not use any expert knowledge or existing prior information.
3. The ALR method is more robust against outliers in the observations than the CL method.

8.4.1 Combined CL and ALR Method: the Model

In the following we assume w.l.o.g. that we use the multivariate CL method for the first K ($K \leq N$) run-off triangles $n=1, \ldots, K$ and the multivariate ALR method for the remaining $N-K$ run-off triangles $n=K+1, \ldots, N$. This means that we have to distinguish between cumulative and incremental claims belonging to run-off triangles for which we use the multivariate CL method and the multivariate ALR method, respectively. Therefore, we introduce a more specific notation. In the following we denote by

$$\mathbf{C}_{i,j}^{\mathrm{CL}} = \left(C_{i,j}^{(1)}, \ldots, C_{i,j}^{(K)}\right)'$$

$$\mathbf{X}_{i,j}^{\mathrm{CL}} = \left(X_{i,j}^{(1)}, \ldots, X_{i,j}^{(K)}\right)'$$

$$\mathbf{F}_{i,j}^{\mathrm{CL}} = \left(C_{i,j}^{(1)}/C_{i,j-1}^{(1)}, \ldots, C_{i,j}^{(K)}/C_{i,j-1}^{(K)}\right)'$$

and

$$\mathbf{C}_{i,j}^{\mathrm{AD}} = \left(C_{i,j}^{(K+1)}, \ldots, C_{i,j}^{(N)}\right)'$$

$$\mathbf{X}_{i,j}^{\mathrm{AD}} = \left(X_{i,j}^{(K+1)}, \ldots, X_{i,j}^{(N)}\right)'$$

for all $i \in \{0, \ldots, I\}$ and $j \in \{0, \ldots, J\}$ the cumulative/incremental claims belonging to run-off triangles for which we use the multivariate CL method and the multivariate ALR method, respectively. In particular, this means that the cumulative/incremental claims for accident year i and development year j of the whole portfolio are given by

$$\mathbf{C}_{i,j} = \begin{pmatrix} \mathbf{C}_{i,j}^{\mathrm{CL}} \\ \mathbf{C}_{i,j}^{\mathrm{AD}} \end{pmatrix} \quad \text{and} \quad \mathbf{X}_{i,j} = \begin{pmatrix} \mathbf{X}_{i,j}^{\mathrm{CL}} \\ \mathbf{X}_{i,j}^{\mathrm{AD}} \end{pmatrix}$$

Moreover, we define

$$\mathcal{B}_k^K = \left\{ \mathbf{C}_{i,j}^{\mathrm{CL}};\ i+j \le I \text{ and } 0 \le j \le k \right\}$$

for $k \in \{0, \ldots, J\}$. This set consists of all K-dimensional random variables of cumulative claims up to development year k which are observed at time I in the first K run-off triangles (cf. (8.1)).

The following multivariate time series model is a combination of the multivariate CL Time Series Model 8.11 and the multivariate ALR Time Series Model 8.22.

Model Assumptions 8.37 (combined CL and ALR time series model)

- Incremental claims $\mathbf{X}_{i,j}$ of different accident years i are independent.
- There are constants $\mathbf{f}_j = \left(f_j^{(1)}, \ldots, f_j^{(K)}\right)'$ and $\boldsymbol{\sigma}_j^{\mathrm{CL}} = \left(\sigma_j^{(1)}, \ldots, \sigma_j^{(K)}\right)'$ with $f_j^{(k)} > 0$, $\sigma_j^{(k)} > 0$ and variables $\boldsymbol{\varepsilon}_{i,j+1}^{\mathrm{CL}} = \left(\varepsilon_{i,j+1}^{(1)}, \ldots, \varepsilon_{i,j+1}^{(K)}\right)'$, such that for all $i \in \{0, \ldots, I\}$ and $j \in \{0, \ldots, J-1\}$ we have

$$\mathbf{C}_{i,j+1}^{\mathrm{CL}} = \mathrm{D}(\mathbf{f}_j)\ \mathbf{C}_{i,j}^{\mathrm{CL}} + \mathrm{D}\left(\mathbf{C}_{i,j}^{\mathrm{CL}}\right)^{1/2}\ \mathrm{D}\left(\boldsymbol{\varepsilon}_{i,j+1}^{\mathrm{CL}}\right)\ \boldsymbol{\sigma}_j^{\mathrm{CL}} \tag{8.64}$$

- There are constants $\mathbf{m}_j = \left(m_j^{(1)}, \ldots, m_j^{(N-K)}\right)'$ and $\boldsymbol{\sigma}_{j-1}^{\mathrm{AD}} = \left(\sigma_{j-1}^{(K+1)}, \ldots, \sigma_{j-1}^{(\mathrm{N})}\right)'$ with $\sigma_{j-1}^{(\mathrm{n})} > 0$ and random variables $\boldsymbol{\varepsilon}_{i,j}^{\mathrm{AD}} = \left(\varepsilon_{i,j}^{(K+1)}, \ldots, \varepsilon_{i,j}^{(\mathrm{N})}\right)'$, such that for all $i \in \{0, \ldots, I\}$ and $j \in \{1, \ldots, J\}$ we have

$$\mathbf{X}_{i,j}^{\mathrm{AD}} = \mathrm{V}_i\ \mathbf{m}_j + \mathrm{V}_i^{1/2}\ \mathrm{D}\left(\boldsymbol{\varepsilon}_{i,j}^{\mathrm{AD}}\right)\ \boldsymbol{\sigma}_{j-1}^{\mathrm{AD}} \tag{8.65}$$

  where $\mathrm{V}_0, \ldots, \mathrm{V}_I$ are deterministic positive definite symmetric $(N-K) \times (N-K)$-matrices.
- The random variables

$$\boldsymbol{\varepsilon}_{\mathrm{i,j+1}} = \begin{pmatrix} \boldsymbol{\varepsilon}_{i,j+1}^{\mathrm{CL}} \\ \boldsymbol{\varepsilon}_{i,j+1}^{\mathrm{AD}} \end{pmatrix} \quad \text{and} \quad \boldsymbol{\varepsilon}_{\mathrm{k},l+1} = \begin{pmatrix} \boldsymbol{\varepsilon}_{\mathrm{k},l+1}^{\mathrm{CL}} \\ \boldsymbol{\varepsilon}_{\mathrm{k},l+1}^{\mathrm{AD}} \end{pmatrix}$$

  are independent for $i \neq k$ or $j \neq l$, with $E\left[\boldsymbol{\varepsilon}_{i,j+1}\right] = \mathbf{0}$ and positive definite

$$\mathrm{Cov}\left(\boldsymbol{\varepsilon}_{i,j+1}, \boldsymbol{\varepsilon}_{i,j+1}\right) = E\left[\boldsymbol{\varepsilon}_{i,j+1}\ \boldsymbol{\varepsilon}_{i,j+1}'\right] = \begin{pmatrix} 1 & \rho_j^{(1,2)} & \cdots & \rho_j^{(1,N)} \\ \rho_j^{(2,1)} & 1 & \cdots & \rho_j^{(2,N)} \\ \vdots & \vdots & \ddots & \vdots \\ \rho_j^{(N,1)} & \rho_j^{(N,2)} & \cdots & 1 \end{pmatrix}$$

  for fixed $\rho_j^{(n,m)} \in (-1, 1)$ for $n \neq m$. □

We use the following notation:

$$\boldsymbol{\sigma}_j = \begin{pmatrix} \boldsymbol{\sigma}_j^{\mathrm{CL}} \\ \boldsymbol{\sigma}_j^{\mathrm{AD}} \end{pmatrix}$$

$$\Sigma_j = E\left[\mathrm{D}(\boldsymbol{\varepsilon}_{i,j+1}) \cdot \boldsymbol{\sigma}_j \cdot \boldsymbol{\sigma}_j' \cdot \mathrm{D}(\boldsymbol{\varepsilon}_{i,j+1})\right]$$

$$\Sigma_j^{(\mathrm{C})} = E\left[\mathrm{D}(\boldsymbol{\varepsilon}_{i,j+1}^{\mathrm{CL}}) \cdot \boldsymbol{\sigma}_j^{\mathrm{CL}} \cdot (\boldsymbol{\sigma}_j^{\mathrm{CL}})' \cdot \mathrm{D}(\boldsymbol{\varepsilon}_{i,j+1}^{\mathrm{CL}})\right]$$

$$\Sigma_j^{(\mathrm{A})} = E\left[\mathrm{D}(\boldsymbol{\varepsilon}_{i,j+1}^{\mathrm{AD}}) \cdot \boldsymbol{\sigma}_j^{\mathrm{AD}} \cdot (\boldsymbol{\sigma}_j^{\mathrm{AD}})' \cdot \mathrm{D}(\boldsymbol{\varepsilon}_{i,j+1}^{\mathrm{AD}})\right]$$

$$\Sigma_j^{(\mathrm{C,A})} = E\left[\mathrm{D}(\boldsymbol{\varepsilon}_{i,j+1}^{\mathrm{CL}}) \cdot \boldsymbol{\sigma}_j^{\mathrm{CL}} \cdot (\boldsymbol{\sigma}_j^{\mathrm{AD}})' \cdot \mathrm{D}(\boldsymbol{\varepsilon}_{i,j+1}^{\mathrm{AD}})\right]$$

$$\Sigma_j^{(\mathrm{A,C})} = E\left[\mathrm{D}(\boldsymbol{\varepsilon}_{i,j+1}^{\mathrm{AD}}) \cdot \boldsymbol{\sigma}_j^{\mathrm{AD}} \cdot (\boldsymbol{\sigma}_j^{\mathrm{CL}})' \cdot \mathrm{D}(\boldsymbol{\varepsilon}_{i,j+1}^{\mathrm{CL}})\right] = \left(\Sigma_j^{(\mathrm{C,A})}\right)' \tag{8.66}$$

Thus, we have

$$\Sigma_j = \mathrm{D}(\boldsymbol{\sigma}_j)\ \mathrm{Cov}(\boldsymbol{\varepsilon}_{i,j+1}, \boldsymbol{\varepsilon}_{i,j+1})\ \mathrm{D}(\boldsymbol{\sigma}_j)$$

$$= \begin{pmatrix} (\sigma_j^{(1)})^2 & \sigma_j^{(1)}\sigma_j^{(2)}\rho_j^{(1,2)} & \cdots & \sigma_j^{(1)}\sigma_j^{(N)}\rho_j^{(1,N)} \\ \sigma_j^{(2)}\sigma_j^{(1)}\rho_j^{(2,1)} & (\sigma_j^{(2)})^2 & \cdots & \sigma_j^{(2)}\sigma_j^{(N)}\rho_j^{(2,N)} \\ \vdots & \vdots & \ddots & \vdots \\ \sigma_j^{(\mathrm{N})}\sigma_j^{(1)}\rho_j^{(N,1)} & \sigma_j^{(\mathrm{N})}\sigma_j^{(2)}\rho_j^{(N,2)} & \cdots & (\sigma_j^{(\mathrm{N})})^2 \end{pmatrix}$$

$$= \begin{pmatrix} \Sigma_j^{(\mathrm{C})} & \Sigma_j^{(\mathrm{C,A})} \\ \Sigma_j^{(\mathrm{A,C})} & \Sigma_j^{(\mathrm{A})} \end{pmatrix}$$

Moreover, we define the K-dimensional and $(N-K)$-dimensional column vector consisting of 1's, $\mathbf{1}_K \in \mathbb{R}^K$ and $\mathbf{1}_{N-K} \in \mathbb{R}^{N-K}$, respectively, such that the N-dimensional column vector consisting of 1's is given by $\mathbf{1} = (\mathbf{1}_K', \mathbf{1}_{N-K}')'$.

Remarks 8.38

- The combined CL and ALR Time Series Model 8.37 is suitable for run-off portfolios of N correlated subportfolios in which the first K subportfolios satisfy the homogeneity assumptions of the (multivariate) CL method (cf. Subsection 8.2.3), and the other $N-K$ subportfolios satisfy the homogeneity assumptions of the (multivariate) ALR method (cf. Subsection 8.3.1).
- Under Model Assumptions 8.37 the properties of cumulative claims $\left(\mathbf{C}_{i,j}^{\mathrm{CL}}\right)_{i,j}$ and incremental claims $\left(\mathbf{X}_{i,j}^{\mathrm{AD}}\right)_{i,j}$ are consistent with the assumptions of the multivariate CL Time Series Model 8.11 and the multivariate ALR Time Series Model 8.22, respectively.
- Analogous to the pure multivariate CL and ALR time series model in Subsection 8.2.3 and 8.3.1, respectively, we restrict any assumptions regarding the correlation between the N subportfolios to each of the corresponding development years $j = 1, \ldots, J$ in the N run-off triangles. Matrix $\Sigma_{j-1}^{(\mathrm{C})}$ reflects the correlation structure between the cumulative claims of development year j in the first K subportfolios (i.e. $\Sigma_{j-1}^{(\mathrm{C})}$ corresponds to (8.18))

and matrix $\Sigma_{j-1}^{(A)}$ the correlation structure between the incremental claims of development year j in the last $N-K$ subportfolios (i.e. $\Sigma_{j-1}^{(A)}$ corresponds to (8.47)). The matrices $\Sigma_{j-1}^{(C,A)}$ and $\Sigma_{j-1}^{(A,C)}$ reflect the the correlation structure between the cumulative claims of development year j in the first K subportfolios and the incremental claims of development year j in the last $N-K$ subportfolios.

- For $K=N$ and $K=0$ the model assumptions of the combined Model 8.37 reduce to the model assumptions of the multivariate CL Time Series Model 8.11 and the multivariate ALR Time Series Model 8.22, respectively.

In the following we estimate the cumulative claims $\mathbf{C}_{i,j}^{CL}$ of the first K run-off triangles and the cumulative claims $\mathbf{C}_{i,j}^{AD}$ of the last $N-K$ run-off triangles for $i+j>I$ by the multivariate CL estimators

$$\widehat{\mathbf{C}_{i,j}}^{CL} = \left(\widehat{C_{i,j}^{(1)}}^{CL}, \ldots, \widehat{C_{i,j}^{(K)}}^{CL}\right)' = \widehat{E}\left[\mathbf{C}_{i,j}^{CL} \middle| \mathcal{D}_I^N\right] = \prod_{l=I-i}^{j-1} \mathrm{D}(\widehat{\mathbf{f}}_l)\, \mathbf{C}_{i,I-i}^{CL} \tag{8.67}$$

and the multivariate ALR estimators

$$\widehat{\mathbf{C}_{i,j}}^{AD} = \left(\widehat{C_{i,j}^{(K+1)}}^{AD}, \ldots, \widehat{C_{i,j}^{(N)}}^{AD}\right)'$$

$$= \widehat{E}\left[\mathbf{C}_{i,j}^{AD} \middle| \mathcal{D}_I^N\right] = \mathbf{C}_{i,I-i}^{AD} + \mathrm{V}_i \sum_{l=I-i+1}^{j} \widehat{\mathbf{m}}_l \tag{8.68}$$

respectively (cf. Estimators 8.4 and 8.25). This means that we predict the N-dimensional ultimate claim $\mathbf{C}_{i,J}$ by $\widehat{\mathbf{C}_{i,J}} = \left((\widehat{\mathbf{C}_{i,J}}^{CL})', (\widehat{\mathbf{C}_{i,J}}^{AD})'\right)'$.

ESTIMATOR 8.39 (combined CL and ALR estimator) *The combined CL and ALR estimator for $E\left[\mathbf{C}_{i,j} \middle| \mathcal{D}_I^N\right]$ is for $i+j>I$ given by*

$$\widehat{\mathbf{C}_{i,j}} = \left(\widehat{C_{i,j}^{(1)}}^{CL}, \ldots, \widehat{C_{i,j}^{(K)}}^{CL}, \widehat{C_{i,j}^{(K+1)}}^{AD}, \ldots, \widehat{C_{i,j}^{(N)}}^{AD}\right)' = \widehat{E}\left[\mathbf{C}_{i,j} \middle| \mathcal{D}_I^N\right]$$

$$= \begin{pmatrix} \prod_{l=I-i}^{j-1} \mathrm{D}(\widehat{\mathbf{f}}_l)\, \mathbf{C}_{i,I-i}^{CL} \\ \\ \mathbf{C}_{i,I-i}^{AD} + \mathrm{V}_i \sum_{l=I-i+1}^{j} \widehat{\mathbf{m}}_l \end{pmatrix}$$

Thereby, the estimates of the K-dimensional age-to-age factors $\mathbf{f}_j$ and the estimates of the $(N-K)$-dimensional incremental loss ratios $\mathbf{m}_j$ are given by

$$\widehat{\mathbf{f}}_j = \left(\widehat{f}_j^{(1)}, \ldots, \widehat{f}_j^{(K)}\right)' = \left(\sum_{i=0}^{I-j-1} \mathrm{D}(\mathbf{C}_{i,j}^{CL})^{1/2} \left(\Sigma_j^{(C)}\right)^{-1} \mathrm{D}(\mathbf{C}_{i,j}^{CL})^{1/2}\right)^{-1}$$

$$\times \sum_{i=0}^{I-j-1} \mathrm{D}(\mathbf{C}_{i,j}^{CL})^{1/2} \left(\Sigma_j^{(C)}\right)^{-1} \mathrm{D}(\mathbf{C}_{i,j}^{CL})^{-1/2}\, \mathbf{C}_{i,j+1}^{CL} \tag{8.69}$$

for $j=0,\ldots,J-1$, and

$$\widehat{\mathbf{m}}_j=\left(\widehat{m}_j^{(1)},\ldots,\widehat{m}_j^{(N-K)}\right)'$$
$$=\left(\sum_{i=0}^{I-j}\mathbf{V}_i^{1/2}\left(\Sigma_{j-1}^{(A)}\right)^{-1}\mathbf{V}_i^{1/2}\right)^{-1}\sum_{i=0}^{I-j}\mathbf{V}_i^{1/2}\left(\Sigma_{j-1}^{(A)}\right)^{-1}\mathbf{V}_i^{-1/2}\,\mathbf{X}_{i,j}^{\mathrm{AD}} \tag{8.70}$$

for $j=1,\ldots,J$, respectively (cf. (8.4) and (8.48)).

LEMMA 8.40 *Under Model Assumptions 8.37 we have*

(a) *given $\mathbf{C}_{i,I-i}$, the estimator $\widehat{\mathbf{C}_{i,J}}$ is an unbiased estimator for $E\left[\mathbf{C}_{i,J}|\mathcal{D}_I^N\right]=E\left[\mathbf{C}_{i,J}|\mathbf{C}_{i,I-i}\right]$,*
(b) *$\widehat{\mathbf{C}_{i,J}}$ is (unconditionally) unbiased for $E[\mathbf{C}_{i,J}]$.*

Proof (a) This follows immediately from Lemma 8.6(d) and Lemma 8.27(e).
(b) This is a direct consequence of(a). □

Remarks 8.41

- Note that Lemma 8.40(a) shows that we have unbiased estimators of the conditionally expected ultimate claims $E\left[\mathbf{C}_{i,J}|\mathcal{D}_I^N\right]$.
- Lemma 8.40(a) implies that the estimator of the aggregated ultimate claim

$$\sum_{n=1}^{K}\widehat{C_{i,J}^{(n)}}^{\mathrm{CL}}+\sum_{n=K+1}^{N}\widehat{C_{i,J}^{(n)}}^{\mathrm{AD}}=\mathbf{1}'\,\widehat{\mathbf{C}_{i,J}}=\mathbf{1}_K'\,\widehat{\mathbf{C}_{i,J}}^{\mathrm{CL}}+\mathbf{1}_{N-K}'\,\widehat{\mathbf{C}_{i,J}}^{\mathrm{AD}} \tag{8.71}$$

  is, given $\mathbf{C}_{i,I-i}$, an unbiased estimator for $\sum_{n=1}^{N}E\left[C_{i,J}^{(n)}\middle|\mathbf{C}_{i,I-i}\right]$.
- Note that the parameters for the CL method are estimated independently from the observations belonging to the ALR method and vice versa. That is, here we could even go one step beyond and learn from ALR method observations for CL parameters, and vice versa. We omit these derivations since formulas get more involved and neglect the fact that one may even improve parameter estimators. We also note that such an improvement often has only a marginal influence on the overall claims reserves and the corresponding MSEP (this has been seen in the multivariate Examples 8.21 and 8.36). Our goal here is to give an estimate for the overall MSEP for the present parameter estimators (8.69) and (8.70).

In the following subsections we derive an estimate for the conditional MSEP of estimator (8.71).

$$\mathrm{msep}_{\sum_{n=1}^{N}C_{i,J}^{(n)}|\mathcal{D}_I^N}\left(\sum_{n=1}^{K}\widehat{C_{i,J}^{(n)}}^{\mathrm{CL}}+\sum_{n=K+1}^{N}\widehat{C_{i,J}^{(n)}}^{\mathrm{AD}}\right)$$
$$=\mathrm{msep}_{\sum_{n=1}^{K}C_{i,J}^{(n)}|\mathcal{D}_I^N}\left(\sum_{n=1}^{K}\widehat{C_{i,J}^{(n)}}^{\mathrm{CL}}\right)+\mathrm{msep}_{\sum_{n=K+1}^{N}C_{i,J}^{(n)}|\mathcal{D}_I^N}\left(\sum_{n=K+1}^{N}\widehat{C_{i,J}^{(n)}}^{AD}\right)$$

$$+2\,E\left[\left(\sum_{n=1}^{K}\widehat{C_{i,J}^{(n)}}^{\text{CL}}-\sum_{n=1}^{K}C_{i,J}^{(n)}\right)\left(\sum_{n=K+1}^{N}\widehat{C_{i,J}^{(n)}}^{\text{AD}}-\sum_{n=K+1}^{N}C_{i,J}^{(n)}\right)\middle|\,\mathcal{D}_I^N\right] \tag{8.72}$$

The first two terms on the right-hand side of (8.72) are the conditional MSEP for single accident years $i \in \{1, \ldots, I\}$ if we use the multivariate CL method for the first K run-off triangles (numbered by $n = 1, \ldots, K$) and the multivariate ALR method for the last $N - K$ run-off triangles (numbered by $n = K + 1, \ldots, N$), respectively. Estimators for these two conditional MSEP are given by Estimators 8.15 and 8.32, respectively.

Moreover, now we have to estimate the cross product terms between the CL estimators and the ALR estimators:

$$\begin{aligned}
&E\left[\left(\sum_{n=1}^{K}\widehat{C_{i,J}^{(n)}}^{\text{CL}}-\sum_{n=1}^{K}C_{i,J}^{(n)}\right)\left(\sum_{n=K+1}^{N}\widehat{C_{i,J}^{(n)}}^{\text{AD}}-\sum_{n=K+1}^{N}C_{i,J}^{(n)}\right)\middle|\,\mathcal{D}_I^N\right]\\
&\quad=\mathbf{1}_K'\ \text{Cov}\left(\mathbf{C}_{i,J}^{\text{CL}},\mathbf{C}_{i,J}^{\text{AD}}\middle|\,\mathcal{D}_I^N\right)\ \mathbf{1}_{N-K}\\
&\qquad+\mathbf{1}_K'\left(\widehat{\mathbf{C}_{i,J}}^{\text{CL}}-E\left[\mathbf{C}_{i,J}^{\text{CL}}\middle|\,\mathcal{D}_I^N\right]\right)\left(\widehat{\mathbf{C}_{i,J}}^{\text{AD}}-E\left[\mathbf{C}_{i,J}^{\text{AD}}\middle|\,\mathcal{D}_I^N\right]\right)'\ \mathbf{1}_{N-K}
\end{aligned} \tag{8.73}$$

The first term on the right-hand side of (8.73) originates from the part of the stochastic movement of the ultimate claim $\mathbf{C}_{i,J} = \left(\mathbf{C}_{i,J}^{\text{CL}\prime}, \mathbf{C}_{i,J}^{\text{AD}\prime}\right)'$ which is caused by the fact that $\mathbf{C}_{i,J}^{\text{CL}}$ and $\mathbf{C}_{i,J}^{\text{AD}}$ are correlated. The second term originates from the fact that we have to estimate the conditionally expected ultimate claims $E\left[\mathbf{C}_{i,J}^{\text{CL}}\middle|\,\mathcal{D}_I^N\right]$ and $E\left[\mathbf{C}_{i,J}^{\text{AD}}\middle|\,\mathcal{D}_I^N\right]$ by the estimators $\widehat{\mathbf{C}_{i,J}}^{\text{CL}}$ and $\widehat{\mathbf{C}_{i,J}}^{\text{AD}}$, respectively. Moreover, their estimation errors may also be correlated. Therefore, in the following we refer to both these terms as (conditional) cross process variance and (conditional) cross estimation error for single accident years, respectively.

8.4.2 Conditional Cross Process Variance

In this subsection we derive an estimate of the conditional cross process variance. We obtain the following result:

LEMMA 8.42 (Cross process variance for single accident years) *Under Model Assumptions 8.37 the conditional cross process variance for the ultimate claim* $\mathbf{C}_{i,J} = \left(\mathbf{C}_{i,J}^{\text{CL}\prime}, \mathbf{C}_{i,J}^{\text{AD}\prime}\right)'$ *of accident year* $i > 0$*, given the observations* $\mathcal{D}_I^N$*, is given by*

$$\mathbf{1}_K'\ \text{Cov}\left(\mathbf{C}_{i,J}^{\text{CL}},\mathbf{C}_{i,J}^{\text{AD}}\middle|\,\mathcal{D}_I^N\right)\ \mathbf{1}_{N-K}=\mathbf{1}_K'\sum_{j=I-i+1}^{J}\prod_{l=j}^{J-1}\text{D}(\mathbf{f}_l)\ \Sigma_{i,j-1}^{\mathbf{CA}}\ \mathbf{1}_{N-K} \tag{8.74}$$

where

$$\Sigma_{i,j-1}^{\mathbf{CA}}=E\left[\text{D}\left(\mathbf{C}_{i,j-1}^{\text{CL}}\right)^{1/2}\ \Sigma_{j-1}^{(\text{C,A})}\middle|\,\mathbf{C}_{i,I-i}\right]\ \text{V}_i^{1/2} \tag{8.75}$$

Proof By induction we prove that

$$\text{Cov}\left(\mathbf{C}_{i,k}^{\text{CL}}, \mathbf{X}_{i,j}^{\text{AD}} \middle| \mathbf{C}_{i,I-i}\right) = \prod_{l=j}^{k-1} \text{D}(\mathbf{f}_l)\ \boldsymbol{\Sigma}_{i,j-1}^{\text{CA}} \tag{8.76}$$

where $\boldsymbol{\Sigma}_{i,j-1}^{\text{CA}}$ is defined by (8.75) for all $k \geq j \geq I-i+1$ and $i = 1, \ldots, I$.

(a) Assume that $k = j$. Then, using (8.66), we have

$$\begin{aligned}
&\text{Cov}\left(\mathbf{C}_{i,j}^{\text{CL}}, \mathbf{X}_{i,j}^{\text{AD}} \middle| \mathbf{C}_{i,I-i}\right) \\
&= \text{Cov}\left(\mathbf{C}_{i,j}^{\text{CL}}, \text{V}_i^{1/2}\ \text{D}(\boldsymbol{\varepsilon}_{i,j}^{\text{AD}})\ \boldsymbol{\sigma}_{j-1}^{\text{AD}} \middle| \mathbf{C}_{i,I-i}\right) \\
&= E\left[\text{D}(\mathbf{C}_{i,j-1}^{\text{CL}})^{1/2}\ \text{D}(\boldsymbol{\varepsilon}_{i,j}^{\text{CL}})\ \boldsymbol{\sigma}_{j-1}^{\text{CL}}\ \left(\text{V}_i^{1/2}\ \text{D}(\boldsymbol{\varepsilon}_{i,j}^{\text{AD}})\ \boldsymbol{\sigma}_{j-1}^{\text{AD}}\right)' \middle| \mathbf{C}_{i,I-i}\right] \\
&= E\left[\text{D}(\mathbf{C}_{i,j-1}^{\text{CL}})^{1/2}\ E\left[\text{D}(\boldsymbol{\varepsilon}_{i,j}^{\text{CL}})\ \boldsymbol{\sigma}_{j-1}^{\text{CL}}\ \left(\text{V}_i^{1/2}\ \text{D}(\boldsymbol{\varepsilon}_{i,j}^{\text{AD}})\ \boldsymbol{\sigma}_{j-1}^{\text{AD}}\right)' \middle| \mathbf{C}_{i,j-1}\right] \middle| \mathbf{C}_{i,I-i}\right] \\
&= E\left[\text{D}(\mathbf{C}_{i,j-1}^{\text{CL}})^{1/2}\ \boldsymbol{\Sigma}_{j-1}^{(\text{C,A})} \middle| \mathbf{C}_{i,I-i}\right]\ \text{V}_i^{1/2} = \boldsymbol{\Sigma}_{i,j-1}^{\text{CA}}
\end{aligned}$$

This completes the proof for $k = j$.

(b) Induction step. Assume that the claim is true for $k \geq j$. We proof that it is also true for $k+1$. Using the induction step, we have conditional on $\mathbf{C}_{i,l}$, $l \leq k$, in the first step

$$\text{Cov}\left(\mathbf{C}_{i,k+1}^{\text{CL}}, \mathbf{X}_{i,j}^{\text{AD}} \middle| \mathbf{C}_{i,I-i}\right) = \text{D}(\mathbf{f}_k)\text{Cov}\left(\mathbf{C}_{i,k}^{\text{CL}}, \mathbf{X}_{i,j}^{\text{AD}} \middle| \mathbf{C}_{i,I-i}\right) + \mathbf{0} = \prod_{l=j}^{k} \text{D}(\mathbf{f}_l)\boldsymbol{\Sigma}_{i,j-1}^{\text{CA}}$$

This finishes the proof of claim (8.76). Furthermore, using the independence of the accident years and result (8.76) we obtain

$$\begin{aligned}
\mathbf{1}_K'\ \text{Cov}\left(\mathbf{C}_{i,J}^{\text{CL}}, \mathbf{C}_{i,J}^{\text{AD}} \middle| \mathcal{D}_I^N\right)\ \mathbf{1}_{N-K} &= \mathbf{1}_K' \sum_{j=I-i+1}^{J} \text{Cov}\left(\mathbf{C}_{i,J}^{\text{CL}}, \mathbf{X}_{i,j}^{\text{AD}} \middle| \mathcal{D}_I^N\right)\ \mathbf{1}_{N-K} \\
&= \mathbf{1}_K' \sum_{j=I-i+1}^{J} \text{Cov}\left(\mathbf{C}_{i,J}^{\text{CL}}, \mathbf{X}_{i,j}^{\text{AD}} \middle| \mathbf{C}_{i,I-i}\right)\ \mathbf{1}_{N-K} \\
&= \mathbf{1}_K' \sum_{j=I-i+1}^{J} \prod_{l=j}^{J-1} \text{D}(\mathbf{f}_l)\ \boldsymbol{\Sigma}_{i,j-1}^{\text{CA}}\ \mathbf{1}_{N-K}
\end{aligned} \tag{8.77}$$

This completes the proof of Lemma 8.42. □

Remarks 8.43

- From (8.77) we obtain the following recursive formula for the conditional cross process variance for a single accident year $i > 0$, $j > I - i$,

$$\begin{aligned}
&\mathbf{1}_K'\ \text{Cov}\left(\mathbf{C}_{i,j}^{\text{CL}}, \mathbf{C}_{i,j}^{\text{AD}} \middle| \mathcal{D}_I^N\right)\ \mathbf{1}_{N-K} \\
&= \mathbf{1}_K' \left(\boldsymbol{\Sigma}_{i,j-1}^{\text{CA}} + \text{D}(\mathbf{f}_{j-1})\ \text{Cov}\left(\mathbf{C}_{i,j-1}^{\text{CL}}, \mathbf{C}_{i,j-1}^{\text{AD}} \middle| \mathcal{D}_I^N\right)\right)\ \mathbf{1}_{N-K}
\end{aligned}$$

with $\text{Cov}\left(\mathbf{C}_{i,I-i}^{\text{CL}}, \mathbf{C}_{i,I-i}^{\text{AD}} \middle| \mathcal{D}_I^N\right) = \mathbf{0}$.

- If we replace parameters $\mathbf{f}_l$ and $\Sigma^{CA}_{i,j-1}$ in (8.74) by their estimates (cf. Subsection 8.4.5, below), we obtain an estimator of the conditional cross process variance for a single accident year.

8.4.3 Conditional Cross Estimation Error for Single Accident Years

In this subsection we deal with the second term on the right-hand side of (8.73)

$$\mathbf{1}'_K \left(\widehat{\mathbf{C}_{i,J}}^{CL} - E\left[\mathbf{C}^{CL}_{i,J}\middle|\mathcal{D}^N_I\right]\right)\left(\widehat{\mathbf{C}_{i,J}}^{AD} - E\left[\mathbf{C}^{AD}_{i,J}\middle|\mathcal{D}^N_I\right]\right)' \mathbf{1}_{N-K}$$

Using Lemmas 8.3 and 8.24, as well as definitions (8.67) and (8.68), we obtain for the cross estimation error of accident year $i > I-J$ the representation:

$$\begin{aligned}
&\mathbf{1}'_K \left(\widehat{\mathbf{C}_{i,J}}^{CL} - E\left[\mathbf{C}^{CL}_{i,J}\middle|\mathcal{D}^N_I\right]\right)\left(\widehat{\mathbf{C}_{i,J}}^{AD} - E\left[\mathbf{C}^{AD}_{i,J}\middle|\mathcal{D}^N_I\right]\right)' \mathbf{1}_{N-K}\\
&\quad= \mathbf{1}'_K \left(\prod_{j=I-i}^{J-1} \mathrm{D}(\widehat{\mathbf{f}}_j) - \prod_{j=I-i}^{J-1} \mathrm{D}(\mathbf{f}_j)\right) \mathbf{C}^{CL}_{i,I-i} \left(\sum_{j=I-i+1}^{J} \left(\widehat{\mathbf{X}_{i,j}}^{AD} - E\left[\widehat{\mathbf{X}_{i,j}}^{AD}\right]\right)\right)' \mathbf{1}_{N-K}\\
&\quad= \mathbf{1}'_K\, \mathrm{D}\left(\mathbf{C}^{CL}_{i,I-i}\right) \left(\widehat{\mathbf{g}}_{i|J} - \mathbf{g}_{i|J}\right) \left(\sum_{j=I-i+1}^{J} (\widehat{\mathbf{m}}_j - \mathbf{m}_j)\right)' \mathrm{V}_i\, \mathbf{1}_{N-K}
\end{aligned} \tag{8.78}$$

where $\widehat{\mathbf{g}}_{i|j}$ and $\mathbf{g}_{i|j}$ are, for $j = I-i+1, \ldots, J$, defined as in (8.16).

In order to derive an estimator of the conditional cross estimation error we use the conditional resampling approach (see Approach 3 in Subsection 3.2.3) to quantify the fluctuations of the estimators $\widehat{\mathbf{f}}_0, \ldots, \widehat{\mathbf{f}}_{J-1}$ and $\widehat{\mathbf{m}}_1, \ldots, \widehat{\mathbf{m}}_J$ around the true CL factors and $\mathbf{f}_0, \ldots, \mathbf{f}_{J-1}$ and the true incremental loss ratios $\mathbf{m}_1, \ldots, \mathbf{m}_J$, respectively (see also Subsection 8.2.3). This means that, given $\mathcal{D}^N_I$, we generate 'new' observations $\widetilde{\mathbf{C}}^{CL}_{i,j+1}$ and $\widetilde{\mathbf{X}}^{AD}_{i,j+1}$ for $i \in \{0, \ldots, I\}$ and $j \in \{0, \ldots, J-1\}$ using the formulas

$$\widetilde{\mathbf{C}}^{CL}_{i,j+1} = \mathrm{D}(\mathbf{f}_j)\, \mathbf{C}^{CL}_{i,j} + \mathrm{D}\left(\mathbf{C}^{CL}_{i,j}\right)^{1/2} \mathrm{D}\left(\widetilde{\boldsymbol{\varepsilon}}^{CL}_{i,j+1}\right) \boldsymbol{\sigma}^{CL}_j \tag{8.79}$$

and

$$\widetilde{\mathbf{X}}^{AD}_{i,j+1} = \mathrm{V}_i\, \mathbf{m}_{j+1} + \mathrm{V}_i^{1/2}\, \mathrm{D}\left(\widetilde{\boldsymbol{\varepsilon}}^{AD}_{i,j+1}\right) \boldsymbol{\sigma}^{AD}_j \tag{8.80}$$

where $\sigma^{(1)}_j, \ldots, \sigma^{(N)}_j > 0$ and

$$\widetilde{\boldsymbol{\varepsilon}}_{i,j+1} = \begin{pmatrix} \widetilde{\boldsymbol{\varepsilon}}^{CL}_{i,j+1} \\ \widetilde{\boldsymbol{\varepsilon}}^{AD}_{i,j+1} \end{pmatrix}, \quad \boldsymbol{\varepsilon}_{i,j+1} = \begin{pmatrix} \boldsymbol{\varepsilon}^{CL}_{i,j+1} \\ \boldsymbol{\varepsilon}^{AD}_{i,j+1} \end{pmatrix} \tag{8.81}$$

are independent and identically distributed copies, given $\mathcal{B}^K_0$.

We define

$$\mathrm{W}_j = \left(\sum_{k=0}^{I-j-1} \mathrm{D}\left(\mathbf{C}^{CL}_{k,j}\right)^{1/2} \left(\Sigma^{(C)}_j\right)^{-1} \mathrm{D}\left(\mathbf{C}^{CL}_{k,j}\right)^{1/2}\right)^{-1}$$

and

$$\mathrm{U}_j = \left(\sum_{k=0}^{I-j-1} \mathrm{V}_k^{1/2} \left(\Sigma_j^{(\mathrm{A})}\right)^{-1} \mathrm{V}_k^{1/2} \right)^{-1}$$

The resampled representations for the estimates of the multivariate CL factors and the incremental loss ratios are then given by (see (8.4) and (8.48))

$$\widehat{\mathbf{f}}_j = \mathbf{f}_j + \mathrm{W}_j \sum_{i=0}^{I-j-1} \mathrm{D}(\mathbf{C}_{i,j}^{\mathrm{CL}})^{1/2} \left(\Sigma_j^{(C)}\right)^{-1} \mathrm{D}(\widetilde{\boldsymbol{\varepsilon}}_{i,j+1}^{\mathrm{CL}})\, \boldsymbol{\sigma}_j^{\mathrm{CL}} \tag{8.82}$$

and

$$\widehat{\mathbf{m}}_{j+1} = \mathbf{m}_{j+1} + \mathrm{U}_j \sum_{i=0}^{I-j-1} \mathrm{V}_i^{1/2} \left(\Sigma_j^{(\mathrm{A})}\right)^{-1} \mathrm{D}(\widetilde{\boldsymbol{\varepsilon}}_{i,j+1}^{\mathrm{AD}})\, \boldsymbol{\sigma}_j^{\mathrm{AD}} \tag{8.83}$$

Remark In (8.82) and (8.83), as well as in the following exposition, we use the previous notations $\widehat{\mathbf{f}}_j$ and $\widehat{\mathbf{m}}_{j+1}$ for the resampled estimates of the multivariate CL factors $\mathbf{f}_j$ and the incremental loss ratios $\mathbf{m}_{j+1}$, respectively, to avoid an overloaded notation.

As in Subsections 3.2.3 (conditional estimation error in the univariate CL method) and 8.2.3 (conditional estimation error in the multivariate CL method) we denote the conditional probability measure of these resampled multivariate estimates by $P^*_{\mathcal{D}_I^N}$. For a more detailed discussion of this resampling approach we refer to Subsection 3.2.3. We obtain the following lemma (see also Lemma 8.13):

LEMMA 8.44 *Under the resampling assumptions* (8.79)–(8.81) *we have*

(a) *estimators* $\widehat{\mathbf{f}}_0, \ldots, \widehat{\mathbf{f}}_{J-1}$ *are independent w.r.t.* $P^*_{\mathcal{D}_I^N}$, *estimators* $\widehat{\mathbf{m}}_1, \ldots, \widehat{\mathbf{m}}_J$ *are independent w.r.t.* $P^*_{\mathcal{D}_I^N}$, *and estimators* $\widehat{\mathbf{f}}_j$ *and* $\widehat{\mathbf{m}}_k$ *are independent w.r.t.* $P^*_{\mathcal{D}_I^N}$ *if* $k \neq j+1$;

(b) $E^*_{\mathcal{D}_I^N}\left[\widehat{\mathbf{f}}_j\right] = \mathbf{f}_j$ *and* $E^*_{\mathcal{D}_I^N}\left[\widehat{\mathbf{m}}_{j+1}\right] = \mathbf{m}_{j+1}$ *for* $0 \le j \le J-1$;

(c) $E^*_{\mathcal{D}_I^N}\left[\widehat{f}_j^{(m)}\ \widehat{m}_{j+1}^{(n)}\right] = f_j^{(m)}\ m_{j+1}^{(n)} + \mathrm{T}_j(m,n)$, *where* $\mathrm{T}_j(m,n)$ *is the entry* (m,n) *of the* $K \times (N-K)$ *matrix*

$$\mathrm{T}_j = \mathrm{W}_j \sum_{i=0}^{I-j-1} \mathrm{D}(\mathbf{C}_{i,j}^{\mathrm{CL}})^{1/2} \left(\Sigma_j^{(\mathrm{C})}\right)^{-1} \Sigma_j^{(\mathrm{C,A})} \left(\Sigma_j^{(\mathrm{A})}\right)^{-1} \mathrm{V}_i^{1/2}\, \mathrm{U}_j \tag{8.84}$$

Proof (a) This follows from (8.82) and (8.83) and the fact that $\widetilde{\boldsymbol{\varepsilon}}_{i,j+1}, \widetilde{\boldsymbol{\varepsilon}}_{i,k+1}$ are independent for $j \neq k$.
(b) This follows from (8.82) and (8.83) and the fact that $E^*_{\mathcal{D}_I^N}\left[\widetilde{\boldsymbol{\varepsilon}}_{i,j+1}\right] = \mathbf{0}$.
(c) Using the independence of different accident years we obtain

$$\mathrm{Cov}_{P^*_{\mathcal{D}_I^N}}\left(\widehat{\mathbf{f}}_j, \widehat{\mathbf{m}}_{j+1}\right) = \mathrm{W}_j \sum_{i=0}^{I-j-1} \mathrm{D}(\mathbf{C}_{i,j}^{\mathrm{CL}})^{1/2} \left(\Sigma_j^{(\mathrm{C})}\right)^{-1}$$

$$\times \operatorname{Cov}_{P^*_{\mathcal{D}_I^N}}\left(D(\widetilde{\varepsilon}^{CL}_{i,j+1})\, \sigma_j^{CL}, D(\widetilde{\varepsilon}^{AD}_{i,j+1})\, \sigma_j^{AD}\right) (\Sigma_j^{(A)})^{-1} V_i^{1/2} U_j$$

$$= W_j \sum_{i=0}^{I-j-1} D(C^{CL}_{i,j})^{1/2} (\Sigma_j^{(C)})^{-1} \Sigma_j^{(C,A)} (\Sigma_j^{(A)})^{-1} V_i^{1/2} U_j = T_j$$

Hence,

$$E^*_{\mathcal{D}_I^N}\left[\widehat{f}_j^{(m)}\ \widehat{m}_{j+1}^{(n)}\right] = f_j^{(m)}\ m_{j+1}^{(n)} + \operatorname{Cov}_{P^*_{\mathcal{D}_I^N}}\left(\widehat{f}_j^{(m)}, \widehat{m}_{j+1}^{(n)}\right)$$
$$= f_j^{(m)}\ m_{j+1}^{(n)} + T_j(m, n)$$

where $T_j(m, n)$ is the entry (m, n) of the $K \times (N-K)$ matrix T_j. This completes the proof of Lemma 8.44. □

Using Lemma 8.44 we choose the following estimator for the conditional cross estimation error (8.78)

$$\mathbf{1}'_K\ D(C^{CL}_{i,I-i})\ E^*_{\mathcal{D}_I^N}\left[(\widehat{\mathbf{g}}_{i|J} - \mathbf{g}_{i|J}) \left(\sum_{j=I-i+1}^{J} (\widehat{\mathbf{m}}_j - \mathbf{m}_j)\right)'\right] V_i\ \mathbf{1}_{N-K}$$
$$= \mathbf{1}'_K\ D(C^{CL}_{i,I-i})\ \operatorname{Cov}_{P^*_{\mathcal{D}_I^N}}\left(\widehat{\mathbf{g}}_{i|J}, \sum_{j=I-i+1}^{J} \widehat{\mathbf{m}}_j\right) V_i\ \mathbf{1}_{N-K} \tag{8.85}$$

We define the matrix

$$\Psi_{k,i} = \left(\Psi_{k,i}^{(m,n)}\right)_{m,n} = \operatorname{Cov}_{P^*_{\mathcal{D}_I^N}}\left(\widehat{\mathbf{g}}_{k|J}, \sum_{j=I-i+1}^{J} \widehat{\mathbf{m}}_j\right) = \sum_{j=I-i+1}^{J} \operatorname{Cov}_{P^*_{\mathcal{D}_I^N}}\left(\widehat{\mathbf{g}}_{k|J}, \widehat{\mathbf{m}}_j\right) \tag{8.86}$$

for all $k, i \in \{1, \ldots, I\}$. The following result hold for its components $\Psi_{k,i}^{(m,n)}$:

LEMMA 8.45 *Under the resampling assumptions* (8.79)–(8.81) *we have for* $m = 1, \ldots, K$ *and* $n = 1, \ldots, N-K$

$$\Psi_{k,i}^{(m,n)} = \sum_{j=(I-i+1)\vee(I-k+1)}^{J} \prod_{r=I-k}^{J-1} f_r^{(m)}\ \frac{1}{f_{j-1}^{(m)}}\ T_{j-1}(m, n)$$

Proof The components $\Psi_{k,i}^{(m,n)}$ are defined by (8.86). Hence, we calculate the terms

$$\operatorname{Cov}_{P^*_{\mathcal{D}_I^N}}\left(\widehat{\mathbf{g}}_{k|J}, \widehat{\mathbf{m}}_j\right) = E^*_{\mathcal{D}_I^N}\left[\widehat{\mathbf{g}}_{k|J}\ \widehat{\mathbf{m}}'_j\right] - E^*_{\mathcal{D}_I^N}\left[\widehat{\mathbf{g}}_{k|J}\right]\ E^*_{\mathcal{D}_I^N}\left[\widehat{\mathbf{m}}'_j\right]$$

This expression is equal to 0 (i.e. the $K \times (N-K)$ matrix consisting of zeros) for $j-1 < I-k$. Hence

$$\Psi_{k,i} = \left(\Psi_{k,i}^{(m,n)}\right)_{m,n} = \sum_{j=(I-i+1)\vee(I-k+1)}^{J} \operatorname{Cov}_{P^*_{\mathcal{D}_I^N}}\left(\widehat{\mathbf{g}}_{k|J}, \widehat{\mathbf{m}}_j\right)$$

Using Lemma 8.44 we have, for $j-1 \geq I-k$, that the (m, n) – component of the covariance matrix on the right-hand side of the above equality is

$$\prod_{r=I-k}^{j-2} f_r^{(m)} \left(f_{j-1}^{(m)} \, m_j^{(n)} + \mathrm{T}_{j-1}(m,n) \right) \prod_{r=j}^{J-1} f_r^{(m)} - \prod_{r=I-k}^{J-1} f_r^{(m)} \, m_j^{(n)}$$

$$= \prod_{r=I-k}^{J-1} f_r^{(m)} \, \frac{1}{f_{j-1}^{(m)}} \, \mathrm{T}_{j-1}(m,n)'$$

Hence the claim of Lemma 8.45 follows. □

Putting (8.72), (8.73), (8.74), (8.85) and Lemma 8.45 together and replacing the parameters by their estimates (cf. Subsection 8.4.5, below) we obtain the following estimator for the conditional MSEP of a single accident year in the combined method:

ESTIMATOR 8.46 (MSEP for single accident years, conditional version) *Under Model Assumptions 8.37 we have the following estimator for the conditional MSEP of the ultimate claim for a single accident year* $i \in \{1, \ldots, I\}$

$$\widehat{\mathrm{msep}}_{\sum_{n=1}^{N} C_{i,J}^{(n)} | \mathcal{D}_I^N} \left(\sum_{n=1}^{K} \widehat{C_{i,J}^{(n)}}^{\mathrm{CL}} + \sum_{n=K+1}^{N} \widehat{C_{i,J}^{(n)}}^{\mathrm{AD}} \right)$$

$$= \widehat{\mathrm{msep}}_{\sum_{n=1}^{K} C_{i,J}^{(n)} | \mathcal{D}_I^N} \left(\sum_{n=1}^{K} \widehat{C_{i,J}^{(n)}}^{\mathrm{CL}} \right) + \widehat{\mathrm{msep}}_{\sum_{n=K+1}^{N} C_{i,J}^{(n)} | \mathcal{D}_I^N} \left(\sum_{n=K+1}^{N} \widehat{C_{i,J}^{(n)}}^{\mathrm{AD}} \right)$$

$$+ 2 \, \mathbf{1}_K' \sum_{j=I-i+1}^{J} \prod_{l=j}^{J-1} \mathrm{D}(\widehat{\mathbf{f}}_l) \, \widehat{\Sigma}_{i,j-1}^{\mathrm{CA}} \, \mathbf{1}_{N-K}$$

$$+ 2 \, \mathbf{1}_K' \, \mathrm{D}(\mathbf{C}_{i,I-i}^{\mathrm{CL}}) \left(\widehat{\Psi}_{i,i}^{(m,n)} \right)_{m,n} \mathrm{V}_i \mathbf{1}_{N-K}$$

with

$$\widehat{\Sigma}_{i,j-1}^{\mathrm{CA}} = \mathrm{D}\left(\widehat{\mathbf{C}_{i,j-1}}^{\mathrm{CL}}\right)^{1/2} \widehat{\Sigma}_{j-1}^{(\mathrm{C,A})} \, \mathrm{V}_i^{1/2}$$

and

$$\widehat{\Psi}_{k,i}^{(m,n)} = \widehat{g}_{k|J}^{(m)} \sum_{j=(I-i+1)\vee(I-k+1)}^{J} \frac{1}{\widehat{f}_{j-1}^{(m)}} \, \widehat{\mathrm{T}}_{j-1}(m,n)$$

Thereby, $\widehat{g}_{k|J}^{(m)}$ *denotes the mth coordinate of* $\widehat{\mathbf{g}}_{k|J}$ *and the parameter estimates* $\widehat{\Sigma}_{j-1}^{(\mathrm{C,A})}$ *as well as* $\widehat{\mathrm{T}}_{j-1}(m,n)$ *(entry* (m,n) *of the estimate* $\widehat{\mathrm{T}}_{j-1}$ *for the* $K \times (N-K)$ *matrix* T_{j-1}*) are given in Subsection 8.4.5, below.*

Remark The first two terms on the right-hand side of Estimator 8.46 are the estimators of the conditional MSEP for a single accident year $i > 0$ if we use the multivariate CL for the first K run-off subportfolios and the multivariate ALR method for the last $N-K$ run-off subportfolios, respectively. These two estimates are given by Estimators 8.15 and 8.32.

8.4.4 Conditional MSEP, Aggregated Accident Years

Now, we derive an estimator of the conditional MSEP for aggregated accident years. To this end we consider two different accident years $1 \le i < k \le I$. Analogous to the multivariate CL and ALR methods, we know that the ultimate claims $\mathbf{C}_{i,J}$ and $\mathbf{C}_{k,J}$ are indeed independent but we also know that we have to take into account the dependence of the estimators $\widehat{\mathbf{C}_{i,J}}$ and $\widehat{\mathbf{C}_{k,J}}$. The conditional MSEP for two aggregated accident years i and k is given by

$$\begin{aligned}
&\mathrm{msep}_{\sum_{n=1}^{N}(C_{i,J}^{(n)}+C_{k,J}^{(n)})|\mathcal{D}_I^N}\left(\sum_{n=1}^{K}\widehat{C_{i,J}^{(n)}}^{\mathrm{CL}}+\sum_{n=K+1}^{N}\widehat{C_{i,J}^{(n)}}^{\mathrm{AD}}+\sum_{n=1}^{K}\widehat{C_{k,J}^{(n)}}^{\mathrm{CL}}+\sum_{n=K+1}^{N}\widehat{C_{k,J}^{(n)}}^{\mathrm{AD}}\right)\\
&=\mathrm{msep}_{\sum_{n=1}^{N}C_{i,J}^{(n)}|\mathcal{D}_I^N}\left(\sum_{n=1}^{K}\widehat{C_{i,J}^{(n)}}^{\mathrm{CL}}+\sum_{n=K+1}^{N}\widehat{C_{i,J}^{(n)}}^{\mathrm{AD}}\right)\\
&+\mathrm{msep}_{\sum_{n=1}^{N}C_{k,J}^{(n)}|\mathcal{D}_I^N}\left(\sum_{n=1}^{K}\widehat{C_{k,J}^{(n)}}^{\mathrm{CL}}+\sum_{n=K+1}^{N}\widehat{C_{k,J}^{(n)}}^{\mathrm{AD}}\right)\\
&+2E\left[\left(\sum_{n=1}^{K}\widehat{C_{i,J}^{(n)}}^{\mathrm{CL}}+\sum_{n=K+1}^{N}\widehat{C_{i,J}^{(n)}}^{\mathrm{AD}}-\sum_{n=1}^{N}C_{i,J}^{(n)}\right)\right.\\
&\times\left.\left(\sum_{n=1}^{K}\widehat{C_{k,J}^{(n)}}^{\mathrm{CL}}+\sum_{n=K+1}^{N}\widehat{C_{k,J}^{(n)}}^{\mathrm{AD}}-\sum_{n=1}^{N}C_{k,J}^{(n)}\right)\middle|\,\mathcal{D}_I^N\right]
\end{aligned}\tag{8.87}$$

The first two terms on the right-hand side of (8.87) are the conditional prediction errors for the two accident years $1 \le i < k \le I$, respectively, which we estimate by Estimator 8.46.

For the third term on the right-hand side of (8.87) we obtain the decomposition

$$\begin{aligned}
&E\left[\left(\sum_{n=1}^{K}\widehat{C_{i,J}^{(n)}}^{\mathrm{CL}}-\sum_{n=1}^{K}C_{i,J}^{(n)}\right)\left(\sum_{n=K+1}^{N}\widehat{C_{k,J}^{(n)}}^{\mathrm{AD}}-\sum_{n=K+1}^{N}C_{k,J}^{(n)}\right)\middle|\,\mathcal{D}_I^N\right]\\
&+E\left[\left(\sum_{n=K+1}^{N}\widehat{C_{i,J}^{(n)}}^{\mathrm{AD}}-\sum_{n=K+1}^{N}C_{i,J}^{(n)}\right)\left(\sum_{n=1}^{K}\widehat{C_{k,J}^{(n)}}^{\mathrm{CL}}-\sum_{n=1}^{K}C_{k,J}^{(n)}\right)\middle|\,\mathcal{D}_I^N\right]\\
&+E\left[\left(\sum_{n=1}^{K}\widehat{C_{i,J}^{(n)}}^{\mathrm{CL}}-\sum_{n=1}^{K}C_{i,J}^{(n)}\right)\left(\sum_{n=1}^{K}\widehat{C_{k,J}^{(n)}}^{\mathrm{CL}}-\sum_{n=1}^{K}C_{k,J}^{(n)}\right)\middle|\,\mathcal{D}_I^N\right]\\
&+E\left[\left(\sum_{n=K+1}^{N}\widehat{C_{i,J}^{(n)}}^{\mathrm{AD}}-\sum_{n=K+1}^{N}C_{i,J}^{(n)}\right)\left(\sum_{n=K+1}^{N}\widehat{C_{k,J}^{(n)}}^{\mathrm{AD}}-\sum_{n=K+1}^{N}C_{k,J}^{(n)}\right)\middle|\,\mathcal{D}_I^N\right]
\end{aligned}\tag{8.88}$$

Using the independence of different accident years, we obtain for the first two terms on the right-hand side of (8.88)

$$\begin{aligned}
&E\left[\left(\sum_{n=1}^{K}\widehat{C_{i,J}^{(n)}}^{\mathrm{CL}}-\sum_{n=1}^{K}C_{i,J}^{(n)}\right)\left(\sum_{n=K+1}^{N}\widehat{C_{k,J}^{(n)}}^{\mathrm{AD}}-\sum_{n=K+1}^{N}C_{k,J}^{(n)}\right)\middle|\,\mathcal{D}_I^N\right]\\
&=\mathbf{1}_K'\left(\widehat{\mathbf{C}_{i,J}}^{\mathrm{CL}}-E\left[\mathbf{C}_{i,J}^{\mathrm{CL}}\middle|\,\mathcal{D}_I^N\right]\right)\left(\widehat{\mathbf{C}_{k,J}}^{\mathrm{AD}}-E\left[\mathbf{C}_{k,J}^{\mathrm{AD}}\middle|\,\mathcal{D}_I^N\right]\right)'\mathbf{1}_{N-K}
\end{aligned}$$

$$= \mathbf{1}_K' \left(\prod_{j=I-i}^{J-1} \mathrm{D}(\widehat{\mathbf{f}}_j) - \prod_{j=I-i}^{J-1} \mathrm{D}(\mathbf{f}_j) \right) \mathbf{C}_{i,I-i}^{\mathrm{CL}} \left(\sum_{j=I-k+1}^{J} \left(\widehat{\mathbf{X}_{k,j}}^{\mathrm{AD}} - E\left[\widehat{\mathbf{X}_{k,j}}^{\mathrm{AD}} \right] \right) \right)' \mathbf{1}_{N-K}$$

$$= \mathbf{1}_K' \, \mathrm{D}\left(\mathbf{C}_{i,I-i}^{\mathrm{CL}}\right) \left(\widehat{\mathbf{g}}_{i|J} - \mathbf{g}_{i|J}\right) \left(\sum_{j=I-k+1}^{J} \left(\widehat{\mathbf{m}}_j - \mathbf{m}_j\right) \right)' \mathrm{V}_k \, \mathbf{1}_{N-K}$$

and analogously

$$E\left[\left(\sum_{n=K+1}^{N} \widehat{C_{i,J}^{(n)}}^{\mathrm{AD}} - \sum_{n=K+1}^{N} C_{i,J}^{(n)} \right) \left(\sum_{n=1}^{K} \widehat{C_{k,J}^{(n)}}^{\mathrm{CL}} - \sum_{n=1}^{K} C_{k,J}^{(n)} \right) \middle| \mathcal{D}_I^N \right]$$

$$= \mathbf{1}_K' \, \mathrm{D}\left(\mathbf{C}_{k,I-k}^{\mathrm{CL}}\right) \left(\widehat{\mathbf{g}}_{k|J} - \mathbf{g}_{k|J}\right) \left(\sum_{j=I-i+1}^{J} \left(\widehat{\mathbf{m}}_j - \mathbf{m}_j\right) \right)' \mathrm{V}_i \, \mathbf{1}_{N-K}$$

With the conditional resampling measure $P^*_{\mathcal{D}_I^N}$, these two terms are estimated by (see also Lemma 8.45), $s = i, k$ and $t = k, i$,

$$\mathbf{1}_K' \, \mathrm{D}\left(\mathbf{C}_{s,I-s}^{\mathrm{CL}}\right) E^*_{\mathcal{D}_I^N} \left[\left(\widehat{\mathbf{g}}_{s|J} - \mathbf{g}_{s|J}\right) \left(\sum_{j=I-t+1}^{J} \left(\widehat{\mathbf{m}}_j - \mathbf{m}_j\right) \right)' \right] \mathrm{V}_t \, \mathbf{1}_{N-K}$$

$$= \mathbf{1}_K' \, \mathrm{D}\left(\mathbf{C}_{s,I-s}^{\mathrm{CL}}\right) \left(\Psi_{s,t}^{(m,n)} \right)_{m,n} \mathrm{V}_t \, \mathbf{1}_{N-K}$$

Now we consider the third term on the right-hand side of (8.88). Again, using the independence of different accident years we obtain

$$E\left[\left(\sum_{n=1}^{K} \widehat{C_{i,J}^{(n)}}^{\mathrm{CL}} - \sum_{n=1}^{K} C_{i,J}^{(n)} \right) \left(\sum_{n=1}^{K} \widehat{C_{k,J}^{(n)}}^{\mathrm{CL}} - \sum_{n=1}^{K} C_{k,J}^{(n)} \right) \middle| \mathcal{D}_I^N \right]$$

$$= \mathbf{1}_K' \left(\widehat{\mathbf{C}_{i,J}}^{\mathrm{CL}} - E\left[\mathbf{C}_{i,J}^{\mathrm{CL}} \middle| \mathcal{D}_I^N \right] \right) \left(\widehat{\mathbf{C}_{k,J}}^{\mathrm{CL}} - E\left[\mathbf{C}_{k,J}^{\mathrm{CL}} \middle| \mathcal{D}_I^N \right] \right)' \mathbf{1}_K$$

$$= \mathbf{1}_K' \, \mathrm{D}\left(\mathbf{C}_{i,I-i}^{\mathrm{CL}}\right) \left(\widehat{\mathbf{g}}_{i|J} - \mathbf{g}_{i|J}\right) \left(\widehat{\mathbf{g}}_{k|J} - \mathbf{g}_{k|J}\right)' \mathrm{D}\left(\mathbf{C}_{k,I-k}^{\mathrm{CL}}\right) \mathbf{1}_K$$

This term is estimated by, see (8.34),

$$\mathbf{1}_K' \, \mathrm{D}\left(\mathbf{C}_{i,I-i}^{\mathrm{CL}}\right) E^*_{\mathcal{D}_I^N} \left[\left(\widehat{\mathbf{g}}_{i|J} - \mathbf{g}_{i|J}\right) \left(\widehat{\mathbf{g}}_{k|J} - \mathbf{g}_{k|J}\right)' \right] \mathrm{D}\left(\mathbf{C}_{k,I-k}^{\mathrm{CL}}\right) \mathbf{1}_K$$

$$= \mathbf{1}_K' \, \mathrm{D}\left(\mathbf{C}_{i,I-i}^{\mathrm{CL}}\right) \left(\Delta_{i,J}^{(n,m)} \right)_{1 \le n,m \le N} \mathrm{D}\left(\mathbf{C}_{k,I-k}^{\mathrm{CL}}\right) \prod_{j=I-k}^{I-i-1} \mathrm{D}(\mathbf{f}_j) \, \mathbf{1}_K$$

Finally, we obtain for the last term on the right-hand side of (8.88)

$$E\left[\left(\sum_{n=K+1}^{N} \widehat{C_{i,J}^{(n)}}^{\mathrm{AD}} - \sum_{n=K+1}^{N} C_{i,J}^{(n)} \right) \left(\sum_{n=K+1}^{N} \widehat{C_{k,J}^{(n)}}^{\mathrm{AD}} - \sum_{n=K+1}^{N} C_{k,J}^{(n)} \right) \middle| \mathcal{D}_I^N \right]$$

$$= \mathbf{1}_{N-K}' \left(\widehat{\mathbf{C}_{i,J}}^{\mathrm{AD}} - E\left[\mathbf{C}_{i,J}^{\mathrm{AD}} \middle| \mathcal{D}_I^N \right] \right) \left(\widehat{\mathbf{C}_{k,J}}^{\mathrm{AD}} - E\left[\mathbf{C}_{k,J}^{\mathrm{AD}} \middle| \mathcal{D}_I^N \right] \right)' \mathbf{1}_{N-K}$$

which is estimated by, see (8.59),

$$\mathbf{1}'_{N-K}\, E\left[\left(\widehat{\mathbf{C}_{i,J}}^{\mathrm{AD}} - E\left[\mathbf{C}^{\mathrm{AD}}_{i,J}\middle|\mathcal{D}^N_I\right]\right)\left(\widehat{\mathbf{C}_{k,J}}^{\mathrm{AD}} - E\left[\mathbf{C}^{\mathrm{AD}}_{k,J}\middle|\mathcal{D}^N_I\right]\right)'\right]\mathbf{1}_{N-K}$$

$$= \mathbf{1}'_{N-K}\, \mathrm{V}_i \left[\sum_{j=I-i+1}^{J}\left(\sum_{l=0}^{I-j} \mathrm{V}_l^{1/2}\left(\Sigma^{(\mathrm{A})}_{j-1}\right)^{-1}\mathrm{V}_l^{1/2}\right)^{-1}\right]\mathrm{V}_k\,\mathbf{1}_{N-K}$$

Putting all the terms together and replacing the parameters by their estimates (see Subsection 8.4.5, below) we obtain the following estimator:

ESTIMATOR 8.47 (MSEP aggregated accident years, conditional version) *Under Model Assumptions 8.37 we have the following estimator for the conditional MSEP of the ultimate claim for aggregated accident years*

$$\widehat{\mathrm{msep}}_{\sum_i\sum_n C^{(n)}_{i,J}|\mathcal{D}^N_I}\left(\sum_{i=1}^{I}\sum_{n=1}^{K}\widehat{C^{(n)}_{i,J}}^{\mathrm{CL}} + \sum_{i=1}^{I}\sum_{n=K+1}^{N}\widehat{C^{(n)}_{i,J}}^{\mathrm{AD}}\right)$$

$$= \sum_{i=1}^{I}\widehat{\mathrm{msep}}_{\sum_n C^{(n)}_{i,J}|\mathcal{D}^N_I}\left(\sum_{n=1}^{K}\widehat{C^{(n)}_{i,J}}^{\mathrm{CL}} + \sum_{n=K+1}^{N}\widehat{C^{(n)}_{i,J}}^{\mathrm{AD}}\right)$$

$$+2\sum_{1\le i<k\le I}\mathbf{1}'_K\,\mathrm{D}(\mathbf{C}^{\mathrm{CL}}_{i,I-i})\left(\widehat{\Psi}^{(m,n)}_{i,k}\right)_{m,n}\mathrm{V}_k\,\mathbf{1}_{N-K}$$

$$+2\sum_{1\le i<k\le I}\mathbf{1}'_K\,\mathrm{D}(\mathbf{C}^{\mathrm{CL}}_{k,I-k})\left(\widehat{\Psi}^{(m,n)}_{k,i}\right)_{m,n}\mathrm{V}_i\,\mathbf{1}_{N-K}$$

$$+2\sum_{1\le i<k\le I}\mathbf{1}'_K\,\mathrm{D}(\mathbf{C}^{\mathrm{CL}}_{i,I-i})\left(\widehat{\Delta}^{(m,n)}_{i,J}\right)_{m,n}\mathrm{D}(\mathbf{C}^{\mathrm{CL}}_{k,I-k})\prod_{j=I-k}^{I-i-1}\mathrm{D}(\widehat{\mathbf{f}}_j)\,\mathbf{1}_K$$

$$+2\sum_{1\le i<k\le I}\mathbf{1}'_{N-K}\,\mathrm{V}_i\sum_{j=I-i+1}^{J}\left(\sum_{l=0}^{I-j}\mathrm{V}_l^{1/2}\left(\widehat{\Sigma}^{(\mathrm{A})}_{j-1}\right)^{-1}\mathrm{V}_l^{1/2}\right)^{-1}\mathrm{V}_k\mathbf{1}_{N-K}$$

where all the estimators are provided in Estimators 8.17, 8.33 and 8.46.

Similar estimators for the covariance matrices $\Sigma_j^{(\mathrm{C})}$ and $\Sigma_j^{(\mathrm{A})}$ for the multivariate CL method and the multivariate ALR method, respectively, have already been provided above, but we still need to estimate the off-diagonal covariance matrix part, $\Sigma_j^{(\mathrm{C,A})}$, of the combined model (see next subsection).

8.4.5 Parameter Estimation

For the practical application of our estimators of the conditional MSEP we need estimates of parameters $\mathbf{f}_0, \ldots, \mathbf{f}_{J-1}$ and $\mathbf{m}_1, \ldots, \mathbf{m}_J$ as well as of matrices $\Sigma_j^{(\mathrm{C})}$, $\Sigma_j^{(\mathrm{A})}$ and $\Sigma_j^{(\mathrm{C,A})}$ for $j \in \{0, \ldots, J-1\}$. We propose the iterative estimation procedures given in Subsections

8.2.5 and 8.3.5 to derive estimates $\widehat{\mathbf{f}}_j$, $\widehat{\Sigma}_j^{(C)}$, $\widehat{\mathbf{m}}_j$, $\widehat{\Sigma}_j^{(A)}$ and $\widehat{\Sigma}_j^{(C,A)}$ respectively. Motivated by estimators (8.39)–(8.40) and (8.62) we propose for $j=0,\ldots,J-1$ and $k\geq 1$

$$\widehat{\Sigma}_j^{(C)(k)} = Q_{j+1} \odot \sum_{i=0}^{I-j-1} \mathrm{D}(\mathbf{C}_{i,j}^{\mathrm{CL}})^{1/2} \left(\mathbf{F}_{i,j+1}^{\mathrm{CL}} - \widehat{\mathbf{f}}_j^{(k-1)}\right) \left(\mathbf{F}_{i,j+1}^{\mathrm{CL}} - \widehat{\mathbf{f}}_j^{(k-1)}\right)' \mathrm{D}(\mathbf{C}_{i,j}^{\mathrm{CL}})^{1/2} \tag{8.89}$$

where

$$Q_{j+1} = \left(\frac{1}{I-j-2+w_{j+1}^{(n,m)}}\right)_{1\leq n,m\leq K} \qquad \text{with } w_{j+1}^{(n,m)} = \frac{\left(\sum_{l=0}^{I-j-1}\sqrt{C_{l,j}^{(n)}}\sqrt{C_{l,j}^{(m)}}\right)^2}{\sum_{l=0}^{I-j-1} C_{l,j}^{(n)} \sum_{l=0}^{I-j-1} C_{l,j}^{(m)}}$$

as estimator of the $(K\times K)$-dimensional parameter $\Sigma_j^{(C)}$, and

$$\widehat{\Sigma}_j^{(A)(k)} = \frac{1}{I-j-1} \sum_{i=0}^{I-j-1} \mathrm{V}_i^{-1/2}\left(\mathbf{X}_{i,j+1}^{\mathrm{AD}} - \mathrm{V}_i\widehat{\mathbf{m}}_{j+1}^{(k-1)}\right)\left(\mathbf{X}_{i,j+1}^{\mathrm{AD}} - \mathrm{V}_i\widehat{\mathbf{m}}_{j+1}^{(k-1)}\right)' \mathrm{V}_i^{-1/2} \tag{8.90}$$

as estimator of the $[(N-K)\times(N-K)]$-dimensional parameter $\Sigma_j^{(A)}$ and

$$\widehat{\Sigma}_j^{(C,A)} = \frac{1}{I-j-1} \sum_{i=0}^{I-j-1} \mathrm{D}(\mathbf{C}_{i,j}^{\mathrm{CL}})^{1/2} \left(\mathbf{F}_{i,j+1}^{\mathrm{CL}} - \widehat{\mathbf{f}}_j^{(0)}\right) \left(\mathbf{X}_{i,j+1}^{\mathrm{AD}} - \mathrm{V}_i\, \widehat{\mathbf{m}}_{j+1}^{(0)}\right)' \mathrm{V}_i^{-1/2}$$

as estimator of the $[K\times(N-K)]$-dimensional parameter $\Sigma_j^{(C,A)}$.

With these we obtain, as estimates of matrices $\Sigma_{i,j}^{\mathbf{CA}}$ and T_j,

$$\widehat{\Sigma_{i,j}^{\mathbf{CA}}} = \mathrm{D}(\widehat{\mathbf{C}_{i,j}^{\mathrm{CL}}})^{1/2}\, \widehat{\Sigma}_j^{(C,A)}\, \mathrm{V}_i^{1/2}$$

$$\widehat{\mathrm{T}}_j = \widehat{\mathrm{W}}_j \sum_{i=0}^{I-j-1} \mathrm{D}(\mathbf{C}_{i,j}^{\mathrm{CL}})^{1/2}\, (\widehat{\Sigma}_j^{(C)})^{-1}\, \widehat{\Sigma}_j^{(C,A)}\, (\widehat{\Sigma}_j^{(A)})^{-1}\, \mathrm{V}_i^{1/2}\, \widehat{\mathrm{U}}_j$$

where

$$\widehat{\mathrm{W}}_j = \left(\sum_{k=0}^{I-j-1} \mathrm{D}(\mathbf{C}_{k,j}^{\mathrm{CL}})^{1/2}\, (\widehat{\Sigma}_j^{(C)})^{-1}\, \mathrm{D}(\mathbf{C}_{k,j}^{\mathrm{CL}})^{1/2}\right)^{-1}$$

and

$$\widehat{\mathrm{U}}_j = \left(\sum_{k=0}^{I-j-1} \mathrm{V}_k^{1/2}\, (\widehat{\Sigma}_j^{(A)})^{-1}\, \mathrm{V}_k^{1/2}\right)^{-1}$$

Matrices $\widehat{\Sigma}_j^{(C)}$ and $\widehat{\Sigma}_j^{(A)}$ are the resulting estimates in the iterative estimation procedure for the parameters $\Sigma_j^{(C)}$ and $\Sigma_j^{(A)}$ (cf. (8.89) and (8.90)).

Remark If we do not have enough data (i.e. $I = J$) we are not able to estimate the parameters $\Sigma_{J-1}^{(C)}$, $\Sigma_{J-1}^{(A)}$ and $\Sigma_{J-1}^{(C,A)}$ by means of the proposed estimators. For example, in this case we can derive estimates of these parameters by extrapolation. For more details see Remarks 8.20 and 8.35.

We close the section with an example.

Example 8.48 (MSEP in the combined multivariate model)

We illustrate the combined multivariate CL and ALR method using the same data of general and auto liability business as in Examples 8.21 and 8.36. In contrast to Example 8.36 we now assume that we only have *a priori* estimates V_i of the ultimate claims for subportfolio A. Therefore, we use the ALR method only for portfolio A (cf. Table 8.1) and the CL method for portfolio B (cf. Table 8.2). This means that we have $K = N - K = 1$, and parameters $\mathbf{f}_j$, $\mathbf{m}_j$, $\Sigma_j^{(C)}$, $\Sigma_j^{(A)}$, $\Sigma_j^{(C,A)}$, as well as *a priori* estimates V_i of the ultimate claims in the different accident years i in portfolio A, are scalars. Moreover, it holds that $\Sigma_j^{(C)} = \left(\boldsymbol{\sigma}_j^{\mathrm{CL}}\right)^2$, $\Sigma_j^{(A)} = \left(\boldsymbol{\sigma}_j^{\mathrm{AD}}\right)^2$ and $\Sigma_j^{(C,A)} = \boldsymbol{\sigma}_j^{\mathrm{CL}}\, \boldsymbol{\sigma}_j^{\mathrm{AD}}\, \rho_j^{(1,2)}$.

Since it holds that $I = J = 13$, we do not have enough data to derive estimates of the parameters $\Sigma_{12}^{(C)}$, $\Sigma_{12}^{(A)}$ and $\Sigma_{12}^{(C,A)}$ by means of the proposed estimators. Therefore, we use the extrapolations

$$\widehat{\Sigma}_{12}^{(C)} = \min\left\{\widehat{\Sigma}_{10}^{(C)}, \left(\widehat{\Sigma}_{11}^{(C)}\right)^2 / \widehat{\Sigma}_{10}^{(C)}\right\}$$

$$\widehat{\Sigma}_{12}^{(A)} = \min\left\{\widehat{\Sigma}_{10}^{(A)}, \left(\widehat{\Sigma}_{11}^{(A)}\right)^2 / \widehat{\Sigma}_{10}^{(A)}\right\}$$

to derive estimates of $\Sigma_{12}^{(C)}$ and $\Sigma_{12}^{(A)}$, respectively. Moreover, in analogy to Example 8.36, we estimate $\Sigma_{11}^{(A)}$ by

$$\widehat{\Sigma}_{11}^{(A)} = \min\left\{\widehat{\Sigma}_{9}^{(A)}, \left(\widehat{\Sigma}_{10}^{(A)}\right)^2 / \widehat{\Sigma}_{9}^{(A)}\right\}$$

The last two covariances, $\Sigma_{12}^{(C,A)}$, $\Sigma_{11}^{(C,A)}$, are estimated by the conservative estimates

$$\widehat{\Sigma}_{12}^{(C,A)} = \widehat{\Sigma}_{11}^{(C,A)} = \left|\widehat{\Sigma}_{10}^{(C,A)}\right|$$

Note that $\left|\Sigma_0^{(C,A)}\right|, \left|\Sigma_1^{(C,A)}\right|, \ldots, \left|\Sigma_{12}^{(C,A)}\right|$ is usually a decreasing series, too.

Table 8.16 shows the estimates for the parameters and Table 8.17 shows the estimates of the ultimate claims for subportfolios A and B, as well as estimates for the whole portfolio consisting of both subportfolios.

Final comments

- We have calculated the total ultimate claim prediction and the MSEP for the sum of two correlated subportfolios using different claims reserving methods on the subportfolios. The resulting reserves do not differ between the sum of the univariate methods and the multivariate method (since we use univariate parameter estimators in the multivariate case). But in the MSEP estimates we observe substantial differences between the independent consideration of the univariate methods $((216\,613)^2 + (162\,874)^2)^{1/2} = 271\,015)$ and

Table 8.16 Estimates $\widehat{\mathbf{m}}_j$, $\widehat{\mathbf{f}}_j$, $\left(\widehat{\Sigma}_j^{(A)}\right)^{1/2}$, $\left(\widehat{\Sigma}_j^{(C)}\right)^{1/2}$ and $\widehat{\Sigma}_j^{(C,A)}$ for the parameters $\mathbf{m}_j$, $\mathbf{f}_j$, $\left(\Sigma_j^{(A)}\right)^{1/2}$, $\left(\Sigma_j^{(C)}\right)^{1/2}$ and $\Sigma_j^{(C,A)}$

Portfolio A/B	0	1	2	3	4	5	6	7	8	9	10	11	12	13
$\widehat{\mathbf{m}}_j$		0.19969	0.20638	0.17528	0.12117	0.08466	0.04852	0.02474	0.01403	0.01186	0.00606	0.00428	0.00529	0.00371
$\widehat{\mathbf{f}}_j$	2.22582	1.26945	1.12036	1.06676	1.03542	1.01677	1.00968	1.00006	1.00374	0.99946	1.00387	0.99891	0.99972	
$\left(\widehat{\Sigma}_j^{(A)}\right)^{1/2}$	31.58	20.03	14.42	18.92	13.64	13.91	5.79	7.15	12.21	6.09	1.84	0.56	0.17	
$\left(\widehat{\Sigma}_j^{(C)}\right)^{1/2}$	105.38	24.64	17.94	19.07	12.50	5.55	4.52	2.13	5.14	1.40	3.21	1.37	0.58	
$\widehat{\Sigma}_j^{(C,A)}$	−661.28	349.61	148. 48	117.50	46.70	24.65	−2.15	11.39	20.71	5.62	−0.84	0.84	0.84	
$\widehat{\rho}_j^{(1,2)}$	−0.19874	0.70835	0.57411	0.32569	0.27382	0.31925	−0.08215	0.74851	0.32998	0.66028	−0.14250	0.14250	0.14250	

Comments

- Table 8.16 contains the resulting parameter estimates. The one-dimensional estimates $\widehat{\mathbf{m}}_j$ and $\left(\widehat{\Sigma}_j^{(A)}\right)^{1/2}$ coincide with the parameter estimates $\widehat{m}_j^{(1)(0)}$ and $\widehat{\sigma}_j^{(1)(1)}$ used in the multivariate ALR method applied to the individual subportfolio A in the first iteration (cf. Table 8.10). Analogously, the one-dimensional estimates $\widehat{\mathbf{f}}_j$ and $\left(\widehat{\Sigma}_j^{(C)}\right)^{1/2}$ coincide with the parameter estimates $\widehat{f}_j^{(2)(0)}$ and $\widehat{\sigma}_j^{(2)(1)}$ used in the multivariate CL method applied to the individual subportfolio B in the first iteration (cf. Table 8.3).
- From the estimates $\widehat{\Sigma}_j^{(C,A)}$ of the covariances $\Sigma_j^{(C,A)}$, we obtain estimates $\widehat{\rho}_j^{(1,2)}$ of the correlation coefficients $\rho_j^{(1,2)}$ by $\widehat{\Sigma}_j^{(C,A)} / \sqrt{\widehat{\Sigma}_j^{(A)}\,\widehat{\Sigma}_j^{(C)}}$. Note that we again have negative correlations in development years 0, 6 and 10, which is similar to Tables 8.10 and 8.3.

Table 8.17 Estimates of the ultimate claims for subportfolio A (ALR method), subportfolio B (CL method) and the whole portfolio (combined method)

i	Subportfolio A		Subportfolio B	Portfolio
	V_i	$\widehat{C_{i,J}}^{AD}$	$\widehat{C_{i,J}}^{CL}$	$\widehat{\mathbf{C}_{i,J}}$
0	510 301	549 589	391 428	941 017
1	632 897	564 740	483 839	1 048 579
2	658 133	608 104	540 002	1 148 107
3	723 456	795 248	486 227	1 281 475
4	709 312	783 593	508 744	1 292 337
5	845 673	837 088	552 825	1 389 913
6	904 378	938 861	639 113	1 577 973
7	1 156 778	1 098 200	658 410	1 756 610
8	1 214 569	1 154 902	684 719	1 839 620
9	1 397 123	1 431 409	845 543	2 276 952
10	1 832 676	1 735 433	962 734	2 698 167
11	2 156 781	2 065 991	1 169 260	3 235 251
12	2 559 345	2 660 561	1 474 514	4 135 075
13	2 456 991	2 274 941	1 426 060	3 701 001
Total	17 758 413	17 498 658	10 823 418	28 322 077

Table 8.18 Claims reserves

i	Subportfolio A reserves ALR method	Subportfolio B reserves CL method	Portfolio reserves ALR method	Portfolio reserves CL method	Portfolio reserves combined method
1	2348	−135	2206	1810	2213
2	5923	−740	5176	4655	5183
3	9608	1211	10 801	11 827	10 819
4	13 717	992	14 610	16 212	14 709
5	26 386	3132	29 541	29 120	29 518
6	40 906	3661	44 149	45 793	44 567
7	80 946	10 045	91 032	86 004	90 991
8	143 915	21 567	164 973	157 165	165 482
9	283 823	54 642	339 448	344 301	338 465
10	594 362	118 575	705 513	679 812	712 937
11	1 077 515	254 151	1 313 272	1 287 458	1 331 666
12	1 806 833	565 448	2 374 947	2 453 038	2 372 281
13	2 225 221	1 031 063	3 263 516	3 101 679	3 256 284
Total	6 311 503	2 063 612	8 359 183	8 218 874	8 375 115

Comment

The first two columns of Table 8.18 show for each accident year the reserves for subportfolios A and B estimated by the (univariate) ALR method and the (univariate) CL method, respectively. The column 'Portfolio reserves ALR method' shows the reserves for the whole portfolio consisting of subportfolios A and B estimated by the multivariate ALR method (cf. Table 8.11, iteration $k = 1$). The column 'Portfolio reserves CL method' shows the reserves for the whole portfolio estimated by the multivariate CL method (cf. Table 8.4, iteration $k = 1$). The last column, denoted by 'Portfolio reserves combined method', shows the claims reserves when estimating the reserves for subportfolio A and B with the (univariate) ALR method and the (univariate) CL method, respectively. In this example the combined method leads to the most conservative total reserves of 8 375 115.

Table 8.19 Estimated conditional process standard deviations

i	Subportfolio A		Subportfolio B		Portfolio		Portfolio		Portfolio	
	$\widehat{\text{Var}}(C_{i,J}^{\text{AD}}\|\mathcal{D}_I)^{1/2}$		$\widehat{\text{Var}}(C_{i,J}^{\text{CL}}\|\mathcal{D}_I)^{1/2}$		$\widehat{\text{Var}}(\mathbf{C}_{i,J}\|\mathcal{D}_I^N)^{1/2}$		$\widehat{\text{Var}}(\mathbf{C}_{i,J}\|\mathcal{D}_I^N)^{1/2}$		$\widehat{\text{Var}}(\mathbf{C}_{i,J}\|\mathcal{D}_I^N)^{1/2}$	
	ALR method		CL method		ALR method		CL method		combined method	
1	133	5,7%	404	−299,8%	483	21,9%	1289	71,2%	1055	47,7%
2	471	7,9%	1091	−147,5%	1289	24,9%	5966	128,2%	1849	35,7%
3	1640	17,1%	2461	203,2%	2783	25,8%	7290	61,6%	3122	28,9%
4	5381	39,2%	2708	273,1%	6420	43,9%	9801	60,5%	6638	45,1%
5	12 669	48,0%	4750	151,7%	14 781	50,0%	16 143	55,4%	14 840	50,3%
6	14 763	36,1%	5384	147,1%	17 227	39,0%	19 120	41,8%	17 482	39,2%
7	17 819	22,0%	6577	65,5%	20 537	22,6%	21 910	25,5%	20 601	22,6%
8	23 840	16,6%	8127	37,7%	27 112	16,4%	28 933	18,4%	27 309	16,5%
9	30 227	10,6%	14 609	26,7%	36 978	10,9%	39 281	11,4%	36 894	10,9%
10	43 067	7,2%	24 366	20,5%	53 848	7,6%	63 663	9,4%	55 200	7,7%
11	51 294	4,8%	33 227	13,1%	67 390	5,1%	99 918	7,8%	70 190	5,3%
12	64 413	3,6%	47 888	8,5%	91 552	3,9%	199 543	8,1%	96 243	4,1%
13	80 204	3,6%	117 293	11,4%	107 567	3,3%	316 020	10,2%	144 203	4,4%
Total	131 444	2,1%	134 676	6,5%	174 596	2,1%	396 731	4,8%	202 846	2,4%

Comment

Table 8.19 shows for each accident year the estimates for the conditional process standard deviations and the corresponding estimates for the variational coefficients. The first two columns of Table 8.19 contain the values for the individual subportfolios A and B calculated by the (univariate) ALR method and the (univariate) CL method, respectively. The column 'portfolio ALR method' shows the estimated conditional process standard deviations and variational coefficients for the portfolio consisting of subportfolios A and B if we use the multivariate ALR method (cf. Table 8.12, iteration $k=1$). The column 'Portfolio CL method' shows the estimates for the whole portfolio estimated by the multivariate CL method (cf. Table 8.5, iteration $k=1$). The last column, denoted by 'Portfolio combined method', shows the results when estimating the reserves for subportfolios A and B with the (univariate) ALR method and the (univariate) CL method, respectively. Except for accident year $i=9$ the combined method leads to estimatess that are between those calculated by the multivariate ALR method and those calculated by the multivariate CL method.

Table 8.20 Square roots of estimated conditional estimation errors

i	Subportfolio A		Subportfolio B		Portfolio		Portfolio		Portfolio	
	$\widehat{\text{Var}}\left(\widehat{C_{i,J}}^{AD}\middle|\mathcal{D}_I\right)^{1/2}$		$\widehat{\text{Var}}\left(\widehat{C_{i,J}}^{CL}\middle|\mathcal{D}_I\right)^{1/2}$		$\widehat{\text{Var}}\left(\widehat{\mathbf{C}_{i,J}}\middle|\mathcal{D}_I^N\right)^{1/2}$		$\widehat{\text{Var}}\left(\widehat{\mathbf{C}_{i,J}}\middle|\mathcal{D}_I^N\right)^{1/2}$		$\widehat{\text{Var}}\left(\widehat{\mathbf{C}_{i,J}}\middle|\mathcal{D}_I^N\right)^{1/2}$	
	ALR method		CL method		ALR method		CL method		combined method	
1	149	6,3%	449	−333,3%	549	24,9%	1320	72,9%	1173	53,0%
2	375	6,3%	934	−126,3%	1103	21,3%	4533	97,4%	1718	33,1%
3	1074	11,2%	1556	128,5%	1809	16,7%	6087	51,5%	2263	20,9%
4	2916	21,3%	1708	172,2%	3515	24,1%	7032	43,4%	3855	26,2%
5	6710	25,4%	2606	83,2%	7810	26,4%	9791	33,6%	7950	26,9%
6	7859	19,2%	3115	85,1%	9087	20,6%	11 726	25,6%	9452	21,2%
7	10 490	13,0%	3570	35,5%	11 887	13,1%	13 978	16,3%	12 065	13,3%
8	12 953	9,0%	4144	19,2%	14 510	8,8%	16 624	10,6%	14 758	8,9%
9	16 473	5,8%	6980	12,8%	19 523	5,8%	22 749	6,6%	19 621	5,8%
10	24 583	4,1%	11 022	9,3%	28 861	4,1%	34 081	5,0%	29 681	4,2%
11	30 469	2,8%	15 669	6,2%	36 975	2,8%	51 355	4,0%	38 531	2,9%
12	38 904	2,2%	23 625	4,2%	50 834	2,1%	99 845	4,1%	52 909	2,2%
13	42 287	1,9%	47 683	4,6%	54 274	1,7%	131 682	4,2%	66 406	2,0%
Total	172 174	2,7%	91 599	4,4%	207 119	2,5%	313 122	3,8%	223 970	2,7%

Comment

Table 8.20 shows the square roots of estimated conditional estimation errors. The first two columns contain the estimates for the individual subportfolios A and B calculated by the (univariate) ALR method and the (univariate) CL method, respectively. Columns 'Portfolio ALR method' and 'Portfolio CL method', show the estimated conditional estimation errors for the whole portfolio consisting of subportfolios A and B if we use the multivariate ALR method and the multivariate CL method, respectively (cf. Tables 8.13 and 8.6, iteration $k=1$). Again, the last column shows the estimates for the combined method, which are between those calculated by the multivariate ALR method and those calculated by the multivariate CL method.

Table 8.21 Estimated prediction standard errors

i	Subportfolio A		Subportfolio B		Portfolio		Portfolio		Portfolio	
	$\widehat{\text{msep}}^{1/2}_{C^{AD}_{i,J}\mid\mathcal{D}_I}$		$\widehat{\text{msep}}^{1/2}_{C^{CL}_{i,J}\mid\mathcal{D}_I}$		$\widehat{\text{msep}}^{1/2}_{\mathbf{C}_{i,J}\mid\mathcal{D}^N_I}$		$\widehat{\text{msep}}^{1/2}_{\mathbf{C}_{i,J}\mid\mathcal{D}^N_I}$		$\widehat{\text{msep}}^{1/2}_{\mathbf{C}_{i,J}\mid\mathcal{D}^N_I}$	
	ALR method		CL method		ALR method		CL method		combined method	
1	200	8,5%	604	−448,2%	731	33,1%	1845	101,9%	1578	71,3%
2	602	10,2%	1436	−194,2%	1696	32,8%	7493	161,0%	2523	48,7%
3	1961	20,4%	2912	240,4%	3319	30,7%	9497	80,3%	3856	35,6%
4	6120	44,6%	3202	322,8%	7319	50,1%	12 063	74,4%	7676	52,2%
5	14 337	54,3%	5418	173,0%	16 717	56,6%	18 880	64,8%	16 835	57,0%
6	16 724	40,9%	6221	169,9%	19 477	44,1%	22 429	49,0%	19 873	44,6%
7	20 677	25,5%	7483	74,5%	23 729	26,1%	25 989	30,2%	23 873	26,2%
8	27 131	18,9%	9123	42,3%	30 751	18,6%	33 369	21,2%	31 042	18,8%
9	34 424	12,1%	16 191	29,6%	41 815	12,8%	45 393	13,2%	41 788	12,3%
10	49 589	8,3%	26 742	22,6%	61 094	8,7%	72 212	10,6%	62 674	8,8%
11	59 660	5,5%	36 737	14,5%	76 868	5,9%	112 343	8,7%	80 070	6,0%
12	75 250	4,2%	53 399	9,4%	104 718	4,4%	223 129	9,1%	109 827	4,6%
13	90 670	4,1%	126 615	12,3%	120 484	3,7%	342 358	11,0%	158 759	4,9%
Total	216 613	3,4%	162 874	7,9%	270 891	3,2%	505 412	6,1%	302 174	3,6%

Comment

Table 8.21 contains for each accident year the estimated prediction standard errors and the corresponding estimates for the variational coefficients. The first two columns contain the estimates for the individual subportfolios A and B calculated by the (univariate) ALR method and the (univariate) CL method, respectively. The last three columns show the estimates of the prediction standard errors for the portfolio consisting of subportfolios A and B resulting in the multivariate ALR method (cf. Table 8.14, iteration $k = 1$), the multivariate CL method (cf. Table 8.7, iteration $k = 1$) and the combined method. Table 8.21 shows that in this example, except for accident year $i = 9$, the prediction standard errors of the combined method are between those calculated by the multivariate ALR method and those calculated by the multivariate CL method.

the multivariate correlated consideration (302 174), see Table 8.21. This clearly indicates that one needs to carefully study correlated portfolios

- Note that there are substantial differences in the MSEP estimates for the three different methods, which highlight that one has to specify an appropriate model for a specific data set very carefully. In the present outline we have not touched the question about model choice. Indeed we apply the three different multivariate ALR, CL and combined method to the same data set. Of course, this leads to some kind of contradiction since the same data set can hardly come from different model assumptions. We only do this analysis for illustrative purposes and omit the question about the correct model choice. The question about model choices and model error are probably the most difficult ones and often there are no statistical methods that would answer such questions. That is, expert opinion and long-term experience about claims development results are in most cases the only indicators for a 'good' model choice. □

9

Selected Topics I: Chain-Ladder Methods

The previous chapters of this book have outlined the classical stochastic claims reserving models and techniques. These include the CL model, BF techniques, GLM techniques, Bayesian models, as well as numerical methods such as the MCMC method and the bootstrap. In the next two chapters we give an outlook on recent developments on specific claims reserving problems. This outlook partly consists of existing results but also of proposals for possible future research.

In the current chapter we present problems and methods that are closely related to the distribution-free CL method. The next chapter then outlines different approaches that lead to the study of individual claims data.

9.1 MUNICH CHAIN-LADDER

In practice one often has the situation that different sources of information are given to predict the ultimate claim. For example, one has cumulative payments and claims-incurred data to estimate the ultimate claim. Usually, the CL method is then applied to both cumulative payments and claims-incurred data, independently. Since in both approaches one predicts the same total ultimate claim amount one hopes that the CL method can lead to a similar estimate for both cumulative payments data and claims-incurred data. However, in practice, this is seldom the case – that is, the estimates based on the different information (payments and claims incurred) may substantially differ.

Halliwell (1997) is probably one of the first who has investigated this problem from a statistical point of view. Recently Quarg and Mack (2004) have introduced the Munich chain-ladder (MCL) model, which aims to reduce the gap between the claims reserves based on cumulative payments data and on claims-incurred data within a CL framework. In the present section we describe the MCL in detail.

In the following we denote by $C_{i,j}^{\mathrm{Pa}}$, f_j^{Pa} and $(\sigma_j^{\mathrm{Pa}})^2$ the cumulative payment data and the corresponding CL parameters, and with $C_{i,j}^{\mathrm{In}}$, f_j^{In} and $(\sigma_j^{\mathrm{In}})^2$ the claims-incurred figures and their corresponding CL parameters. The cumulative payments, the claims incurred, as well as the joint cumulative payments and claims incurred, respectively, observed at time I, are then given by the sets

$$\mathcal{D}_I^{\mathrm{Pa}} = \{C_{i,j}^{\mathrm{Pa}};\ 0 \le i+j \le I\}$$

$$\mathcal{D}_I^{\mathrm{In}} = \{C_{i,j}^{\mathrm{In}};\ 0 \le i+j \le I\}$$

$$\widetilde{\mathcal{D}}_I = \mathcal{D}_I^{\mathrm{Pa}} \cup \mathcal{D}_I^{\mathrm{In}}$$

We use the tilde notation $\widetilde{\mathcal{D}}_I$ to indicate that this information differs from the information $\mathcal{D}_I$ studied in the previous chapters.

Moreover, we define

$$\mathcal{G}_j^{\text{Pa}} = \left\{C_{i,k}^{\text{Pa}};\ k \le j,\ 0 \le i \le I\right\}$$
$$\mathcal{G}_j^{\text{In}} = \left\{C_{i,k}^{\text{In}};\ k \le j,\ 0 \le i \le I\right\}$$
$$\widetilde{\mathcal{G}}_j = \left\{C_{i,k}^{\text{Pa}}, C_{i,k}^{\text{In}};\ k \le j,\ 0 \le i \le I\right\}$$

the paid, incurred and joint paid and incurred claim data, respectively, up to development year j.

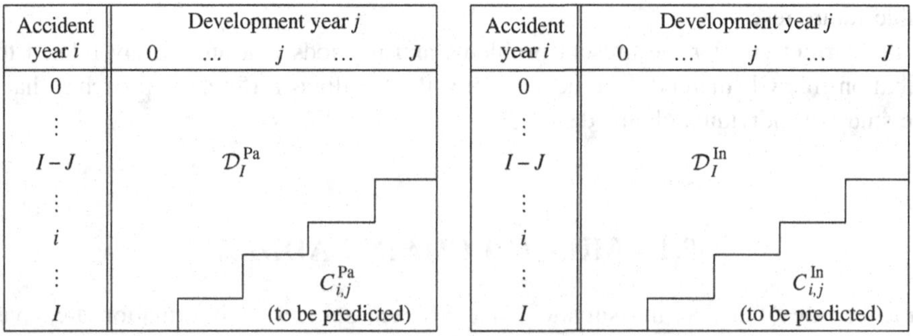

Figure 9.1 Observed cumulative payments $\mathcal{D}_I^{\text{Pa}}$ and observed claims incurred $\mathcal{D}_I^{\text{In}}$ at time I

If we assume that both cumulative payments $C_{i,j}^{\text{Pa}}$ and claims incurred $C_{i,j}^{\text{In}}$, respectively, satisfy the CL Model Assumptions 3.2, we can independently predict the ultimate claim of accident year i by (see estimators (3.4))

$$\widehat{C_{i,J}^{\text{Pa}}}^{\text{CL}} = \widehat{E}\left[C_{i,J}^{\text{Pa}} \middle| \mathcal{D}_I^{\text{Pa}}\right] = C_{i,I-i}^{\text{Pa}} \prod_{j=I-i}^{J-1} \widehat{f_j^{\text{Pa}}}$$

and

$$\widehat{C_{i,J}^{\text{In}}}^{\text{CL}} = \widehat{E}\left[C_{i,J}^{\text{In}} \middle| \mathcal{D}_I^{\text{In}}\right] = C_{i,I-i}^{\text{In}} \prod_{j=I-i}^{J-1} \widehat{f_j^{\text{In}}}$$

with estimated age-to-age factors

$$\widehat{f_j^{\text{Pa}}} = \frac{\sum_{i=0}^{I-j-1} C_{i,j+1}^{\text{Pa}}}{\sum_{i=0}^{I-j-1} C_{i,j}^{\text{Pa}}} \qquad \text{and} \qquad \widehat{f_j^{\text{In}}} = \frac{\sum_{i=0}^{I-j-1} C_{i,j+1}^{\text{In}}}{\sum_{i=0}^{I-j-1} C_{i,j}^{\text{In}}}$$

for $j=0,\ldots,J-1$. Unbiased estimates for the variance parameters $(\sigma_j^{\mathrm{Pa}})^2$ and $(\sigma_j^{\mathrm{In}})^2$ are given by (see estimators (3.4))

$$(\widehat{\sigma_j^{\mathrm{Pa}}})^2=\frac{1}{I-j-1}\sum_{i=0}^{I-j-1} C_{i,j}^{\mathrm{Pa}}\left(\frac{C_{i,j+1}^{\mathrm{Pa}}}{C_{i,j}^{\mathrm{Pa}}}-\widehat{f_j^{\mathrm{Pa}}}\right)^2$$

and

$$(\widehat{\sigma_j^{\mathrm{In}}})^2=\frac{1}{I-j-1}\sum_{i=0}^{I-j-1} C_{i,j}^{\mathrm{In}}\left(\frac{C_{i,j+1}^{\mathrm{In}}}{C_{i,j}^{\mathrm{In}}}-\widehat{f_j^{\mathrm{In}}}\right)^2$$

Since we predict the same random variable twice, namely the ultimate claim $C_{i,J}=C_{i,J}^{\mathrm{Pa}}=C_{i,J}^{\mathrm{In}}$ of accident year i, we expect that the two independently calculated predictors $\widehat{C_{i,J}^{\mathrm{Pa}}}^{\mathrm{CL}}$ and $\widehat{C_{i,J}^{\mathrm{In}}}^{\mathrm{CL}}$ are close to each other. In practice, it often turns out that this is not the case. Observe that we use 'disjoint' (possibly dependent) information for the prediction. It is the goal of the MCL method introduced by Quarg and Mack (2004) to combine both $\mathcal{D}_I^{\mathrm{Pa}}$ and $\mathcal{D}_I^{\mathrm{In}}$ to get reasonable unified predictors for the ultimate claims that are based on the aggregate information $\widetilde{\mathcal{D}}_I$.

9.1.1 The Munich Chain-Ladder Model

The crucial idea in the MCL model proposed by Quarg and Mack (2004) is to combine the information coming from cumulative payments and claims incurred data. This is done using paid/incurred ratios and incurred/paid ratios, that is, we consider

$$Q_{i,j}=\frac{C_{i,j}^{\mathrm{Pa}}}{C_{i,j}^{\mathrm{In}}} \quad \text{and} \quad Q_{i,j}^{-1}=\frac{C_{i,j}^{\mathrm{In}}}{C_{i,j}^{\mathrm{Pa}}} \tag{9.1}$$

These ratios are used to smooth the predictors in the sense that a paid/incurred ratio $Q_{i,j}$ that is below average (above average) leads to an above average (below average) paid development factor and/or a below average (above average) incurred development factor. The same applies analogously to the incurred/paid ratios $Q_{i,j}^{-1}$. Formally, the implementation of these two ratios lead to additional model assumptions/structures in the MCL method compared to the usual CL Model Assumptions 3.2 made in Mack's model.

The assumptions of the MCL model proposed by Quarg and Mack (2004) are:

Model Assumptions 9.1 (MCL model)

- Cumulative payments $C_{i,j}^{\mathrm{Pa}}$ of different accident years are independent. Claims incurred $C_{i,j}^{\mathrm{In}}$ of different accident years are independent.
- There exist factors $f_0^{\mathrm{Pa}},\ldots,f_{J-1}^{\mathrm{Pa}}>0$, $f_0^{\mathrm{In}},\ldots,f_{J-1}^{\mathrm{In}}>0$ and variance parameters $\sigma_0^{\mathrm{Pa}},\ldots,\sigma_{J-1}^{\mathrm{Pa}}>0$, $\sigma_0^{\mathrm{In}},\ldots,\sigma_{J-1}^{\mathrm{In}}>0$ such that for all $0\le i\le I$ and $1\le j\le J$ we have

$$E\left[C_{i,j}^{\mathrm{Pa}}\middle|\mathcal{G}_{j-1}^{\mathrm{Pa}}\right]=f_{j-1}^{\mathrm{Pa}}\,C_{i,j-1}^{\mathrm{Pa}} \quad \text{and} \quad \mathrm{Var}\left(C_{i,j}^{\mathrm{Pa}}\middle|\mathcal{G}_{j-1}^{\mathrm{Pa}}\right)=\left(\sigma_{j-1}^{\mathrm{Pa}}\right)^2 C_{i,j-1}^{\mathrm{Pa}} \tag{9.2}$$

$$E\left[C_{i,j}^{\mathrm{In}}\middle|\mathcal{G}_{j-1}^{\mathrm{In}}\right]=f_{j-1}^{\mathrm{In}}\,C_{i,j-1}^{\mathrm{In}} \quad \text{and} \quad \mathrm{Var}\left(C_{i,j}^{\mathrm{In}}\middle|\mathcal{G}_{j-1}^{\mathrm{In}}\right)=\left(\sigma_{j-1}^{\mathrm{In}}\right)^2 C_{i,j-1}^{\mathrm{In}} \tag{9.3}$$

- There are constants λ^{Pa}, λ^{In} such that for all $0 \le i \le I$ and $1 \le j \le J$ we have

$$E\left[\frac{C_{i,j}^{\mathrm{Pa}}}{C_{i,j-1}^{\mathrm{Pa}}}\middle|\widetilde{\mathcal{G}}_{j-1}\right]$$
$$= f_{j-1}^{\mathrm{Pa}} + \lambda^{\mathrm{Pa}}\,\mathrm{Var}\left(\frac{C_{i,j}^{\mathrm{Pa}}}{C_{i,j-1}^{\mathrm{Pa}}}\middle|\mathcal{G}_{j-1}^{\mathrm{Pa}}\right)^{1/2}\frac{Q_{i,j-1}^{-1} - E\left[Q_{i,j-1}^{-1}\middle|\mathcal{G}_{j-1}^{\mathrm{Pa}}\right]}{\mathrm{Var}\left(Q_{i,j-1}^{-1}\middle|\mathcal{G}_{j-1}^{\mathrm{Pa}}\right)^{1/2}} \tag{9.4}$$

and

$$E\left[\frac{C_{i,j}^{\mathrm{In}}}{C_{i,j-1}^{\mathrm{In}}}\middle|\widetilde{\mathcal{G}}_{j-1}\right]$$
$$= f_{j-1}^{\mathrm{In}} + \lambda^{\mathrm{In}}\,\mathrm{Var}\left(\frac{C_{i,j}^{\mathrm{In}}}{C_{i,j-1}^{\mathrm{In}}}\middle|\mathcal{G}_{j-1}^{\mathrm{In}}\right)^{1/2}\frac{Q_{i,j-1} - E\left[Q_{i,j-1}\middle|\mathcal{G}_{j-1}^{\mathrm{In}}\right]}{\mathrm{Var}\left(Q_{i,j-1}\middle|\mathcal{G}_{j-1}^{\mathrm{In}}\right)^{1/2}} \tag{9.5}$$

- Different accident years across both cumulative payments $C_{i,j}^{\mathrm{Pa}}$ and claims incurred $C_{i,j}^{\mathrm{In}}$ are independent, i.e. the sets

$$\left\{C_{0,j}^{\mathrm{Pa}}, C_{0,j}^{\mathrm{In}};\ j=0,\ldots,J\right\},\ldots,\left\{C_{I,j}^{\mathrm{Pa}}, C_{I,j}^{\mathrm{In}};\ j=0,\ldots,J\right\}$$

are independent.

Remarks 9.2

- The first two bullets in Model Assumptions 9.1 are the classical CL assumptions for cumulative payments and claims incurred, respectively. The additional assumptions (9.4)–(9.5) do not contradict these assumptions. That is

$$E\left[\frac{C_{i,j}^{\mathrm{Pa}}}{C_{i,j-1}^{\mathrm{Pa}}}\middle|\mathcal{G}_{j-1}^{\mathrm{Pa}}\right] = E\left[E\left[\frac{C_{i,j}^{\mathrm{Pa}}}{C_{i,j-1}^{\mathrm{Pa}}}\middle|\widetilde{\mathcal{G}}_{j-1}\right]\middle|\mathcal{G}_{j-1}^{\mathrm{Pa}}\right] = f_{j-1}^{\mathrm{Pa}} \tag{9.6}$$

and a similar equality holds true for claims incurred.
- The two parameters λ^{Pa} and λ^{In} are conditional correlation coefficients. We show that in general they are constants, given $\mathcal{G}_{j-1}^{\mathrm{Pa}}$ and $\mathcal{G}_{j-1}^{\mathrm{In}}$, that is, λ^{Pa} and λ^{In} are $\mathcal{G}_{j-1}^{\mathrm{Pa}}$-measurable and $\mathcal{G}_{j-1}^{\mathrm{In}}$-measurable, respectively. W.l.o.g. we prove this claim for cumulative payments. We obtain from assumptions (9.2), (9.4) and (9.6) that

$$E\left[\frac{\frac{C_{i,j}^{\mathrm{Pa}}}{C_{i,j-1}^{\mathrm{Pa}}} - E\left[\frac{C_{i,j}^{\mathrm{Pa}}}{C_{i,j-1}^{\mathrm{Pa}}}\middle|\mathcal{G}_{j-1}^{\mathrm{Pa}}\right]}{\mathrm{Var}\left(\frac{C_{i,j}^{\mathrm{Pa}}}{C_{i,j-1}^{\mathrm{Pa}}}\middle|\mathcal{G}_{j-1}^{\mathrm{Pa}}\right)^{1/2}}\middle|\widetilde{\mathcal{G}}_{j-1}\right] = \lambda^{\mathrm{Pa}}\,\frac{Q_{i,j-1}^{-1} - E\left[Q_{i,j-1}^{-1}\middle|\mathcal{G}_{j-1}^{\mathrm{Pa}}\right]}{\mathrm{Var}\left(Q_{i,j-1}^{-1}\middle|\mathcal{G}_{j-1}^{\mathrm{Pa}}\right)^{1/2}} \tag{9.7}$$

Multiplying both sides of equality (9.7) by the term

$$\frac{Q_{i,j-1}^{-1} - E\left[Q_{i,j-1}^{-1}\middle|\mathcal{G}_{j-1}^{\mathrm{Pa}}\right]}{\mathrm{Var}\left(Q_{i,j-1}^{-1}\middle|\mathcal{G}_{j-1}^{\mathrm{Pa}}\right)^{1/2}}$$

using the $\widetilde{\mathcal{G}}_{j-1}$-measurability of $Q_{i,j-1}^{-1}$ and taking the conditional expectation $E[\cdot \mid \mathcal{G}_{j-1}^{\text{Pa}}]$ on both sides, leads to

$$\text{Cor}\left(Q_{i,j-1}^{-1}, \frac{C_{i,j}^{\text{Pa}}}{C_{i,j-1}^{\text{Pa}}} \middle| \mathcal{G}_{j-1}^{\text{Pa}}\right) = \text{Cor}\left(C_{i,j-1}^{\text{In}}, C_{i,j}^{\text{Pa}} \middle| \mathcal{G}_{j-1}^{\text{Pa}}\right) = \lambda^{\text{Pa}} \tag{9.8}$$

Particularly, this means that in the MCL model of Quarg and Mack (2004) it is assumed that the conditional correlation coefficients are independent of the development year j, nor do they depend on the observations $\mathcal{G}_{j-1}^{\text{Pa}}$ (note, to derive (9.8) we only need $\mathcal{G}_{j-1}^{\text{Pa}}$ – measurability of λ^{Pa}).

- In order to get a better understanding for the model, we rewrite model assumption (9.4) as follows:

$$E\left[C_{i,j}^{\text{Pa}} \mid \widetilde{\mathcal{G}}_{j-1}\right] = C_{i,j-1}^{\text{Pa}} f_{j-1}^{\text{Pa}} + \lambda^{\text{Pa}} \text{Var}\left(C_{i,j}^{\text{Pa}} \middle| \mathcal{G}_{j-1}^{\text{Pa}}\right)^{1/2} \frac{C_{i,j-1}^{\text{In}} - E\left[C_{i,j-1}^{\text{In}} \middle| \mathcal{G}_{j-1}^{\text{Pa}}\right]}{\text{Var}\left(C_{i,j-1}^{\text{In}} \middle| \mathcal{G}_{j-1}^{\text{Pa}}\right)^{1/2}} \tag{9.9}$$

which means that for a positive correlation coefficient λ^{Pa} between $C_{i,j-1}^{\text{In}}$ and $C_{i,j}^{\text{Pa}}$, given $\mathcal{G}_{j-1}^{\text{Pa}}$, the paid CL estimate $f_{j-1}^{\text{Pa}}\, C_{i,j-1}^{\text{Pa}}$ for $C_{i,j}^{\text{Pa}}$ is smoothed into the direction of the deviation $C_{i,j-1}^{\text{In}} - E\left[C_{i,j-1}^{\text{In}} \middle| \mathcal{G}_{j-1}^{\text{Pa}}\right]$ and vice versa for a negative conditional correlation coefficient λ^{Pa}. The same applies analogously to the model assumption (9.5).

- The last independence assumption in the MCL Model 9.1 is stronger than the first one. However, this assumption is only needed for the motivation and derivation of appropriate estimators for the conditional moments of the ratios

$$E\left[Q_{i,j-1}^{-1} \middle| \mathcal{G}_{j-1}^{\text{Pa}}\right], \text{Var}\left(Q_{i,j-1}^{-1} \middle| \mathcal{G}_{j-1}^{\text{Pa}}\right) \quad \text{and} \quad E\left[Q_{i,j-1} \middle| \mathcal{G}_{j-1}^{\text{In}}\right], \ \text{Var}\left(Q_{i,j-1} \middle| \mathcal{G}_{j-1}^{\text{In}}\right)$$

on the right-hand side of (9.4) and (9.5), respectively (cf. Subsection 9.1.3, below).

In Quarg and Mack (2004) the model assumptions (9.4)–(9.5) are motivated by a data analysis and statistical diagnostics based on observed correlations between the individual paid ($C_{i,j}^{\text{Pa}} / C_{i,j-1}^{\text{Pa}}$) and incurred ($C_{i,j}^{\text{In}} / C_{i,j-1}^{\text{In}}$) development factors and the preceding incurred/paid ratios $Q_{i,j-1}^{-1}$ and paid/incurred ratios $Q_{i,j-1}$, respectively. The (assumed) dependence of the individual paid and incurred development factors is described from the preceding incurred/paid ratios and paid/incurred ratios, respectively. The MCL estimators of $E\left[C_{i,j}^{\text{Pa}} \middle| \widetilde{\mathcal{G}}_{j-1}\right]$ and $E\left[C_{i,j}^{\text{In}} \middle| \widetilde{\mathcal{G}}_{j-1}\right]$ are then obtained by replacing iteratively all parameters in (9.4)–(9.5) by appropriate estimators and multiplying both sides by $C_{i,j-1}^{\text{Pa}}$ and $C_{i,j-1}^{\text{In}}$, respectively (see Quarg and Mack 2004 and Subsection 9.1.3, below). In the following subsection we give a credibility approach to the MCL method which indicates that the MCL can be derived from the classical distribution-free CL model without making extra assumptions. Extra assumptions are only needed if we want to have stronger independence assumptions on the conditional correlation coefficients (9.8).

9.1.2 Credibility Approach to the MCL Method

In Sections 4.5 and 4.6 we have already used credibility methods to derive credibility predictors for the ultimate claims. In this subsection we consider the credibility approach proposed by Merz and Wüthrich (2006). In the framework of the classical distribution-free CL

Model 3.2, the resulting credibility predictors lead to the same estimators as the MCL model of Quarg and Mack (2004) presented in the last subsection. Indeed, we drop the additional MCL assumptions (9.4)–(9.5) but therefore we use a linear credibility approach in an enlarged σ-algebra containing both cumulative payments and claims-incurred information. More precisely, we show that the two assumptions (9.4)–(9.5) are equivalent to a linear credibility approach in which the conditional moments

$$E\left[C_{i,j}^{\mathrm{Pa}}\big|\,\widetilde{\mathcal{G}}_{j-1}\right] \quad \text{and} \quad E\left[C_{i,j}^{\mathrm{In}}\big|\,\widetilde{\mathcal{G}}_{j-1}\right]$$

are approximated by the best affine-linear estimators within the linear subspaces

$$L\left(C_{i,j-1}^{\mathrm{In}}, 1\right) = \left\{a_{i,0} + a_{i,1}\, C_{i,j-1}^{\mathrm{In}};\ a_{i,0}, a_{i,1} \in \mathbb{R}\right\} \tag{9.10}$$

and

$$L\left(C_{i,j-1}^{\mathrm{Pa}}, 1\right) = \left\{a_{i,0} + a_{i,1}\, C_{i,j-1}^{\mathrm{Pa}};\ a_{i,0}, a_{i,1} \in \mathbb{R}\right\} \tag{9.11}$$

given the information $\mathcal{G}_{j-1}^{\mathrm{Pa}}$ and $\mathcal{G}_{j-1}^{\mathrm{In}}$, respectively. The factors $a_{i,0}$ and $a_{i,1}$ are understood as $\mathcal{G}_{j-1}^{\mathrm{Pa}}$- and $\mathcal{G}_{j-1}^{\mathrm{In}}$-measurable constants in (9.10) and (9.11), respectively. Observe, the fact that the subspaces $L\left(C_{i,j-1}^{\mathrm{In}}, 1\right)$ and $L\left(C_{i,j-1}^{\mathrm{Pa}}, 1\right)$ do not contain $C_{k,j-1}^{\mathrm{In}}$ and $C_{k,j-1}^{\mathrm{Pa}}$, respectively, with $k \neq i$, is motivated by the last assumption in the MCL Model Assumptions 9.1.

Given the information $\mathcal{G}_{j-1}^{\mathrm{Pa}}$ and $\mathcal{G}_{j-1}^{\mathrm{In}}$ with $j > I - i$, our goal is to derive estimators $\widehat{Z_{i,j}^{\mathrm{Pa}}} \in L\left(C_{i,j-1}^{\mathrm{In}}, 1\right)$ and $\widehat{Z_{i,j}^{\mathrm{In}}} \in L\left(C_{i,j-1}^{\mathrm{Pa}}, 1\right)$ of $E\left[C_{i,j}^{\mathrm{Pa}}\big|\,\widetilde{\mathcal{G}}_{j-1}\right]$ and $E\left[C_{i,j}^{\mathrm{In}}\big|\,\widetilde{\mathcal{G}}_{j-1}\right]$, respectively, that minimize the conditional expected squared loss among all estimators that are affine-linear in the observation $C_{i,j-1}^{\mathrm{In}}$ and $C_{i,j-1}^{\mathrm{Pa}}$, respectively. That is, we have to solve the optimization problems

$$\widehat{Z_{i,j}^{\mathrm{Pa}}} = \operatorname{argmin}_{Z \in L(C_{i,j-1}^{\mathrm{In}}, 1)} E\left[\left(E\left[C_{i,j}^{\mathrm{Pa}}\big|\,\widetilde{\mathcal{G}}_{j-1}\right] - Z\right)^2\bigg|\, \mathcal{G}_{j-1}^{\mathrm{Pa}}\right]$$

and

$$\widehat{Z_{i,j}^{\mathrm{In}}} = \operatorname{argmin}_{Z \in L(C_{i,j-1}^{\mathrm{Pa}}, 1)} E\left[\left(E\left[C_{i,j}^{\mathrm{In}}\big|\,\widetilde{\mathcal{G}}_{j-1}\right] - Z\right)^2\bigg|\, \mathcal{G}_{j-1}^{\mathrm{In}}\right]$$

for $j > I - i$. The use of the conditional expected squared loss instead of the unconditional one is motivated by the fact that optimality is desired only with regard to the information provided by the past, that is $a_{i,0}$ and $a_{i,1}$ in (9.10) and (9.11) are $\mathcal{G}_{j-1}^{\mathrm{Pa}}$- and $\mathcal{G}_{j-1}^{\mathrm{In}}$-measurable, respectively.

The estimators $\widehat{Z_{i,j}^{\mathrm{Pa}}}$ and $\widehat{Z_{i,j}^{\mathrm{In}}}$ are called best affine-linear one-step estimators of $E\left[C_{i,j}^{\mathrm{Pa}}\big|\,\widetilde{\mathcal{G}}_{j-1}\right]$ and $E\left[C_{i,j}^{\mathrm{In}}\big|\,\widetilde{\mathcal{G}}_{j-1}\right]$ given $\mathcal{G}_{j-1}^{\mathrm{Pa}}$ and $\mathcal{G}_{j-1}^{\mathrm{In}}$, respectively. It can be shown that the estimators $\widehat{Z_{i,j}^{\mathrm{Pa}}}$ and $\widehat{Z_{i,j}^{\mathrm{In}}}$ exist and are unique almost surely (a.s.) (cf. Theorem 2.3.1 in Brockwell and Davis 1991). Furthermore, $\widehat{Z_{i,j}^{\mathrm{Pa}}}$ satisfies the (conditional) normal equations

$$E\left[\left(E\left[C_{i,j}^{\mathrm{Pa}}\big|\,\widetilde{\mathcal{G}}_{j-1}\right] - \widehat{Z_{i,j}^{\mathrm{Pa}}}\right) 1 \bigg|\, \mathcal{G}_{j-1}^{\mathrm{Pa}}\right] = 0 \quad \text{a.s.}$$

$$E\left[\left(E\left[C_{i,j}^{\mathrm{Pa}}\big|\,\widetilde{\mathcal{G}}_{j-1}\right] - \widehat{Z_{i,j}^{\mathrm{Pa}}}\right) C_{i,j-1}^{\mathrm{In}} \bigg|\, \mathcal{G}_{j-1}^{\mathrm{Pa}}\right] = 0 \quad \text{a.s.} \tag{9.12}$$

(cf. Theorem 3.15 in Bühlmann and Gisler 2005). The same equations apply analogously to $\widehat{Z_{i,j}^{\mathrm{In}}}$. Based on (9.12) we obtain the following representation for $\widehat{Z_{i,j}^{\mathrm{Pa}}}$ and $\widehat{Z_{i,j}^{\mathrm{In}}}$:

THEOREM 9.3 (best affine-linear one-step estimators) *Under the first two assumptions of the MCL Model 9.1 the best affine-linear one-step estimators $\widehat{Z_{i,j}^{\mathrm{Pa}}} \in L(C_{i,j-1}^{\mathrm{In}}, 1)$ and $\widehat{Z_{i,j}^{\mathrm{In}}} \in L(C_{i,j-1}^{\mathrm{Pa}}, 1)$ for $E\left[C_{i,j}^{\mathrm{Pa}} \middle| \widetilde{\mathcal{G}}_{j-1}\right]$ and $E\left[C_{i,j}^{\mathrm{In}} \middle| \widetilde{\mathcal{G}}_{j-1}\right]$ given the information $\mathcal{G}_{j-1}^{\mathrm{Pa}}$ and $\mathcal{G}_{j-1}^{\mathrm{In}}$, respectively, are given by*

$$\widehat{Z_{i,j}^{\mathrm{Pa}}} = f_{j-1}^{\mathrm{Pa}}\, C_{i,j-1}^{\mathrm{Pa}} + \lambda^{\mathrm{Pa}}\, \mathrm{Var}\left(C_{i,j}^{\mathrm{Pa}} \middle| \mathcal{G}_{j-1}^{\mathrm{Pa}}\right)^{1/2} \frac{C_{i,j-1}^{\mathrm{In}} - E\left[C_{i,j-1}^{\mathrm{In}} \middle| \mathcal{G}_{j-1}^{\mathrm{Pa}}\right]}{\mathrm{Var}\left(C_{i,j-1}^{\mathrm{In}} \middle| \mathcal{G}_{j-1}^{\mathrm{Pa}}\right)^{1/2}}$$

and

$$\widehat{Z_{i,j}^{\mathrm{In}}} = f_{j-1}^{\mathrm{In}}\, C_{i,j-1}^{\mathrm{In}} + \lambda^{\mathrm{In}}\, \mathrm{Var}\left(C_{i,j}^{\mathrm{In}} \middle| \mathcal{G}_{j-1}^{\mathrm{In}}\right)^{1/2} \frac{C_{i,j-1}^{\mathrm{Pa}} - E\left[C_{i,j-1}^{\mathrm{Pa}} \middle| \mathcal{G}_{j-1}^{\mathrm{In}}\right]}{\mathrm{Var}\left(C_{i,j-1}^{\mathrm{Pa}} \middle| \mathcal{G}_{j-1}^{\mathrm{In}}\right)^{1/2}}$$

with

$$\lambda^{\mathrm{Pa}} = \mathrm{Cor}\left(C_{i,j}^{\mathrm{Pa}}, C_{i,j-1}^{\mathrm{In}} \middle| \mathcal{G}_{j-1}^{\mathrm{Pa}}\right) \quad \text{and} \quad \lambda^{\mathrm{In}} = \mathrm{Cor}\left(C_{i,j}^{\mathrm{In}}, C_{i,j-1}^{\mathrm{Pa}} \middle| \mathcal{G}_{j-1}^{\mathrm{In}}\right)$$

for $0 \le i \le I$ and $1 \le j \le J$.

Proof W.l.o.g. we prove the claim for the cumulative payments $C_{i,j}^{\mathrm{Pa}}$. Since $\mathcal{G}_{j-1}^{\mathrm{Pa}} \subseteq \widetilde{\mathcal{G}}_{j-1}$ we obtain from (9.12)

$$E\left[C_{i,j}^{\mathrm{Pa}} \middle| \mathcal{G}_{j-1}^{\mathrm{Pa}}\right] = E\left[\widehat{Z_{i,j}^{\mathrm{Pa}}} \middle| \mathcal{G}_{j-1}^{\mathrm{Pa}}\right] \quad \text{a.s.} \tag{9.13}$$

and

$$E\left[E\left[C_{i,j}^{\mathrm{Pa}} \middle| \widetilde{\mathcal{G}}_{j-1}\right] C_{i,j-1}^{\mathrm{In}} \middle| \mathcal{G}_{j-1}^{\mathrm{Pa}}\right] = E\left[\widehat{Z_{i,j}^{\mathrm{Pa}}}\, C_{i,j-1}^{\mathrm{In}} \middle| \mathcal{G}_{j-1}^{\mathrm{Pa}}\right] \quad \text{a.s.} \tag{9.14}$$

Using $\widehat{Z_{i,j}^{\mathrm{Pa}}} \in L(C_{i,j-1}^{\mathrm{In}}, 1)$ and $a_{i,0}, a_{i,1} \in \mathcal{G}_{j-1}^{\mathrm{Pa}} \subseteq \widetilde{\mathcal{G}}_{j-1}$ we have

$$a_{i,0} = E\left[C_{i,j}^{\mathrm{Pa}} \middle| \mathcal{G}_{j-1}^{\mathrm{Pa}}\right] - a_{i,1}\, E\left[C_{i,j-1}^{\mathrm{In}} \middle| \mathcal{G}_{j-1}^{\mathrm{Pa}}\right] \quad \text{a.s.}$$

and, using (9.13)–(9.14), we obtain a.s.

$$\begin{aligned} &\mathrm{Cov}\left(E\left[C_{i,j}^{\mathrm{Pa}} \middle| \widetilde{\mathcal{G}}_{j-1}\right], C_{i,j-1}^{\mathrm{In}} \middle| \mathcal{G}_{j-1}^{\mathrm{Pa}}\right) \\ &= E\left[\widehat{Z_{i,j}^{\mathrm{Pa}}} C_{i,j-1}^{\mathrm{In}} \middle| \mathcal{G}_{j-1}^{\mathrm{Pa}}\right] - E\left[C_{i,j}^{\mathrm{Pa}} \middle| \mathcal{G}_{j-1}^{\mathrm{Pa}}\right] E\left[C_{i,j-1}^{\mathrm{In}} \middle| \mathcal{G}_{j-1}^{\mathrm{Pa}}\right] \\ &= \mathrm{Cov}\left(\widehat{Z_{i,j}^{\mathrm{Pa}}}, C_{i,j-1}^{\mathrm{In}} \middle| \mathcal{G}_{j-1}^{\mathrm{Pa}}\right) = a_{i,1}\, \mathrm{Var}\left(C_{i,j-1}^{\mathrm{In}} \middle| \mathcal{G}_{j-1}^{\mathrm{Pa}}\right) \end{aligned} \tag{9.15}$$

Moreover, since $C^{\text{In}}_{i,j-1} \in \widetilde{\mathcal{G}}_{j-1}$ we obtain a.s.

$$E\left[E\left[C^{\text{Pa}}_{i,j}\middle|\widetilde{\mathcal{G}}_{j-1}\right] C^{\text{In}}_{i,j-1}\middle|\mathcal{G}^{\text{Pa}}_{j-1}\right] = E\left[E\left[C^{\text{Pa}}_{i,j}\, C^{\text{In}}_{i,j-1}\middle|\widetilde{\mathcal{G}}_{j-1}\right]\middle|\mathcal{G}^{\text{Pa}}_{j-1}\right]$$
$$= E\left[C^{\text{Pa}}_{i,j}\, C^{\text{In}}_{i,j-1}\middle|\mathcal{G}^{\text{Pa}}_{j-1}\right] \tag{9.16}$$

and therefore from (9.15)–(9.16)

$$a_{i,1} = \frac{\text{Cov}\left(C^{\text{Pa}}_{i,j}, C^{\text{In}}_{i,j-1}\middle|\mathcal{G}^{\text{Pa}}_{j-1}\right)}{\text{Var}\left(C^{\text{In}}_{i,j-1}\middle|\mathcal{G}^{\text{Pa}}_{j-1}\right)} \quad \text{a.s.}$$

Finally, this, together with the second assumption of the MCL Model 9.1, leads to the following representation, a.s.

$$\begin{aligned}
\widehat{Z^{\text{Pa}}_{i,j}} &= a_{i,0} + a_{i,1}\, C^{\text{In}}_{i,j-1} \\
&= E\left[C^{\text{Pa}}_{i,j}\middle|\mathcal{G}^{\text{Pa}}_{j-1}\right] + \frac{\text{Cov}\left(C^{\text{Pa}}_{i,j}, C^{\text{In}}_{i,j-1}\middle|\mathcal{G}^{\text{Pa}}_{j-1}\right)}{\text{Var}\left(C^{\text{In}}_{i,j-1}\middle|\mathcal{G}^{\text{Pa}}_{j-1}\right)} \left(C^{\text{In}}_{i,j-1} - E\left[C^{\text{In}}_{i,j-1}\middle|\mathcal{G}^{\text{Pa}}_{j-1}\right]\right) \\
&= f^{\text{Pa}}_{j-1}\, C^{\text{Pa}}_{i,j-1} + \frac{\text{Cov}\left(C^{\text{Pa}}_{i,j}, C^{\text{In}}_{i,j-1}\middle|\mathcal{G}^{\text{Pa}}_{j-1}\right)}{\text{Var}\left(C^{\text{In}}_{i,j-1}\middle|\mathcal{G}^{\text{Pa}}_{j-1}\right)} \left(C^{\text{In}}_{i,j-1} - E\left[C^{\text{In}}_{i,j-1}\middle|\mathcal{G}^{\text{Pa}}_{j-1}\right]\right)
\end{aligned}$$

This finishes the proof of Theorem 9.3. □

Remarks 9.4

- This shows that the best affine-linear one-step estimators $\widehat{Z^{\text{Pa}}_{i,j}}$ and $\widehat{Z^{\text{In}}_{i,j}}$, given $\mathcal{G}^{\text{Pa}}_{j-1}$ and $\mathcal{G}^{\text{In}}_{j-1}$, lead to the same estimators of $E\left[C^{\text{Pa}}_{i,j}\middle|\widetilde{\mathcal{G}}_{j-1}\right]$ and $E\left[C^{\text{In}}_{i,j}\middle|\widetilde{\mathcal{G}}_{j-1}\right]$ as the assumptions of the MCL method (cf. (9.9)). The only difference is that we do not require the conditional correlation coefficients λ^{Pa} and λ^{In} to be constants.
- Moreover, this shows that the MCL Model 9.1 introduced by Quarg and Mack (2004) is a natural extension of the classical distribution-free CL Model 3.2 to a multivariate setup. The credibility view proposed by Merz and Wüthrich (2006) also shows that the MCL estimators are locally optimal affine-linear estimators. This means that the MCL estimator for accident year i and development year j in the paid (incurred) triangle minimizes the conditional MSEP to the cumulative payments (claims incurred) in accident year i after development year j, given the information in the paid (incurred) triangle after development year $j-1$.
- Note, that we have derived the best affine-linear estimators $\widehat{Z^{\text{Pa}}_{i,j}} \in L(C^{\text{In}}_{i,j-1}, 1)$ and $\widehat{Z^{\text{In}}_{i,j}} \in L(C^{\text{Pa}}_{i,j-1}, 1)$ given the information $\mathcal{G}^{\text{Pa}}_{j-1}$ and $\mathcal{G}^{\text{In}}_{j-1}$, respectively. In this way we ensure that the affine-linear estimators $\widehat{Z^{\text{Pa}}_{i,j}}$ and $\widehat{Z^{\text{In}}_{i,j}}$ use the information in $\mathcal{G}^{\text{Pa}}_{j-1}$ and $\mathcal{G}^{\text{In}}_{j-1}$ in the form of Bayes estimators $E\left[C^{\text{Pa}}_{i,j}\middle|\mathcal{G}^{\text{Pa}}_{j-1}\right]$ and $E\left[C^{\text{In}}_{i,j}\middle|\mathcal{G}^{\text{In}}_{j-1}\right]$, respectively.
- Observe, that Theorem 9.3 is valid without the last assumption of the MCL Model 9.1. However, this assumption is needed for the derivation of appropriate estimators for the conditional moments (cf. Subsection 9.1.3, below) and motivates our definition of the linear subspaces $L(C^{\text{In}}_{i,j-1}, 1)$ and $L(C^{\text{Pa}}_{i,j-1}, 1)$, otherwise it would be natural to extend the set of information to other accident years.

- This credibility approach can be extended in a natural way to additional sources of information, that is, the linear subspaces $L\left(C^b_{i,j-1}, 1\right)$, $b = \text{Pa}, \text{In}$, can, for example, be extended to

$$L\left(\mathbf{C}_{i,j-1}, 1\right) = \left\{ a_{i,0} + \sum_{n=1}^{N} a_{i,n}\ C^n_{i,j-1};\ a_{i,0}, a_{i,1}, \ldots, a_{i,N} \in \mathbb{R} \right\}$$

where $\mathbf{C}_{i,j-1} = (C^1_{i,j-1}, \ldots, C^N_{i,j-1})$ are N different sources of information. That is, this leads to a natural extension of the MCL to arbitrary sources of information.

- Under the assumptions of Theorem 9.3 it also holds that

$$\widehat{Z^{\text{Pa}}_{i,j}} = \operatorname{argmin}_{Z \in \overline{L^{\text{In}}_{i,j-1}}} E\left[\left(C^{\text{Pa}}_{i,j} - Z\right)^2\right]$$

and

$$\widehat{Z^{\text{In}}_{i,j}} = \operatorname{argmin}_{Z \in \overline{L^{\text{Pa}}_{i,j-1}}} E\left[\left(C^{\text{In}}_{i,j} - Z\right)^2\right]$$

where

$$\overline{L^{\text{Pa}}_{i,j-1}} = \left\{ Z;\ \text{there is } (Z_n)_{n\in\mathbb{N}} \subset L^{\text{Pa}}_{i,j-1} \text{ with } \lim_{n\to\infty} E\left[(Z - Z_n)^2\right] = 0 \right\}$$

$$\overline{L^{\text{In}}_{i,j-1}} = \left\{ Z;\ \text{there is } (Z_n)_{n\in\mathbb{N}} \subset L^{\text{In}}_{i,j-1} \text{ with } \lim_{n\to\infty} E\left[(Z - Z_n)^2\right] = 0 \right\}$$

with

$$L^{\text{In}}_{i,j-1} = \left\{ Z;\ Z = A_{i,0} + A_{i,1} C^{\text{In}}_{i,j-1} \text{ with } A_{i,0}, A_{i,1} \text{ are } \mathcal{G}^{\text{Pa}}_{j-1}\text{-measurable} \right\}$$

$$L^{\text{Pa}}_{i,j-1} = \left\{ Z;\ Z = A_{i,0} + A_{i,1} C^{\text{Pa}}_{i,j-1} \text{ with } A_{i,0}, A_{i,1} \text{ are } \mathcal{G}^{\text{In}}_{j-1}\text{-measurable} \right\}$$

(see Merz and Wüthrich 2006). This means that under the first two assumptions of the MCL Model 9.1, the MCL estimators $\widehat{Z^{\text{Pa}}_{i,j}}$ minimize the unconditional MSEP to the cumulative payments $C^{\text{Pa}}_{i,j}$ within the subspace of all random variables that are at the limit of a sequence $(Z_n)_{n\in\mathbb{N}} \subset L^{\text{In}}_{i,j-1}$ of affine-linear estimators in $C^{\text{In}}_{i,j-1}$. Moreover, by the requirement that $A_{i,0}$, $A_{i,1}$ are $\mathcal{G}^{\text{Pa}}_{j-1}$-measurable random variables we ensure that the affine-linear estimator $\widehat{Z^{\text{Pa}}_{i,j}}$ of $C^{\text{Pa}}_{i,j}$ use the information given by $\mathcal{G}^{\text{Pa}}_{j-1}$. The same applies analogously to $\widehat{Z^{\text{In}}_{i,j}}$, $C^{\text{In}}_{i,j}$ and $L^{\text{Pa}}_{i,j-1}$.

The following result is obvious:

COROLLARY 9.5 *Under the assumptions of Theorem 9.3 we have: Given $\mathcal{G}^{\text{Pa}}_{j-1}$ and $\mathcal{G}^{\text{In}}_{j-1}$, the estimators $\widehat{Z^{\text{Pa}}_{i,j}}$ and $\widehat{Z^{\text{In}}_{i,j}}$ are unbiased estimators for $E\left[C^{\text{Pa}}_{i,j} \middle| C^{\text{Pa}}_{i,j-1}\right]$ and $E\left[C^{\text{In}}_{i,j} \middle| C^{\text{In}}_{i,j-1}\right]$, respectively.*

9.1.3 MCL Parameter Estimation

In order to perform the MCL method we need to estimate/predict the two correlation coefficients λ^{Pa} and λ^{In} as well as the four conditional moments $E\left[Q_{i,j-1}\middle|\mathcal{G}_{j-1}^{\mathrm{In}}\right]$, $\mathrm{Var}\left(Q_{i,j-1}\middle|\mathcal{G}_{j-1}^{\mathrm{In}}\right)$, $E\left[Q_{i,j-1}^{-1}\middle|\mathcal{G}_{j-1}^{\mathrm{Pa}}\right]$ and $\mathrm{Var}\left(Q_{i,j-1}^{-1}\middle|\mathcal{G}_{j-1}^{\mathrm{Pa}}\right)$ (cf. model assumptions (9.4)–(9.5) or estimators from Theorem 9.3).

For the derivation of reasonable estimates we assume:

The conditional expectations

$$E\left[Q_{i,j}^{-1}\middle|\mathcal{G}_j^{\mathrm{Pa}}\right] \quad \text{and} \quad E\left[Q_{i,j}\middle|\mathcal{G}_j^{\mathrm{In}}\right]$$

as well as the conditional variances

$$\mathrm{Var}\left(Q_{i,j}^{-1}\middle|\mathcal{G}_j^{\mathrm{Pa}}\right) \quad \text{and} \quad \mathrm{Var}\left(Q_{i,j}\middle|\mathcal{G}_j^{\mathrm{In}}\right)$$

of the ratios $Q_{i,j}^{-1}$ and $Q_{i,j}$ are constants depending only on $j=0,\ldots,J$. We set

$$\widehat{q}_j = \frac{1}{\sum_{i=0}^{I-j} C_{i,j}^{\mathrm{In}}} \sum_{i=0}^{I-j} C_{i,j}^{\mathrm{In}}\, Q_{i,j} = \frac{\sum_{i=0}^{I-j} C_{i,j}^{\mathrm{Pa}}}{\sum_{i=0}^{I-j} C_{i,j}^{\mathrm{In}}}$$

and

$$\widehat{q_j^{-1}} = \frac{1}{\sum_{i=0}^{I-j} C_{i,j}^{\mathrm{Pa}}} \sum_{i=0}^{I-j} C_{i,j}^{\mathrm{Pa}}\, Q_{i,j}^{-1} = \frac{\sum_{i=0}^{I-j} C_{i,j}^{\mathrm{In}}}{\sum_{i=0}^{I-j} C_{i,j}^{\mathrm{Pa}}} = (\widehat{q}_j)^{-1}$$

for all $j=0,\ldots,J$.

LEMMA 9.6 *Under the assumption that the conditional first moments of the ratios $Q_{i,j}$ and $Q_{i,j}^{-1}$ are constants depending only on j, we have for all $0\le j\le J$*

(a) *given $\mathcal{G}_j^{\mathrm{In}}$, $\widehat{q}_j$ is an unbiased estimator for $q_j=E\left[Q_{i,j}\middle|\mathcal{G}_j^{\mathrm{In}}\right]$ and*

(b) *given $\mathcal{G}_j^{\mathrm{Pa}}$, $\widehat{q_j^{-1}}$ is an unbiased estimator for $q_j^{-1}=E\left[Q_{i,j}^{-1}\middle|\mathcal{G}_j^{\mathrm{Pa}}\right]$.*

Proof W.l.o.g. we prove the claim for $\widehat{q}_j$. We have

$$E\left[\widehat{q}_j\middle|\mathcal{G}_j^{\mathrm{In}}\right] = E\left[\left.\frac{\sum_{i=0}^{I-j} C_{i,j}^{\mathrm{Pa}}}{\sum_{i=0}^{I-j} C_{i,j}^{\mathrm{In}}}\right|\mathcal{G}_j^{\mathrm{In}}\right] = \frac{1}{\sum_{i=0}^{I-j} C_{i,j}^{\mathrm{In}}} \sum_{i=0}^{I-j} C_{i,j}^{\mathrm{In}}\, E\left[Q_{i,j}\middle|\mathcal{G}_j^{\mathrm{In}}\right] = q_j$$

This finishes the proof of the lemma. □

Remark The assumption that the conditional moments are independent of accident year i and do not depend on the filtration $\mathcal{G}$ is in general not fulfilled, since it suggests that $Q_{i,j}$ is constant, which we do not observe in practice (see also Subsection 3.1.2 in Quarg and Mack

(2004)). However, as this assumption is 'only' needed to motivate the parameter estimators via Lemmas 9.6 and 9.7, it should be skipped.

The estimators for the variances $\text{Var}\left(Q_{i,j}\middle|\mathcal{G}_j^{\text{In}}\right)$ and $\text{Var}\left(Q_{i,j}^{-1}\middle|\mathcal{G}_j^{\text{Pa}}\right)$ are given by

$$\widehat{\text{Var}}\left(Q_{i,j}\middle|\mathcal{G}_j^{\text{In}}\right)=\left[\sum_{i=0}^{I-j} C_{i,j}^{\text{In}}-\frac{\sum_{i=0}^{I-j}\left(C_{i,j}^{\text{In}}\right)^2}{\sum_{i=0}^{I-j} C_{i,j}^{\text{In}}}\right]^{-1}\sum_{i=0}^{I-j} C_{i,j}^{\text{In}}\left(Q_{i,j}-\widehat{q}_j\right)^2$$

and

$$\widehat{\text{Var}}\left(Q_{i,j}^{-1}\middle|\mathcal{G}_j^{\text{Pa}}\right)=\left[\sum_{i=0}^{I-j} C_{i,j}^{\text{Pa}}-\frac{\sum_{i=0}^{I-j}\left(C_{i,j}^{\text{Pa}}\right)^2}{\sum_{i=0}^{I-j} C_{i,j}^{\text{Pa}}}\right]^{-1}\sum_{i=0}^{I-j} C_{i,j}^{\text{Pa}}\left(Q_{i,j}^{-1}-\widehat{q_j^{-1}}\right)^2$$

respectively, for all $0\le i\le I$ and $0\le j\le J$.

We can now make a similar (in practice unrealistic) statement as in Lemma 9.6:

LEMMA 9.7 *Under the assumptions of Lemma 9.6 and the additional assumption that* $\text{Cov}\left(Q_{i,j},\widehat{q}_j\middle|\mathcal{G}_j^{\text{In}}\right)$ *and* $\text{Cov}\left(Q_{i,j}^{-1},\widehat{q}_j\middle|\mathcal{G}_j^{\text{Pa}}\right)$ *are constants depending only on j, we have*

(a) *given* $\mathcal{G}_j^{\text{In}}$, $\widehat{\text{Var}}\left(Q_{i,j}\middle|\mathcal{G}_j^{\text{In}}\right)$ *is an unbiased estimator for* $\text{Var}\left(Q_{i,j}\middle|\mathcal{G}_j^{\text{In}}\right)$ *and*
(b) *given* $\mathcal{G}_j^{\text{Pa}}$, $\widehat{\text{Var}}\left(Q_{i,j}^{-1}\middle|\mathcal{G}_j^{\text{Pa}}\right)$ *is an unbiased estimator for* $\text{Var}\left(Q_{i,j}^{-1}\middle|\mathcal{G}_j^{\text{Pa}}\right)$

for all $0\le j\le J$.

Proof W.l.o.g. we prove the claim for $\widehat{\text{Var}}\left(Q_{i,j}\middle|\mathcal{G}_j^{\text{In}}\right)$. We have seen that, given $\mathcal{G}_j^{\text{In}}$, $\widehat{q}_j$ is an unbiased estimator for $E\left[Q_{i,j}\middle|\mathcal{G}_j^{\text{In}}\right]$ (cf. Lemma 9.6 (a)). Hence weobtain

$$E\left[\left(Q_{i,j}-\widehat{q}_j\right)^2\middle|\mathcal{G}_j^{\text{In}}\right]=\text{Var}\left(Q_{i,j}\middle|\mathcal{G}_j^{\text{In}}\right)+\text{Var}\left(\widehat{q}_j\middle|\mathcal{G}_j^{\text{In}}\right)-2\,\text{Cov}\left(Q_{i,j},\widehat{q}_j\middle|\mathcal{G}_j^{\text{In}}\right)$$

The assumption that $\text{Var}\left(Q_{i,j}\middle|\mathcal{G}_j^{\text{In}}\right)$ and $\text{Cov}\left(Q_{i,j},\widehat{q}_j\middle|\mathcal{G}_j^{\text{In}}\right)$ do not depend on i, and the independence of different accident years, implies

$$\text{Var}\left(\widehat{q}_j\middle|\mathcal{G}_j^{\text{In}}\right)=\frac{\sum_{i=0}^{I-j}\left(C_{i,j}^{\text{In}}\right)^2}{\left(\sum_{i=0}^{I-j} C_{i,j}^{\text{In}}\right)^2}\,\text{Var}\left(Q_{i,j}\middle|\mathcal{G}_j^{\text{In}}\right)$$

$$\text{Cov}\left(Q_{i,j},\widehat{q}_j\middle|\mathcal{G}_j^{\text{In}}\right)=\frac{C_{i,j}^{\text{In}}}{\sum_{i=0}^{I-j} C_{i,j}^{\text{In}}}\,\text{Var}\left(Q_{i,j}\middle|\mathcal{G}_j^{\text{In}}\right)$$

The claim then easily follows. □

We remark once more that the assumptions that lead to these parameter estimates are not realistic. However, they still justify in some sense why we choose the estimators defined above.

There remains to estimate the $\widetilde{\mathcal{G}}_{j-1}$-measurable correlation coefficients λ^{Pa} and λ^{In}. Using (9.7) and the model assumptions (9.2)–(9.3) we obtain

$$\lambda^{\text{Pa}} = E\left[\frac{(C^{\text{Pa}}_{i,j}/C^{\text{Pa}}_{i,j-1}) - f^{\text{Pa}}_{j-1}}{\sqrt{(\sigma^{\text{Pa}}_{j-1})^2/C^{\text{Pa}}_{i,j-1}}} \Bigg/ \frac{Q^{-1}_{i,j-1} - E\left[Q^{-1}_{i,j-1}\middle| \mathcal{G}^{\text{Pa}}_{j-1}\right]}{\text{Var}\left(Q^{-1}_{i,j-1}\middle| \mathcal{G}^{\text{Pa}}_{j-1}\right)^{1/2}} \middle| \widetilde{\mathcal{G}}_{j-1} \right] \tag{9.17}$$

and

$$\lambda^{\text{In}} = E\left[\frac{(C^{\text{In}}_{i,j}/C^{\text{In}}_{i,j-1} - f^{\text{In}}_{j-1})}{\sqrt{(\sigma^{\text{In}}_{j-1})^2/C^{\text{In}}_{i,j-1}}} \Bigg/ \frac{Q_{i,j-1} - E\left[Q_{i,j-1}\middle| \mathcal{G}^{\text{In}}_{j-1}\right]}{\text{Var}\left(Q_{i,j-1}\middle| \mathcal{G}^{\text{In}}_{j-1}\right)^{1/2}} \middle| \widetilde{\mathcal{G}}_{j-1} \right] \tag{9.18}$$

Hence we need estimates of the residuals of the ratios $Q^{-1}_{i,j-1}$ and $Q_{i,j-1}$ as well as estimates of the residuals of the individual development factors.

With the help of the estimators of the conditional moments, we define estimates of the residuals of the paid/incurred ratios $Q_{i,j-1}$ and the incurred/paid ratios $Q^{-1}_{i,j-1}$ by

$$\widetilde{Q}_{i,j-1} = \frac{Q_{i,j-1} - \widehat{q}_{j-1}}{\widehat{\text{Var}}\left(Q_{i,j-1}\middle| \mathcal{G}^{\text{In}}_{j-1}\right)^{1/2}} \quad \text{and} \quad \widetilde{Q}^{-1}_{i,j-1} = \frac{Q^{-1}_{i,j-1} - \widehat{q^{-1}_{j-1}}}{\widehat{\text{Var}}\left(Q^{-1}_{i,j-1}\middle| \mathcal{G}^{\text{Pa}}_{j-1}\right)^{1/2}}$$

respectively, for $1 \le i+j \le I$. Estimates of the residuals for the CL factors f^{Pa}_{j-1} and f^{In}_{j-1} are defined by

$$\widetilde{F}^{\text{Pa}}_{i,j} = \frac{(C^{\text{Pa}}_{i,j}/\,C^{\text{Pa}}_{i,j-1}) - \widehat{f^{\text{Pa}}_{j-1}}}{\widehat{\sigma^{\text{Pa}}_{j-1}}/(C^{\text{Pa}}_{i,j-1})^{1/2}} \quad \text{and} \quad \widetilde{F}^{\text{In}}_{i,j} = \frac{(C^{\text{In}}_{i,j}/\,C^{\text{In}}_{i,j-1}) - \widehat{f^{\text{In}}_{j-1}}}{\widehat{\sigma^{\text{In}}_{j-1}}/(C^{\text{In}}_{i,j-1})^{1/2}}$$

We are now able to define estimates of the conditional correlation coefficients λ^{Pa} and λ^{In}. Equalities (9.17)–(9.18) propose the following estimators

$$\widehat{\lambda^{\text{Pa}}} = \frac{1}{\sum_{1\le i+j\le I} \widetilde{Q}^{-1\,2}_{i,j-1}} \sum_{1\le i+j\le I} \widetilde{Q}^{-1\,2}_{i,j-1} \frac{\widetilde{F}^{\text{Pa}}_{i,j}}{\widetilde{Q}^{-1}_{i,j-1}} = \frac{\sum_{1\le i+j\le I} \widetilde{Q}^{-1}_{i,j-1}\, \widetilde{F}^{\text{Pa}}_{i,j}}{\sum_{1\le i+j\le I} \widetilde{Q}^{-1\,2}_{i,j-1}} \tag{9.19}$$

$$\widehat{\lambda^{\text{In}}} = \frac{1}{\sum_{1\le i+j\le I} \widetilde{Q}_{i,j-1}^{2}} \sum_{1\le i+j\le I} \widetilde{Q}_{i,j-1}^{2} \frac{\widetilde{F}^{\text{In}}_{i,j}}{\widetilde{Q}_{i,j-1}} = \frac{\sum_{1\le i+j\le I} \widetilde{Q}_{i,j-1}\, \widetilde{F}^{\text{In}}_{i,j}}{\sum_{1\le i+j\le I} \widetilde{Q}_{i,j-1}^{2}} \tag{9.20}$$

Hence the predictors of the MCL method are given by:

ESTIMATOR 9.8 (MCL estimators) *The MCL estimators are given iteratively by*

$$\widehat{E}\left[C^{\text{Pa}}_{i,j}\middle| \widetilde{\mathcal{D}}_I\right] = \widehat{E}\left[C^{\text{Pa}}_{i,j-1}\middle| \widetilde{\mathcal{D}}_I\right] \left(\widehat{f^{\text{Pa}}_{j-1}} + \widehat{\lambda^{\text{Pa}}} \frac{\widehat{\sigma^{\text{Pa}}_{j-1}}}{\widehat{E}\left[C^{\text{Pa}}_{i,j-1}\middle| \widetilde{\mathcal{D}}_I\right]^{1/2}} \widetilde{Q}^{-1}_{i,j-1} \right)$$

and

$$\widehat{E}\left[C^{\text{In}}_{i,j}\middle| \widetilde{\mathcal{D}}_I\right] = \widehat{E}\left[C^{\text{In}}_{i,j-1}\middle| \widetilde{\mathcal{D}}_I\right] \left(\widehat{f^{\text{In}}_{j-1}} + \widehat{\lambda^{\text{In}}} \frac{\widehat{\sigma^{\text{In}}_{j-1}}}{\widehat{E}\left[C^{\text{In}}_{i,j-1}\middle| \widetilde{\mathcal{D}}_I\right]^{1/2}} \widetilde{Q}_{i,j-1} \right)$$

for $i+j>I$, where we set $\widehat{E}\left[C^{\mathrm{Pa}}_{i,I-i}\middle|\widetilde{\mathcal{D}}_I\right]=C^{\mathrm{Pa}}_{i,I-i}$ and $\widehat{E}\left[C^{\mathrm{In}}_{i,I-i}\middle|\widetilde{\mathcal{D}}_I\right]=C^{\mathrm{In}}_{i,I-i}$. Hence the MCL estimators for the conditionally expected ultimate claims are defined as

$$\widehat{C^{\mathrm{Pa}}_{i,J}}^{\mathrm{MCL}}=\widehat{E}\left[C^{\mathrm{Pa}}_{i,J}\middle|\widetilde{\mathcal{D}}_I\right] \quad \textit{and} \quad \widehat{C^{\mathrm{In}}_{i,J}}^{\mathrm{MCL}}=\widehat{E}\left[C^{\mathrm{In}}_{i,J}\middle|\widetilde{\mathcal{D}}_I\right]$$

Remarks 9.9

- A similar model has been studied by Verdier and Klinger (2005). One difference to the MCL model is that in Verdier and Klinger (2005) it is assumed that only the paid CL can learn from the incurred observations, but not vice versa (which would correspond to setting $\lambda^{\mathrm{In}}=0$ in the MCL model).
- We only give an estimator for the expected liabilities. At this point it would also be interesting to obtain an estimate of the MSEP. However, this is rather difficult since the paid/incurred residuals and the incurred/paid residuals give non-trivial dependence structures between the paid and incurred triangles, and also because we have used various ad-hoc estimators for the parameters.

Example 9.10 (Munich chain-ladder)

We now give an example for the MCL method. We have two sources of data for the estimation of the ultimate claims, namely cumulative payments $C^{\mathrm{Pa}}_{i,j}$ and claims incurred $C^{\mathrm{In}}_{i,j}$ (Tables 9.1 and 9.2; see also Table 9.3).

Remarks 9.11 (see also Table 9.4)

- We see that the estimated ultimates $\widehat{C^{\mathrm{Pa}}_{i,J}}^{\mathrm{CL}}$ and $\widehat{C^{\mathrm{In}}_{i,J}}^{\mathrm{CL}}$ can be rather different depending on accident year i (here the difference is more than 5%). This can have various reasons: e.g. the payments in the last observed diagonal are rather high compared to the claims incurred. Especially, with the claims incurred data, one has to be careful. Do the estimates contain the latest information? Are there any changes in claims reserving guidelines or in the claims reserving department? Is there any change in the claims closing guidelines? Etc. All this (partly subjective) information may have a large influence on claims adjusters' case estimates and hence on claims incurred, whereas, for cumulative payments, changes are only observed over time (i.e. with a time lag).
- In our data set, the CL reserves coming from claims incurred data $C^{\mathrm{In}}_{i,j}$ are rather volatile. This could also come from the fact that the portfolio considered is too small. We also observe that in older accident years the incurred data do not lead to reasonable estimates. This may come from the fact that some claims are still open, though they are already paid, but their estimates are not updated. In practice this is quite often the case that, due to administrative purposes, claims are not immediately closed, but the case estimate is not updated to the latest cumulative payment.

For the estimated correlation coefficients we obtain

$$\widehat{\lambda^{\mathrm{Pa}}}=48.2\% \quad \text{and} \quad \widehat{\lambda^{\mathrm{In}}}=24.0\% \tag{9.21}$$

Table 9.1 Distribution-free CL Model 3.2 for cumulative payments $C_{i,j}^{\mathrm{Pa}}$

	0	1	2	3	4	5	6	7	8	9	10	11	12	13	14	15	16
0	46 726	64 768	65 412	65 663	66 008	66 462	67 208	67 252	67 258	67 279	67 281	67 282	67 292	67 307	67 313	67 331	67 336
1	48 658	71 816	73 514	73 946	74 137	74 254	74 765	74 793	74 820	74 821	74 830	74 901	74 901	74 901	74 901	74 898	
2	53 455	79 454	81 188	82 236	83 203	83 901	84 924	85 387	85 522	86 105	86 106	86 107	86 286	86 286	86 286		
3	61 851	91 040	92 205	93 297	93 375	93 544	93 597	93 647	95 128	95 139	95 201	95 201	95 631	95 675			
4	65 971	89 125	92 019	92 563	92 688	93 713	93 721	93 731	93 690	93 662	93 644	93 644	93 811				
5	64 913	89 369	91 819	92 350	93 306	93 811	93 831	93 841	93 818	93 849	93 844	93 848					
6	64 019	87 951	89 930	92 170	93 606	93 726	93 725	93 658	93 655	93 698	93 702						
7	60 412	86 978	88 988	89 685	89 917	89 896	89 877	89 843	89 832	89 832							
8	60 994	87 799	89 708	90 470	91 300	92 482	92 605	92 829	92 830								
9	82 391	118 384	120 920	121 490	122 399	123 373	123 432	123 446									
10	75 977	109 038	111 630	112 733	112 848	112 968	112 980										
11	74 212	110 220	112 615	113 427	113 777	113 805											
12	65 557	96 596	99 317	102 561	103 019												
13	66 116	100 415	109 417	110 900													
14	66 782	97 728	100 447														
15	71 205	103 052															
16	72 624																
$\widehat{f_j^{\mathrm{Pa}}}$	1.4416	1.0278	1.0112	1.0057	1.0048	1.0025	1.0008	1.0020	1.0010	1.0001	1.0002	1.0019	1.0002	1.0000	1.0001	1.0001	
$\widehat{\sigma_j^{\mathrm{Pa}}}$	11.8749	5.6664	2.5295	1.4271	1.3909	1.3518	0.5373	1.6019	0.6962	0.0829	0.1062	0.5320	0.0649	0.0147	0.0591	0.0147	

Table 9.2 Distribution-free CL Model 3.2 for claims incurred $C_{i,j}^{\mathrm{In}}$

	0	1	2	3	4	5	6	7	8	9	10	11	12	13	14	15	16
0	71 229	71 262	68 803	68 511	67 572	68 448	67 682	67 680	67 670	67 642	67 564	67 526	68 183	68 158	68 162	68 144	68 074
1	86 774	82 525	79 191	77 111	77 776	76 851	76 061	75 507	75 436	75 422	75 385	75 086	75 064	75 046	75 006	74 997	
2	86 064	90 815	88 342	89 265	87 915	87 314	87 903	87 063	86 988	86 651	86 557	86 524	86 420	86 405	86 334		
3	98 419	101 600	99 502	96 215	96 996	96 625	98 179	98 794	98 087	97 998	97 936	97 872	96 041	96 068			
4	106 154	102 136	99 693	98 418	96 443	95 520	95 381	95 349	95 032	95 029	94 656	94 387	94 288				
5	102 815	100 942	100 835	97 769	96 331	95 520	95 268	95 556	95 196	95 148	94 894	94 882					
6	104 442	100 028	98 028	97 167	94 689	94 391	94 091	93 928	93 917	93 777	93 789						
7	102 366	98 160	93 327	92 097	91 215	91 162	91 169	91 123	90 742	90 678							
8	100 672	95 277	96 141	95 002	94 102	94 235	94 208	94 219	94 000								
9	134 428	131 328	127 963	126 999	127 355	126 368	126 068	125 538									
10	125 793	124 528	122 220	121 751	119 238	115 689	115 380										
11	121 351	124 244	120 442	118 423	118 232	116 084											
12	110 666	111 664	111 508	109 246	105 643												
13	119 939	117 876	118 237	117 462													
14	112 185	112 416	107 240														
15	114 117	116 216															
16	119 140																
$\widehat{f_j^{\mathrm{In}}}$	0.9903	0.9787	0.9868	0.9888	0.9917	0.9993	0.9986	0.9973	0.9990	0.9986	0.9986	0.9967	0.9999	0.9995	0.9998	0.9990	
$\widehat{\sigma_j^{\mathrm{In}}}$	9.9537	5.6675	3.5807	4.0395	3.2636	2.2027	1.4005	0.6995	0.3653	0.4297	0.4560	3.0094	0.0833	0.1247	0.0261	0.0055	

Table 9.3 CL reserves in the CL Model 3.2 for cumulative payments $C_{i,j}^{\mathrm{Pa}}$ and claims incurred $C_{i,j}^{\mathrm{In}}$

i	$C_{i,I-i}^{\mathrm{Pa}}$	CL reserves Paid	CL reserves Incurred
0	67 336		
1	74 898	6	22
2	86 286	15	−58
3	95 675	20	232
4	93 811	36	309
5	93 848	213	551
6	93 702	227	−520
7	89 832	226	128
8	92 830	322	330
9	123 446	677	637
10	112 980	712	908
11	113 805	1003	698
12	103 019	1403	322
13	110 900	2153	2712
14	100 447	3100	1909
15	103 052	6139	5509
16	72 624	38 306	37 594
Total		54 559	51 282

This leads to the reserves shown in Table 9.5.

Remarks 9.12

- We see that the overall paid CL reserve of 54 559 becomes smaller and the overall incurred CL reserve of 51 282 becomes larger (difference CL 3277, difference MCL-1593). However, the correction is such that the MCL reserve for paid is smaller than the MCL reserve for incurred.
- If we consider single accident years, sometimes the MCL correction 'overdoes' or even looks unreasonable (see, e.g., accident years 8 and 9).
- If we look at the paid/incurred residuals $\widetilde{Q}_{i,j}$ (see Table 9.6) we see that most of the residuals have a positive sign on the last observed diagonal $i+j=I$. This may suggest that we have trends in the payout behaviour or even a change in the payout administration. In this case, of course, the MCL Model Assumptions 9.1 are not satisfied. □

9.2 CL RESERVING: A BAYESIAN INFERENCE MODEL

The outline of this section is based on Gisler (2006) and Gisler and Wüthrich (2007). We present Bayesian models for the estimation of CL factors. Often, when working with real data, we are confronted with the fact that observed development figures heavily fluctuate. This may have many reasons, such as insufficient data basis, and creates major difficulties producing reliable claims reserves estimates. As we have already seen in Chapter 4, Bayesian methods are often an appropriate tool to combine data with expert opinion, or, in other words, to combine internal data with external information. This external information

Table 9.4 Paid/incurred ratios $Q_{i,j}$ for MCL

	0	1	2	3	4	5	6	7	8	9	10	11	12	13	14	15	16
0(%)	65.6	90.9	95.1	95.8	97.7	97.1	99.3	99.4	99.4	99.5	99.6	99.6	98.7	98.8	98.8	98.8	98.9
1(%)	56.1	87.0	92.8	95.9	95.3	96.6	98.3	99.1	99.2	99.2	99.3	99.8	99.8	99.8	99.9	99.9	
2(%)	62.1	87.5	91.9	92.1	94.6	96.1	96.6	98.1	98.3	99.4	99.5	99.5	99.8	99.9	99.9		
3(%)	62.8	89.6	92.7	97.0	96.3	96.8	95.3	94.8	97.0	97.1	97.2	97.3	99.6	99.6			
4(%)	62.1	87.3	92.3	94.1	96.1	98.1	98.3	98.3	98.6	98.6	98.9	99.2	99.5				
5(%)	63.1	88.5	91.1	94.5	96.9	98.2	98.5	98.2	98.6	98.6	98.9	98.9					
6(%)	61.3	87.9	91.7	94.9	98.9	99.3	99.6	99.7	99.7	99.9	99.9						
7(%)	59.0	88.6	95.4	97.4	98.6	98.6	98.6	98.6	99.0	99.1							
8(%)	60.6	92.2	93.3	95.2	97.0	98.1	98.3	98.5	98.8								
9(%)	61.3	90.1	94.5	95.7	96.1	97.6	97.9	98.3									
10(%)	60.4	87.6	91.3	92.6	94.6	97.6	97.9										
11(%)	61.2	88.7	93.5	95.8	96.2	98.0											
12(%)	59.2	86.5	89.1	93.9	97.5												
13(%)	55.1	85.2	92.5	94.4													
14(%)	59.5	86.9	93.7														
15(%)	62.4	88.7															
16(%)	61.0																
$\widehat{q}_j$(%)	60.7	88.3	92.7	94.9	96.6	97.7	98.0	98.2	98.7	98.9	99.0	99.0	99.5	99.5	99.6	99.4	98,9
$\widehat{q_j^{-1}}$	1.6486	1.1330	1.0792	1.0540	1.0357	1.0232	1.0203	1.0180	1.0134	1.0115	1.0102	1.0104	1.0050	1.0047	1.0044	1.0064	1.0110
$\widehat{\mathrm{Var}}(Q_{i,j}\|\mathcal{G}_j^{\mathrm{In}})^{1/2}$	0.02406	0.01720	0.01633	0.01481	0.01316	0.00871	0.01175	0.01362	0.00807	0.00892	0.00919	0.00955	0.00428	0.00484	0.00647	0.00750	
$\widehat{\mathrm{Var}}(Q_{i,j}^{-1}\|\mathcal{G}_j^{\mathrm{Pa}})^{1/2}$	0.06652	0.02200	0.01908	0.01649	0.01410	0.00913	0.01231	0.01428	0.00832	0.00916	0.00943	0.00980	0.00433	0.00490	0.00655	0.00761	

Table 9.5 Reserves in CL Model 3.2 and in the MCL Model 9.1 for cumulative payments and incurred claims data

i	$C^{Pa}_{i,I-i}$	CL reserves		MCL reserves	
		Paid	Incurred	Paid	Incurred
0	67 336				
1	74 898	6	22	5	22
2	86 286	15	−58	9	−57
3	95 675	20	232	18	233
4	93 811	36	309	36	309
5	93 848	213	551	220	534
6	93 702	227	−520	99	−223
7	89 832	226	128	179	237
8	92 830	322	330	281	405
9	123 446	677	637	603	736
10	112 980	712	908	724	937
11	113 805	1003	698	808	899
12	103 019	1403	322	858	864
13	110 900	2153	2712	2335	2539
14	100 447	3100	1909	2458	2534
15	103 052	6139	5509	5717	5842
16	72 624	38 306	37 594	37 813	37 944
Total		54 559	51 282	52 162	53 755

could be an expert opinion but it could also be industry-wide data. For example, for the developments of new solvency guidelines, regulators have estimated industry-wide claims development patterns. Our goal here is to combine this external information with our internal data – that is, we adjust industry behaviour with internal observations for CL factors (or vice versa).

In Chapter 3 we have studied different approaches in order to quantify the parameter estimation uncertainty. Choosing one specific approach meant choosing one specific approximation or estimation method. In a Bayesian context this question does not arise because parameters also appear within the stochastic framework which allows for statistical inference on the unknown parameters. In that sense the estimation method is chosen by placing appropriate stochastic model assumptions on the unknown parameters.

In Chapter 4 we have applied Bayesian inference methods directly to the incremental claims $X_{i,j}$ (see Section 4.3). Here we apply Bayesian inference to the age-to-age factor estimates $\hat{f}_j$, that is, we use a Bayesian approach to model our uncertainties about the 'true' unknown CL factors f_j. This exactly expresses our uncertainties in the choice of the CL factors.

Recall that under the CL Model Assumptions 3.2 we can calculate the claims reserves iteratively by, see (2.1),

$$E\left[C_{i,j+1}\middle| C_{i,0},\ldots,C_{i,j}\right]=E\left[C_{i,j+1}\middle| C_{i,j}\right]=f_j\, C_{i,j}$$

Table 9.6 Paid/incurred residuals $\widetilde{Q}_{i,j}$

	0	1	2	3	4	5	6	7	8	9	10	11	12	13	14	15
0	2.0545	1.5244	1.4738	0.6492	0.8626	−0.7263	1.0986	0.8318	0.8809	0.6691	0.6429	0.6954	−1.9005	−1.6220	−1.2503	−0.7410
1	−1.9042	−0.7208	0.1020	0.6846	−0.9347	−1.2749	0.2438	0.6029	0.6220	0.3768	0.2990	0.8172	0.6491	0.5583	0.4580	0.6733
2	0.6042	−0.4499	−0.4669	−1.8598	−1.4528	−1.8827	−1.1911	−0.1163	−0.4540	0.5643	0.5323	0.5692	0.7925	0.6717	0.5893	0.8059
3	0.9094	0.7805	0.0016	1.4088	−0.2156	−1.0552	−2.2776	−2.5295	−2.1025	−2.0019	−1.9385	−1.7844	0.1564	0.1105	0.1153	0.4044
4	0.6191	−0.5832	−0.2217	−0.5605	−0.3376	0.4325	0.2124	0.0503	−0.1157	−0.3420	−0.0634	0.2492	−0.0280	−0.0310	0.0120	0.3168
5	1.0302	0.1575	−0.9837	−0.2861	0.2346	0.5508	0.4100	−0.0208	−0.1583	−0.2599	−0.1043	−0.0679	−0.1364	−0.1229	−0.0551	0.2599
6	0.2657	−0.1961	−0.5667	−0.0161	1.7516	1.7943	1.3632	1.0859	1.2881	1.1769	0.9990	1.0830	1.5855	1.3385	1.0113	1.1641
7	−0.6818	0.2000	1.6454	1.6882	1.5395	1.0087	0.4868	0.2655	0.3918	0.2258	0.2404	0.3931	0.5491	0.4585	0.3690	0.6194
8	−0.0292	2.2594	0.3943	0.2357	0.3584	0.4672	0.2453	0.2132	0.0927	0.0812	0.1073	0.2723	0.3735	0.3098	0.2607	0.5276
9	0.2631	1.0928	1.1218	0.5272	−0.3360	−0.1166	−0.0858	0.0727	0.1190	0.1034	0.1285	0.2925	0.4329	0.3622	0.2998	0.5614
10	−0.1073	−0.4087	−0.8140	−1.5448	−1.4518	−0.0959	−0.0767	−0.0649	−0.0687	−0.0415	−0.0059	0.1693	0.2313	0.1899	0.1735	0.4540
11	0.2069	0.2606	0.5128	0.6076	−0.2423	0.3497	0.1876	0.1302	0.1962	0.1621	0.1827	0.3419	0.5027	0.4212	0.3427	0.5977
12	−0.5894	−1.0219	−2.2028	−0.6750	0.7340	0.8512	0.4022	0.2861	0.4030	0.3183	0.3267	0.4727	0.6919	0.5813	0.4594	0.6965
13	−2.2990	−1.7886	−0.0760	−0.3154	−0.2807	−0.1919	−0.0578	−0.0509	−0.0497	−0.0269	0.0076	0.1817	0.2505	0.2062	0.1855	0.4641
14	−0.4692	−0.7730	0.6136	0.4907	0.3428	0.4512	0.2263	0.1572	0.2300	0.1863	0.2047	0.3614	0.5199	0.4349	0.3524	0.6056
15	0.7230	0.2378	0.1153	0.1360	0.0727	0.1768	0.1078	0.0710	0.1151	0.0994	0.1245	0.2884	0.4137	0.3450	0.2868	0.5501
16	0.1247	0.1342	0.0743	0.1064	0.0500	0.1535	0.0978	0.0637	0.1055	0.0921	0.1178	0.2823	0.4057	0.3383	0.2820	0.5461

One main difficulty in the determination of the CL reserves was the estimation of the CL factors f_j. The individual development factors $F_{i,j+1}$ were defined by

$$F_{i,j+1} = \frac{C_{i,j+1}}{C_{i,j}}, \qquad \text{that is,} \qquad C_{i,j+1} = C_{i,j}\, F_{i,j+1}$$

Then the age-to-age factor estimates $\widehat{f}_j$ were determined by taking volume-weighted averages of the individual development factors (see (3.6)).

To model the uncertainties in our choice of CL factors we use the following model assumptions.

Model Assumptions 9.13 (Bayesian CL model)

- Conditional on $\boldsymbol{\Theta} = (\Theta_0, \ldots, \Theta_{J-1})$, the random variables $C_{i,j}$ belonging to different accident years are independent.
- Conditional on $\boldsymbol{\Theta}$, $(C_{i,j})_{j\geq 0}$ is a Markov chain.
- For $j = 1, \ldots, J$, conditional on $\boldsymbol{\Theta}$ and $C_{i,j-1}$, the individual development factor $F_{i,j}$ has an EDF distribution with

$$F_{i,j|\{\boldsymbol{\Theta}, C_{i,j-1}\}} \overset{(d)}{\sim} a\left(y, \frac{C_{i,j-1}}{\sigma_{j-1}^2}\right) \exp\left\{\frac{y\, \Theta_{j-1} - b(\Theta_{j-1})}{\sigma_{j-1}^2 / C_{i,j-1}}\right\} d\nu(y)$$

  for all $i \in \{0, \ldots, I\}$ and $j \in \{1, \ldots, J\}$, where $\nu(\cdot)$ is an appropriate measure on $\mathbb{R}_+$, σ_{j-1}^2 is a positive constant and $b(\cdot)$ is a real-valued twice differentiable function.
- The vector $\boldsymbol{\Theta} = (\Theta_0, \ldots, \Theta_{J-1})$ has density $u_{\boldsymbol{\Theta}}$. □

Remarks 9.14

- The vector $\boldsymbol{\Theta}$ characterizes the unknown CL factors. This is described in detail below, see (9.22)–(9.23).
- In the following the measure ν is given by the Lebesgue measure or by the counting measure. Note that we need to assume that ν only lives on the strictly positive real line $\mathbb{R}_+$. That is, the individual development factors need to stay strictly positive in order that the Markov chain $(C_{i,j})_{j\geq 0}$ can be further developed.
- We will study the model for two different prior densities $u_{\boldsymbol{\Theta}}$, namely non-informative priors and associate conjugate priors. Associate conjugate priors were already defined and studied in Section 4.3.
- The Gaussian model and the Gamma model studied in Gisler (2006) are special cases of the EDF defined above. However, the domain of the Gaussian model needs to be restricted to strictly positive outcomes $F_{i,j}$.
- The model is formulated in terms of individual development factors $F_{i,j}$. However, we could also formulate it in terms of cumulative claims $C_{i,j}$. Then, for a given $\boldsymbol{\Theta}$, we would obtain a time series CL model similar to Model Assumptions 3.9.

9.2.1 Prediction of the Ultimate Claim

We define the conditional expectation (see also Theorem 4.39)

$$F_j(\Theta_j) = E\left[F_{i,j+1}\middle|\, \boldsymbol{\Theta}, C_{i,j}\right] = b'(\Theta_j) \tag{9.22}$$

Hence, for a given $\boldsymbol{\Theta}$ we have

$$\begin{aligned} E\left[C_{i,j+1}\middle|\, \boldsymbol{\Theta}, C_{i,0}, \ldots, C_{i,j}\right] &= E\left[C_{i,j+1}\middle|\, \boldsymbol{\Theta}, C_{i,j}\right] \\ &= C_{i,j}\; E\left[F_{i,j+1}\middle|\, \boldsymbol{\Theta}, C_{i,j}\right] \\ &= F_j(\Theta_j)\; C_{i,j} \end{aligned} \tag{9.23}$$

which corresponds to the CL iteration (2.1) with f_j replaced by $F_j(\Theta_j)$. For the variance function we define (see (6.19))

$$V\big(F_j(\Theta_j)\big) = b''\left((b')^{-1}\left(F_j(\Theta_j)\right)\right) = b''\left(\Theta_j\right) \tag{9.24}$$

Hence, we see that Model Assumptions 9.13 correspond to (see also Theorem 4.39)

$$E\left[F_{i,j+1}\middle|\, \boldsymbol{\Theta}, C_{i,j}\right] = F_j(\Theta_j) \quad \text{and} \quad \operatorname{Var}\left(F_{i,j+1}\middle|\, \boldsymbol{\Theta}, C_{i,j}\right) = \frac{\sigma_j^2}{C_{i,j}}\; V\big(F_j(\Theta_j)\big) \tag{9.25}$$

Note that this is similar to the CL model considered in Section 3.4, see (3.56)–(3.57). However, the programme in this section will differ from the outline in Section 3.4. With the help of appropriate prior distributions for $\boldsymbol{\Theta}$ we calculate posterior distributions and estimate parameters using Bayesian inference.

9.2.2 Likelihood Function and Posterior Distribution

We define the vectors of observed individual CL factors related to $\mathcal{D}_I$ by

$$\mathbf{y}_j = \left(F_{0,j+1}, \ldots, F_{I-j-1,j+1}\right)'$$

for $j = 0, \ldots, J-1$. Vector $\mathbf{y}_j$ is the jth observed column of individual claims development factors in the claims development triangle $\mathcal{D}_I$. Conditional on $\boldsymbol{\Theta}$ and $\mathcal{B}_0$, the likelihood function of the observations $(\mathbf{y}_0, \ldots, \mathbf{y}_{J-1})$ is then given by

$$h_{\boldsymbol{\Theta},\mathcal{B}_0}(\mathbf{y}_0, \ldots, \mathbf{y}_{J-1}) = \prod_{\substack{i+j\le I\\ 1\le j\le J}} a\left(F_{i,j}, \frac{\sigma_{j-1}^2}{C_{i,j-1}}\right) \exp\left\{\frac{F_{i,j}\;\Theta_{j-1} - b(\Theta_{j-1})}{\sigma_{j-1}^2 / C_{i,j-1}}\right\} \tag{9.26}$$

where $C_{i,j} = C_{i,j-1}\; F_{i,j} = C_{i,0}\; F_{i,1} \cdots F_{i,j}$. Next we rearrange the terms of the product of the last terms in (9.26). This gives

$$\prod_{\substack{i+j\le I\\ 1\le j\le J}} \exp\left\{\frac{F_{i,j}\ \Theta_{j-1} - b(\Theta_{j-1})}{\sigma_{j-1}^2/C_{i,j-1}}\right\}$$

$$= \exp\left\{\sum_{\substack{i+j\le I\\ 1\le j\le J}} \frac{C_{i,j-1}}{\sigma_{j-1}^2}\left(F_{i,j}\ \Theta_{j-1} - b(\Theta_{j-1})\right)\right\}$$

$$= \exp\left\{\sum_{j=1}^{J}\left[\frac{\Theta_{j-1}}{\sigma_{j-1}^2}\sum_{i=0}^{I-j} C_{i,j} - \frac{b(\Theta_{j-1})}{\sigma_{j-1}^2}\sum_{i=0}^{I-j} C_{i,j-1}\right]\right\}$$

$$= \prod_{j=1}^{J} \exp\left\{\frac{\Theta_{j-1}}{\sigma_{j-1}^2}\sum_{i=0}^{I-j} C_{i,j} - \frac{b(\Theta_{j-1})}{\sigma_{j-1}^2}\sum_{i=0}^{I-j} C_{i,j-1}\right\}$$

This implies that, conditional on $\boldsymbol{\Theta}$ and $\mathcal{B}_0$, the vector $(\mathbf{y}_0, \ldots, \mathbf{y}_{J-1})$ has the likelihood function

$$h_{\boldsymbol{\Theta},\mathcal{B}_0}(\mathbf{y}_0, \ldots, \mathbf{y}_{J-1}) \propto \prod_{j=1}^{J} \exp\left\{\frac{\Theta_{j-1}}{\sigma_{j-1}^2}\sum_{i=0}^{I-j} C_{i,j} - \frac{b(\Theta_{j-1})}{\sigma_{j-1}^2}\sum_{i=0}^{I-j} C_{i,j-1}\right\}$$

where $\propto$ means that we only consider the relevant terms that contain $\boldsymbol{\Theta}$. Next, we construct the posterior distribution $u(\boldsymbol{\theta}|\mathcal{D}_I)$ of $\boldsymbol{\Theta}$, given the observations $\mathcal{D}_I$, for different prior densities $u_{\boldsymbol{\Theta}}$. This is given by

$$u(\boldsymbol{\theta}|\mathcal{D}_I) \propto \prod_{j=1}^{J} \exp\left\{\frac{\theta_{j-1}}{\sigma_{j-1}^2}\sum_{i=0}^{I-j} C_{i,j} - \frac{b(\theta_{j-1})}{\sigma_{j-1}^2}\sum_{i=0}^{I-j} C_{i,j-1}\right\}\ u_{\boldsymbol{\Theta}}(\boldsymbol{\theta}) \tag{9.27}$$

with $\boldsymbol{\theta} = (\theta_0, \ldots, \theta_{J-1})$

Below, we consider two different types of prior distribution $u_{\boldsymbol{\Theta}}$: (i) conjugate prior distributions that we have already considered in Section 4.3; (ii) non-informative priors that will lead to the classical CL estimators.

Associate Conjugate Priors

Model Assumptions 9.15 (associated conjugate)

The random variables $\Theta_0, \ldots, \Theta_{J-1}$ are independent with densities

$$\Theta_j \overset{(d)}{\sim} d(f_j^{(0)}, \tau_j^2)\ \exp\left\{\frac{\theta\ f_j^{(0)} - b(\theta)}{\tau_j^2}\right\} d\theta \tag{9.28}$$

and $\exp\left\{(\theta f - b(\theta))/\tau^2\right\}$ disappears on the boundary of the domain of Θ_j for all f and $\tau^2 > 0$. □

Under Model Assumptions 9.13 and 9.15 the posterior distribution (9.27) is proportional to

$$\propto \prod_{j=1}^{J} \exp\left\{\frac{\theta_{j-1}}{\sigma_{j-1}^2}\sum_{i=0}^{I-j} C_{i,j} - \frac{b(\theta_{j-1})}{\sigma_{j-1}^2}\sum_{i=0}^{I-j} C_{i,j-1}\right\} \exp\left\{\frac{\theta_{j-1}\ f_j^{(0)} - b(\theta_{j-1})}{\tau_j^2}\right\}$$

This can be rewritten as follows

$$u(\boldsymbol{\theta}|\mathcal{D}_I) \propto \prod_{j=1}^{J} \exp\left\{\frac{\theta_{j-1}\,\widetilde{f}_{j-1} - b(\theta_{j-1})}{\alpha_{j-1}\,\sigma_{j-1}^2/S_{j-1}^{[I-j]}}\right\} \tag{9.29}$$

where we have defined

$$\widetilde{f}_{j-1} = \alpha_{j-1}\,\widehat{f}_{j-1} + \left(1-\alpha_{j-1}\right)\,f_{j-1}^{(0)}$$

$$\alpha_{j-1} = \frac{S_{j-1}^{[I-j]}\,\tau_{j-1}^2}{S_{j-1}^{[I-j]}\,\tau_{j-1}^2 + \sigma_{j-1}^2} = \frac{S_{j-1}^{[I-j]}}{S_{j-1}^{[I-j]} + \sigma_{j-1}^2/\tau_{j-1}^2}$$

$$S_{j-1}^{[I-j]} = \sum_{i=0}^{I-j} C_{i,j-1} \tag{9.30}$$

Estimators $\widetilde{f}_{j-1}$ and $\widehat{f}_{j-1}$ are the Bayesian estimator for $F_{j-1}(\Theta_{j-1})$ and the classical age-to-age factor estimate defined in (2.4), respectively.

Remarks 9.16

- We obtain a credibility weighted average $\widetilde{f}_{j-1}$ between a prior estimate $f_{j-1}^{(0)}$ for the CL factor f_{j-1} and the purely observation based age-to-age factor estimate $\widehat{f}_{j-1}$ from (2.4).
- If we choose $\alpha_{j-1} = 1$, i.e. choose $\kappa_{j-1} = \sigma_{j-1}^2/\tau_{j-1}^2 = 0$, then we have the classical age-to-age factor estimate from the CL method.
- This way we can estimate credibility weighted claims development patterns, that is, the observations $\widehat{f}_{j-1}$ are smoothed with the help of external data or expert opinion reflected by $f_{j-1}^{(0)}$. The credibility weights α_{j-1} describe the degree of smoothing.

COROLLARY 9.17 *Under Model Assumptions 9.13 and 9.15 we have*

$$E\left[F_j(\Theta_j)\middle|\,\mathcal{D}_I\right] = E\left[b'(\Theta_j)\middle|\,\mathcal{D}_I\right] = \widetilde{f}_j$$

Moreover, conditionally given $\mathcal{D}_I$, the $F_j(\Theta_j)$ are independent.

Proof The proof follows from Theorem 4.39. □

This implies the following corollary:

COROLLARY 9.18 *Under Model Assumptions 9.13 and 9.15 we have*

$$\widehat{C}_{i,J}^{BCL} = E\left[C_{i,J}\middle|\,\mathcal{D}_I\right] = C_{i,I-i}\prod_{j=I-i}^{J-1}\widetilde{f}_j$$

Proof We easily see that

$$E\left[C_{i,J}\middle|\,\mathcal{D}_I\right] = E\left[E\left[C_{i,J}\middle|\,\boldsymbol{\Theta}, C_{i,I-i}\right]\middle|\,\mathcal{D}_I\right] = C_{i,I-i}\,E\left[\prod_{j=I-i}^{J-1} F_j(\Theta_j)\middle|\,\mathcal{D}_I\right]$$

which completes the proof in view of Corollary 9.17. □

Non-informative Priors

Model Assumptions 9.19 (non-informative prior)

The random variables $\Theta_0, \ldots, \Theta_{J-1}$ are i.i.d. with uniform distribution $\mathcal{U}(-a, a)$ on the interval $(-a, a)$. □

Under Model Assumptions 9.13 and 9.19 the posterior distribution of $\boldsymbol{\Theta}$, given the observations $\mathcal{D}_I$, is given by

$$u(\boldsymbol{\theta}|\mathcal{D}_I) \propto \prod_{j=1}^{J} \exp\left\{ \frac{\theta_{j-1}}{\sigma_{j-1}^2} \sum_{i=0}^{I-j} C_{i,j} - \frac{b(\theta_{j-1})}{\sigma_{j-1}^2} \sum_{i=0}^{I-j} C_{i,j-1} \right\} 1_{(-a,a)}(\theta_{j-1})$$

If we now consider the limiting posterior distribution for $a \to \infty$ we obtain

$$\begin{aligned} u(\boldsymbol{\theta}|\mathcal{D}_I) &\propto \prod_{j=1}^{J} \exp\left\{ \frac{\theta_{j-1}}{\sigma_{j-1}^2} \sum_{i=0}^{I-j} C_{i,j} - \frac{b(\theta_{j-1})}{\sigma_{j-1}^2} \sum_{i=0}^{I-j} C_{i,j-1} \right\} \\ &= \prod_{j=1}^{J} \exp\left\{ \frac{\theta_{j-1}\widehat{f}_{j-1} - b(\theta_{j-1})}{\sigma_{j-1}^2 / S_{j-1}^{[I-j]}} \right\} \end{aligned}$$

That is, the posterior distribution of $F_{j-1}(\Theta_{j-1}) = b'(\Theta_{j-1})$ has an expected value $\widehat{f}_{j-1}$, which is the classical estimate of the age-to-age factor f_{j-1}. In other words, this Bayesian inference model with non-informative priors gives a further stochastic model that explains the CL algorithm. We immediately have the following corollary:

COROLLARY 9.20 *Under Model Assumptions 9.13 and 9.19 we have*

$$\lim_{a\to\infty} E\left[F_j(\Theta_j)\middle|\mathcal{D}_I\right] = \lim_{a\to\infty} E\left[b'(\Theta_j)\middle|\mathcal{D}_I\right] = \widehat{f}_j$$

Conditional on $\mathcal{D}_I$, the $F_j(\Theta_j)$ are independent. Moreover, we have

$$\widehat{C}_{i,J}^{\mathrm{ACL}} = \lim_{a\to\infty} E\left[C_{i,J}\middle|\mathcal{D}_I\right] = C_{i,I-i} \prod_{j=I-i}^{J-1} \widehat{f}_j$$

Proof The proof is similar to the proof of Corollary 9.18. Note that $\exp\{(\theta f - b(\theta))/\tau^2\}$ needs to disappear on $\pm\infty$ for all f and τ^2. □

9.2.3 Mean Square Error of Prediction

We estimate the uncertainties of the predictors $\widehat{C}_{i,J}^{BCL}$ and $\widehat{C}_{i,J}^{\mathrm{ACL}}$ for the ultimate claim $C_{i,J}$. We measure this uncertainty again in terms of the conditional MSEP. It is given by

$$\mathrm{msep}_{C_{i,J}|\mathcal{D}_I}\left(\widehat{C}_{i,J}^{\mathrm{ACL}}\right) = E\left[\left(C_{i,J} - \widehat{C}_{i,J}^{\mathrm{ACL}}\right)^2\middle|\mathcal{D}_I\right] = \mathrm{Var}\left(C_{i,J}\middle|\mathcal{D}_I\right)$$

and

$$\text{msep}_{C_{i,J}|\mathcal{D}_I}\left(\widehat{C}_{i,J}^{BCL}\right) = E\left[\left(C_{i,J} - \widehat{C}_{i,J}^{BCL}\right)^2 \middle| \mathcal{D}_I\right] = \text{Var}\left(C_{i,J} \middle| \mathcal{D}_I\right)$$

respectively, where the first line only holds true in an asymptotic sense. Observe that now we have put the parameter uncertainty into the distribution of Θ_j. In this perspective the MSEP defined above contains a component for the parameter uncertainty.

In the following we consider $\widehat{C}_{i,J}^{BCL}$. If we choose $\alpha_j = 1$, this corresponds to the MSEP of the classical age-to-age factor estimate $\widehat{f}_j$ (motivated by our Bayesian Model Assumptions 9.13; cf. Remarks 9.16). For $\alpha_j < 1$ we assume that the parameters $f_j^{(0)}$, τ_j^2 and σ_j^2 are given constants.

Associate Conjugate Priors

We write $F_j = F_j(\Theta_j)$. Observe that we have the following recursive formula for the conditional variances

$$\begin{aligned}
&\text{Var}\left(C_{i,J} \middle| \Theta, \mathcal{D}_I\right)\\
&\quad = E\left[\text{Var}\left(C_{i,J} \middle| \Theta, C_{i,J-1}\right) \middle| \Theta, \mathcal{D}_I\right] + \text{Var}\left(E\left[C_{i,J} \middle| \Theta, C_{i,J-1}\right] \middle| \Theta, \mathcal{D}_I\right)\\
&\quad = \sigma_{J-1}^2 \; V(F_{J-1}) \; E\left[C_{i,J-1} \middle| \Theta, \mathcal{D}_I\right] + F_{J-1}^2 \; \text{Var}\left(C_{i,J-1} \middle| \Theta, \mathcal{D}_I\right)\\
&\quad = \sigma_{J-1}^2 \; \frac{V(F_{J-1})}{F_{J-1}} \; C_{i,I-i} \prod_{j=I-i}^{J-1} F_j + F_{J-1}^2 \; \text{Var}\left(C_{i,J-1} \middle| \Theta, \mathcal{D}_I\right)
\end{aligned}$$

Using Corollary 9.17 this implies that we obtain the following recursive formula

$$\begin{aligned}
&\text{Var}\left(C_{i,J} \middle| \mathcal{D}_I\right)\\
&\quad = E\left[\text{Var}\left(C_{i,J} \middle| \Theta, \mathcal{D}_I\right) \middle| \mathcal{D}_I\right] + \text{Var}\left(E\left[C_{i,J} \middle| \Theta, \mathcal{D}_I\right] \middle| \mathcal{D}_I\right)\\
&\quad = \sigma_{J-1}^2 \; C_{i,I-i} \; E\left[\frac{V(F_{J-1})}{F_{J-1}} \prod_{j=I-i}^{J-1} F_j \middle| \mathcal{D}_I\right] + \text{Var}\left(F_{J-1} \; C_{i,J-1} \middle| \mathcal{D}_I\right)\\
&\quad = \sigma_{J-1}^2 \; C_{i,I-i} \; E\left[V(F_{J-1}) \middle| \mathcal{D}_I\right] \prod_{j=I-i}^{J-2} \widetilde{f}_j + \text{Var}\left(F_{J-1} \; C_{i,J-1} \middle| \mathcal{D}_I\right) \qquad (9.31)
\end{aligned}$$

We see that the conditional MSEP decouples again into two terms. If we iterate this procedure for the last term on the right-hand side of (9.31) we obtain

$$\begin{aligned}
\text{Var}\left(C_{i,J} \middle| \mathcal{D}_I\right) = {} & C_{i,I-i} \sum_{j=I-i}^{J-1} \prod_{n=j+1}^{J-1} E\left[F_n^2 \middle| \mathcal{D}_I\right] \; \sigma_j^2 \; E\left[V(F_j) \middle| \mathcal{D}_I\right] \prod_{m=I-i}^{j-1} \widetilde{f}_m\\
& + C_{i,I-i}^2 \; \text{Var}\left(\prod_{j=I-i}^{J-1} F_j \middle| \mathcal{D}_I\right) \qquad (9.32)
\end{aligned}$$

The second term on the right-hand side of (9.32) corresponds to the conditional parameter estimation error in the CL method (see also (3.26)).

In the classical CL approach the first term on the right-hand side of (9.32) corresponds to the conditional process variance. Here, it corresponds to the conditional process variance plus a term that is similar to the parameter prediction error from Section 3.4. This means that this model does not lead to such a clear distinction between the parameter error terms as the one studied in Section 3.4.

Note that conditionally, given $\mathcal{D}_I$, the F_j's are independent, i.e. the last term in (9.32) can easily be calculated and we obtain a multiplicative structure as in the conditional resampling approach in Subsection 3.2.3 for the classical CL method (see also the derivation of formula (3.26)).

Using (9.22) and Corollary 9.17 we have

$$E\left[F_j(\Theta_j)^2 \middle| \mathcal{D}_I\right] = E\left[\left(b'(\Theta_j)\right)^2 \middle| \mathcal{D}_I\right]$$

and

$$v_j(\mathcal{D}_I) \overset{def.}{=} \text{Var}\left(F_j(\Theta_j) \middle| \mathcal{D}_I\right) = E\left[\left(b'(\Theta_j) - \widetilde{f}_j\right)^2 \middle| \mathcal{D}_I\right]$$

Hence, we obtain

$$v_j(\mathcal{D}_I) = \frac{\alpha_j\,\sigma_j^2}{S_j^{[I-j-1]}}\, E\left[b''(\Theta_j) \middle| \mathcal{D}_I\right] = \frac{\alpha_j\,\sigma_j^2}{S_j^{[I-j-1]}}\, E\left[V(F_j(\Theta_j)) \middle| \mathcal{D}_I\right] \tag{9.33}$$

where we have used the explicit form of the posterior distribution – see (9.29) – (4.41) and (9.24) and partial integration (note that we now need the assumption that $b'(\theta)$ times the posterior density of Θ_j disappears on the boundary of the domain of Θ_j). This immediately leads to the following corollary:

COROLLARY 9.21 *Under Model Assumptions 9.13 and 9.15 we have that the conditional MSEP of the ultimate claim for a single accident year $i \in \{1, \ldots, I\}$ is given by*

$$\text{msep}_{C_{i,J}|\mathcal{D}_I}\left(\widehat{C}_{i,J}^{BCL}\right) = \text{Var}\left(C_{i,J} \middle| \mathcal{D}_I\right) = C_{i,I-i}\,\Gamma_{I-i}^{B} + C_{i,I-i}^2\,\Delta_{I-i}^{B}$$

where

$$\Gamma_{I-i}^{B} = \sum_{j=I-i}^{J-1} \prod_{n=j+1}^{J-1} \left(v_n(\mathcal{D}_I) + \widetilde{f}_n^2\right) \frac{S_j^{[I-j-1]}\; v_j(\mathcal{D}_I)}{\alpha_j} \prod_{m=I-i}^{j-1} \widetilde{f}_m$$

$$\Delta_{I-i}^{B} = \prod_{j=I-i}^{J-1} \left(v_j(\mathcal{D}_I) + \widetilde{f}_j^2\right) - \prod_{j=I-i}^{J-1} \widetilde{f}_j^2$$

Remarks 9.22

- Observe that the term Γ_{I-i}^{B} has a similar structure as in the classical conditional process variance term in the distribution-free CL model (see (3.10)). However, the single terms differ due to the fact that we also consider fluctuations in the CL factors $F_j(\Theta_j)$. This corresponds to the parameter prediction error considered in Section 3.4.

- The term Δ^B_{I-i} has the same multiplicative structure as in the conditional resampling approach for the classical CL method, see (3.26).
- The difficulty for the interpretation now is that there is no longer a strict distinction between conditional process variance and conditional estimation error, note that Γ^B_{I-i} also contains fluctuations in $F_j(\Theta_j)$ (not only Δ^B_{I-i}).
- For the special case where

$$b(\theta)=\frac{\theta^2}{2} \tag{9.34}$$

i.e. Gaussian case, we see that the conditional variance of $F_{i,j+1}$, given $\mathbf{\Theta}$ and $C_{i,j}$, does not depend on Θ_j, i.e. we have

$$\mathrm{Var}\left(F_{i,j+1}\middle|\,\mathbf{\Theta},C_{i,j}\right)=\frac{\sigma_j^2}{C_{i,j}} \qquad \text{and} \qquad v_j(\mathcal{D}_I)=\frac{\alpha_j\,\sigma_j^2}{S_j^{[I-j-1]}}$$

(cf. (9.24)–(9.25) and (9.33)). Under the Gaussian assumption this implies that

$$\mathrm{msep}_{C_{i,J}|\mathcal{D}_I}\left(\widehat{C}_{i,J}^{BCL}\right)=\mathrm{Var}\left(C_{i,J}\middle|\,\mathcal{D}_I\right)=C_{i,I-i}\,\Gamma_{I-i}^{B,*}+C_{i,I-i}^2\,\Delta_{I-i}^{B,*}, \tag{9.35}$$

where

$$\Gamma_{I-i}^{B,*}=\sum_{j=I-i}^{J-1}\prod_{n=j+1}^{J-1}\left(\frac{\alpha_n\,\sigma_n^2}{S_n^{[I-n-1]}}+\widetilde{f}_n^2\right)\sigma_j^2\prod_{m=I-i}^{j-1}\widetilde{f}_m$$

$$\Delta_{I-i}^{B,*}=\prod_{j=I-i}^{J-1}\left(\frac{\alpha_j\,\sigma_j^2}{S_j^{[I-j-1]}}+\widetilde{f}_j^2\right)-\prod_{j=I-i}^{J-1}\widetilde{f}_j^2$$

Note, however, that we need to carefully consider the Gaussian case, since it allows for negative individual development factors. That is, for mathematical correctness we need to restrict the Gaussian distribution to the region where it has a positive support (which changes the results since Model Assumptions 9.15 are no longer fulfilled), or we only use it for an approximation (with a very small probability of becoming negative).

- For aggregated accident years, one obtains

$$\mathrm{msep}_{\sum_i C_{i,J}|\mathcal{D}_I}\left(\sum_{i=1}^{I}\widehat{C}_{i,J}^{BCL}\right) \tag{9.36}$$

$$=\sum_{i=1}^{I}\mathrm{msep}_{C_{i,J}|\mathcal{D}_I}\left(\widehat{C}_{i,J}^{BCL}\right)+2\sum_{1\le i<k\le I}C_{i,I-i}\,\widehat{C}_{k,I-i}^{BCL}\,\Delta_{I-i}^{B}$$

- Note that we cannot only calculate the conditional MSEP from (9.29); indeed, we obtain the whole distribution that allows us to calculate the posterior distribution of

$$C_{i,I-i}\prod_{j=I-i}^{J-1}F_j(\Theta_j)$$

given $\mathcal{D}_I$, since the posterior distribution of $(\Theta_{I-i}, \ldots, \Theta_{J-1})$ is the appropriate marginal of $u(\boldsymbol{\theta}|\mathcal{D}_I)$. Under some distributional assumptions this can be done analytically, otherwise we need to apply MCMC methods.

Non-informative Priors

The case of non-informative priors is just a special instance of the case with associate conjugate priors, set $\alpha_j = 1$. Nevertheless, we should discuss that case since it leads to the classical age-to-age factor estimates $\widehat{f}_j$ for f_j and $F_j(\Theta_j)$, respectively. Completely analogously, as in Corollary 9.21, we obtain the following corollary:

COROLLARY 9.23 *Under Model Assumptions 9.13 and 9.19 we have that the conditional MSEP of the ultimate claim for a single accident year $i \in \{1, \ldots, I\}$ is asymptotically for $a \to \infty$ given by*

$$\mathrm{msep}_{C_{i,J}|\mathcal{D}_I}\left(\widehat{C}_{i,J}^{\mathrm{ACL}}\right) = \mathrm{Var}\left(C_{i,J}\middle|\mathcal{D}_I\right) = C_{i,I-i}\,\Gamma_{I-i}^A + C_{i,I-i}^2\,\Delta_{I-i}^A$$

where

$$\Gamma_{I-i}^A = \sum_{j=I-i}^{J-1}\prod_{n=j+1}^{J-1}\left(v_n(\mathcal{D}_I) + \widehat{f}_n^2\right)\, S_j^{[I-j-1]}\, v_j(\mathcal{D}_I)\prod_{m=I-i}^{j-1}\widehat{f}_m$$

$$\Delta_{I-i}^A = \prod_{j=I-i}^{J-1}\left(v_j(\mathcal{D}_I) + \widehat{f}_j^2\right) - \prod_{j=I-i}^{J-1}\widehat{f}_j^2$$

For aggregated accident years one obtains

$$\begin{aligned}\mathrm{msep}_{\sum_i C_{i,J}|\mathcal{D}_I}&\left(\sum_{i=1}^{I}\widehat{C}_{i,J}^{\mathrm{ACL}}\right)\\ &= \sum_{i=1}^{I}\mathrm{msep}_{C_{i,J}|\mathcal{D}_I}\left(\widehat{C}_{i,J}^{\mathrm{ACL}}\right) + 2\sum_{1\le i<k\le I} C_{i,I-i}\,\widehat{C}_{k,I-i}^{\mathrm{ACL}}\,\Delta_{I-i}^A\end{aligned}$$

Consider the special case of the Gaussian variance function given in (9.34). Then we obtain asymptotically

$$\mathrm{Var}\left(\widehat{f}_j\middle|\boldsymbol{\Theta}, \mathcal{B}_j\right) = \frac{\sigma_j^2}{S_j^{[I-j-1]}}$$

and

$$\mathrm{Var}\left(F_j(\Theta_j)\middle|\mathcal{D}_I\right) = v_j(\mathcal{D}_I) = \frac{\sigma_j^2}{S_j^{[I-j-1]}}$$

(cf. (9.33)). This means that in this special case the estimated CL factors $\widehat{f}_j$ as well as the CL factors $F_j(\Theta_j)$ have the same variances under the appropriate conditional distributions.

As a consequence we obtain the same formula for Δ_{I-i}^{A} as for the conditional estimation error in the conditional resampling approach (see Estimator 3.11). For the term Γ_{I-i}^{A} we obtain in this special Gaussian case

$$\begin{aligned}\Gamma_{I-i}^{A,*} &= \sum_{j=I-i}^{J-1} \prod_{n=j+1}^{J-1} E\left[F_n(\Theta_n)^2 \middle| \mathcal{D}_I\right] \sigma_j^2 \prod_{m=I-i}^{j-1} \widehat{f}_m \\ &= \sum_{j=I-i}^{J-1} \prod_{n=j+1}^{J-1} \left(v_n(\mathcal{D}_I)+\widehat{f}_n^2\right) S_j^{[I-j-1]}\, v_j(\mathcal{D}_I) \prod_{m=I-i}^{j-1} \widehat{f}_m \\ &= \sum_{j=I-i}^{J-1} \prod_{n=j+1}^{J-1} \left(\frac{\sigma_n^2}{S_n^{[I-n-1]}}+\widehat{f}_n^2\right) \sigma_j^2 \prod_{m=I-i}^{j-1} \widehat{f}_m \end{aligned} \tag{9.37}$$

That is, for the conditional MSEP we obtain asymptotically in the Gaussian model

$$\mathrm{msep}_{C_{i,J}|\mathcal{D}_I}\left(\widehat{C}_{i,J}^{\mathrm{ACL}}\right) = \mathrm{Var}\left(C_{i,J}\middle| \mathcal{D}_I\right) = C_{i,I-i}\, \Gamma_{I-i}^{A,*} + C_{i,I-i}^2\, \Delta_{I-i}^{A,*}$$

with

$$\Delta_{I-i}^{A,*} = \prod_{j=I-i}^{J-1} \left(\frac{\sigma_j^2}{S_j^{[I-j-1]}}+\widehat{f}_j^2\right) - \prod_{j=I-i}^{J-1} \widehat{f}_j^2 \tag{9.38}$$

Observe that $\Gamma_{I-i}^{A,*}$ differs from the conditional process variance obtained in Estimator 3.11. The reason is that in Estimator 3.11 we assume that $F_n(\Theta_n)$ is a constant, which implies that $E\left[F_n(\Theta_n)^2 \middle| \mathcal{D}_I\right]$ is also a constant. Whereas in (9.37) we obtain an additional variance term (which also corresponds to the CL factor parameter prediction uncertainties). Hence, $\Gamma_{I-i}^{A,*}$ becomes larger than the pure conditional process variance term in Estimator 3.11.

9.2.4 Credibility Chain-Ladder

In the Bayesian set-up – Model Assumptions 9.13 as well as 9.15 and 9.19, respectively – one needs to know the whole distribution of $\boldsymbol{\Theta}$ and the conditional distributions of $C_{i,j}$, given $\boldsymbol{\Theta}$. This is often very restrictive for practical applications and, therefore, one introduces linear credibility estimators. The model at hand is the Bühlmann–Straub model, as in Section 4.5.

Model Assumptions 9.24

- Conditionally, given $\boldsymbol{\Theta}$, the random variables $C_{i,j}$ belonging to different accident years i are independent.
- Conditionally, given $\boldsymbol{\Theta}$, $(C_{i,j})_{j\geq 0}$ is a Markov chain. Moreover, we have

$$E\left[F_{i,j+1}|\boldsymbol{\Theta}, C_{i,j}\right] = F_j(\Theta_j)$$
$$\mathrm{Var}\left(F_{i,j+1}|\boldsymbol{\Theta}, C_{i,j}\right) = \frac{\sigma_j^2(\Theta_j)}{C_{i,j}}$$

  for all $i=0,\ldots,I$ and $j=0,\ldots,J-1$.
- The random variables $\Theta_0,\ldots,\Theta_{J-1}$ are independent.

Observe that Θ_j does not depend on $\mathcal{B}_j$ owing to the assumption that $C_{i,j}$ depends on Θ_{j-1}. Otherwise we would get a contradiction to the assumption that the Θ_j's are independent.

Note that Model Assumptions 9.13 with independent $\Theta_0, \ldots, \Theta_{J-1}$ satisfy Model Assumptions 9.24 (Bühlmann–Straub conditions).

Our goal is to find the credibility estimator $\widehat{F}_j^{\text{cred}}$ for $F_j(\Theta_j)$, given $\mathcal{B}_j$. That is

$$\widehat{F}_j^{\text{cred}} = \text{argmin}_{\widetilde{F} \in L^{(j)}(\mathbf{F},1)} E\left[\left(F_j(\Theta_j) - \widetilde{F}\right)^2 \middle| \mathcal{B}_j \right]$$

where

$$L^{(j)}(\mathbf{F}, 1) = \left\{ \widetilde{F};\ \widetilde{F} = a_0 + \sum_{i=0}^{I-j-1} a_i\, F_{i,j+1} \quad \text{with } a_i \in \mathbb{R} \right\}$$

This means that $\mathcal{B}_j$ acts for the estimation of $F_j(\Theta_j)$ as a fixed volume measure.

THEOREM 9.25 (Bühlmann–Straub) *Under Model Assumptions 9.24 the credibility estimator $\widehat{F}_j^{\text{cred}}$ is given by*

$$\widehat{F}_j^{\text{cred}} = \alpha_j\, \widehat{f}_j + (1-\alpha_j)\, f_j^{(0)}$$

where $\widehat{f}_j$ is the classical CL estimator given in (2.4) *and*

$$\begin{aligned} f_j^{(0)} &= E\left[F_j(\Theta_j)\right] \\ \sigma_j^2 &= E\left[\sigma_j^2(\Theta_j)\right] \\ \tau_j^2 &= \text{Var}\left(F_j(\Theta_j)\right) \\ \alpha_j &= \frac{S_j^{[I-j-1]}}{S_j^{[I-j-1]} + \sigma_j^2/\tau_j^2} \end{aligned}$$

The conditional MSEP is given by

$$\begin{aligned} \text{msep}_{F_j(\Theta_j)|\mathcal{B}_j}\left(\widehat{F}_j^{\text{cred}}\right) &= E\left[\left(\widehat{F}_j^{\text{cred}} - F_j(\Theta_j)\right)^2 \middle| \mathcal{B}_j \right] \\ &= \alpha_j\, \frac{\sigma_j^2}{S_j^{[I-j-1]}} = (1-\alpha_j)\, \tau_j^2 \end{aligned}$$

Proof See Chapter 4 in Bühlmann and Gisler (2005). □

Note that $\widehat{F}_j^{\text{cred}}$ has exactly the same form as the Bayesian estimator $\widetilde{f}_j$, see (9.30). This motivates the following credibility-based prediction for the total ultimate claim $C_{i,J}$

$$\widehat{C}_{i,J}^{\text{CCL}} = \widehat{E}\left[C_{i,J} \middle| \mathcal{D}_I\right] = C_{i,I-i} \prod_{j=I-i}^{J-1} \widehat{F}_j^{\text{cred}}$$

One should highlight here that $\widehat{C}_{i,J}^{\text{CCL}}$ is a credibility-based estimator, due to the fact that it is based on credibility estimators $\widehat{F}_j^{\text{cred}}$ for the CL factors f_j. However, $\widehat{C}_{i,J}^{\text{CCL}}$ is not a credibility predictor for $C_{i,J}$. As immediately seen below, this has the consequence that the derivation of properties of $\widehat{C}_{i,J}^{\text{CCL}}$ are rather difficult. If, for example, we consider the conditional MSEP we obtain

$$\begin{aligned}\text{msep}_{C_{i,J}|\mathcal{D}_I}\left(\widehat{C}_{i,J}^{\text{CCL}}\right) &= E\left[\left(C_{i,J}-\widehat{C}_{i,J}^{\text{CCL}}\right)^2\middle|\mathcal{D}_I\right]\\ &= E\left[\operatorname{Var}\left(C_{i,J}\middle|\boldsymbol{\Theta},\mathcal{D}_I\right)\middle|\mathcal{D}_I\right]\\ &\quad + E\left[\left(E\left[C_{i,J}\middle|\boldsymbol{\Theta},\mathcal{D}_I\right]-\widehat{C}_{i,J}^{\text{CCL}}\right)^2\middle|\mathcal{D}_I\right]\end{aligned}$$

Both terms cannot be calculated explicitly; for example, the second term corresponds to (we multiply both sides by $C_{i,I-i}^{-2}$)

$$\begin{aligned}&C_{i,I-i}^{-2}\, E\left[\left(E\left[C_{i,J}\middle|\boldsymbol{\Theta},\mathcal{D}_I\right]-\widehat{C}_{i,J}^{\text{CCL}}\right)^2\middle|\mathcal{D}_I\right]\\ &= E\left[\left(\prod_{j=I-i}^{J-1}F_j(\Theta_j)-\prod_{j=I-i}^{J-1}\widehat{F}_j^{\text{cred}}\right)^2\middle|\mathcal{D}_I\right]\\ &= \operatorname{Var}\left(\prod_{j=I-i}^{J-1}F_j(\Theta_j)\middle|\mathcal{D}_I\right)+\left(E\left[\prod_{j=I-i}^{J-1}F_j(\Theta_j)\middle|\mathcal{D}_I\right]-\prod_{j=I-i}^{J-1}\widehat{F}_j^{\text{cred}}\right)^2\end{aligned}$$

Observe that the last term compares the Bayesian estimator with the credibility estimator. Under our general Model Assumptions 9.24 we are not able to calculate the Bayesian estimator (otherwise we would not need the credibility-based estimator). Therefore, one often does the following approximation/estimation (motivated by (9.35), see also Gisler and Wüthrich 2007).

$$\widehat{\text{msep}}_{C_{i,J}|\mathcal{D}_I}\left(\widehat{C}_{i,J}^{\text{CCL}}\right)=C_{i,I-i}\,\Gamma_{I-i}^{C,*}+C_{i,I-i}^2\,\Delta_{I-i}^{C,*}$$

where

$$\Gamma_{I-i}^{C,*}=\sum_{j=I-i}^{J-1}\prod_{n=j+1}^{J-1}\left(\frac{\alpha_n\,\sigma_n^2}{S_n^{[I-n-1]}}+\left(\widehat{F}_n^{\text{cred}}\right)^2\right)\sigma_j^2\prod_{m=I-i}^{j-1}\widehat{F}_m^{\text{cred}}$$

$$\Delta_{I-i}^{C,*}=\prod_{j=I-i}^{J-1}\left(\frac{\alpha_j\,\sigma_j^2}{S_j^{[I-j-1]}}+\left(\widehat{F}_j^{\text{cred}}\right)^2\right)-\prod_{j=I-i}^{J-1}\left(\widehat{F}_j^{\text{cred}}\right)^2$$

For aggregated accident years one obtains

$$\widehat{\text{msep}}_{\sum_i C_{i,J}|\mathcal{D}_I}\left(\sum_{i=1}^{I}\widehat{C}_{i,J}^{\text{CCL}}\right)=\sum_{i=1}^{I}\widehat{\text{msep}}_{C_{i,J}|\mathcal{D}_I}\left(\widehat{C}_{i,J}^{\text{CCL}}\right)+2\sum_{1\le i<k\le I}C_{i,I-i}\,\widehat{C}_{k,I-i}^{\text{CCL}}\,\Delta_{I-i}^{C,*}$$

9.2.5 Examples

We present an example for the Bayesian CL method. We calculate the Gaussian case (9.34) for two versions: (i) with associate conjugate priors, (ii) with non-informative priors.

Example 9.26 (associate conjugate priors)

To apply the theory to a data set we need an external expert opinion that determines the prior CL pattern $f_j^{(0)}$ and the variance parameters τ_j^2. These two parameter sets depend on the external information.

For the explicit application here, we revisit Example 3.4.7, in which we have two portfolios: Portfolio A was given by Table 3.12 and Portfolio B was given by Table 3.18. Moreover, we know that both portfolios contain the same line of business and that Portfolio A has about twice the size of Portfolio B.

Now we choose the set-up as follows: Portfolio A plays the role of the expert, that is, for $f_j^{(0)}$ we choose the CL factors of Portfolio A. Then we apply the Bayesian CL method to Portfolio B. The only parameter for which we do not have sufficient data for the estimation is τ_j^2. Therefore, τ_j^2 is given a reasonable value using external expert opinion only.

The parameters are then given by Table 9.7.

Table 9.7 Prior parameters: $f_j^{(0)}$ are the CL factors from Portfolio A, τ_j is determined using expert opinion only

$j=$	0	1	2	3	4	5	6	7	8	9
$f_j^{(0)}$	1.4416	1.0278	1.0112	1.0057	1.0048	1.0025	1.0008	1.0020	1.0010	1.0001
τ_j	0.0144	0.0093	0.0081	0.0070	0.0060	0.0050	0.0040	0.0030	0.0020	0.0010

This leads to the following parameter estimates for Portfolio B (see Table 9.8). Note that σ_j^2 is estimated with the classical variance estimator given by formula (3.4).

Table 9.8 Parameters for the Bayesian CL method applied to Portfolio B

$j=$	0	1	2	3	4	5	6	7	8	9
$f_j^{(0)}$	1.4416	1.0278	1.0112	1.0057	1.0048	1.0025	1.0008	1.0020	1.0010	1.0001
$\widehat{f}_j$	1.4405	1.0331	1.0117	1.0063	1.0046	1.0041	1.0010	1.0003	1.0009	1.0000
$\widetilde{f}_j$	1.4409	1.0307	1.0116	1.0063	1.0046	1.0038	1.0010	1.0003	1.0009	1.0000
τ_j	0.0144	0.0093	0.0081	0.0070	0.0060	0.0050	0.0040	0.0030	0.0020	0.0010
σ_j	13.0026	10.8936	3.5471	2.2520	2.3583	2.6386	1.1066	0.3060	0.6908	0.0559
α_j(%)	61.0	55.1	89.4	93.6	90.0	81.6	93.4	98.9	87.4	99.6

In Table 9.8 we see that the age-to-age factor estimates $\widehat{f}_j$ of Portfolio B are smoothed with the help of the prior parameters $f_j^{(0)}$. This leads to the Bayesian estimators $\widetilde{f}_j$ for Portfolio B. All credibility weights α_j for the smoothing are larger than 50% (for our specific choice of τ_j^2), i.e. for this parameter set we give more weight to the observations. Here we could question the choice of τ_j^2 because α_j could also be decreasing for higher j since the estimate is based on fewer observations.

Now, we can calculate the three different estimators for the conditionally expected ultimate claim, given $\mathcal{D}_I$:

$$\widehat{C}_{i,J}^{(0)} = C_{i,I-i} \prod_{j=I-i}^{J-1} f_j^{(0)} \qquad \text{prior estimate}$$

$$\widehat{C_{i,J}}^{\text{CL}} = C_{i,I-i} \prod_{j=I-i}^{J-1} \widehat{f}_j \qquad \text{CL estimate}$$

$$\widehat{C}_{i,J}^{BCL} = C_{i,I-i} \prod_{j=I-i}^{J-1} \widetilde{f}_j \qquad \text{Bayes CL estimate}$$

This leads to the reserves given in Table 9.9. Moreover, Table 9.9 provides the estimates for the conditional MSEP in the Bayesian CL method (Gaussian model) and for the CL method (conditional approach).

Table 9.9 Reserves and conditional MSEP for Portfolio B: Bayesian CL method (associate conjugate priors) and CL method

i	Reserves			Bayes			CL		
	Prior $f_j^{(0)}$	CL $\widehat{f}_j$	Bayes $\widetilde{f}_j$	Process std dev.	Estimation error$^{1/2}$	msep$^{1/2}$	Process std dev.	Estimation error$^{1/2}$	msep$^{1/2}$
7	9	−4	−4	18	7	19	18	7	19
8	113	91	92	228	77	240	228	82	242
9	457	166	170	293	117	316	293	124	319
10	580	319	322	520	194	555	520	202	558
11	973	960	916	1159	384	1221	1159	419	1233
12	1474	1444	1407	1382	419	1444	1382	452	1454
13	2591	2650	2601	1737	561	1826	1738	599	1838
14	3641	3748	3701	2057	587	2139	2058	625	2151
15	7409	8225	7859	4555	1031	4670	4557	1295	4738
16	45 244	45 929	45 616	6024	1287	6160	6033	1631	6249
Total	62 490	63 530	62 681	8243	3516	8962	8251	4037	9186

We conclude that the CL parameters are more conservative since they lead to slightly higher reserves. Pay attention to the fact that we compare volume-weighted quantities which usually make interpretations more difficult. This means that with the same CL parameters we could come to a different conclusion if the weights of the accident years were different.

The conditional MSEPs in Table 9.9 are calculated with formulas (9.35)–(9.36) for the Bayesian CL method and with the conditional resampling approach for the CL method (see Estimator 3.14).

We see that the MSEP results for the two methods mainly differ in the term that corresponds to the parameter estimation error in the CL method and $\Delta_{I-i}^{B,*}$ in the Bayesian CL method, respectively. The main difference is that the Bayesian CL method scales these error terms with the credibility weights α_j ($< 100\%$), which leads to a smaller value. □

Example 9.27 (non-informative priors)

We use the same data set as in Example 9.26; that is, we calculate the reserves for Portfolio B of Example 3.4.7. For the non-informative prior case, Portfolio A is not relevant because we do not rely on prior information.

The reserves $\widehat{C}_{i,J}^{ACL}$ are equal to the CL reserves $\widehat{C_{i,J}}^{CL}$ and for the calculation of the conditional MSEP we use formulas (9.37)–(9.38). The results are provided in Table 9.10.

Table 9.10 Reserves and conditional MSEP for Portfolio B: Bayesian CL method (non-informative priors) and CL method

i	Reserves	Non-informative			CL		
		Process std dev.	Estimation error$^{1/2}$	msep$^{1/2}$	Process std dev.	Estimation error$^{1/2}$	msep$^{1/2}$
7	−4	17.9	7	19	17.9	7	19
8	91	227.7	82	242	227.7	82	242
9	166	293.4	124	319	293.4	124	319
10	319	519.7	202	558	519.7	202	558
11	960	1 159.2	419	1233	1 159.2	419	1233
12	1444	1 382.1	452	1454	1 382.1	452	1454
13	2650	1 737.6	599	1838	1 737.6	599	1838
14	3748	2 057.8	625	2151	2 057.8	625	2151
15	8225	4 557.3	1295	4738	4 557.3	1295	4738
16	45 929	6 033.1	1 631	6250	6 032.9	1631	6249
Total	63 530	8 251.3	4 037	9186	8 251.1	4037	9186

The conditional estimation errors are equal, due to the fact that we use the same multiplicative structure for its calculation, that is, $\Delta_{I-i}^{A,*}$ for the non-informative prior case and the conditional resampling approach for the CL method (formula (3.27)).

On the other hand, the term for the conditional process variance differs, compare $\Gamma_{I-i}^{A,*}$ and (3.10). The difference lies in the terms

$$\prod_{n=j+1}^{J-1}\left(\frac{\sigma_n^2}{S_n^{[I-n-1]}}+\widehat{f}_n^2\right)$$

for the non-informative prior case, and

$$\prod_{n=j+1}^{J-1}\widehat{f}_n^2$$

for the process variance in the CL method. However, Table 9.10 shows that this difference is of negligible order for our data set. This comes from the fact that for typical data sets

$$\widehat{f}_j^2 \gg \frac{\sigma_j^2}{S_j^{[I-j-1]}}$$

□

9.2.6 Markov Chain Monte Carlo Methods

We close this section with some remarks on MCMC methods. In view of Model Assumptions 9.13 and 9.15 there are different possibilities that require the application of MCMC methods:

- One reason could be that the prior density u_Θ of $\boldsymbol{\Theta}=(\Theta_0,\ldots,\Theta_{J-1})$ does not fit the distribution of the individual CL factors $F_{i,j}$ given in Model Assumptions 9.13. This can have various reasons; for example, we want to have different tails in the distribution of Θ_j or we want to model dependencies between the different risk characteristics $\Theta_0,\ldots,\Theta_{J-1}$. In that case we take the posterior distribution given in (9.27) and apply the MCMC method as described in Section 4.4 (MH algorithm). For an example with dependent CL factors we refer to Section 11.2.
- We would like to have distributions for the individual development factors $F_{i,j}$ different from the conditional EDF distributions (see Model Assumptions 9.13). In that case the likelihood function of the problem changes and the posterior distribution given in (9.27) need to be adjusted accordingly. Then we apply the MH algorithm to the new likelihood function as described in Section 4.4.
- If we assume Model Assumptions 9.13 and 9.15, we can calculate the posterior distribution of $\boldsymbol{\Theta}=(\Theta_0,\ldots,\Theta_{J-1})$. This is given by (9.29). But then for solvency purposes, for instance, we would also like to calculate the posterior distribution of

$$\widehat{C}_{i,J}(\boldsymbol{\Theta},\mathcal{D}_I)=E\left[C_{i,J}\middle|\boldsymbol{\Theta},\mathcal{D}_I\right]=C_{i,I-i}\prod_{j=I-i}^{J-1}F_j(\Theta_j)$$

given $\mathcal{D}_I$, with $F_j(\Theta_j)=b'(\Theta_j)$. Note that this can take non-trivial forms, so that the distribution of $\widehat{C}_{i,J}(\boldsymbol{\Theta},\mathcal{D}_I)$ can only be calculated numerically. Henceforth, one needs to apply the MCMC method to this situation. Of course the conditional expectation, given $\mathcal{D}_I$, is given by $\widehat{C}_{i,J}^{BCL}=E[C_{i,J}|\mathcal{D}_I]$

Moreover, observe that the second conditional moment is given by

$$\operatorname{Var}\left(\widehat{C}_{i,J}(\boldsymbol{\Theta},\mathcal{D}_I)\middle|\mathcal{D}_I\right)=C_{i,I-i}^2\,\Delta_{I-i}^B \tag{9.39}$$

Below we numerically calculate the conditional distribution of $\widehat{C}_{i,J}(\boldsymbol{\Theta},\mathcal{D}_I)$, given $\mathcal{D}_I$, which specifies the parameter estimation error.

We can also calculate the conditional distribution of the random variables $\{F_{i,j};\ i+j>I\}$, given $\mathcal{D}_I$. The joint likelihood function of $\{F_{i,j};\ i+j>I\}$ and $\boldsymbol{\Theta}$, given $\mathcal{D}_I$, is given by

$$\prod_{i+j>I} a\left(F_{i,j},\frac{\sigma_{j-1}^2}{C_{i,j-1}}\right)\exp\left\{\frac{F_{i,j}\,\Theta_{j-1}-b(\Theta_{j-1})}{\sigma_{j-1}^2/C_{i,j-1}}\right\}\;u(\boldsymbol{\Theta}|\mathcal{D}_I) \tag{9.40}$$

From this we can numerically determine the conditional distribution of the ultimate claim

$$\sum_{i=1}^{I}C_{i,J}\qquad\text{with}\qquad C_{i,J}=C_{i,I-i}\prod_{j=I-i+1}^{J}F_{i,j}$$

Below we calculate an example with Gamma distributions. In this example we can explicitly calculate the underlying distribution, so that we can apply the Monte Carlo method for an empirical approximation of the aggregate claims distribution. In cases where we cannot explicitly determine the underlying distributions we apply MCMC methods.

Example 9.26

We revisit the data set Portfolio B given in Example 3.4.7, Table 3.18, and we assume that Model Assumptions 9.13 and 9.15 are satisfied. We choose all prior parameters according to Example 9.26 (see Table 9.7). The parameters of the posterior distribution of $\boldsymbol{\Theta}$, given $\mathcal{D}_I$, are then provided in Table 9.8.

We assume that the domain of the risk characteristic Θ_j is the negative half-line and that $b(\theta) = -\log(-\theta)$, that is, we assume independent Gamma distributions for the priors. Hence, for the posterior of $\boldsymbol{\Theta}$ we have

$$u(\boldsymbol{\theta}|\mathcal{D}_I) \propto \prod_{j=1}^{J} \left(-\theta_{j-1}\right)^{\frac{S_{j-1}^{[I-j]}}{\alpha_{j-1}\sigma_{j-1}^2}} \exp\left\{\frac{\widetilde{f}_{j-1} S_{j-1}^{[I-j]}}{\alpha_{j-1}\sigma_{j-1}^2}\,\theta_{j-1}\right\} \tag{9.41}$$

(cf. (9.29)), which, of course, is again a Gamma distribution (this already follows from Lemma 4.37). Therefore, in this example we can explicitly calculate the normalizing constants. This directly allows for the application of simulations of independent Gamma random variables and for the calculation of the posterior distribution of

$$\widehat{C}_{i,J}(\boldsymbol{\Theta}, \mathcal{D}_I) = E\left[C_{i,J}\middle|\boldsymbol{\Theta}, \mathcal{D}_I\right] = C_{i,I-i} \prod_{j=I-i}^{J-1} \frac{-1}{\Theta_j}$$

which implies

$$\widehat{C}_{i,J}^{BCL} = C_{i,I-i} E\left[\prod_{j=I-i}^{J-1} \frac{-1}{\Theta_j}\middle| \mathcal{D}_I\right] = C_{i,I-i} \prod_{j=I-i}^{J-1} E\left[\frac{-1}{\Theta_j}\middle| \mathcal{D}_I\right] = C_{i,I-i} \prod_{j=I-i}^{J-1} \widetilde{f}_j$$

For the conditional distribution of $F_{i,j}$, given $\boldsymbol{\Theta}$ and $C_{i,j-1}$, we also assume a Gamma distribution with parameters $C_{i,j-1}/\sigma_{j-1}^2$ and $-\Theta_{j-1}C_{i,j-1}/\sigma_{j-1}^2$. Note that this is in line with Model Assumptions 9.13. Hence we can numerically calculate the posterior of the ultimate claim $\sum_{i=1}^{I} C_{i,J}$, given $\mathcal{D}_I$.

The key figures are then given by

$$\begin{aligned}
\mathrm{Vco}(\Theta_j|\mathcal{D}_I) &= \left(1 + \frac{S_{j-1}^{[I-j]}}{\alpha_{j-1}\sigma_{j-1}^2}\right)^{-1/2} \\
E[C_{i,j}|\boldsymbol{\Theta}, C_{i,j-1}] = C_{i,j-1}\ E[F_{i,j}|\boldsymbol{\Theta}, C_{i,j-1}] &= -C_{i,j-1}/\Theta_{j-1} \\
\mathrm{Var}(C_{i,j}|\boldsymbol{\Theta}, C_{i,j-1}) = C_{i,j-1}^2 \mathrm{Var}(F_{i,j}|\boldsymbol{\Theta}, C_{i,j-1}) &= \sigma_{j-1}^2 C_{i,j-1}/\Theta_{j-1}^2 \\
\mathrm{Vco}(C_{i,j}|\boldsymbol{\Theta}, C_{i,j-1}) = \mathrm{Vco}(F_{i,j}|\boldsymbol{\Theta}, C_{i,j-1}) &= \sigma_{j-1}\, C_{i,j-1}^{-1/2}
\end{aligned}$$

(cf. (9.22)–(9.25)). Now we apply the MCMC method described in Section 4.4 to (9.40)–(9.41). For the following empirical results we have used 30 000 simulations, and this gives the results presented in Table 9.11. Note that we need to have that $E[\Theta_j^{-2}|D_I] < \infty$, which is the case for our data set since $S_j^{[I-j]} > \alpha_j \sigma_j^2$ for all j.

Note that these numerical results are in line with Table 9.9. The reserves $\widehat{C}_{i,J}^{BCL} - C_{i,I-i}$ slightly differ due to the fact that in Table 9.11 they are obtained numerically whereas those in Table 9.9 are exact. The uncertainty measures differ due to the fact that we have different distributional assumptions (Gauss and Gamma in Table 9.9 and Table 9.11, respectively).

Table 9.11 Reserves and conditional MSEP for Portfolio B: Bayesian CL method under Gamma assumptions

	Bayesian reserves	Process std dev.	Estimation error$^{1/2}$	msep$^{1/2}$
	$\widehat{C}_{i,J}^{BCL} - C_{i,I-i}$	$(C_{i,I-i}\Gamma_{I-i}^{B})^{1/2}$	$(C_{i,I-i}^{2}\Delta_{I-i}^{B})^{1/2}$	
7	−4	18	7	19
8	93	228	77	241
9	171	291	117	314
10	322	517	195	553
11	913	1160	387	1223
12	1409	1384	421	1447
13	2602	1756	565	1845
14	3699	2083	593	2166
15	7862	4672	1060	4791
16	45 618	7462	1559	7623
Total	62 684	9443	3655	10 125

We denote

$$R_I = \sum_{i=7}^{16} \left(C_{i,J} - C_{i,I-i}\right) \quad \text{and} \quad \widehat{R} = \widehat{R}_{\Theta,\mathcal{D}_I} = \sum_{i=7}^{16} \left(\widehat{C}_{i,J}(\Theta, \mathcal{D}_I) - C_{i,I-i}\right)$$

Note that for the total portfolio over all accident years we have

$$\text{msep}_{R_I|\mathcal{D}_I}\left(\sum_{i=7}^{16} \left(\widehat{C}_{i,J}^{BCL} - C_{i,I-i}\right)\right) = \text{Var}(R_I|\mathcal{D}_I)$$

and, moreover, the estimation error over all accident years, see (9.39) and Corollary 9.21, is given by

$$\text{Var}\left(\widehat{R}\middle|\mathcal{D}_I\right)$$

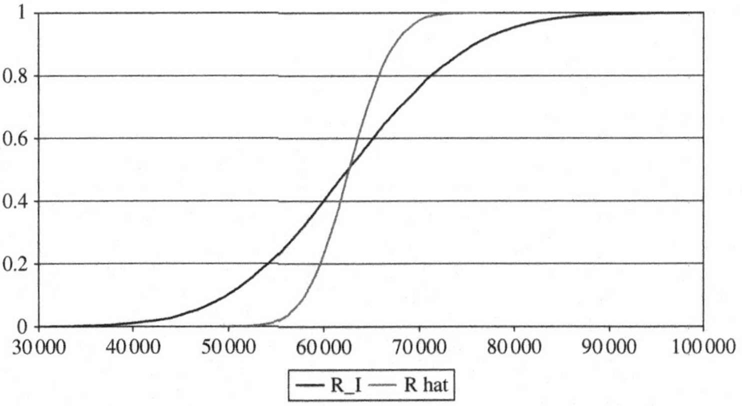

Figure 9.2 Conditional distributions for R_I and $\widehat{R}$, given $\mathcal{D}_I$ (from 30 000 simulations)

Figure 9.2 shows the conditional distributions for R_I and $\widehat{R}$ (given $\mathcal{D}_I$) obtained from 30 000 simulations, from which the error terms in Table 9.11 were calculated (row 'Total').

Of course, since we have now the whole distribution of R_I and $\widehat{R}$ we can easily determine higher moments, quantiles, Value-at-Risk, etc. Table 9.12 provides some key figures, and compares these figures by the same figures if we fit a Gamma and a Gauss distribution to the overall reserves such that the first two moments are equal.

Table 9.12 Key figures of R_I and $\widehat{R}$ compared to Gamma and Gauss distributions with the same first two moments

	Empirical distribution		Gamma approximation		Gauss approximation	
	$\widehat{R}$	R_I	$\widehat{R}$	R_I	$\widehat{R}$	R_I
Mean	62 684	62 715	62 684	62 715	62 684	62 715
Std. dev.	3655	10 125	3655	10 125	3655	10 125
Vco	5.83%	16.15%	5.83%	16.15%	5.83%	16.15%
Skewness	0.027	0.086	0.117	0.323	0.000	0.000
90% VaR	4725	12 957	4728	13 276	4684	12 976
95% VaR	6044	16 975	6131	17 531	6012	16 655
99% VaR	8559	24 149	8816	25 927	8503	23 555

For Value-at-Risk (VaR) we consider the distance between the quantile and the expected value. The skewness of a random variable X is given by

$$\gamma(X) = \frac{E\left[\left(X - E[X]\right)^3\right]}{\mathrm{Var}(X)^{3/2}}$$

Note that the skewness of the overall Gamma distribution (with the first two moments equal to R_I) is larger than the skewness of the empirical distribution of R_I. Moreover, the VaR of R_I is smaller than the approximation by an overall Gamma distribution (see Table 9.12).

The slight difference $\mathrm{E}[\widehat{R}]$ and $E[R_I]$ comes from the fact that we use numerical simulations and empirical distributions in order to determine the values. □

10 Selected Topics II: Individual Claims Development Processes

In Section 1.2 we introduced the different classes into which claims reserves could be subdivided. That is, one should clearly distinguish between IBNeR claims (reported claims), IBNyR claims (incurred but not yet reported claims) and UPR claims (claims that correspond to the unearned premium reserves). So far, none of the methods presented in these chapters have made this clear distinction. In the present chapter we give mathematical ideas on how one can model the different classes and how one could study development processes for individual claims. This is in the spirit of Arjas (1989) and Norberg (1993, 1999). Most of the research on individual claims development process modelling is probably still in its infancy; that is, such developments mainly study mathematical and statistical properties of the models and they are, currently, seldom used in practice in a mathematically consistent way. There are many methods in place that separate IBNeR and IBNyR claims but this is often an ad-hoc separation.

Section 10.1 presents the mathematical framework for modelling individual claims. This is done with the help of stochastic processes such as marked Poisson point processes. In order to have well-parametrized models and nice statistical properties, one then needs to pool claims in an appropriate way so that, for example, we have a law of large numbers or a central limit theorem. If we do a rough pooling that models reported claims under the CL hypothesis and uses a BF or GLM approach for IBNyR claims, we arrive at the model introduced by Schnieper (1991), which is the topic studied in Section 10.2.

10.1 MODELLING CLAIMS DEVELOPMENT PROCESSES FOR INDIVIDUAL CLAIMS

In Section 1.2 we defined a structural framework for the claims reserving problem. This framework was based on the stochastic claims settlement processes $(T_{i,j}, I_{i,j}, X_{i,j})_{j\geq 0}$ for individual claims $i = 1, \ldots, N$ that occur within a fixed time period. These processes have enabled us to define the different classes of claims reserves. The main conclusions were (see p. 10) that one should estimate the reserves for reported claims individually and the reserves for IBNyR claims on a collective basis. The main reason for this conclusion was based on the fact that on reported claims we have individual observations (individual claims parameters such as degree of damage, estimated recovery time, etc.), whereas for IBNyR claims we only have collective (external) information such as weather conditions, catastrophic events, inflation rate, etc.

The base points of the analysis of the settlement processes were the reporting dates $T_i = T_{i,0}$, and we have ordered the claims according to those dates, i.e., $T_i < T_{i+1}$ for all $i \geq 1$.

A statistical background would state that this is the best way to look at the problem, because the T_i's are the flow of observable events at the insurance company. On the other hand, we have also seen that ordering according to reporting dates introduces certain difficulties for the estimation of IBNyR reserves (see, e.g., (1.10) and the subsequent remark). That is, the reporting date does not clearly distinguish between UPR liabilities and IBNyR claims. Moreover, for a reasonable premium analysis one needs to clearly link premium income with claims exposures, which is difficult when one works with the reporting dates as base points for the claims settlement processes.

Therefore, in this section we slightly change the set-up, and will look at the problem according to accident date orderings. For this analysis we closely follow Norberg (1993, 1999). The initial date is the accident date, denoted (in this section) by S_i, and we will order the claims according to $S_i < S_{i+1}$ for all $i \geq 1$.

From a practical point of view, it is important to see that the accident date is the crucial date that determines whether there is a liability for the insurance company; this is exactly how it is stated in the insurance contracts. Below, we see that the accident date ordering plays a dual role from a mathematical point of view, and this means that it is not important whether we mark claims according to the notification date or the accident date, but we have to apply the methodology consistently to all claims. We believe that it is easier to think in terms of the accident date. The reason for this is that the accident date is directly linked to the insurance premium, the insurance contract and the claims exposure. In particular, for a more explicit description of the unearned premium reserve we refer to p. 376.

10.1.1 Modelling Framework

The following implementation is based on Norberg (1993, 1999). We define $w(t) \geq 0$ to be the risk exposure per time. This is the exposure rate at time $t \geq 0$. We assume that the total exposure W satisfies

$$W = \int_0^\infty w(t)\; dt\; < \infty \tag{10.1}$$

Interpretation

The typical situation we consider is that we are at a (fixed) time point $\tau \geq 0$ and are interested in solvency considerations at that specific time. This means that we consider no new contracts signed after time τ, i.e. our total liabilities after time τ are only contracts signed before time τ (this is the so-called run-off situation). That is, our exposure eventually goes to zero, and a possible example for the exposure $w(t)$ is $(t \geq 0)$

$$w(t) = \begin{cases} w_0 + t\; a & t \in [0, \tau] \\ \max\{w_0 + \tau\; a - (t - \tau)\; b\; ;\; 0\} & t > \tau \end{cases}$$

where $w_0 > 0$, $a > 0$ and $b > 0$ are fixed constants. This means that we start with an initial exposure rate w_0, then continuously increase our portfolio exposure at slope a until τ, and after τ we consider the run-off situation; the rate decreases with slope $-b$ since we do not sign any new contracts after time τ (cf. Figure 10.1). An exposure pattern that is constant in time is often called *pro rata temporis* exposure (see also Subsection 1.1.1). We especially obtain a *pro rata temporis* exposure if there are no seasonal effects.

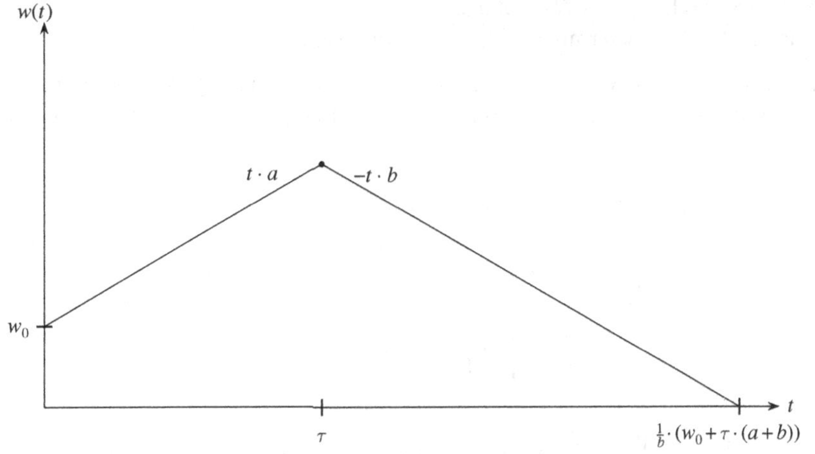

Figure 10.1 Risk exposure per time

We assume that the claims for the total exposure W arrive at times S_i (accident dates). Moreover, we assume that no two claims occur simultaneously. Then, we order the labelling of our claims according to $S_i < S_{i+1}$, for all $i \geq 1$. Note that this leads to a different ordering compared to Section 1.2. We define the claims arrival/counting process by

$$N(t) = \sum_{i\geq 1} 1_{\{S_i \leq t\}}$$

and the total number of claims for the exposure W is given by

$$N = \lim_{t\to\infty} N(t)$$

Observe that this definition of N coincides with the definition of N in Section 1.2, but the claims counting process $\left(N(t)\right)_{t\geq 0}$ differs from the claims reporting process $(N_t)_{t\geq 0}$ defined in (1.7).

Model Assumptions 10.1

We assume that the claims counting process $\left(N(t)\right)_{t\geq 0}$ is an inhomogeneous Poisson point process with intensity $w(t)$ that satisfies (10.1). □

Remarks 10.2

- This means that $\left(N(t)\right)_{t\geq 0}$ has independent increments with, for $s < t$,

$$N(t) - N(s) \overset{(d)}{\sim} \text{Poisson}\left(\int_s^t w(u)\, du\right)$$

see, for example, Ross (1985), Section 5.4.1. If we define the operational time $W(t) = \int_0^t w(s)\, ds$ and its (generalized) inverse $W^{-1}(u) = \inf\{t;\; W(t) = u\}$, then the counting process $N\left(W^{-1}(u)\right)$ is a homogeneous Poisson point process with constant intensity 1.

- Since $W < \infty$ we have that $N < \infty$, a.s.
- Of course, $(N(t))_{t\geq 0}$ determines $(S_i)_{i\geq 1}$ and vice versa.

The statement $X \in dx$ denotes that X takes its values in a dx neighbourhood around x. The joint probability distribution of the counting process and the arrival times is given by (set $0 = t_0 < t_1 < \cdots$)

$$\begin{aligned}
P[N = n,\ S_i \in dt_i \text{ for all } i = 1, \ldots, n] \\
&= \prod_{i=1}^{n} \exp\left\{-\int_{t_{i-1}}^{t_i} w(t)\, dt\right\} w(t_i)\, dt_i \left\{-\int_{t_n}^{\infty} w(t)\, dt\right\} \\
&= \exp\left\{-\int_0^{\infty} w(t)\, dt\right\} \prod_{i=1}^{n} w(t_i)\, dt_i \\
&= \exp(-W)\, \frac{W^n}{n!}\, n! \prod_{i=1}^{n} \frac{w(t_i)}{W}\, dt_i
\end{aligned} \tag{10.2}$$

Hence, we see that the claims arrival process $(S_i)_{i\geq 1}$ has two stages: firstly, we generate the total number N of claims from a Poisson distribution with mean W; secondly, we distribute them over time with intensity $w(t)/W$ and order them according to their arrival time. Of course, these are well-known properties of Poisson point processes.

Now, we are ready to define the claims settlement process. Assume that $S \in [0, \infty)$ denotes the accident date, and that T denotes the reporting date of a claim at the insurance company. A claim is a pair

$$\text{CLA} = (S, Z),$$

where $Z = (U, V, C, \widetilde{C})$ is the mark describing the settlement process and

$U = T - S \in [0, \infty)$ is the reporting delay,

$V \in [0, \infty)$ is the waiting time until final settlement after T,

$C \in [0, \infty)$ is the ultimate claim size,

$\widetilde{C} = \left\{(C(v))_{0\leq v\leq V};\ C(V) = C\right\}$ is the cumulative claims payment process.

Note that in general the mark Z has even more components such as a claims adjusters' case estimate, and parameters describing the claim (bodily injury claim, fire claim, whiplash claim, etc.).

We denote by $\mathcal{Z}$ the space of possible claims settlement processes $Z = (U, V, C, \widetilde{C})$; hence a claim CLA is a random element in the set $\mathcal{C} \stackrel{def.}{=} [0, \infty) \times \mathcal{Z}$.

DEFINITION 10.3 *A marked Poisson point process with intensity $(w(t))_{t\geq 0}$ and position-dependent marks is a process*

$$((S_i, Z_i))_{i=1,\ldots,N}$$

where the claims counting process $N(t)$ is an inhomogeneous Poisson point process with intensity $w(t)$, arrival times S_i and marks $Z_i = Z_{S_i} \in \mathcal{Z}$. The marks satisfy the following assumptions: $(Z_t)_{t>0}$ is a family of random elements in $\mathcal{Z}$ that are mutually independent, are independent of the Poisson point process $N(\cdot)$ and have time-dependent probability distributions $Z_t \overset{(d)}{\sim} P_{Z|t}$. □

We write

$$\big((S_i, Z_i)\big)_{i=1,\dots,N} \quad \overset{(d)}{\sim} \quad \text{Poisson}\big(w(t), P_{Z|t}\big)$$

Model Assumptions 10.4

We assume that the marked Poisson point process $\big((S_i, Z_i)\big)_{i=1,\dots,N}$ with distribution $\text{Poisson}\big(w(t), P_{Z|t}\big)$ satisfies (10.1). □

PROPOSITION 10.5 *Assume that the marked Poisson point process $\big((S_i, Z_i)\big)_{i=1,\dots,N}$ satisfies Model Assumptions 10.4. Then we have for $t_1 < t_2 < \cdots$*

$$\begin{aligned} &P[N=n,\ (S_i, Z_i) \in (dt_i, dz_i) \text{ for all } i=1,\dots,n] \\ &\quad = \exp(-W) \prod_{i=1}^{n} w(t_i)\ dt_i\ dP_{Z|t_i}(z_i) \\ &\quad = \exp(-W)\ \frac{W^n}{n!}\ n! \prod_{i=1}^{n} \frac{w(t_i)}{W}\ dt_i\ dP_{Z|t_i}(z_i) \end{aligned}$$

Proof The proof is straightforward similar to (10.2). For more details see Norberg (1993, 1999). □

Our goal is to study the claims reserving problem on different classes of claims. That is, reported claims, IBNyR claims, UPR claims. We therefore consider partitions of $\mathcal{C}$. Assume that $\mathcal{C}^g$, $g=1,\dots,h \le \infty$, gives a partition of $\mathcal{C}$. Let us introduce, for $t \ge 0$,

$$\mathcal{Z}_t^g = \big\{z \in \mathcal{Z};\ (t, z) \in \mathcal{C}^g\big\}$$

that is, the possible settlement processes in $\mathcal{C}^g$ for claims that have occurred at time $t \ge 0$. Moreover, we define the set of possible occurrence times in $\mathcal{C}^g$ by

$$\mathcal{T}^g = \big\{t \in [0, \infty);\ P_{Z|t}[\mathcal{Z}_t^g] > 0\big\}$$

Now, we consider the subprocess of the marked Poisson point process that only considers the claims in $\mathcal{C}^g$, i.e.

$$\big((S_i^g, Z_i^g)\big)_{i=1,\dots,N^g} \tag{10.3}$$

with

$$N^g = \sum_{i=1}^{N} 1_{\{(S_i, Z_i) \in \mathcal{C}^g\}} \tag{10.4}$$

We omit the explicit definition of (10.3)–(10.4) since it is straightforward how the appropriate re-labelling needs to be done. Because we have taken a partition, we have following statement

$$N = \sum_{g=1}^{h} N^g$$

PROPOSITION 10.6 *Assume that the marked Poisson point process* $((S_i, Z_i))_{i=1,\ldots,N}$ *satisfies Model Assumptions 10.4. Then we have the following properties*

(a) $((S_i^g, Z_i^g))_{i=1,\ldots,N^g}$ *for* $g = 1, \ldots, h$ *are independent marked Poisson point processes with intensities*

$$w^g(t) = w(t)\ P_{Z|t}\,[\mathcal{Z}_t^g]$$

and time-dependent probability distributions

$$P_{Z|t}^g(dz) = \frac{P_{Z|t}(dz)}{P_{Z|t}\left[\mathcal{Z}_t^g\right]}\ 1_{\mathcal{Z}_t^g}(z)$$

(b) *The sum/amalgamation of finitely many independent marked Poisson point processes satisfying Model Assumptions 10.4 is again a marked Poisson point process satisfying Model Assumptions 10.4.*

Proof The proof follows from Proposition 10.5 (this is a basic property of the Poisson point process with mutually independent marks). For further details we refer to Norberg (1999) Theorems 2 and 3. □

Hence, Proposition 10.6 states that we can study the claims reserving problem in appropriate subclasses. In the following, we assume that the distribution $P_{Z|t}$ has density $p_{Z|t}$. Marginal densities are denoted, for example, by $p_{U,V|t}(u, v)$ and conditional densities are denoted, for example, by $p_{U|t,V}(u)$.

Decomposition by Occurence/Accident Year

For $k \geq 1$ we define the partition

$$\mathcal{C}^k = \{(s, z) \in \mathcal{C};\ k-1 < s \leq k\}$$

The intensities of the decomposed claims are given by

$$w^k(s) = w(s)\ 1_{(k-1,k]}(s)$$

with total exposure

$$W^k = \int_{k-1}^{k} w(s)\ ds$$

We define for the ultimate claim C

$$P_C^k(c) = \frac{1}{W^k} \int_{k-1}^{k} w(s)\ P_{C|s}(c)\ ds$$

Then, the total claim amount of accident year k has a compound Poisson distribution with an expected number of claims given by W^k and independent claims severities with distribution P_C^k. This means that for future accident years we consider a compound Poisson distribution, which is a well-known approach in risk theory (see, e.g., Mikosch 2004).

Decomposition by Accident Year and Reporting Delay

For $k \geqslant 1$, $j \geq 0$ we define the partition

$$\mathcal{C}^{k,j} = \left\{(s, z) \in \mathcal{C}^k;\ k + j - 1 \leq s + u \leq k + j\right\}$$

Recall that $z = (u, v, c, \tilde{c})$ and $t = s + u$ is the reporting time T. The total exposure is given by

$$W^{k,j} = \int_{k-1}^{k} w(s) \int_{k+j-1-s}^{k+j-s} p_{U|s}(u)\ du\ ds$$

We define the ultimate claims density for C by

$$p_C^{k,j}(c) = \frac{1}{W^{k,j}} \int_{k-1}^{k} w(s) \int_{k+j-1-s}^{k+j-s} p_{U,C|s}(u, c)\ du\ ds$$

Then, the total claim amount of accident year k with reporting year $k + j$ has a compound Poisson distribution with expected number of claims given by $W^{k,j}$ and independent claims severities with distribution $P_C^{k,j}$ which gives again a compound Poisson distribution.

Process of Reported Claims

As already mentioned, the reporting time is given by $T = S + U$. We could consider new marks $Z^{(r)} = (S, V, C, \widetilde{C})$ and a new process

$$\left(\left(T_i, Z_i^{(r)}\right)\right)_{i=1,\ldots,N}$$

with elements in $[0, \infty) \times \mathcal{Z}^{(r)}$ which is now ordered according to the reporting time T (with the obvious definition for $\mathcal{Z}^{(r)}$). This is exactly the situation considered in Section 1.2. Then (see Norberg 1999, Theorem 4) $\left(\left(T_i, Z_i^{(r)}\right)\right)_{i=1,\ldots,N}$ is under our model assumptions a marked Poisson point process with intensity (we use the notation $t = s + u$ for the reporting time T)

$$w^{(r)}(t) = \int_0^t w(s)\ p_{U|s}(t - s)\ ds$$

and time-dependent marks, $z^{(r)} = (s, v, c, \tilde{c})$,

$$P^{(r)}_{Z^{(r)}|t}(dz^{(r)}) = \frac{w(s)\ p_{U|s}(t-s)\ ds}{W}\ P_{V,C,\tilde{C}|s,U=t-s}(dv, dc, d\tilde{c})$$

This immediately shows that we can work in both frameworks, based on accident date or reporting date.

10.1.2 Claims Reserving Categories

In this subsection we consider a different partition of $\mathcal{C}$. This partition is crucial for considering claims according to their current claims development status.

Assume that we are at time $\tau \geq 0$ and that we want to estimate claims reserves. At time τ we define the following claims categories:

$$\mathcal{C}^{\text{set}} = \{(s, z) \in \mathcal{C};\ s+u+v \leq \tau\} \quad \text{the settled claims,}$$

$$\mathcal{C}^{\text{IBNeR}} = \{(s, z) \in \mathcal{C};\ s+u \leq \tau < s+u+v\} \quad \text{the reported open claims,}$$

$$\mathcal{C}^{\text{IBNyR}} = \{(s, z) \in \mathcal{C};\ s \leq \tau < s+u\} \quad \text{the incurred but not yet reported claims,}$$

$$\mathcal{C}^{\text{UPR}} = \{(s, z) \in \mathcal{C};\ \tau < s\} \quad \text{the covered but not yet incurred claims}$$

$\mathcal{C}^{\text{UPR}}$ contains the claims that have not yet incurred but are covered via the insurance contract (premium liability). If we are at time τ the reserve for these claims is exactly the unearned premium reserve (UPR) at time τ, as described in Subsection 1.1.1.

The total liability for the N claims now splits into four different classes, $Z_i = (U_i, V_i, C_i, \tilde{C}_i)$,

$$C = \sum_{i=1}^{N} C_i = C^{\text{set}} + C^{\text{IBNeR}} + C^{\text{IBNyR}} + C^{\text{UPR}}$$

with

$$C^g = \sum_{i=1}^{N^g} C_i^g$$

where $\left((S_i^g, Z_i^g)\right)_{i=1,\ldots,N^g}$ corresponds to the marked Poisson point process with $g =$ set, IBNeR, IBNyR, UPR. At time τ certain parts of these total liabilities are paid, namely

$$C(\tau) = C^{\text{set}} + \sum_{i=1}^{N^{\text{IBNeR}}} C_i^{\text{IBNeR}}\left(\tau - T_i^{\text{IBNeR}}\right)$$

where $T_i^{\text{IBNeR}} = S_i^{\text{IBNeR}} + U_i^{\text{IBNeR}}$ is the reporting time of the ith reported open claim. The outstanding liabilities at time τ are then given by

$$\begin{aligned} R(\tau) &= C - C(\tau) \\ &= \left(C^{\text{IBNeR}} - \sum_{i=1}^{N^{\text{IBNeR}}} C_i^{\text{IBNeR}}\left(\tau - T_i^{\text{IBNeR}}\right)\right) + C^{\text{IBNyR}} + C^{\text{UPR}} \end{aligned}$$

We define the outstanding liablities for the different subclasses

$$R(\tau)^{\text{rep}} = C^{\text{IBNeR}} - \sum_{i=1}^{N^{\text{IBNeR}}} C_i^{\text{IBNeR}}\left(\tau - T_i^{\text{IBNeR}}\right)$$

$$R(\tau)^{\text{IBNyR}} = C^{\text{IBNyR}}$$

Observe that

$$R(\tau) = R(\tau)^{\text{rep}} + R(\tau)^{\text{IBNyR}} + C^{\text{UPR}}$$

If we compare this to Section 1.2, we see that $C(\tau)$ is the same as in (1.1) for $t=\tau$.

As in Section 1.2, we denote by $\mathcal{F}_\tau$ the information available at time τ. Assume that it consists of the histories of all claims available at time τ (these are exactly the reported claims and their claims settlement processes up to time τ). We want to calculate the distributions of C^g, given the information $\mathcal{F}_\tau$.

Due to Proposition 10.6, we see that this problem decouples into four independent problems, given $\mathcal{F}_\tau$. The settled claims payments C^{set} are simply a deterministic number at time τ, and, of course, the reserves for these claims are zero (otherwise they wouldn't be settled).

Predicting Reported Open Claims

For reported open claims we know the accident date $S_i \le \tau$ and the reporting delay $U_i \le \tau - S_i$. Moreover, the total number of reported claims N^{IBNeR} is known. Hence, the conditional distribution of

$$C^{\text{IBNeR}} = \sum_{i=1}^{N^{\text{IBNeR}}} C_i^{\text{IBNeR}}$$

given $\mathcal{F}_\tau$, is the convolution of N^{IBNeR} independent conditional distributions

$$P_{C_i,\tilde{C}_i|S_i,U_i,\{C_i(v);v\le\tau-T_i^{\text{IBNeR}}\}} \qquad \text{for } i=1,\ldots,N^{\text{IBNeR}}$$

We define $\tau_i = \tau - T_i^{\text{IBNeR}}$; this is the time passed between the reporting data T_i^{IBNeR} and today τ. These conditional distributions have, in general, a very complex structure, i.e. future payments may depend on the total history of such claims. In order to determine claims reserves for reported open claims, one needs to choose additional structure for these distributions $P_{C_i;\tilde{C}_i|S_i,U_i,\{C_i(v);v\le\tau_i\}}$ – for example, Markov properties, etc. If we assume that

$$P_{C_i|S_i,U_i,\{C_i(v);v\le\tau_i\}} \overset{(d)}{=} P_{C_i|S_i,U_i,C_i(\tau_i)}$$

then the problem is substantially simplified and one can estimate claims reserves with the information S_i, U_i, $C_i(\tau_i)$. In practical applications, one often even assumes that these conditional distributions do not depend on U_i and that we can introduce a yearly grid for the accident year. This then implies that we can apply the claims triangle methods, where the data is adjusted such that IBNyR claims are not contained in the data, e.g. do a CL assumption and perform the CL method on all claims that have a reporting delay of less than 2 years, and start this CL analysis only with development year 2.

Predicting IBNyR Claims

Observe that C^{IBNyR} is independent of $\mathcal{F}_\tau$. Applying Proposition 10.6, we see that $\left(\left(S_i^{\text{IBNyR}}, Z_i^{\text{IBNyR}}\right)\right)_{i=1,\ldots,N^{\text{IBNyR}}}$ is a marked Poisson point processes with intensity

$$w^{\text{IBNyR}}(t) = w(t)\; P_{U|t}\left[\tau < t + U\right]\; 1_{\{t \le \tau\}}$$

The total exposure is given by

$$W^{\text{IBNyR}} = \int_0^\tau w(t)\; P_{U|t}\left[U > \tau - t\right] dt$$

Define the density

$$p_{C|\tau}^{\text{IBNyR}}(c) = \frac{1}{W^{\text{IBNyR}}} \int_0^\tau w(t) \int_{\tau-t}^{\infty} p_{U,C|t}(u, c)\; du\; dt$$

Then, C^{IBNyR} is a compound Poisson distribution with an expected number of claims equal to W^{IBNyR} and a claims severity distribution $P_{C|\tau}^{\text{IBNyR}}$. There are various different ways to calculate distributions of compound Poisson, such as the Panjer algorithm or the fast Fourier transform (see, e.g., Panjer 2006).

Predicting UPR Claims

The prediction of UPR claims is completely analogous to the prediction of IBNyR claims. Observe that C^{UPR} is independent of $\mathcal{F}_\tau$. Applying Proposition 10.6, we see that $\left(\left(S_i^{\text{UPR}}, Z_i^{\text{UPR}}\right)\right)_{i=1,\ldots,N^{\text{UPR}}}$ is a marked Poisson point processes with intensity

$$w^{\text{UPR}}(t) = w(t)\; 1_{\{t > \tau\}}$$

The total exposure is given by

$$W^{\text{UPR}} = \int_\tau^\infty w(t)\; dt$$

Define the density

$$p_{C|\tau}^{\text{UPR}}(c) = \frac{1}{W^{\text{UPR}}} \int_\tau^\infty w(t)\; p_{C|t}(c)\; dt$$

Then, C^{UPR} is a compound Poisson distribution with an expected number of claims equal to W^{UPR} and a claims severity distribution of $P_{C|\tau}^{\text{UPR}}$.

Remark With Proposition 10.6 (b) we could also consider IBNyR and UPR claims simultaneously. However, we have chosen to consider them individually, because the risk factors for these two risk classes are not completely the same. This is similar to the fact that, for solvency calculations, the regulator considers two different risk classes for insurance risks: (i) premium liability risks, (ii) claims reserving risks (see, e.g., SST 2006, Sandström 2005).

Parameter Modelling

If we choose distributions for the time-dependent marks and for the inhomogeneous Poisson process there are several parameters involved. So far, we have assumed that they are known. However, for two reasons we could also assume that they depend on latent variables: (i) we do not know the true parameters and need to estimate them, and in a Bayesian context we would model such parameters as random variables coming from prior distributions; (ii) we predict future parameters that are, from today's view point, random variables (and may randomly change over time).
Formally, let us assume that the claims frequency has the following structure

$$w(t)\ \Theta_t$$

where $\{\Theta_t\}_{t\geq 0}$ is a positive stochastic process. On the prediction of the IBNeR reserves this new structure has no influence, since the number of reported open claims is fixed. But the prediction of the IBNyR and the UPR claims becomes more complicated, because $\mathcal{F}_\tau$ contains partial information about Θ_t; moreover, the frequencies of N^{IBNyR} and N^{UPR} are then no longer necessarily independent and, in general, they also depend on $\mathcal{F}_\tau$.

We could also do similar considerations for the distributions of the marks (claims severities). However, this gets even more complicated because latent factors may also have an influence on settled claims or on the definition what a settled claim is. Assume that we have a latent variable for legal changes. Now, if jurisdiction changes, we may have to re-open several old claims (which try to fall under the new jurisdiction if this is more favourable for the injured). According to such considerations we have to carefully choose the distribution of V, and we also need to decide which latent factors have an influence on the claims closings process and which do not.

General remark This approach, modelling single claims, becomes immediately complicated when one introduces latent variables and dependencies. Explicit examples are only poorly understood, and most of them have strong assumptions on independencies. We do not give explicit examples here, but refer to some papers in the literature: Hachemeister (1980), Norberg (1993, 1999), Arjas (1989), Neuhaus (2004), Taylor *et al.* (2006) or Larsen (2007). For those interested in the modelling of IBNyR claims and reporting delays, we refer to Jewell (1989, 1990) and Herbst (1999).

10.2 SEPARATING IBNER AND IBNYR CLAIMS

In this section we present a CL-based model that aims to separate IBNeR and IBNyR reserves. This model was introduced by Schnieper (1991). The remarkable fact about the Schnieper model is that it was the basis of the famous Mack paper (1993). Schnieper developed an approximation to the conditional MSEP using Taylor series approximations. Mack's paper adapts these ideas for the pure CL case. However, for the specialized pure CL case things are easier and Taylor series approximations can be replaced by more exact procedures (as stated in Mack 1993, p. 214).

In our view, we see the Schnieper model as a first step towards separating reserves for reported claims from reserves for IBNyR claims. We derive formulas for the conditional MSEP using the conditional resampling approach (see Section 3.2.3). Similar derivations are also found in a recent paper by Liu and Verrall (2007).

In this subsection the cumulative claim $C_{i,j}$ is understood to be claims incurred. The change in claims incurred from the end of period j to the end of period $j+1$, that is, from $C_{i,j}$ to $C_{i,j+1}$, has two components:

(i) change of $C_{i,j}$ due to new information available at the end of period $j+1$ (i.e., updating the σ-field on reported claims) and
(ii) new claims reported within the period $j+1$.

That is, we have

$$C_{i,j} \quad \longmapsto \quad C_{i,j+1} = \left(C_{i,j} + D_{i,j+1}\right) + Y_{i,j+1}$$

where $Y_{i,j+1}$ denotes the claims incurred for claims reported within the development period $j+1$ (i.e. newly reported IBNyR claims within the development year $j+1$), and $D_{i,j+1}$ denotes the changes in claims incurred in the period $j+1$ for claims reported before the end of period j.

Analogously, as in the CL model we denote

$$\mathcal{D}_I = \left\{C_{i,j}, D_{i,j}, Y_{i,j};\ i+j \le I\right\} \tag{10.5}$$

$$\mathcal{B}_k = \left\{C_{i,j}, D_{i,j}, Y_{i,j};\ i+j \le I, j \le k\right\} \subseteq \mathcal{D}_I \tag{10.6}$$

Observe that these definitions differ from (1.16) and (2.6). In (10.5) and (10.6) we require stronger assumptions on the data structures/data warehouse. In order to avoid overloading the notation we use the same symbols. Moreover, we define

$$\mathcal{G}_k = \left\{C_{i,j}, D_{i,j}, Y_{i,j}; j \le k\right\}$$

Observe that $\mathcal{B}_k \subseteq \mathcal{G}_k$, and that $\mathcal{G}_k$ contains all information up to development period k (not only the information in the upper triangle).

We have already seen different forms of exposures, for example, in Section 2.3 we had an exposure μ_i which stood for the total ultimate claim amount of accident year i, or, in Subsection 5.2.5, we had an exposure w_i which played the role of a volume measure. In this section we denote the (deterministic) exposure of accident year i by e_i which plays the role of a volume measure for IBNyR claims. Then we consider the following model:

Model Assumptions 10.7 (Schnieper 1991)

- Claim variables $C_{i,j}$, $D_{i,j}$ and $Y_{i,j}$ of different accident years i are independent.
- Conditionally, given $\mathcal{G}_{j-1}$, $D_{i,j}$ and $Y_{i,j}$ are independent.
- There exist factors $\lambda_0, \ldots, \lambda_{J-1}$ and $\delta_0, \ldots, \delta_{J-1}$ such that

$$E\left[D_{i,j} \middle| \mathcal{G}_{j-1}\right] = \delta_{j-1}\ C_{i,j-1}$$

$$E\left[Y_{i,j} \middle| \mathcal{G}_{j-1}\right] = \lambda_{j-1}\ e_i$$

- There exist factors $\sigma_0^2, \ldots, \sigma_{J-1}^2 > 0$ and $\tau_0^2, \ldots, \tau_{J-1}^2 > 0$ such that

$$\mathrm{Var}\left(D_{i,j} \middle| \mathcal{G}_{j-1}\right) = \tau_{j-1}^2\ C_{i,j-1}$$

$$\mathrm{Var}\left(Y_{i,j} \middle| \mathcal{G}_{j-1}\right) = \sigma_{j-1}^2\ e_i$$

□

Note that Model Assumptions 10.7 can also be seen as a mixture of a CL model (cf. Model Assumptions 3.2) and a (univariate) ALR model (cf. (8.44)–(8.45)). For changes in claims incurred of reported claims $D_{i,j}$, one has a CL assumption, whereas for the newly reported IBNyR claims $Y_{i,j}$, one has a ALR assumption. That is, the first two moments of the IBNyR claim $Y_{i,j}$ do not depend on the observations prior to development period j.

LEMMA 10.8 *Under Model Assumptions 10.7 we have*

$$E\left[C_{i,J}\middle|\mathcal{D}_I\right]=C_{i,I-i}\prod_{j=I-i}^{J-1}\left(1+\delta_j\right)+e_i\sum_{j=I-i}^{J-1}\lambda_j\prod_{k=j+1}^{J-1}\left(1+\delta_k\right) \tag{10.7}$$

for all $1\leq i\leq I$

Proof Due to the independence of different accident years we have

$$E\left[C_{i,J}\middle|\mathcal{D}_I\right]=E\left[C_{i,J}\middle|\mathcal{B}_{I-i}\right]=E\left[C_{i,J}\middle|\mathcal{G}_{I-i}\right]$$

Moreover, using the properties of conditional expectations, we have

$$\begin{aligned}E\left[C_{i,J}\middle|\mathcal{G}_{I-i}\right]&=E\left[E\left[C_{i,J}\middle|\mathcal{G}_{J-1}\right]\middle|\mathcal{G}_{I-i}\right]\\&=E\left[E\left[C_{i,J-1}+D_{i,J}+Y_{i,J}\middle|\mathcal{G}_{J-1}\right]\middle|\mathcal{G}_{I-i}\right]\\&=E\left[(1+\delta_{J-1})\,C_{i,J-1}+\lambda_{J-1}\,e_i\middle|\mathcal{G}_{I-i}\right]\\&=(1+\delta_{J-1})\,E\left[C_{i,J-1}\middle|\mathcal{G}_{I-i}\right]+\lambda_{J-1}\,e_i\end{aligned}$$

This immediately implies the recursive formula for the conditionally expected ultimate claim and completes the proof. □

Next we need to estimate the unknown model parameters λ_j, δ_j, σ_j^2 and τ_j^2.

$$\widehat{\delta}_j=\frac{\sum_{i=0}^{I-j-1}D_{i,j+1}}{\sum_{i=0}^{I-j-1}C_{i,j}} \tag{10.8}$$

$$\widehat{\lambda}_j=\frac{\sum_{i=0}^{I-j-1}Y_{i,j+1}}{\sum_{i=0}^{I-j-1}e_i} \tag{10.9}$$

$$\widehat{\tau}_j^2=\frac{1}{I-j-1}\sum_{i=0}^{I-j-1}C_{i,j}\left(\frac{D_{i,j+1}}{C_{i,j}}-\widehat{\delta}_j\right)^2 \tag{10.10}$$

$$\widehat{\sigma}_j^2=\frac{1}{I-j-1}\sum_{i=0}^{I-j-1}e_i\left(\frac{Y_{i,j+1}}{e_i}-\widehat{\lambda}_j\right)^2 \tag{10.11}$$

We obtain the following result for the properties of the estimates:

LEMMA 10.9 *Under Model Assumptions 10.7 we have*

(a) *given $\mathcal{B}_j$, the estimators $\widehat{\delta}_j$ and $\widehat{\lambda}_j$ are conditional independent;*
(b) *given $\mathcal{B}_j$, the estimators $\widehat{\delta}_j$ and $\widehat{\sigma}_j^2$ are conditional independent;*
(c) *given $\mathcal{B}_j$, the estimators $\widehat{\tau}_j^2$ and $\widehat{\lambda}_j$ are conditional independent;*
(d) *given $\mathcal{B}_j$, the estimators $\widehat{\tau}_j^2$ and $\widehat{\sigma}_j^2$ are conditional independent;*
(e) *estimator $\widehat{\delta}_j$ is the $\mathcal{B}_{j+1}$-measurable unbiased estimator for δ_j, which has minimal conditional variance among all unbiased linear combinations of the unbiased estimators $\left(D_{i,j+1}/C_{i,j}\right)_{0\le i\le I-j-1}$ for δ_j, conditional on $\mathcal{B}_j$, i.e.*

$$\mathrm{Var}\left(\widehat{\delta}_j|\mathcal{B}_j\right) = \min_{\substack{\alpha_i\in\mathbb{R}\\ \sum_i \alpha_i=1}} \mathrm{Var}\left(\left.\sum_{i=0}^{I-j-1} \alpha_i \frac{D_{i,j+1}}{C_{i,j}}\right|\mathcal{B}_j\right)$$

(f) *estimator $\widehat{\lambda}_j$ is the $\mathcal{B}_{j+1}$-measurable unbiased estimator for λ_j, which has minimal variance among all unbiased linear combinations of the unbiased estimators $\left(Y_{i,j+1}/e_i\right)_{0\le i\le I-j-1}$ for λ_j, i.e.*

$$\mathrm{Var}\left(\widehat{\delta}_j|\mathcal{B}_j\right) = \min_{\substack{\alpha_i\in\mathbb{R}\\ \sum_i \alpha_i=1}} \mathrm{Var}\left(\sum_{i=0}^{I-j-1} \alpha_i \frac{Y_{i,j+1}}{e_i}\right)$$

(g) *the (conditional) variances of the estimators $\widehat{\delta}_j$ and $\widehat{\lambda}_j$ are given by*

$$\mathrm{Var}\left(\widehat{\delta}_j|\mathcal{B}_j\right) = \tau_j^2 \Big/ \sum_{i=0}^{I-j-1} C_{i,j}$$

$$\mathrm{Var}\left(\widehat{\lambda}_j\right) = \sigma_j^2 \Big/ \sum_{i=0}^{I-j-1} e_i$$

Proof The proof of claims (a)–(d) follows immediately from the conditional independence of $D_{i,j}$ and $Y_{i,j}$, given $\mathcal{G}_{j-1}$. The proof of claims (e)–(g) is completely analogous to the proof of Lemma 3.3. □

The estimators $\widehat{\tau}_j^2$ and $\widehat{\sigma}_j^2$ are (unconditionally) unbiased:

LEMMA 10.10 *Under Model Assumptions 10.7 we have*

(a) *given $\mathcal{B}_j$, $\widehat{\tau}_j^2$ is an unbiased estimator for τ_j^2, i.e. $E\left[\widehat{\tau}_j^2\middle|\mathcal{B}_j\right] = \tau_j^2$;*
(b) *$\widehat{\sigma}_j^2$ is an (unconditionally) unbiased estimator for σ_j^2, i.e. $E\left[\widehat{\sigma}_j^2\right] = \sigma_j^2$.*

Proof The proof is analogous to the proof of Lemma 3.5. □

We define the following estimator for the conditionally expected ultimate claim:

ESTIMATOR 10.11 *The estimator for* $E\left[C_{i,J}\middle|\mathcal{D}_I\right]$ *is given by*

$$\widehat{C}_{i,J}^{\text{Sch}}=\widehat{E}\left[C_{i,J}\middle|\mathcal{D}_I\right]=C_{i,I-i}\prod_{j=I-i}^{J-1}\left(1+\widehat{\delta}_j\right)+e_i\sum_{j=I-i}^{J-1}\widehat{\lambda}_j\prod_{k=j+1}^{J-1}\left(1+\widehat{\delta}_k\right)$$

for all $1\le i\le I$

The following result holds:

LEMMA 10.12 *Under Model Assumptions 10.7 estimator* $\widehat{C}_{i,J}^{\text{Sch}}$ *is conditionally unbiased for* $E\left[C_{i,J}\middle|\mathcal{D}_I\right]$, *given* $C_{i,I-i}$.

Proof The claim easily follows from the conditional unbiasedness of the estimators (which also implies the uncorrelatedness of the estimators). For details we refer to the proof of Lemma 2.5. □

In the following we derive an estimate for the conditional MSEP of $\widehat{C}_{i,J}^{\text{Sch}}$. Notice that, due to the $\mathcal{D}_I$-measurability of $\widehat{C}_{i,J}^{\text{Sch}}$, we have the decomposition

$$\begin{aligned}\operatorname{msep}_{C_{i,J}|\mathcal{D}_I}\left(\widehat{C}_{i,J}^{\text{Sch}}\right)&=E\left[\left(\widehat{C}_{i,J}^{\text{Sch}}-C_{i,J}\right)^2\middle|\mathcal{D}_I\right]\\&=\operatorname{Var}\left(C_{i,J}\middle|\mathcal{D}_I\right)+\left(E\left[C_{i,J}\middle|\mathcal{D}_I\right]-\widehat{C}_{i,J}^{\text{Sch}}\right)^2\end{aligned}\tag{10.12}$$

The first term on the right-hand side of (10.12) is the conditional process variance and the second term corresponds to the conditional estimation error (for more details to the conditional MSEP and its components see Section 3.1).

Conditional Process Variance

In this subsection we calculate the conditional process variance. Similarly as in the classical CL model, we derive a recursive formula ($i\ge 1$)

$$\begin{aligned}\operatorname{Var}\left(C_{i,J}\middle|\mathcal{D}_I\right)=&E\left[\operatorname{Var}\left(C_{i,J}\middle|\mathcal{D}_I,\mathcal{G}_{J-1}\right)\middle|\mathcal{D}_I\right]\\&+\operatorname{Var}\left(E\left[C_{i,J}\middle|\mathcal{D}_I,\mathcal{G}_{J-1}\right]\middle|\mathcal{D}_I\right)\end{aligned}\tag{10.13}$$

Moreover, for the first term on the right-hand side of (10.13) we have, using the conditional independence of $D_{i,J}$ and $Y_{i,J}$,

$$\begin{aligned}&E\left[\operatorname{Var}\left(C_{i,J}\middle|\mathcal{D}_I,\mathcal{G}_{J-1}\right)\middle|\mathcal{D}_I\right]\\&\quad=E\left[\operatorname{Var}\left(C_{i,J-1}+D_{i,J}+Y_{i,J}\middle|\mathcal{G}_{J-1}\right)\middle|\mathcal{D}_I\right]\\&\quad=E\left[\operatorname{Var}\left(D_{i,J}\middle|\mathcal{G}_{J-1}\right)+\operatorname{Var}\left(Y_{i,J}\middle|\mathcal{G}_{J-1}\right)\middle|\mathcal{D}_I\right]\\&\quad=\tau_{J-1}^2\,E\left[C_{i,J-1}\middle|\mathcal{D}_I\right]+\sigma_{J-1}^2\,e_i\\&\quad=C_{i,I-i}\,\tau_{J-1}^2\prod_{j=I-i}^{J-2}\left(1+\delta_j\right)+e_i\,\tau_{J-1}^2\sum_{j=I-i}^{J-2}\lambda_j\prod_{k=j+1}^{J-2}\left(1+\delta_k\right)+\sigma_{J-1}^2\,e_i\end{aligned}$$

Using (10.7), this last expression can also be written as

$$\frac{\tau_{J-1}^2}{1+\delta_{J-1}} \left(E\left[C_{i,J}\middle|\mathcal{D}_I\right] - \lambda_{J-1}\, e_i\right) + \sigma_{J-1}^2\, e_i$$

For the second term on the right-hand side of (10.13) we obtain

$$\begin{aligned}
&\operatorname{Var}\left(E\left[C_{i,J}\middle|\mathcal{D}_I, \mathcal{G}_{J-1}\right]\middle|\mathcal{D}_I\right)\\
&\quad= \operatorname{Var}\left(E\left[C_{i,J-1} + D_{i,J} + Y_{i,J}\middle|\mathcal{D}_I, \mathcal{G}_{J-1}\right]\middle|\mathcal{D}_I\right)\\
&\quad= \operatorname{Var}\left((1+\delta_{J-1})\, C_{i,J-1} + \lambda_{J-1}\, e_i\middle|\mathcal{D}_I\right)\\
&\quad= (1+\delta_{J-1})^2 \operatorname{Var}\left(C_{i,J-1}\middle|\mathcal{D}_I\right)
\end{aligned}$$

Hence we obtain the following recursive formula:

LEMMA 10.13 *Under Model Assumptions* 10.7, *the conditional process variance for the ultimate claim of a single accident year* $i \in \{1, \ldots, I\}$ *is given by*

$$\operatorname{Var}\left(C_{i,J}\middle|\mathcal{D}_I\right) = \tau_{J-1}^2\, E\left[C_{i,J-1}\middle|\mathcal{D}_I\right] + \sigma_{J-1}^2\, e_i + (1+\delta_{J-1})^2 \operatorname{Var}\left(C_{i,J-1}\middle|\mathcal{D}_I\right)$$

If we replace the unknown parameters τ_{J-1}^2, σ_{J-1}^2 and δ_{J-1} with its estimates we obtain an estimator for the conditional process variance.

Conditional Estimation Error, Single Accident Years

For the conditional estimation error of a single accident year $i \in \{1, \ldots, I\}$ we need to estimate the term

$$\left(E\left[C_{i,J}\middle|\mathcal{D}_I\right] - \widehat{C}_{i,J}^{\text{Sch}}\right)^2 \tag{10.14}$$

which is equal to

$$\begin{aligned}
C_{i,I-i}^2 &\left(\prod_{j=I-i}^{J-1} (1+\delta_j) + e_i \sum_{j=I-i}^{J-1} \lambda_j \prod_{k=j+1}^{J-1} (1+\delta_k)\right.\\
&\left. - \prod_{j=I-i}^{J-1} \left(1+\widehat{\delta}_j\right) + e_i \sum_{j=I-i}^{J-1} \widehat{\lambda}_j \prod_{k=j+1}^{J-1} \left(1+\widehat{\delta}_k\right)\right)^2
\end{aligned} \tag{10.15}$$

(cf. (10.7) and Estimator 10.11). Our goal is to apply Approach 3 (conditional resampling) from Subsection 3.2.3 to derive an estimate for (10.14). That is, as in (3.18), we denote the measure for the conditional resampling by $P^*_{\mathcal{D}_I}$, and conditionally, given $\mathcal{D}_I$, we resample new observations as follows: $\widetilde{D}_{i,j+1}$ and $\widetilde{Y}_{i,j+1}$ are resampled values for $D_{i,j+1}$ and $Y_{i,j+1}$, respectively, where the observations in $\mathcal{B}_j \subseteq \mathcal{D}_I$ serve as fixed volume measures.

Hence, under the measure $P^*_{\mathcal{D}_I}$ the random variables $\widehat{\delta}_0, \ldots, \widehat{\delta}_{J-1}, \widehat{\lambda}_0, \ldots, \widehat{\lambda}_{J-1}$ are independent with

$$E^*_{\mathcal{D}_I}\left[\widehat{\delta}_j\right]=\delta_j \qquad \text{and} \qquad E^*_{\mathcal{D}_I}\left[\widehat{\lambda}_j\right]=\lambda_j$$

and

$$\mathrm{Var}_{P^*_{\mathcal{D}_I}}\left(\widehat{\delta}_j\right)=\frac{\tau_j^2}{\sum_{i=0}^{I-j-1} C_{i,j}}=\frac{\tau_j^2}{S_j^{[I-j-1]}}$$

$$\mathrm{Var}_{P^*_{\mathcal{D}_I}}\left(\widehat{\lambda}_j\right)=\frac{\sigma_j^2}{\sum_{i=0}^{I-j-1} e_i}$$

Henceforth, the term in the round brackets in (10.15) is estimated by

$$\begin{aligned}
E^*_{\mathcal{D}_I}\Bigg[\Bigg(&\prod_{j=I-i}^{J-1}(1+\delta_j)+e_i\sum_{j=I-i}^{J-1}\lambda_j\prod_{k=j+1}^{J-1}(1+\delta_k)\\
&-\prod_{j=I-i}^{J-1}\left(1+\widehat{\delta}_j\right)+e_i\sum_{j=I-i}^{J-1}\widehat{\lambda}_j\prod_{k=j+1}^{J-1}\left(1+\widehat{\delta}_k\right)\Bigg)^2\Bigg]\\
&=\mathrm{Var}_{P^*_{\mathcal{D}_I}}\left(\prod_{j=I-i}^{J-1}\left(1+\widehat{\delta}_j\right)+e_i\sum_{j=I-i}^{J-1}\widehat{\lambda}_j\prod_{k=j+1}^{J-1}\left(1+\widehat{\delta}_k\right)\right)
\end{aligned}\tag{10.16}$$

This is equal to

$$\begin{aligned}
&\mathrm{Var}_{P^*_{\mathcal{D}_I}}\left(\prod_{j=I-i}^{J-1}\left(1+\widehat{\delta}_j\right)+e_i\sum_{j=I-i}^{J-1}\widehat{\lambda}_j\prod_{k=j+1}^{J-1}\left(1+\widehat{\delta}_k\right)\right)\\
&=\mathrm{Var}_{P^*_{\mathcal{D}_I}}\left(\prod_{j=I-i}^{J-1}\left(1+\widehat{\delta}_j\right)\right)+e_i^2\,\mathrm{Var}_{P^*_{\mathcal{D}_I}}\left(\sum_{j=I-i}^{J-1}\widehat{\lambda}_j\prod_{k=j+1}^{J-1}\left(1+\widehat{\delta}_k\right)\right)\\
&\quad+2\,e_i\,\mathrm{Cov}_{P^*_{\mathcal{D}_I}}\left(\prod_{j=I-i}^{J-1}\left(1+\widehat{\delta}_j\right),\sum_{j=I-i}^{J-1}\widehat{\lambda}_j\prod_{k=j+1}^{J-1}\left(1+\widehat{\delta}_k\right)\right)
\end{aligned}\tag{10.17}$$

Therefore, we need to calculate the three terms on the right-hand side of (10.17). The first term, using the independence of the estimators $\widehat{\delta}_0,\ldots,\widehat{\delta}_{J-1}$ under the probability law $P^*_{\mathcal{D}_I}$, gives

$$\begin{aligned}
&\mathrm{Var}_{P^*_{\mathcal{D}_I}}\left(\prod_{j=I-i}^{J-1}\left(1+\widehat{\delta}_j\right)\right)\\
&=\prod_{j=I-i}^{J-1}E^*_{\mathcal{D}_I}\left[\left(1+\widehat{\delta}_j\right)^2\right]-\prod_{j=I-i}^{J-1}E^*_{\mathcal{D}_I}\left[1+\widehat{\delta}_j\right]^2\\
&=\prod_{j=I-i}^{J-1}\left(\mathrm{Var}_{P^*_{\mathcal{D}_I}}\left(1+\widehat{\delta}_j\right)+(1+\delta_j)^2\right)-\prod_{j=I-i}^{J-1}(1+\delta_j)^2
\end{aligned}$$

$$= \prod_{j=I-i}^{J-1} \left(\frac{\tau_j^2}{\sum_{i=0}^{I-j-1} C_{i,j}} + (1+\delta_j)^2 \right) - \prod_{j=I-i}^{J-1} (1+\delta_j)^2$$

$$\approx \prod_{j=I-i}^{J-1} (1+\delta_j)^2 \sum_{j=I-i}^{J-1} \frac{\tau_j^2/(1+\delta_j)^2}{S_j^{[I-j-1]}}$$

where in the last step we have done the same linear approximation as in (3.31). For the second term we have

$$\begin{aligned}
&\mathrm{Var}_{P^*_{\mathcal{D}_I}} \left(\sum_{j=I-i}^{J-1} \widehat{\lambda}_j \prod_{k=j+1}^{J-1} \left(1+\widehat{\delta}_k\right) \right) \\
&= \mathrm{Cov}_{P^*_{\mathcal{D}_I}} \left(\sum_{j=I-i}^{J-1} \widehat{\lambda}_j \prod_{k=j+1}^{J-1} \left(1+\widehat{\delta}_k\right), \sum_{l=I-i}^{J-1} \widehat{\lambda}_l \prod_{m=l+1}^{J-1} \left(1+\widehat{\delta}_m\right) \right) \\
&= \sum_{j=I-i}^{J-1} \sum_{l=I-i}^{J-1} \mathrm{Cov}_{P^*_{\mathcal{D}_I}} \left(\widehat{\lambda}_j \prod_{k=j+1}^{J-1} \left(1+\widehat{\delta}_k\right), \widehat{\lambda}_l \prod_{m=l+1}^{J-1} \left(1+\widehat{\delta}_m\right) \right)
\end{aligned} \tag{10.18}$$

For $j = l$, using the independence of $\widehat{\lambda}_j, \widehat{\delta}_{j+1}, \ldots, \widehat{\delta}_{J-1}$ under the probability law $P^*_{\mathcal{D}_I}$, a summand of the sum on the right-hand side of (10.18) is equal to,

$$\begin{aligned}
&\mathrm{Var}_{P^*_{\mathcal{D}_I}} \left(\widehat{\lambda}_j \prod_{k=j+1}^{J-1} \left(1+\widehat{\delta}_k\right) \right) \\
&= \left(\mathrm{Var}_{P^*_{\mathcal{D}_I}} (\widehat{\lambda}_j) + \lambda_j^2 \right) \prod_{k=j+1}^{J-1} \left(\mathrm{Var}_{P^*_{\mathcal{D}_I}} \left(1+\widehat{\delta}_k\right) + (1+\delta_k)^2 \right) \\
&\quad - \lambda_j^2 \prod_{k=j+1}^{J-1} (1+\delta_k)^2 \\
&\approx \lambda_j^2 \prod_{k=j+1}^{J-1} (1+\delta_j)^2 \left(\frac{\sigma_j^2/\lambda_j^2}{\sum_{i=0}^{I-j-1} e_i} + \sum_{k=j+1}^{J-1} \frac{\tau_k^2/(1+\delta_k)^2}{S_k^{[I-k-1]}} \right)
\end{aligned}$$

For $l > j$ we obtain

$$\begin{aligned}
&\mathrm{Cov}_{P^*_{\mathcal{D}_I}} \left(\widehat{\lambda}_j \prod_{k=j+1}^{J-1} \left(1+\widehat{\delta}_k\right), \widehat{\lambda}_l \prod_{m=l+1}^{J-1} \left(1+\widehat{\delta}_m\right) \right) \\
&= \lambda_j \, \lambda_l \prod_{k=j+1}^{l} (1+\delta_k) \, \mathrm{Var}_{P^*_{\mathcal{D}_I}} \left(\prod_{m=l+1}^{J-1} \left(1+\widehat{\delta}_m\right) \right) \\
&\approx \lambda_j \, \lambda_l \prod_{k=j+1}^{l} (1+\delta_k) \prod_{m=l+1}^{J-1} (1+\delta_m)^2 \sum_{m=l+1}^{J-1} \frac{\tau_m^2/(1+\delta_m)^2}{S_m^{[I-m-1]}}
\end{aligned}$$

This implies that the variance term in (10.18) is approximated by

$$\operatorname{Var}_{P^*_{\mathcal{D}_I}}\left(\sum_{j=I-i}^{J-1} \widehat{\lambda}_j \prod_{k=j+1}^{J-1}\left(1+\widehat{\delta}_k\right)\right)$$

$$\approx \sum_{j=I-i}^{J-1} \lambda_j^2 \prod_{k=j+1}^{J-1} (1+\delta_j)^2 \left(\frac{\sigma_j^2/\lambda_j^2}{\sum_{i=0}^{I-j-1} e_i} + \sum_{k=j+1}^{J-1} \frac{\tau_k^2/(1+\delta_k)^2}{S_k^{[I-k-1]}}\right)$$

$$+2 \sum_{j=I-i}^{J-1} \sum_{l=j+1}^{J-1} \lambda_j \lambda_l \prod_{k=j+1}^{l} (1+\delta_k) \prod_{m=l+1}^{J-1} (1+\delta_m)^2 \sum_{m=l+1}^{J-1} \frac{\tau_m^2/(1+\delta_m)^2}{S_m^{[I-m-1]}} \tag{10.19}$$

Thus, there remains to estimate the covariance terms in (10.17). We have

$$\operatorname{Cov}_{P^*_{\mathcal{D}_I}}\left(\prod_{j=I-i}^{J-1}\left(1+\widehat{\delta}_j\right), \sum_{j=I-i}^{J-1} \widehat{\lambda}_j \prod_{k=j+1}^{J-1}\left(1+\widehat{\delta}_k\right)\right)$$

$$= \sum_{j=I-i}^{J-1} \operatorname{Cov}_{P^*_{\mathcal{D}_I}}\left(\prod_{l=I-i}^{J-1}\left(1+\widehat{\delta}_l\right), \widehat{\lambda}_j \prod_{k=j+1}^{J-1}\left(1+\widehat{\delta}_k\right)\right)$$

$$= \sum_{j=I-i}^{J-1} \lambda_j \prod_{l=I-i}^{j} (1+\delta_l) \operatorname{Var}_{P^*_{\mathcal{D}_I}}\left(\prod_{k=j+1}^{J-1}\left(1+\widehat{\delta}_k\right)\right)$$

$$\approx \sum_{j=I-i}^{J-1} \lambda_j \prod_{l=I-i}^{j} (1+\delta_l) \prod_{k=j+1}^{J-1} (1+\delta_k)^2 \sum_{k=j+1}^{J-1} \frac{\tau_k^2/(1+\delta_k)^2}{S_k^{[I-k-1]}}$$

Henceforth, we obtain the following linear approximation:

ESTIMATOR 10.14 (conditional estimation error, single accident year) *Under Model Assumptions 10.7 we obtain the following estimator for the conditional estimation error of a single accident year* $i \in \{1, \ldots, I\}$

$$C_{i,I-i}^2 \operatorname{Var}_{P^*_{\mathcal{D}_I}}\left(\prod_{j=I-i}^{J-1}\left(1+\widehat{\delta}_j\right) + e_i \sum_{j=I-i}^{J-1} \widehat{\lambda}_j \prod_{k=j+1}^{J-1}\left(1+\widehat{\delta}_k\right)\right)$$

$$\approx C_{i,I-i}^2 \prod_{j=I-i}^{J-1} (1+\delta_j)^2 \sum_{j=I-i}^{J-1} \frac{\tau_j^2/(1+\delta_j)^2}{S_j^{[I-j-1]}}$$

$$+ C_{i,I-i}^2\, e_i^2 \sum_{j=I-i}^{J-1} \lambda_j^2 \prod_{k=j+1}^{J-1} (1+\delta_j)^2 \left(\frac{\sigma_j^2/\lambda_j^2}{\sum_{n=0}^{I-j-1} e_n} + \sum_{k=j+1}^{J-1} \frac{\tau_k^2/(1+\delta_k)^2}{S_k^{[I-k-1]}}\right)$$

$$+2\, C_{i,I-i}^2\, e_i^2 \sum_{j=I-i}^{J-1} \sum_{l=j+1}^{J-1} \lambda_j \lambda_l \prod_{k=j+1}^{l} (1+\delta_k) \prod_{m=l+1}^{J-1} (1+\delta_m)^2 \sum_{m=l+1}^{J-1} \frac{\tau_m^2/(1+\delta_m)^2}{S_m^{[I-m-1]}}$$

$$+2\, C_{i,I-i}^2\, e_i \sum_{j=I-i}^{J-1} \lambda_j \prod_{l=I-i}^{j} (1+\delta_l) \prod_{k=j+1}^{J-1} (1+\delta_k)^2 \sum_{k=j+1}^{J-1} \frac{\tau_k^2/(1+\delta_k)^2}{S_k^{[I-k-1]}} \tag{10.20}$$

If we now replace the unknown parameters in (10.20) by the estimates we obtain an estimator for the conditional estimation error. Henceforth, Lemma 10.13 and Estimator 10.14 provide an estimator for the conditional MSEP of a single accident year $i \in \{1, \ldots, I\}$ given by

$$\mathrm{msep}_{C_{i,J}|\mathcal{D}_I}\left(\widehat{C}_{i,J}^{\mathrm{Sch}}\right)$$

Conditional Estimation Error, Aggregated Accident Years

For *aggregated* accident years one needs to be careful, since the same parameter estimates (and, hence, the same observations) are used for different accident years. We have

$$\begin{aligned}
\mathrm{msep}_{\sum_i C_{i,J}|\mathcal{D}_I}\left(\sum_{i=i}^{I} \widehat{C}_{i,J}^{\mathrm{Sch}}\right) &= \sum_{i=1}^{I} \mathrm{msep}_{C_{i,J}|\mathcal{D}_I}\left(\widehat{C}_{i,J}^{\mathrm{Sch}}\right) + \\
&\quad + 2 \sum_{1 \le i < k \le I} \left(E\left[C_{i,J}\middle|\mathcal{D}_I\right] - \widehat{C}_{i,J}^{\mathrm{Sch}}\right)\left(E\left[C_{k,J}\middle|\mathcal{D}_I\right] - \widehat{C}_{k,J}^{\mathrm{Sch}}\right)
\end{aligned} \tag{10.21}$$

So, we need to treat the covariance terms on the right-hand side of (10.21). We assume that $i < k$ and estimate these covariance terms by

$$\begin{aligned}
C_{i,I-i}\, C_{k,I-k}\, \mathrm{Cov}_{P^*_{\mathcal{D}_I}}\Bigg(& \prod_{j=I-i}^{J-1}\left(1+\widehat{\delta}_j\right) + e_i \sum_{j=I-i}^{J-1} \widehat{\lambda}_j \prod_{l=j+1}^{J-1}\left(1+\widehat{\delta}_l\right), \\
& \prod_{j=I-k}^{J-1}\left(1+\widehat{\delta}_j\right) + e_k \sum_{j=I-k}^{J-1} \widehat{\lambda}_j \prod_{l=j+1}^{J-1}\left(1+\widehat{\delta}_l\right)\Bigg)
\end{aligned} \tag{10.22}$$

(cf. (10.14)–(10.15) and (10.16)–(10.17)). If we decouple these covariance terms we obtain the expressions

$$\begin{aligned}
& \mathrm{Cov}_{P^*_{\mathcal{D}_I}}\left(\prod_{j=I-i}^{J-1}\left(1+\widehat{\delta}_j\right), \prod_{j=I-k}^{J-1}\left(1+\widehat{\delta}_j\right)\right) \\
& + e_i\, \mathrm{Cov}_{P^*_{\mathcal{D}_I}}\left(\sum_{j=I-i}^{J-1} \widehat{\lambda}_j \prod_{l=j+1}^{J-1}\left(1+\widehat{\delta}_l\right), \prod_{j=I-k}^{J-1}\left(1+\widehat{\delta}_j\right)\right) \\
& + e_k\, \mathrm{Cov}_{P^*_{\mathcal{D}_I}}\left(\prod_{j=I-i}^{J-1}\left(1+\widehat{\delta}_j\right), \sum_{j=I-k}^{J-1} \widehat{\lambda}_j \prod_{l=j+1}^{J-1}\left(1+\widehat{\delta}_l\right)\right) \\
& + e_i\, e_k\, \mathrm{Cov}_{P^*_{\mathcal{D}_I}}\left(\sum_{j=I-i}^{J-1} \widehat{\lambda}_j \prod_{l=j+1}^{J-1}\left(1+\widehat{\delta}_l\right), \sum_{j=I-k}^{J-1} \widehat{\lambda}_j \prod_{l=j+1}^{J-1}\left(1+\widehat{\delta}_l\right)\right)
\end{aligned} \tag{10.23}$$

All terms in (10.23) can now be calculated as in the last section. The assumption $i < k$ implies $I - k < I - i$, and we obtain for the first term

$$
\begin{aligned}
&\mathrm{Cov}_{P^*_{\mathcal{D}_I}}\left(\prod_{j=I-i}^{J-1}\left(1+\widehat{\delta}_j\right), \prod_{j=I-k}^{J-1}\left(1+\widehat{\delta}_j\right)\right)\\
&= \prod_{j=I-k}^{I-i-1}(1+\delta_j)\ \mathrm{Var}_{P^*_{\mathcal{D}_I}}\left(\prod_{j=I-i}^{J-1}\left(1+\widehat{\delta}_j\right)\right)\\
&\approx \prod_{j=I-k}^{I-i-1}(1+\delta_j)\ \prod_{j=I-i}^{J-1}(1+\delta_j)^2 \sum_{j=I-i}^{J-1}\frac{\tau_j^2/(1+\delta_j)^2}{S_j^{[I-j-1]}}
\end{aligned}
\tag{10.24}
$$

For the second term in (10.23) we have, $i<k$,

$$
\begin{aligned}
&e_i\ \mathrm{Cov}_{P^*_{\mathcal{D}_I}}\left(\sum_{j=I-i}^{J-1}\widehat{\lambda}_j \prod_{l=j+1}^{J-1}\left(1+\widehat{\delta}_l\right), \prod_{j=I-k}^{J-1}\left(1+\widehat{\delta}_j\right)\right)\\
&= e_i \sum_{j=I-i}^{J-1}\lambda_j \prod_{m=I-k}^{j}(1+\delta_m)\ \mathrm{Var}_{P^*_{\mathcal{D}_I}}\left(\prod_{l=j+1}^{J-1}\left(1+\widehat{\delta}_l\right)\right)\\
&\approx e_i \sum_{j=I-i}^{J-1}\lambda_j \prod_{m=I-k}^{j}(1+\delta_m)\ \prod_{l=j+1}^{J-1}(1+\delta_l)^2 \sum_{l=j+1}^{J-1}\frac{\tau_l^2/(1+\delta_l)^2}{S_l^{[I-l-1]}}
\end{aligned}
\tag{10.25}
$$

For the third term we have, $i<k$,

$$
\begin{aligned}
&e_k\ \mathrm{Cov}_{P^*_{\mathcal{D}_I}}\left(\prod_{j=I-i}^{J-1}\left(1+\widehat{\delta}_j\right), \sum_{j=I-k}^{J-1}\widehat{\lambda}_j \prod_{l=j+1}^{J-1}\left(1+\widehat{\delta}_l\right)\right)\\
&= e_k \sum_{j=I-k}^{J-1}\lambda_j\ \mathrm{Cov}_{P^*_{\mathcal{D}_I}}\left(\prod_{l=I-i}^{J-1}\left(1+\widehat{\delta}_l\right), \prod_{l=j+1}^{J-1}\left(1+\widehat{\delta}_l\right)\right)\\
&= e_k \sum_{j=I-k}^{J-1}\lambda_j \prod_{m=(j+1)\wedge(I-i)}^{(I-i-1)\vee j}(1+\delta_m)\ \mathrm{Var}_{P^*_{\mathcal{D}_I}}\left(\prod_{l=(I-i)\vee(j+1)}^{J-1}\left(1+\widehat{\delta}_l\right)\right)\\
&\approx e_k \sum_{j=I-k}^{J-1}\lambda_j \prod_{m=(j+1)\wedge(I-i)}^{(I-i-1)\vee j}(1+\delta_m) \prod_{l=(I-i)\vee(j+1)}^{J-1}(1+\delta_l)^2 \sum_{l=(I-i)\vee(j+1)}^{J-1}\frac{\tau_l^2/(1+\delta_l)^2}{S_l^{[I-l-1]}}
\end{aligned}
\tag{10.26}
$$

And, for the last term in (10.23), we have, $i<k$,

$$
\begin{aligned}
&e_i\ e_k\ \mathrm{Cov}_{P^*_{\mathcal{D}_I}}\left(\sum_{j=I-i}^{J-1}\widehat{\lambda}_j \prod_{l=j+1}^{J-1}\left(1+\widehat{\delta}_l\right), \sum_{j=I-k}^{J-1}\widehat{\lambda}_j \prod_{l=j+1}^{J-1}\left(1+\widehat{\delta}_l\right)\right)\\
&= e_i\ e_k \sum_{j=I-i}^{J-1}\sum_{l=I-k}^{J-1}\mathrm{Cov}_{P^*_{\mathcal{D}_I}}\left(\widehat{\lambda}_j \prod_{n=j+1}^{J-1}\left(1+\widehat{\delta}_n\right), \widehat{\lambda}_l \prod_{m=l+1}^{J-1}\left(1+\widehat{\delta}_m\right)\right)\\
&= e_i e_k \sum_{j=I-i}^{J-1}\sum_{l=I-k}^{I-i-1}\mathrm{Cov}_{P^*_{\mathcal{D}_I}}\left(\widehat{\lambda}_j \prod_{n=j+1}^{J-1}\left(1+\widehat{\delta}_n\right), \widehat{\lambda}_l \prod_{m=l+1}^{J-1}\left(1+\widehat{\delta}_m\right)\right)
\end{aligned}
$$

$$+ e_i e_k \sum_{j=I-i}^{J-1} \sum_{l=I-i}^{J-1} \mathrm{Cov}_{P^*_{\mathcal{D}_I}} \left(\widehat{\lambda}_j \prod_{n=j+1}^{J-1} \left(1+\widehat{\delta}_n\right), \widehat{\lambda}_l \prod_{m=l+1}^{J-1} \left(1+\widehat{\delta}_m\right) \right)$$

$$= e_i\, e_k \sum_{j=I-i}^{J-1} \sum_{l=I-k}^{I-i-1} \lambda_j\, \lambda_l \prod_{m=l+1}^{j} (1+\delta_m)\, \mathrm{Var}_{P^*_{\mathcal{D}_I}} \left(\prod_{n=j+1}^{J-1} \left(1+\widehat{\delta}_n\right) \right)$$

$$+ e_i\, e_k\, \mathrm{Var}_{P^*_{\mathcal{D}_I}} \left(\sum_{j=I-i}^{J-1} \widehat{\lambda}_j \prod_{n=j+1}^{J-1} \left(1+\widehat{\delta}_n\right) \right) \tag{10.27}$$

Note that the last term on the right-hand side of (10.27) has been calculated in formula (10.19).

ESTIMATOR 10.15 (conditional estimation error, aggregation) *Under Model Assumptions 10.7 we obtain for the covariance term, $i < k$,*

$$\left(E\left[C_{i,J} \middle| \mathcal{D}_I\right] - \widehat{C}^{\mathrm{Sch}}_{i,J}\right) \left(E\left[C_{k,J} \middle| \mathcal{D}_I\right] - \widehat{C}^{\mathrm{Sch}}_{k,J}\right)$$

estimator (10.22)*, where the single terms are given in* (10.23) *and estimated in* (10.24)–(10.27).

Concluding Remarks

We see that this (slightly) more complicated claims reserving model leads to rather complicated formulas both for the expected ultimate claim and the conditional MSEP. The predictor for the ultimate claim can still be implemented on a single spreadsheet, but for the implementation of the formulas for the conditional MSEP one has to be rather careful (see Lemma 10.13 and Estimator 10.14 for a single accident year i). Hence, we come to a similar conclusion as Mack (1993), p. 214, that the things become easier when one considers the pure CL case (see Chapter 3). But we believe that the Schnieper (1991) model is still important and possible for calculations.

Moreover in practice, we have observed that actuaries use models that are closely related to Schnieper's model. They often lead to more elaborated claims reserves due to the fact that one is able to include more expert opinion for sensitive structural parameters (see (10.8) and (10.9)). That is, very often δ_j and λ_j are not estimated mechanically using (10.8) and (10.9), but therefore they are adjusted 'by hand' using expert opinion. For example, there are good reasons for changing λ_0 appropriately due to external knowledge such as year end constellation of public holidays, weather conditions during the last days before the end of the development period, etc. Often, $Y_{i,1}$ acts very sensitively to such events, and adjusting the parameters 'by hand' leads to more reasonable reserves.

On the other hand, we should mention that many claims reserving models are close to being overparametrized. Perhaps the use of an extensive number of parameters can lead to very accurate backtesting results, but in general, this does not mean that the power for predicting future behaviour is better. From this point of view one should rather prefer easy models, which also allow for easy formulas of the conditional MSEP. Hence, we are confronted with the well-known trade-off situation of, simplicity vs accuracy, and only an experienced actuary can decide which is the more appropriate method for his dataset.

11
Statistical Diagnostics

In the present outline we have mainly studied the claims reserving problem from a probability theory point of view. This means that we have defined stochastic models and have demonstrated the properties that these models possess. To a large extent we have omitted statistical questions about model fitting, model errors, backtesting, etc. Unfortunately, this also holds true to a large extent for the present actuarial literature to claims reserving. Model testing in claims reserving has only been partially investigated and documented, although some statistical work can be found in Venter (1998), Barnett and Zehnwirth (2000), Mack (1994, 1997), Murphy (1994) or in England and Verrall (2001). Some work on model errors can also be found in Gigante and Sigalotti (2005) and Cairns (2000).

In this chapter we investigate some of these basic statistical diagnostics.

11.1 TESTING AGE-TO-AGE FACTORS

In this section we consider three different models for the incremental claims $X_{i,j}$.

Model Assumptions 11.1

- Incremental claims $X_{i,j}$ of different accident years i are independent.
- There exist positive constants $\sigma_0, \ldots, \sigma_{J-1} > 0$ and independent standard normally distributed random variables $\varepsilon_{i,j} \stackrel{(d)}{\sim} \mathcal{N}(0, 1)$ such that for all $i = 0, \ldots, I$ and $j = 1, \ldots, J$ we obtain the following three models for incremental claims:

  (M1) There are constants g_j such that

  $$X_{i,j} = g_{j-1}\, C_{i,j-1} + \sigma_{j-1}\, \sqrt{C_{i,j-1}}\; \varepsilon_{i,j}$$

  (M2) There are constants g_j and δ_j such that

  $$X_{i,j} = \delta_{j-1} + g_{j-1}\, C_{i,j-1} + \sigma_{j-1}\, \sqrt{C_{i,j-1}}\; \varepsilon_{i,j}$$

  (M3) There are constants g_j, u_i and $c_{i,j} \geq 0$ such that

  $$X_{i,j} = g_{j-1}\, u_i + \sigma_{j-1}\, \sqrt{c_{i,j-1}}\; \varepsilon_{i,j}$$

□

Remarks 11.2

- Theoretically, we could get negative values for the cumulative claims $C_{i,j}$ in Models (M1)–(M2) which makes it impossible to continue the time series, but this problem is not further investigated here. For a discussion we refer to Remarks 3.10.
- Of course, the assumption of Gaussian residuals $\varepsilon_{i,j}$ is not imperative. However, many of the calculations below are exact for Gaussian residuals, whereas for other distributions we only get asymptotic equalities.
- Model (M1) leads to the CL model for cumulative claims with $f_j = g_j + 1$, i.e.

$$C_{i,j} = X_{i,j} + C_{i,j-1} = (g_{j-1} + 1)\ C_{i,j-1} + \sigma_{j-1} \sqrt{C_{i,j-1}}\ \varepsilon_{i,j} \tag{11.1}$$

  see also Model Assumptions 3.9.
- Model (M2) is the CL model where we also allow for an intercept $\delta_j \neq 0$ in the incremental claims. This model was proposed by Murphy (1994). Note that the Bayesian model from the EDF with its associated conjugates has the structure of Model (M2), see ((4.50)), which means that the incremental claim $X_{i,j}$ partly depends on the cumulative claims $C_{i,j-1}$ and partly on δ_{j-1}, which could be expert opinion.
- Model (M3) is a GLM-type model where future incremental claims are independent from past observations. This is more in the spirit of additive models (cf. (8.44)). It can also be viewed as a BF-type model (cf. Remarks 6.23).

We define

$$\mu_{i,j+1} = \begin{cases} g_j\ C_{i,j} & \text{Model (M1)} \\ g_j\ C_{i,j} + \delta_j & \text{Model (M2)} \\ g_j\ u_i & \text{Model (M3)} \end{cases}$$

$$\tau^2_{i,j+1} = \begin{cases} \sigma_j^2\ C_{i,j} & \text{Model (M1) and (M2)} \\ \sigma_j^2\ c_{i,j} & \text{Model (M3)} \end{cases}$$

Hence, the MLE function for the observations $\mathcal{D}_I$ is given by

$$L^{(k)}_{\mathcal{D}_I}\left(\mu_{i,j};\ 0 \le i+j \le I\right) = \prod_{0\le i+j\le I} \frac{1}{\sqrt{2\pi}\tau_{i,j}}\ \exp\left\{-\frac{1}{2\tau^2_{i,j}}\ \left(X_{i,j} - \mu_{i,j}\right)^2\right\}$$

where $k = 1, 2, 3$ denotes the model chosen.

The MLEs for $\mu_{i,j}$ are then easily obtained using that for all $0 \le i+j \le I$

$$\frac{\partial}{\partial \alpha} \log L^{(k)}_{\mathcal{D}_I}\left(\mu_{i,j};\ 0 \le i+j \le I\right) = \sum_{0\le i+j\le I} \frac{1}{\tau^2_{i,j}}\ \left(X_{i,j} - \mu_{i,j}\right)\ \frac{\partial \mu_{i,j}}{\partial \alpha} \overset{!}{=} 0$$

where $\alpha = g_{j-1}, \delta_{j-1}, \mu_i$.

In Model (M1) this leads to the CL factor estimates minus 1, i.e. we have

$$\widehat{g}_j^{\text{MLE}} = \widehat{f}_j - 1 = \frac{\sum_{i=0}^{I-j-1} X_{i,j+1}}{\sum_{i=0}^{I-j-1} C_{i,j}} \tag{11.2}$$

For Model (M2) we have to solve the following system of equations

$$\sum_{i=0}^{I-j} \left(X_{i,j} - g_{j-1}\, C_{i,j-1} - \delta_{j-1} \right) = 0$$

$$\sum_{i=0}^{I-j} \frac{1}{C_{i,j-1}} \left(X_{i,j} - g_{j-1}\, C_{i,j-1} - \delta_{j-1} \right) = 0$$

This gives for Model (M2) the following MLE

$$\widehat{g}_j^{\text{MLE}} = \frac{\sum_{i=0}^{I-j-1} \frac{X_{i,j+1}}{C_{i,j}} - \sum_{i=0}^{I-j-1} \frac{1}{C_{i,j}} \sum_{i=0}^{I-j-1} \frac{X_{i,j+1}}{I-j}}{(I-j) - \sum_{i=0}^{I-j-1} \frac{1}{C_{i,j}} \sum_{i=0}^{I-j-1} \frac{C_{i,j}}{I-j}} \tag{11.3}$$

$$\widehat{\delta}_j^{\text{MLE}} = \sum_{i=0}^{I-j-1} \frac{X_{i,j+1}}{I-j} - \widehat{g}_j^{MLE} \sum_{i=0}^{I-j-1} \frac{C_{i,j}}{I-j} \tag{11.4}$$

Finally, in Model (M3) we have to solve the system of equations:

$$g_j = \frac{\sum_{i=0}^{I-j-1} \frac{u_i\, X_{i,j+1}}{\sigma_j^2\, c_{i,j}}}{\sum_{i=0}^{I-j-1} \frac{u_i^2}{\sigma_j^2\, c_{i,j}}}$$

$$u_i = \frac{\sum_{j=0}^{I-i-1} \frac{g_j\, X_{i,j+1}}{\sigma_j^2\, c_{i,j}}}{\sum_{i=0}^{I-i-1} \frac{g_j^2}{\sigma_j^2\, c_{i,j}}}$$

which can, for example, be solved with the Newton–Raphson algorithm.

In the following we denote the MLE of $\mu_{i,j}$ by $\widehat{\mu}_{i,j}^{\text{MLE}(k)}$ for Models (Mk), $k = 1, 2, 3$.

Example 11.4

We revisit the data set given in Example 2.7 in order to compare the results from Models (M1) and (M2). Notice that for Model (M2) we cannot estimate the last two parameters g_{J-1} and δ_{J-1} since we have only one observation $X_{0,J}$ in the last development period. Hence, for the last development period we simply set the intercept δ_{J-1} equal to 0, which is Model (M1) for the last development year (see Table 11.1).

We observe that negative intercepts in Model (M2) are compensated by a larger value for g_j compared to Model (M1), and vice versa. This leads to the claims reserves given in Table 11.2.

We see in Table 11.2 that the model with intercept (M2) leads to approximately 5% higher claims reserves than Model (M1) for this specific data set. The question that remains is: Which model gives a better fit? □

Table 11.1 MLE for Models (M1) and (M2)

Dev. year j	Model (M1)	Model (M2)	
	$\widehat{g}_j^{\text{MLE}}$	$\widehat{g}_j^{\text{MLE}}$	$\widehat{\delta}_j^{\text{MLE}}$
0	0.46898	0.68399	−1 118 277
1	0.07541	0.15403	−675 137
2	0.02346	−0.02621	477 258
3	0.01484	−0.01580	308 170
4	0.00697	−0.03442	424 693
5	0.00515	0.01527	−105 925
6	0.00108	0.00997	−95 906
7	0.00105	−0.00106	22 970
8	0.00142	0.00142	0

Table 11.2 Reserves for Models (M1) and (M2)

i	$C_{i,I-i}$	Reserves (M1)	Reserves (M2)
0	11 148 124	0	0
1	10 648 192	15 126	15 126
2	10 635 751	26 257	26 771
3	9 724 068	34 538	27 511
4	9 786 916	85 302	72 090
5	9 935 753	156 494	160 736
6	9 282 022	286 121	326 915
7	8 256 211	449 167	607 047
8	7 648 729	1 043 242	1 115 379
9	5 675 568	3 950 815	3 954 604
Total		6 047 061	6 306 177

11.1.1 Model Choice

Sum of Squared Errors

There are various methods for the comparison of these three models. The first statistics we look at is the so-called sum of squared errors, SSE, defined by, $k = 1, 2, 3$,

$$\text{SSE}(k) = \sum_{0 \le i+j \le I} \left(X_{i,j} - \widehat{\mu}_{i,j}^{\text{MLE}(k)} \right)^2$$

This is an aggregate measure that determines how much the observations deviate around the regression lines. Observe that the more parameters we have the smaller becomes the SSE. On the other hand, to more parameters we estimate the larger is the disadvantage for prediction. Hence in order to compare Model (M1) to (M2) one needs to adjust the SSE by the number of parameters chosen. Usually, one compares the scaled SSE

$$\widetilde{\text{SSE}}(k) = \frac{1}{N - p(k)} \text{SSE}(k) \tag{11.5}$$

where $N = |\mathcal{D}_I|$ is the number of observations and $p(k)$ denotes the number of parameters in Model (Mk). Then, the model that minimizes (11.5) is preferred.

Remark One could also think of other adjustment factors for the number of parameters involved. There is no unique method that is generally accepted. Note that we have already used such an adjustment factor in the framework of GLMs, see (7.21).

Akaike Information Criterion

Another criterion that is often studied is the so-called Akaike information criterion (AIC). For the AIC we study the adjusted log-likelihood function

$$\mathrm{AIC}(k) = -2 \ \log L^{(k)}_{\mathcal{D}_I}\left(\mu_{i,j};\ 0 \le i+j \le I\right) + 2\ p(k) \tag{11.6}$$

A (partly heuristical) entropy argument says that the model that minimizes (11.6) should be favoured.

Example 11.4 (revisited)

If we consider the data set given in Example 2.7 we find Table 11.3. From this analysis we see that we would (slightly) prefer the CL model without an intercept δ_j (i.e. Model (M1)). The picture for single development years is rather different; there we would prefer the model with intercept. Observe that this ambiguity between single development years and overall estimate comes from the scaling factor for the number of parameters estimated.

Table 11.3 Scaled SSE for Models (M1) and (M2): Overall and for single development years

	Overall	0	1	2	3	4	5	6	7	8
$\widetilde{\mathrm{SSE}}(1)^{1/2}$	179 299	360 909	104 784	50 144	62 757	29 627	6 495	2 716	724	NA
$\widetilde{\mathrm{SSE}}(2)^{1/2}$	179 836	342 743	95 063	43 375	67 948	19 282	3 431	1 610	NA	NA

If we consider the AIC we find Table 11.4. In contrast to the (scaled) SSE analysis we see that we would prefer the model with intercepts. □

Table 11.4 Akaike information criterion for Models (M1) and (M2): overall and for single development periods

	Overall	0	1	2	3	4	5	6	7	8
AIC(1)	1084	255.7	207.3	171.2	149.6	117.2	81.6	55.9	32.0	13.4
AIC(2)	1077	254.6	206.2	170.0	150.3	115.5	80.1	55.3	32.0	13.4

11.1.2 Age-to-Age Factors

Significance of CL Factors

In this subsection we concentrate on the CL models, i.e. Models (M1) and (M2). Under Model (M1) we see that the conditional distribution of $\widehat{g}_j^{\mathrm{MLE}}$, given $\mathcal{B}_j$, is

$$\widehat{g}_j^{\mathrm{MLE}} \overset{(d)}{\sim} \mathcal{N}\left(g_j, \frac{\sigma_j^2}{\sum_{i=0}^{I-j-1} C_{i,j}}\right)$$

(cf. (11.2)). Is g_j significantly different from zero? If we consider a two-sided confidence interval for the probability 95%, we have the question whether holds

$$\widehat{g}_j^{\mathrm{MLE}} \notin \left[-1.96\sqrt{\frac{\sigma_j^2}{\sum_{i=0}^{I-j-1} C_{i,j}}}, 1.96\sqrt{\frac{\sigma_j^2}{\sum_{i=0}^{I-j-1} C_{i,j}}}\right]$$

For Model (M2) we rewrite the MLE as follows

$$\widehat{g}_j^{\mathrm{MLE}} = \frac{\sum_{i=0}^{I-j-1}\left(\frac{1}{C_{i,j}} - \frac{\sum_{i=0}^{I-j-1} C_{i,j}^{-1}}{I-j}\right) X_{i,j+1}}{\sum_{i=0}^{I-j-1}\left(\frac{1}{C_{i,j}} - \frac{\sum_{i=0}^{I-j-1} C_{i,j}^{-1}}{I-j}\right) C_{i,j}}$$

(cf. (11.3)). Thus, $\widehat{g}_j^{\mathrm{MLE}}$ is a weighted average of $X_{i,j+1}/C_{i,j}$ and it is conditionally normally distributed with variance

$$\begin{aligned}
v_j &= \sigma_j^2 \frac{\sum_{i=0}^{I-j-1}\left(\frac{1}{C_{i,j}} - \frac{\sum_{k=0}^{I-j-1} C_{k,j}^{-1}}{I-j}\right)^2 C_{i,j}}{\left(\sum_{i=0}^{I-j-1}\left(\frac{1}{C_{i,j}} - \frac{\sum_{k=0}^{I-j-1} C_{k,j}^{-1}}{I-j}\right) C_{i,j}\right)^2} \\
&= \sigma_j^2 \frac{\sum_{i=0}^{I-j-1} C_{i,j}^{-1}}{\sum_{i=0}^{I-j-1} C_{i,j}^{-1} \sum_{i=0}^{I-j-1} C_{i,j} - (I-j)^2}
\end{aligned}$$

The estimator $\widehat{\delta}_j^{\mathrm{MLE}}$ is conditionally normally distributed with variance

$$t_j = \sigma_j^2 \sum_{i=0}^{I-j-1}\left(\frac{1}{I-j} - \frac{\sum_{k=0}^{I-j-1} C_{k,j}}{I-j} \frac{\frac{1}{C_{i,j}} - \frac{\sum_{k=0}^{I-j-1} C_{i,j}^{-1}}{I-j}}{\sum_{l=0}^{I-j-1}\left(\frac{1}{C_{l,j}} - \frac{\sum_{k=0}^{I-j-1} C_{k,j}^{-1}}{I-j}\right) C_{l,j}}\right)^2 C_{i,j}$$

(cf. (11.4)).

Example 11.5

Going back to Example 2.7, we see that all parameters g_j are significantly different from zero. This means that on a 95% confidence level the CL factors estimates $\widehat{f}_j = \widehat{g}_j^{\text{MLE}} + 1$ differ from 1 (see Table 11.5).

Table 11.5 MLE for parameters and their standard deviations

	0	1	2	3	4	5	6	7	8
Model (M1)									
$\widehat{g}_j^{\text{MLE}}$	0.4690	0.0754	0.0235	0.0148	0.0070	0.0051	0.0011	0.0010	0.0014
$\text{std}(\widehat{g}_j^{\text{MLE}})$	0.0187	0.0040	0.0019	0.0026	0.0013	0.0003	0.0001	0.0000	0.0000
$\widehat{g}_j^{\text{MLE}}/\text{std}$	25.14	18.77	12.28	5.81	5.35	16.64	7.47	22.25	81.02
Model (M2)									
$\widehat{g}_j^{\text{MLE}}$	0.6840	0.1540	−0.0262	−0.0158	−0.0344	0.0153	0.0100	−0.0011	0.0014
$v_j^{1/2}$	0.0848	0.0033	0.0011	0.0026	0.0006	0.0000	0.0000	0.0000	0.0000
$\widehat{g}_j^{\text{MLE}}/v_j^{1/2}$	8.07	46.66	23.17	6.16	55.56	364.27	206.76	238.70	81.02
$\widehat{\delta}_j^{\text{MLE}}$	−1 118 277	−675 137	477 258	308 170	424 693	−105 925	−95 906	22 970	
$t_j^{1/2}$	1 697 191	70 634	49 289	87 456	52 113	17 094	24 985	11 488	
$\widehat{\delta}_j^{\text{MLE}}/t_j^{1/2}$	0.66	9.56	9.68	3.52	8.15	6.20	3.84	2.00	

Observe that on a 95% confidence interval we have no significance difference of $\widehat{\delta}_0^{\text{MLE}}$ from 0. That is, under this analysis we need not necessarily introduce an intercept for the first development period $j = 0$, we also refer to Figure 11.1. □

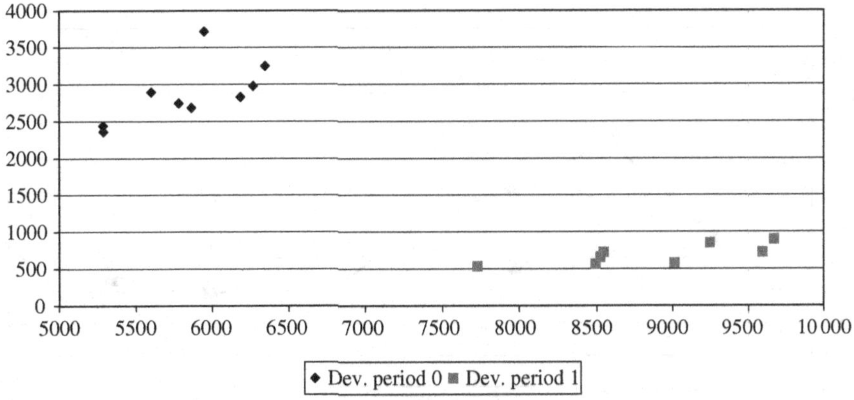

Figure 11.1 $X_{i,j+1}$ vs $C_{i,j}$ for Example 2.7 and $j = 0, 1$

Volume assumptions

In the CL model we assume that the conditional expected incremental claims $E[X_{i,j+1}|C_{i,j}]$ are proportional to the preceding cumulative observations $C_{i,j}$. A simple diagnostic is to plot $X_{i,j+1}$ vs $C_{i,j}$ to see whether we observe a linear connection. □

Example 11.6

If we plot $X_{i,j+1}$ vs $C_{i,j}$ for development periods $j=0,1$ in Example 2.7 we obtain Figure 11.1. A first glance at Figure 11.1 does not reject the assumption of this linear connection. □

11.1.3 Homogeneity in Time and Distributional Assumptions

We have assumed that accident years i are independent. If we look at Model (M1) then the individual CL factors are, conditional on $C_{i,j}$, given by (set $f_j = g_j + 1$)

$$F_{i,j+1} = \frac{C_{i,j+1}}{C_{i,j}} \overset{(d)}{\sim} \mathcal{N}\left(f_j, \frac{\sigma_j^2}{C_{i,j}}\right)$$

(cf. (11.1)). Using the appropriate scaling we obtain the residuals

$$\varepsilon_{i,j} = \frac{F_{i,j+1} - f_j}{\sigma_j / C_{i,j}^{1/2}} \tag{11.7}$$

which are, under the assumptions of Model (M1), i.i.d. standard normally distributed. This means that we should not observe trends over time i in these residuals $\varepsilon_{i,j}$.

Example 11.7

We go back to Example 2.7. Note that the residuals in (11.7) are not observable (since the model parameters are not known). If we replace the unknown parameters by estimators we obtain observable residuals (see also Section 7.4). Plotting the observable residuals we obtain Figure 11.2 for development periods $j=0,1,2$.

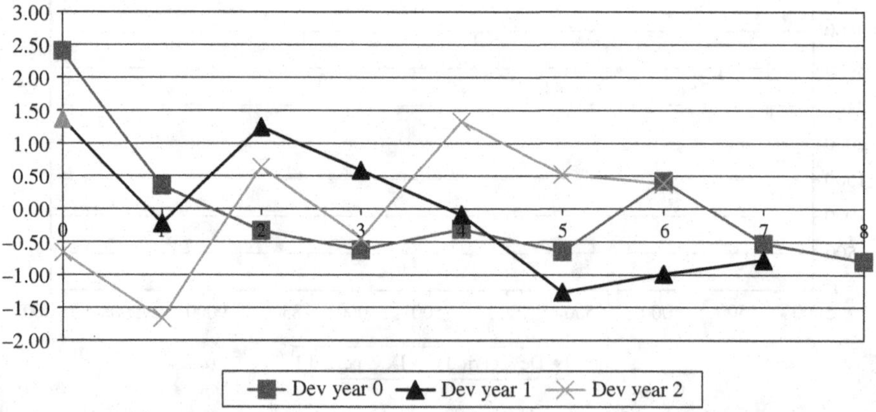

Figure 11.2 Observable residuals as a function of accident year i for Example 2.7 and development periods $j=0,1,2$

We see that, probably, the stationarity assumption is violated in all three development periods (see Figure 11.2). In development periods $j=0,1$ we observe a negative trend in the individual development factors, whereas for $j=2$ we observe a positive trend. If we make a regression analysis we find the results in Table 11.6. From this point of view it is questionable to apply the CL method to the unadjusted data.

Table 11.6 Results of a regression analysis for linear trends in the individual development factors $F_{i,j}$ of development years $j = 0, 1, 2$

	Dev year 0	Dev year 1	Dev year 2
Slope	−0.2327	−0.3223	0.2933
Std dev.	0.12910	0.13750	0.15430
90% confidence interval	±0.2123	±0.2262	± 0.2538

Though not imperative, we have done the Gaussian assumption for the residuals in this section. If we plot the observable residuals against the standard Gaussian distribution we obtain the Q–Q plot obtained in Figure 11.3. Observe that the empirical distribution has lighter tails than the Gaussian distribution. However, there is one (heavy) outlier, which corresponds to the individual development factor $F_{0,1}$. This means that the oldest accident year $C_{0,1}/C_{0,0}$, somehow, does not fit into our distributional picture. Observe that this accident year $i = 0$ is also one of the main reasons why we obtain a negative slope in Figure 11.2.

□

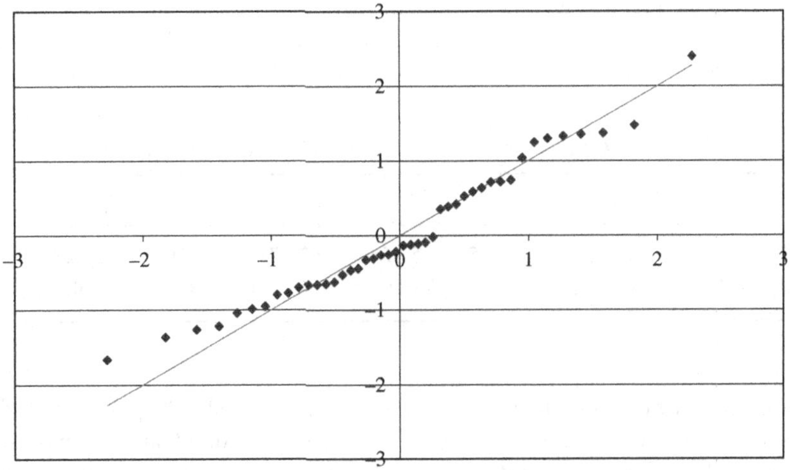

Figure 11.3 Q–Q plot for empirical distribution of the observable residuals against the standard Gaussian distribution

11.1.4 Correlations

One of the main features of the CL model is that individual development factors are uncorrelated, but the squares of two successive individual development factors are negatively correlated, i.e. we have that (see also Lemmas 2.5 and 3.8)

$$\mathrm{Cor}\left(F_{i,j}, F_{i,j+1} \middle| C_{i,j-1}\right) = 0$$
$$\mathrm{Cor}\left(F_{i,j}^2, F_{i,j+1}^2 \middle| C_{i,j-1}\right) < 0$$

Hence, we estimate these correlations from our observations. Observe that

$$\begin{aligned}\mathrm{Cor}\left(F_{i,j}, F_{i,j+1}\middle| C_{i,j-1}\right) &= \frac{\mathrm{Cov}\left(F_{i,j}, F_{i,j+1}\middle| C_{i,j-1}\right)}{\mathrm{Var}\left(F_{i,j}\middle| C_{i,j-1}\right)^{1/2}\ \mathrm{Var}\left(F_{i,j+1}\middle| C_{i,j-1}\right)^{1/2}} \\ &= \frac{\mathrm{Cov}\left(F_{i,j}, F_{i,j+1}\middle| C_{i,j-1}\right)}{\left(\sigma_{j-1}/C_{i,j-1}^{1/2}\right)\ E\left[\sigma_j^2/C_{i,j}\middle| C_{i,j-1}\right]^{1/2}} \\ &\approx \frac{\mathrm{Cov}\left(F_{i,j}, F_{i,j+1}\middle| C_{i,j-1}\right)}{\sigma_{j-1}/C_{i,j-1}^{1/2}\ \sigma_j/C_{i,j}^{1/2}}\end{aligned} \tag{11.8}$$

Hence, if we replace that individual development factors by the (observable) residuals, we obtain an estimator for the correlations.

Example 11.8

Unfortunately, the analysis for the data in Example 2.7 does not give a clear picture as Table 11.7 shows. Quite often, we observe this phenomenon in claims reserving that reliable correlation estimates are difficult to obtain and data give unreasonable values. One reason for this difficulty is probably that a lot of effects are, unintentionally, smoothed over time. This comes from the fact that it is, in general, difficult to find the truth within the observable random variables because one often does not observe the true facts but only those facts that are already based on estimates.

Table 11.7 Correlation estimates for individual development factors

	1	2	3	4	5	6	7
$\widehat{\mathrm{Cor}}\left(F_{i,j}, F_{i,j+1}\middle| C_{i,j-1}\right)$	41.08%	−16.95%	57.54%	62.77%	−27.09%	52.28%	−40.60%
$\widehat{\mathrm{Cov}}\left(F_{i,j}^2, F_{i,j+1}^2\middle| C_{i,j-1}\right)$	1.69E-03	−4.38E-05	7.65E-05	4.78E-05	−2.07E-06	3.16E-07	−2.68E-08

Hence, from this point of view, this analysis does not really help in the decision of model choices. Observe that if the correlation of successive individual development factors is (clearly) negative, this means that one should reject the CL method. It would mean that a large development factor $F_{i,j}$ is compensated by a small factor $F_{i,j+1}$ and vice versa. For cumulative claims, such a behaviour can have several reason, for example:

1. If we consider the LoB private property, we usually observe a very rapid claims development. Private property is usually exposed to winter storm events. If we have a large winter storm on 31 December (and we close our books on 31 December), we observe that $F_{i,1}$ has a value that is larger than the average. However, if all these claims are immediately settled, $F_{i,2}$ is probably below average, because this winter storm event has no influence on the settlement of the other claims within this LoB.
2. Due to several reasons at the year end constellation (Sundays, Christmas days, etc.), it may happen that the year end payouts differ from year to year; for example, it can happen that in one year claims are settled on both 30 and 31 December, whereas in other years

these claims are shifted to the next accounting year. Such behaviors may have a disturbing effect on payout patterns and contradict the CL assumptions. □

11.1.5 Diagonal Effects

We have always assumed that the accident years are independent. However, one crucial time axis in claims development triangles are the diagonals which constitute accounting years. Accounting year payments, for example, are characterized by the fact that they are done at the same point in time (for different accident years). If we have external factors as, for example, legal chances, high inflation, etc., we usually observe such phenomena on the accounting diagonals. This means that the independence assumption between accident years is violated. Moreover, such external factors may have very different effects on different claims figures such as claims payments and claims incurred.

We come back to Model (M3)

$$X_{i,j} = g_{j-1}\ u_i + \sigma_{j-1}\ \sqrt{c_{i,j-1}}\ \varepsilon_{i,j}$$

Accounting year effects mean that we should introduce additional parameters: we define Model (M4) by

$$X_{i,j} = g_{j-1}\ u_i\ \psi(i+j) + \sigma_{j-1}\ \sqrt{c_{i,j-1}}\ \varepsilon_{i,j}$$

where $\psi(i+j)$ measures such diagonal effects as inflation. At first sight, this looks convincing and promising, but observe that we often have too many parameters, i.e. the model is overparametrized. One way to reduce the number of parameters is to choose a parametric assumption on inflation, for example, we could set

$$\psi(i+j) = \left(1+\widetilde{\psi}\right)^{i+j}$$

Then, $\widetilde{\psi}$ is the only inflation parameter that needs to be estimated. Another way to reduce parameters would also be to introduce a parameteric form for the claims development pattern. This was previously discussed in Chapter 6 and is also subject of the next section. Concluding, diagonal effects are probably the most important uncertainties that are only barely studied in classical stochastic reserving problems. Here, future research needs to be done for obtaining sound methods that allow for the study of diagonal effects.

11.2 NON-PARAMETRIC SMOOTHING

We have already mentioned several times that the models we consider have a rather high number of parameters. That is, overparametrization is always a central topic in all these models. Usually, one proposal to reduce the number of parameters is to introduce a parametric curve for the parameters, for example, the Hoerl curve in equation (4.76) or other parameteric shapes (see, e.g., Clark 2003). This approach of choosing a parametric curve is often too rigid and England and Verrall (2001) proposed the use of non-parametric smoothing.

We consider parametric smoothing for the CL Model (M1) (see also Verdier and Klinger 2005)

$$C_{i,j} = f_{j-1}\, C_{i,j-1} + \sigma_{j-1}\, \sqrt{C_{i,j-1}}\, \varepsilon_{i,j}$$

(cf. (11.1)). We now introduce a linear state space model which allows for smoothing of the CL factors f_j. Define the linear transition equations

$$f_j = f_{j-1} + \Theta_j \tag{11.9}$$

where Θ_j are independent centred normally distributed random variables with $\text{Var}\left(\Theta_j\right) = v_j^2$. For the time being we neglect the question about positivity. This means that CL factors are random variables with some prior distribution u_Θ. This is exactly as in the Bayesian context, cf. Section 9.2. In Section 9.2 the CL factors were independent random variables, whereas here the CL factors are time series that satisfy

$$E\left[f_j \middle| f_{j-1}\right] = f_{j-1}$$

This means that $(f_j)_{j\geq 0}$ is a random walk, whose jump sizes are determined by Θ_j. Observe that the likelihood function of the prior distribution of $f_0, \ldots, f_{J-1}$ is given by

$$L_\Theta(f_0, \ldots, f_{J-1}) = \prod_{j=0}^{J-2} \frac{1}{\sqrt{2\pi}\, v_{j+1}} \exp\left\{ -\frac{1}{2\, v_{j+1}^2} \left(f_{j+1} - f_j\right)^2 \right\}$$

where we have assumed that there is no constraint on f_0 (non-informative prior). For given CL factors, the likelihood function of the data distribution $\mathcal{D}_I$, given $\mathcal{B}_0$, is given by

$$L_{\mathcal{D}_I}(f_0, \ldots, f_{J-1}) = \prod_{i+j\leq I, j\geq 1} \frac{1}{\sqrt{2\pi}\, \sigma_{j-1}\, C_{i,j-1}^{-1/2}} \exp\left\{ -\frac{C_{i,j-1}}{2\sigma_{j-1}^2} \left(\frac{C_{i,j}}{C_{i,j-1}} - f_{j-1} \right)^2 \right\}$$

This implies that, conditionally given $\mathcal{B}_0$, the joint log-likelihood function is given by

$$\begin{aligned} \log L(f_0, \ldots, f_{J-1}) &= \log L_{\mathcal{D}_I}(f_0, \ldots, f_{J-1}) + \log L_\Theta(f_0, \ldots, f_{J-1}) \\ &\propto - \sum_{i+j\leq I, j\geq 1} \frac{C_{i,j-1}}{2\sigma_{j-1}^2} \left(\frac{C_{i,j}}{C_{i,j-1}} - f_{j-1} \right)^2 - \sum_{j=0}^{J-2} \frac{1}{2 v_{j+1}^2} \left(f_{j+1} - f_j\right)^2 \end{aligned} \tag{11.10}$$

That is, in addition to the classical CL term we obtain an additional penalty term which disappears for $v_j = \infty$ (no smoothing). For other forms of smoothing we refer to England and Verrall (2001), Section 3.

We can now apply Bayesian methods and calculate posterior distributions of the CL parameters (using for instance MCMC methods which also enable to consider different priors and quantify uncertainties, this is exactly what is done in Subsection 9.2.6) or we can simply calculate MLE which leads to the following system of linear equations

$$\frac{\partial}{\partial f_0} \log L(f_0, \ldots, f_{J-1}) = \sum_{i=0}^{I-1} \frac{C_{i,0}}{\sigma_0^2} \left(F_{i,1} - f_0\right) + \frac{f_1 - f_0}{v_1^2} = 0$$

$$\frac{\partial}{\partial f_{J-1}} \log L(f_0, \ldots, f_{J-1}) = \sum_{i=0}^{I-J} \frac{C_{i,J-1}}{\sigma_{J-1}^2} \left(F_{i,J} - f_{J-1}\right) - \frac{f_{J-1} - f_{J-2}}{v_{J-1}^2} = 0$$

and

$$\frac{\partial}{\partial f_j} \log L(f_0, \ldots, f_{J-1}) = \sum_{i=0}^{I-j-1} \frac{C_{i,j}}{\sigma_j^2} \left(F_{i,j+1} - f_j\right) - \frac{f_j - f_{j-1}}{v_j^2} + \frac{f_{j+1} - f_j}{v_{j+1}^2} = 0$$

for $j = 1, \ldots, J-2$. We introduce the following $J \times J$ matrix

$$A = \begin{pmatrix} \frac{S_0}{\sigma_0^2} + v_1^{-2} & -v_1^{-2} & 0 & 0 & \cdots & 0 \\ -v_1^{-2} & \frac{S_1}{\sigma_1^2} + v_1^{-2} + v_2^{-2} & -v_2^{-2} & 0 & \cdots & 0 \\ 0 & -v_2^{-2} & \frac{S_2}{\sigma_2^2} + v_2^{-2} + v_3^{-2} & -v_3^{-2} & \cdots & 0 \\ \vdots & \vdots & & & & \vdots \\ 0 & \cdots & 0 & 0 & -v_{J-1}^{-2} & \frac{S_{J-1}}{\sigma_{J-1}^2} + v_{J-1}^{-2} \end{pmatrix}$$

where $S_j = S_j^{[I-j-1]} = \sum_{i=0}^{I-j-1} C_{i,j}$ was defined in (3.20). Hence, this implies that we have to solve the system

$$A\,(f_0, \ldots, f_{J-1})' = \left(\sum_{i=0}^{I-1} \frac{C_{i,1}}{\sigma_0^2}, \ldots, \sum_{i=0}^{I-J} \frac{C_{i,J}}{\sigma_{J-1}^2} \right)'$$

This then gives the MLE

$$\left(\widehat{f}_0^{\mathrm{MLE}}, \ldots, \widehat{f}_{J-1}^{\mathrm{MLE}}\right)'$$

Example 11.9

If we revisit the data set given in Example 2.7 we obtain Figure 11.4 (where also the expert choice for v_j is provided).

We see that this smoothing does not look too convincing for this specific data set. All CL factor estimates $\widehat{f}_j^{\mathrm{MLE}}$ are lower than the unsmoothed ones $\widehat{f}_j$. Hence, for applications in practice one needs to choose other types of random walks in (11.9). Another example would be

$$f_j = f_{j-1} + c_j + \Theta_j,$$

where c_j is a known prior difference between f_{j-1} and f_j. This also leads to a way of including expert opinions in the CL estimates. □

	v_j	Unsmoothed CL factors	Smoothed CL factors
0	1.000	1.49524	1.49165
1	0.050	1.07776	1.06430
2	0.050	1.02287	1.01985
3	0.050	1.01484	1.00955
4	0.050	1.00697	1.00560
5	0.050	1.00515	1.00507
6	0.050	1.00108	1.00106
7	0.050	1.00105	1.00104
8	0.050	1.00142	1.00142

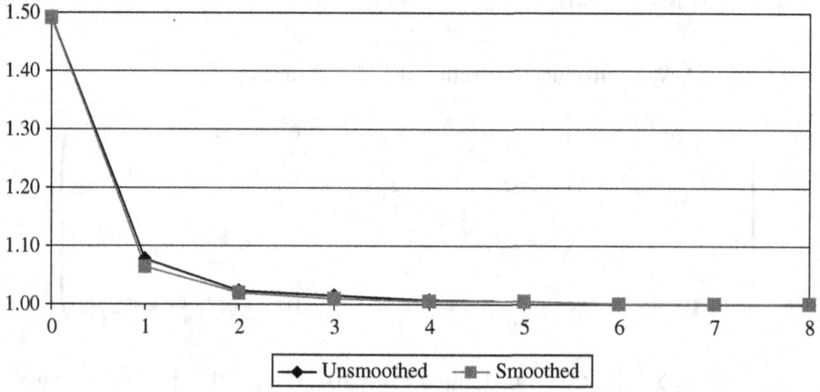

Figure 11.4 Smoothed CL factor estimates

Appendix A
Distributions

A.1 DISCRETE DISTRIBUTIONS

A.1.1 Binomial Distribution

For $n \in \mathbb{N}$ and $p \in (0, 1)$ the Binomial distribution $\mathrm{Bin}(n, p)$ is defined to be discrete with a probability function

$$f_{n,p}(x) = \binom{n}{x} p^x (1-p)^{n-x}$$

for all $x \in \{0, \ldots, n\}$ (Table A.1).

Table A.1 Expectation, variance and variational coefficient of a $\mathrm{Bin}(n, p)$-distributed random variable X

$\mathrm{E}(X)$	$\mathrm{Var}(X)$	$\mathrm{Vco}(X)$
np	$np(1-p)$	$\sqrt{(1-p)/np}$

A.1.2 Poisson Distribution

For $\lambda \in (0, \infty)$ the Poisson distribution, $\mathrm{Poisson}(\lambda)$, is defined to be discrete with a probability function

$$f_\lambda(x) = \exp(-\lambda) \frac{\lambda^x}{x!}$$

for all $x \in \mathbb{N}_0$ (Table A.2).

Table A.2 Expectation, variance and variational coefficient of a $\mathrm{Poisson}(\lambda)$-distributed random variable X

$\mathrm{E}(X)$	$\mathrm{Var}(X)$	$\mathrm{Vco}(X)$
λ	λ	$1/\sqrt{\lambda}$

A.1.3 Negative-Binomial Distribution

For $r \in (0, \infty)$ and $p \in (0, 1)$ the Negative-Binomial distribution $\mathrm{NB}(r, p)$ is defined to be discrete with a probability function

$$f_{r,p}(x) = \binom{r+x-1}{x} p^r (1-p)^x$$

for all $x \in \mathbb{N}_0$ (Table A.3).

For $\alpha \in \mathbb{R}$ and $n \in \mathbb{N}_0$, the generalized binomial coefficient is defined to be

$$\binom{\alpha}{n} = \frac{\alpha\,(\alpha-1)\,\cdots\,(\alpha-n+1)}{n!} = \prod_{k=1}^{n} \frac{\alpha-k+1}{k}$$

Table A.3 Expectation, variance and variational coefficient of a NB(r, p)-distributed random variable X

E(X)	Var(X)	Vco(X)
$r\,\dfrac{1-p}{p}$	$r\,\dfrac{1-p}{p^2}$	$\dfrac{1}{\sqrt{r(1-p)}}$

A.2 CONTINUOUS DISTRIBUTIONS

A.2.1 Uniform Distribution

For $a, b \in \mathbb{R}$ with $a < b$ the Uniform distribution $\mathcal{U}(a, b)$ is defined to be continuous with a density (Table A.4)

$$f_{a,b}(x) = \frac{1}{b-a}\, 1_{[a,b]}(x)$$

Table A.4 Expectation, variance and variational coefficient of a $\mathcal{U}(a, b)$-distributed random variable X

E(X)	Var(X)	Vco(X)
$\dfrac{a+b}{2}$	$\dfrac{(b-a)^2}{12}$	$\dfrac{b-a}{\sqrt{3}(a+b)}$

A.2.2 Normal Distribution

For $\mu \in \mathbb{R}$ and $\sigma^2 > 0$ the Normal/Gaussian distribution $\mathcal{N}(\mu, \sigma^2)$ is defined to be continuous with density (Table A.5)

$$f_{\mu,\sigma^2}(x) = \frac{1}{\sqrt{2\pi\sigma^2}}\, \exp\left(-\frac{(x-\mu)^2}{2\sigma^2}\right)$$

Table A.5 Expectation, variance and variational coefficient of a $\mathcal{N}(\mu, \sigma^2)$-distributed random variable X

E(X)	Var(X)	Vco(X)
μ	σ^2	σ/μ

A.2.3 Log-Normal Distribution

For $\mu \in \mathbb{R}$ and $\sigma^2 > 0$ the Log-normal distribution $\mathcal{LN}(\mu, \sigma^2)$ is defined to be continuous with a density (Table A.6)

$$f_{\mu,\sigma^2}(x) = \frac{1}{\sqrt{2\pi\,\sigma^2}\,x}\ \exp\left(-\frac{(\log(x)-\mu)^2}{2\sigma^2}\right)\ 1_{(0,\infty)}(x)$$

Table A.6 Expectation, variance and variational coefficient of a $\mathcal{LN}(\mu, \sigma^2)$-distributed random variable X

E(X)	Var(X)	Vco(X)
$e^{\mu+\frac{\sigma^2}{2}}$	$e^{2\mu+\sigma^2}\left(e^{\sigma^2}-1\right)$	$\sqrt{e^{\sigma^2}-1}$

A.2.4 Gamma Distribution

For $\gamma, c \in (0, \infty)$ the Gamma distribution $\Gamma(\gamma, c)$ is defined to be continuous with a density

$$f_{\gamma,c}(x) = \frac{c^\gamma}{\Gamma(\gamma)}\ x^{\gamma-1}\ \exp(-cx)\ 1_{(0,\infty)}(x)$$

The parameters γ and c are called shape and scale, respectively. The Gamma function $\Gamma\colon (0,\infty) \rightarrow (0,\infty)$ is given by the map

$$\Gamma(\gamma) = \int_0^\infty u^{\gamma-1}\ \exp(-u)\,du$$

The Gamma function has the following properties (Table A.7):

(1) $\Gamma(1) = 1$.
(2) $\Gamma(1/2) = \sqrt{\pi}$.
(3) $\Gamma(\gamma+1) = \gamma\ \Gamma(\gamma)$.

Table A.7 Expectation, variance and variational coefficient of a $\Gamma(\gamma, c)$-distributed random variable X

E(X)	Var(X)	Vco(X)
$\frac{\gamma}{c}$	$\frac{\gamma}{c^2}$	$\frac{1}{\sqrt{\gamma}}$

A.2.5 Beta Distribution

For $a, b \in (0, \infty)$ the Beta distribution, Beta(a, b), is defined to be continuous with a density

$$f_{a,b}(x) = \frac{1}{\mathrm{B}(a, b)}\, x^{a-1}\, (1-x)^{b-1}\, 1_{(0,1)}(x)$$

The map B: $(0, \infty) \times (0, \infty) \rightarrow (0, \infty)$ given by

$$\mathrm{B}(a, b) = \int_0^1 u^{a-1}\, (1-u)^{b-1}\, du = \frac{\Gamma(a)\, \Gamma(b)}{\Gamma(a+b)}$$

is called a Beta function (Table A.8).

Table A.8 Expectation, variance and variational coefficient of a Beta(a, b)-distributed random variable X

E(X)	Var(X)	Vco(X)
$\frac{a}{a+b}$	$\frac{a\, b}{(a+b)^2\, (a+b+1)}$	$\sqrt{\frac{b}{a\, (a+b+1)}}$

Bibliography

Abraham, B. and Ledolter, J. (1983). *Statistical Methods for Forecasting.* John Wiley & Sons, Inc., New York.

Ajne, B. (1994). Additivity of chain-ladder projections. *Astin Bulletin* 24/2, 311–318.

Alai, D.H., Merz, M. and Wüthrich, M.V. (2007). Mean square error of prediction in the Bornhuetter-Ferguson claims reserving method. Submitted preprint, ETH Zürich.

Alba de, E. (2002). Bayesian estimation of outstanding claim reserves. *North American Actuarial J.* 6/4, 1–20.

Alba de, E. (2006). Claims reserving when there are negative values in the runoff triangle: Bayesian analysis using the three-parameter log-normal distribution. *North American Actuarial J.* 10/3, 45–59.

Alba de, E. and Corzo, M.A.R. (2006). Bayesian claims reserving when there are negative values in the runoff triangle. *Actuarial Research Clearing House*, Jan 01, 2006.

Arjas, E. (1989). The claims reserving problem in non-life insurance: some structural ideas. *Astin Bulletin* 19/2, 139–152.

Barnett, G. and Zehnwirth, B. (1998). Best estimate for reserves. *CAS Forum* (Fall), 1–54.

Barnett, G. and Zehnwirth, B. (2000). Best estimates for reserves. *Proc. CAS*, Vol. LXXXVII, 245–321.

Beaumont, M.A., Zhang, W. and Balding, D.J. (2002). Approximate Bayesian computation in population genetics. *Genetics* 162, 2025–2035.

Benktander, G. (1976). An approach to credibility in calculating IBNR for casualty excess reinsurance. *The Actuarial Review*, April 1976, Vol. 312, 7.

Bernardo, J.M. and Smith, A.F.M. (1994). *Bayesian Theory.* John Wiley & Sons Ltd, Chichester.

Bornhuetter, R.L. and Ferguson, R.E. (1972). The actuary and IBNR. *Proc. CAS*, Vol. LIX, 181–195.

Braun, C. (2004). The prediction error of the chain ladder method applied to correlated run-off triangles. *Astin Bulletin* 34/2, 399–423.

Brehm, P.J. (2002). Correlation and the aggregation of unpaid loss distributions. *CAS Forum* (Fall), 1–24.

Brockwell, P.J. and Davis, R.A. (1991). *Time Series: Theory and Methods*, 2nd edition. Springer, Berlin.

Buchwalder, M., Bühlmann H., Merz, M. and Wüthrich, M.V. (2005). Legal valuation portfolio in non-life insurance. Conference paper. *36th Astin Colloquium 2005*, Zürich, Switzerland.

Buchwalder, M., Bühlmann H., Merz, M. and Wüthrich, M.V. (2006a). Estimation of unallocated loss adjustment expenses. *Schweiz. Aktuarver. Mitt.* 2006/1, 43–53.

Buchwalder, M., Bühlmann H., Merz, M. and Wüthrich, M.V. (2006b). The mean square error of prediction in the chain ladder reserving method (Mack and Murphy revisited). *Astin Bulletin* 36/2, 521–542.

Buchwalder, M., Bühlmann H., Merz, M. and Wüthrich, M.V. (2007). Valuation portfolio in non-life insurance. *Scand. Actuarial J.* 2007/2, 108–125.

Bühlmann, H. (1983). Estimation of IBNR reserves by the methods chain ladder, Cape Cod and complimentary loss ratio. International Summer School 1983, unpublished.

Bühlmann, H. (1992). Stochastic discounting. *Insurance: Math. Econom.* 11/2, 113–127.

Bühlmann, H. (1995). Life insurance with stochastic interest rates. In: *Financial Risk in Insurance*, G. Ottaviani (Ed.). Springer, Berlin, pp. 1–14.

Bühlmann, H. and Gisler, A. (2005). *A Course in Credibility Theory and its Applications*. Springer, Berlin.

Bühlmann, H. and Merz, M. (2007). The valuation portfolio. *Schweiz. Aktuarver. Mitt.* 2007/1, 69–84.

Cairns, A.J.G. (2000). A discussion of parameter and model uncertainty in insurance. *Insurance: Math. Econom.* 27/3, 313–330.

Casualty Actuarial Society (CAS) (1989). *Foundations of Casualty Actuarial Science*. 4th edition. Arlington.

Chip, S. and Greenberg, E. (1995). Understanding the Metropolis-Hastings algorithm. *The American Statistician* 49/4, 327–335.

Clark, D.R. (2003). LDF curve-fitting and stochastic reserving: a maximum likelihood approach. *CAS Forum* (Fall), 41–92.

Clark, D.R. (2006). Variance and covariance due to inflation. *CAS Forum* (Fall), 61–95.

Cordeiro, G.M. and McCullagh, P. (1991). Bias correction in generalized linear models. *J. Royal Statist. Soc. B* 53/3, 629–643.

Davison, A.C. and Hinkley, D.V. (1997). *Bootstrap Methods and their Application.* Cambridge University Press, Cambridge.

Dunn, P.K. and Smyth, G.K. (2005). Series evaluation of Tweedie exponential dispersion model densities. *Statistics and Computing* 15/4, 267–280.

Efron, B. (1979). Bootstrap methods: another look at the jackknife. *Ann. Statist.* 7/1, 1–26.

Efron, B. and Tibshirani, R.J. (1993). *An Introduction to the Bootstrap*. Chapman & Hall, NY.

Embrechts, P., Klüppelberg, C. and Mikosch, T. (1997). *Modelling Extremal Events for Insurance and Finance*. Springer, Berlin.

England, P.D. (2002). Addendum to 'Analytic and bootstrap estimates of prediction errors in claims reserving'. *Insurance: Math. Econom.* 31/3, 461–466.

England, P.D. and Verrall, R.J. (1999). Analytic and bootstrap estimates of prediction errors in claims reserving. *Insurance: Math. Econom.* 25/3, 281–293.

England, P.D. and Verrall, R.J. (2001). A flexible framework for stochastic claims reserving. *Proc. CAS*, Vol. LXXXVIII, 1–38.

England, P.D. and Verrall, R.J. (2002). Stochastic claims reserving in general insurance. *British Actuarial J.* 8/3, 443–518.

England, P.D. and Verrall, R.J. (2007). Predictive distributions of outstanding liabilities in general insurance. *Ann. Actuarial Science* 1/2, 221–270.

Fahrmeir, L. and Tutz, G. (2001). *Multivariate Statistical Modelling Based on Generalized Linear Models*, 2nd edition. Springer, NY.

Feldblum, S. (2002). Completing and using schedule P. *CAS Forum* (Fall), 353–590.

Finney, D.J. (1941). On the distribution of a variate whose algorithm is normally distributed. *JRSS Suppl.* 7, 155–161.

Fortuin, C.M., Kasteleyn, P.W. and Ginibre, J. (1971). Correlation inequalities on some partially ordered sets. *Comm. Math. Phys.* 22/2, 89–103.

Gelman, A., Gilks, W.R. and Roberts, G.O. (1997). Weak convergence and optimal scaling of random walks metropolis algorithm. *Ann. Appl. Prob.* 7/1, 110–120.

Gerber, H.U. and Jones, D.A. (1975). Credibility formulas of the updating type. In: *Credibility: Theory and Applications*, P.M. Kahn (Ed.). Academic Press, NY, pp. 89–105.

Gigante, P. and Sigalotti, L. (2005). Model risk in claims reserving with generalized linear models. *Giornale dell'Istituto Italiano degli Attuari*, Vol. LXVIII, 55–87.

Gilks, W.R., Richardson, S. and Spiegelhalter, D.J. (1996). *Markov Chain Monte Carlo in Practice.* Chapman & Hall, London.

Gisler, A. (2006). The estimation error in the chain-ladder reserving method: a Bayesian approach. *Astin Bulletin* 36/2, 554–565.

Gisler, A. and Wüthrich, M.V. (2007). Credibility for the chain ladder reserving method. Conference paper, 37th Astin Colloquium 2007, Orlando, USA.

Gogol, D. (1993). Using expected loss ratios in reserving. *Insurance: Math. Econom.* 12/3, 297–299.

Haastrup, S. and Arjas, E. (1996). Claims reserving in continuous time; a nonparametric Bayesian approach. *Astin Bulletin* 26/2, 139–164.

Hachemeister, C.A. (1975). Credibility for regression models with application to trend. In: *Credibility: Theory and Applications*, P.M. Kahn (Ed.). Academic Press, NY, pp. 129–163.

Hachemeister, C.A. (1980). A stochastic model for loss reserving. *Transactions of the 21st international Congress of Actuaries*, 185–194.

Hachemeister, C.A. and Stanard, J.N. (1975). IBNR claims count estimation with static lag functions. *Astin Colloquium 1975*, Portimão, Portugal.

Halliwell, L.J. (1997). Conjoint prediction of paid and incurred losses. *CAS Forum* (Summer), 1, 241–379.

Hastings, W.K. (1970). Monte Carlo sampling methods using Markov chains and their applications. *Biometrika* 57, 97–109.

Herbst, T. (1999). An application of randomly truncated data models in reserving IBNR claims. *Insurance: Math. Econom.* 25/2, 123–131.

Hertig, J. (1985). A statistical approach to the IBNR-reserves in marine insurance. *Astin Bulletin* 15/2, 171–183.

Hess, K.T., Schmidt, K.D. and Zocher, M. (2006). Multivariate loss prediction in the multivariate additive model. *Insurance: Math. Econom.* 39/2, 185–191.

Hesselager, O. (1991). Prediction of outstanding claims: a hierarchical credibility approach. *Scand. Actuarial J.* 1, 25–47.

Hesselager, O. and Witting, T. (1988). A credibility model with random fluctutations in delay probabilities for the prediction of IBNR claims. *Astin Bulletin* 18/1, 79–90.

Hoedemakers, T., Beirlant, J., Goovaerts, M.J. and Dhaene, J. (2003). Confidence bounds for discounted loss reserves. *Insurance: Math. Econom.* 33/2, 297–316.

Hoedemakers, T., Beirlant, J., Goovaerts, M.J. and Dhaene, J. (2005). On the distribution of discounted loss reserves using generalized linear models. *Scand. Actuarial J.* 1, 25–45.

Hogg, R.V. and Craig, A.T. (1995). *Introduction to Mathematical Statistics.* Prentice Hall, Upper Saddle River, NJ.

Houltram, A. (2003). Reserving Judgement. Presented at the Institute of Actuaries of Australia. *XIVth General Insurance Seminar 2003.*

Hovinen, E. (1981). Additive and continuous IBNR. *Astin Colloquium 1981*, Loen, Norway.

Hürlimann, W. (2005). Approximate bounds for the IBNR claims reserves based on the bivariate chain-ladder model. *Belgian Actuarial Bulletin* 5/1, 46–51.

Jewell, W.S. (1976). Two classes of covariance matrices giving simple linear forecasts. *Scand. Actuarial J.* 15–29.

Jewell, W.S. (1989). Predicting IBNYR events and delays I. Continuous time. *Astin Bulletin* 19/1, 25–55.

Jewell, W.S. (1990). Predicting IBNYR events and delays II. Discrete time. *Astin Bulletin* 20/1, 93–111.

Johnson, W. (1989). Determination of outstanding liabilities for unallocated loss adjustment expenses. *Proc. CAS*, Vol. LXXVI, 111–125.

Jones, A.R., Copeman, P.J., Gibson, E.R., Line, N.J.S., Lowe, J.A., Martin, P., Matthews, P.N. and Powell, D.S. (2006). A change agenda for reserving. *Report of the General Insurance Reserving Issues Taskforce* (GRIT). Institute of Actuaries and Faculty of Actuaries.

Jong De, P. (2006). Forecasting runoff triangles. *North American Actuarial J.* 10/2, 28–38.

Jong De, P. and Zehnwirth, B. (1983). Claims reserving, state-space models and the Kalman filter. *J. Institute Actuaries* 110, 157–182.

Jørgensen, B. (1997). *The Theory of Dispersion Models*. Chapman & Hall/CRC, Boca Raton.

Jørgensen, B. and de Souza, M.C.P. (1994). Fitting Tweedie's compound Poisson model to insurance claims data. *Scand. Actuarial J.*1, 69–93.

Keller, P. (2007). Internal models for the Swiss Solvency Test. *Schweiz. Aktuarver. Mitt.* 1, 53–68.

Kirkpatrick, S., Gelatt, C.D. and Vecci, M.P. (1983). Optimization by simulated annealing. *Science* 220, 671–680.

Kirschner, G.S., Kerley, C. and Isaacs, B. (2002). Two approaches to calculating correlated reserve indications across multiple lines of business. *CAS Forum* (Fall), 211–246.

Kittel, J. (1981). Unallocated loss adjustment expense reserves in an inflationary economic environment. *CAS Discussion Paper Program*, 311–331.

Klemmt, H.J. (2004). Trennung von Schadenarten und Additivität bei Chain Ladder Prognosen. Paper presented at the 2004 Fall Meeting of the German Astin Group in Munich.

Kremer, E. (1982). IBNR-claims and the two-way model of ANOVA. *Scand. Actuarial J.* 47–55.

Kremer, E. (1985). *Einführung in die Versicherungsmathematik*. Vandenhoek & Ruprecht, Göttingen.

Lambrigger, D.D., Shevchenko, P.V. and Wüthrich, M.V. (2007). The quantification of operational risk using internal data, relevant external data and expert opinion. *J. Op. Risk* 2/3, 3–27.

Larsen, C.R. (2007). An individual claims reserving model. *Astin Bulletin* 37/1, 113–132.

Lehmann, E.L. (1983). *Theory of Point Estimation*. John Wiley & Sons, Inc., New York.

Liu, H. and Verrall, R.J. (2007). Predictive distributions for reserves which separate true IBNR and IBNER claims. Conference paper. *37th Astin Colloquium 2007*, Orlando, USA.

Lowe, J. (1994). A practical guide to measuring reserve variability using: bootstrapping, operational time and a distribution-free approach. *General Insurance Convention*, Institute of Actuaries and Faculty of Actuaries.

Lyons, G., Forster, W., Kedney, P., Warren, R. and Wilkinson, H. (2002). Claims reserving working party paper. *General Insurance Convention*. Institute of Actuaries and Faculty of Actuaries.

Mack, T. (1990). Improved estimation of IBNR claims by credibility theory. *Insurance: Math. Econom.* 9/1, 51–57.

Mack, T. (1991). A simple parametric model for rating automobile insurance or estimating IBNR claims reserves. *Astin Bulletin* 21/1, 93–109.

Mack, T. (1993). Distribution-free calculation of the standard error of chain ladder reserve estimates. *Astin Bulletin* 23/2, 213–225.

Mack, T. (1994). Measuring the variability of chain ladder reserve estimates. *CAS Forum* (Spring), 101–182.

Mack, T. (1997). *Schadenversicherungsmathematik*. Verlag Versicherungswirtschaft, Karlsruhe.

Mack, T. (2000). Credible claims reserves: the Benktander method. *Astin Bulletin* 30/2, 333–347.

Mack, T. (2006). Parameter estimation for Bornhuetter/Ferguson. *CAS Forum* (Fall), 141–157.

Mack, T. and Venter, G. (2000). A comparison of stochastic models that reproduce chain ladder reserve estimates. *Insurance: Math. Econom.* 26/1, 101–107.

Mack, T., Quarg, G. and Braun, C. (2006). The mean square error of prediction in the chain ladder reserving method – a comment. *Astin Bulletin* 36/2, 543–552.

Marjoram, P., Molitor, J., Plagnol, V. and Tavaré, S. (2003). Markov chain Monte Carlo without likelihoods. *Proc. National Academy of Science, USA* 100, 15'324–15'328.

McCullagh, P. and Nelder, J.A. (1989). *Generalized Linear Models*. 2nd Edition. Chapman & Hall, London.

McNeil A.J., Frey, R. and Embrechts, P. (2005). *Quantitative Risk Management: Concepts, Techniques and Tools*. Princeton University Press, Princeton.

Merz, M. and Wüthrich, M.V. (2006). A credibility approach to the Munich chain-ladder method. *Blätter DGVFM* XXVII, 619–628.

Merz, M. and Wüthrich, M.V. (2007a). Prediction error of the expected claims development result in the chain ladder method. *Schweiz. Aktuarver. Mitt.* 2007/1, 117–137.

Merz, M. and Wüthrich, M.V. (2007b). Prediction error of the chain ladder reserving method applied to correlated run off triangles. Accepted for publication in *Ann. Actuarial Science.*

Merz, M. and Wüthrich, M.V. (2007c). Prediction error of the multivariate chain ladder reserving method. Accepted for publication in *North American Actuarial J.*

Merz, M. and Wüthrich, M.V. (2007d). Prediction error of the multivariate additive loss reserving method for dependent lines of business. Submitted preprint, ETH Zürich.

Merz, M. and Wüthrich, M.V. (2008). Combining chain-ladder and additive loss reserving method for dependent lines of business. Submitted preprint, ETH Zürich.

Metropolis, N., Rosenbluth, A.W., Rosenbluth, M.N., Teller, A.H. and Teller, E. (1953). Equation of state calculations by fast computing machines. *J. Chem. Phys.* 21/6, 1087–1092.

Mikosch, T. (2004). *Non-Life Insurance Mathematics: An Introduction with Stochastic Processes.* Springer, Berlin.

Mildenhall, S.J. (2006). A multivariate Bayesian claim count development model with closed form posterior and predictive distibutions. *CAS Forum* (Winter), 451–493.

Murphy, D.M. (1994). Unbiased loss development factors. *Proc. CAS*, Vol. LXXXI, 154–222.

Neuhaus, W. (1992). Another pragmatic loss reserving method or Bornhuetter-Ferguson revisited. *Scand. Actuarial J.* 2, 151–162.

Neuhaus, W. (2004). On the estimation of outstanding claims. Conference paper, *35th Astin Colloquium 2004*, Bergen, Norway.

Norberg, R. (1993). Prediction of outstanding liabilities in non-life insurance. *Astin Bulletin* 23/1, 95–115.

Norberg, R. (1999). Prediction of outstanding liabilities II. Model variations and extensions. *Astin Bulletin* 29/1, 5–25.

Ntzoufras, I. and Dellaportas, P. (2002). Bayesian modelling of outstanding liabilities incorporating claim count uncertainty. *North American Actuarial J.* 6/1, 113–128.

Panjer, H.H. (2006). *Operational Risk: Modeling Analytics.* John Wiley & Sons, Inc., New Jersey.

Partrat, C., Pey, N. and Schilling, J. (2005). Delta method and reserving. Conference paper, *36th Astin Colloquium 2005*, Zürich, Switzerland.

Peters, G.W. and Sisson S.A. (2006). Bayesian inference, Monte Carlo sampling and operational risk. *J. Op. Risk* 1/3, 27–50.

Pfanzagl, J. (1994). *Parametric Statistical Theory.* De Gruyter, Berlin.

Pinheiro, P.J.R., Andrade e Silva, J.M. and de Lourdes Centeno, M. (2003). Bootstrap methodology in claim reserving. *J. Risk Insurance*, 70/4, 701–714.

Pröhl, C. and Schmidt, K.D. (2005). Multivariate chain-ladder. *Dresdner Schriften zur Versicherungsmathematik* 3/2005.

Quarg, G. and Mack, T. (2004). Munich chain ladder. *Blätter DGVFM* XXVI, 597–630.

Radtke, M. and Schmidt, K.D. (2004). *Handbuch zur Schadenreservierung.* Verlag Versicherungswirtschaft, Karlsruhe.

Renshaw, A.E. (1989). Chain ladder and interactive modelling (claims reserving and GLIM). *J. Institute Actuaries* 116, 559–587.

Renshaw, A.E. (1994). Claims reserving by joint modelling. *Actuarial Research Paper* no. 72, Department of Actuarial Sciences and Statistics, City University, London.

Renshaw, A.E. (1995). Claims reserving by joint modelling. *Astin Colloquium 1995*, Leuven, Belgium.

Renshaw, A.E. and Verrall, R.J. (1998). A stochastic model underlying the chain-ladder technique. *British Actuarial J.* 4/4, 903–923.

Robert, C.P. and Casella, G. (2004). *Monte Carlo Statistical Methods*, 2nd edition. Springer, NY.

Roberts, G.O. and Rosenthal, J.S. (2001). Optimal scaling for various Metropolis-Hastings algorithms. *Stat. Science* 16/4, 351–367.

Ross, S.M. (1985). *Introdution to Probability Models*, 3rd edition. Academic Press, Orlando.

Sandström, A. (2005). *Solvency: Models, Assessment and Regulation.* Chapman & Hall/CRC, Boca Raton.

Sandström, A. (2007). Solvency – a historical review and some pragmatic solutions. *Schweiz. Aktuarver. Mitt.* 1, 11–34.

Schmidt, K.D. (2006a). Methods and models of loss reserving based on run-off triangles: a unifying survey. *CAS Forum* (Fall), 269–317.

Schmidt, K.D. (2006b). Optimal and additive loss reserving for dependent lines of business. *CAS Forum* (Fall), 319–351.

Schmidt, K.D. and Schnaus, A. (1996). An extension of Mack's model for the chain ladder method. *Astin Bulletin* 26/2, 247–262.

Schnieper, R. (1991). Separating true IBNR and IBNER claims. *Astin Bulletin* 21/1, 111–127.

Scollnik, D.P.M. (2001). Actuarial modeling with MCMC and BUGS. *North American Actuarial J.* 5/2, 96–124.

Scollnik, D.P.M. (2002). Implementation of four models for outstanding liabilities in WinBUGS: a discussion of a paper by Ntzoufras and Dellaportas. *North American Actuarial J.* 6/1, 128–136.

Shevchenko, P.V. and Wüthrich, M.V. (2006). The structural modeling of operational risk via Bayesian inference. *J. Op. Risk* 1/3, 3–26.

Smyth, G.K. and Jørgensen, B. (2002). Fitting Tweedie's compound Poisson model to insurance claims data: dispersion modelling. *Astin Bulletin* 32/1, 143–157.

Spiegelhalter, D.J., Thomas, A., Best, N.G. and Gilks, W.R. (1995). *BUGS: Bayesian Inference Using Gibbs Sampling, Version 0.5.* MRC Biostatistics Unit, Cambridge.

Srivastava, V.K. and Giles, D.E.A. (1987). *Seemingly Unrelated Regression Equation Models: Estimation and Inference.* Dekker, NY.

Swiss Solvency Test (2006). *BPV SST Technisches Dokument, Version 2.* October 2006. Available under www.bpv.admin.ch

Taylor, G. (2000). *Loss Reserving: An Actuarial Perspective.* Kluwer Academic Publishers, Boston.

Taylor, G. and McGuire, G. (2005). Synchronous bootstrapping of seemingly unrelated regressions. Conference paper, *36th Astin Colloquium 2005*, Zürich, Switzerland.

Taylor, G. and McGuire, G. (2007). A synchronous bootstrap to account for dependencies between lines of business in the estimation of loss reserve prediction error. *North American Actuarial J.* 11/3, 70–88.

Taylor, G., McGuire, G. and Sullivan, J. (2006). Individual claim loss reserving conditioned by case estimates. Submitted preprint.

Taylor, G.C. (1987). Regression models in claims analysis I: theory. *Proc. CAS*, Vol. LXXIV, 354–383.

Taylor, G.C. (2004). Risk and discounted loss reserves. *North American Actuarial J.* 8/1, 37–44.

Taylor, G.C. and Ashe, F.R. (1983). Second moments of estimates of outstanding claims. *J. Econometrics* 23, 37–61.

Tweedie, M.C.K. (1984). An index which distinguishes between some important exponential families. In *Statistics: Applications in New Directions. Proceeding of the Indian Statistical Institute Golden Jubilee International Conference*, J.K. Ghosh and J. Roy (eds), Indian Statistical Institute, Calcutta, pp. 579–604.

Venter, G.G. (1998). Testing the assumptions of age-to-age factors. *Proc. CAS*, Vol. LXXXV, 807–847.

Venter, G.G. (2006). Discussion of mean square error of prediction in the chain ladder reserving method. *Astin Bulletin* 36/2, 566–571.

Verdier, B. and Klinger, A. (2005). JAB Chain: a model-based calculation of paid and incurred loss development factors. Conference paper. *36th Astin Colloquium 2005*, Zürich, Switzerland.

Verrall, R.J. (1989). A state space representation of the chain ladder linear model. *J. Institute Actuaries* 116, 589–609.

Verrall, R.J. (1990). Bayes and empirical Bayes estimation for the chain ladder model. *Astin Bulletin* 20/2, 217–243.

Verrall, R.J. (1991). On the estimation of reserves from loglinear models. *Insurance: Math. Econom.* 10/1, 75–80.

Verrall, R.J. (2000). An investigation into stochastic claims reserving models and the chain-ladder technique. *Insurance: Math. Econom.* 26/1, 91–99.

Verrall, R.J. (2004). A Bayesian generalized linear model for the Bornhuetter–Ferguson method of claims reserving. *North American Actuarial J.* 8/3, 67–89.

Verrall, R.J. (2007). Obtaining predictive distributions for reserves which incorporate expert opinion. *Variance* 1/1, 53–80.

Verrall, R.J. and England, P.D. (2000). Comments on: 'A comparison of stochastic models that reproduce chain ladder reserve estimates', by Mack and Venter. *Insurance: Math. Econom.* 26/1, 109–111.

Verrall, R.J. and England, P.D. (2006). Incorporating expert opinion into a stochastic model for the chain-ladder technique. *Insurance: Math. Econom.* 37/2, 355–370.

Vylder De, F. (1982). Estimation of IBNR claims by credibility theory. *Insurance: Math. Econom.* 1/1, 35–40.

Vylder De, F. and Goovaerts, M.J. (1979). *Proceedings of the First Meeting of the Contact Group 'Actuarial Sciences'*. KU Leuven, Belgium.

Witting, H. (1985). *Mathematische Statistik I.* Teubner, Stuttgart.

Wood, S.N. (2006). *Generalized Additive Models: An Introduction.* Chapman & Hall/CRC, Boca Raton.

Wright, E.M. (1933). On the coefficients of power series having essential singularities. *J. Lond. Math. Soc.* 8, 71–79.

Wright, E.M. (1935). On asymptotic expansions of generalized Bessel functions. *Proc. Lond. Math. Soc.* 38, 257–270.

Wright, T.S. (1990). A stochastic method for claims reserving in general insurance. *J. Institute Actuaries* 117, 677–731.

Wüthrich, M.V. (2003). Claims reserving using Tweedie's compound Poisson model. *Astin Bulletin* 33/2, 331–346.

Wüthrich, M.V. (2006). Premium liability risks: modeling small claims. *Schweiz. Aktuarver. Mitt.* 2006/1, 27–38.

Wüthrich, M.V. (2007). Using Bayesian models for claims reserving. *Variance* 1/2, 292–311.

Wüthrich, M.V. (2008). Prediction error in the chain ladder method. *Insurance: Math. Econom.* 42/1, 378–388.

Wüthrich, M.V., Merz, M. and Bühlmann, H. (2007a). Bounds on the estimation error in the chain ladder method. Accepted for publication in *Scand. Actuarial J.*

Wüthrich, M.V., Merz, M. and Lysenko, N. (2007b). Uncertainty of the claims development result in the chain ladder method. Accepted for publication in *Scand Actuarial J.*

Wüthrich, M.V., Bühlmann, H. and Furrer, H. (2008). *Market-Consistent Actuarial Valuation.* Springer, Berlin.

Zehnwirth, B. (1998). *ICRFS-Plus 8.3 Manual.* Insureware Pty Ltd, St Kilda, Australia.

Zellner, A. (1962). An efficient method of estimating seemingly unrelated regressions and tests for aggregation bias. *J. American Statist. Assoc.* 57, 348–368.

Index

Printed in the United States
By Bookmasters